Handbook of
Building Security
Planning and Design

Other McGraw-Hill Handbooks of Interest

Aljian · Purchasing Handbook
Azad · Industrial Wastewater Management Handbook
Baumeister and Marks · Standard Handbook for Mechanical Engineers
Brady · Materials Handbook
Callender · Time-Saver Standards for Architectural Design Data
Conover · Grounds Maintenance Handbook
Considine · Energy Technology Handbook
Crocker and King · Piping Handbook
Croft, Carr, and Watt · American Electricians' Handbook
DeChiara and Callender · Time-Saver Standards for Building Types
Fink and Carroll · Standard Handbook for Electrical Engineers
Foster · Handbook of Municipal Administration and Engineering
Harris · Dictionary of Architecture and Construction
Harris · Handbook of Noise Control
Harris and Crede · Shock and Vibration Handbook
Hicks · Standard Handbook and Engineering Calculations
Juran · Quality Control Handbook
Karassik, Krutzsch, Fraser, and Messina · Pump Handbook
LaLonde and Janes · Concrete Engineering Handbook
Lewis · Management Handbook for Plant Engineers
Lewis and Marron · Facilities and Plant Engineering Handbook
Maynard · Handbook of Business Administration
Maynard · Industrial Engineering Handbook
Merritt · Building Construction Handbook
Merritt · Standard Handbook for Civil Engineers
Morrow · Maintenance Engineering Handbook
O'Brien · Scheduling Handbook
Perry · Engineering Manual
Smeaton · Switchgear and Control Handbook
Stubbs · Handbook of Heavy Construction
Tuma · Engineering Mathematics Handbook
Tuma · Handbook of Physical Calculations
Tuma · Technology Mathematics Handbook
Urquhart · Civil Engineering Handbook
Woods · Highway Engineering Handbook

Handbook of Building Security Planning and Design

PETER S. HOPF *Editor*
A.I.A.

McGRAW-HILL BOOK COMPANY

New York St. Louis San Francisco Auckland Bogotá
Düsseldorf Johannesburg London Madrid Mexico
Montreal New Delhi Panama Paris São Paulo
Singapore Sydney Tokyo Toronto

Library of Congress Cataloging in Publication Data

Main entry under title:

Handbook of building security planning and design.

Bibliography: p.
Includes index.
1. Burglary protection. 2. Public buildings—
Security measures. 3. Dwellings—Security measures.
I. Hopf, Peter S., date.
TH9720.H35   690   78-21636
ISBN 0-07-030316-9

1234567890   KPKP   78765432109

*The editors for this book were Harold B. Crawford and Lester Strong,
the designer was Naomi Auerbach, and the production supervisor
was Thomas G. Kowalczyk. It was set in Baskerville by
University Graphics, Inc.
Printed and bound by The Kingsport Press.*

Contents

Contributors   vii
Preface   ix

PART ONE   Design Considerations

1. The Need for Security 1-3
2. Security of Property and Person 2-1
3. Security in the Neighborhood 3-1
4. Building Security Codes 4-1
5. Selecting a Security Consultant 5-1

PART TWO   Security from Natural Disasters

6. Earthquakes 6-3
7. Hurricanes, Tornadoes, and Extreme Winds 7-1
8. Floods 8-1

PART THREE   Security Components

9. An Overview of Protection Systems 9-3
10. Site Protection 10-1
11. Electronic Security Systems 11-1
12. Glass and Glazing 12-1
13. Doors and Windows 13-1
14. Lighting 14-1
15. Locks and Keying 15-1
16. Surveillance Cameras 16-1
17. Safes, Vaults, and Money Collection Areas 17-1
18. Security Personnel 18-1
19. Fire Alarm Communications 19-1
20. Sprinkler Systems 20-1

PART FOUR   Building Types—Special Security Provisions

21. Banks 21-3
22. Cargo Storage 22-1
23. Computer Power Security 23-1
24. Educational Facilities 24-1
25. Health Care Facilities 25-1
26. High-Rise Office Buildings 26-1
27. Industrial Plants 27-1
28. Libraries 28-1
29. Multiple Housing 29-1
30. Public Buildings 30-1
31. Single Family Homes 31-1

Appendix A. Security Product Directory A-1

Appendix B. Directory of Security Consultants B-1

Bibliography   BB-1
Index follows Bibliography

Contributors

ALAN B. ABRAMSON, P.E.   *Senior Staff Engineer, Syska & Hennessy, Inc., Engineers*

RALPH M. BALL, A.I.A.   *Chairman of the Board, HTB, Inc.*

REX M. BALL, F.A.I.A., A.I.P.   *President, HTB, Inc.*

MICHAEL B. BARKER   *Administrator, Department of Environment and Design, American Institute of Architects*

ROBERT BARRY   *Product Manager, The Mosler Safe Company*

RAY A. BRAY   *Senior Consultant, California Commission on Peace Officer Standards and Training*

RICHARD G. BRIGHT   *Center for Fire Research, National Bureau of Standards*

JAMES L. BRODIE, M.P.A.   *Director of Public Safety, Oak Forest Hospital*

RICHARD W. BUKOWSKI   *Center for Fire Research, National Bureau of Standards*

LUCIUS W. BURTON   *Security Advisor, City of Alexandria Public Schools*

RICHARD L. P. CUSTER   *Center for Fire Research, National Bureau of Standards*

JAMES M. DALEY, P. E.   *Product Manager, Automatic Switch Co.*

CHARLES E. GAYLORD   *Johnson Controls, Inc.*

RAYMOND J. GEORGES   *President, Lancaster Sprinkler Company*

DR. CHARLES M. GIRARD   *Partner, Koepsell-Girard and Associates*

OSCAR S. GLASBERG   *Publisher and Editor,* Glass Digest

LESLIE W. GRAHAM, P.E.   *Partner, Graham & Kellam, Structural Engineers*

RICHARD J. HEALY   *Head, Security and Safety Department, The Aerospace Corporation*

JERRY W. HICKLIN   *President, Hicklin Security Service, Inc.*

RAYMOND M. HOLT   *Library Consultant*

ED HUDGINS, A.I.A.   *Secretary, HTB, Inc.*

JOHN E. HUNTER   *Staff Curator, American Association of State and Local History*

ARTHUR A. KINGSBURY   *Associate Dean, Business/Public Service Departments, Macomb County Community College*

DR. JAMES R. McDONALD   *Dept. of Civil Engineering, Texas Tech University*

A. M. MARZANO   *Product Manager, The Mosler Safe Company*

DR. KISHOR C. MEHTA *Dept. of Civil Engineering, Texas Tech University*

DR. JOSEPH E. MINOR *Director, Institute for Disaster Research*

RONALD MOWATT *Product Manager, The Mosler Safe Company*

JOHN W. POWELL *President, John W. Powell Consultants, Inc.*

DR. GEORGE RAND *School of Architecture & Urban Planning, UCLA*

DOUGLAS E. ROUDABUSH *Executive Vice President, The Mentoris Company*

JOHN R. SHEAFFER *President, Sheaffer & Roland, Inc.*

RONALD SILVERS *Product Manager, The Mosler Safe Company*

HARDY STORMES, JR. *Crime Prevention Officer, Concord Police Department*

J. E. THORSEN *Editor-in-Chief,* Security World *Magazine*

TIMOTHY J. WALSH *President, Harris & Walsh Management Consultants, Inc., New Rochelle, NY*

WILLIAM A. WEIBEL, P.E., F.I.E.S. *Lighting Consultant*

ROBERT A. WILGUS *Market Support Manager, Diebold, Inc.*

GEORGE E. WHEATLEY, D.A.H.C. *Campbell Hardware, Inc.*

RONALD S. WOODRUFF *Chief of Security, Mentor-Towmotor Corporation*

Preface

When the editors of McGraw-Hill suggested to me that they felt there was a need for a building security handbook for the design professions, my first question to them was, "What do you mean by security?"

"Oh," was the reply, "the usual things an architect might be interested in, such a burglar alarms, sprinklers, and so forth. Anything dealing with making buildings more secure." The response seemed simple enough. But where to begin?

Security has been, historically, quite low on the architect's list of priorities, with subjects such as aesthetics, construction costs, new technologies, professional liability, and energy conservation being among those deemed much more important. In fact, some architects consider security as anathema, seeing it as restricting their freedom of design—and yet, security *is* a functional element of design which should not be neglected if competent professional services are to be provided for one's client.

Through my own architectural/engineering practice for close to twenty years, I was aware that most architects are woefully ignorant on the general subject of security as it impacts their projects. My own firm, for example, tended to let lock suppliers provide basic guidance in specifying hardware without our own recognition of the choices and options available; we relied on our mechanical engineers or on sprinkler companies for advice on fire protection systems, considering it beneath our dignity to become too involved in the selection and design of such systems; and we often left it to the initiative of our clients to suggest the need for security provisions that might be required or desired.

In the research for this volume, I became increasingly aware of the dearth of design-oriented security information. While there are organizations like the National Fire Protection Association with their excellent *Fire Protection Handbook* and other publications, most other existing material on security deals largely with management concepts, organizational principles, and operations strategy—all of which are too broadly based to be of much practical value to the building design professions.

Furthermore, while there is available a considerable amount of literature on the subject of security, most architects will have difficulty in locating this material because much of it is published by government sources or by smaller publishers, and appears in specialized trade publications usually not available to them. A search through almost any library catalog by the interested reader will quickly reveal a very limited shelf stock on the subject (I am delighted that some of the authors who *are* listed in the catalogs are also represented herein).

My initial question to the publisher as to what they meant by "security" answered itself quite rapidly, and the objective of this book quickly began to clarify itself: to assemble the specific material on the broad subject of security about which the design profession should be knowledgeable in order to round out the professional services offered to a client. It was not to be a duplication of the details appearing in existing codes and regulations but, rather, would contain the basic data with which the designer should be familiar in order to fill a frequent gap in the design of all types of structures.

The book has been organized into four major sections: "Design Considerations" provides the conceptual approaches for incorporating security into building design; "Security from Natural Disasters" should be of interest to all architects, but especially to those who undertake projects in parts of the country that may be subject to hazards that are normally not encountered in their more normal area of practice; "Security Components" describes the specific building elements which will probably be incorporated into the facility—in effect, the "hardware" section of the book; "Building Types—Special Security Provisions" concerns itself with those security provisions that are unique to individual building types.

The authors of the individual chapters represent a broad segment of persons concerned with the subject of security, and I am grateful that so many knowledgeable persons have consented to contribute their talents to this volume. The authors include university professors, law enforcement personnel, members of government agencies, manufacturers, architects, engineers, and private security consultants. In addition to these contributors, numerous individuals were most helpful in suggesting the most appropriate authors for the various chapters. Many government and private organizations were most cooperative, either in suggesting potential material or by providing data for inclusion herein. They include:

American Association for State and Local History

American Institute of Architects

American Library Association

American Society for Industrial Security

California Crime Prevention Institute

California Crime Technological Research Foundation

Commission on Peace Officer Standards and Training, State of California

Concord Police Department

Defense Civil Preparedness Agency
Door and Hardware Institute
Federal Disaster Assistance Administration
Illuminating Engineering Society
Institute for Disaster Research
National Association of School Security Directors
National Bureau of Standards
National Fire Protection Association
National Law Enforcement Administration
National Oceanic and Atmospheric Administration
Office of Emergency Preparedness, Executive Office of the President
Security World Publishing, Inc.
U.S. Customs Service
U.S. Department of Transportation

Finally, my thanks to my wife Edith for her editorial assistance and for her patience with me through many evenings of "widowhood" while I pored over reams of paper, and to my daughter, Suzanne, for her help with some of the typing chores.

Peter S. Hopf

Handbook of
Building Security
Planning and Design

Part One

Design Considerations

Chapter 1

The Need for Security

DOUGLAS E. ROUDABUSH

**Executive Vice President, The Mentoris Company; Formerly
Executive Director, California Crime Technological Research Foundation**

According to recent opinion polls the problems of crime and building security, as they affect the average citizen, have become one of society's top priorities. Currently the sales and use of our buildings depend on how the owners, management, and users view each structure for its resistance to, or susceptibility to, crime. There is a worldwide trend toward requiring designers, planners, and builders to consider the total structure and its environment, plus social problems in and around it, of which crime is a principal factor. Designers and builders have been concerned for centuries with the physical requirements of loads, occupancy, comfort, and safety in ingress and egress of its users. It is a relatively new requirement for designers to consider building layout, lighting, or entry through doors, windows, etc., with respect to crime.

The benefits of scientific and technological advances have enriched the lives of our citizenry. If our society is to stem and reverse the increasing incidence of crime, it is essential that scientific and technical "know-how" be utilized to the fullest extent in the design of buildings to provide increased security and resistance to crime.

Many of our social problems are first given wide publicity in political campaigns, where candidates promise quick solutions, for example, in the form of laws and stricter requirements, in order to win support at the polls. So it is with crime, but the promised results have been slow to appear. For a number of years our elected officials have debated what action should be taken to reduce crime. The "hardening" of a building to crime is an accepted phrase in law enforcement circles.

There are three basic elements necessary for a person to commit a crime: (1) motive, (2) ability, (3) opportunity. In providing building security by design and by the installation of equipment and systems, we attempt to eliminate or reduce the ability and opportunity to commit a crime, and therefore also to reduce the motive.

DEFINITION OF SECURITY

Security attempts to provide protection against all forms of losses stemming from artificial, natural, or environmental hazards. It is in this context that we will consider building security.

The term "security" is used in many different contexts, such as national security, international security, internal security, private security, retail security, physical security, industrial security, and information security. All of these can be involved in building security, depending on the use and occupancy of the building.

CRIME AND THE NEED FOR PROTECTION

A quick review of crime statistics from California in 1974, which are generally true for the entire United States, indicates that 15.9 percent are crimes against persons and 84.1 percent are property crimes (see Fig. 1). It can be seen that the crime of burglary

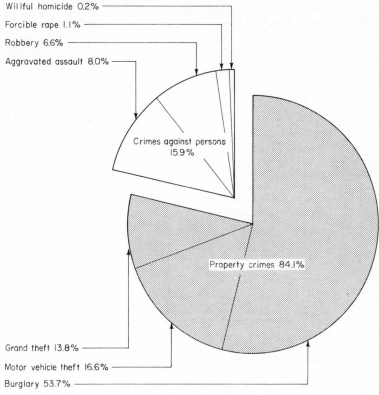

Willful homicide 0.2%

Forcible rape 1.1%

Robbery 6.6%

Aggravated assault 8.0%

Crimes against persons
15.9%

Property crimes 84.1%

Grand theft 13.8%

Motor vehicle theft 16.6%

Burglary 53.7%

Fig. 1   Felony crimes reported, 1974, for seven major offenses. *(Taken from "Crime and Delinquency in California in 1974," Department of Justice, Bureau of Criminal Statistics.)*

represents 53.7 percent of the major offenses as reported by the Federal Bureau of Investigation. Burglary is defined as the "unlawful entry of a structure to commit crime" (and this includes attempted forced entry). From Table 1, Burglary Crimes Reported, it can be seen that in over 70 percent of the cases force or attempted force was used.

The patterns of crime are changing, and crime is increasingly being committed by juveniles. The percentage committed by females is also increasing, as new attitudes and assertiveness become more common among women.

A study of the crime statistics for a particular area reveals that the proportion of day and night burglaries is related to the type of location, type of persons involved, hours worked, and life-style. These factors should all be considered in design and should be based upon data for the area where the building is to be erected.

If we consider forcible entry as a major factor in the crime of burglary, we must consider what type of force is being used and how it is being generated. Table 2 analyzes burglaries in a California study, comparing the type of structure and the percentage of entries where tools were used. To consider adequate design, one must know the type of tools used in burglaries and the quantity of energy or destructive force these tools or physical strength will generate. As one can see from the table, a higher percentage of tools are used on stronger targets in commercial, government, and industrial buildings, as contrasted with residential structures. The type of tool and of burglary threat can be seen in the California Crime Technological Research

TABLE 1   Burglary Crimes Reported, 1969, 1973, and 1974: Type of Entry, Premise, and Time of Day

	Number			Percent			Percent change	
Item	1969*	1973	1974	1969	1973	1974	1969–1974*	1973–1974
Total	320,708	407,375	431,863	100.0	100.0	100.0	34.7	6.0
Force and attempted force	230,239	290,819	308,590	71.8	71.4	71.5	34.0	6.1
No force (unlawful entry)	90,469	116,556	123,273	28.2	28.6	28.5	36.3	5.8
Residence	193,472	269,978	283,735	60.3	66.3	65.7	46.7	5.1
Nonresidence	127,236	137,397	148,128	39.7	33.7	34.3	16.4	7.8
Day	89,769	151,794	159,472	28.0	37.3	36.9	77.6	5.1
Night	122,374	146,988	150,512	38.2	36.1	34.9	23.0	2.4
Unknown	108,565	108,593	121,879	33.9	26.7	28.2	12.3	12.2

*Table 1 data were based on final counts.
Note: Percentages may not total 100 due to rounding.
SOURCE: California Department of Justice, *Crime and Delinquency in California in 1974,* Bureau of Criminal Statistics.

Foundation's (CCTRF) Building Security Standards Report to the Attorney General's Building Security Commission in May 1974. CCTRF attempted to provide test methods and data to measure these threats in engineering terms. Chapter 13 in this book reproduces these data.

As one would suspect, the greatest percentage of burglaries are perpetrated by entering a structure through doors and windows. Table 3 shows data from a California study that are considered typical of crime patterns throughout the United States; doors, being most readily available to enter buildings, are the most frequently used in burglaries.

TABLE 2   Burglaries: Premises and Tools Used

Type of burglary	Hands, feet used, %	Tools used, %	Not specified, %
Total burglaries	3,101*	35	62	3
Residential	2,178*	40	57	3
Commercial	800*	23	74	3
Government or institutional	123*	26	71	3

*Number of burglaries from six California areas, Apr. 1 to Aug. 31, 1972.
SOURCE: California Attorney General's Building Security Commission, *Preliminary Report to the California Legislature: Building Security Standards,* January 1973.

A review of changing historical crime patterns as our society changes its habits and life-styles is also helpful. The writer believes that in the future the study by architects of crime patterns is essential—they must raise their level of knowledge to cope with the ever-changing relationships between society and the criminal.

Figure 2 shows a noticeable change in the patterns of arrests for burglary in California over a period of twelve years. From a statewide ratio of burglary arrests of 61 percent adults to 39 percent juveniles in 1960, the ratio shifted to 49 percent adults and 51 percent juveniles in 1972.

Table 4 shows that 49.4 percent of the offenders selected for this special study are 17 years old and under, 62.7 percent are 19 and under, 82.3 percent are 24 and under, and 91.6 percent are 29 and under. Only eight of each 100 offenders were 30 or older. These age groupings indicate that burglary is definitely a crime of the young offender.

TABLE 3   Burglaries: Premises and Point of Entry

Type of burglary		Doors, %	Windows, %	Other, %
Total burglaries	3,101*	56	38	6
Residential	2,178*	56	40	4
Commercial	800*	58	39	3
Government or institutional	123*	46	43	11

*Number of burglaries from six California areas, Apr. 1 to Aug. 31, 1972.

SOURCE: California Attorney General's Building Security Commission, *Preliminary Report to the California Legislature: Building Security Standards,* January 1973.

Police knowledge of professional burglars indicates that they travel widely in pursuit of their profession. However, the average burglar in the study, according to Table 5, operated in his or her own city and very close to home. Overall, 50.5 percent committed their offense within 1 mile, 71.6 percent within 3 miles, and 81 percent within 5 miles of where they lived at the time of their arrest. Juveniles tended to stay within 1 mile 64.4 percent of the time, and within 3 miles in 85.1 percent of the cases. Young adults operated within 1 mile 38.1 percent of the time, and within 3 miles 59.7 percent of the time. Older adults traveled farther more frequently, but still were within 1 mile 33.4 percent of the time, and within 3 miles 54 percent of the time. The major conclusion of this report is that burglary is primarily a crime of opportunity rather than the work of professionals.

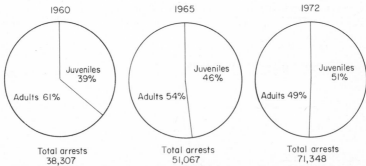

Fig. 2   Burglary arrests in California, 1960, 1965 and 1972. *(From "The Burglar in California: A Profile," Research Report No. 15, California Department of Justice, Division of Law Enforcement, Bureau of Criminal Statistics.)*

The effects of crime against business are major, and our society is just realizing that buildings can be built (and society is willing to pay the price) in such a way that it is more difficult for a person to commit a crime. The Bureau of Domestic Commerce estimates that the cost of "ordinary" crimes against business will have reached $20.3 billion in 1974. This figure represents an increase of about 30 percent over the $15.7 billion cost estimated for 1971. Table 6 lists the commercial burglary rate per 1000 establishments. It can be seen from these data that the crime figures are from 253 per 1000 in San Francisco to 637 per 1000 in Oakland across the bay. (Some of the recent studies on crime indicate that a great percentage of the offenses are not reported to law enforcement officials and therefore do not show up in the crime statistics.)

TABLE 4 Burglary Offenders by Age

Age group	Number	Percent
Total	1,242	100.0
17 and under	613	49.4
18–19	165	13.3
20–24	243	19.6
25–29	116	9.3
30–34	35	2.8
35–39	33	2.7
40–44	17	1.4
45–49	12	0.9
50 and over	8	0.6

SOURCE: California Department of Justice, Division of Law Enforcement, *The Burglar in California: A Profile*, Research Report No. 15, Bureau of Criminal Statistics.

Table 7 contains an estimate of the cost of crime by type of business.

The cost of crimes against business must be passed on to consumers in the form of higher prices or be absorbed as costs by businesses, with resulting lower profits. The estimated total cost of $20.3 billion is equal to $89 for every man, woman, and child in the country; if one considers only the adult population, the per capita cost is $137. Crime-related losses also have a depressing effect on business. The ratio of losses to total capital expenditures is in excess of 16 percent, or equal to about 17 percent of total corporate profits.

Crime can affect businesses regardless of location, although the incidence varies by type of area, as the list below indicates. For example, firms in central-city areas,

TABLE 5 Distance from Burglary Scene to Offender's Residence

Distance	Total	Percent	Juvenile	Percent	18–29	Percent	Adult 30 and over	Percent
Total known	1,220	100.0	600	100.0	518	100.0	102	100.0
Within 1 mile	617	50.5	386	64.4	197	38.1	34	33.4
1–3 miles	257	21.1	124	20.7	112	21.6	21	20.6
3–5 miles	115	9.4	35	5.8	70	13.5	10	9.8
5–10 miles	112	9.2	26	4.3	67	12.9	19	18.6
10 miles and over	119	9.8	29	4.8	72	13.9	18	17.6

Note: Of the total 1,242 offenders, mileage was unknown for 22.

SOURCE: California Department of Justice, Division of Law Enforcement, *The Burglar in California: A Profile*, Research Report No. 15, Bureau of Criminal Statistics.

particularly in low-income sections, have the highest rate of burglaries and robberies by a substantial margin.

Conclusions reported by the U.S. Department of Commerce relating to crime against businesses show that:

- "Ordinary" crimes will cost business more than $20 billion in 1974, up 31 percent over 1971.
- Retail establishments are hardest hit by crime.
- The incidence of crimes against business continues to rise.
- Crime affects firms in all parts of the country.
- Small businesses suffer from crime more than larger firms.
- Crime losses by retailers are expected to reach $5.8 billion for 1974, up 21 percent from 1971.
- Losses by wholesalers in 1974 will total $2.1 billion, up 50 percent from 1971.
- Losses by manufacturers are very difficult to calculate, because of the scarcity of data. However, it is estimated that manufacturers will lose $2.8 billion in 1974, up 60 percent from 1971.
- Service industries will lose an estimated $3.5 billion to criminals in 1974, an increase of about 30 percent over 1971.
- Between 31 percent and 61 percent of the commercial establishments in the largest American cities suffered burglary attempts in 1972.
- In one city, Detroit, 72 percent of the retail stores were burglarized in 1972.
- Losses to business caused through arson reached an estimated $300 million in 1974.
- Businesses spent $3.9 billion in crime prevention programs in 1974.

The magnitude and increasing cost of crimes against business are clearly evident, with such cost being passed on to the customer in the form of higher prices. In order to improve this situation, designers have a great responsibility to provide the best and most cost-effective security system for the structures they design.

TABLE 6   Commercial Burglary Rate per 1,000 Establishments

Boston	576
Buffalo	319
Cincinnati	566
Houston	518
Miami	292
Milwaukee	321
Minneapolis	436
New Orleans	448
Oakland	637
Pittsburgh	293
San Diego	358
San Francisco	253
Washington, D.C.	330

SOURCE: U.S. Department of Justice, Law Enforcement Assistance Administration, *Criminal Victimization Surveys in 13 American Cities,* National Criminal Justice Information and Statistics Service, June 1975.

HOW CAN PROTECTION BE OBTAINED?

The obvious conclusion is that if a building were stronger (or differently designed), potential burglars who live close to it would be deterred from attempting to break in.

Following this reasoning, many progressive states and local governments have enacted crime codes for the purpose of reducing crime in buildings.

A leading state in this effort is California. On November 30, 1971, the Governor signed into law Assembly Bill 3030, which required the Department of Justice to develop and recommend to the Legislature, and thereafter continually review, building security standards for the purpose of reducing the likelihood of burglary.

Even though the need for stronger components can be demonstrated, one cannot expect industry voluntarily to make changes which may affect its profits and ultimately its competitive existence. History has shown that where the vital interests of society are in jeopardy, legislators must take the initiative in (1) designing laws that will protect the citizens and (2) making sure that they are enforced.

TABLE 7   Estimated Cost of "Ordinary" Crime by Sector of Business: 1971, 1973, and 1974 (Billions of Dollars)

Sectors of business	1971	1973	1974
Retailing	4.8	5.2	5.8
Manufacturing	1.8	2.6	2.8
Wholesaling	1.4	1.8	2.1
Services	2.7	3.2	3.5
Transportation	1.5	1.7	1.9
Arson	0.2	0.3	0.3
Preventive measures	3.3	3.5	3.9
	15.7	18.3	20.3

SOURCE: U.S. Department of Commerce, Bureau of Domestic Commerce.

BUILDING SECURITY PROGRAMS

Local Government

In response to the increasing crime problem, individual communities throughout the United States have initiated procedural crime prevention programs. These include such things as marking valuables for identification, organizing neighborhood alert programs, and changing building codes to "harden the target" against unlawful entry. Some of the programs have effected a reduction in the rates of those crimes toward which they were directed. The best-known example is the Oakland Burglary Security Ordinance (see Chapter 4).

In this program, as a burglary prevention measure, the Oakland Municipal Code was amended to require security devices in certain buildings used for business purposes. Provisions include mandatory design features for various building components (e.g., cylinder deadlocks) and authorization for the Chief of Police to require supplemental devices or alarms where the requirements of the code do not adequately secure a particular building. After a two-year period of comparing data on businesses that complied with the ordinance against those that did not, the city was able to demonstrate the value of the ordinance. The major shortcoming in the Oakland program was that the standards were consensus standards written by a committee without the benefit of an engineering test program. Even though some of the standards were impossible to meet with present design and construction practice, the Oakland code was a progressive approach to building security.

It appears that a better way to design and enforce physical building security standards is to set an overall functional requirement of physical strength defined in engineering terms (foot pounds of energy). This is in contrast to setting individual design requirements for each component (lock, door, hinges, windows, etc.), in which case the total assembly is only as strong as the weakest part, and even this strength can be reduced by faulty assembly.

In another example of independent security regulations, the County of Los Angeles has adopted an ordinance which covers both commercial and residential premises. It goes one step beyond Oakland's approach in that it contains actual resistance ratings for sliding doors and windows, an important feature in allowing for proper evaluation of systems that contain several different components. A prominent trade association has adopted similar standards for member and associate groups, and the Los Angeles County efforts have been instrumental in developing testing criteria for certification of products. However, most of the problems evident in Oakland's approach, which was pioneering legislation at the time, are also present in Los Angeles County's standards; that is, they are based upon consensus standards, not a complete engineering test program. In addition, resistance values had to be tempered somewhat because of a general inability of door and window manufacturers to meet an optimum standard that would prevent the average burglar from making forcible entry.

Today, hundreds of cities have included various standards for burglary prevention in their security ordinances or are considering doing so. However, as cited in the above examples, lack of necessary technical input has resulted in a "causal" (limitations on design) approach rather than an "effect" (what a system should do) approach, and it has restricted the development of adequate performance standards. Local governments have lacked the funds, scientific know-how, and facilities to devise a technical program for acquiring scientific data to develop adequate performance standards.

Federal Government

Several government-sponsored groups of national scope have been conducting research and training programs directed toward assisting local units of government combat the rise in the nation's crime rate. Two of the more promising are the National Bureau of Standards Security Program and the National Crime Prevention Institute's Crime Prevention Training Program.

The Law Enforcement Assistance Administration's (LEAA) National Institute for Law Enforcement and Criminal Justice (NILECJ) has a program at the National Bureau of Standards to prepare specifications for security systems. A series of programs have been funded by LEAA to study the security and crime problem.

The National Crime Prevention Institute (NCPI) at the University of Louisville offers crime prevention training, including security systems theory, designed to assist in the development of crime prevention bureaus by local law enforcement agencies. Although it is essentially a nontechnical program, it provides basic information that can be valuable in the administration of procedural building security programs, particularly where provisions for alternative materials or devices require knowledge beyond the scope of normal police experience. The material provided by NCPI is based upon a compilation of data from various expert sources, but it generally does not include verification through testing techniques.

Private Action

Historically, there have been many professional and trade associations in the United States which have developed marketing-oriented standards for nomenclature, design, materials, or quality. Several groups have begun to recognize the validity of the proposition that a new standard should be developed that is based upon optimum performance criteria rather than merely a consensus of member opinions.

The American Society for Testing and Materials (ASTM) is an example of a group currently involved in a project to develop nomenclature, test methods, specifications, and recommended practices for security systems and equipment.

The American Society for Industrial Security (ASIS) is a professional organization whose members and associates are concerned with the protection of personnel, property, and information in industrial and government facilities. The latter are large-scale security products users who are deeply involved in the management and maintenance, as well as selection, of security systems. ASIS is in a unique position to offer expert assistance to a research project involving almost any type, size, or complexity of system. Since ASIS is not a trade or manufacturers' association, standards and recommendations derived from its committees should be based upon optimum needs rather than marketing interests.

The International Conference of Building Officials (ICBO), at 5360 South Workman Mill Road, Whittier, California 90601, has a Fire and Life Safety Committee and a security subcommittee working on the problem of building security. ICBO's Uniform Building Code—generally used in Western states—is the most widely adopted local code in the United States, with about 75 percent of local governments using it. The current California legislation specifies the use of this code and alludes to the security requirements that are being developed by ICBO.

Underwriters' Laboratories, Inc., has been working on standards for key locks and other security hardware. They offer testing and certification service to their standards. The Associated Locksmiths of America (ALOA) also have building security programs under way.

Recognition of the need for building security standards now exists. Many interested groups are working on the problem, and the hoped-for next step is the evolution of uniform standards and nomenclature.

SUMMARY

The nation is confronted with a serious crime problem, and burglary is the commonest offense. The increasingly high proportion of juvenile arrests is an indication that the criminal population and the threat of crime are likely to grow in future years. The failure of law enforcement to effectively control the problem is dramatized by the decreased percentage of "clearance rate" for crimes committed.

Attempts by local governmental agencies to implement burglary prevention standards have been generally limited by a lack of technical input. Research must therefore be conducted to determine how strong building components must be in order to withstand a criminal's efforts to break in.

Architects, buiding developers, and contractors are finding security an important ingredient in successful marketing. Facilities in areas with a high-crime reputation are subject to decreasing property values and loss of revenue.

Naturally, security design involves trade-offs: (1) freedom of movement may be restricted in order to limit access, (2) cost of construction may rise, and (3) type of building layout may be restricted, along with (4) type of components used in doors, windows, hardware, etc. Given the nature of crime and our social problems, professionals must develop the means to design buildings that are cost-effective and have a high degree of security.

Since the patterns of crime and asocial behavior are predictable, these will have to be taken into account in designing buildings for a specific function and location. Where will architects obtain information on which to base design and cost trade-offs? One source would be design guides put out by government and technical societies. For example, *A Design Guide for Improving Residential Security*[7] lists the concepts of defensible space, hardware, electronic security systems, security personnel, etc. A number of local governments in California are requiring building designs and development plans to be reviewed by public safety officers in law enforcement and fire services. Such officials are generally knowledgeable about crime patterns and other social problems unique to their location. The aim is to discover the optimum "trade-off point" in balancing costs for security against the proposed design of a structure.

REFERENCES

1. *Academic Guidelines for Security and Loss Prevention Programs in Community and Junior Colleges,* American Society for Industrial Security, Washington, DC.
2. California Attorney General's Building Commission, *Preliminary Report to the California Legislature: Building Security Standards,* January 1973.
3. California Crime Technological Research Foundation, *Building Security Standards Report to the Attorney General's Building Security Commission,* May 1974.
4. California Department of Justice, Division of Law Enforcement, *The Burglar in California: A Profile,* Research Report No. 15, Bureau of Criminal Statistics.
5. ——, *Crime and Delinquency in California in 1974,* Bureau of Criminal Statistics.
6. U.S. Department of Commerce, *The Cost of Crime against Business,* U.S. Government Printing Office, November 1974.
7. U.S. Department of Housing and Urban Development, Center for Residential Security Design, *A Design Guide for Improving Residential Security,* U.S. Government Printing Office, 1973.
8. U.S. Department of Justice, Law Enforcement Assistance Administration, *Criminal Victimization Surveys in 13 American Cities,* National Criminal Justice Information and Statistics Service, June 1975.

Chapter 2

Security of Property and Person

ARTHUR A. KINGSBURY, Ph. D.

**Associate Dean, Business/Public Service Departments,
Macomb County Community College**

HISTORICAL BACKGROUND

Security and protection systems can usefully be described in terms of their historical background—that is, by referring to historical concepts of security and the administration of justice. Many effective security techniques (physical barriers, manufactured or natural, and other means of protection) were invented and developed long before most of the techniques used by police today.

The protection of people and their property is one of the oldest tasks undertaken in the course of history because it is so closely allied with a basic human instinct: self-preservation. This historical fact was largely neglected until recent years, when historians began tracing the development of law enforcement. The walled cities of Nippon in the Sumerian and Akkadian cultures in 1500 B.C., the Great China Wall erected to guard against a Mongol invasion, use of the crater of Mount Vesuvius as a natural fortress by Spartacus, and the walled city of Trier—the oldest Roman town in Germany—are all examples of the early recognition of the need for security.[16]

It is important to understand why and how the pattern of development in private security differs from what is commonly known as law enforcement. The concept of individual protection and the concept of justice among individuals of very primitive groups is synonymous with the maintenance of community equilibrium. When property was stolen from an individual in a primitive community, the economic equilibrium was unjustly disturbed. Such an act constituted a wrong against the individual, and equilibrium was reestablished by a settlement between the aggrieved person and the wrongdoer. If the thief restored what had been stolen, the injured party was very often satisfied, and no further action was taken. This philosophy has continued with relatively little modification to the present time.[14]

The history of law enforcement follows the flow of legal development, which shifted the primary responsibility for protection and prevention of criminal activities from the private individual to the governmental jurisdiction in which he or she lived. In other words, the individual was no longer legally responsible for protection and prevention, but the public became the aggrieved party and assumed the responsibility for prevention, protection, and apprehension of offenders.[14]

The industrial revolution, with its subsequent growth of urban and suburban communities, saw the beginnings of a shift of total reliance on government resources for security. While on the one hand governmental security agencies increased—often from necessity, at other times through the momentum of a self-perpetuating bureaucracy—it became virtually impossible for private industry to rely exclusively on government resources for its security needs. Not only would the citizenry not support the requisite governmental security forces for financial and social reasons, but industry in the free world has always been understandably reluctant to rely on the government to manage its affairs. Stated differently, if the public were to foot the bill to meet all of industry's security needs, the cost of such security would soon reach an intolerable point. When industry provides for its own security, the cost simply becomes one more small element in the cost of the end product. Industry, as described herein, is intended as a broad term encompassing every segment of the economy, including factories, offices, schools, hospitals, stores, warehouses, and so forth.

Traditionally, the police have had little success in the prevention of crime. On the other hand, the private security sector, with its differing emphasis, has had a substantial influence on the reduction of criminal opportunity.

The average person tends to have a distorted image of the individual employed in the field of security; that is, that all security personnel are elderly and, in some cases, not very competent. On the contrary, the majority of such individuals are capable, and at the senior management level they often equal or exceed their counterparts in other fields in terms of academic degrees and training. Loss prevention, campus security, plant protection, bank security, and retail security are related terms covering a broad range of activities in the security field. There are approximately 800,000 persons in security services, and approximately 400,000 in law enforcement. In 1969, over $8 billion was devoted to security services and equipment (0.85 percent of the gross national product). One in every 250 persons in the entire population was employed in security work, and over $40 per capita was spent on security.[20]

The major concern of many specialists in the security profession focuses on the complex areas of (1) definitions of security; (2) the role of security in our culture; and (3) the application of security processes. A better understanding of security can be achieved by reviewing some of the major definitions of this field.

DEFINITIONS OF SECURITY[14]

The term "security" derives from the Latin word "securus," meaning "safe," "free from danger." It appears in German as "sicher." Related meanings are "protect," "shield from," "guard against," "render safe," and "take effective precautions against."

Original translations of the word "securus" describe basic characteristics which are relevant today. The areas include:
1. Safety
2. Freedom from danger
3. Feeling no care or apprehension
4. Being protected from, or not exposed to, danger
5. Guardianship
6. Freedom from risk
7. Satisfaction

8. Protection

9. Taking effective precautions against

Definitions, of course, tend to be arbitrary, and attempts to classify them may result in overlap. But the definitions of security may be separated into eight categories[14]:

1. *Historical*—a narrative of past events

2. *Psychological*—the study and interpretation of the mind

3. *Sociological*—the study of human social behavior

4. *Functional*—the procedural aspects of social control

5. *Management*—the organizational context of security

6. *Normative*—the presenting of norms and standards

7. *Structural*—security viewed in terms of its parts and inter-relationships

8. *Descriptive*—a collection of different classifications of elements of security

In the context of these categories, the designer of a warehouse, for example, must understand the use of the building in terms of its functional, management, and structural elements. In the functional category would be such elements as public access (pickups and deliveries) and restrictions on movement of personnel and vehicles. Management would include supervision of employees at check-in and check-out times and the monitoring of the movement of goods entering and leaving the facility. Structural considerations would include physical elements such as perimeter security, alarm systems, and physical barriers within the warehouse to limit access to unauthorized persons.

The three processes basic to all security endeavors are[1]:

1. *Physical security.*   The tangible aspects of security—locks, alarms, constructed and natural barriers, and related security equipment.

2. *Personnel security.*   Measures taken through a careful selection process, to obtain trustworthy employees.

3. *Information security.*   The concept of safeguarding information, ideas, correspondence, and the like.

These three processes should be considered inseparable and basic to any security-oriented program.

Most security organizations have a common element and purpose within their corporate and/or individual goals and objectives—namely, *loss prevention*. The major purpose or rationale for the existence of all proprietary security is the denial or prevention of loss—whether of human origin or environmental. It must be noted, of course, that security is a philosphy of self-defense for both individuals and organizations, and, like other needs, it should be kept in its proper perspective at all times. For example, a designer would rarely want to spend $1,000 to secure $100. Hence, security will be but one of the many considerations in the planning and implementing of any given project.

PLANNING SECURITY PROCEDURES

Before any security program is adopted, a "needs analysis" should be performed, as is the case with most other disciplines. An example would be the area of management and program needs analysis. The only difference is in the actual implementation; whereas a management study may be done in an office atmosphere, the security survey is performed in the field.

An understanding of the planning process prior to and during a survey is essential for success. General management planning processes should be considered in preparing a workable survey instrument or model. The traditional steps in planning include[8]:

1. Recognizing a need

2. Stating objectives

3. Gathering significant/relevant data

4. Developing alternatives
5. Preparing a course of action
6. Analyzing capabilities
7. Reviewing the plan
8. Implementing the plan

A security or physical security survey is "a critical on-site examination and analysis of an industrial plant, business, home, public or private institution, to ascertain the present security status, to identify deficiencies or excesses, to determine the protection needed, and to make recommendations to improve the over-all security."

The sequence of the tasks involved in carrying out the actual design of a model survey, from the first stages of planning to the preparation of the final report, is extracted from materials presented in Ref. 8* and presented here as a guide.

Designing a Sample Survey Model

A major requirement of developing a survey instrument is the preparing of a topical outline depicting the major areas of concentration. Subject areas of interest or topics to be surveyed should be listed under the three major categories described earlier—physical security, personnel security, and information security.

Topics to Consider Major considerations or topics in the development of a survey instrument fall into four general areas of consideration: (a) planning (purpose), (b) responsibilities, (c) area (duties), and (d) issues (policy-procedure).

A. Planning (purpose): *What and how much security?*
    1. Physical security (property, etc.)
    2. Personnel (background, etc.)
    3. Information (files, records, etc.)
    4. Security survey/consultant
B. Responsibilities: *Who?*
    1. Administrative authority (vice president level, etc.)—security organization
    2. Budget/scheduling
C. Area (duties): *Where* will the security emphasis be placed?
    1. Parking
    2. Visitor control
    3. Hazards (human and environmental)
    4. Employee pilferage
    5. Outside losses
    6. Disaster planning/civil disturbance
    7. Fire/safety responsibility
    8. Special events
D. Issues (policy-procedure): *When? Why?*
    1. Legal basis
    2. Education/training
    3. Manuals (general/specific)
    4. Intelligence gathering
    5. Contract guard vs. in-house
    6. Side arms vs. none
    7. Extra chores
        a. Escort
        b. Lock-up
        c. Room checks
        d. Protect transfer of monies
    8. Guard force vs. hardware

*Courtesy Charles C. Thomas, publishers.

  9. Uniform vs. nonuniform
10. Contract with local law enforcement
11. Security cadets
12. Consultant (outside)
13. Consultant (staff member)—contract guard

The use of more than one individual in preparing and implementing a security or crime prevention survey is recommended in order to obtain the benefit of new and varied viewpoints, as well as a more solid and objective survey.

Security Survey Outline

Each organization or facility is unique, which makes it difficult to establish a universal checklist.[11] The following brief topical outline gives an example of categories to be considered.

A. General
  1. The purpose of the survey
  2. Name of the plant/organization
  3. Location (street address, city, county, state)
  4. Jurisdiction (city, county, federal)
  5. Security responsibility (private or governmental agency)
  6. Names of the principal officers and their duties (attach as an exhibit an official roster of the installation if readily available)
  7. Type of business
  8. Product or service rendered
  9. Brief history of plant and products
  10. Size and physical characteristics of the plant and labor force
  11. Statement of hazards caused by type of industry, neighborhood, and terrain
  12. Previous surveys, including the date and conducting agency, and a statement of the corrective action taken.[11]

B. Sociopolitical considerations
  1. Radical or reactionary groups
  2. Local power structures
  3. Primary political opinions
  4. Economic progress of area

C. Physical security
  1. Perimeter barriers
    a. Natural barriers
    b. Structural barriers
    c. Human barriers
    d. Animal barriers
    e. Energy barriers
  2. Protective lighting
  3. Alarm procedures
  4. Entrances
    a. Vehicle
    b. Personnel

D. Personnel security
  1. Key personnel
  2. Security clearances of employee (if applicable)
  3. Disaster and emergency plans
  4. Morale (employees)

E. Information security
  1. Classified information available (if applicable)

   2. Areas where important documents are kept
      a. Safes
      b. Cash registers, etc.
   3. Destruction of documents
      a. Employee payroll records
      b. Canceled checks, etc.
   4. Transmission of documents from one place to another
F. Security education
   1. How much security education?
   2. Who receives security education?
   3. How often given?
G. Fire-fighting facilities
   1. Personnel
   2. Equipment
   3. Alarms

The implementation of a survey should be considered one of the most important tasks the architect undertakes, since the first step in any security, crime prevention, risk identification, or loss control program is the evaluation of the present state of affairs. This, of course, means a thorough and objective survey. The critical on-site examination and analysis of any facility (home, business, etc.) will, in effect, dictate the future course of action regarding its security.

The designer should consult the bibliography which accompanies this chapter and become familiar with the literature in the field of planning and implementation of security processes. The next step is exploration of the major "prevention" techniques. Later chapters in this book describe in detail the techniques and processes of providing security.

REFERENCES

1. Blanchard, Robert E., *Introduction to the Administration of Justice*, Wiley, New York, 1975.
2. Cole, Richard B., *The Application of Security Systems and Hardware*, Charles C. Thomas, Springfield, IL, 1970.
3. ———, *Protect Your Property: The Applications of Burglar Alarm Hardware*, Charles C. Thomas, Springfield, IL, 1971.
4. Curtis, S. J., *Security Control—External Theft*, Chain Store Age Publishing Corp., New York, 1971.
5. Davis, John Richelieu, *Industrial Plant Protection*, Charles C. Thomas, Springfield, IL, 1957.
6. Gocke, B. W., *Practical Plant Protection and Policing*, Charles C. Thomas, Springfield, IL, 1957.
7. Healy, Richard J., *Design for Security*, Wiley, New York, 1968.
8. Kingsbury, Arthur A., *Introduction to Security and Crime Prevention Surveys*, Charles C. Thomas, Springfield, IL, 1973.
9. Liechtenstein, Michael and William Fairley, *Improving Public Safety in Urban Apartment Dwellings: Security Concepts and Experimental Design for N.Y. City Housing Authority Buildings*, New York City Rand Institute, New York, 1971.
10. Mathematica, Incorporated, *An Evaluation of Policy—Related Research*, Prepared for National Science Foundation, 1974.
11. Momboisse, Raymond M., *Industrial Security for Strikes, Riots, and Disasters*, Charles C. Thomas, Springfield, IL, 1968.
12. Newman, Oscar, *Defensible Space*, Collier Books, New York, 1973 (paperback edition).
13. Oliver, Eric and John Wilson, *Security Manual*, Gower, London, 1969.
14. Post, Richard S. and Arthur A. Kingsbury, *Security Administration: An Introduction*, Charles C. Thomas, Springfield, IL, 1976.
15. ———, *Determing Security Needs*, Oak Security Publications, Madison, WI, 1973.
16. Rowan, Richard W., *Secret Service: 33 Centuries of Espionage*, New York, 1967.

17. Tobias, Marc Weber, *Locks, Safes and Security: A Handbook for Law Enforcement Personnel,* Charles C. Thomas, Springfield, IL, 1971.

18. U.S. Department of Housing and Urban Development, Center for Residential Security Design, *A Design Guide for Improving Residential Security,* U.S. Government Printing Office, Washington, DC, 1973.

19. U.S. Department of Justice, Law Enforcement Assistance Administration, *Residential Security,* U.S. Government Printing Office, Washington, DC, 1974.

20. ——, *Private Police in the U.S.: Findings and Recommendations,* National Institute of Law Enforcement and Criminal Justice, 1, R-869/DOJ, 1971.

Chapter 3

Security in the Neighborhood

MICHAEL B. BARKER

Administrator, Department of Environment and Design,
American Institute of Architects

ASPECTS OF THE NEIGHBORHOOD CONCEPT

The "Good" Neighborhood

We often hear it said that one particular place is a good neighborhood and another is a bad neighborhood. Usually the speaker is summarizing a broad range of impressions that have to do with the attractiveness of a location, its exposure to nuisances such as noise and fumes, the characteristics of the people who occupy the area (poor, rich, white, black, young, or old), and finally, and perhaps most importantly, the individuals' projected sense of security, both for themselves and their property. These characteristics vary in importance over the years as public opinions and public concerns shift and change. Today few would disagree that uppermost in the public mind is the fear of crime, particularly crimes against persons, more specifically street crimes. A "good" neighborhood today has to be a secure neighborhood.

Neighborhood as Setting

Contemporary neighborhood design is both an art and a science. Each year dozens of publications come out on the various aspects of neighborhood design. None has focused on security. Many would argue that "good" neighborhood design, whether intentionally structured to obtain security or not, would in fact achieve a secure environment because of the effective functioning of the neighborhood. While this view has considerable merit, it is not very helpful to the designer of an individual building in a specific location. Very seldom is there an opportunity to make major modifications to neighborhoods which would improve overall security, let alone to design a neighborhood from scratch. This chapter is structured to provide building designers with insights into how their projects will perform in the long run, within a given neighborhood setting. It is not a manual for neighborhood design.

The Design and the Community

The designer of a building will probably be interested in two things—(1) the impact of the neighborhood on his or her project initially and over a period of time, and (2) the impact of the projected building on the neighborhood.

The building designer's interests are not always the same as those of the larger community. Consider, for example, community reactions against half-way houses located in residential neighborhoods. The residents of the neighborhood fear that the half-way house will attract undesirable and dangerous individuals to the community. Yet the designer's responsibility is to produce a design that meets the client's needs, usually *after* the site has been selected. The designer's understanding of differing points of view can serve to strengthen a proposed design and prepare both designer and client to answer questions raised by the community. In some situations a particular project could make a substantial contribution to the security of a particular neighborhood—for example, the addition of a fire station or police station.

Another important consideration is the performance of individual buildings and neighborhoods over a long period of time. Neighborhoods change from "good" to "bad" and from "bad" to "good" as demographic, economic, and other factors change over the years. A sense of how things are likely to change is important for both designer and client.

Neighborhood: A Definition

What is a neighborhood? Architects and town planners have been writing on this question for millennia. For the purpose of this chapter we will adopt a rather simple definition: A neighborhood is the immediate setting in which a building functions. The geographic size of a residential neighborhood can range from as small as perhaps two or three acres for high-rise inner-city-type development to well over several hundred acres for single-family detached suburban areas. A somewhat loose geographic definition will be sufficient for our purposes. It is important to note, however, that "neighborhood" is much more than a physical concept. For a person living or working in a neighborhood it represents a life- or work-style, a set of city services, numerous patterns of social and economic interactions, a transportation system, and the like.

Crime and Accessibility

Crime is a behavioral concept, one not rooted geographically but carried around by the potential criminal. Crimes does, however, occur in time and physical space, thus providing at least a physical parameter for target location. For example, if a neighborhood is highly accessible through public transportation or other means to populations which are characteristically high risks for criminal behavior, mere physical distance should not be excluded from the idea of neighborhood considerations.

Crime Deterrents in the Planning Stage

User Characteristics   Who do you anticipate will be using the environs of your building during the daytime, evening, nighttime, and early morning? What is the exposure level of your project to crimes against people and crimes against property? Will your facility bring people to the neighborhood who may cause security problems? Will your project provide positive security benefits like natural surveillance? It is no longer sufficient to make guesses, particularly if the building you are designing is by its nature a potential target for vandalism, theft, and employee victimization. It is important for you to know the characteristics of the users in your project's neighborhood.

Will the occupants of your building tend to stabilize the neighborhood environment, or will they introduce a new element of risk? Frequently, community groups resist new housing for fear of increasing exposure to potential criminal activity. For the same reason these groups also frequently resist commercial and institutional development in residential areas. What are the facts in your case? Crucial in determining whether a particular project will be designed to properly integrate into a neighborhood is the designer's sensitivity to these factors. The client will be able to advise on the characteristics of those who are expected to use the building. It may be necessary to sharpen the questions so that your design can reflect the client's security needs and those of the people who will actually live in the building. The perceptions of need of the landlord are not always the same as those of the tenant.

User characteristics for a neighborhood are difficult to come by. In most cases the designer will be required to spend a substantial amount of time in the neighborhood, assessing its present users as well as potential future users. In addition to the designer's assessment, other sources of information are the neighborhood residents themselves, other building owners, and various municipal agencies such as the Planning Commission and the Police Department. The checklist at the end of this chapter provides a convenient method of recording these evaluations. More explicit information related to this will be found in the section on nonphysical parameters of security in the material which follows.

Urban Frame   Residential areas run the gamut from high-rise inner-city to sprawling suburban, each with its own set of unique security problems. Two principal elements of concern, regardless of residential density, are user characteristics and accessibility, of which the accessibility dimension is the most important in considering the urban frame. The designer should be alert to changes in the neighborhood which make building sites more or less accessible to potential criminals—new or improved arterial streets, public transit facilities, adjacent developments, and the like.

The only constant in urban neighborhoods is the fact of change. In a security sense, neighborhoods constantly change physically and socially. This directly affects the security of individuals and property for better or worse. Designers must anticipate these shifts, so that their buildings have the flexibility to cope with change. There are no formulas, no easy answers to these questions. The sensitivity and insight of the designer are crucial.

ELEMENTS FOR CONSIDERATION IN DESIGN AND PLANNING

Zoning, Density, Transportation, and Urban Planning

Make a visit to local planning authorities to determine what the city's general plan says about the neighborhood and its future. Examine the existing and proposed transportation systems and the planning of any other major facilities which will have an impact upon accessibility or users of the area.

For years there has been a resistance to mixed uses in residential areas, i.e., to having commercial and industrial activities in residential areas and vice versa. Many citywide general plans reflect this concept. The common assumption is that the most profitable and best land use is a single-family detached residence on an individual lot. The introduction of commercial facilities and apartments is seen as bringing in undesirable transient people and creating traffic. Increased density and a mixture of uses do attract more people and quite frequently do lead to anonymity or a lesser sense of community. On the other hand the presence of people as observers, apart from other considerations, tends to create a system of informal surveillance. This is pointed out in Jane Jacobs' book, *The Death and Life of Great American Cities.*[5] The designer is left with a dilemma. An awareness of local circumstances and a sensitivity to security will enable the designer to produce a building which responds to neighborhood conditions. What works in New York City may not work in Palo Alto.

Block Face Characteristics

The block face is a much smaller piece of urban fabric than a neighborhood. It involves the several hundred feet on either side of the building site. Check the lighting, level of traffic, parking facilities, kind of buildings, alleyways, and so on. All of these physical factors are related to security problems. Lighting, of course, has tended to reduce crime in urban areas. The physical arrangement of buildings and alleys can provide ideal escape routes and hiding places, both of which can increase the probability of crime, particularly if there is an adequate supply of potential victims on hand. A well-thought-out arrangement can facilitate police services. Security concerns have typically been absent in most urban development.

Check out the routes to public transportation and parking for automobiles. Also check out routes to public facilities and commercial facilities. Will residents in the building have to run the gauntlet in a high-risk area?

Within the scope of your project or through public action, can better street lighting, traffic patterns, parking, and public transportation stops be obtained so as to improve the security performance of the block face for the safety of the users of your building? (The checklist on the opposite page can be used to assess block face characteristics.)

Crime Information and Police Services

Architects and engineers would never design a building in an area of questionable soils without test borings for a soils and geological analysis. This research is necessary in order to design the foundations of a building properly and thus ensure the safety of its occupants. When it comes to security against crime, seldom if ever are "test borings" of the social conditions in the neighborhood taken. Yet the designer's concern for safety should go beyond the structural aspects of the building to the total wellbeing of those who use it. Safety from crime can be affected by physical design. In residential projects, the work of Oscar Newman in his book *Defensible Space*[8] demonstrates these relationships conclusively. The seldom-used behavioral "test borings" in the security area are crime statistics and other local intelligence acquired from the police department. Many excellent records kept by police are available to the public. Visit the police station closest to your project site. Find out whether there are problems with street crime, robbery, rape, or vandalism. Are there particularly dangerous areas near your site? If so, what efforts are being made to reduce these problems? Armed with this information, assess the design implications for your project.

Determine what public security services are in use and are available to your site. Check response times and typical patrolling activity. Check future police plans for improving the security in the neighborhoods surrounding your site. Identify your concerns and seek assistance.

CPTED Concepts

The idea of crime prevention through environmental design (CPTED) is quite new and lacks precision. CPTED deals with three factors to reduce crime: (1) physical facilities, (2) police services, and (3) user characteristics and behavior. In residential areas the key idea is to establish a sense of territoriality on both the neighborhood level and dwelling-unit level. The physical structure of a neighborhood provides environmental signals to those who use it. Intruders who may be up to no good should feel they are in someone else's territory. Further, they should feel they are being observed. The idea of natural surveillance is well developed by Jane Jacobs and Oscar Newman.

In an individual building, the physical arrangement can either encourage feelings of community and natural surveillance or hamper these positive forces of crime reduction. Oscar Newman's work provides striking evidence as to the importance of the physical setting in reducing crime.

BUILDING SECURITY CHECKLIST FOR RESIDENTIAL PROJECTS

I. User Characteristics as Conceived by Various Interested Parties	Residents	Landlord	Designer	Planning Commission
A.				
B.				
C.				
D.				
E.				
F.				
G.				
H.				

II. Public Services and Security	Level of quality	Projection improvement	Apparent deterioration	Comments
A. Police				
B. Fire				
C. Sanitation				
D. Water				
E. Sewer				
F. Recreation facilities				
G. Education				

III. Transportation: System and Facilities	Good	Average	Poor	Comments
A. Serves residents' needs				
B. Discourages through-traffic				
C. Minimizes conflicts between pedestrian and vehicular traffic				
D. Remote enough from arterial streets and public transportation to discourage impulse crime				

IV. Block Face Characteristics Consistent with a Secure Residential Neighborhood
A. Lighting
B. Level of traffic
C. Parking
D. Kinds of buildings
E. Alleyways
F. Public transportation stops
G. Potential for natural surveillance

V. Police Services as Crime Deterrents
A. Frequency and thoroughness of patrolling activity
B. Response times

VI. Crime Statistics as Related to a Secure Residential Neighborhood	Good	Average	Poor	Comments
A. Street crime				
B. Robbery				
C. Rape				
D. Vandalism				

VII. Designer's Analysis:

3-5

The objectives of CPTED are (1) to prevent crime through natural surveillance and (2) to discourage crime by increasing the risks of apprehension of criminals. This latter objective requires close cooperation between police, tenants, and, possibly, private security. While the physical aspects are important, CPTED depends on the unique interactions between the physical environment and the users. The chapter entitled "Multiple Housing" provides a comprehensive approach to this concept.

Public Processes

As important as the physical aspects of the neighborhood is the quality of services that will be provided by the local public authorities. Before any site is selected, it is well to examine the level of quality of public services and their projected long-run improvement or deterioration. Police services, sanitation, water supply, sewer facilities, recreation, and education fall into this service category. It should be remembered that it is not only the presence of police which deters crime. A sanitation worker, meter reader, recreation supervisor, and street repair worker are all community employees who may contribute to neighborhood security.

REFERENCES

1. Booth, Alan, Susan Welch, and David Richard Johnson, "A Reply to Higgins, Richards, and Swan," *Urban Affairs Quarterly,* vol. 11, no. 3, March 1976. (See Ref. 4.)
2. The Center for Residential Security Design, New York, *A Design Guide for Improving Residential Security,* U.S. Government Printing Office, Washington, DC, 1973.
3. Cruickshank, Dan, "Developers as Vandals," in Colin Ward (ed.), *Vandalism,* Van Nostrand, New York, 1973.
4. Higgins, Paul C., Pamela J. Richards, and James H. Swan, "Crowding and Urban Crime Rates," *Urban Affairs Quarterly,* vol. 11, no. 3, March 1976.
5. Jacobs, Jane, *The Death and Life of Great American Cities,* Random House, New York, 1961.
6. Liechtenstein, Michael, "Designing for Security" (P-4633, Paper presented for the AIAA Urban Technology Conference, New York, May 24–26, 1971), The New York City Rand Institute, New York.
7. National Advisory Commission on Criminal Justice Standards and Goals, *A National Strategy to Reduce Crime,* U.S. Government Printing Office, Washington, DC, 1973.
8. Newman, Oscar, *Defensible Space,* Macmillan, New York, 1972 (hardback edition).
9. ——— and S. Johnsten, *Model Security Code for Residential Areas,* Institute for Community Design Analysis, New York, 1974.
10. Reppetto, Thomas A., *Residential Crime,* Ballinger Publishing Co., Cambridge, MA, 1974.
11. Taylor, Laurie, "The Meaning of the Environment," in Colin Ward (ed.), *Vandalism* (see Ref. 3).
12. Ward, Colin, "Planners as Vandals," in Colin Ward (ed.), *Vandalism* (see Ref. 3).
13. Westinghouse Electric Corporation, *Crime Prevention Through Environmental Design (CPTED),* with annotated bibliography, Westinghouse Corporation, Arlington, VA, 1975.
14. Wood, Elizabeth, "Housing Design, A Social Theory," New York Citizens' Housing and Planning Council, 1961. [Reprinted in Gwen Bell and Jaqueline Tyrwhitt (eds.), *Human Identity in the Urban Environment,* Penguin Books, Baltimore, 1972, pp. 327–351.]
15. Wright, Roger, *The Impact of Street Lighting on Street Crime,* National Institute of Law Enforcement and Criminal Justice, Washington, DC, 1974.

Chapter 4

Building Security Codes

HARDY STORMES, JR.

Crime Prevention Officer, Concord Police Department, Concord, California;
Vice President, Northern California Crime Prevention Officers Association

SECURITY CODES: A NEW APPROACH

In November 1972 Concord, California, adopted a building security code which imposed minimum standards governing locks and security precautions on doors, windows, and other potential points of illegal entry on all new or substantially remodeled structures within the city. Compelled by a rising incidence of burglary, growing density, and forthcoming developments, this middle-class suburban community responded to its problems in a manner which is rapidly becoming a trend across the nation. Based on the same legal considerations that support state and local fire and building regulations, local governments—and in some cases states—are exercising their delegated power to establish minimum standards of design, construction, and quality of materials used as security devices or for security precautions.

The net result of these legislative enactments has drawn criticism and revolt from developers and builders, who find the provisions an added expense and another troublesome procedure to cope with in competitively marketing their product. Many cannot understand the rationale used by proponents of building security codes and argue that they should not be compelled to provide protective devices which, even when used, will not stop illegal entry by a knowledgeable or determined thief.

Critics of building security codes, like most people today, are very often ignorant of the nature of burglary, the burglar, and what they as individuals can do to protect themselves against being victimized. Their misconceptions and preconceived ideas have created an atmosphere in which the lack of positive protective action and a defeatist attitude have done much to perpetuate the crime of burglary. As the problem increases, especially at its present volume, it disporportionately taxes our coping ability and faith in social values. To address the true nature of the problem, we must attack it from a realistic viewpoint and divorce ourselves from the stereotyping created by our previous conception of a burglar.

Insight into the burglary problem should provide a justification for building security codes and, it is hoped, stimulate an appreciation for the specific provisions to encourage their use even when legal compulsion is not there. It should also provide the designer with the knowledge necessary to compensate for the weaknesses in physical design outlined in the codes.

CHIEF PURPOSES OF CODES

First of all, the building security code is not intended to prevent a determined and knowledgeable thief from entering a building or structure if he or she wishes to do so. The principle of minimum standards does not imply an intensified effort at resisting forced entry. The purpose of minimum standards derives from an understanding of the relationship between opportunity and criminal behavior and a realization of the ineffectiveness of traditional security devices. The provisions are intended to make illegal entry more difficult, thereby preventing opportunistic burglaries.

In order for a crime to take place, three elements must be present—desire, ability, and opportunity; furthermore, all three must be in existence *at the same time*. It is not sufficient for a person to have the ability and opportunity to commit a theft if the desire is not also present. Similarly, if the person has the desire and ability without the opportunity, no theft can occur. Thus, if it is our intention to reduce the occurrence of crime, we must remove one or more of the "necessary, but not sufficient" elements.

Opportunity and ability are elements grossly abused because erroneous interpretation of the burglary threat will not permit a logical understanding of their importance. In 1970 and 1971 the California Bureau of Criminal Statistics (BCS) took a close look at what is generally considered to be the professionally committed burglary and the professional burglar in two publications, "Safe Burglaries in California" and "Safe Burglars, Part II." In these studies, the crime of safe burglary was probed. It was found that this particular offense was only the tip of the iceberg, representing about 1 percent of the total burglaries reported. The studies concluded that there was a gradual decline in occurrence of this offense in relation to other property crimes. Professionals, then, would seem to account for only a small proportion of the burglaries committed in California.

To answer the question of who *was* in fact committing the burglaries in California, the BCS initiated a study to draw a profile of the average burglar in California. The 1972 publication, "The Burglar in California: A Profile," came to the major conclusion that "burglary is primarily a crime of opportunity rather than the work of professionals." It noted that patterns of burglary arrests since 1960 had changed from predominantly adult arrests to current ratios of about half adults and half juveniles (under 18 years of age).

The ratio of adult to juvenile offenders will naturally differ from community to community. As an example, in Concord it was found that approximately 77 percent of the reported burglaries were committed by youthful offenders. While this does little to establish the relative skill possessed by offenders, it does paint a more realistic picture of the burglary threat.

Experience has demonstrated that measures aimed at "hardening the target" are effective deterrents. This is not to say that the physical resistance of most devices will prevent illegal entry, but it is indicative of the displacement effect known to occur when target hardening is not universal. The opportunist burglar seeks out a target by locating an obviously unoccupied structure which will accommodate that individual's mode of entry in the swiftest and easiest way. By restricting the ability and limiting possible victims, the opportunist is forced to take risks greater than his or her personal reward factor will permit.

Since the building security code's purpose is to prevent opportunistic burglaries, it can have a major impact on the incidence of professional burglaries as well. Often, skillful burglars will use the weaknesses of adjoining buildings to assist them in attacking well-protected buildings. This assistance might be in the form of roof access, basement access, or concealment while forcing entry through a door or wall. Like opportunist criminals, skilled burglars know that the longer it takes them to get inside or the more noise they must make, the greater is the risk of detection and apprehension. These facts also demonstrate the substantial interest any given structure has in a neighboring structure's security.

Legislative provisions establishing minimum standards for security devices and precautions would hardly be necessary if the average citizen realized the meaning of adequate security. Many find out too late and, once informed, find the replacement cost for inadequate doors, windows, and locks prohibitive. Most assumed that they were receiving adequate protection from a quality product when they purchased their structure. Builders themselves may or may not be aware of the quality of the security devices they use; yet all too often their concern is more in the direction of profit margin. Either way, the building security code ensures that reasonable protection will be provided and that the devices installed will be quality products.

The cost of installing security devices at the time of construction is small when compared with the total cost of a home, office, or commercial building. In Concord, it was found that the additional costs of meeting the residential requirements averaged from $60 to $150 per unit, depending upon the kind of materials previously used by the builder. This is a relatively small cost which the average buyer would be more than willing to accept if he or she were aware of the alternatives

THE FAILURE OF TRADITIONAL SECURITY DEVICES

How are our traditional security devices failing? What are the alternatives?

So far, we have delved into conceptual justification and presumptive value for a building security code. We discussed opportunity and how it affects vulnerability. Still, a firm grasp of these concepts cannot be absorbed without examining the traditional security devices and learning the weaknesses which burglars have found rewarding.

First of all, consider the basic key-in-knob lock used on most doors, especially residential dwellings. There are several basic weaknesses of this lock. The first lies in the fact that the locking cylinder is in the knob (whence the name), and once the knob is twisted or broken off, the lock has been defeated. A pipe wrench, channel lock pliers, and a piece of diesel exhaust pipe are popular tools used by burglars to capitalize on this weakness.

Another weakness of the key-in-knob lock is the beveled spring-loaded latch which protrudes into the strike on the door jamb and holds the door closed. The first problem created by the spring latch has to do with the distance the latch extends. The most expensive spring latches have a maximum $5/8$-in throw, with the more common having about $1/2$- to $3/8$-in throws. The importance of maximum bolt projection in protecting the door against forced opening becomes readily apparent when considering tolerances of door fittings, the usual contraction of wood, and the flexibility of the door frame. A screwdriver, pry bar, or tire iron wedged between the door and the jamb easily develops the leverage needed to overcome the short distance these latches extend. A bumper jack inserted within the outside door frame will easily spread the frame enough to pop the door open.

The final major weakness of the spring latch is found in the type that has no deadlocking trigger bolt. This bolt is a feature mounted on the flat side of the spring latch. When the door is closed, the strike holds the trigger bolt in, thereby locking the spring latch. Locks without this trigger bolt are vulnerable because the spring latch is not locked, and a piece of celluloid or a credit card can be slipped between the door and the frame, forcing the spring latch back into the door.

Special note should be taken of the methods outlined above, as these are the more common ways in which burglars take advantage of our traditional locking devices; such techniques provide swift, quiet circumvention without the use of sophisticated tools.

Another area in which traditional locking devices and security precautions create vulnerability is that inherent in the type of door or window to be used. For instance, doors that open toward the outside generally have hinges mounted so that the pins are exteriorly exposed. Removal of the hinge pins will allow the door to be opened or removed in most cases, even when a good locking device is used on the other side.

Aluminum-frame sliding doors and windows, especially the latter, are coming to dominate the market. Their vulnerability lies in their light aluminum construction, which, if not reinforced, cannot provide its locking mechanism with the strength to withstand the force developed by a screwdriver, pry bar, buck knife, or tire iron. Many of the sliding-type doors and windows have an appreciable amount of vertical freedom which enables the door or window to be lifted in and out of the guide track. This movement also permits manipulation of the sliding section into positions that can disengage the locking device.

The once popular louvered window permits easy removal of the glass panes without the use of special tools, even in some cases without the use of any tool. Fortunately, the cost of louvered windows has kept their use to a minimum, and the building security code's restrictive provision should lessen their number even further.

Commercial structures often suffer the same vulnerable weak points as residential dwellings. The point least recognized is that commercial burglaries are often committed through points of entry other than the doors and windows. Attention must also be given to commercial buildings without consideration for their intended use. Although the use will many times dictate the potential threat, and although the building security code has special provisions for establishments with specific types of inventories, it is not uncommon for a new user to move into an existing structure and completely change the vulnerability factor. A good example would be a coin shop moving into what was once a barber shop. Minimum standards should apply uniformly so that the structure will provide a certain level of protection recognized as necessary for all.

Inadequate design of a commercial building can create security problems or negate many of the provisions which the building security code addresses. For example, accessible windows not visible from the street must be protected. Since the requirements for protecting windows can be costly, it would be well to keep the number of accessible windows not visible from the street to a minimum. Glass in or next to a door is another feature requiring burglar-resistant material or a specific kind of protection. A good rule of thumb is to keep glass at least 40 inches away from the door.

Rooftops provide many access points for illegal entry. Today's concern for aesthetics has created the need to design roofs in a manner which hides unsightly air-conditioning units and other equipment on the roof. This concealment is favorable to thieves because it provides them with the protection they need to remove an air-duct cover, hatchway cover, or skylight.

Thus, the first means of protection for the roof should be a limited-access situation—that is, one where it is difficult to get on the roof. Ladders required by building or fire regulations should be guarded or, if possible, mounted on the interior. Elements such as trellis supports or terraces should not be included if they provide easy roof access.

In many cases, air ducts, skylights, or exhaust vents are large enough to permit easy access into a building. Limiting the size of ducts and vents to under 8 by 12 in, or multiples thereof, will eliminate the need for further security measures. Should a large opening be required, a security grating in the duct interior can be provided as an effective barrier to further penetration by a burglar. Skylights should be limited in design to be long and narrow, not more than 8 inches wide. Alarms should be provided for larger openings.

These basic weaknesses in building design provide opportunities that permit an unskilled burglar to effect illegal entry. Accepting the fact that improved hardware and special security precautions will provide a reasonable level of protection is a step toward changing the trend of criminal activity.

THE BUILDING SECURITY CODE

The building security code places the responsibility for compliance on the owner of a building. Generally, the builder is charged with the task of meeting the specifications set forth in the code at the time of construction. Security can be addressed much more sensibly at the early stages of a development instead of as an afterthought.

Many other factors can and should be considered in order to provide a better knowledge of crime prevention through physical planning. In Concord, planners recognized the advantages (and even the necessity) of having law enforcement personnel become involved in the planning process and responded by including a police representative on their staff. After all, who is in a better position to respond to questions concerning criminal activity?

The building security code was not designed or intended to provide a level of security which would make illegal entry impossible. The specific provisions were conceived by law enforcement personnel from first-hand knowledge of the crime of burglary. Buildings and structures should have a minimum level of security, and codes at least establish a standard which is far better than we have had in the past.

It is hoped that the work of such agencies as the California Crime Technological Research Foundation will raise the standards to a more satisfactory level and provide the pressure on manufacturers of building materials to become more security-conscious. (The reader is referred to Chapter 13, "Doors and Windows," where some of these standards are described.)

* * * * *

OAKLAND MODEL BURGLARY SECURITY CODE
Minimum Standards

I. Purpose. The purpose of this Code is to provide minimum standards to safeguard property and public welfare by regulating and controlling the design, construction, quality of materials, use and occupancy, location and maintenance of all buildings and structures within a city and certain equipment specifically regulated herein.

II. Development of Model Code. The following City Ordinances were used as guides in developing the model code: General Ordinance No. 25, 1969, as amended, City of Indianapolis, Indiana—Section 605-3—F211 Housing Inspection and Code Enforcement, Trenton, New Jersey—Section 23-405 of the Arlington Heights Village, Illinois, Code—Section 614.46 Chapter 3 of the Arlington County, Virginia, Building Code—Section H-323.4 of the Prince George's County, Maryland Housing Code—City of Oakland, California Building Code—Burglary Prevention Ordinance, Oakland, California.

III. Scope. The provisions of the Code shall apply to new construction and to buildings or structures to which additions, alterations or repairs are made except as specifically provided in this Code. When additions, alterations or repairs within any 12-month period exceed 50 per cent of the replacement value of the existing building or structure, such building or structure shall be made to conform to the requirements for new buildings or structures.

IV. Applications to Existing Buildings. (It is the Committee's recommendation that the Code apply only to new construction, additions, alterations or repairs. However, some cities may wish to include present structures. If so, the following paragraph may be substituted for III. above.)

All existing and future buildings in the city shall, when unattended, be so secured as to prevent unauthorized entry, in accordance with specifications for physical security of accessible openings as provided in this Code.

V. Alternate Materials and Methods of Construction. The provisions of this Code are not intended to prevent the use of any material or method of construction not specifically prescribed by this Code, provided any such alternate has been approved, nor is it the intention of this Code to exclude any sound method of structural design or analysis not specifically provided for in this Code. Structural design limitations given in this Code are to be used as a guide only, and exceptions thereto may be made if substantiated by calculations or other suitable evidence prepared by a qualified person.

The enforcing authority may approve any such alternate provided he finds the proposed design is satisfactory and the material, method or work offered is, for the purpose intended, at least equivalent of that prescribed in this Code in quality, strength, effectiveness, burglary resistance, durability and safety.

VI. Tests. Whenever there is insufficient evidence of compliance with the provisions of this Code or evidence that any material or any construction does not conform to the requirements of this Code, or in order to substantiate claims for alternate materials or methods of construction, the enforcing authority may require tests as proof of compliance to be made at the expense of the owner or his agent by an approved agency.

VII. Enforcement. The Multiple Dwelling and Private Dwelling Ordinances shall be included in the Building Code and enforced by the Building Official. The Commercial Ordinance shall be administered and enforced by the Chief of Police.

VIII. Responsibility for Security. The owner or his designated agent shall be responsible for compliance with the specifications set forth in this Code.

IX. Violations and Penalties. It shall be unlawful for any person, firm, or corporation to erect, construct, enlarge, alter, repair, move, improve, remove, convert or demolish, equip, use, occupy or maintain any building or structure in the city, or cause the same to be done, contrary to or in violation of any of the provisions of this Code.

Any person, firm, or corporation violating any of the provisions of this Code shall be deemed guilty of a misdemeanor and shall be punishable by a fine of not more than $500, or by imprisonment for not more than six months, or by both such fine and imprisonment.

X. Appeals. In order to prevent or lessen unnecessary hardship or practical difficulties in exceptional cases where it is difficult or impossible to comply with the strict letter of this Code, and in order to determine the suitability of alternate materials and types of construction and to provide for reasonable interpretations of the provisions of this Code, there shall be created a Board of Examiners and Appeals (if none exist). The Board shall exercise its powers on these matters in such a way that the public welfare is secured, and substantial justice done most nearly in accord with the intent and purpose of this Code.

Model Commercial Burglary Security Ordinance
Minimum Standards

I. All Exterior Doors Shall Be Secured As Follows:

    A. A single door shall be secured with either a double cylinder deadbolt or a single cylinder deadbolt without a turnpiece with a minimum throw of one inch. A hook or expanding bolt may have a throw of $3/4$ inch. Any deadbolt must contain hardened material to repel attempts at cutting through the bolt.

    B. On pairs of doors, the active leaf shall be secured with the type lock required for single doors in (A) above. The inactive leaf shall be equipped with flush bolts protected by hardened material with a minimum throw of $5/8$ inch at head and foot. Multiple point locks, cylinder activated from the active leaf and satisfying (I, A and B) above may be used in lieu of flush bolts.

C. Any single or pair of doors requiring locking at the bottom or top rail shall have locks with a minimum ⅝ inch throw bolt at both the top and bottom rails.

D. Cylinders shall be so designed or protected so they cannot be gripped by pliers or other wrenching devices.

E. Exterior sliding commercial entrances shall be secured as in (A, B & D) above, with special attention given to safety regulations.

F. Rolling overhead doors, solid overhead swinging, sliding or accordion garage-type doors shall be secured with a cylinder lock or padlock on the inside, when not otherwise controlled or locked by electric power operation. If a padlock is used, it shall be of hardened steel shackle, with minimum five pin tumbler operation with non-removable key when in an unlocked position.

G. Metal accordion grate or grill-type doors shall be equipped with metal guide track at top and bottom, and a cylinder lock and/or padlock with hardened steel shackle and minimum five pin tumbler operation with non-removable key when in an unlocked position. The bottom track shall be so designed that the door cannot be lifted from the track when the door is in a locked position.

H. Outside hinges on all exterior doors shall be provided with nonremovable pins when using pin-type hinges.

I. Doors with glass panels and doors that have glass panels adjacent to the door frame shall be secured as follows:
  1. Rated burglary-resistant glass or glass-like material, or
  2. The glass shall be covered with iron bars of at least one half-inch round or 1″ × ¼″ flat steel material, spaced not more than five inches apart, secured on the inside of the glazing, or
  3. Iron or steel grills of at least ⅛″ material of 2″ mesh secured on the inside of the glazing.

J. Inswinging doors shall have rabbeted jambs.

K. Wood doors, not of solid core construction, or with panels therein less than 1⅜″ thick, shall be covered on the inside with at least 16 gauge sheet steel or its equivalent attached with screws on minimum six inch centers.

L. Jambs for all doors shall be so constructed or protected so as to prevent violation of the function of the strike.

M. All exterior doors, excluding front doors, shall have a minimum of 60-watt bulb over the outside of the door. Such bulb shall be protected with a vapor cover or cover of equal breaking resistant material.

II. Glass Windows:

A. Accessible rear and side windows not viewable from the street shall consist of rated burglary resistant glass or glass-like material. Fire Department approval shall be obtained on type of glazing used.

B. If the accessible side or rear window is of the openable type it shall be secured on the inside with a locking device capable of withstanding a force of 300 pounds applied in any direction.

C. Louvered windows shall not be used within eight feet of ground level, adjacent structures or fire escapes.

D. Outside hinges on all accessible side and rear glass windows shall be provided with non-removable pins. If the hinge screws are accessible the screws shall be of the non-removable type.

III. Accessible Transoms:

All exterior transoms exceeding 8″ × 12″ on the side and rear of any building or premises used for business purposes shall be protected by one of the following:
  1. Rated burglary-resistant glass or glass-like material, or
  2. Outside iron bars of at least ½″ round or 1″ × ¼″ flat steel material, spaced no more than 5″ apart, or
  3. Outside iron or steel grills of at least ⅛″ material but not more than 2″ mesh

    4. The window barrier shall be secured with rounded-head flush bolts on the outside.

IV. Roof Openings:

  A. All glass skylights on the roof of any building or premises used for business purposes shall be provided with:

    1. Rated burglary-resistant glass or glass-like material meeting Code requirements, or

    2. Iron bars of at least ½″ round or 1″ × ¼″ flat steel material under the skylight and securely fastened, or

    3. A steel grill of at least ⅛″ material of 2″ mesh under the skylight and securely fastened.

  B. All hatchway openings on the roof of any building or premises used for business purposes shall be secured as follows:

    1. If the hatchway is of wooden material, it shall be covered on the inside with at least 16 gauge sheet steel or its equivalent attached with screws.

    2. The hatchway shall be secured from the inside with a slide bar or slide bolts. The use of crossbar or padlock must be approved by the Fire Marshal.

    3. Outside hinges on all hatchway openings shall be provided with non-removable pins when using pin-type hinges.

  C. All air duct or air vent openings exceeding 8″ × 12″ on the roof or exterior walls of any building or premise used for business purposes shall be secured by covering the same with either of the following:

    1. Iron bars of at least ½″ round or 1″ × ¼″ flat steel material spaced no more than 5″ apart and securely fastened, or

    2. A steel grill of at least ⅛″ material of 2″ mesh and securely fastened.

    3. If the barrier is on the outside, it shall be secured with rounded head flush bolts on the outside.

V. Special Security Measures:

  A. Safes: Commercial establishments having $1,000 or more in cash on the premises after closing hours shall lock such money in a Class "E" safe after closing hours.

  B. Office Buildings (Multiple Occupancy): All entrance doors to individual office suites shall have a deadbolt lock with a minimum one inch throw bolt which can be opened from the inside.

VI. Intrusion Detection Devices:

  A. If it is determined by the enforcing authority of this ordinance that the security measures and locking devices described in this ordinance do not adequately secure the building, he may require the installation and maintenance of an intrusion detection device (Burglar Alarm System).

  B. Establishments having specific type inventories shall be protected by the following type alarm service:

    1. Silent Alarm—Central Station—Supervised Service
      a. Jewelry store—Mfg., wholesale, and retail
      b. Guns and ammo shops
      c. Wholesale liquor
      d. Wholesale tobacco
      e. Wholesale drugs
      f. Fur stores

    2. Silent Alarm
      a. Liquor stores
      b. Pawn shops
      c. Electronic equipment
      d. Wig stores
      e. Clothing (new)
      f. Coins and stamps
      g. Industrial tool supply houses

       h. Camera stores
       i. Precious metal storage facility
    3. Local Alarm (Bell outside premise)
       a. Antique dealers
       b. Art galleries
       c. Service stations

VII. Exceptions:

No portion of this Code shall supersede any local, state or Federal laws, regulations, or codes dealing with the life-safety factor.

Enforcement of this ordinance should be developed with the cooperation of the local fire authority to avoid possible conflict with fire laws.

Model Private Dwelling Security Ordinance
Minimum Standards

I. Exterior Doors:

  A. Exterior doors and doors leading from garage areas into private family dwellings shall be of solid core no less than 1¾ inches thick.

  B. Exterior doors and doors leading from garage areas into private family dwellings shall have self-locking (dead latch) devices with a minimum throw of one-half inch.

  C. Vision panels in exterior doors or within reach of the inside activating device must be of burglary-resistant material or equivalent as approved by the Building Official.

  D. Exterior doors swinging out shall have non-removable hinge pins.

  E. In-swinging exterior doors shall have rabbeted jambs.

  F. Jambs for all doors shall be so constructed or protected so as to prevent violation of the function of the strike.

II. Sliding Patio-Type Doors Opening Onto Patios or Balconies Which Are Less Than One Store Above Grade or Are Otherwise Accessible from the Outside:

  A. All single sliding patio doors shall have the movable section of the door sliding on the inside of the fixed portion of the door.

  B. Dead locks shall be provided on all single sliding patio doors. The lock shall be operable from the outside by a key utilizing a bored lock cylinder of pin tumbler construction. Mounting screws for the lock case shall be inaccessible from the outside. Lock bolts shall be of hardened steel or have hardened steel inserts and shall be capable of withstanding a force of 800 pounds applied in any direction. The lock bolt shall engage the strike sufficiently to prevent its being disengaged by any possible movement of the door within the space or clearances provided for installation and operation. The strike area shall be reinforced to maintain effectiveness of bolt strength.

  C. Double sliding patio doors must be locked at the meeting rail and meet the locking requirements of "B" above.

III. Window Protection:

  A. Windows shall be so constructed that when the window is locked it cannot be lifted from the frame.

  B. Window locking devices shall be capable of withstanding a force of 300 pounds applied in any direction.

  C. Louvered windows shall not be used within eight feet of ground level.

IV. It Shall Be Unlawful to Furnish Overhead Garage Doors with Bottom Vents.

V. Exceptions:

No portion of this Code shall supersede any local, state or Federal laws, regulations, or codes dealing with the life-safety factor.

Enforcement of this ordinance should be developed with the cooperation of the local fire laws.

Model Multiple-Dwelling Security Ordinance
Minimum Standards

I. Exterior Doors:

    A. Exterior doors and doors leading from garage areas into multiple-dwelling buildings and doors leading into stairwells below the sixth-floor level shall have self-locking (dead latch) devices, allowing egress to the exterior of the building or into the garage area, or stairwell, but requiring a key be used to gain access to the interior of the building from the outside or garage area or into the hallways from the stairwell.

    B. Exterior doors and doors leading from the garage areas into multiple-dwelling buildings and doors leading into stairwells shall be equipped with self-closing devices, if not already required by other regulations, ordinance, or code.

II. Garage Doors:

    Whenever parking facilities are provided, either under or within the confines of the perimeter walls of any multiple dwelling, such facility shall be fully enclosed and provided with a locking device.

III. All Swinging Doors to Individual Motel, Hotel, and Multi-Family Dwellings:

    A. All wood doors shall be of solid core with a minimum thickness of 1¾ inches.

    B. Swinging entrance doors to individual units shall have deadbolts with one-inch minimum throw and hardened steel inserts in addition to deadlatches with half-inch minimum throw. The locks shall be so constructed that both deadbolt and deadlatch can be retracted by a single action of the inside door knob. Alternate devices to equally resist illegal entry may be substituted subject to prior approval of the Police Department.

    C. An interviewer or peephole shall be provided in each individual unit entrance door.

    D. Door closers will be provided on each individual entrance door.

    E. Doors swinging out shall have non-removable hinge pins.

    F. In-swinging exterior doors shall have rabbeted jambs.

    G. Jambs for all doors shall be so constructed or protected so as to prevent violation of the function of the strike.

IV. Sliding Patio-Type Doors Opening onto Patios or Balconies Which Are Less Than One Store above Grade Or Are Otherwise Accessible from the Outside:

    A. All single sliding patio doors shall have the movable section of the door slide on the inside of the fixed portion of the door.

    B. Dead locks shall be provided on all single sliding patio doors. The lock shall be operable from the outside by a key utilizing a bored lock cylinder of pin tumbler construction. Mounting screws for the lock case shall be inaccessible from the outside. Lock bolts shall be of hardened material or have hardened steel inserts and shall be capable of withstanding a force of 800 pounds applied in any direction. The lock bolts shall engage the strike sufficiently to prevent its being disengaged by any possible movement of the door within the space or clearances provided for installation and operation. The strike area shall be reinforced to maintain effectiveness of bolt strength.

    C. Double sliding patio doors must be locked at the meeting rail and meet the locking requirements of "B" above.

V. Window Protection:

    A. Windows shall be so constructed that when the window is locked it cannot be lifted from the frame.

    B. Window locking devices shall be capable of withstanding a force of 300 pounds applied in any direction.

C. Louvered windows shall not be used within eight feet of ground level, adjacent structures, or fire escapes.

VI. Exceptions:

No portion of this Code shall supersede any local, state or Federal laws, regulations, or codes dealing with the life-safety factors.

Enforcement of this ordinance should be developed with the cooperation of the local fire authority to avoid possible conflict with fire laws.

*   *   *   *   *

COUNTY OF LOS ANGELES

Chapter 67: Security Provisions

Section 6701: Purpose. The purpose of this chapter is to set forth minimum standards of construction for resistance to unlawful entry.

Section 6702: Scope. The provisions of this chapter shall apply to enclosed Group F, G, H, I, and J Occupancies regulated by this Code. EXCEPTION: The requirements shall not apply to enclosed Group J Occupancies having no opening to an attached building or which are completely detached.

Section 6703: Limitations. No provision of this Chapter shall require or be construed to require devices on exit doors contrary to the requirements specified in Chapter 33.

Section 6704: Alternate Security Provisions. The provisions of this Chapter are not intended to prevent the use of any device or method of construction not specifically prescribed by this Code when such alternate provides equivalent security based upon a recommendation of the County Sheriff.

Section 6705: Definitions. For the purpose of this Chapter, certain terms are defined as follows:

1. **Cylinder guard** is a hardened ring surrounding the exposed portion of the lock cylinder or other device which is so fastened as to protect the cylinder from wrenching, prying, cutting or pulling by attack tools.
2. **Deadlocking latch** is a latch in which the latch bolt is positively held in the projected position by a guard bolt, plunger, or auxiliary mechanism.
3. **Deadbolt** is a bolt which has no automatic spring action and which is operated by a key cylinder, thumbturn, or lever, and is positively held fast when in the projected position.
4. **Latch** is a device for automatically retaining the door in a closed position upon its closing.

Section 6706: Tests. Sliding Glass Doors. Panels shall be closed and locked. Tests shall be performed in the following order:

a. TEST A: With the panels in the normal position, a concentrated load of 300 pounds shall be applied separately to each vertical pull stile incorporating a locking device at a point on the stile within six inches of the locking device in the direction parallel to the plane of glass that would tend to open the door.
b. TEST B: Repeat Test A while simultaneously adding a concentrated load of 150 pounds to the same area of the same stile in a direction perpendicular to the plane of glass toward the interior side of the door.
c. TEST C: Repeat Test B with the 150 pound force in the reversed direction towards the exterior side of the door.
d. TESTS D, E, and F: Repeat A, B, and C with the movable panel lifted upwards to its full limit within the confines of the door frame.

Section 6707: Tests. Sliding Glass Windows. Sash shall be closed and locked. Tests shall be performed in the following order:

    a. TEST A: With the sliding sash in the normal position, a concentrated load of 150 pounds shall be applied separately to each sash member incorporating a locking device at a point on the sash member within six (6) inches of the locking device in the direction parallel to the plane of glass that would tend to open the window.

    b. TEST B: Repeat Test A while simultaneously adding a concentrated load of 75 pounds to the same area of the same sash member in the direction perpendicular to the plane of glass toward the interior side of the window.

    c. TEST C: Repeat Test B with the 75 pound force in the reversed direction towards the exterior side of the window.

    d. TESTS D, E, and F: Repeat Tests A, B, and C with the movable sash lifted upwards to its full limit within the confines of the window frame.

Section 6708: Doors—General. A door forming a part of the enclosure of a dwelling unit or of an area occupied by one tenant of a building shall be constructed, installed, and secured as set forth in Sections 6709, 6710, 6711, and 6712, when such door is directly reachable or capable of being reached from a street, highway, yard, court, passageway, corridor, balcony, patio, breezeway, private garage, portion of the building which is available for use by the public or other tenants, or similar area. A door enclosing a private garage with an interior opening leading directly to a dwelling unit shall also comply with said Sections 6709, 6710, 6711, and 6712.

Section 6709: Doors—Swinging Doors

    a. Swinging wooden doors, openable from the inside without the use of a key and which are either of hollow-core construction or less than $1\frac{3}{8}$ inches in thickness, shall be covered on the inside face with 16 gauge sheet metal attached with screws at six (6) inch maximum centers around the perimeter or equivalent. Lights in doors shall be as set forth in Sections 6714 and 6715.

    b. A single swinging door, the active leaf of a pair of doors, and the bottom leaf of Dutch doors shall be equipped with a deadbolt and a deadlocking latch. The deadbolt and latch may be activated by one lock or by individual locks. Deadbolts shall contain hardened inserts or equivalent, so as to repel cutting-tool attack. The lock or locks shall be key-operated from the exterior side of the door and engaged or disengaged from the interior side of the door by a device not requiring a key or special knowledge or effort. EXCEPTION:

      (1) The latch may be omitted from doors in Group F and G occupancies.

      (2) Locks may be key or otherwise operated from the inside when not prohibited by Chapter 33 or other laws and regulations.

      (3) A swinging door of width greater than five (5) feet may be secured as set forth in Section 6711. A straight deadbolt shall have a minimum throw of one inch and the embedment shall be not less than $\frac{5}{8}$ inch into the holding device receiving the projected bolt; a hook shape or expanding lug deadbolt shall have a minimum throw of $\frac{3}{4}$ inch. All deadbolts of locks which automatically activate two or more deadbolts shall embed at least $\frac{1}{2}$ inch but need not exceed $\frac{3}{4}$ inch into the holding devices receiving the projected bolts.

    c. The inactive leaf of a pair of doors and the upper leaf of Dutch doors shall be equipped with a deadbolt or deadbolts as set forth in Subsection (b). EXCEPTION:

      (1) The bolt or bolts need not be key operated, but shall not be otherwise activated from the exterior side of the door.

      (2) The bolt or bolts may be engaged or disengaged automatically with the deadbolt or by another device on the active leaf or lower leaf.

      (3) Manually operated hardened bolts at the top and bottom of the leaf and which embed a minimum of $\frac{1}{2}$ inch into the device receiving the projected bolt may be used when not prohibited by Chapter 33 or other laws and regulations.

    d. Door stops on wooden jambs for in-swinging doors shall be of one piece construction with the jamb or joined by a rabbet.

    e. Nonremovable pins shall be used in pin-type hinges which are accessible from the outside when the door is closed.

    f. Cylinder guards shall be installed on all mortise or rim-type cylinder locks installed in hollow metal doors whenever the cylinder projects beyond the face of the door or is otherwise accessible to gripping tools.

Section 6710: Doors—Sliding Glass Doors. Sliding glass doors shall be equipped with locking devices and shall be so installed that, when subjected to tests specified in Section 6706, remain intact and engaged. Movable panels shall not be rendered easily openable or removable from the frame during or after the tests. Cylinder guards shall be installed on all mortise or rim-type cylinder locks installed in hollow metal doors whenever the cylinder projects beyond the face of the door or is otherwise accessible to gripping tools.

Section 6711: Doors—Overhead and Sliding Doors. Metal or wooden overhead and sliding doors shall be secured with a cylinder lock, padlock with a hardened steel shackle, metal slide bar, bolt or equivalent when not otewise locked by electric power operation.

Cylinder guards shall be installed on all mortise or rim-type cylinder locks installed in hollow metal doors whenever the cylinder projects beyond the face of the door or is otherwise accessible to gripping tools.

Section 6712: Doors—Metal Accordion Grate or Grille-Type Doors. Metal accordion grate or grille-type doors shall be equipped with metal guides at top and bottom, and cylinder lock or padlock and hardened steel shackle shall be provided. Cylinder guards shall be installed on all mortise or rim-type cylinder locks installed in hollow metal doors whenever the cylinder projects beyond the face of the door or is otherwise accessible to gripping tools.

Section 6713: Lights—General. A window, skylight, or other light forming a part of the enclosure of a dwelling unit or of an area occupied by one tenant of a building shall be constructed, installed and secured as set forth in Sections 6714 and 6715, when the bottom of such window, skylight or light is not more than sixteen (16) feet above the grade of a street, highway, yard, court, passageway, corridor, balcony, patio, breezeway, private garage, portion of the building which is available for use by the public or other tenants, or similar area.

A window enclosing a private garage with an interior opening leading directly to a dwelling unit shall also comply with said Sections 6714 and 6715.

Section 6714: Lights—Material. Lights within forty (40) inches of a required locking device on a door when in the closed and locked position and openable from the inside without the use of a key, and lights with a least dimension greater than six (6) inches but less than forty-eight (48) inches in F and G Occupancies, shall be of fully tempered glass or approved burglary-resistant material or guarded by metal bars, screens or grilles in an approved manner.

Section 6715: Lights—Locking Devices

 a. Sliding glass windows shall be provided with locking devices that, when subjected to the tests specified in Section 6707, remain intact and engaged. Movable panels shall not be rendered easily openable or removable from the frame during or after the tests.

 b. Other openable windows shall be provided with substantial locking devices which render the building as secure as the devices required by this section. In Group F and G Occupancies, such devices shall be a glide bar, bolt, cross bar, and/or padlock with hardened steel shackle.

 c. Special louvered windows, except those above the first story in Group H and I Occupancies which cannot be reached without a ladder, shall be of material or guarded as specified in Section 6714, and individual panes shall be securely fastened by mechanical fasteners requiring a tool for removal and not accessible from the outside when the window is in the closed position.

Section 6716: Other Openings—General. Openings, other than doors or lights, which form a part of the enclosure, or portion thereof, housing a single occupant, and the bottom of which is not more than sixteen (16) feet above the grade of a street, highway, yard, court, passageway, corridor, balcony, patio, breezeway, or similar area, or from a private garage, or from a portion of the building which is occupied, used or available for use by the public or other tenants, or an opening enclosing a private garage attached to a dwelling unit with openings therein shall be constructed, installed and secured as set forth in Section 6717.

Section 6717: Hatchways, Scuttles, and Similar Openings

a. Wooden hatchways of less than 1¾ inch thick solid wood shall be covered on the inside with 16 gage sheet metal attached with screws at six (6) inch maximum centers around perimeter.

b. The hatchway shall be secured from the inside with a slide bar, slide bolts, and/or padlock with a hardened steel shackle.

c. Outside pin-type hinges shall be provided with nonremovable pins.

d. Other openings exceeding ninety-six (96) square inches with a least dimension exceeding eight (8) inches shall be secured by metal bars, screens, or grilles in an approved manner.

*   *   *   *   *

CONCORD MUNICIPAL CODE

Article III
Chapter 9 (1)
Building Security*

Section 3920: Purpose. The purpose of this Chapter is to provide minimum safe standards to safeguard property and public welfare by regulating and controlling the design, construction, quality of materials, use and occupancy, location and maintenance of all buildings and structures within the City of Concord and certain equipment specifically regulated here.   (Ord. 919)

Section 3921: Scope. The provisions of the Chapter shall apply to all new construction and to buildings and structures to which additions, alterations or repairs are made except as specifically provided in this Chapter. When additions, alterations or repairs within any twelve (12) month period exceed fifty per cent (50%) of the replacement value of the existing building or structure, such building or structure shall be made to conform to the new requirements for new buildings or structures.   (Ord. 919)

Section 3922: Enforcement. This Chapter shall be administered and enforced by the Building Official.   (Ord. 919)

Section 3923: Responsibility for Security. The owner or his designated agent shall be responsible for compliance with the specifications set forth in this Chapter.   (Ord. 919)

Section 3924: Right of Entry. With the consent of the owner, his agent, the tenant, or person in charge of the building, employees or agents of the City designated to make inspections herein may enter or go upon or about any building or premises used for business purposes at any reasonable hour for the purpose of inspecting the physical exterior accessible openings of such building or premises or for any other purpose consistent herewith. Such employee or agent shall identify themselves by exhibiting a badge or other evidence of their identity and authority. If the City representative is refused admittance a search warrant may be procured.   (Ord. 919)

Section 3925: Violation. It shall be unlawful for any person to fail to provide such security devices, as hereinafter defined for the protection of their building.   (Ord. 919)

Section 3926: Appeal. Any interested person may appeal the decision of the Building Official to the Board of Appeals.   (Ord. 919)

(a) **Filing.** The notice of appeal must be in writing and filed with the Secretary of the Board of Appeals, within seven (7) calendar days of the decision from which the appeal is taken.   (Ord. 919)

(b) **Form.** The notice of appeal shall set forth in concise language the following: (Ord. 919)

---

*Concord's Building Security Code was written by Officer Raymond A. Bray under the direction of Chief James L. Chambers, Concord Police Department.

(1) Date of appeal. (Ord. 919)
(2) Name of appellant. (Ord. 919)
(3) Individual representing appellant. (Ord. 919)
(4) Address to which notices shall be sent. (Ord. 919)
(5) Telephone number of representative. (Ord. 919)
(6) Name of applicant, if different from appellant. (Ord. 919)
(7) Date of action or decision from which appeal is taken. (Ord. 919)
(8) Action or decision being appealed (Ord. 919)
(9) Grounds for appeal. (Ord. 919)
(10) Estimated time required by appellant to present appeal. (Ord. 919)
(11) Address and description of real property involved. (Ord. 919)

(c) No filing fee shall be required for an appeal under this section. (Ord. 919)

(d) Notifying Board. The Secretary of the Board of Appeals shall place the matter of the Notice of Appeal on the Agenda of the meeting of the Board of Appeals, the preparation of which Agenda immediately follows filing of Notice of Appeal. (Ord. 919)

(e) Hearing. The Board of Appeals may hear the matter at the first meeting at which the appeal has been placed on the Agenda or may, at the request of appellant or other interested persons on good cause being shown, or on its own motion, continue the hearing. (Ord. 919)

(f) Manner of Notice. Notice of hearing shall be mailed to the appellant and any person specifically requesting notice at least five (5) calendar days before the hearing. (Ord. 919)

Section 3927: Exceptions. No portion of this Chapter shall supersede any local, state, or Federal laws, regulations, or codes dealing with the life-safety factor. Enforcement of this Chapter will be in cooperation with the local fire authority to avoid possible conflict with fire laws. (Ord. 919)

Section 3928: Definitions. For the purpose of this Chapter, certain terms are defined as follows: (Ord. 919)

(a) Cylinder Guard is a hardened ring surrounding the exposed portion of the lock cylinder or other device which is so fastened as to protect the cylinder from wrenching, prying, cutting or pulling by attack tools. (Ord. 919)

(b) Deadlatch is a latch in which the latch bolt is positively held in the projected position by guardbolt, plunger, or auxiliary mechanism. (Ord. 919)

(c) Insert is a hardened steel roller inside unhardened bolts to prevent bolt cutting or sawing with common tools. (Ord. 919)

(d) Deadbolt is a bolt which has no automatic spring action and is operated by a key cylinder, thumbturn or lever. (Ord. 919)

(e) Commercial Building is any building used by any person for the purpose of conducting, managing, or carrying on any business. Storage of any merchandise, household goods or product shall be included as a business. (Ord. 919)

Section 3929: Commercial Building Security Provisions.

(a) Minimum Standards. (Ord. 919)

(1) All exterior doors shall be secured as follows: (Ord. 919)

a. A single door shall be secured with either a double cylinder deadbolt or a single cylinder deadbolt without a turnpiece with a minimum throw of one (1) inch. A hook or expanding bolt may have a throw of three-fourths (¾) inch. Any deadbolt must contain an insert of hardened material to repel attempts at cutting through the bolt and must have a minimum of 6,000 possible key changes or locking combinations. (Ord. 919)

b. On pairs of doors, the active leaf shall be secured with the type of lock required for single doors in *a.* above. The inactive leaf shall be equipped with flush bolts protected by hardened material with a minimum throw of five-eights (⅝) inch at head and foot. Multiple point locks, cylinder activated from the active leaf and satisfying (1)a. and b. above, may be used in lieu of flush bolts. (Ord. 919)

c. Any single or pair of doors requiring locking at the bottom or top rail shall have locks with a minimum five-eights (⅝) inch throw bolt at both the top and bottom rails. (Ord. 919)

d. Cylinders shall be so designed or protected that they cannot be gripped by pliers or other wrenching devices. (Ord. 919)

e. Exterior sliding commercial entrances shall be secured as in a. b. & d. above with special attention given to safety regulations. (Ord. 919) *f.* Rolling overhead doors, solid overhead swinging, sliding or accordion garage-type doors shall be secured with a cylinder lock or a padlock on the inside when not otherwise controlled or locked by electric power operation. If a padlock is used, it shall be of hardened steel shackle, with a minimum of five pin tumbler operation with non-removable key when it is in an unlocked position.   (Ord.919)

g. Metal accordion grate or grill type doors shall be equipped with metal guide track, top and bottom, and a cylinder lock and/or padlock with hardened steel shackle and minimum five pin tumbler operation with non-removable key when in an unlocked position. The bottom track shall be so designed that the door cannot be lifted from the track when the door is in a locked position.   (Ord. 919)

h. Outside hinges on all exterior doors shall be provided with non-removable pins or hinges of the interlocking stud type when using pin-type hinges.   (Ord. 919)

i. Doors with glass panels and doors that have glass panels adjacent to the door frame shall be secured as follows: (Ord. 919)

1. Rated burglary resistant glass or glass-like material, or   (Ord. 919)

2. The glass shall be covered with iron bars of at least one half ($\frac{1}{2}$) inch round or one inch by one-fourth inch (1″ × $\frac{1}{4}$″) flat steel material mortised, spaced not more than five (5) inches apart, secured on the inside of the glazing, or   (Ord. 919)

3. Iron or steel grills of at least one-eighth inch ($\frac{1}{8}$) material of two (2) inch mesh secured on inside of the glazing.   (Ord. 919)

j. Inswinging doors shall have rabbeted jambs.   (Ord. 919)

k. Wood doors, not of solid core construction, or with panels therein less than one and three-eights inch ($1\frac{3}{8}$″) thick, shall be covered on the inside with at least 16 gauge sheet steel or its equivalent attached with screws on minimum six (6) inch centers. (Ord. 919)

l. Jambs for all doors shall be so constructed or protected so as to prevent violation of the function of the strike.   (Ord. 919)

m. All exterior doors shall have a minimum of 60 watt bulb over the outside of the door. Such bulb shall be protected with a vapor cover or cover of equal breaking resistant material.   (Ord. 919)

(2) ALTERNATIVES. Nothing contained in this Chapter shall be deemed to prohibit the use of alternate materials, devices or measures when such alternate provisions are deemed by the Building Official as providing equivalent security.   (Ord. 919)

(b) Glass Windows.   (Ord. 919)

(1) Accessible rear and side windows not viewable from the street shall consist of rated burglary resistant glass or glass-like material.*   (Ord. 919)

*Exception: Window openings required by Building Code for access by fire department shall be protected by a material approved by the fire department.   (Ord. 919)

Protection of these window openings should be by a glass, i.e., tempered glass, which may be broken without unnecessary delay and use of specialized equipment.   (Ord. 919)

(2) If the accessible side or rear window is of the openable type, it shall be secured on the inside with a locking device capable of withstanding a force of three hundred (300) pounds applied in any direction.   (Ord. 919)

(3) Louvered windows shall not be used within eight (8) feet of ground level, adjacent structures or fire escapes.   (Ord. 919)

(4) Outside hinges on all accessible side and rear glass windows shall be provided with non-removable pins. If the hinge screws are accessible, the screws shall be of the non-removable type.   (Ord. 919)

(c) Accessible Transoms. All exterior transoms exceeding eight (8) inches by twelve (12) inches on the side and rear of any building or premises used for business purposes shall be protected by one of the following: (Ord. 919)

(1) Rated burglary resistant glass or glass-like material, or   (Ord. 919)

(2) Outside iron bars of at least one half inch ($\frac{1}{2}$) round or one inch by one-fourth inch (1 × $\frac{1}{4}$) flat steel material, spaced no more than five (5) inches apart, or   (Ord. 919)

(3) Outside iron or steel grills of at least one-eighth ($\frac{1}{8}$) inch material but not more than two (2) inch mesh.   (Ord. 919)

(4) The window barrier shall be secured with rounded head flush bolts on the outside.   (Ord. 919)

(d) Roof Openings.   (Ord. 919)

(1) All glass skylights on the roof of any building or premises used for business purposes shall be provided with: (Ord. 919)

    a. Rated burglary resistant glass or glass-like material meeting building code requirements, or   (Ord. 919)

    b. Iron bars of at least one-half (½) inch round or one inch by one-fourth inch (1″ × ¼″) flat steel material under the skylight and securely fastened, or   (Ord. 919)

    c. A steel grill of at least one-eighth (⅛) inch material of two (2) inch mesh under the skylight and securely fastened.   (Ord. 919)

    (2) All hatchway openings on the roof of any building or premises used for business purposes shall be secured as follows: (Ord. 919)

    a. If the hatchway is of wooden material, it shall be covered on the inside with at least 16 gauge sheet steel or its equivalent attached with screws.   (Ord. 919)

    b. The hatchway to be secured from the inside with a slide bar or slide bolts. The use of crossbar or padlock must be approved by the Fire Marshal.   (Ord. 919)

    c. Outside hinges on all hatchway openings shall be provided with non-removable pins when using pin-type hinges.   (Ord. 919)

    (3) All air duct or air vent openings exceeding eight (8) inches by twelve (12) inches on the roof or exterior walls of any building or premise used for business purposes shall be secured by covering the same with either of the following: (Ord. 919)

    a. Iron bars of at least one half (½) inch round or one inch by one-fourth inch (1″ × ¼″) flat steel material, spaced no more than five (5) inches apart and securely fastened, or   (Ord. 919)

    b. A steel grill of at least one-eighth (⅛) inch material of two (2) inch mesh and securely fastened.   (Ord. 919)

    c. If the barrier is on the outside, it shall be secured with rounded head flush bolts on the outside.   (Ord. 919)

    (4) LADDERS. Any ladder excluding fire escapes, located on the exterior of any building which could provide access to the roof shall be protected from such access by a continuous piece of wood or metal covering the rungs. The wood or metal shall be locked with a padlock. The padlock shall have a minimum of five (5) pin tumblers and be of case-hardened steel. Hinges used on the covering shall be of a non-removable pin type. The wood or metal barrier shall be a minimum of eight (8) feet continuous covering of not less than one half (½) inch thickness and located four (4) feet from ground level or be secured in a manner approved by the Building Official.   (Ord. 919)

(e) Special Security Measures.   (Ord. 919)

    (1) SAFES. Commercial establishments having one thousand dollars ($1,000.00) or more in cash on the premises after closing hours shall lock such money in at least a Class "E" or higher rated safe after closing hours.   (Ord. 919)

    (2) OFFICE BUILDINGS (MULTIPLE OCCUPANCY). All entrance doors to individual office suites shall have a deadbolt lock with a minimum one (1) inch throw bolt which can be opened from the inside.   (Ord. 919)

(f) Intrusion Detection Devices.   (Ord. 919)

    (1) If it is determined by the enforcing authority of this Chapter that the security measures and locking devices described in this Chapter do not adequately secure the building, he may require the installation and maintenance of an intrusion detection device (Burglar Alarm System).   (Ord. 919)

    (2) Establishments having specific type inventories shall be protected by the following type alarm service: (Ord. 919)

    a. Silent Alarm—Central Station—Supervised Service.   (Ord. 919)

        1. Jewelry Store—Manufacturing, Wholesale and Retail.   (Ord. 919)

        2. Guns and ammunition.   (Ord. 919)

        3. Wholesale liquor.   (Ord. 919)

        4. Wholesale tobacco.   (Ord. 919)

        5. Wholesale drugs.   (Ord. 919)

        6. Fur stores.   (Ord. 919)

    b. Silent Alarm.   (Ord. 919)

        1. Liquor stores.   (Ord. 919)

        2. Pawn shops.   (Ord. 919)

        3. Electronic equipment including musical instrument stores.   (Ord. 919)

        4. Wig stores.   (Ord. 919)

        5. Clothing (new).   (Ord. 919)

        6. Coins and stamps.   (Ord. 919)

7. Industrial tool supply houses.	(Ord. 919)
8. Camera stores.	(Ord. 919)
9. Precious metal storage facility.	(Ord. 919)
10. Drug stores.	(Ord. 919)
c. Local Alarm (Bell outside premise).	(Ord. 919)
1. Antique dealers.	(Ord. 919)
2. Art galleries.	(Ord. 919)
3. Service stations.	(Ord. 919)

(a) Purpose. The purpose of this section is to set forth minimum standards of construction for resistance to unlawful entry to the residential structures located in the City of Concord. (Ord. 919)

(b) Alternatives. Nothing contained in this Chapter shall be deemed to prohibit the use of alternate materials, devices or measures when such alternate provisions are deemed by the Building Official as providing equivalent security. (Ord. 919)

(c) Tests. (Ord. 919)

(1) SLIDING GLASS DOORS. Panels shall be closed and locked. Tests shall be performed in the following order: (Ord. 919)

a. TEST A: With the panels in the normal position a concentrated load of three hundred (300) pounds shall be applied separately to each vertical pull stile incorporating a locking device at a point on the stile within six (6) inches of the locking device, in the direction parallel to the plane of glass that would tend to open the door. (Ord. 919)

b. TEST B: Repeat Test A while simultaneously adding a concentrated load of one hundred fifty (150) pounds to the same area of the same stile in a direction perpendicular to the plane of glass toward the interior side of the door. (Ord. 919)

c. TEST C: Repeat Test B with the one hundred fifty (150) pound force in the reversed direction towards the exterior side of the door. (Ord. 919)

d. TESTS D, E, AND F: Repeat Tests A, B. and C with the movable panel lifted upwards to its full limit within the confines of the door frame. (Ord. 919)

(2) SLIDING GLASS WINDOWS. Sash shall be closed and locked. Tests shall be performed in the following order: (Ord. 919)

a. TEST A: With the sliding sash in the normal position, a concentrated load of one hundred fifty (150) pounds shall be applied separately to each sash member within six (6) inches of the locking device, in the direction parallel to the plane of glass that would tend to open the window. (Ord. 919)

b. TEST B: Repeat Test A while simultaneously adding a concentrated load of seventy five (75) pounds to the same area of the same sash member in the direction perpendicular to the plane of glass toward the interior side of the window. (Ord. 919)

c. TEST C: Repeat Test B with the seventy-five (75) pounds force in the reversed direction towards the exterior side of the window. (Ord. 919)

d. TESTS D, E, AND F: Repeat Tests A, B and C with the movable sash lifted upwards to its full limit within the confines of the window frame. (Ord. 919)

(3) TESTING AGENCY. All tests shall be performed by an approved independent testing agency. Written reports shall be submitted to the Building Official. (Ord. 919)

(d) Doors—General. A door forming a part of the enclosure of a dwelling unit shall be of solid core construction installed and secured as set forth in paragraphs (e), (f) and (g), when such door is accessible from a street, highway, yard, court, passageway, corridor, balcony, patio, breezeway, private garage, portion of the building which is available for use by the public or other tenants, or similar area. A door enclosing a private garage with an interior opening leading directly to a dwelling unit shall also comply with said paragraphs (e), (f) and (g) of Section 3930. (Ord. 919)

(e) Doors—Swing Doors. (Ord. 919)

(1) A single swing door, the active leaf of a pair of doors and the bottom leaf of dutch doors shall be equipped with a deadbolt with a minimum throw of one (1) inch and a deadlocking latch. Deadbolts shall contain hardened inserts, or equivalent, so as to repel cutting tool attack. The lock or locks shall be key-operated from the exterior side of the door and engaged or disengaged from the interior side of the door by a device not requiring a key or special knowledge or effort. (Ord. 919)

(2) Flushbolts with a minimum throw of five-eights (⅝) inch shall be provided at the head and foot (floor and ceiling) of the inactive leaf of double doors, and at the top and bottom of the upper leaf of dutch doors. (Ord. 919)

(3) Door stops on wooden jambs for in-swinging doors shall be of one (1) piece construction with the jamb or joined by a rabbet. (Ord. 919)

(4) Non-removable pins or interlocking stud type hinges shall be used in pin-type hinges which are accessible from the outside when the door is closed. (Ord. 919)

(5) Cylinder guards shall be installed on all mortise or rim-type cylinder locks whenever the cylinder projects beyond the face of the door or is otherwise accessible to gripping tools. (Ord. 919)

(f) Doors—Sliding Glass. (Ord. 919)

(1) Sliding glass doors shall be equipped with locking devices and shall be so installed that, when subject to tests specified in paragraph (c), they remain intact and engaged. Movable panels shall not be rendered easily openable or removable from the frame during or after the tests. (Ord. 919)

(2) Cylinder guards shall be installed on all mortise or rim-type cylinder locks which project beyond the face of the door or are otherwise accessible to gripping tools. (Ord. 919)

(g) Doors—Overhead and Sliding. (Ord. 919)

(1) Metal or wooden overhead and sliding doors shall be secured with a cylinder lock, padlock with a hardened steel shackle, metal slide bar, bolt or equivalent on the inside when not otherwise locked by electric power operation. In the event that this type door provides the only entrance to a garage, the cylinder lock or padlock may be on the outside. (Ord. 919)

(2) Cylinder guards shall be installed on all mortise or rim-type cylinder locks which project beyond the face of the door or are otherwise accessible to gripping tools. (Ord. 919)

(h) Windows—General. A window, skylight or other light forming a part of the enclosure of a dwelling unit shall be constructed, installed and secured as set forth in paragraphs (i) and (j), when such window, skylight or light is not more than twelve (12) feet above the grade of a street, highway, yard, court, passageway, corridor, balcony, patio, breezeway, private garage, portion of the building which is available for use by the public or other tenants, or similar area. A window enclosing a private garage with an interior opening leading directly to a dwelling unit shall also comply with said paragraphs (i) and (j). (Ord. 919)

(i) Windows—Locking Devices. (Ord. 919)

(1) Sliding glass windows shall be provided with locking devices that, when subjected to the tests specified in paragraph (c) remain intact and engaged. (Ord. 919)

(2) Movable panels shall not be rendered easily openable or removable from the frame during or after the tests. (Ord. 919)

(3) Other openable windows shall be provided with substantial locking devices which the Building Official finds render the building as secure as the devices required by this section. (Ord. 919)

(4) Louvered windows, except those above the first story, shall not be permitted. (Ord. 919)

(j) Lighting parking lots (Ord. 919)

Open parking lots (including lots having carports) providing more than ten (10) parking spaces shall be provided with a maintained minimum of three (3) foot candles of light on the parking surface during hours of darkness. (Ord. 919)

Chapter **5**

Selecting a Security Consultant

PETER S. HOPF, AIA

G. EDITH HOPF

THE SELECTION PROCESS

The selection of a security consultant is as important as that of any other professional—a doctor, attorney, or architect, for example—and should follow several well-planned steps so as to ensure that the security needs of a given building or installation are most appropriately met. Ideally, the process involves both client and building designer in at least some of the steps.

In general, the steps involved in organizing the selection process are these:

1. Prepare a checklist of needs.
2. Select a reputable and dependable source of potential candidates.
3. Check several individuals' credentials of past performance as it relates to the priority needs.
4. Interview one or more candidates.

PREPARING A CHECKLIST OF NEEDS

In order to find the most competent individual or firm, it is important to first analyze the particular set of security needs which a given building is expected to have. These may be related to building construction, building use, user population, and/or general community location. The checklists given in Chapter 3, "Security in the Neighborhood," and Chapter 30, "Public Buildings," have been designed with this in mind and can serve as a departure point, with more items added as the designer and client see fit.

WHERE TO FIND POTENTIAL CANDIDATES

There are numerous sources from which candidates can be selected. The checklist of needs will assist in narrowing the field somewhat by making evident a set of priority needs. The search can then be directed toward specialized experts in the areas of priority.

Names of recognized authorities in the various aspects of security planning and implementation are available from a variety of sources in addition to this handbook.

Security Associations

There are a number of associations specializing in the field of security. Probably the most comprehensive permanently based national organization is the American Society for Industrial Security, whose members include thousands of persons competent in virtually every aspect of the security field. The society publishes an annual directory of members, which can serve as a resource file for locating a specialized expert in a given geographical area. Individual members who do not provide consulting services will ususally be helpful in recommending specialists in their particular field of security.

At the end of this book, in Appendix B, is a list of security associations, including those of a more specialized nature. Where addresses are not noted, the associations generally do not have a permanent mailing address due to the practice of periodically changing officeholders.

Government Agencies

Local, county, and state law enforcement agencies often have a crime prevention department and willingly provide helpful security suggestions. A potential building operator need not be reluctant to contact such agencies since they will normally be most cooperative, especially when consulted during the early design stages.

Locally, these agencies are normally administered by the police department. At the state level, they often operate under the Attorney General. In Washington, the Law Enforcement Assistance Administration (LEAA) can provide a wide range of security information. The Department of Justice, of which the LEAA is a branch, publishes a directory of security consultants which is available from the Superintendent of Documents, Government Printing Office.

Publications

Security publications, such as *Security Management* and *Security World,* contain excellent articles by security experts, many of whom are private consultants. Several of the chapters in this handbook were written by security experts who are available for private consultation.

Manufacturers and Distributors

Sales representatives will often provide a great deal of helpful information. The client's overall needs must be considered, however, to avoid having the building's security compromised, either in planning or implementation, by overzealous salespeople. Data and information received from manufacturers can be most useful but should not be accepted as providing the total security solution without weighing a variety of choices available. In this respect, information from manufacturers and distributors is no substitute for the services of an independent, objective, and carefully selected security consultant.

Personal Recommendation

Perhaps the best method of selecting a consultant is to seek personal recommendations from trusted business associates, other building owners, managers, or security directors of similar installations. This type of recommendation can make available a wide range of information about the prospective candidate's performance and background that is not generally readily available through review of written material or interview.

CHECKING CREDENTIALS

When one or more candidates have been selected and contacted for interview, reference lists will provide the names of previous clients who can be contacted for their opinions regarding the nature and competence of the consultant's prior performance.

This should be done with specific reference to the security needs checklist and the order of priorities already established by client and building designer. Special attention should be given to recommendations by prior clients who have had installation and surveillance needs similar to the existing ones.

INTERVIEWING THE CONSULTANT

The last and possibly most important step in selection is the interview. This is the time for discussing with the candidates the breadth of their experience and background as these relate to current needs. At this time, an effort can be made to assess each consultant's level of competence and the degree to which he or she understands and can satisfy the specific security needs of the project more deeply than another individual.

This is also the time to pay particular attention to the potential for communication and rapport between the consultant and others responsible for the successful implementation of the project. Is the individual under consideration able to communicate ideas articulately and concisely? More important, are the consultant's problem-solving ideas, the means and tools by which he or she proposes a plan for security, relevant to the project being undertaken, as conceived and understood by the hiring agents? Is there a consensus, among those individuals present, of the existing priorities? Can the candidate listen as well as propose? Does it appear that this person can function as a member of a team rather than as an independent agent? Can he or she bring fresh ideas to the project in a manner that will be acceptable to the other persons responsible for implementation? Is the candidate able to deal with and carry out responsibilities in the expected manner, both qualitatively and quantitatively?

When all these questions can be answered in the affirmative, the designer and client may be assured that they have selected an expert, dependable, and effective security consultant.

DIRECTORY OF SECURITY CONSULTANTS

Appendix B in this volume contains a listing of security consultants extracted from the *Directory of Security Consultants* prepared for the National Institute of Law Enforcement and Criminal Justice, Law Enforcement Assistance Administration, U.S. Department of Justice, by Elizabeth Robertson and John V. Fechter. The material was prepared by the Law Enforcement Standards Laboratory of the National Bureau of Standards under the direction of Lawrence K. Eliason, Manager, Security Systems Program, and Jacob J. Diamond, Chief of LESL.

No directory such as this can, of course, be all-inclusive. Names, organizations, and addresses change periodically, and there are probably hundreds of other individuals and firms across the United States that can provide equally competent consulting services; however, the guidelines in this chapter should be useful in selecting a consultant. It is also the authors' hope that this chapter and the valuable resource material included in Appendix B will be of assistance in the task of selecting the security consulting services best suited for the job at hand.

Part Two

Security from Natural Disasters

Chapter **6**

Earthquakes

LESLIE W. GRAHAM

Partner, Graham & Kellam, Structural Engineers, San Francisco

HISTORICAL ASPECTS

Over the years, numerous theories have evolved as to the causes of earthquakes. Primitive people attributed them to volcanic phenomena or subterranean winds in caverns, and as late as the eighteenth century the most common belief was that earthquakes were caused by subterranean fires.

It was not until early in this century, however, that reliable instrumentation for recording seismic events was developed. Therefore, the earlier records, catalogs, and intensity scales were based on personal reactions, although these older catalogs are still very important in the field of seismology and earthquake engineering. With their judicious use, the instrumental records of recent modern times can be extended back so that the locations, time of occurrence, and relative magnitudes of the largest earthquakes can be derived with some degree of certainty. As an example, in 1924 de Montessus de Ballore published a very extensive study of historical earthquakes, comprising about 160,000 different occurrences, which endeavored to go back to the dawn of recorded history.

Turning to the modern instrumental records, a number of catalogs have been prepared. The largest of these is the *Bulletin of the International Seismological Center,* Edinburgh, which in 1964 replaced the *International Seismological Summary.* Other international lists of earthquakes are the *Bulletin Mensuel du Bureau Central Seismologique,* Strasbourg, and the catalogs of the United States Coast and Geodetic Survey, Washington, D.C. In recent years, because of the increasing interest in earthquake investigation and design, many scientific and technical organizations devoted to seismological and earthquake engineering research have come into being and have published a great number of very valuable lists, technical articles, and proceedings of their meetings. Among those bodies active in the United States are the Seismological Society of America and the Earthquake Engineering Research Institute.

THEORIES OF EARTHQUAKE CAUSES

Crustal Movements   In the nineteenth century, theories began to appear in which mechanical sources were considered. These sources included the sudden flexure and constraint of the earth's crust and the sudden relief of this constraint by the withdrawal of the forces or by the crustal materials giving way and becoming fractured. Attempts were made to explain these movements as being caused by radial expansion or contraction of the earth as a whole, or by isostatic compensations in the crust between adjacent mountains and plains.

Another theory to explain earthquake phenomena was the so-called "elastic rebound theory." This became widely accepted after studies of the 1906 California earthquake and is credited to Professor H.F. Reid (1911). After the 1906 California earthquake, very obvious large-scale and continuous fault ruptures could be observed. In addition, surveys showed horizontal displacements of the ground surface parallel to the San Andreas Fault and relative displacement of distant points on opposite sides of the fault, in the order of 10 to 11 ft. Reid stated, "It is impossible for rock to rupture without first being subjected to elastic strains greater than it can endure. We conclude that the crust in many parts of the earth is being slowly displaced and the difference between displacements in neighboring regions sets up elastic strains, which may become larger than the rock can endure. A rupture then takes place and the then strained rock rebounds under its own elastic stresses, until the strain is largely or wholly relieved. In the majority of cases, the elastic rebounds on opposite sides of the fault are in opposite directions."

Plate Tectonics   In recent years the theory of plate tectonics has gained widespread adherence, but similar theories were proposed much earlier. In 1620, Francis Bacon examined the possibility that the Western Hemisphere had once been joined to Europe and Africa. In 1668, P. Placet wrote an imaginative article entitled "The corruption of the great and little world, where it is shown that before the deluge, America was not separated from the other parts of the world." In 1858, Antonio Snider proposed that all the continents were once part of a single land mass. His paper is called "The Creation and Its Mysteries Revealed." By the end of the nineteenth century, the Austrian Eduard Suess proposed that the land masses of the Southern Hemisphere had once been a single continent which he called Gondwanaland.

F.B. Taylor of the United States in 1908 and Alfred L. Wegener of Germany in 1910–1912 independently proposed a theory which would account for large lateral displacements of the earth's crust and thus show how continents might move apart or come together. Wegener's work became the center of debate which has continued to the present, but intensive worldwide research in a variety of fields has tended to support his hypotheses more and more. These hypotheses are strengthened by recent studies of the thicknesses of the sediments of the ocean floor and the continental masses, carbon dating of the rocks, matching of fossils in various continents, and the arrangement of varying adjacent belts of residual magnetism in the rock mantle in the ocean floor.

The implied relationships of sea-floor spreading, continental drift, and seismic belts are strong, and at the present time they are believed to afford the most reasonable explanation of seismic phenomena. In general, the plate tectonic theory can be simplified to state that the outer shell (lithosphere) of the earth is made up of a number of rigid plates resting on the underlying asthenosphere and that the outer-shell plates move with respect to each other.

Plate boundaries are both at continental edges and at mid-ocean rises or rifts (see Fig. 1). The mid-ocean ridges coincide with regions of upwelling of material from below. Due to the upwelling, the sea-floor materials spread away from the mid-ocean rifts and ridges and then, still in motion, tend to pass under the seaward edges of the

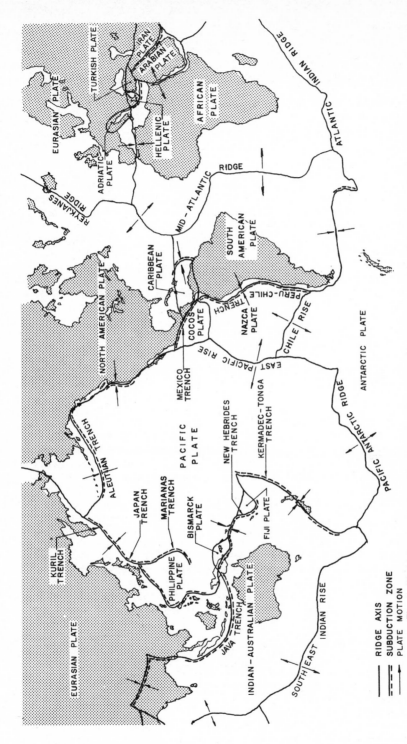

Fig. 1 World map showing plate boundaries, direction of plate drift, mid-ocean ridges, and subduction zones.

—————— RIDGE AXIS
- - - - - - SUBDUCTION ZONE
———→ PLATE MOTION

6-5

continental masses, forming the so-called "subduction zones" or sinks, whereupon they are fused into the asthenosphere and mesosphere below. This passing of an oceanic plate under a continental plate tends to buckle the contact edges of the land mass, forming the oceanic trenches and mountain chains, with resulting seismic activity being caused by the deforming movements imposed upon the materials of the two plates (see Fig. 2).

LOCATIONS OF HIGH SEISMICITY

An examination of records of seismicity throughout the world indicates widespread occurrence of earthquake activity, but the records also tend to indicate that the majority of seismic activity is concentrated in relatively well-defined zones (see Fig. 3).

An examination of the seismic activity map (Fig. 3) clearly shows two global belts of high seismicity. These are the Pacific Rim Belt circling the Pacific Ocean and the Alpide Belt running roughly in an east-west direction from the Mediterranean into Asia. The locations of these belts of activity coincide very closely with either the subduction zones of the various impinging lithosphere plates or the locations of the mid-ocean rifts or rises. The belt around the Pacific coincides with the subduction zones between oceanic and continental plates, while at least a major part of the Alpide zone corresponds with the subduction zones of colliding continental plates.

DISTRIBUTION OF EARTHQUAKES WITH DEPTH

The major portion (more than 75 percent) of the average annual seismic energy is released by relatively shallow-focus earthquakes, that is, with foci less than 60 km (36 mi) deep. In certain continental regions, no earthquakes with foci deeper than 20 to 40 km (12 to 24 mi) have been observed. Very deep-focus earthquakes are known to have occurred in only a few regions, such as the Andes, the Japan Sea, Indonesia, and the New Hebrides.

The distribution of seismic activity can best be explained by the subduction theory of plate tectonics (see Fig. 2).

There is intense earthquake activity at shallow depths where the edges of the rigid plates are in contact with each other. Many of the greatest earthquakes such as Kamchatka 1952, Chile 1960, and Alaska 1964 occur along the shear plane between the oceanic and continental lithosphere. Some shallow earthquakes also occur on the ocean side of the oceanic trench caused by subduction and are believed to be caused by arching of the ocean plate.

The deep- and intermediate-focus earthquakes are believed to occur in the coolest region of the interior of the descending plate. These are thought to be caused by gravitational forces acting on the relatively dense interior of the descending slab and by the resistance of the surrounding mantle to the descending slab's penetration. The cool and rigid interior of the descending slab acts as a conductor to transmit stresses caused by the penetration.

The absence of earthquakes below 700 km (435 mi) can be explained by the theory that the descending lithosphere heats up below that depth to the point where it cannot behave rigidly and be subject to faulting or brittle fracture. Stresses may also be relieved by slow plastic deformation.

EARTHQUAKE WAVE MOTIONS

Types of Waves   The discussion in this section is intended to briefly cover the behavior of elastic waves generated by earthquakes. It does not include nonelastic behavior, such as movements due to sliding, slumping, or soil liquefaction. Also, the

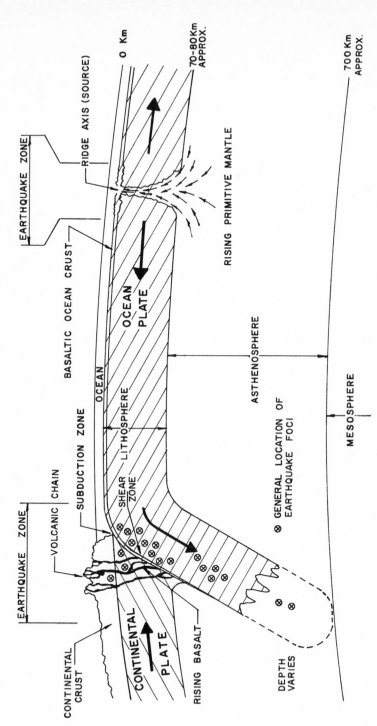

Fig. 2 Idealized section through crust and mantle showing motion of adjacent plates, subduction zone, and areas of major earthquake activity.

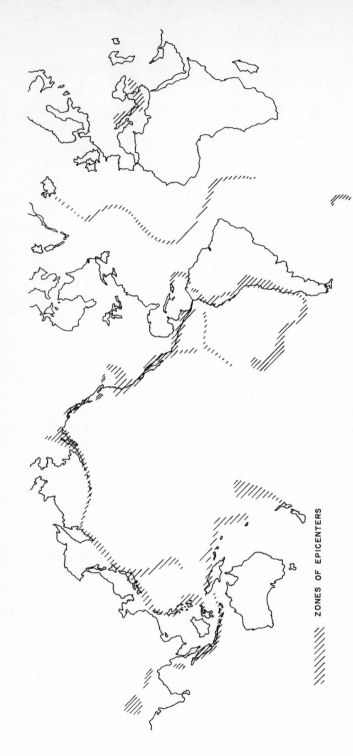

Fig. 3 Major earthquake zones of the world.

ZONES OF EPICENTERS

subject of wave propagation, transmission, and absorption is a very complex one which cannot be adequately treated in a short chapter. The reader is referred to the many excellent books and research papers exhaustively treating this subject.

The elastic-rebound theory of earthquake generation indicates that the displacement is suddenly initiated at a relatively small point. The region in the earth at which the displacement is initiated is called the "focus," and the corresponding point immediately above it on the earth's surface is called the "epicenter."

The depth of the focus affects the spectrum of the elastic waves in a number of ways. In major earthquakes, the travel of the disturbance along the length of the fault may produce a series of irregular steps. The rupture may begin suddenly and spread with varying periods of acceleration and retardation along the fault zone. In the most extreme case, a series of separate movements may occur in succession along the fault. The starting and stopping phases will give rise to varying wave pulses.

The motions existing in the wave structure are of various forms. Waves which penetrate through the main body of the earth are of two types. One is the compression (P) wave, in which the particular motion is in the direction of the wave; the other is the shear (S) wave, in which the motion is at right angles to the line of travel.

In addition to the body waves, longer-period surface waves (Rayleigh and Love waves) are also generated. Rayleigh waves move in a vertical plane, with any given surface particle in the path of the wave moving with a retrograde motion in an elliptical orbit. In the Love wave, the motion of the particle is in a horizontal plane and at right angles to the direction in which the wave is propagated.

Though the Rayleigh and Love waves move on the earth simultaneously, the two waves are not associated in any way. These surface waves are of a characteristically long period because the shorter-period components of the original disturbance tend to be damped out by surface-layer discontinuities, for example. Some theoretical work has indicated that the amplitude of the Rayleigh surface wave is insignificant compared to P and S waves out to distances from the epicenter in the order of five times the focal depth of the earthquake. Beyond this distance the Rayleigh waves become very prominent.

It is therefore evident that at any point on the earth's surface near the fault the wave motion may be quite complex. The duration of the shaking at the point under consideration will depend roughly on the linear extent of the fault rupture and on the amount of displacement. Variation in intensity of shaking during the earthquake will depend on the smoothness of the rupturing surface and on the position of the observation point on the surface relative to the fault break. Thus, if the fault rupture moves toward the observation point and then away, the intensity may grow and then decline. In the epicentral area the energy represented by waves with a period shorter than 1 s may be high. At long distances from the epicenter, only waves with a period of 5 s or more may be detected. Thus, if the distance from the point of observation to the point of rupture varies, the makeup of the wave trains passing under the point of observation will change.

Starting in 1932, the United States Coast and Geodetic Survey instituted a program of installing strong-motion seismographs. The program has been continued and amplified, but at the time of writing there are still gaps in the records taken at varying distances from the earthquakes in the ranges of practical interest to engineers.

The influence of local ground characteristics is very great. The depth to bedrock and the kind(s) of overburden will materially affect the characteristics of the energy input into the structures of human origin with which we are concerned.

Based on existing records for earthquakes of magnitude 5, 6, and 7 and for sites on rock and competent soil at distances greater than 10, 20, and 40 km (6, 12, and 24 mi), respectively, it may be concluded that peak ground acceleration increases with magnitude and decreases with distance from the site. A similar attenuation of peak horizontal ground velocity may also be observed, but the rate of attenuation is somewhat less.

Intensity Scales   Attempts to record and judge relative sizes of earthquakes have led to the formulation of many types of scales of intensity. The scaling of "intensity" came into being first because intensity does not require instrumental observation and can be based on human observation. The scaling of "magnitude" (to be discussed later) requires recorded instrumentation. Over the years and in different countries, many different intensity scales have been established.

One of the earliest scales of this type was developed in 1811 by Jared Brooks. In the period from 1873 to 1883, the DeRossi, the Forel, and the Mercalli scales were developed independently. The DeRossi and Forel scales were combined in 1883. Many other scales have been proposed since then.

In general, these scales attempt to describe the effects of the disturbance on the observer's surroundings, the effect on the composure of the observer, and the effects on certain types of structures. Necessarily, to be of any consistent value, the structures selected as a measure must be of a type of construction which is common to a particular region.

Ideally, the intensity rating should be assigned by an experienced observer on the site at the time of the event, which is usually not possible, but the use of such a comparative scale based in familiar terms has the advantage that after an event reports can be gathered from inexperienced persons in the area at the time, the reports can be processed and evaluated by experienced persons, and a relatively reliable intensity rating can be derived. In the United States data for these ratings are routinely gathered after an event by the United States Coast and Geodetic Survey.

In this country the most widely used intensity scale is the Modified Mercalli Intensity Scale. The ratings vary from I to XII. The scale is reproduced on the following pages, with the Rossi-Forel equivalent indicated.

COMPARATIVE SCALES OF INTENSITY
(Description Edited)

Rossi-Forel	(Description Edited)	Modified Mercalli (1931)
I	Not felt except by a very few under especially favorable circumstances.	I
I to II	Felt only by a few persons at rest, especially on upper floors of buildings. Delicately suspended objects may swing.	II
III	Felt noticeably indoors, especially on upper floors of buildings, but many people do not recognize it as an earthquake. Standing motor cars may rock slightly. Vibration like passing of truck. Duration estimated.	III
IV to V	During the day felt indoors by many, outdoors by few. At night some awakened. Dishes, windows, doors disturbed, walls make creaking sound. Sensation like heavy truck striking building. Standing motor cars rocked noticeably.	IV
V to VI	Felt by nearly everyone; many awakened. Some dishes, windows, etc., broken; a few instances of cracked plaster; unstable objects overturned. Disturbances of trees, poles, and other tall objects sometimes noticed. Pendulum clocks may stop.	V
VI to VII	Felt by all; many frightened and run outdoors. Some heavy furniture moved; a few instances of fallen plaster or damaged chimneys. Damage slight.	VI

VIII minus	Everybody runs outdoors. Damage negligible in buildings of good design and construction; slight to moderate in well-built ordinary structures; considerable in poorly built or badly designed structures; some chimneys broken. Noticed by persons driving cars.	VII
VIII plus to IX minus	Damage slight in specially designed structures; considerable in ordinary substantial buildings, with partial collapse; great in poorly built structures. Panel walls thrown out of frame structures. Fall of chimneys, factory stacks, columns, monuments, walls. Heavy furniture overturned. Sand and mud ejected in small amounts. Changes in well water. Disturbs persons driving motor cars.	VIII
IX plus	Damage considerable in specially designed structures; well-designed frame structures thrown out of plumb; damage great in substantial buildings, with partial collapse. Buildings shifted off foundations. Ground cracked conspicuously. Underground pipes broken.	IX
X	Some well-built wooden structures destroyed; most masonry and frame structures destroyed with foundations; ground badly cracked. Rails bent. Landslides considerable from river banks and steep slopes. Shifted sand and mud. Water splashed (slopped) over banks.	X
None	Few, if any (masonry) structures remain standing. Bridges destroyed. Broad fissures in ground. Underground pipelines completely out of service. Earth slumps and land slips in soft ground. Rails bent greatly.	XI
None	Damage total. Waves seen on ground surfaces. Lines of sight and level distorted. Objects thrown upward into the air.	XII

Magnitude Scales   Magnitude scales differ from intensity scales in that they are derived from instrumental records. Many magnitude scales have been used throughout the world, and they differ widely. This sometimes leads to what appear to be conflicting magnitudes for the same earthquake.

Probably the most widely used magnitude scale in the United States is that developed by C.F. Richter. The magnitude number assigned is defined as the logarithm (to base 10) of the maximum amplitude (in microns) traced by a standard Wood-Anderson seismograph at a distance of 100 km (62 mi) from the epicenter. This approach is based on the principle that the amplitudes of ground surface movements, as reflected by seismographs, will provide an estimate of the seismic energy released by an earthquake. However, local crustal conditions and other influences may make this difficult to apply in practice. With scales of this type there is no largest or smallest limit. Using this basis, magnitudes may be derived varying from the order of -1.0 to $+8.0$ to $+9.0$.

Maximum Possible Energy Release   At the present time there is evidence leading to the conclusion that the largest earthquake which can occur under the earth's geological conditions would have a Richter magnitude no greater than 9.0.

The finite strength of crustal rocks limits the strain energy which they can store. Because, under present theories, the earthquake energy comes from strain energy stored in the rocks, the total seismic energy released may be judged to be proportional to the area of fault which ruptures. In very large shallow-focus earthquakes the depth of dislocation is small compared to the observed length of rupture. The total energy release, therefore, is believed to be bounded by the length of fault possible to rupture. The California earthquake of 1906 had a fault rupture estimated to be approximately 270 mi long. The 1960 Chilean and 1964 Alaskan earthquakes' fault ruptures were estimated to be some 500 mi long.

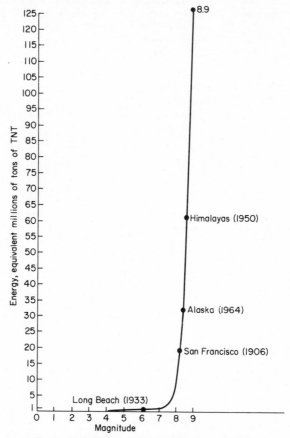

Fig. 4   Magnitude number—equivalent energy level.

It is possible to work out empirical formulas linking magnitude and energy release. For shallow earthquakes such as those that occur in California, the formula $\log_{10} E = 11.4 + 1.5\,M$ is in common use, where E is the energy in ergs and M is the Richter magnitude. A study of this expression indicates that an increase of a unit of *magnitude* represents an increase in *energy* of approximately 32 times. It is obvious, then, that there is an enormous spread of energy release between the largest and smallest earthquakes. (See Fig. 4 for a graphic illustration of this spread.)

The use of magnitude alone is a misleading quantity when applied to planning and engineering design. Due consideration must be given to the splitting of the energy into various wave frequencies depending on the variations in the rock and soil properties, the size of the area over which the energy is released, the response characteristics of various types of structures, and the duration of the shock.

Structures of human origin have various natural periods of their own. When excited by earthquake disturbances, they will respond strongly to waves of the same period. In the case of low-rise structures, which respond with relatively short natural periods, these will be most affected by that part of the earthquake which has similar periods. Due to relative attenuation and dissipation in the various strata of the earth, waves with shorter periods tend to lose their energy with a longer length of travel of the waves, so that those coming from distant parts of the rupture will be mainly of longer period. Accordingly, we would expect taller high-rise buildings to respond more strongly to the longer-frequency waves which might be predominant as the result of a far distant earthquake, while the relatively low-rise, shorter-period structures might be expected to respond more strongly to waves rich in shorter periods and coming from a closer source.

LOCATION CONSIDERATIONS

It would obviously be advantageous to locate all of our buildings outside regions of high seismic activity, but as a practical matter this is of course impossible. Many influences—geographic, economic, and the like—result in high population concentrations, along with their coincident concentrations of buildings at locations which may be subject to high seismic activity.

We must recognize this, and endeavor to design and build our structures, when necessary, with due regard to the effects of earthquake activity. This regard can be, and has been, channeled in a number of ways. These include special design provisions in building codes and proper enforcement of the building code requirements; the initiation of seismic zoning maps; the prohibition of human-inhabited structures in certain narrow areas obviously subject to surface ruptures due to fault traces and similar movements; the furnishing of geologic site surveys and hazard reports for key structures; and the introduction of the relatively new "importance concept" to building structures. This concept leads to the conclusion that certain types of structures which must be required to remain functional after an earthquake, such as hospitals, police and fire stations, and power plants, should be designed and constructed to satisfy more stringent requirements than other types of structures. The regulations covering atomic power plant design and construction are classic examples of special requirements being established for a structure which would be particularly hazardous if damaged by an earthquake.

The preparation and use of seismic zoning maps is a comparatively new development. The Seismic Risk Map of the United States currently being included in the Uniform Building Code is an example of this type of control. It should be pointed out that various types of criteria for the establishment of the contour lines drawn on maps of this kind can be applied, such as acceleration, velocity, intensity, or frequency of occurrence. In many areas the assignment of the seismic risk is a difficult task owing to lack of dependable and/or extensive data and because the assignment of contours of risk to an area on a smoothing basis transcends political boundaries and can result in difficulties of administration within political subdivisions or between adjacent political subdivisions.

Seismic safety through land use regulations requires a thorough study of the various hazards associated with earthquakes. These criteria must include consideration of the numerous modes of failure which can occur during an earthquake. Equally important are the density and location of buildings, and the criteria to be utilized in the design of new structures and in the evaluation of existing ones. A brief consideration of modes of failure of the supporting earth structure follows.

Ground Shaking   Most of the damage to buildings attributed to earthquakes is caused by earth vibration. This damage is a function of the resistance of the structure and the characteristics and duration of the ground movement. In a severe and prolonged earthquake, variations in damage within an area of strong shaking can be caused by differences in intensity and types of vibration due to soil conditions, distance and direction to the epicenter, direction and extent of faulting, and soil-structure interaction; these in turn will cause differences in response of various types of structures supported in the various soils. It is obvious that given this number of variables, risks in a comparatively small area can vary greatly.

Up to the present time, most United States codes have not made much effort to account for differences in soil-structure interaction, although the trend now is moving in that direction. In order to account for the differences, it will be necessary to have a great deal more information regarding the response characteristics of the soils and the seismic velocity profiles of the varying areas than is presently available generally. If this information were at hand, risk maps for local areas could be made. It should be pointed out that such a code would be very complex and, because of the microzoning, extremely difficult to enforce.

Permanent Ground Movement   Permanent ground movements caused by earthquakes should be a serious consideration in the preparation of any document controlling building safety. The damage potentials inherent in areas subject to movements of this kind should be recognized, and local building codes should provide for this since prohibition of certain types of construction may be necessary in areas known to be subject to such movement.

Permanent ground movements may be itemized as follows:

Landslides and Lurching.   If the areas of potential instability are known, local landslides can be effectively controlled by properly prepared and properly administered grading codes and land use regulations. Code requirements requiring engineering measures to be applied to soil compaction and foundation design will minimize damage due to settlement or movement of filled-in soil. However, potential for large-scale landslides in natural soils, and movements such as those that occurred during the Turnagain Arm slide of Anchorage in the 1964 shock and the San Fernando earthquake of February 9, 1971, may not always be apparent, and it may not be possible to protect against them. However, where known, the potential for damage from movement of this type on a larger-scale areal basis should be recognized in codes, and provision should be made for green belts or open spaces with the prohibition of critical structures within such known areas.

Faulting.   One of the most spectacular and obvious causes of damage to buildings is that of surface fault ruptures. If the fault ruptures extend through the buildings, severe damage usually results. It is generally not considered economically feasible to design structures to resist these movements. If possible, potentially dangerous faults should be located and avoided, but the present state of the art does not enable us to locate all of these areas. Also, the task of mapping potentially hazardous surface areas throughout the country would be tremendous and impractical. Some active faults are also covered by considerable depths of overburden, and in this case it would be very difficult to predict where a surface break due to the buried fault would intercept the surface.

In the case of public utilities systems, potential breakage due to faulting is critical, and in this case adequate planning to the greatest extent possible is essential. Where such systems cross known active faults, there should be provisions for either prevention of, or isolation and rapid repair of, damage due to differential movement.

Liquefaction.   The phenomenon known as liquefaction can occur where the earth vibrations cause saturated, silty sand soils to subside and flow laterally. These phenomena occur quite rapidly. A spectacular instance of this type of failure occurred in Niigata, Japan, in 1964. Land control measures for this type of failure may include the prohibition of the subject area for use, or the requirement of specific and better engineering design practices, or the limitation for use of this area to types of structures which can accept the resulting considerable movement and damage.

Effects of Water   These may be itemized as follows:

Floods.   Among the more obvious causes of failure of human structures resulting from water are floods caused by dam failure.

Rarely, if ever, in the United States has a modern engineered earth-fill or concrete dam failed owing to earthquake effects. Older dams which have been placed by the hydraulic fill method have demonstrated their vulnerability to damage caused by earthquake movements. The near catastrophic failure of the Van Norman Dam in the 1971 San Fernando earthquake is one of the more recent instances of this type of potential failure. At the present time, many old hydraulic-fill dams or dams formed from mine tailings, etc., exist on waterways above large centers of population, with the waterways flowing through the populated areas below. There is a high potential for damage and great loss of life in the areas below resulting from failures of these structures. It is obvious that these structures should be identified and either removed or strengthened.

Tsunami. A tsunami is a type of sea wave produced by large submarine earthquakes whose epicenters are near a coastal area, by large submarine landslides, or by volcanic eruption. The first recorded tsunami dates back to 1400 B.C., when it destroyed the town of Amnisos in Crete. Recent examples have occurred in the Hawaiian Islands, in Chile, and in Alaska. Losses resulting from this phenomenon can be minimized by (1) *zoning regulations* which would prevent the building of important structures in areas known to be subject to tsunamis; (2) *building regulations* which would require structures in these subject areas to be specially designed to withstand and minimize the effects of tsunamis; and (3) the installation of *sea wave warning systems.* Such a system was installed in 1948 by the United States Coast and Geodetic Survey, and since then it has been expanded to most of the Pacific nations.

It should be pointed out that many of the known hazardous locations include existing industrialized waterfront areas. The retroactive imposition of such building restrictions on existing structures would be very expensive and difficult.

DESIGN CRITERIA

General Considerations   It is strongly emphasized that a proper structural design requires a good deal of engineering judgment, experience, and thoughtful study of the actual performance of buildings subjected to past earthquakes.

The performance of a building during an earthquake can be profoundly influenced by decisions made by the owner, architect, and engineer in the early stages of the design process. Adverse effects of earthquakes can be minimized by the proper application of a series of basic preliminary structural design considerations, and the recommendations of the engineer should be given equal consideration with those from persons concerned with other aspects of the building.

Site Location.   The proper selection of a building site by the owner can have a great influence on the ultimate safety of a project, although in today's social and economic framework it is not always possible to choose the most satisfactory site from a seismic performance viewpoint. Where a number of site choices are available, adequate comparative geologic studies considering site response and site hazards should be made in addition to the customary soil capacity investigation, in order to select the most favorable site.

Symmetry.   In the determination of the preliminary layout and framing scheme for the structure, careful consideration should be given to the factors influencing the dynamic force resistance of the structure. Symmetry of the structural frame and of seismic-resisting elements has a very significant influence on the satisfactory performance of a structure when it is subjected to dynamic forces.

Symmetry and regularity should apply not only to the plan layout of the building but to story heights, distribution of the masses throughout the height of the building, location of the resisting elements, continuity of the form and type of the resisting elements throughout the height of the building, continuity of the same materials used in the resisting elements throughout the building, minimizing of openings in floor diaphragms, and the careful placing of these openings so as not to isolate vertical resisting elements or promote rotation or deflections in the horizontal elements. The materials used, and the connections of nonstructural elements such as interior partitions and exterior screen walls, should be such as to avoid providing incidental noncalculated, unsymmetrical resistance against seismic forces. If it is not possible to avoid providing this incidental resistance, such effects should be considered in the design of the seismic-resisting system. The choice of materials and connections for these should be such as to provide for adequate accommodation to story drifts or other deflections.

Load Paths.   Detailed design of the structure should include careful consideration of the deflected behavior of the structure itself, with conservatively designed diaphragm chords, adequate inter-ties between various plan sections of the building, and conservatively designed collectors ("drag struts") or other adequate connections between the horizontal diaphragms (floors) and the vertical resisting elements (shear walls, frames, etc.). Component parts of the structure, as well as nonstructural elements, must be interconnected to transmit seismic forces through to the resisting elements. In precast concrete construction this is a major consideration.

Actual Forces on the Building.   The designer should always keep in mind that in an earthquake the building is being subjected to forces along more than one axis, that there are probably vertical accelerations and displacements imposed on the building, and that the characteristics of the energy input throughout the structure may not be uniform over the whole area of the building. Designers should also recognize that the forces computed on the basis of present code loadings will probably be exceeded in a major earthquake.

Ductility.   Because of the possibility of excessive force levels being imposed on the structure, one of the most important properties to be provided in seismic design is ductility in the seismic-resisting frame. The use of ductile materials and the proper detailing of connections to allow ductile behavior provide an extra capacity for the absorption of excess energy input imposed on the building by earthquake forces. Details should be developed which guard against brittle behavior and the incorporation of excessive locked-in stresses.

Structural Elements

General.   For the purposes of this book, the discussion of any one topic of earthquake engineering must necessarily be very brief and very elementary. This is particularly true regarding the design of the seismic force–resisting system of a building. For a complete treatment of the dynamic behavior of structures, the reader is referred to the many excellent books on seismology and dynamics.

In the United States, because of the seismicity of the Pacific coast region, a major portion of seismological research and the development of practical engineering design requirements has been concentrated there, with California being particularly active in this work. Other areas of the United States have suffered earthquakes, some of major proportions, but practical interest in this field did not develop in the rest of the nation until comparatively recently. The Structural Engineers Association of California, being made up of members actively engaged in the practical design of earthquake-resistant structures, early began to be a major contributor to work in this field. The result of its interest was embodied in the first earthquake codes developed, such as those of the Uniform Building Code, Title 21 of the California Administrative Code, and the codes of such cities as San Francisco and Los Angeles. These documents have influenced the thinking on this subject in other parts of the world, and a great number of provisions developed in them have been incorporated into other codes. It must be stated, however, that differing approaches have been taken in certain other countries.

History.   With the above in mind, a brief history of the development of earthquake provisions in California follows.

After the San Francisco earthquake of 1906, reconstruction was carried out under a code which required a uniform 30-lb/ft² wind force to be applied to the structure to take care of both wind and earthquake forces. No other required earthquake design provision was in existence in San Francisco for a number of years, but during this time some leading structural engineers in the area employed the concept in their design work of subjecting the building to equivalent static horizontal earthquake forces applied in proportion to the localized masses of the building.

After the 1925 Santa Barbara earthquake, the United States Coast and Geodetic Survey was directed to make studies in the field of seismology. This work has continued to the present day. In 1927, the Uniform Building Code published an Appendix containing suggested earthquake design provisions which could be adopted by the local political jurisdiction at its option. In 1928, the California State Chamber of Commerce commissioned a study of building-code earthquake design provisions. This study formed the basis for many of the provisions of subsequent codes.

In 1933, the Long Beach earthquake destroyed many private buildings and public school buildings. As a result of this, the California state legislature adopted the Field Act, in which responsibility for the administration of public school construction was given to the Division of Architecture, State Department of Public Works. This body established lateral-force design provisions, as well as procedures for reviewing and approving the construction documents and for supervising the construction inspection. In 1937, 1941, and 1953, these lateral-force design provisions underwent various revisions and amplifications. The present requirements are given in Title 21, California Administrative Code.

Also in 1933, the California state legislature adopted the Riley Act, which required all buildings except certain private dwellings and farm buildings to be designed for a minimal lateral force of 2 percent of the vertical design load. In 1953, this was revised to increase the requirement to 3 percent for buildings less than 40 ft in height and 2 percent for those over 40 ft in height.

In 1933, the City of Los Angeles revised its building code to include seismic design requirements utilizing a fixed percentage (8 percent) of the sum of the dead load plus half the live load of the building applied as a static horizontal force. At that time the Los Angeles Building Code also had a maximum height limit of 160 ft or thirteen stories. In 1935 this coefficient was also adopted by the Uniform Building Code, with the added requirement that the seismic coefficient be increased for structures located on weaker soils. In 1943, the City of Los Angeles recognized the influence of flexibility of the structure by making the lateral-force coefficients a function of the number of stories in the building. Until 1947, San Francisco had no more stringent earthquake design requirements than those of the Riley Act. In 1947, more restrictive requirements were added, the seismic design coefficients varying with the number of stories and with variations in soil conditions.

In 1948, a "Joint Committee on Lateral Forces" was formed, consisting of members of the San Francisco Section, American Society of Civil Engineers, and the Structural Engineers Association of Northern California. The work of this committee was a landmark in seismic design recommendations. It proposed lateral-force coefficients based on the fundamental period of a typical symmetrical building, and it recommended that the computed total lateral force be distributed up the height of the building in a triangular manner, thus endeavoring to simulate the effects of the primary modes of vibration (see Fig. 5). This was a first attempt to simulate the dynamic behavior of a building by equivalent static design forces. The report of this committee was published as Separate 66 of Volume 77, dated April 1951, of the American Society of Civil Engineers.

In 1957, the Structural Engineers Association of California formed a statewide Seismology Committee to develop seismic recommendations acceptable to all practicing engineers throughout the state of California. The committee submitted its final report in 1959, and this has become the basis for most current codes in the United States. Reminiscent of the 1948 joint committee's report, the 1959 document recommended an "equivalent static force" procedure, approximating the dynamic characteristics of the building. It also included coefficients dependent on the type of seismic-resisting system. The equivalent static force for the seismic analysis is determined by the equation

$$V = KCW$$

where V is the seismic base shear, K a factor varying from 0.67 to 1.33, introduced to account for the relative behavior of various building systems during earthquakes, C a multiplying factor dependent on a computation for the period of the building, and W

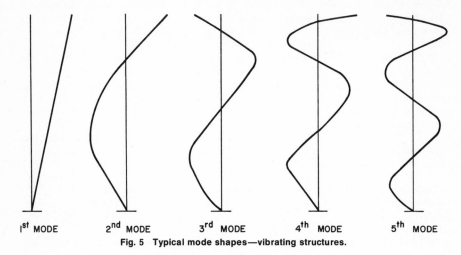

1st MODE   2nd MODE   3rd MODE   4th MODE   5th MODE

Fig. 5   Typical mode shapes—vibrating structures.

the dead load on the building (plus certain specified live loads). In adopting the provisions of the report for use in their code, the International Conference of Building Officials (ICBO) added the multiplier Z to the above expression to account for seismic zoning, and as a result it was necessary to add a seismic zoning map to the Uniform Building Code.

The basic goals of these code provisions were that (1) little structural damage should occur during relatively moderate earthquakes, but some damage to nonstructural items could occur; and (2) in very strong earthquake movements some structural damage could occur, but the probability of structural collapse would be minimal.

Methods of Analysis. During the period of development of what might be called "equivalent static force" design provisions, a vast amount of research was being done on the actual response of structures. As a result, other concepts have been gradually introduced into the Structural Engineers Association's "Recommended Lateral Force Requirements and Commentary," and then into the Uniform Building Code. The influence of the ground motion at the site and the soil-structure interaction on the forces generated in the building, the concept of the ductility of the structure as an energy absorber, and the relatively new concept of an "importance factor" for critical buildings have been subject to considerable study and debate. The capacity to be provided for connections, etc., of various parts or elements of a structure has also been gradually included in codes.

Equivalent Static Force. The 1976 edition of the Uniform Building Code represents the most up-to-date requirements for the equivalent static force design of seismically resistant structures as developed in the United States. This code has been adopted by the ICBO and has been strongly influenced by the above-mentioned 1974 publication, "Recommended Lateral Force Requirements and Commentary." The reader is urged to study both documents—the code for design provisions and the commentary for background thinking.

In the 1976 code it will be noted that the base shear formula has now been expanded to the expression

$$V = ZIKCSW$$

where Z is determined from the seismic zoning map, I is the occupancy importance factor, K reflects the type and characteristics of the resisting frame, C reflects the

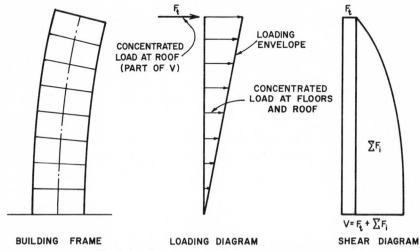

BUILDING FRAME   LOADING DIAGRAM   SHEAR DIAGRAM
Fig. 6   Loading as per 1976 Uniform Building Code.

period of the building, S represents the site structure resonance effect, and W is the total dead load (plus certain live loads) of the structure being designed. The resulting shear is distributed up the height of the building in a triangular fashion, with a part of the base shear concentrated at the roof as a special load. The loads are regarded as static forces and are applied at floor levels, much the same as wind loads. The resulting loads and stresses in the resisting elements are determined by standard methods of statics (see Fig. 6). It will also be noted that the expression for the lateral force generated by elements or parts or portions of the structure follows basically the same format as that for the main structure.

It should be pointed out that the foregoing design requirements are basically developed for structures of uniform dynamic stiffness, relatively uniform distribution of masses, and uniform dynamic "drift." It is tacitly expected that they can be applied to structures with characteristics moderately different from the above assumptions. However, with buildings that have varying structural features (for example, large setbacks), with buildings irregular in plan, or with dynamically irregular buildings, it is required that a dynamic analysis as outlined below be made.

In the San Fernando earthquake of 1971, some major hospital buildings suffered extensive structural as well as nonstructural damage. As a result, it became apparent that because hospitals must be available to provide emergency services to casualties after a severe earthquake, additional more stringent design requirements against earthquake forces should be instituted for hospitals. Accordingly, in 1973, a California state law was passed requiring that the design and construction of hospital buildings should comply with Title 24 of the California Administrative Code in general and with Division T17, Part 6, in particular. Three analysis procedures were set up: two methods—dynamic (Method A) or static (Method B)—for essential hospital facilities, and one method—static (Method C)—for satellite structures not required for the complete functioning of a hospital after a disaster.

In 1976, these requirements were restated. Two alternate methods of analysis were required for all hospital structures.

1. *A dynamic analysis* which is based upon the ground motion prescribed for the site in a special geotechnic report. The report must consider a seismic event which may be postulated with a reasonable confidence level within a 100 year period. The dynamic analysis may be based either on an appropriate time history or on an appropriate response spectra with damping.

2. *An equivalent static lateral force analysis.* Any structure which does not have a highly irregular shape, large differences in lateral resistance or stiffnesses between adjacent stories, or other unusual structural features which could significantly affect the dynamic response may be designed using the static lateral force as set forth in the Code. These forces are considerably larger than static code forces specified for the design of other non-essential buildings.

In actual enforcement of these design provisions, a dynamic analysis is usually required for other than very regular structures.

With the increasing importance of more sophisticated dynamic analysis, the two most widely used methods should be briefly discussed.

Response Spectrum Analysis.   A response spectrum is a plot of the maximum responses of different vibrating bodies with corresponding varying fundamental periods to a given input motion. The plots can show acceleration, velocity, and deflection responses. Plots are usually provided corresponding to varying amounts of viscous damping. Spectra can be developed for vibrating systems behaving elastically or inelastically, for those having other types of damping, and for either single or "multi" degrees of freedom (see Fig. 5). They can also be prepared showing the response to actual earthquakes or to various "standard earthquakes." Steps in the analysis using this approach may be outlined as follows:

- Determine the mathematical model that represents the proposed building.
- Determine the period and the mode shapes of the first several modes of vibration of the mathematical model.
- Determine the modal participation factors describing the portion of the total mass of the building exerted with each mode.
- Determine the base shear and distribution of shears throughout the structure for each mode, spectral value, and specified degree of damping.
- Combine the responses of the various modes.

(The maximum responses do not occur at the same point in time. Therefore, for purposes of design, they must be combined in a reasonable manner. The usual means of doing this is by using the square root of the sum of the squares of the individual modal effects.)

In some ways this method of analysis can be considered an equivalent semistatic approach, because time is not a variable. The time and number of high-amplitude cycles is not specified. It should be recognized that if the response is in the elastic range, the number of cycles has no significance, but should inelastic deformations occur, the number of cycles of high acceleration would make a difference in the extent of damage.

Time-History Response Analysis.   In this method, the time-history record used for input can be that of an actual earthquake or a predetermined or modified so-called "standard earthquake." A choice of damping value is made, and the appropriate mathematical model of the structure is set up. Approximate inelastic as well as elastic behavior can be mathematically modeled. Using the equations of motion, suitably small increments of time on the record are used, and the sequential responses of the assumed mathematical model to the earthquake motions in the very small increments of time are determined.

It is possible to use the ground input characteristics at the foundation level of the building and consider the structure only, or, if the characteristics of the base rock and the supporting soil are able to be determined accurately, a composite model made up of both the supporting soils above the rock and the structure itself can be set up. The characteristics of the motion at the base rock can be assigned, and by using the finite-element method the response of the total composite model can be investigated.

It should be pointed out that a great number of uncertainties exist as far as the selection of the earthquake to be used and the selection of the mathematical model of the building and/or supporting soils are concerned. A complete analysis using this method is both time-consuming and expensive, and it is not always prudent to assume that a time-history response analysis provides the engineer with a more reliable design than might be obtained by other methods.

Nonstructural Elements

General.   A study of earthquake design provisions in many building codes of the past shows that the requirements for lateral bracing and/or connections of nonstructural elements during earthquakes was in general ignored, or that the requirements were very minimal. Experience during recent earthquakes has drawn attention to the overall inadequacies of many of the anchorage systems of nonstructural elements. Accordingly, as codes have been revised in the recent past or as new codes have been produced, more requirements have been progressively introduced covering this field.

These criteria are particularly important in the case of essential structures such as hospitals, police and fire stations, power plants, and electrical switching yards. In California, in the case of schools, seismic-resistance requirements for anchorage of ceilings, lights, shelving, etc., have been in effect for some time. Requirements for hospitals in California (Titles 17 and 24) recently have become even more stringent. The Veterans Administration has also introduced stringent requirements for the design of its hospitals.

In the past, customary procedure in the allocating of design responsibilities has led to virtually no attention being given to the design of these nonstructural elements. Thus, the interconnection and anchorage of these elements have often been left to standard trade practices, putting them in the hands of the manufacturers and installers. Since standard trade practice is not based on earthquake considerations, little provision is usually made for connection, or anchorage against earthquake forces. It is therefore imperative that the member of the design team most qualified to cope with these considerations lead in preparing the necessary design details, and it is equally essential for them to be adequately shown in the contract documents. It is not sufficient, however, to merely prepare and supply adequate details in the contract documents. Careful field follow-up must make sure that all the details are executed in accordance with the contract requirements.

The following discussion represents a broad overview of the basic elements which have performed badly in the past when subjected to earthquake disturbances:

Elevators.   Elevators in taller buildings (over three stories) are generally of the traction type. Hydraulic elevators, because of their speed and design, are usually installed in lower buildings (from two to three stories). As a general statement, because of their configurations, hydraulic elevators, dumbwaiters, and escalators survive with only relatively small damage.

Vulnerable components of traction-type elevators may be listed as follows:

COUNTERWEIGHTS: When subjected to earthquake motion, heavy counterweights tend to bend or break their roller guides and deform their guide rails. As a result of this deformation, they very often become derailed during the earthquake and, as the earthquake progresses, become free-swinging, inflicting damage on spreader beams, brackets, guide rails, and cars. It is a comparatively simple matter to strengthen the guide rails to withstand computed earthquake forces and to install safety shoes on the counterweights. These shoes can be designed to allow the shoe to contact the rail during the earthquake and carry the lateral forces to the guide rail.

GUIDE RAILS FOR COUNTERWEIGHTS: Guide rails should be designed to withstand the computed earthquake forces imposed upon them by the counterweights and by their own weight and should be designed to span to adequate brackets, which generally should be spaced close together and should be heavier than is customary today. These brackets should again be designed to withstand the calculated forces brought to them by the guide rails and in turn should be connected in a logical structural manner to the main building frame, which in turn should be capable of absorbing and dissipating the forces transmitted by the brackets.

ELEVATOR CARS: In general, the cars themselves have performed relatively well during seismic disturbances. Damage to them has resulted from their being struck by the swinging counterweights or from derailment due to excessive deformation of their guide rail system. Consideration should be given to the installation of seismic override switches to shut down the elevator during an earthquake. Manual override switches should also be provided to be used for slow-speed operation after the quake until the system can be more adequately investigated.

GUIDE RAILS FOR ELEVATOR CARS: Surveys of earthquake damage to the car guide rails show that in general they have performed relatively well because they are designed to withstand loads imposed upon them by the car. However, in all cases, they should be adequately analyzed and engineered to withstand operational and seismic forces.

HOISTWAY AND CABLES: The hoistway itself is subject to the deflections of the building structure. Due regard should be given in the design of door frames to accommodate predicted maximum story deflections. The various cables in the hoistway are subject to considerable induced movement during the earthquake. Manufacturers should be required to develop designs that restrain or do away with loose traveling cables in hoistways.

ELEVATOR DRIVING MECHANISMS: Motor generators are usually mounted on vibration isolator mounts. Mounts of this kind should be specially designed not only to screen out vibration and noise resulting from operation but to restrain the machine against movements arising from earthquake forces.

ELECTRICAL CONTROL PANELS: These should be adequately braced and connected both to the floor and/or the ceiling above. These braces should be designed against specified seismic forces.

DRIVE MOTORS, ETC: These motors are generally securely mounted on bases which in turn are bolted to the floor; in general the unit itself is afforded adequate anchorage, but the internal design of the equipment itself should render it capable of withstanding the internal inertia forces generated by an earthquake.

Mechanical Systems.   Mechanical systems such as boilers and flues, fans and ducts, compressors and chillers, cooling towers, etc., resist earthquakes with varying degrees of success. If the equipment itself is internally designed to adequately resist the generated seismic forces and the equipment itself is adequately bolted to a competent base structure, usually little damage results. If the equipment is not adequately bolted down, it may shift or overturn, with resulting damage to appurtenant pipes, ducts, satellite equipment, and so on. In the past, if the equipment has been mounted upon vibrator isolators which are not designed and constructed to furnish resistance against sliding and overturning forces, heavy damage has occurred to the equipment and to its related piping, ducting, and other service connections. In many cases, the requirements for vibration isolation and acoustical control are in conflict with those of adequate anchorage to resist earthquake forces.

The designer should also be aware that the characteristics of the energy input to equipment mounted in the basement may vary considerably from the input into equipment mounted high up in the structure. In general, vibration isolators may be expected to lower the natural frequency of the equipment assembly. The possibility of resonant response of the equipment with the structure when the predominant period of the structure approaches that of the equipment assembly should be given serious consideration.

Tanks.   Tanks containing liquids have traditionally behaved poorly during earthquakes. Unanchored tanks are susceptible to overturning and lateral shifting. Any movement of this kind can cause secondary damage to connected piping, and if the tanks are large and move off their bases and fall, they can cause structural damage to the surrounding floor systems.

General guidelines for lateral support of tanks may be summarized as follows:

- Horizontal tanks should be adequately connected to their saddles to prevent horizontal movement, and the saddles should be bolted to the structural framing.
- Ceiling-mounted tanks should be connected tightly against the overhead supporting structural members.
- The suspended equipment should be braced on all four sides.
- Elevated tanks supported on frames resting on the structural floor must be provided with adequate bracing and anchors to the structural floor and/or walls.

Piping Systems.   There have been long-standing criteria for bracing fire sprinkler piping, but until quite recently little thought has been given to code requirements for the anchoring of piping against seismic forces.

In general, recommendations for anchoring piping may be summarized as follows:

- Piping is damaged when a part of a main header pipe run is free to move and small branch lines are not, being clamped to the structural frame. Accordingly, all pipe runs should have a system of longitudinal and transverse sway bracing.
- Where piping passes through seismic or expansion joints, or where rigidly supported pipes connect to equipment mounted on vibration isolators, flexible joints should be supplied in the line.
- Where piping passes through walls or floors and anticipated wall or floor movements may occur, provide pipe sleeves with ample clearances.
- For vertical piping, provide adequate lateral guides at regular intervals.

Air Handling Systems.   Duct work, grilles, ceiling diffusers, etc., are analogous in their behavior to piping.

Design requirements for bracing against horizontal forces can be summarized as follows:

- Provide adequate sway bracing properly connected to a competent part of the structural frame.
- Support duct runs at the closest possible adequate structural members.
- Ensure that ceiling and wall registers and duct work are adequately connected to the ceiling suspension systems or to the wall framing, preferably by carefully installed sheet metal screws of proper size.
- Have vertical duct runs adequately braced to the shaft walls, which in turn should be adequately connected to the structural system and/or floor openings.
- Provide for movement at seismic joints with flexible joints or sections.

Flues and Chimneys.   Heavy unreinforced masonry chimneys have traditionally performed poorly in earthquakes. Modern-day codes now require relatively high seismic-design coefficients for these items. Free-standing stacks or chimneys should be regarded as structures within themselves and designed as such. Flues and stacks passing up through the building should be designed to span between floors, and they should be adequately connected to the floors and roof of the buildings if these are part of the bracing system of the building itself. Patent flues (double-wall) are usually of lightweight construction and, if adequately connected, generally perform reasonably well. Again, careful consideration should be given to the furnaces and water heaters to allow for differential movement between either the flue or the equipment itself.

Light Fixtures.   Light fixtures may be divided into three types—recessed, surface-mounted, and pendant fixtures; each behaves differently during seismic disturbances.

Recessed fixtures, in general, are mounted in T-bar ceilings. If they are supported by, and secured directly to, the main runners of the ceiling support system, their performance in general has been adequate. Where they have been supported by cross runners or light furring, in many instances they have pounded the surrounding ceiling elements and have slid or jumped off their supports.

Recessed fixtures should also be provided with independent secondary supports. These are generally in the form of two wire hangers at diagonal corners of each fixture. The wires should be independently attached to the fixture housing and to the building structure above, and they should be capable of safely supporting a large percentage overload.

Surface-mounted fixtures generally require relatively secure attachments to the ceiling system. Damage may occur where support clamps open or clips to the T-bar ceiling member loosen. In all cases, positive locking devices between the fixture and the main runners of the ceiling system should be provided. It is recommended that direct attachments be made to the building structure, if possible.

Pendant fixtures have not had good performance records since they have an inherent tendency to be set into resonance by the predominant frequencies of an earthquake. In general, their supports have failed at the ceiling connections, at the swivel joints, at the fixture housing, and in the supporting stems or chains. It is recommended that, in general, additional safety wires be attached to the fixture canopy and to an adequate member of the ceiling support system. This will prevent the fixture from falling but not from being damaged due to lateral movement. Pendant fixtures with long steel-rod stems or hanger chains are often damaged when they strike each other or adjacent objects. Failures also occur when supporting chains jump out of open support hooks, or the supporting chains break. In addition, movement can cause failures to occur at outlet box connections. The use of adequate-capacity chains and large safety hooks is recommended.

Ceiling systems are greatly varied, including, for example, those with exposed T-bar supports and drop-in tile; those with a concealed spline system; and luminous ceilings, which are essentially a combination of surface-mounted lamps on one ceiling plane and a suspended ceiling with diffusers on a lower plane. These systems generally are hung on suspender wires. The concealed-spline installations are inherently more stable than the exposed T-bar system, and they have generally sustained less damage. The tiles are relatively better keyed together by the splines, and the entire ceiling plane is more rigid. Another system of ceiling construction employs wood joists with wood hangers attached to the overhead structural system. The ceiling element for this system may be either gypsum board or nailed-on or glued-on tiles.

Until recently, wire hanger and T-bar systems did not have bracing systems incorporated in their construction and were free to swing on their suspension wires and batter against adjacent partitions and walls. To provide adequately against horizontal forces induced by seismic disturbances, the ceiling-grid T-bar systems should be adequately braced against lateral and vertical movements by adequately designed and detailed diagonal bracing, located at regular intervals. The ceiling system should not be fastened to the surrounding walls or partitions. Main and cross runners should have hangers at the perimeter, so that the wall trim angles do not support the ceiling but are large enough to allow for lateral differential movement on the outstanding leg of the angle without coming off the leg. Cross runners should be fastened to the main runners using locking clips or similar devices.

In the case of ceilings composed of a system of wood joists and wood hangers, adequate bracing in both directions in the form of wood diagonals connected to the structural frame above should be provided. Because of the form of construction, this type of framing inherently offers better resistance and more opportunities to brace the system easily.

General recommendations for all types of ceilings are as follows:
- In ceilings with an irregularly shaped plan, adequate provisions should be made to tie the reentrant corners, etc., into the main body of the ceiling.
- If large ceiling areas are separated into smaller parts by rows of light fixtures, etc., the separated areas should be adequately held together with rigid ties.
- Ceiling light fixtures are usually quite heavy with respect to the ceiling construction; the "battering" effect of the fixture should be recognized and provision made for adequate anchorage and dissipation of the fixture-generated lateral loads.
- At intersections of walls and ceilings, the ceilings should be free to move with respect to the walls.

CONSTRUCTION

The preparation of adequate drawings and specifications is only one step in the process by which an earthquake-resistant structure comes into being. Proper monitoring of the construction processes is essential in order that all parties may be reasonably assured that the as-built structure incorporates all the requirements of the contract documents. Experience on the Pacific coast has clearly shown that the contractor cannot be expected to fully interpret and carry out the requirements of the contract documents without the support of monitoring.

Testing   Adequate testing of the component materials by a competent impartial testing agency, to ensure their conformance with the specifications, should be carried out from the beginning of the job and should be continuously performed through the construction period.

Shop Details   The detailing of moment-resisting connections should be the responsibility of the structural design office and should be carefully prepared, with complete details appearing on the contract drawings. This is true regardless of the material in which the design is being executed, and it is particularly applicable in the case of ductile frames, whether of steel or concrete. It is, of course, mandatory that these design details be accurately transferred to the shop details. To ensure this, the design structural engineer's office should routinely and carefully review the shop details as they are prepared, and well before any fabrication takes place. This procedure not only helps to guard against field errors but ensures that the design engineer is afforded a "second look" at the contract drawings before the details are executed.

Field Inspection   Experience in the state of California on the design of schools and hospitals has demonstrated the value of a competent full-time inspector on the job. This individual should have some grounding in design, should be experienced in construction procedures in all types of materials, and should be carefully selected so that the responsible engineer can have confidence in the inspector's integrity, intelligence, and diligence.

Construction Support   In addition, the design engineer should regularly visit the site at frequent intervals in order to furnish construction support, both to the inspector and to the contractor, and to obtain personal assurance that the intent of the drawings and specifications is being adequately carried out.

Chapter **7**

Hurricanes, Tornadoes, and Extreme Winds

JOSEPH E. MINOR, P.E., Ph.D.

JAMES R. MCDONALD, P.E., Ph.D.

KISHOR C. MEHTA, P.E., Ph.D.

Institute for Disaster Research, Texas Tech University

The understanding of mechanisms through which extreme winds affect structures has advanced significantly in recent years. Extensive studies of the effects of hurricanes, tornadoes, and other windstorms on buildings and other structures have led engineers and architects to conclude that shelters can be constructed to protect people from the severe environment presented by severe windstorms. Shelters have been designed and constructed in residences, schools, and public buildings which will assure virtually 100 percent survivability in the event of a tornado, hurricane, or extreme windstorm, if a minimum warning time of approximately two minutes is assumed.

EXTREME WINDS

Persons concerned with life safety in environments subject to severe windstorms must be familiar with the features of these natural hazards. The following sections present information on the tornado, the hurricane, and other severe windstorms ("foehn" winds, severe thunderstorms, frontal passages, etc.).

A major finding affecting life safety is that maximum values of wind speeds in the several types of storms are well within the range of manageability. The recent consensus among meteorologists and engineers is that tornadic wind speeds near ground level (30 feet and less) do not exceed 300 mi/h, and many responsible viewpoints hold that 250 mi/h may well be a limiting value. Hurricane winds seldom exceed 200 mi/h near ground level over land, and winds in other types of windstorms rarely exceed a 110- to 125-mi/h range. Hence, engineers and architects who address the extreme wind hazards presented by windstorms peculiar to their geographic regions of interest can begin with the knowledge that design values for maximum wind speeds are in a range of manageability both technically and economically.

Tornadoes

Tornadoes are violent, narrow-pathed windstorms. They create loadings on structures through three interrelated phenomena: wind velocity, atmospheric pressure change, and missile impact. These three types of loadings and combinations thereof must be considered in the design of tornado-resistant structures.

The design of such structures generally involves three tasks: (1) the establishment of a so-called "design-basis tornado" (DBT), (2) the conversion of the tornado wind and pressure effects into equivalent design loads on the structure, and (3) the design of the individual structural components. Since tornadoes vary in frequency, size, and intensity, it is desirable to establish the DBT relative to the geographical location under consideration. The DBT specifies tornado parameters (which identify wind speed characteristics) and atmospheric pressure-change parameters and establishes postulated missile criteria. In converting the wind and pressure effects into design loads, the structure size and geometry must be taken into account, as well as local features such as gables and overhangs. The remainder of this subsection is devoted to the general nature of tornadoes.

Physical Description

Among the many natural phenomena over which human beings have no control, tornadoes are the most violent. Relatively short-lived and limited in size, they travel a narrow path on the ground, leaving a wake of almost total destruction. Their most frequent occurrence is in the Middle Plains states of the United States, although they are reported in all other states.

Many statistical data have been collected on tornadoes concerning location, duration, translational speed, dimensions of path, damage, and loss of life. Many of these data can be found in the references at the end of this chapter. Every year we can be sure that millions of dollars in property destruction will take place, as has been the case in years past.

Tornadoes are generally quite small; the vast majority are less than a mile in diameter, and many damage paths are less than 100 yd wide. They appear as funnels which dip downward from the base of existing clouds and approach the ground in an irregular fashion. A fully developed tornado can have a variety of shapes. Sometimes it looks like an ordinary funnel, wide at the top and tapering to a small diameter at ground level. At times the tornado is a large cylinder whose diameter is constant between the cloud base and the ground. The funnel may be either vertical or inclined.

The tornado funnel one actually sees is a cloud of water droplets mixed with dust and other debris. Above the ground, water droplets cause the outline of the funnel cloud. The droplets form because low atmospheric pressure in the funnel causes an expansion and cooling of the air, which leads to an increase of the relative humidity and condensation. Thus a vertical tube, with a wall consisting of a mass of air rotating counterclockwise at very high speed, touches the ground. At ground level the air moves radially toward the circular base of the tube. As it approaches the circle, the air is rotating counterclockwise, as is the tube. The air on the right side of the funnel, looking in the direction of translational movement, has a higher velocity than that on the left side. Combined with the high rotational winds, the water vapor forms a barrier that prevents air from moving across it. There is no clear agreement concerning the flow of air within the funnel itself. Three types of inner funnel motion are mathematically possible:

    1. The radial velocity component is directed inward along the ground surface

with an upward component along the axis of the vortex resulting in turbulent flow (referred to as a one-cell model).

2. There is a downward motion on the central axis with a radial velocity component directed outward near the surface.

3. The radial velocity component is directed inward along the surface with a downward component on the axis and a compensating outflow at an intermediate angle (referred to as a two-cell model).

The major flow of air at ground level is circular and translational at the same time. The translational speed of a tornado is considered to be a well-known quantity, since the measurement is not too difficult to make. The time that the storm passes specific points along the path can be determined by stopped clocks. The range of translational speed varies from 5 to 70 mi/h, with an average of 45 mi/h.

Maximum wind velocities in tornadoes are not recorded, because anemometers in a position to make the measurements are not likely to survive. Recent studies of tornado damage have led tornado experts to estimate maximum velocity to be approximately 300 mi/h.

Values of tornado wind forces are estimated by one or more of the following methods:

1. Analysis of a damaged structure
2. Analysis of ground marks
3. Examination of motion pictures of tornado funnels
4. Statistical analysis of window-glass breakage in tall buildings
5. Analysis of funnel shapes

Caution must always be exercised in applying the damage analysis technique in predicting wind velocities. "Freak" exhibitions of tremendous forces can often be explained in some rational manner.

One common feature of all tornadoes is the low pressure at the center of the storm. As in the case of wind velocity, little is known about the magnitude of the pressure drop. The probability of a small tornado funnel passing directly over a barograph is remote. Even if the instrument were not destroyed, the values would be subject to question because most barographs are not designed to respond to the rapid pressure variations produced by a moving tornado. This problem was particularly true in years past before the advent of modern transducers. A vast network of closely spaced pressure sensing units has been proposed, but because of the large number of recording units necessary to obtain data in a reasonable amount of time, and the expense involved, this project has not been carried out. The National Severe Storms Laboratory at Norman, Oklahoma, does have a mesoscale network of a limited size in southwestern Oklahoma.

Recorded pressure drop in the center of a tornado is about 2.5 in Hg (1.2 lb/in^2), although some unofficial records place it higher. The exploding of buildings from low atmospheric (as opposed to wind or dynamic) pressure has perhaps been grossly overstated. Examples of such explosions can be found, but their occurrence is rare.

One characteristic of all tornado damage is the large number of missiles and amount of debris present. Missiles range in size from roof gravel and twigs to power poles and tumbling automobiles. A missile is considered to be any type of object that is accelerated by the wind forces. Missiles may be carried parallel to the ground surface, or they may be lifted to high elevations and then fall to the ground under the influence of gravity. Missiles cause damage from two principal effects: (1) local effects from penetration or perforation and (2) instability effects caused by the impact of massive objects.

Debris comes from destroyed building components, such as walls and roofs, or from building contents. Debris loadings may be significant when part of a facility is hardened against tornadoes and another part is not. Destruction of the nonhardened building may create debris loads on the hardened facility.

Meteorological Conditions

There are generally three separate synoptic weather situations which tend to spawn tornadoes in the United States: one is most common to the Great Plains, one to the Gulf Coast area, and the third to the Pacific Coast.

The first and by far the most common synoptic tornado weather pattern is the squall line. A line of thunderstorms, some of which may be severe, forms ahead of a surface cold front, along a surface or upper-air cold front, or in a low-pressure trough. Squall-line tornadoes frequently form in families or groups. They are more numerous in the afternoon but may occur at any hour. Damage swaths from these storms are normally longer and wider than tornadoes characteristic of other conditions.

The second synoptic situation responsible for tornado generation is most common when warm moist air travels northward from the Gulf of Mexico and is overrun by cool dry air from the west or southwest. Although many thunderstorms may be present in the air mass, only one will normally breed a tornado. If more than one tornado develops, they will usually be more than 100 mi apart. These storms are usually slow-moving and short-lived, and they produce short and narrow damage paths.

The third, and least common, tornado-bearing stiuation is restricted to the Pacific Coast region, where cold moist air prevails from the surface to great altitudes. Funnel clouds are often seen aloft. When they do touch ground, they are often short-lived. Damage is normally confined to an area which is small in both length and width. The storms more often occur singly than in families and are associated with isolated thunderstorms which are embedded in scattered rainshowers.

Common in all three synoptic situations listed above are the following three meteorological conditions necessary for producing tornadoes:

1. A low-level layer of moist air surmounted by an upper-level layer of dry air
2. Narrow bands of strong winds in both low-level and upper-level air layers
3. A triggering mechanism

Conditions 1 and 2, when met, represent a potentially unstable atmospheric situation which, when disturbed by condition 3, produces interlayer mixing. This instability results in the generation of a severe storm. A squall line, a cold front, movement of the dry line, or unequal heating at the ground surface can each serve as the mechanism which produces instability from a potentially unstable situation.

Geographical Distribution and Intensity

A great deal of time and effort during the past 70 years has been spent in collecting and evaluating statistical data on tornadoes. Most of the collecting has been done by meteorologists rather than by engineers. Much of the information needed for tornado force evaluation is still lacking or is in a form that is not conveniently interpreted by the engineer.

Until recently there has been no real systematic approach to the gathering of data about tornadoes. The efforts of Dr. T. T. Fujita at the University of Chicago and Mr. Allen D. Pearson at the National Severe Storms Forecast Center at Kansas City, Missouri, have produced a systematic collection of tornado data, however. Data are gradually accumulating that will be useful in the estimation of tornado occurrence and intensity based on probabilistic methods.

Despite some inconsistencies in acquiring tornado data, there is a great deal of information available on the frequency of occurrence, geographical distribution, and severity of tornadoes. Table 1 enumerates a selected list of sources of tornado records and other information.

Tornado data are presented in a variety of different forms. Geographical distributions are often presented as contour maps in which the average number of tornadoes per year is plotted for annual probability of tornado occurrence. Sometimes the number of occurrences in a given period is tabulated for various geographical units such as counties, states, or 1° squares.

The frequency of tornado occurrence is expressed in terms of a "tornado day," which is defined by the National Severe Storms Forecast Center as a day on which one or more tornadoes are reported within a certain geographical boundary. Tornado

TABLE 1   Sources of Tornado Records

Data	Source	Type of data
1. "Tornado Occurrences in the United States 1916–1958"	Department of Commerce, Environmental Data Service, NOAA (National Oceanic and Atmospheric Administration), Weather Bureau Technical Paper No. 20 (Revised)	Statistical data on tornado frequencies and occurrences
2. Climatology Data, National Summary	Department of Commerce, NOAA	Reports of tornado occurrences 1950–1958
3. "Severe Local Storm Occurrences 1955–1967"	See Bibliography (Pautz, 1969)	Statistical data on frequency and geographical distribution of tornadoes
4. *Storm Data*	Department of Commerce, Environmental Data Service, NOAA, Asheville, NC	Monthly publications; lists by state all tornadoes, funnel clouds, wind, hail and ice storms. Began publication in 1959.
5. Computer records of all tornadoes since 1950	Department of Commerce, NOAA, National Severe Storms Forecast Center, Kansas City, MO	A computer tape listing of all known tornadoes is maintained. Information includes location, time, length and width of damage path and F-scale rating. Data is not 100 percent complete prior to 1970.
6. F-scale classification of tornadoes: 1971–present	Satellite and Mesometeorology Research Project, University of Chicago	Since 1971 tornadoes are classified according to FPP scales.
7. Records from each state	Department of Commerce, NOAA, National Weather Service	The office of state climatologist was eliminated in 1972. However, there is generally one individual in each state who is responsible for keeping tornado records.
8. Monthly weather publications	*Weatherwise, Monthly Weather Review, Bulletin of American Meteorological Society*	National summaries, details of specific storms, reports of tornado research

days are divided into eight mutually exclusive classes as days with one, two, three, four, five, six to ten, eleven to twenty, and more than twenty tornadoes. A "family outbreak" is the term used when six or more tornadoes take place on a given day. With six to ten occurrences, it is called a *small* family outbreak; eleven to twenty is a *moderate* family outbreak, and more than twenty constitute a *large* family outbreak. Geographic distribution is not considered in the family outbreak definition.

In the last 50 years there has been a great increase in the number of reported tornado occurrences, as shown in certain weather summaries. The increase largely results from a better system of reporting rather than from a change in climatic conditions.

For a tornado to be "confirmed" and included in the National Oceanic and Atmospheric Administration (NOAA) records, an official observer must sight a funnel cloud on the ground and judge the extent and type of damage caused by the tornado. Official observers may be National Weather Service personnel, law enforcement officers, or trained citizen weather observers. Local confirmation of tornadoes is forwarded to the National Climatic Center (NOAA) in Asheville, North Carolina. The data are then recorded in *Storm Data*.

Fig. 1   Tornado occurence map: number of tornadoes per 10,000 mi² per year.

For years the state of Kansas had the dubious distinction of being the "cyclone state." Innocently bestowed by *The Wizard of Oz* and statistically merited until 1961, this title conveyed for Kansas an image of a dusty plain incessantly lashed by these awesome storms. Curiously, with the advent of a better reporting system, both Texas and Oklahoma were found to exceed Kansas in total number of tornadoes and number of tornadoes per unit area, respectively.

Figure 1 shows the average number of tornadoes per year per 10,000 mi². Clearly, almost all tornado activity occurs east of the Rocky Mountains. Central Oklahoma has the highest concentration of tornadoes. Other high-incident cells are centered in the Midwest (Illinois, Indiana, Ohio, and Michigan) and the Southeast (Mississippi, Georgia, and Alabama). Quite a number of hurricane-spawned tornado occurrences are reported along the Eastern seaboard from Florida to New England.

It is possible to calculate the possibility of a tornado striking a particular location in a given geographical region.

$$\text{Probability} = \frac{\text{average damage-path area} \times \text{frequency}}{\text{geographical area}}$$

The average damage-path area is estimated by some researchers to be 2.8 mi². In lieu of this value, an average damage-path area can be determined from the records of tornadoes in the region. As an example, suppose five tornadoes have struck a 1° square having 4200 mi² in a given year. The probability of any point within the 1° square being struck by a tornado in a year is

$$P = \frac{2.8\,(5)}{4200} = 0.0336$$

The inverse of the above value gives the mean recurrence interval between tornado occurrences. The recurrence interval in this example is 298 years. In terms of tornado probabilities, this is a relatively short recurrence interval. For example, most nuclear power plant locations in the United States have tornado recurrence intervals from 1000 to 6000 years.

Although the probability of occurrence cited here accounts for damage-path area, it does not portray the effects of tornado intensity, which are most important to the design engineer. More useful approaches to the calculation of tornadic wind occurrences are available.

Tornadoes have been recorded in every month of the year. The peak season varies in different locations. Generally, April through July represents the peak season. Table 2 and Fig. 2 illustrate the seasonal distribution of tornadoes in the period 1955–1967. Table 3 contains an important analysis of tornado intensity distributions. Note that almost 90 percent of all 1971 and 1972 tornadoes had maximum wind speeds of less than 160 mi/h.

Hurricanes

Hurricanes are tropical cyclones whose maximum sustained winds reach or exceed a threshold speed of 74 mi/h. The winds circulate in a large spiral around a relatively calm center called the core (eye).

Hurricanes are tropical cyclones, but all tropical cyclones are not hurricanes. Sometimes they begin as a tropical disturbance. As they gain progressively in intensity, they become known as a tropical disturbance, a tropical depression (wind of 32 to 38 mi/h), a tropical storm (wind of 39 to 74 mi/h), and finally a hurricane. Tropical storms form over the oceans from about 5 to 15° of latitude from the equator. Many details of the formation and maintenance of a tropical storm are still not completely known.

Hurricanes begin to weaken and die when their source of energy is diminished. This usually occurs when the hurricane encounters land, where, in addition to the lack of energy, frictional forces alter the momentum, resulting in a rapid decrease of wind velocity. The mature hurricane may consist of a relatively cloud-free, calm eye with low pressure averaging 15 mi (24 km) in diameter; around it, winds of hurricane intensity cover on the average an area 100 mi (160 km) in diameter. Clouds and rain are organized in spiral bands around the storm and may extend several hundred miles.

The characteristics of hurricanes are described in the paragraphs below in terms of wind, atmospheric pressure change, translational speed, size, life span, and frequency of occurrence.

The wind field in the hurricane is a function of the radius of maximum wind, the central pressure difference, the translational speed, and the geographical location of the hurricane. The maximum wind occurs along the rim of the eye near the wall cloud, forward and to its right, looking along the direction of translation.

The elevation of the wind velocity instrument, its accuracy, and the terrain roughness upwind from the instrument significantly affect its measurements. Wind gusts within the hurricane may exceed sustained winds by 30 to 50 percent. Wind maxima typically found near the center of a hurricane result from the development of strong pressure gradients which accelerate the flow of mass radially, causing the wind speeds to increase inward due to angular momentum considerations. As the acceleration of

TABLE 2 Frequencies of Tornado Days, 1955–1967

Month	Class (Tornadoes per tornado day)								Total	Avg. no. tornado days/ mo.	% of days with tornadoes
	1	2	3	4	5	6–10	11–20	21+			
Jan.	32	9	2	4	0	4	4	1	56	4.3	14
Feb.	31	12	7	3	4	9	9	2	77	5.9	21
Mar.	42	26	16	17	12	15	15	3	146	11.2	36
Apr.	47	33	29	17	20	45	30	18	239	18.4	61
May	53	44	43	19	22	65	46	34	326	25.0	81
Jun.	28	51	60	37	32	89	53	9	359	27.6	92
Jul.	97	58	41	50	36	58	13	1	354	27.3	88
Aug.	104	61	44	26	18	21	5	0	279	21.4	69
Sep.	83	46	15	12	12	17	2	4	191	14.7	49
Oct.	58	21	7	9	2	8	3	2	110	8.5	27
Nov.	34	15	8	6	0	9	7	3	82	6.3	21
Dec.	22	6	3	2	4	6	2	2	47	3.6	12
TOTAL	631	382	275	202	162	346	189	79	2266	174.3	
% of tornado days	27.9	16.9	12.1	8.9	7.1	15.3	8.4	3.4			48

source: "Severe Local Storm Occurrences 1955–1967," ESSA Technical Memorandum, WBTM FCST 12, Office of Meteorological Operations, Weather Analysis and Prediction Division, Silver Spring, MD.

mass (energy) is increased or decreased, so is the central pressure. The effect of the atmospheric pressure drop as force on a structure is not as significant as it is in the case of tornadoes, because the rate of change of atmospheric pressure, as the hurricane moves over a given point, is small relative to that in a tornado.

The size of a hurricane is conventionally expressed in terms of the diameter of the region of hurricane winds (greater than 74 mi/h) or of the region of gale-force winds

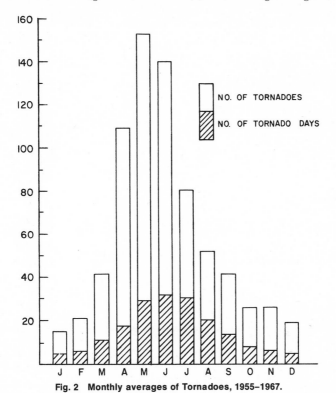

Fig. 2 Monthly averages of Tornadoes, 1955–1967.

(above 40 mi/h). A typical hurricane will have hurricane-force winds over an area 100 mi (161 km) in diameter, and the gales may cover an area 350 to 400 mi (563 to 587 km) in diameter.

The movement of a hurricane is a result of its interaction, throughout the vertical extent of the storm system, with the wind regime in which it is embedded. Forward translational speeds may vary from near 0 to 60 mi/h. Typical translational speeds range from average values of 10 mi/h in the Gulf of Mexico and along the Florida east coast. They increase linearly to the north, reaching a mean value of 32 mi/h, for example, at the latitudes of New York State. The average life of a hurricane is about 9 days, although it may vary from less than 1 to more than 12 days.

In the period 1901–1958 there were 459 tropical storms recorded. Of these, 261 reached hurricane intensity. Twenty-five percent or more approach close enough to the coastline of the continental United States to bring hurricane winds. No state except Florida averages one full hurricane per year. An average of six Atlantic hurricanes occur per year. However, there are significant deviations from this average.

Landfall probabilities have been determined for 50-mi sectors along the United States coast. The range-of-return period for a hurricane of any intensity varies from 1 in 6 years in southeast Florida to 1 in 85 years along the New England coast. The probability of a "great" hurricane (a hurricane possessing wind speeds of 125 mi/h or greater) ranges from 1 in 15 years to 1 in 50 along Florida and the Gulf Coast and is smaller to the north.

There are numerous related features which accompany hurricanes; among these are tides, storm surges, wave action, floods, tornadoes, and heavy rainfall. Only the effects of tornadoes are included in the scope of this discussion. There are many instances of tornado occurrences associated with hurricanes. In general they have been observed in the forward semicircle or along the advancing periphery of the storm, and they occur just prior to and during landfall. They are generally less severe than those associated with extratropical cyclones.

TABLE 3   Intensity Distribution of Tornadoes, 1971 and 1972

Estimated wind speed,* mi/h	No. of tornadoes	Percent	Cumulative percent
40–72	352	21.6	21.6
73–112	718	44.1	65.7
113–157	410	25.2	90.9
158–206	113	7.0	97.9
207–260	33	2.0	99.9
261–318	2	0.1	100.0
	1628		

*From aerial inspection of damage.
SOURCE: T. T. Fujita and A. D. Pearson, "Results of FPP Classification of 1971 and 1972 Tornadoes," Preprint Volume, Eighth Conference on Severe Local Storms, American Meteorological Society, Boston, MA, 1973.

Other Extreme Windstorms

The winds of the tornado and tropical cyclone (hurricanes) have been discussed in previous sections. Other extreme winds may be created in cyclones outside the tropics (extratropical), in thunderstorms, and as orographic lee winds.

Orographic winds are the winds that form in the lee of mountains and mountain ranges. They are the cold "bora" and the warm "foehn," or mixtures of the two. Often they are associated with fronts accompanying the eastward travel of large cyclones and anticyclones. There are also the devastating valley, gorge, or fjord winds, which may create more destruction when mixed with the "bora" or "foehn" winds. Additionally, the lee winds can be associated with the winds along fronts or squall lines.

SHELTERS FOR PROTECTION FROM EXTREME WINDS

The explosion of research and technical literature addressing the tornado, the hurricane, and other extreme windstorms has provided engineers and architects with a sound technical basis for developing shelter designs. The consensus that maximum wind speeds in these storms are, indeed, manageable and the observation that the vast majority of such storms are much less severe than the worst incidents of record have brought forth a "risk-oriented" approach to the design of shelters for extreme winds. This approach was followed in the examples presented below, which are intended for residential shelters and shelters for schools and public buildings.

Residential Shelters

Shelters contained within the residence (called "in-residence shelters") can promise excellent protection against severe winds. More than 3 billion worker-hours are spent annually in the United States under tornado watches. Tornadoes cause more than $75 million in property damage and kill more than 125 people in the United States each year.

Until recently most people thought that the forces of a tornado were so awesome that nothing could be done to provide safety above ground economically. Basements, cellars, and some community shelters can be found, but not in numbers or locations to offer protection to most people.

Because of the cost of making the entire structure safe against extreme winds, and the resulting unattractive appearance, the concept of a protective module *within* the home was introduced. A small interior room such as a closet or bathroom, readily accessible from all parts of the house, can be the storm shelter. The idea is applicable to existing residences, although of course it is most readily applicable to new construction. All parts of the module—walls, ceilings, doors, and openings—must be properly designed to provide occupants protection even if the surrounding structure is severely damaged or destroyed.

The accessibility of an in-residence shelter near the center of the house at the "living level" gives it a great advantage over a cellar or community shelter. There is extreme danger of being struck by flying debris in trying to reach a shelter outside the house. The in-residence shelter idea permits a family to continue regular living patterns during a weather watch, knowing that a safe place is only a few seconds away. It does little to reduce property damage to other portions of a residence, but it does ensure safety; further, the shelter module has a daily usefulness. Its protective features can be visually and functionally blended to fit the residence.

Basements offer adequate shelter from storms and are readily accessible, but their high cost prevents widespread use. Also, the in-residence shelter can be economically constructed within an existing house, whereas a basement cannot.

Shelter Concept

The shelter's structural integrity is the primary design consideration. In a storm, it must be able to withstand the direct forces of the wind and secondary forces such as those imposed by the collapse of the house onto the shelter. Direct forces from winds can be estimated with reasonable confidence—loads up to 140 lb/ft^2 (683 kg/m^2) are possible on some surfaces. Secondary loads are more difficult to predict and are likely to be more localized than direct wind loads. Venting can be provided to relieve pressure differentials.

Of prime importance to structural integrity are adequate fasteners. The ceiling must be securely connected to the walls, the walls to each other, and the walls to the floor or foundation. This can be done by bolting units to the floor slab, drilling into existing slabs, or using vertical reinforcing bars to lock floor, walls, and ceiling together.

Large factors of safety for collapse from wind loads can be used without seriously affecting costs. A small room properly fastened and designed to resist penetration by missiles inherently possesses great structural integrity.

Walls, doors, and ceilings of the shelter must also be able to prevent penetration by missiles. The mechanics of penetration are not well understood in the case of a windborne missile impacting a wall section built of typical construction materials. Intuitively, the energy at impact would seem to be an important measure of the missile's ability to penetrate, while mass, shear strength, and ductility of the shield (wall, ceiling, or door) would seem important in resisting penetration of a missile.

In-residence Shelter in New Construction

The concept of an in-residence shelter module, as suggested by Dr. E.W. Kiesling of Texas Tech University, is that of a strengthened interior space which ensures protection from the effects of extreme winds. Strengthening an entire residence to resist tornadic winds, even in new construction, usually is impractical due to high cost and resulting appearance of the residence. The shelter module is a reasonable and possibly more acceptable alternative.

The in-residence shelter module is a sturdy space, such as a bathroom, utility room, den, hallway, or storage space, whose construction is stronger than that of other portions of the residence and is also independent of them (see Fig. 3). There are

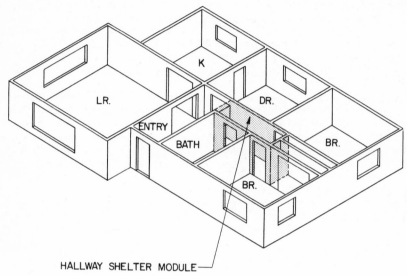

Fig. 3   In-residence shelter concept.

many possible locations for the shelter module within a residence. Here are some guidelines for the selection:

1. Interior spaces are best.
2. The space selected should be rather small, such as a bathroom, utility room, or dressing room–closet combination.
3. Allow few door openings into the space. A single door is preferred.
4. Construction should be independent of other portions of the residence.

Interior spaces are best because penetration by airborne debris is less likely. Small spaces gain greater strength than larger spaces with the same construction. Economy is also a factor in making the space small. Door openings into the shelter module can be a weakness if not protected by adjoining or baffle walls, or if the door is not made heavier. Roof construction also must be sufficient to resist missile penetration. Independent construction reduces the possibility that failure of other portions of the residence will cause failure of the shelter module. For example, if the roof of the residence is torn off, this could expose occupants of the shelter module as well.

Modification of Existing Space

Modification of existing space will be the only realistic approach for many home-owners to gain some protection from extreme winds and tornadoes. This concept, like that of the in-residence shelter module, essentially provides occupant safety in one place rather than protection throughout the residence. Modification of existing space is most reasonably applied to a selected space within the residence rather than to the entire house. The concept does not consider wind damage to other portions of the residence.

Modification can be done to varying degrees, with the resulting safety depending upon the strength of the existing construction and the extent of modification.

In discussing application of the concept to existing construction, several assumptions are made; the following are among the most likely situations. We assume a residence with (1) a wood-framed roof, either flat or sloped; (2) interior partitions of wood-stud construction covered with gypsum board; and (3) exterior walls either of wood framing and wood sheathing, or of brick or block masonry.

Factors to be considered in modification of existing space include:
1. Interior space location
2. Rigidity to resist collapse should the surrounding residence fail
3. Tie-down of roof or other overhead construction above the protected space
4. Sufficient wall strength to resist penetration of airborne debris
5. Shielded openings into the space, or strengthening of door(s)

Sometimes the strength of existing construction is difficult to assess, especially when it is covered with finish materials. For a proper assessment of interior framing, or to strengthen it, some surface coverings may have to be removed. Key items to check are (1) wall bracing in all directions and (2) secure connections—particularly tie-downs to resist uplift and overturning.

Roof tie-down is likely to be inadequate for most residences that are subject to extreme winds, unless special precautions are taken. Not only must the roof be securely fastened to the walls, but the walls must be secured to the foundations or, if slab-on-grade construction is used, to the floor.

Wall strength to resist airborne debris may require additional wall material over, or in place of, gypsum board.

Upgrading of Overall Construction

The concept of strengthened construction throughout is aimed primarily at reducing wind damage to residences even from winds not classified as extreme. Occupant safety will be improved through the application of this concept, although that is not the basic objective. Severe damage can be avoided merely by insisting upon adequately designed bracing, connections, and anchorage. Shortcuts in construction must be avoided. Even code-required minimum standards should be checked to determine whether additional strength is needed. The additional cost of bracing, tie-downs, and anchors is minimal in comparison with losses experienced in many windstorms.

Suggestions for reducing wind damage to residences include:
- Anchorage of walls and floor plates to foundations.
- Bracing of walls in all directions by means of plywood diaphragms or strap bracing.
- Tie-down of roof to walls.
- Strong eave and ridge connections to transfer localized loadings which are greater than overall surface loadings.
- Uplift resistance for overhangs and cantilevered roofs and porches.
- Proper types of anchorage for wood sheathing and sheet metal to resist outward-acting forces on exterior surfaces.
- Vertical and horizontal reinforcement in masonry walls subject to bending or overturning forces. Through-ties between roof plate and foundation may be necessary to transfer uplift forces in masonry walls.

Not only are the indicated connections needed, but they also should be sufficiently strong if wind-induced damage is to be reduced. As noted in earlier sections, sufficient strength is dependent upon the wind speed as the basis for design.

Some kinds of wind-induced damage are very difficult to eliminate, largely because of the anchorage problems associated with some materials. Roofing materials are an example. Tearing of asphalt shingles and asphaltic-felt membranes probably cannot be stopped in extreme winds. Even wood shingles usually will not be secure in extreme winds.

Future Innovations

In the future, factory-built bathrooms with plumbing, wiring, and fixtures already installed and with walls capable of repelling a missile might possibly be produced and made available as "off-the-shelf" items. The advantages of the in-residence shelter might then be combined with the advantages of mass production at little or no additional cost over conventional construction. At present, an in-residence shelter can offer, at very little cost, protection from tornadoes and, only slightly less important, freedom from the anxiety caused by a severe weather watch.

Shelters in Schools and Public Buildings

Specific criteria have been developed to govern the design of shelter space in schools and public buildings. Engineers and architects can use these criteria to develop specific designs for modules within buildings which they are designing.

Tornadic effects that are reflected as winds and changes in atmospheric pressure cause structural damage through three principal mechanisms:

1. Pressure forces created by air flowing around the structure
2. Pressure forces created by relatively rapid changes in atmospheric pressure
3. Impact forces created by missiles

A tornado-resistant design must consider all three of the damaging mechanisms listed above.

A wind speed of 260 mi/h should be kept in mind when designing protection for building occupants. The atmospheric pressure change may occur in as little as 3 seconds, and the reduced atmospheric pressure may prevail for an extended period. (Pressures induced by change in atmospheric pressure are not to be confused with wind-induced pressures.)

Wind-induced Forces

Wind-induced design pressures for various parts of a vented shelter module should be as follows:

- Windward wall design pressure of 138 lb/ft² acting inward.
- Leeward wall design pressure of 87 lb/ft² acting outward.
- Sidewalls design pressure of 121 lb/ft² acting outward.
- Flat roof design pressure of 121 lb/ft² acting outward.
- Wall corners local design pressure of 347 lb/ft² acting outward on vertical strips of width $0.1\ w$, where w is the least width of the shelter area. This design pressure is not to be included in the overall wind loads.
- Roof eaves local design pressure of 415 lb/ft² acting outward on strips of width $0.1\ w$, where w is the least width of the shelter area. This design pressure is not to be included in the overall wind loads.
- Roof corners local design pressure of 865 lb/ft² acting outward on an area of $0.1\ w \times 0.1\ w$, where w is the least width of the shelter area. This design pressure is not to be included in the overall wind loads.

If the design wind pressure for a structure or a structural component is not given above, the same can be obtained by multiplying an *effective velocity pressure* of 173 lb/ft² by the appropriate pressure coefficients from the American National Standards Institute's *Building Code Requirements for Minimum Design Loads in Buildings and Other Structures,* ANSI A58.1-1972.

Forces Induced by Atmospheric Pressure

Design pressures of 205 lb/ft² acting outward on all surfaces should be used unless venting is provided. If adequate venting is provided, the atmospheric-pressure-change forces will not exist. The design pressures due to atmospheric pressure change may be created in as little as 3 seconds; however, they will not create any dynamic load effect for most stiff structures.

Missiles

The design missile is a 2 by 4 in by 12-ft-long piece of lumber. The missile is assumed to be traveling on end at 100 mi/h. The Amirikian–Modified Petry Formula should be used to calculate depth of penetration in the shelter walls and roof slabs. The missile should be assumed to strike normal to the plane of the wall or roof slab.

Load Combinations

If the designer uses maximum values of design-basis forces resulting from wind, atmospheric pressure change, and missiles, as suggested in these criteria, each can be assumed to act separately. The forces given in these guidelines are ultimate loads; hence, ultimate-strength design concepts could be used.

The occupant shelter area should be designed independently for normal dead and live loads in addition to the loads mentioned in these guidelines.

Venting

Design pressures induced by atmospheric pressure change can be deleted if adequate venting to accomplish escape of air is provided. The venting area necessary to limit escaping air velocity to 25 mi/h can be determined using the following formula:

$$A_v = 0.00098 \times V$$

where A_v is the area of venting in square feet and V is the volume of shelter to be vented in cubic feet.

Venting can be provided through windows or doors. A structural screen wall should be provided in front of windows or doors to prevent missiles from entering the shelter area.

Location of Shelter Area

The shelter area should be located in a basement below grade, or in an interior hallway above grade. To meet the definitions of an interior hallway, sidewalls of the shelter hallway shall not be exterior walls, and at least one conventionally designed wall shall be placed between the shelter area walls and the outside of the building. A typical module design which meets these criteria is presented in Fig. 4.

EMERGENCY PLANNING AND INSTRUCTIONS

Life safety considerations require that responsible administrators concern themselves with planning for extreme windstorms and with developing appropriate instructions for people within their areas of responsibility. Where time and resources do not permit the construction of shelters, the decision maker (head of household, school principal, employer, civil defense official, etc.) must determine individually the best available space within the buildings at his or her disposal. Further, the person in charge must develop specific instructions to govern emergency actions in the face of an impending windstorm strike. The following paragraphs address these two aspects of life safety.

A procedure has been developed to assist in a systematic review of a building to find the best available shelter space against severe winds. It is not intended to imply that these spaces guarantee safety during a storm, but that they are the safest available in the building.

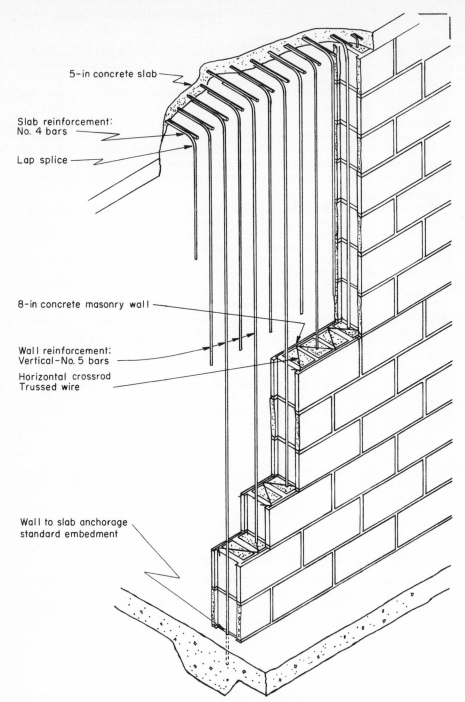

5-in concrete slab

Slab reinforcement:
No. 4 bars

Lap splice

8-in concrete masonry wall

Wall reinforcement:
Vertical-No. 5 bars

Horizontal crossrod
Trussed wire

Wall to slab anchorage
standard embedment

Fig. 4 Wall and overhead slab design which meet tornado design criteria.

The space per person depends on the size of the people and their degree of mobility. Small children require only 3 ft² per person. Usually 5 to 6 ft² per person is adequate for adults. However, nursing home or hospital patients will require much more space.

An emergency plan is almost worthless if it is not tested and understood by the people it is intended to protect. A good plan has the following features:

- It identifies one or more spotters who are responsible for prompt and accurate visual identification of an approaching storm.
- It provides for a prompt, clear warning that will be readily understood by all.

The emergency plan should be recorded and made known to all concerned, so that everyone knows where to go and what to do in an emergency.

Building Survey
Check completely around the building. Look for and record the location of the following:

- Potential missiles, such as site equipment, nearby buildings, automobiles, and other debris especially on the south and west sides
- Ground embankment against the buildings
- Mechanical equipment on the roof
- Entry point of electrical service
- High building elements, such as chimneys and high portions of the building
- Changes in roof level

Take a long look from each direction, particularly from the south and west, noting building entrances, windows, and construction features.

Spaces to Avoid
Carefully identify the following spaces as the most hazardous locations. Avoid locations where roofs are likely to be blown off, as they may fall in on the occupants. Missiles also have direct access to the interior. Portions of roofs most likely to be blown off are:

- Windward edges (usually south and west)
- Long spans
- Portions with load-bearing wall supports
- Portions with overhangs on the windward sides

Avoid exterior walls that are most likely to be partially or completely destroyed. Damage will probably occur, *although not always,* in the following order, to these walls:

- South
- West
- East
- North

Avoid corridors and ends of corridors with exterior doors allowing direct exit (no turns) to the outside. Avoid locations with windows facing likely storm approach direction. Assume that the windows will blow *in* on the south and west sides of the building, and occasionally on the east and north.

Avoid, whenever possible, portions of buildings that contain load-bearing walls. If such a wall collapses, the roof or floor will fall in.

Best Available Space
Generally, the best available spaces are:

1. *The lowest floor.* If a building has a basement, or a partial basement, it is probably the safest space in the structure.

2. *Interior spaces.* These are spaces that have no walls on the exterior of the building. However, avoid interior spaces with large spans.

3. *Short spans.* It is difficult to find one space, with the exception of a basement, that will offer a high degree of protection to all of the building occupants. Therefore, seek out a number of smaller spaces.

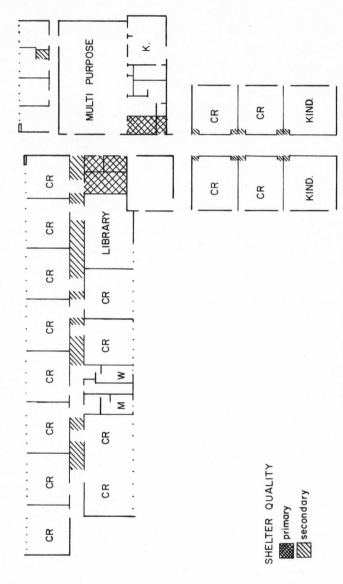

SHELTER QUALITY
■ primary
▨ secondary

Fig. 5   Best available shelter space in a typical elementary school.

4. The portions of buildings supported by *rigid structural frames,* such as steel, concrete, or wood, rather than those portions that have load-bearing walls.

It is essential that spaces selected be the very best available. Often poor (relatively hazardous) spaces exist within generally safe areas. These poor spaces must either be avoided or occupied as a last resort:

- Avoid spaces opposite doorways or openings into rooms that have windows in the exterior walls, particularly those facing south or west.
- Avoid interior locations that contain windows such as display cases, transoms above doors, and door sidelights.
- Avoid interior locations under skylights.
- Avoid locations where interior doors swing. When the storm hits, the doors are likely to swing violently.
- Avoid spaces within the falling radius of higher building elements, such as chimneys or upper walls enclosing higher roof areas. Assume that the falling radius is approximately equal to the height of the higher building element above the roof.

Often the best available shelter spaces in a building *cannot* be occupied during emergencies for various reasons. Consideration of the following will help determine whether the spaces can be occupied:

- What portion of the space is usable? Permanent equipment and furniture reduce the usable space.
- Which good spaces are often inaccessible in an emergency? Many fine spaces normally are locked, with few people having keys.
- Which good spaces are unsuitable for occupancy because of operational reasons? Many secure spaces offer excellent protection but operationally are not feasible owing to the need to retain security over records, equipment, or money.
- Where are the building's first aid kit or medical supplies? They should be in one of the safest places.
- Would protection levels increase significantly and movement time to the shelter decrease significantly if people were jammed in at lower square-foot-per-person ratios? This is a valid alternative in lieu of using a lower quality of protection, with more space per person.

Figure 5 illustrates the best available space in a school building that was severely damaged by a tornado.

BEYOND DESIGN

This chapter has dealt with design criteria as they are affected by hurricanes, tornadoes, and other extreme windstorms. In addition to the building designer, however, the homeowner, business person, educator, social scientist, and economist can, in their own areas of activity, arm themselves and society with valuable and possibly life-saving information by becoming acquainted with this technology. For additional literature on this subject, see the references below.

REFERENCES

1. Defense Civil Preparedness Agency, Department of Defense, *Protecting Mobile Homes from High Winds,* U.S. Army A.G. Publication Center, Civil Defense Board [2800 Easter Blvd. (Middle River), Baltimore, MD 21220], February 1974.
2. Executive Office of the President, Office of Emergency Preparedness, *Disaster Preparedness— Report to Congress,* Government Printing Office, January 1974.
3. U.S. Department of Commerce, National Oceanic and Atmospheric Administration, *Hurricane, the Greatest Storm on Earth,* U.S. Government Printing Office, Washington, D.C.
4. ———, *Severe Local Storm Warning Service and Tornado Statistics 1953–73.*
5. ———, *Spotter's Guide for Identifying and Reporting Severe Local Storms,* 1971.
6. ———, *Tornado,* 1970.
7. ———, *Tornado Preparedness Planning,* 1970.

Chapter 8

Floods

JOHN R. SHEAFFER, Ph.D.

**President, Sheaffer & Roland, Inc., Environmental Planning &
Engineering, Solar Energy, Resources Management**

Although flooding can occur from any accumulation or rise of water on land areas, this chapter concerns itself principally with river floods, since they occur frequently. In popular usage, "river flood" describes an overflow of water onto normally dry land. More professionally, hydrologists consider a river to be "in flood" when its waters have risen to an elevation ("flood stage") at which damage can occur in the absence of protective works.

Floods can, and do, occur in almost every part of the United States. Certain areas, such as the Pacific Northwest, the Rocky Mountain and Great Basin areas, and parts of Southern California, experience floods only during well-defined seasons. On the other hand, along the Southeastern and Gulf Coasts, floods occur without any pronounced seasonal pattern. There are also some areas in which a great flood may occur at any time of year, but in which most of the floods occur during a fairly well-defined period. These are in the Northeast and in the basins of the Ohio and upper Mississippi Rivers, as well as the lower Mississippi. Flash floods have occurred in almost every region of the United States, but the areas most susceptible are the upper reaches of streams and creeks which receive the torrential rains associated with the thunderstorms experienced most frequently in the spring and summer (see Fig. 1).

The statistics associated with river flooding are impressive. Annual losses have been variously estimated between $1.5 billion and $2 billion (see Fig. 2). An estimated 50 million acres in the United States are subject to flooding, and although this is only 2.5 percent of the total land area, most of it is densely settled and of high value. Approximately 10 million people live in the significantly defined flood plains, and another 25 million nearby can be indirectly affected. For the United States as a whole, during the period 1955 through 1969, the average annual loss of life was 83 persons.

Annual flood losses in the United States are estimated to have been $4.5 billion in 1977, of which $1.5 billion were classified as urban flood losses. A survey of urban areas showed that 19.7 percent of the total land area was in the Special Flood Hazard Area (SFHA), or below the base flood elevation (the 100-year flood). The floodplains

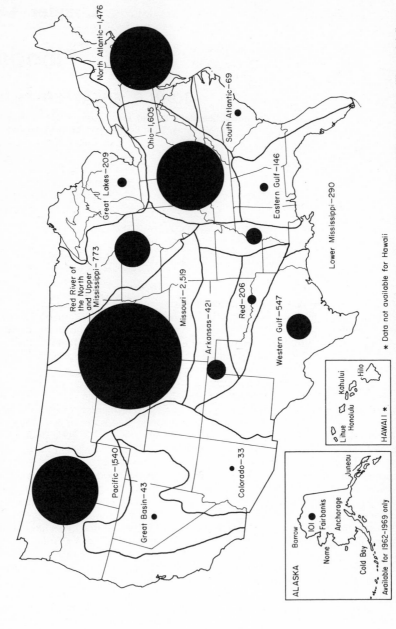

Fig. 1 Distribution of estimated flood losses in the United States by major river systems, 1925–1969. Losses in millions of dollars; areas of circles proportional to those losses. *(From "Climatological Data, National Summary, 1970.")*

North Atlantic—1,476

South Atlantic—69

Ohio—1,605

Great Lakes—209

Eastern Gulf—146

Red River of the North and Upper Mississippi—773

Lower Mississippi—290

Missouri—2,519

Arkansas—421

Red—206

Western Gulf—547

Pacific—1,540

Great Basin—43

Colorado—33

* Data not available for Hawaii

Lihue Kahului Hilo
Honolulu

HAWAII *

ALASKA

Barrow

Nome Fairbanks
101
Anchorage Juneau

Cold Bay

Available for 1962–1969 only

8-2

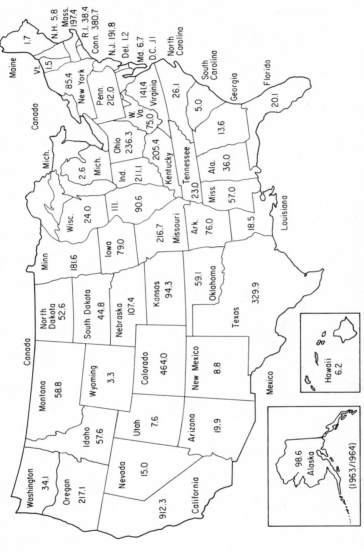

Fig. 2 Flood damage estimates by states, 1965–1969. Totals by millions of dollars. (*From "Climatological Data, National Summary, 1970."*)

were 17.8 percent developed for urban purposes, in contrast to the nonhazard areas which were 29.4 percent developed. This indicates that the perception of flood hazard has deterred, to a degree, the development of flood hazard areas.

It is estimated that 13.8 percent of the nation's population, and 13.5 percent of the nation's housing units, are in the Special Flood Hazard Area. However, because of the existence of housing units which are elevated above the level of the base flood, only 7.9 percent of the population and 7.2 percent of all housing units are actually at risk from the 100-year flood event. Thus, in 1975 there were an estimated 24,146,000 persons living in the Special Flood Hazard Area of which 13,342,000 were at risk from the 100-year floodplain. The developed floodplain acreage in 1975 was estimated at 4,342,000 acres.

FLOODPROOFING DECISIONS*

Floodproofing of a building, when properly accomplished, will allow occupancy of a flood hazard site without vulnerability to unacceptable flood risk. In addition, floodproofing provides the following benefits:

1. A building manager is able to act quickly and independently in implementing a desired level of flood protection.

2. Floodproofing gives a higher level of protection than community-wide flood control.

3. The cost of federal flood insurance is reduced markedly if the floodproofing is designed so that water is kept out of the building under 100-year flood conditions.

The protection of property from flood losses depends, in part, upon the designer's and the manager's awareness of the flood hazard and their willingness to do something about it. To arrive at a feasible decision on floodproofing, potential flood problems and their related effects must be recognized. This knowledge can be obtained in several ways.

In a way, the most cogent, though the worst method, is personal experience—to have seen one's own building damaged and its contents ruined. There are other ways, however: Awareness of a flood hazard can be gained from a "near miss," i.e., when a flood almost causes a catastrophe. If a flood occurred before a current occupant was located on the site, local government officials and others occupying nearby areas can provide useful information.

In the United States, the area of special flood hazard is the land subject to inundation from the base flood, which is the flood having a 1 percent chance of being equaled or exceeded in any given year (the 100-year flood).

The Federal Insurance Administration has the responsibility for pinpointing special flood hazard areas. Hazard areas are delineated either on the Flood Hazard Boundary Map (FHBM) or on a Flood Insurance Rate Map (FIRM). On the Flood Hazard Boundary Map, the special-hazard area is designated as a single zone (Zone A). The Flood Insurance Rate Map divides the special-hazard area into risk premium zones for flood insurance purposes (Zones A, A0, A1-99). Figure 3 presents examples of such maps.

During early 1977 there were over 14,000 communities participating in the Emergency Flood Insurance Program, in which all flood insurance rates are subsidized. The "regular program" communities number 1035. In these communities, detailed flood insurance rate maps are available, and rates for new construction reflect the flood risk.

Maps for a specific community or site can be obtained from the Federal Insurance Administrator, Department of Housing and Urban Development, Washington, DC

---

*The spelling of the term "floodproof" as one word in this chapter, a style based solely on editorial considerations of uniformity and consistency, does not imply its preference over the two-word spelling "flood proof," which is used in many government and private publicatons.

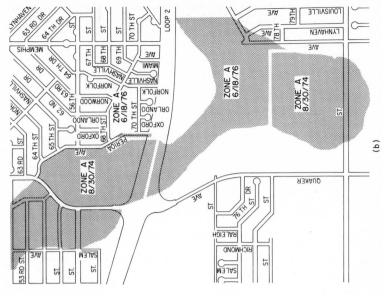

(b)

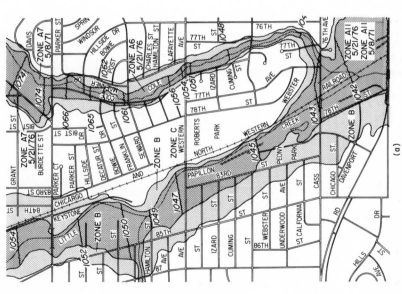

(a)

Fig. 3 (a) Sample flood insurance rate map (FIRM) for a part of Omaha, Nebraska; (b) sample flood hazard boundary map for Lubbock, Texas.

20410. Toll-free telephone numbers [(800)424-8872 or (800)424-8873] have been established to expedite the exchange of information. Other sources of information on the flood hazard can be obtained from the district offices of the Corps of Engineers, Floodplain Management Services Branch, or from the Tennessee Valley Authority.

When exploring the possibilities of floodproofing, one should seek the help of professionals who have a working knowledge of structures and who have had experience in floodproofing. Qualified professional engineering and architectural personnel should begin by examining the building. Its structural soundness must be established and related to the depth and duration of flooding and to the soil foundation conditions.

The National Flood Insurance Rules and Regulations (Federal Register, Vol. 41, No. 207—Tuesday, October 26, 1976) establish minimum criteria, as directed by Congress. These criteria require that where floodproofing is utilized for a particular structure, a registered professional engineer or architect shall certify that the flood-proofing methods are adequate to withstand the flood depths, pressures, velocities, impact and uplift forces, and other factors associated with the base (100-year) flood. A record of such certificates, indicating the specific elevation (in relation to mean sea level) to which such structures are floodproofed, shall be maintained with the official designated by the community; or a certified copy of a local regulation containing detailed floodproofing specifications which satisfy the watertight performance standards required shall be submitted to the Flood Insurance Administrator for approval.

When developing a floodproofing design, a number of publications should be consulted, and these are listed in the References at the end of this chapter.

THE ECONOMICS OF FLOODPROOFING

The planning considerations for flood-prone areas associated with the flood insurance program call for a community to permit only that development which (1) is appropriate in light of the probability of flood damage and the need to reduce flood losses, (2) is an acceptable social and economic use of the land in relation to the hazards involved, and (3) does not increase the danger to human life. When either existing or proposed development meets these criteria, communities are urged to consider the encouragement of floodproofing to reduce flood damage.

The actuarial rate structure in effect for flood insurance encourages floodproofing of new structures. In some instances, existing structures on the subsidized rates may find that it is economically advantageous to floodproof and pay the actuarial rates.

An example of how flood insurance premiums encourage floodproofing is presented in a publication entitled "Economic Justification of Flood Proofing: Analysis of a New Commercial Structure" (HUD, Office of Policy Development and Research, 1977).

In this publication, general designs for five building types were developed. The basic design was for a commercial structure of conventional construction, having no special treatment with respect to flood hazards, to provide a basis of comparison for evaluating the costs and benefits of floodproofed structures. The second design was for a "wet-floodproofed" structure at grade that permits entry of flood waters. Although contrary to National Flood Insurance Program requirements, this design was included in order to permit evaluation of the comparative costs and benefits of a structure designed according to the wet-floodproofing criteria developed by a local Urban Renewal Authority.

The last three designs were for a building floodproofed to meet the minimum requirements of the National Flood Insurance Program. Two designs were flood-proofed to 1 ft above the base flood level [base flood = 551 mean sea level (MSL)], of which one was accomplished by raising it on fill and equipping it with watertight closures. Although the structure on fill alone need not have been above the base flood elevation, in order to compare buildings with equivalent levels of potential flood inundation, the study chose the same designed elevation as for the fill-plus-closure structure (which must be floodproofed to 1 ft above the base flood level to be insured at rates for the base flood elevation). The third design was floodproofed through elevation on columns; so that the space beneath the elevated building might be used for parking and delivery, this design was raised one full story, to a height of 6 ft above the base flood level. The three floodproofed designs provide a basis for the comparative evaluation of various construction approaches that can be used to conform with flood insurance program requirements.

The major objectives in the design of the floodproofed structures were:

    1. To protect the structure and contents from damages due to the base flood and all floods of lesser magnitude

    2. To reduce losses from floods of greater magnitude (lesser frequency)

    3. To reduce flood insurance premium costs

All relevant national and local codes, ordinances, and acts were observed in the design of all five building types.

The relative costs and benefits for each design alternative were analyzed from two perspectives: (1) construction requirements and associated costs and benefits, and (2) insurance premium costs. The building with conventional construction was used as the basic building for purposes of comparison, and the costs and benefits for all alternatives were defined in relation to the cost and performance characteristics of the basic building. To facilitate comparisons among all aspects of cost and benefit, all quantifiable costs and benefits were calculated on an average annual dollar basis.

It was assumed that each building would be insured against flood losses at actuarial rates and that each building would be insured to the maximum value allowed under the rules and regulations of the National Flood Insurance Program, i.e., $200,000 for the structure and $200,000 for the contents.

The rates used were those for a two-story nonresidential structure with no basement and were taken from rate tables included in the Flood Insurance Manual (National Flood Insurers Association, Arlington, VA, 1975). The rates are correlated to the elevation of the floodproofed level of each building. The rates for the basic building and the wet-floodproofed building, both at grade, were taken for the −6-ft elevation; those for the building potentially raised on fill and equipped for watertight closure were taken for the base flood elevation; those for the building raised on fill were taken for the +1-ft elevation; and those for the building elevated on columns were taken for the +6-ft elevation.

In accordance with the policies of the National Flood Insurers Association, an expense constant of $15 was added to the first-layer premium because actuarial rates were used in determining the premium.

A reduction in flood insurance premium was considered a benefit of elevation. A benefit-to-cost ratio for each building type other than the basic building was determined by dividing the reduction in annual insurance premiums by the average annual increase in building costs of each floodproofed building compared with the basic building.

Diagrams for the floodproofed building alternatives are presented in Figs. 4, 5, and 6.

Table 1 details the construction costs associated with each building type. Costs are presented in terms of total building costs, per-square-foot costs, and average annual costs. While construction costs in various parts of the country vary, and inflation tends to increase costs on a continuing basis, the various unit costs provide valuable comparative data.

The total construction cost for the basic building is estimated at $562,812, or an average annual cost of $52,398 over a 20-year period. On a square-foot basis these costs total $25.01, or $2.33 annually for the 20 years.

TABLE 1   Construction Costs of Various Floodproofing Alternatives

	No floodproofing	Wet- floodproofing	Raised on fill	Raised, with watertight closures	Raised on columns
Basic building cost	$562,812	$562,812	$562,812	$562,812	$562,812
per square foot*	$ 25.01	$ 25.01	$ 25.01	$ 25.01	$ 25.01
Net costs associated with flood- proofing	. . .	$ 46,915	$ 35,912	$ 89,732	$ 87,923
per square foot	. . .	$ 2.09	$ 1.60	$ 3.99	$ 3.91
Total cost	$562,812	$609,727	$598,724	$652,544	$650,735
per square foot	$ 25.01	$ 27.10	$ 26.61	$ 29.00	$ 28.92
Average Annual Costs†					
Basic building cost	$ 52,398	$ 52,398	$ 52,398	$ 52,398	$ 52,398
per square foot	$ 2.33	$ 2.33	2.33	$ 2.33	2.33
Net costs associated with flood- proofing	. . .	$ 4,368	$ 3,343	$ 8,354	$ 8,186
per square foot	. . .	$ 0.19	$ 0.15	$ 0.37	$ 0.36
Total cost	$ 52,398	$ 56,766	$ 55,741	$ 60,752	$ 60,584
per square foot*	$ 2.33	$ 2.52	$ 2.48	$ 2.70	2.69

*Area of building is 22,500 ft².

†Assuming: (1) A 20-year life of improvements with no salvage value, and (2) 100 percent financing of all improvements at a 7 percent interest rate per year for 20 years at a constant payment rate (debt retirement rate) of 9.31 percent per year.

For the wet-floodproofed building, the two major additive costs are for glazed concrete block partitions in lieu of metal stud and drywall ($14,400) and the premium for installing a waterproofed pit and hoistway-type elevator and associated penthouse in lieu of a hydraulic elevator ($10,000). In total, such wet-floodproofing adds $46,915 to the cost of the total structure, or $2.09 per square foot (when dispersed over the total square footage of the building). Since many of the floodproofing costs are incurred only for the ground floor construction, the taller and larger the building the less floodproofing adds to the square-foot cost of the building.

For the building raised to 1 ft above the base flood on fill, the two major additive costs are for the imported compacted fill material at $3.50 per cubic yard (a total of $12,530) and the addition of curved approach ramps with handrailings and retaining walls ($9,000). In total, this method of compliance with the minimum rules and

Fig. 4   Perspective of floodproofed building raised on fill.

regulations of the National Flood Insurance Program adds $35,912 to the cost of the total structure, or $1.60 per square foot.

For the raised building with watertight closures, the primary additive cost is for a 30-in mat slab on fill in lieu of the 6-in slab on grade ($33,750). The other relatively major additive cost is for a 3-in layer of troweled asphalt waterproofing below the mat slab ($11,250). The actual bulkheading adds only a $5,000 cost to the total structure.

When the building is elevated to 6 ft above the base flood on columns, certain cost items are added, but others are subtracted. The largest additive cost is for the metal-pan-formed concrete suspended slab, including formwork, bracing, reinforcement, and finish ($41,250). Other major additional costs are for extending the building core to the parking area at the ground level, including stairs and elevator extension ($20,000), the premium for installing a waterproofed pit and hoistway-type elevator with associated penthouse in lieu of a hydraulic elevator ($10,000), and the increased cost of foundations ($10,000). Costs which are deducted from the basic structure, on the other hand, are for the slab on grade ($12,000) and one set of entranceway stairs ($5,000). Overall, the cost of the structure is increased by $87,923, or $3.91 per square foot. For each of the elevated structures, the additional cost per square foot is also reduced when costs are dispersed over a larger building. Even though the costs of elevation might increase for larger structures, the square-foot cost of elevation, when amortized over the greater square footage of the large structure would decrease.

In terms of additional construction cost, therefore, raising on fill proved to be the least costly method of complying with the minimum regulations for the proposed building.

Equipping the building with watertight closures was, in this case, also more expensive, primarily because waterproofing the foundation made the building buoyant, requiring use of a heavier, thicker slab. Indeed, if watertight closures had been installed on a building at grade rather than raising the building 3 ft on fill, the cost would have been virtually prohibitive, because of the thick concrete slab required to counteract the buoyancy. As building size and weight increase, a structure eventually supplies sufficient dead load to counteract buoyancy without added depth and expense in the floor slab. In the example discussed here, the relatively small size of the proposed commercial structure became a critical factor in determining the most economical method of complying with National Flood Insurance Regulations.

Actuarial insurance rates are determined by the height of the first-floor elevation of a structure. Since wet-floodproofing does not change the first-floor elevation of the structure, the insurance premiums for the basic building (no floodproofing) and the wet-floodproofed building were the same.

The annual insurance premiums for the five buildings are detailed in Table 2. The annual insurance premiums for maximum coverage in the regular program at actuarial rates are $20,795 for the buildings at grade; $1215 for the building partially raised on fill and floodproofed to 1 ft above base flood levels; $575 for the building raised on fill to 1 ft above the base flood level; and $235 for the building elevated on columns to 6 ft above the base flood level. Thus, it can be seen that floodproofing through elevation or watertight closures significantly reduces insurance premiums.

These reductions, furthermore, are dramatically greater than the increases in average annual building costs for the elevated buildings. The benefit-to-cost ratios calculated on this basis are presented in Table 3. While the benefit-to-cost ratios for all three elevated buildings are good, the most favorable ratio is for the building raised on fill. Thus, from the perspective of flood insurance, construction of the building raised on fill would be recommended at this site.

The benefits to an owner who floodproofs a structure are dramatic. Without floodproofing, the annual cost of insurance, based on actuarial rates, would be $20,795, or nearly $1.00 a square foot. For the building with watertight closures to 1 ft above the base flood, the premium decreases to $1,215 or approximately $0.05 per square foot, a reduction of approximately 94 percent. The building raised on fill to 1

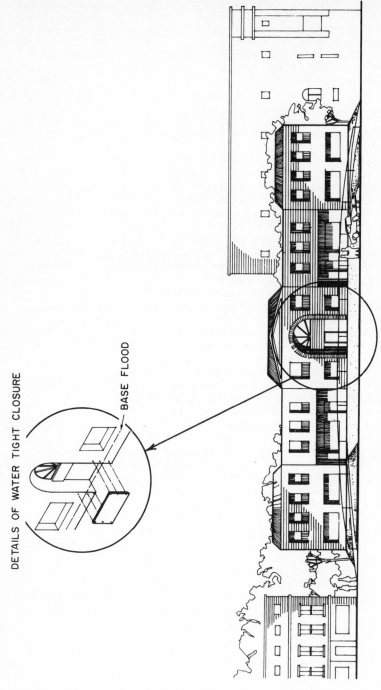

DETAILS OF WATER TIGHT CLOSURE

BASE FLOOD

Fig. 5 Floodproofed building partially raised on fill and equipped with watertight closure.

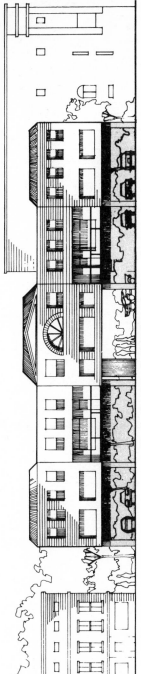

Fig. 6 Floodproofed building raised on columns.

ft above the base flood shows premium reductions to $575, or less than $0.03 per square foot. This results in a benefit-to-cost ratio of 5.96 for the building raised on fill and 2.31 for the one with watertight closures. For the building elevated on columns, with its first floor 6 ft above the base flood, the insurance premium would be only $235, or approximately $0.01 per square foot (with a benefit-to-cost ratio of 2.48).

There are several additional benefits of floodproofing. These include shorter business disruptions, enhanced marketability, potential for multiple use of the struc-

TABLE 2   Annual Insurance Costs

	Basic building with no floodproofing	Raised on fill	Raised with watertight closures	Raised on columns
First-layer coverage (first $100,000 of coverage) Structure:				
Rate per $100	$ 3.64	$ 0.10	$ 0.22	$ 0.01
Annual cost	$ 3,640	$ 100	$ 220	$ 10
Expense constant	$ 15	$ 15	$ 15	$ 15
Contents:				
Rate per $100	$ 6.75	$ 0.18	$ 0.38	$ 0.10
Cost	$ 6,750	$ 180	$ 380	$ 100
Subtotal	$ 10,405	$ 295	$ 615	$ 125
Second-layer coverage (second $100,000 of coverage) Structure:				
Rate per $100	$ 3.64	$ 0.10	$ 0.22	$ 0.01
Annual cost	$ 3,640	$ 100	$ 220	$ 10
Contents:				
Rate per $100	$ 6.75	$ 0.18	$ 0.38	$ 0.10
Cost	$ 6,750	$ 180	$ 380	$ 100
Subtotal	$ 10,390	$ 280	$ 600	$ 110
TOTAL ANNUAL COST	$ 20,795	$ 575	$ 1,215	$ 235
TOTAL PRESENT VALUE*	$220,302	$6,092	$12,872	$2,490

NOTE: Wet-floodproofing does not entail a reduction in flood insurance premium.

*Assuming 20 annual payments at 7 percent interest per year with a present-value factor of 10.594 times annual insurance payment.

TABLE 3   Floodproofing Benefits Derived from Reduced Insurance Costs

	Wet-floodproofing	Raised on fill	Raised, with watertight closures	Raised on columns
Cost of floodproofing	$46,915	$ 35,912	$ 89,732	$ 87,923
Present value of reduced insurance costs	0	$214,210	$207,430	$217,812
Benefit/cost ratio	. . .	5.96	2.31	2.48
Payment period in years*	. . .	3.4	8.7	8.1

*Payment period in years is 20 years divided by the benefit/cost ratio.

ture and its environs, potential for aesthetic innovations, and reduced need for emergency and disaster relief efforts.

Raising on fill was the most cost-effective solution for floodproofing the proposed commercial structure. The reasons for its advantage are specific to the site and the design of the building—a light, low-rise building on a site with poor soil-bearing capacity in an area of modest development density.

Changes in any of several conditions—conditions which can vary by region and even from block to block—might make any one of the floodproofing techniques more appropriate for another building at another site. Factors which should be considered in the selection of floodproofing approaches include topography, soil conditions, development density, construction budget, building function, architectural style, and the type of flood event to be avoided.

FLOODPROOFING PROCEDURES AND EXAMPLES

Several general procedures to achieve floodproofing are discussed in this section. These procedures include site planning, raising buildings, and preventing the entry of water into a building. Most procedures will apply to either existing structures or new structures when they are determined to be a proper use of a flood-plain site.

Site Planning

The practice of "clustering" buildings is prevalent in planned unit developments. This clustering permits buildings to be attractively grouped on parts of a site which are above flood levels and reserves the low-lying sections as landscaped green areas and parking facilities.

The use of the higher ground for development allows streams and other natural lowland features to be kept intact as scenic elements, for recreational purposes, and for fish and wildlife habitats. For example, low-lying swampy areas can be transformed into permanent lakes that provide opportunities for water-oriented recreation and modest amounts of flood-water storage as well.

Where natural high ground does not exist, sites can be raised by filling, provided the fill does not interfere with the flow of flood waters. The concept of clustering buildings on higher ground, elevated by filling, is especially useful in metropolitan areas where a shortage of land may force the development of areas subject to low-stage flooding.

In flood fringe areas, raising the site only a few feet may achieve the desired results—placing the buildings above the design flood stage. Constructing new buildings without basements would facilitate floodproofing of this type since problems associated with groundwater pressure can be avoided.

Floodproofing measures can be designed to blend with the overall appearance of a structure. When this is done, a structure's appearance can be preserved and in some cases even enhanced by floodproofing.

Raising the Buildings

The practice of elevating a building on "stilts" to provide an "open" effect at ground level can also reduce the flood hazard. If some means of access is maintained and utilities can continue to function, activities will not be interrupted during floods.

This raising of the main floor level is practiced in much new construction throughout the country; there are numerous examples of residential, commercial, recreational, and industrial buildings that follow this design, especially where land is at a premium, as in central business districts. Parking facilities are on the ground level in such instances.

As may be seen in Fig. 7, desirable aesthetic effects—such as the creation of upper-level pedestrian plazas above utilitarian lower-level parking areas—can be integrated into a flood-protective scheme in which the lower level can be flooded without affecting the pedestrian areas and buildings. Similarly, the contemporary practice of placing mechanical equipment on upper levels of multistoried buildings will minimize potential damage of valuable equipment and interruption of service during floods. Techniques designed for the more normal locations can be applied with little modification to buildings in flood plains, resulting in structures which will suffer little damage.

The Farnsworth House in Plano, Illinois (Fig. 8), is an example of this approach to flood protection. The house is on the banks of the Fox River and was designed by Mies van der Rohe with the floor level of the home raised on columns to place it at an elevation above known flood heights, thus permitting the use of a scenic riverfront

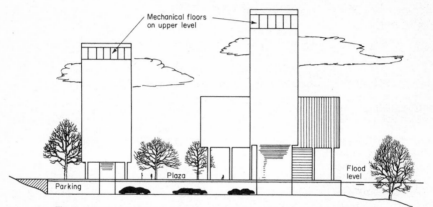

Fig. 7   Urban development that is compatible with a flood-plain location.

site for a house location. When the record flood of 1960 occurred, the house proved to be above the flood waters. Figure 9 presents two other houses that demonstrate architectural styles used to elevate houses above the flood levels.

Figure 10 shows another type of building elevated on columns. The floor elevation of the Manker Patten Tennis Center, at the University of Chattanooga, is approximately 1 ft above the maximum known flood as regulated by the TVA reservoir system. The floor was placed at this elevation to reduce flood risk and to serve as an observation deck. The picture was taken when the flood of March 14, 1963, was 0.3 ft below its crest.

Preventing the Entry of Water

Existing structures can be raised also. An example of raising a private residence is described in a recently issued report of the Corps of Engineers.* Another example of raising private residences is found at Wayne Township, New Jersey. There, some fifty houses were raised from 2 to 7.5 ft to mitigate the flood hazard. Some structures in built-up urban areas are exposed to flood waters. In such circumstances, the building owner, architect, or engineer is faced with the job of designing floodproofing measures to prevent the entry of water. A total plan must be developed for such structures which will withstand flooding from groundwater seepage, sewer backup,

*S. R. McKeever, *Flood Proofing: Example of Raising a Private Residence,* South Atlantic Division, Corps of Engineers, Atlanta, 1977.

and overland flow from a design flood stage. Floodproofing such buildings can incorporate many contemporary design features, such as large window areas, pedestrian arcades, open floor space, and curtain wall panels.

Another example of successful floodproofing of an existing structure is the Stanley House in La Grange, Illinois (Fig. 11). The house is located on a scenic site overlook-

Fig. 8   Farnsworth House, Plano, Illinois. Mies van der Rohe designed this house to avoid damage from Fox River flooding. The lower photograph, taken during the 1960 Fox River flood, shows the success of the design. *(Top photograph reproduced courtesy Bill Hedrich, Hedrich-Blessing.)*

ing a golf course. After an experience with high water, the owner constructed a brick wall to close off the front and back porch areas and added aluminum flood shields to close off the entranceways. The owner, an artist, says the additions have not detracted from the home's appearance and have kept the house completely dry when there was water 2 ft deep all around it. Further details of the Stanley House are presented in Fig. 12.

In designing new structures, or in altering existing ones, thought should be given to the use of receding flood shields, which are normally hidden from view but can be easily lowered or slid into place when there is a flood warning. Such semi-fixed shields also escape the hazard of being misplaced.

When flood shields must be mounted on the street side of an opening, the brackets to which they would be bolted can be concealed with easily removed aluminum strips or "skins." Figure 13 shows a department store entrance that has been modernized and floodproofed at the same time. The installation required for mounting the shield is indistinguishable from the building rim.

Figure 14 shows flood shields which protect the loading-dock area at a department store. These shields are hinged on top and can be lowered (flap down) into position

Fig. 9   Elevated houses. The above photographs show two houses of this architectural style. The raised effect can be readily adapted to a floodproofing design. *(Photos by D. J. Volk.)*

against the loading dock after the wooden bumpers have been removed and then bolted into place. Ropes or chains used to lower the shields are attached to the large rings above them. At some doorways it is possible to design lightweight aluminum flood shields which hinge on the sides and close like any other door (Fig. 15). The shields in this illustration also serve as a fireproof door. Heavy shields can be designed to move on overhead tracks to facilitate opening and closing.

Openings which are no longer necessary, such as old coal chutes, windows into storage and basement areas, or unused doorways, can be permanently closed and

Fig. 10   The Manker Patten Tennis Center, University of Chattanooga. This building was raised to provide flood protection and to be used as an observation deck. *(Photo by Chattanooga Free Press.)*

Fig. 11   E. Lee Stanley House, LaGrange, Illinois. *(Photo by E. Lee Stanley.)*

(a)

(b)

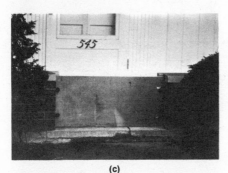

(c)

Fig. 12   Floodproofing at the Stanley House. (a)
Front entrance. Brick wall was added to close
off much of the front porch. The brackets or
flanges on the edge of the brick are used to
secure the aluminum flood shield which closes
off the opening during floods. (b) Aluminum
flood shield. A 1-in thick slab of aluminum that is
about to be bolted on to the flanges in anticipation of a flood. (c) Flood shield in place. This
shield is designed to withstand a flood stage of
2.5 ft. *(Photos by E. Lee Stanley.)*

(a)

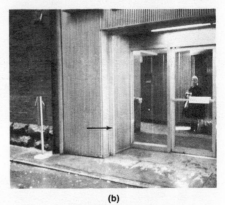

(b)

Fig. 13   Floodproofed department store entrance.
(a) Remodeled store entrance incorpora-
ting glass doors and aluminum sheeting in the
design. (b) Bracket for flood shield covered with
removable trim so as not to detract from the
appearance.

Fig. 14   Flood shields at a loading dock. These shields hinge from the top and drop down to prevent entry of water. The insert illustrates how the shields can be put in place. *(Photo by Horne Department Store, Pittsburgh, Pennsylvania.)*

Fig. 15   Hinged flood shields which also serve as a fireproof door.

sealed up by masonry or reinforced glass block construction. Masonry enclosures should be "keyed" into existing masonry in a manner similar to the original construction (Fig. 16).

Continuing Essential Systems

Unless a building is to be completely evacuated during a flood, provision should be made for continuing essential building systems, at least on a limited basis. First consideration should go to locating central telephone equipment and electrical transformers above flood level. In addition, auxiliary generators should be available to provide energy during a power failure for emergency lights, vital pumps to control seepage, and elevator operation.

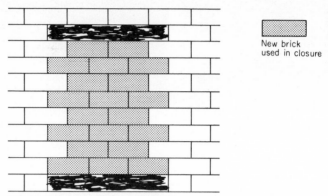

New brick used in closure

Fig. 16   Masonry closure for unnecessary windows. The closure is keyed into the existing masonry to provide strength.

Sewer systems can be kept in operation through the use of cut-off valves to prevent backup. Pumps within a building should be provided to remove seepage from the building if outlets are provided which extend above anticipated flood stages. Check valves, vacuum breakers, or air gaps should be installed to prevent back siphoning (see Fig. 17).

Water mains are normally kept under sufficient pressure to avoid contamination by flood waters, but pressure should be increased during floods to compensate for the increased head acting on the mains. If the pumping station is flooded, pressure will be reduced and contamination can occur. This suggests an internal water supply, perhaps a roof storage tank, to keep buildings in operation during floods. It is also advisable to provide cutoff valves to isolate portions of a building which may be flooded to prevent contamination by back siphonage into those parts which are not inundated. Where water wells are located on flood plains, their casings should be sealed and extended above anticipated flood levels to prevent the entry of polluted flood waters.

Storage tanks may contain products necessary for a building's operation. They should be anchored and weighted down or else raised above flood levels to prevent flotation and loss or damage to other items during floods.

Floodproofed Building Program

Each floodproofed building should have a total plan, such as that illustrated in Fig. 18, to show the relationships among the various protection measures. In addition, costs should be associated with each of the measures depicted and alternative financial solutions defined to determine both feasibility and the optimal amortization schedule.

(a)

(b)

Fig. 17 Cutoff valves for sewers. These types of valves can be used to control the problem of flooding from sewer backup. (a) Cylindrical plus valve; (b) cross section of plug valve; (c) flanged end gate valve.

(c)

An evaluation of such plans would assist in determining the adequacy of a flood-proofing program.

Floodproofing of selected buildings can be an effective means of reducing potential flood losses. It merits consideration when plans are being formulated for flood plain management. The fact that floodproofing is available broadens the range of choice that property owners can consider when faced with the need for taking action to reduce flood risks.

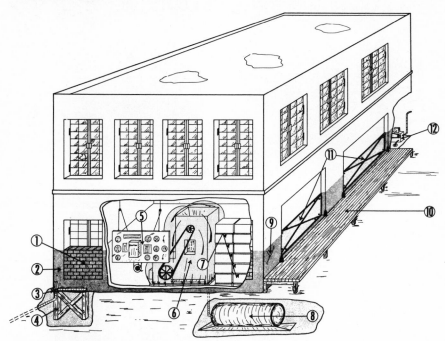

Fig. 18   A floodproofed structure. This sketch illustrates the many items that must be employed to floodproof a structure. (1) Permanent closure of opening with masonry; (2) Thoroseal coating to reduce seepage; (3) valve on sewer line; (4) underpinning; (5) instrument panel raised above expected flood level; (6) machinery protected with polyethylene covering; (7) strips of polyethylene between layers of cartons; (8) underground storage tank properly anchored; (9) cracks sealed with hydraulic cement; (10) rescheduling has emptied the loading dock; (11) steel bulkheads for doorways; (12) sump pump and drain to eject seepage.

REFERENCES

1. McKeever, S. R., *Flood Proofing: Example of Raising a Private Residence,* South Atlantic Division, Corps of Engineers, Atlanta, 1977.
2. Sheaffer, J. R., *Flood Proofing: An Element in a Flood Damage Reduction Program,* Department of Geography, Research Paper No. 65, University of Chicago, 1960.
3. ———— et al., *Introduction to Flood Proofing: An Outline of Principles and Methods,* Center for Urban Studies, University of Chicago, 1967.
4. Sheaffer & Roland, Inc., *Economic Justification of Flood Proofing: Analysis of a New Commercial Structure,* Sheaffer & Roland, Inc., Chicago, 1977.
5. U.S. Army Corps of Engineers, *Flood Proofing Regulations,* Office of the Chief of Engineers, Washington, D.C., 1972.
6. U.S. Department of Housing and Urban Development, Flood Insurance Administration, *Elevated Residential Structures,* Washington, D.C., September 1976.
7. James F. MacLaren Limited, *Flood Proofing: A Component of Flood Damage Reduction,* 2 vols., Ontario, Canada, March 1978.

Part Three
Security Components

Chapter 9

An Overview of
Protection Systems

TIMOTHY J. WALSH

**President, Harris & Walsh Management Consultants, Inc.,
New Rochelle, New York**

PROTECTION SYSTEMS

Let us start by defining "protection" and "system."

Protection may be considered as the state or condition in which the risk of a likely loss event is eliminated or reduced, or in which the consequences of that event are controlled in such a way as to prevent or reduce the loss.

A *system* is any integrated combination of resources operating in designed interrelationship for the achievement of a predetermined objective.

It follows that a *protection system* is a design-integrated combination of resources operating in mutual support for the purposes of preventing or deterring loss events and avoiding or reducing losses. The term "loss event" is used here to provide a broadly based definition of a pure risk event, such as fire or theft, as contrasted with a speculative risk loss, such as failure to sell a product in a competitive market.

WAYS IN WHICH PROTECTION CAN BE ACHIEVED

Protection can be achieved in any one or a combination of the following ways:

1. Prevent the loss event from occurring in the first place.
2. Remove the asset at risk from the effect of the loss event.
3. Increase the time over which the loss event must operate.
4. Halt the loss event after it has started.

Illustrations of these four approaches to protection can be seen in considering a single asset, say, an amount of cash exposed in a desk drawer. To prevent the loss event from occurring would require security countermeasures sufficient to ensure that a potential thief could not get at the cash. That might involve locking the desk and the office, alarms on doors, identity check on persons seeking admittance, and a host of other precautions.

To approach protection in the second way would involve merely the removal of the cash from the desk to some other location. To approach it in the third way would mean to select one or more of those precautions or countermeasures which might also be appropriate for the first approach (e.g., locks) and depend upon them to delay completion of the event but not completely prevent it.

To approach protection in the last way would be to fix on some method for knowing when a loss event was taking place and responding before it could be completed. Intrusion alarms would be the classical countermeasure under this approach.

Which method or methods of approach will be chosen is determined by three factors: (1) the value (monetary or otherwise) of the asset at risk; (2) the reliability required or failure rate accepted of the protection scheme; and (3) the relationship between the cost of the protection and the cost of the loss.

POINTS AT WHICH PROTECTION MAY BE APPLIED

It is useful to think of the places or locations at which protective systems or measures may be applied as being successively closer to the asset at risk. The asset itself may be anything from the cash considered in the previous section to the building in which it is located. When dealing with disaster, or with pure risks (like fire, natural catastrophe, explosion, and so on), the focus is often upon the larger asset or concentration of assets, such as the building. When dealing with pure-risk losses involving theft or other crime, the focus is more often on the smaller, high-value asset, such as a product, or tools, or cash. However, the technique of regarding protection points as successively closer to the asset involved is helpful in both cases.

The first point for protection is the most remote from the asset. In a typical situation this will be the property line or boundary. Another writer has referred to this as the "first line of defense."* The kinds of protective measures usually encountered at this point are fences, exterior illumination, guard patrols, and alarms. Increasingly, remote surveillance via closed-circuit television is also being employed.

The second point, or "second line of defense," is closer to the asset. For assets vulnerable to theft it is often the building wall. Measures applied here include those used at the first line and also locks of mechanical, electrical, or electromechanical varieties.

The third point or line is the interior space which houses the asset. This may be considered as a floor, suite, or office. In addition to the countermeasures noted for the other two points, the activities of people in using, watching, or otherwise affecting the asset now take on protective importance. The aspect of "procedural security" becomes significant here.

The fourth point of protection is the precise location of the asset. This may be at a point of use, as with equipment and tools, or a point of storage, as with finished goods or materials.

THE KIND OF PROTECTION TO BE APPLIED

This handbook discusses many forms of security protection and many individual protective resources. How does the designer determine which of these resources to use? The answer depends in part on whether the system is intended to achieve prevention of the loss event, or merely prevention of the loss. But whichever approach is taken, the system designer must first know those actual risks which threaten the facility for which the system is being planned.

*R. J. Healy, "Design for Security," Wiley, New York, 1968.

The Risk Logic Tree

Efficient risk analysis can be promoted by the use of *risk* or *loss logic trees.* These are devices for organizing in clusters of progressively more significant impact those events, circumstances, and conditions which can or must exist or occur in order for the loss to occur. Figure 1 illustrates the risk logic tree technique applied to the consideration of a single risk or loss event, namely, the theft of cash from an office safe located in a typical office building.

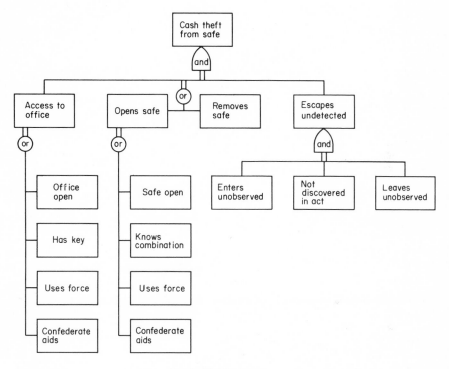

Fig. 1   Risk logic tree.

As the diagram shows, the risk logic tree breaks down the individual events or conditions that precede the successful theft of cash in the safe. This is the result of analysis which seeks to plot the flow of those events in their necessary sequence. It is important to break compound events into single elements. Thus, the ultimate risk is that the cash will be stolen from the safe. But for that to happen, the thief must (1) gain access to the office, *and* (2) open or remove the safe, *and* (3) escape undetected. If he (or she) fails *at any one* of these, the attempted theft fails of its objective. Said another way, the cash will not be stolen from the safe if the security system reliably prevents access to the office, *or* ensures that the safe cannot be opened or removed, *or* detects the thief before a successful escape.

Reading further down the tree, we can see that for each of these second-level conditions to occur, there are still other events or circumstances that must be true. Thus, in order to achieve an undetected escape, the thief must (1) not be observed entering the office, (2) not be seen or discovered in the office, *and* (3) not be observed leaving. Again, the conditions are joined by the word "and," i.e., they must all be true.

On the other hand, in order to gain access to the office, the thief could do so by having a key, *or* by finding the office open, *or* by using force, *or* by having a confederate open it. Any one of these conditions will permit access to the office.

It is clear that fewer security resources will be needed if they are placed at those *"and"* connections between events. Thus, the system designer may decide either to prevent access to the office, or to make the safe difficult to remove or open (if that is possible), or to ensure that undetected escape is not possible. But, although any one of those countermeasures would prevent the theft, it is apparent that to prevent access to the office would require many physical and procedural countermeasures, because access is possible in a multitude of independent ways. With regard to the safe, too, the thief has several options, and the security countermeasures would have to neutralize all of them. While this might theoretically be done in some situations, the probability of system failure will be greatly increased because there will be that many more devices or protection points at which failure can occur.

Looking at the last of the three necessary conditions to theft, we see that all of its subconditions must also exist together. If a countermeasure can be used which will make it impossible or very difficult for the thief to enter, remain in, or leave the office undetected, the theft can be defeated. We have thus *identified the kind of protection to be applied and the place at which to apply it.* The kind of protection will be an alarm or surveillance device, and the place of application will be the office itself.

Multiple Countermeasures

Although the primary resource is identified as indicated in the preceding section, the designer of an effective system will not place exclusive reliance upon that one measure. He or she will consider whether a second or third countermeasure would not be justified as contributing to an even further reduction of the probability of loss. In the example chosen, the safe would also be locked, as might be the office itself. However, in making any determination of countermeasures it is indispensable to first recognize the conditions which will lead to loss and to understand their interrelationships. Only in this way will the system design take advantage of all options.

In the example, we have suggested that one kind of countermeasure, at the fourth line of defense or point of protection, would be a key countermeasure in preventing the loss. Note that the loss event might occur, i.e., the thief might gain access to the office and might even start to remove or open the safe. But the actual loss would not occur until the safe or contents were removed and an undetected escape was made. The key countermeasure would prevent that last condition.

In actual fact, any but the simplest security or protective systems will be redundant in providing protection—partly because individual countermeasures, designed primarily to prevent one kind of loss, will have an adjunct effect on other exposures. Also, certain assets will be so important or certain kinds of losses so unacceptable that several primary countermeasures will be adopted to prevent or reduce them.

The Specific Countermeasure

Selection of the specific measure (e.g., what kind of alarm or what kind of lock?) is the next task after determining the kinds and points of protection. Whoever makes this choice must not only be familiar with security practice and technology but must understand that, at best, security is a relative concept that depends upon probabilities of success or failure. The probability that a security countermeasure will succeed or fail, in turn, is related to the validity and reliability of that countermeasure.

Validity of the Countermeasure

This term refers to the security resource's *capability to do the exact task* for which it has been selected. If, for example, closed-circuit television were selected for surveillance of a parking lot so that, should suspicious movements of cars occur, the vehicles could be observed and identified, it would have to be considered whether identification was to be made solely by make and model of car or by license plate number. If those were the only parameters, then a camera of sufficiently high resolution and sufficiently bright compatible light would be the prime requisites of the installation. But if, in more distant or angular observations, it was planned to identify the vehicles by their color and the states of registration by license plate color, then color television would be required. Black and white television would not be a *valid* resource for the color identification because it would be incapable of performing that task.

The same point can be developed with another example. It is frequently said that water-flow alarms on sprinkler and stand-pipe riser systems are fire alarms (in other words, that water flowing in the system is flowing because a sprinkler head or hose valve has been opened to respond to a fire condition). Strictly speaking, that is not necessarily correct. A water-flow alarm indicates only that (1) water is flowing or (2) the system has malfunctioned and an improper alarm is being received. It does not indicate the presence of fire. That is an inductive conclusion reached from the fact of water flow, which is associated with the idea of fire. A broken pipe or leaking valve could (and often does) produce water flow in sprinkler systems. So, while a water-flow alarm might be acceptable as a fire signal, it would not validly indicate fire but only water flow. If the system in question had to detect the presence of fire, not merely provide automatic extinguishing, it would have to use other means of detection. If the acceptable failure rate were zero, there might have to be multiple other means.

Reliability of the Countermeasure

In the example of the water-flow alarm, we noted that the cause could be a malfunction in the system. That is, it might function at a time when it was not designed to or might fail to function at a time when it *was* designed to. *Reliability is the quality of doing the design job at a predictable rate.* If the system will tolerate one failure or error in ten performances, it is 90 percent reliable. If it permits one failure in a hundred, it is 99 percent reliable. But if it will tolerate only one failure in a million occurrences, it is 99.9999 percent reliable. There is generally a close correlation between the degree or level of reliability and the cost of the countermeasure. Achieving an additional 0.1 percent reliability may prove to be very expensive. Yet in some situations there may be a very high reliability demand.

REDUNDANT DESIGN

The most generally followed method of achieving high reliability at acceptable cost is that of designing redundant performance at critical system locations. For example, if detection of fire is particularly critical in a given system (a point which will be decided for each system by the application of the "protective purpose" test suggested earlier), multiple fire-sensing detectors might be planned for the same fire exposure area. There might be a heat-actuated device (HAD) of some kind *plus* a products-of-combustion (POC) detector. Or the mix might be a POC and a flame (ultraviolet) detector. Another alternative might be a conventional sprinkler water-flow alarm reinforced with one or more of the other detectors.

The point is that multiple detectors, particularly when they operate on different principles, are much more likely to perform reliably than any one alone. This would be true even though the individual reliability of any one might not be high enough to meet the system criteria. A quick look at some principles of probability theory will show why this is true.

Assume that all of the sensors or detectors used have individual reliability levels of 0.90, i.e., one failure in ten; such a low reliability for a security system would not typically be acceptable. However, if we have three devices sensing the same area for fire, and if we are willing to consider an alarm by any one of the sensors a true fire signal, at least for the purpose of initial response, then in a given case only one of the three devices need function. Probability theory says that for the simultaneous occurrence of a number of independent and equally probable events, the probability (P) is equal to the product of the probabilities of the individual events:

$$P = P_1 \times P_2 \times P_3 \quad \text{or} \quad P = 0.10 \times 0.10 \times 0.10$$

In this case we see that the simultaneous failure of all three devices would have a probability of 0.001. In effect, the reliability of the *system of three* has been raised to 99.999 percent from what would have been 90 percent.

If the cost of individual sensing devices operating at the 90 percent level of reliability were, let us say, $50 for the POC, $3.50 for the HAD, and $20 for the ultraviolet, the combined cost for the subsystem of three would be $73.50. This would be far less than the cost for any one device with a reliability of 99.999 percent, if such a single device could be found.

But two other advantages are apparent from this redundant-design approach. Assume that, in a given system, reliable functioning of the HAD is enough and there is no requirement for additional sensing through the different principles underlying the POC and UV. (There are many applications for which the HAD detection would be sufficient, if it were reliable.) By using three HADs at a combined cost of $10.50, it would be possible to achieve 99.999 percent reliability. If that approach is applied to other subsystems (intrusion detection, surveillance, etc.), the economies in system design become quite apparent.

The other advantage to a redundant-design system employing multiple principles (or multiple detectors operating on the same principle) is the highly increased probability that what has been reported by the system is, in fact, the phenomenon which the system was designed to detect. Again, with the fire example, if three (or two, or any multiple) detectors report the presence of fire in the same area, the report is more reliable than if only one reported it. The same reason applies as cited before. The probability of simultaneous malfunction for multiple devices, each equally likely to malfunction, is the *product of the individual probabilities.*

There is a common application of this factor in the "dual logic" grids commonly employed with products-of-combustion detectors used to actuate automatic extinguishing systems of CO^2 or Freon 1301. One detector reporting an alarm will annunciate, but it requires two, detecting in different zones, to release the extinguishing agent.

Using the advantage of redundancy, derived from devices and resources themselves valid and each meeting a minimum reliability test, a highly reliable *system* can be designed whose *performance specification* can *exceed the performance ratings of its individual components.* This is a prime objective of security system design effort.

Another advantage of the system approach is that the high reliability can be achieved at no more, and often significantly less, cost than would be generated by nonsystematic efforts at security coverage. Designers must live with the cost constraints imposed on their projects. Historically in the security field this has led to elimination of protection that was really required.

A third advantage, perhaps the most valuable from the design point of view, is that with the variety of options offered by a systematic approach to protection, no single protective technique need be mandated. This often permits a scope and range of design freedom essential to a result which will meet functional and aesthetic requirements. Serious disputes can be avoided by allowing the designer to *respond to a security functional requirement rather than incorporate a piece of security hardware.* In some cases the hardware will be self-evident (as when the requirement calls for real-time remote surveillance, such as closed-circuit television), but there will be many other situations in which greater freedom will be possible.

A REVIEW OF SECURITY TECHNOLOGY

Until the mid-1960s the typical security installation was not designed as a system but was developed incrementally and often disjointedly, and would involve direct connections between sensing devices and the annunciation or terminal equipment. These "hard-wired" systems were fairly reliable in that each device was individually connected to an annunciator. Barring some failure of the device or the terminal equipment, the transmission paths or circuits would generally function as intended. Electrical supervision on those circuits would permit continuous (or intermittent) monitoring of that functional continuity, and the failure of any one device or its annunciator would not affect other devices as they did not share circuit paths.

The Loop Circuit

An exception to this was the so-called "loop circuit." This is a technique for combining many devices, separated by long distances, into a common network. The loop is a continuous wire path to which are attached at various points either individual devices or, more often, clusters of devices such as the variety of intrusion- or burglary-type alarms which might be found in a conventional industrial facility. Each cluster would be attached through a local control unit, and thereafter alarms from any of that cluster would be characteristically indicated at the terminal or annunciating equipment. Numbers of such clusters could be included on a single loop, each with a characteristic signature to distinguish its alarms from those in other clusters on the same loop.

The advantage of the loop was the reduced cost in providing alarm protection. Before it came into general use, in many cases if protection had to be procured at the higher costs of individual or "hard-wired" installation, some or all of it would be eliminated.

From the protection point of view, however, there are important disadvantages to the loop configuration. First, as many users share a common wire path, they are all subject to the results of loss of that path. Most loops (except those entirely proprietary and contained within a single installation) involve telephone company wire connections. For a variety of reasons those connections often fail. Installers' mistakes, changes in relative humidity, accidents, and deliberate sabotage have all affected loop circuits.

The McCulloh Feature

In an effort to assure high reliability, a circuit configuration referred to as a "McCulloh feature" was added to loops. This feature utilized a common neutral and circuit switching (manual or automatic) which permitted the continued transmission of alarms in the event of a single "open" or a single "ground," or a combination of those circuit faults. It did this by changing the circuit paths, when such faults were detected, so as to transmit around the faulted loop in two directions from the source of electrical energy to the last device on either side of the open or ground. In this way, given a single "open," every device or cluster of devices on the loop might still function if the "open" lay between them. However, if two "opens" occurred, the section of loop between them would be eliminated. Other devices and clusters would continue to function, but the section between the "opens" would be dropped. In practical application, it would be very difficult to determine exactly what section of the loop was affected unless tests could be made from every device and cluster on the loop (the nonfunctional being recognized through the failure to test), or the electrical characteristics of various sections of the loop could be carefully measured. In practice, location and correction of loop faults might be a matter of hours or days. In the interim, a loop subscriber might not know whether he or she was protected. So, even though the McCulloh loop concept added a great deal to the capacity of alarm circuits to afford protection, there were still significant problems.

Multiplexing Circuits

A great stride forward has been the provision of multiplex circuits for alarm and security signal transmissions. Multiplexing is the technique which uses a common carrier (wire or radio frequency) to transmit multiple signals. This is done by assigning different time periods to the transmission of different signals, or by transmitting different signals on different frequencies. Although there is a real interval of time between the different signals, it is so short as to be virtually inaudible or at least indistinguishable to the human ear (as in the case of FM stereo radio broadcasting), and thus it will not affect the processing of the received signals at the annunciating or control end of the system.

Most modern integrated security systems feature multiplexing circuits.

Digital Encoding

Another major improvement in security systems was the change from analog to digital data transmissions. Although the basic fact reported on the system would be the same, e.g., door open–door closed or movement–no movement, the report would be in digital form. This made it possible to apply the data-handling capabilities of digital computers to security system signal inputs. This, in turn, permitted programming, first of the nonvariable and later of the stored-memory variable type. With programming, and especially variable programming, modern security systems can now control major activities such as access, in which thousands of different people require selective admittance to many different locations over varying time frames. By assigning a unique digital code to each person to be controlled and a unique digital code to each control point, and by storing the various permutations of who was to be admitted at what point and when on some form of readily accessible memory storage device (tape, disk, etc.), it is possible to make the determinations at the speed of computer operations whenever a controlled person addresses the system for admittance. Not only can the decision be made in milliseconds but, because each system component has been uniquely identified, the entire transaction can be recorded. By adding a real-time clock to the system, the transaction can be accomplished and the information recorded in real time, thus establishing a serial time log of all events. Moreover, as all the transaction data can themselves be stored in the computer, data can later be retrieved in any combination or sequence in which they would be useful. Thus, the whole area of management reporting, data analysis, and trend plotting is opened for security application. The ultimate in the modern security system carries this process one step further. It processes all the alarm and security signal inputs, analyzes the trends, and, based upon programs prepared in anticipation of possible trends, adjusts itself (and field conditions) to respond to the trends. Such performance would simply not be possible with earlier systems.

KEY POINTS IN CONCEIVING THE SECURITY SYSTEM

By putting together what has been said so far, we can formulate the following *Designer's Guide to a Security System:*

1. *Determine the protective objective.* (Prevent or delay loss event. Prevent or delay loss. Control or reduce loss.)

2. *Determine the point at which to apply protection.* (How close to or remote from the asset at risk?)

3. *Determine the kind of protection.* (From analysis of risk logic tree relationships and the maximum use of "leverage" or risk control through breaking required combinations of conditions.)

4. *Decide the level of required reliability.* (From the impact of failure or nonfunction.)

5. *Consider achieving reliability through redundancy.* (By use of multiple, lower-cost resources in lieu of single, high-cost resources.)

6. *Take advantage of current technology.* (To permit system tasks not previously possible and to avoid former dangers of nonfunction or malfunction.)

SPECIFYING THE SECURITY SYSTEM

Most designers are not personally familiar with all the available security equipment or even all the conceptual approaches which different systems could take to the same objectives. Under these circumstances it is a needless limitation for the designer to specify *equipment.* Although one can consult Sweet's catalog and similar architectural and engineering reference sources and draw from them a hardware specification, unfamiliarity with the field might easily lead the designer astray if he or she were to select equipment merely because it was listed in a brochure. For designers who are not themselves familiar with the security field, a better approach is to prepare a *functional specification* and then solicit responses from qualified suppliers who will enter into a technical as well as a cost competition to meet the system task requirements. By utilizing qualified suppliers, and by developing a very precise functional specification, the designer will have an opportunity to review the latest technology and still make a rational comparison among potential suppliers because all are addressing the same tasks.

IDENTIFYING THE SYSTEM TASKS

The security system will often have been considered by the project owner or manager even before the designer or architect is asked to submit a proposal or begin work. If this is not evident from the state of the project program, the designer's and the client's best interests will be served by requesting that the security requirements be established in the form of architectural or design criteria *before the design concept is perfected.* Such criteria should be included in the scope of work in the same way that functional and aesthetic criteria are included and should be couched in performance terms rather than design terms. The following statements can be regarded as security design criteria which pose targets for the designer but do not limit freedom of design in any specific way. Every security function which has an impact on design can become the subject of a criterion and should be considered only as representative of the elements to be considered.

Access Control

1. No person shall be able to (enter, leave) the (complex, building, floor, suite, office, etc.) without having to pass (one, two, three, etc.) control point(s).

2. No vehicle shall be able to (enter, leave) the (complex, court, garage, driveway, etc.) without (stopping, passing x control points, etc.).

3. Elevators shall be so positioned that access to any car or cab must be via an access route on which a (single, double, etc.) control point can monitor all movements.

Site Hardening

No (exterior, interior) wall or surface of the (building, structure, etc.) accessible from grade to a height of (x ft) shall be constructed of any materials other than those which will resist impacts of (x ft.·lb) applied at the rate of (number of times) over (time period) without shattering, breaking, or losing their structural integrity.

DESIRED CONTROL FUNCTION	Total complex	Building	Floor	Suite	Office	Windows	Courtyards	Garage	Storage stacks	Driveway	Elevators	Storage and work areas	Valuable goods	Computer areas	(Continue list of facility components as appropriate)					
Entering persons	X					X						X	X	X						
Leaving persons	X				X	X			X			X	X	X						
One control point		X							X											
Additional control points	X																			
Monitoring	X	X				X			X	X	X	X	X	X						
Stopping	X											X	X	X						
Passing																				
Breakability						X						X	X							
Vehicular passage										X										
Visibility			X																	
Removal of goods	X								X			X	X	X						

Fig. 2   Security system tasks: an example of a checklist for establishing security criteria.

(A useful method of reviewing security elements for a given facility is to develop a checklist. An example of such a checklist is shown in Fig. 2. The structure in this example is a library building.)

JUSTIFYING THE COST OF THE SECURITY SYSTEM

When the system has been conceived and specified, and the qualified suppliers have proposed their versions and their prices, the decision will be taken as to which approach to follow and how much to invest. The amount of investment must bear a reasonable relationship to the cost of loss without the system and the cost of loss with any other system. Cost of loss thus becomes a key ingredient in the justification formula; it may be regarded as that cost most likely to be incurred from a loss event. The happening of a loss event involves the measurement of probability, and its cost involves measurement of criticality or impact. Normally, that impact involves (1) a permanent replacement cost for a totally lost asset, (2) temporary replacement cost if such replacement is needed, (3) related cost, as when a lost asset produces idle time or holds up other work at some cost penalty, and (4) discounted cash cost, when the money required to be diverted or spent on the first three cost elements is unable to earn return as a short-term investment. From the sum of these costs, or the sum of as many as are relevant to the asset loss involved, would be subtracted any indemnification available from insurance, hold harmless agreements, or otherwise. The remainder, the unreimbursed costs resulting from the loss, would be the measure of that loss's impact or criticality. All loss criticality measurements considered together, when related to assets which could be protected by a single integrated security system, become the cost risk. The actual cost (procurement and operation) of the security system is then considered over some agreed period of time. The difference between the cost risk and the system cost is the cost benefit. This will determine the appropriate amount of investment in the security system.

Chapter **10**

Site Protection

RICHARD J. HEALY

Head, Security and Safety Department, The Aerospace Corporation

SITE CONSIDERATIONS

Site selection and the layout of facilities on a site can have a significant influence on the cost which an organization may have to pay for security or a lack of it. Two financial benefits can usually be realized if effective security planning is done at an early stage. The first is a reduction in the cost of losses that threaten every organization, regardless of size or type. Some examples of such losses are fraud, theft, terrorism, sabotage, and disasters of all types. The second benefit that can be realized is a reduction in costs required to provide adequate security for the protection of assets and personnel.

Those involved in the selection and planning of a site give great emphasis, as they should, to a host of requirements dictated by the user. These include such items as appearance and convenience for personnel—both employees and others—as well as the efficiency of the layout to accommodate work to be done. Because of the priority given to such requirements, security is often not considered, except for such obvious items as keys and locks, until the facility is completed and almost ready for occupancy. Then, because of design errors having an adverse effect on security that could have been avoided with proper planning, an attempt is often made to provide protection with the use of guards.

Although guards are frequently necessary as an element in security planning, using them is one of the most costly means of providing protection. Everyone, of course, recognizes that costs for personnel have been skyrocketing in recent years. However, in many cases the real impact of guard costs is not appreciated because management may overlook the fact that a facility or item must be protected twenty-four hours a day, seven days a week. Three shifts of guards must be used for such protection. This does not mean that three guards can do the job. Instead, when vacations, sickness, and other absences are considered, at least $4\frac{1}{2}$ guards must be scheduled to cover one post around the clock for seven days.

The significance that guard costs can have on an organization's overall cost of doing business is evident from the fact that the average annual cost of one guard in the

United States in 1978 was estimated to be $8000. Multiplying this by the number of guards required to cover one post results in a cost of $36,000 for each guard post. If company-employed guards are utilized, the cost will be a great deal more. If adequate safeguards are to be maintained, the costs for guards will continue during the entire life of the facility.

If guards are not used in an effort to provide protection, an optional solution is to make construction changes to correct the security design mistakes. This solution can represent a costly capital expenditure and therefore is not likely to be favorably received, especially if the construction budget for the facility has overrun, a frequent occurrence in times of escalating costs. Still another solution would be to take a calculated risk, disregard the potential threats, not do any construction alterations, and not use guards. Such a decision would represent not merely a bad business decision but an irresponsible gamble, because losses that might result, given the pervasively threatening present-day environment, could seriously damage the enterprise or, worse still, force it out of existence. Consequently, making security a basic element in the planning and design of a facility is essential if adequate protection is to be obtained at a reasonable cost. Items that should be given attention during the planning stage will be discussed in the remainder of this chapter.

SITE SELECTION

The first consideration is the location of the site, as this can have a profound effect on protective measures that may be required. The three main items that may have an effect on protection requirements are physical, social, and political influences (see Table 1). An analysis of an area may indicate possible problems involving any or all of these factors, but this does not necessarily mean that plans to occupy the site should be abandoned. Instead, if the problems are recognized in advance, plans to develop the site can be implemented if appropriate protective measures are made a part of the planning and design so that the potential threats that have been identified can be neutralized.

Physical Factors

A physical analysis of an area should include (but not be limited to) the neighborhood adjoining the site, as well as potential environmental problems that might represent threats to the area, such as floods, tornadoes, and earthquakes. With reference to the neighborhood, it is important to know what kinds of work or processes are carried on in adjoining facilities and whether there are any hazards that might threaten the site being considered—for example, the use of potentially dangerous explosive material or components, chemicals, or other processes in neighboring facilities that might constitute a hazard in the event of an accident. Such potential problems would not necessarily result in a decision not to develop the site. Instead, through placement of structures on the site and by planning other protective measures such as barriers into the design of the site, countermeasures could be developed that would provide reasonably secure protection of the facility.

One nationally recognized pharmaceutical company did not consider security in the location of a major drug distribution center in a large population area. After the center, which was known to stock drugs attractive to addicts, was constructed and occupied, it was found that the methadone clinic for that major population center was in the adjoining building. As a result, hundreds of drug addicts were being attracted to that area at all times of the day and night because of the methadone center. The result was that additional security measures which had not been budgeted for in the planning had to be added to the distribution center to ensure protection against these addicts. The installation of these measures was a great deal more costly at that point than if they had been installed as a part of the site construction. Top management of that organization, recognizing that a major error in site selection had been made, then adopted a policy that the security director of the organization was to be included in the selection and planning of all future sites.

Social Factors

When social influences are being considered, some items to be analyzed would be the crime rate, the level of income, and the community interest indicated by residents. If

TABLE 1   Major Elements Affecting Protection Requirements

	Physical factors
COMPOSITION:	Material, mass, weight
CLIMATE:	Temperature, range and mean; relative humidity, mean and range; rainfall; snowfall; onset and end of freezing
GEOGRAPHY:	Latitude, longitude, elevation
LOCATION:	Neighboring exposures; sheltered or unsheltered; environment controlled or uncontrolled
CONDITIONS OF USE:	Times, processes, procedures

	Political factors
GOVERNMENT UNIT:	City, town, village
GENERAL TONE:	Conservative, liberal, major parties, minor parties, mixed, apolitical
ATTITUDES:	Tightly organized, loosely organized, no neighborhood organization, competitive organizations, dominant group(s)
POLITICAL AREA:	Single election or congressional district, multiple districts, identities and affiliations of federal, state, and local legislators

	Social factors
ETHNIC IDENTITY:	Population mix and distribution
AGE GROUPS:	Children, adolescents, young adults, middle adults, aging, old and infirm
INCOME LEVELS:	Blue collar, white collar, unemployed and welfare recipients, wealthy
NEIGHBORHOOD:	Percent residential, business, industrial, institutional, recreational, undeveloped deteriorated
SOCIAL HISTORY:	Peace, local incidents, major disturbances; chronology of significant events
PLANNING:	Reconstruction, rehabilitation, extension, rezoning
CRIME:	High crime, moderate crime, low crime; types of crime—organized or random; police relations—amount and frequency of patrol

it is determined that there is a high crime rate in the area, greater than normal protective measures and control would be indicated as a part of the site development plan. With regard to those living in the area, if the level of income is reasonably high and the appearance of residences reflects pride of ownership, it could be anticipated that there would be fewer problems with such neighbors than if the site adjoined a slum. If the site did adjoin such an area, site planning should take into consideration the possibility of vandalism, theft, and perhaps harassment of employees and visitors by the neighborhood residents. As a result, the facility should be designed so that such threats would be minimized.

Political Factors

Political influences involve the attitude, effectiveness, and ability of the various local service agencies in the area. Included would be, for example, the local fire and police services and other enforcement organizations such as prosecutors and the courts. The quality of such services will vary from jurisdiction to jurisdiction. Although normally it is not possible to correct deficiencies that are recognized, consideration can be given to such items in the planning of the facility, and more protective measures and controls can be included than would be considered otherwise.

SITE PLANNING

After a site has been selected and the three factors just discussed have been carefully considered, the planning of the site to ensure protection at the least cost is the next objective in the design process. The use of physical controls and the location of buildings and other facilities on the site, such as parking lots, should be given emphasis at this stage.

Physical Controls

Physical controls are normally incorporated into the design of a facility to influence the conduct, movements, and activities of people. For example: employees of all classes associated with the enterprise; visitors; customers; and others from outside the organization intent on causing harm, such as terrorists, burglars, saboteurs, robbers, and spies. Examples of physical controls are barriers such as fences and walls; locks; bars for windows and doors; protective lighting; vaults; safes; signs; and electronic alarms.

Physical controls, because they often act as psychological deterrents, will normally discourage an undetermined potential intruder. However, it is virtually impossible to design controls that cannot be penetrated if enough time, money, personnel, and planning effort are spent in the attempt. As a result, such controls can only be expected to delay a determined intruder. For that reason, each control should be designed to cause as much delay as possible. With the accumulation of delay resulting from a series of controls, an intruder attempting a penetration should be sufficiently hampered so he or she can be controlled or intercepted. "Security in depth" is a term commonly used to describe the utilization of a series of such controls. As important as the planning of physical controls is in the design of a facility, they cannot be expected to give complete protection, and they must be integrated with other types of controls, such as guards, if adequate protection is to be obtained.

Barriers   Various types of barriers can be utilized to obtain protection. There are two general types, natural and structural. Examples of natural barriers are bodies of water, mountains, deserts, valleys, marshes, or other terrain difficult to traverse. Structural barriers are of human origin and may be constructed from a variety of materials such as wood, metal, plastic, or glass. Examples of structural barriers are building surfaces, fencing, and masonry walls.

Barriers are used to control both foot and vehicular traffic and to discourage penetration of a facility or an area unauthorized by individuals. In addition, barriers are used to prevent penetration into areas or rooms within the facility and to prevent surreptitious listening and visual access. They can be effective in controlling traffic and the movement of material from the inside out. For instance, barriers can be used to prevent individuals working inside from stealing property or other items of value by carrying or throwing such material out through unprotected openings.

Protection planning for the site should also include the installation of barriers to prevent surreptitious entry. If these are properly installed, an intruder has to use force to break in or to penetrate a barrier or barriers to gain access to items being protected. The intruder then has to leave evidence that a penetration has occurred, and it is easier to assess the loss, identify the intruder, and take whatever other action is appropriate. Otherwise, it might be difficult to determine when an incident of penetration occurred as well as difficult or impossible to identify the individual or individuals responsible.

Those responsible for the design and planning of a facility may react negatively to any suggestion that barriers such as fencing or masonry walls be utilized, fearing that they would detract from the appearance of the facility. Such a concern is understandable, because many individuals can only envision a prison- or concentration camp-like appearance resulting from the use of unattractive masonry material or chain link fencing with barbed wire. However, barriers need not present an unsightly appearance if properly integrated into the design of the facility. With modern, attractive building materials now readily available, a knowledgeable, creative architect can incorporate barriers into the design of the site in such a way that they add to the appearance and become an integral part of the facility.

All building surfaces must be considered to be protective barriers—building walls as well as the floors and roofs. Each surface is vulnerable to penetration, and this type of threat must be considered in the facility design. For example, any opening in a building surface which is 96 in² or larger or is less than 18 ft above ground level is vulnerable to penetration. Some examples of areas that might be used by an intruder are ventilation shaft openings; grates, manholes, or chute openings that might lead to a basement area; and elevator penthouses and skylights on the roof. It must also be realized that a determined intruder might cut through a building wall, as well as the floor or the roof, to gain access to a facility. As a result, consideration must be given in the design stage to the fact that the facility will be vulnerable from all angles—sides, top, and bottom. Consequently, appropriate security countermeasures must be included in the overall plan to neutralize all threats of this type.

Door and Window Controls Doors and windows are obviously vulnerable to penetration if they are not properly designed and installed. If the material utilized in their construction is not of sufficient strength to prevent penetration, they should be strengthened with metal bars, screens, security-type glass, or plastic or other reinforcing material to ensure proper protection. Although doors and windows specified in a facility design might be strong enough, there are a number of other factors relating to their installation that might make them vulnerable. For example, the frames used to install both doors and windows must be of sufficient strength and be so installed that they cannot be sprung with the use of a pry bar to gain entrance. The vulnerability of hinges is often overlooked, too. If they are installed so that they can be tampered with from the outside, it is possible for an intruder to remove them to gain entrance.

Lighting The planned use of light is another physical control that should be included in the facility design. Protective lighting within structures as well as for outside areas such as parking lots, storage areas, and other open areas will act as a psychological deterrent. Potential interlopers will be reluctant to penetrate a well-lighted area or otherwise attempt to cause harm if they know that they may be under observation. Another important factor in planning protective lighting for a facility is that at night the enterprise is not usually operating at the same level of activity as during daylight hours and for that reason is more vulnerable. For further details on this subject, refer to Chapter 14, "Lighting."

Guard Towers Guard towers are sometimes included in a site design as another physical control element. However, as with other types of physical controls, guard towers alone cannot be relied on for security.

The height of a tower increases the range of observation during daylight hours and at night with artificial illumination, but during inclement weather and at night without lights, towers lose this advantage and must be supplemented by on-the-ground observation. Psychologically, the elevation of the observer in the tower has an unnerving effect on a potential intruder, but the inactivity of standing watch in a tower tends to lull the guard into a state of drowsiness. Mobile towers are useful in some temporary situations, such as in a large open storage area where there is activity in receiving and storing equipment. Towers may also be integrated into buildings on a site so that they are made a part of the structure. All towers should have a support force available for emergencies, and guards should be rotated at frequent intervals.

Safes and Vaults If safes and vaults are included in the facility design, they can also be used effectively as another type of physcial control. However, the type of protection each is designed to offer must be analyzed when consideration is being given to their use. For example, a safe is normally constructed for either fire protection or security against theft, not for both. A safe constructed primarily for fire protection can be expected to give only minimum protection against forcible entry because of the light steel and insulation utilized in the construction. On the other hand, a safe designed to give protection against penetration will allow a rapid transfer of heat to the interior because of its solid, thick steel walls. This type of safe will provide little or no protection against fire.

Vaults, except for the types designed for installation in financial institutions, are usually designed to give protection against fire only, and so they will be vulnerable to forcible entry. As a result, if a vault of this type is to be used for the storage of negotiable instruments, consideration should be given in the design stage to the installation of a money safe within the vault to ensure proper protection for such valuables.

Location of Facilities on the Site

The location of buildings and areas on a site should be made a fundamental element in the design criteria for the facility, as both the level and the cost of protection can be influenced. For example, the location of buildings on a site can have an effect on the number of access points required, and this in turn will affect their control as well as the cost of protection. Security controls at access points are ordinarily installed for two reasons—control of people and control of assets. As a result, the more access points there are, the more costly it will be to control them; the design objective should be to have a minimum number of regularly used access points.

Interconnecting Buildings One way of accomplishing this objective is to locate buildings on the site properly. If a number of buildings are to be constructed on a site and each structure has an entrance, each may have to be controlled individually. However, if the buildings are located so that they can be interconnected, all the structures on the site can be treated as one building when access controls are being planned. One technique is to incorporate an interconnecting barrier into the design of the facility so that all structures on the site are tied in to form one unit. As suggested earlier in this chapter, material used for the barrier can be planned as a part of the overall design so that it appears to be an integral part of the facility. Connecting tunnels or bridges between structures might also be integrated into the design to eliminate access points.

The appropriate number of emergency exits to meet fire, OSHA (Occupational Safety and Health Administration), and other safety or code requirements must be designed into the facility to supplement the regularly used access points. However, such exits can be reserved for emergency use, and the necessary controls (such as alarms) can be installed to ensure that they are being used for that purpose only. Also, each regularly used access point must be sized and properly designed to accommodate the amount of traffic using it. For example, in a large facility the traffic through access points might be very heavy during shift changes, and a number of channels for entry and exit, as well as guards, might be needed to accommodate the traffic flow. But between shift changes the traffic might decrease to such an extent that most of the access channels could be closed, with the result that a like number of guards could be eliminated. The reduction in guard costs in such a situation could be significant.

Parking Lot Location The location of parking can also have an effect on the number of access points needed as well as on the difficulty of the control of people and assets. Parking should never be allowed within an area being controlled, because it is very difficult to exercise control over people and material going in and out in vehicles. Also, buildings should be located on the site so that all of the parking can be on one side, if possible. This requires access points on only one side, and fewer are needed than if parking is located around the entire perimeter. If parking areas surround the facilities, access points are required on all sides for the convenience of those parking there, which makes it difficult to close any access points during periods of low traffic or during off hours. As a result, more security-controlled access points are required, at additional cost.

Planning for Operational Needs   Planning the location of organizational units and operational needs as a part of the site design is another element that should be included in the layout of the site. Most facilities contain a number of units that have

Fig. 1   An emergency generator inside a security-controlled area enclosed with chain link fencing for protection against sabotage, vandalism, and tampering.

large numbers of visitors but do not usually require security controls—for example, purchasing, personnel, and sales. If these are located outside a security-controlled area, their visitors can come and go without the usual physical controls (badging, escorting, etc.) provided for a controlled area. As a result, visitors as well as the unit's own personnel are less inconvenienced, and the security organization can then concentrate on protective measures for the parts of the facility requiring them. Of course, when such offices are not occupied during nonworking hours, normal protective measures such as alarms and guard patrols usually provided for nonsensitive areas can be planned as a part of the overall facility protection scheme.

On the other hand, there are other organizational units that usually require special protective measures which should be included in the site design. Some of these are computer centers; laboratories or other areas in which sensitive or proprietary work is done; areas in which hazardous processes or operations are carried on; and the utilities for the site.

In the case of computer installations and other sensitive operations, it is normally advisable to place such units in the interior of the facility in a location where there will be no windows or exterior walls. It will then be simpler to install the necessary protective physical controls such as barriers, alarms, etc., to discourage penetration.

With regard to hazardous-type operations, the location on the site and the control of such areas may be important for the protection of those in the area as well as others in adjoining areas. For example, such a unit might be located in a remote part of the site and could be designed with appropriate barriers to ensure protection for the other buildings and personnel on the site in case of an accident.

The location and protection of all utilities being used in the facility should also be given consideration in the site plan. These should be located within the security-controlled area and be protected against sabotage, vandalism, and tampering. Items that require this type of security include transformers; all power controls such as valves, regulators, and main switches; emergency generators; and pump stations. If possible, these should be located within a building that can be locked and controlled. If this is not possible, the areas in which the items are located should be fenced, screened, and lighted at night, and the access points should be locked (see Fig. 1).

THE RELATIONSHIP BETWEEN DESIGN AND SECURITY

Representatives of the architect, contractors, and management of the user enterprise who are responsible for the design of a facility do not usually have sufficient knowledge or experience in the field of security to include the various protection elements discussed here. Therefore, to ensure that cost-effective techniques as well as items to improve protection are properly incorporated into a design, a close relationship must be established between the various individuals responsible for the planning and design of a facility and those responsible for security. This relationship must be established as soon as a decision is made that a facility is to be developed and should continue until it is completed and ready for occupancy. This means that security must be included as an essential design element starting with the development of conceptional planning, even before any designs are rendered, and following with the development of the facility through all design and construction phases to include all changes and revisions.

If a security staff is not available in the user enterprise or if those available are not qualified or are too busy to participate in the planning of a facility, the hiring of a security consultant with experience in this field should be considered. The normal fee for such advice is small in comparison to the large sums that such a consultant can save an enterprise after the construction is completed and the facility is occupied. As previously indicated, these savings can result if attention is given to two areas—reduction in the cost of protection and reduction in losses. Such savings are not of a short-term duration but will be in effect during the lifetime of the facility.

Also, the design-security relationship should be continued after the completion of construction because of changes that can have an influence on the protection of the facility. For example, any rearrangement of construction, movement of personnel, or changes in the work processes might require changes in existing physical controls or the addition of others.

Chapter 11

Electronic Security Systems

ALAN B. ABRAMSON, P. E.

Senior Engineer, Syska & Hennessy, Inc.

Recent studies project that the market for electronic security products and services for commerical, industrial, financial, and institutional customers could reach $1 billion by 1980. This represents an annual growth rate of 10 percent per year. The reasons for this projected meteoric rise are the increasing need for security, the rapidly increasing costs associated with maintaining a security force, and the lower cost and increasing reliability of manufactured electronic equipment. Building owners and tenants who have not been able to afford security programs in the past will find that they have become an operational necessity.

ELECTRONIC VERSUS HUMAN ABILITY

All security programs must involve human ability in the form of human judgment and human responses. Typically, the cost-effectiveness of a security program can be optimized with the judicious application of electronic security equipment.

In some cases, electronic security equipment will outperform the security officers in a particular task. This may free them for other duties, eliminate the need for their posts, or increase the level of protection.

In other cases, where the existing security force is small and efficient or where employee trust is a key element in the personnel policy, the application of electronic security equipment may serve only to demoralize the security force and existing personnel, thereby reducing protection, overall productivity, or efficiency.

MAKING THE BEST CHOICE

Unfortunately, electronic equipment will not solve the majority of security problems. There is no panacea.

Promises of performance are made by equipment manufacturers who tend to neglect the legal, operational, and architectural constraints within which the end user must operate.

When a building owner or tenant considers implementing an electronic security system, he or she should do so by evaluating all types of equipment available and the effect that each might have on the operation being reviewed. Promises of labor savings and an ultimately secure environment should not be accepted without reevaluating the complete security program in the context of future expansion, building operations, management objectives, and hidden but recurring maintenance costs.

Attention should be given to the performance record and future financial outlook of manufacturers whose equipment is under consideration. The importance of such an investigation becomes obvious when factory service or replacement parts are required. Integrated subsystems should be sought wherever possible. Potential purchasers should speak to those who own or operate such systems. They are the best source for information on system performance, limitations, and requisite reliability.

Finally, it must be understood that the electronic security equipment industry is in its infancy. New and improved devices are being manufactured and marketed faster than "old" devices can be purchased and installed. This severe contraction of time makes it very difficult to keep abreast of new developments. It does, however, make this a very attractive field of expertise for the creative security consultant. New and creative applications for this equipment will set standards for the future and will ensure the successful development of newer techniques.

The intent of this chapter is not to provide the type of detailed data that might be found in manufacturers' catalogs, but to provide the designer with the tools to evaluate the system options that exist with regard to overall system design. Stress will be given to the wide range of functional parts that make up the modern electronic security system. These tools will permit the system designer to make the judgments necessary in integrating a cost-effective system.

THE GROWTH OF THE INDUSTRY

The electronic security equipment industry has developed from three separate directions. They are as follows:

- The military and defense industry
- The banking industry
- The process control industry

The military and defense industry's contribution has been in the fields of sensor development, reliability, and telecommunications. The rigorous approach and formalization of experimental and analytical techniques used by the military is well illustrated by their evaluation of various sensors for intrusion detection. Their evaluations examine the performance of selected types of sensors falling within similar functional detection categories. Intruder criteria and evaluation scenarios are developed. The data analyses include the definition of detection probabilities and false-alarm rates versus environmental conditions. Such data and analytical techniques are very helpful in the determination of the use of a particular device. Hopefully, these techniques will eventually be applied to commercially available sensing equipment and the information disseminated for design purposes.

The banking industry was the first customer of the central-station alarm companies in the nineteenth century. Through this industry we have seen the development of line supervision techniques, multipoint annunciation techniques, rudimentary multiplexing techniques, and central-station standards.

The process control industry has been the leader in incorporating state-of-the-art technology into open- and closed-loop monitoring and control systems. These systems have been adapted to commercial buildings and building complexes for the monitoring and control of the mechanical and electrical systems. This application has spawned the development of high-speed, high-volume, computerized data collection and processing control systems. The existence of these systems for monitoring and control, building management, energy management, communications, and fire safety has created a natural environment for the incorporation of electronic security equipment. A further discussion of the technical and functional aspects of this integration is presented in subsequent sections of this chapter.

ELECTRONIC SECURITY SYSTEMS

All security systems must contain three functional parts. They are the *security center,* the *data distribution and processing system,* and the *remote sensors and control points.*

A fully integrated system may be represented by a functional block diagram (Table 1).

TABLE 1

Security Center
Alarm annunciation Secure/access switching Remote controls Video monitors Video controls Audio inputs Audio monitors Audio controls Access system controls Security guard tour programming Radio Communication Controls

Data Processing and Distribution
Data collection and distribution Line supervision Video distribution Audio distribution Radio spectrum System power distribution

Remote Equipment
Detection sensors Remotely controlled devices Surveillance cameras Audio sounding devices Audio detectors Access control stations Security guard tour reporting stations Portable radio equipment

SYSTEM STRUCTURE

Modern electronic security systems are composed of many subsystems which may be integrated from the point of view of both function and hardware. The major subsystems that should be considered for such integration are as follows:

- Access control systems
- Perimeter intrusion detection systems
- Area intrusion detection systems
- Video communication systems

- Audio communication systems
- Radio communication systems
- Emergency reporting systems
- Security guard tour reporting systems
- Fire detection and protection systems
- Life safety systems

These subsystems form the basis for all modern electronic security systems. This permits the security manager to go beyond what has been traditionally included in an "alarm system" to take advantage of available technology, creative application engineering, and modern building operation methods.

All security systems can be classified by the location of their associated alarm-sounding devices. The major classifications and their respective design features are as follows:

1. A *local alarm system* is a system in which the alarm-sounding device is located in the immediate vicinity of the protected area. This is used to let intruders know that they have been detected. Hopefully, they will not stay to complete their intended purpose. In addition, it enables the security force or police, when called, to "follow the alarm" to the breached area. The system is automatic and requires no human intervention for operation. It is the least expensive type of system to install and is usually combined with one of the other types to allow the breach to be signaled at a staffed location for appropriate response.

2. A *proprietary alarm system* is one in which the alarm signal is relayed to a headquarters location owned, staffed, and operated by the proprietor or agents of the proprietor. This is used in places where there is a 24-hour-operated officer dispatch location. Sending devices may be silent or may actuate local alarms. It enables a proprietary security force to be used with maximum effectiveness. A two-way radio system should be incorporated to permit optimal deployment of personnel and minimal response time. Initial cost is high in terms of installation and space requirements, but the system becomes very cost-effective in large buildings, multibuilding complexes, high-security areas, or any other locations with a proprietary security force.

3. A *central-station alarm system* is a system in which the alarm signal is relayed to a remote panel located at some centralized facility owned by an outside agency. This may be a privately owned protection agency or, where permitted, a local police or fire station. The connection to the central station may be by communication lines that are shared by many subscribers or by lines that are "dedicated" to each subscriber. When dedicated lines are used, the system is called a "direct-connect alarm system." A central-station system is often used in conjunction with local or proprietary alarm systems to provide response backup and allow signaling at an off-site auxiliary reporting station. Central-station companies provide a 24-hour monitoring service to their subscribers and will usually install and maintain the sensing equipment in the facility. The cost of such service includes an initial installation charge, recurring subscription charges, and recurring telephone leased-line charges. In high-security applications, where telephone lines can be easily disabled or are subject to compromise, two central-station connections may be maintained. They may go through different telephone exchanges or may incorporate a radio-operated relay to another location or building for connection to a separate set of dedicated lines.

Security system design should begin with the consideration of the remote equipment. What should your system do for you? Remote function selection will now enable you to know the number and types of detection and control points and the extent and nature of the other subsystems.

The required remote functions will have complementary security center functions. Upon consideration of the number and types of subsystems, the physical space requirements of the security center, the level of security desired, the expected number of system operators and officers on duty, the nature of any auxiliary control centers, and governing codes and regulations, the security center can be functionally designed.

The functional link between the security center and the remote equipment is the most important and, in many cases, the most misunderstood part of the system design. This functional link actually represents many subsystem hardware links. A well-designed system is one in which the data processing and distribution systems (1) are economically designed and (2) optimally utilize the remote equipment within the functional requirements of the security center.

SYSTEM RELIABILITY

The most important design criteria for a security system are related to the system's reliability, i.e., its probability of failure. The probability of failure of an individual piece of electronic equipment can usually be obtained from its manufacturer. Standard engineering concepts are available for combining the individual pieces into a complete system that is easily analyzed for its overall failure rate. In addition, good internal design and good quality-assurance procedures help minimize the failure rate. Two further reliability concepts will be discussed. The first concerns only *hardware reliability.* The second concerns *operational reliability.*

Experience with electronic systems has shown that their failure characteristics follow definite patterns (see Fig. 1). When failure rate is considered as a function of time, the life of an electronic component can be divided into three distinct patterns, each corresponding to a particular failure mode. They are as follows:

1. Infant failures
2. Normal failures
3. Aging failures

Infant failures are associated with malfunctions due to poor design, poor workmanship, and poor material quality. This period is characterized by a high failure rate that rapidly decreases with time. Good quality-assurance procedures incorporate a phase of burn-in and operational equipment shock to accelerate the initial equipment life and filter out infant failures. Paradoxical as it may seem, equipment that survives early use or abuse has a greater probability of having a long life than off-the-shelf, untested equipment. Due to the unpredictability of when the period of infant failure will end and when the next stage will begin, equipment guarantees are very important. Guarantee periods of a year's duration are typical and are sufficiently long to cover infant failures.

Normal failures are associated with the random failures that occur during the primary operating life of the equipment. This period is characterized by a relatively constant failure rate over time.

Aging failures are caused by malfunctions due to excessive wear after the expected useful design life of the equipment has been exceeded. This type is characterized by a rapidly increasing rate of failure over time.

In addition to hardware reliability, security system design must address itself to operational reliability. What can be done to maintain system operation, in full or in part, during a hardware failure? The system must be designed with standby, backup, or (to use system engineering terminology) redundancy. Redundancy techniques utilize parallel elements to reduce the probability of total system failure should any system component fail. It must be emphasized that redundancy in a security system must be considered with regard to the trade-off that exists between system integrity and system cost. Only when this trade-off analysis is performed can the economic feasibility of redundancy be determined.

Redundancy considerations will be discussed in terms of the previously developed functional breakdown.

Remote equipment is usually applied utilizing the following criteria:

1. Establish a perimeter at which intrusion detection and access control equipment should be implemented.

2. Select special vulnerable areas in which remote-surveillance or space-intrusion detection equipment should be implemented.

3. Determine communications requirements, and locate equipment for appropriate coverage.

Redundancy must be an important part of equipment selection with regard to all the above criteria. In a high-security application, multiple perimeters of intrusion detection may be required in addition to interior space-intrusion detection and video and audio surveillance. The operational feasibility of such an application will depend to a large extent upon the architectural configuration of the protected area. Very often, primary remote equipment will be located so that it is highly visible and, therefore, its existence serves as a deterrent to the prospective intruder. The redundant equipment will then be located so that it is hidden, therefore performing its

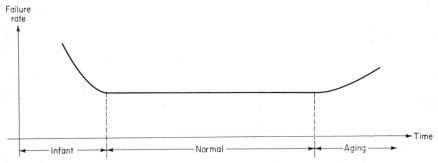

Fig. 1   Failure rates and the aging process for electronic equipment.

function without the knowledge of the intruder. Ultimately, the selection and location of remote equipment will depend upon that ubiquitous determinant, system integrity versus cost.

Redundancy considerations with regard to the security center are critical. The points to be considered are as follows:

1. The numbers, types, and locations of security centers.

2. The capabilities or system information available at each security center.

3. The extent of the printed record and the need for system logging.

4. The criticality of downtime for any piece of security center hardware.

5. The physical effect of equipment redundancy on security center "human engineering."

In facilities with extensive electronic security systems, the key to the facility very often lies in the hands of the operator on duty at the security center. No matter how well paid this operator may be, if the potential reward is high enough, anyone can be bought. Hence the possibility of an "inside job." Multiple security centers minimize the possibility of such an occurrence by increasing the number of people who have a real-time knowledge of the system's operation and the operator's actions.

The primary security center, i.e., the security center at which all system information, all central surveillance equipment, and all operator control and logging functions are available, should be located within the protected area. Auxiliary security centers may be located at remote guard stations, security manager's offices, or at a central station office. Having too many auxiliary security centers reduces system integrity by increasing the number of people who have knowledge of the existence and location of the remote equipment. Good design practice would normally limit the number of centers, with the possible additional insurance afforded by a central-station connection.

One function of the security center may be to establish a log of system operation, operator actions, and access control transactions as these items occur in real time. In addition, operator requests for the present status of devices, access control points, disabled devices, etc., may be required. This type of management information should be duplicated at the security manager's office to minimize the possibility of tampering with the printed record.

As previously discussed, a probability of failure exists for any given piece of equipment. A decision must be made as to how critical each piece of equipment is to the operation of the security system or to the implementation of the security program. An evaluation must be made of how much downtime can be tolerated. Redundant equipment may be switched into operation either automatically (Fig. 2) or

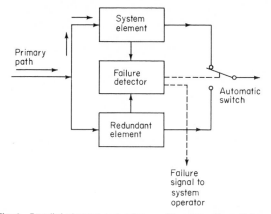

Fig. 2   Parallel element redundancy with automatic switchover.

manually. Automatic switchover requires the presence of failure detection circuitry and internal system diagnostics to isolate the failure and make the system operator aware of its occurrence. Manual switchover can be anything from the simple actuation of a switch to the actual replacement of a part from an on-site inventory of spare parts. The technology will permit any of these configurations. The design decision must be based on an analysis of system integrity versus cost.

The reliability of the data processing and distribution portion of a security system is extremely important. This portion of the system is most vulnerable to failures resulting from attempts to compromise, poor installation, and environmental interference. The fact that these subsystems may be spread out over the entire facility also increases the time necessary to diagnose and localize a failure. A method of ensuring the continuous operation of a system and the integrity of signal transmission is called "line supervision." There are many forms of line supervision, each corresponding to a different level of security. Line supervision is an electronic technique that originates at one end of the protected signal circuit (usually the annunciator section of the security center) and detects a failure or attempted compromise of the circuit and the connected device. Provisions for automatic switchover to an auxiliary circuit can be made. A discussion of the methods of line supervision and their associated technical aspects is given further on in this chapter.

The data collection and processing section of a security system may require computerization for the programmed functions required by data logging, guard's tour functions, access control data storage, or English-language input/output coding. The need for redundant computers or peripherals (input/output terminals) should be studied. The interconnection of these devices and the programmed system modes should also be studied. Fortunately, standard statistical mathematical modeling techniques have been developed to enable the performance of a meaningful, logical analysis of these complex systems.

Redundancy in audio or video distribution systems takes the form of dual distribution systems, with line supervision being used as the primary means of fault detection. In audio systems, multiple amplifier arrangements are often used to increase reliability. Redundant video equipment is usually not considered in security applications due to its high cost and the ease with which its function may be replaced with live personnel during downtime.

The critical redundancy item in radio system design is related to the selection of the frequencies of transmission. A good design will anticipate the usage of a particular frequency and will provide additional frequencies as required.

All electronic security systems require electric power at various points in the system. Failure of power at any point can disable a single device or the entire system, depending upon the point of failure. Some facilities have emergency power systems which start an emergency generator and switch it on line automatically upon sensing a power failure. If the capacity is available, the security system could be powered from this system. These power systems may take from 15 to 60 sec. to come on line. This is sufficient time for someone to make a surreptitious entry while bypassing the alarm system. Almost all remote devices can be bought with built-in battery backup to keep the device active for short periods of time. Battery backup can also be supplied for the security center. If the security center is computerized, an uninterruptible power supply unit would need to be provided to prevent computer shutdown or loss of memory during the power outage. (Refer to Chapter 23, "Computer Power Security.") Systems may also be designed with a separate power distribution system for the security equipment to permit uninterrupted power to be centrally produced and distributed.

REMOTE EQUIPMENT

Security system remote equipment consists of devices placed locally—that is, at the point where detection, access control, communication, etc., take place.

One such equipment classification includes devices for the detection of an undesired intrusion. All detection devices initiate an alarm by the opening or closing of an

Fig. 3 **Proximity-type magnetically actuated reed switch.** (*Photograph courtesy Honeywell, Inc.*)

electrical contact. These devices range in complexity from simple electromechanical switches to sophisticated electronic detectors.

The Switch   The most common alarm-initiating device is the door or window switch. This may be of the limit switch or magnetically held variety. They are manufactured in various shapes and sizes for different applications.

The most reliable of these switches is the proximity-type magnetically actuated reed switch. It consists of two housings, one containing a permanent magnet and the other containing a sealed unit of fine metal reeds which make or break contact in the presence of a magnetic field. Consequently, when these two housings are apart more than ½ to ¾ in, an alarm condition is generated by the making or breaking of the electrical contact.

A variation of the magnetic reed switch is the balanced magnetic reed switch, used in high-security applications where special compromise-resistant protection is required. The difference between this and the nonbalanced reed switch is the existence of a bias magnet in the housing containing the switched contact mechanism. The only time that the switch is in the secure mode is when the bias magnet and the permanent magnet in the other housing present a balanced magnetic field to the reed switch mechanism. Any external magnetic field, such as one that might be used in a compromise attempt, will unbalance the field and initiate the alarm. By adjusting the position of the bias magnet, the sensitivity of the device to external magnetic fields can be made to vary.

Fig. 4   Balanced magnetic reed switch in tamper-resistant housing.   *(Photograph courtesy Honeywell, Inc.)*

The remaining class of door or window switch is the limit switch type. This is an electromechanical device where the opened or closed condition of the electrical contact is determined by the actuation of a mechanical mechanism. It is often called a limit switch because of the limits imposed on the position of its spring-loaded actuating mechanism.

Proper installation of a door or window switch will result when a minimal compromise of the protected opening will trigger the device and when the device-actuating mechanisms or contacts are least susceptible to compromise. For example, a magnetic reed switch on a door should be installed on the protected side of the door, as far from the hinge side as possible, and should be located on the head of the door buck. Limit switches are typically installed in the hinge side of the door buck, in the hinge mechanism, or within the door closer. In general, detection devices whose existence and location are difficult to discern are the most difficult to compromise.

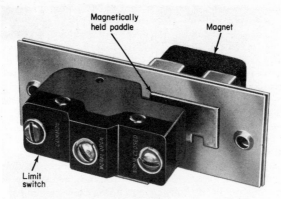

Fig. 5 Magnetically held limit switch. *(Phograph courtesy Honeywell, Inc.)*

Conductive Foil   This device is actually a material applied to glass or other breakable surfaces to detect surreptitious or forced penetrations. It is a common sight in retail stores or shopping centers where large glass display windows are present. Electrically conductive foil, usually less than $\frac{1}{2}$ in wide, is applied to the protected area much like adhesive tape. It is then coated with a clear varnish to assure adherence and make it resistant to false alarm by inadvertent scratching or peeling. The detection principle is based on the fact that the foil will form an electrically conductive loop or closed circuit that opens when the foil and the material to which it adheres are broken. An advantage of foil is that its installation is usually very visible, which serves to deter as well as detect an intrusion. A disadvantage is that false alarms may regularly occur due to cracking and peeling, necessitating replacement of the complete loop. Another disadvantage is that its visibility often offends the aesthetic sense in terms of architectural design. Foil comes in various widths and metallic finishes and may be applied in various patterns. When designing an appropriate foil pattern, all likely stress points and entry points should be covered. A problem with foil is that its application must be made by a skilled technician. Proper foiling and its electrical connection using the correct electrical take-off blocks is a delicate operation. A poor installation will mean many unnecessary and troublesome false alarms and a system difficult to troubleshoot and repair.

An alternative method exists for the protection of glass that provides the advantages of foil without its disadvantages, although it is quite expensive. It involves the imbedding of very fine breakwire, barely visible, in the glass during its fabrication. The high cost of this method results from the required custom fabrication for each application and the extensive quality control required in the fabrication process.

Breakwire   A breakwire detector consists of very fine, electrically conductive wire arrayed in the form of a screen or grid and utilizing a detection principle identical to that of conductive foil, i.e., the breaking of a conductive material whose continuity is required for the maintenance of a secured circuit. Its purpose is to detect intrusion through a building opening, such as an outdoor air duct. Standard-size breakwire screens are commercially available. Careful consideration must be given to potential breakwire applications with regard to the methods of physically securing the breakwire assembly. Breakwire assemblies are often installed in conjunction with magnetic switches whose function is to detect the movement of the entire assembly without breaking the wire.

Positive Beam Interrupt   This type of device consists of a transmitter-receiver pair between which a beam of electromagnetic energy must be maintained. When the beam is interrupted, an alarm contact is activated. The electromagnetic beam is, typically, visible light, noncoherent infrared radiation, or laser (coherent) infrared radiation. The simplest of these systems utilizes a light-bulb transmitter and photocell receiver, with the light being focused by lenses. Since the presence of such a system is readily discernible, and since it is easily compromised by shining an ordinary flashlight on the receiver, low-power infrared radiation that is modulated with a unique code by an electronic circuit is typically used. These systems may be used in a single- or multiple-beam configuration when corresponding transmitters and receivers are carefully focused.

In all beam-interrupt systems, the recommended range over which the system will work must be maintained. Ranges of 100 to 300 ft are available in indoor systems and ranges of up to 1000 ft in outdoor applications. Outdoor applications of beam-interrupt systems must be engineered very carefully, with attention given to the terrain of the selected detection zone and the areas of entry on the detection perimeter. False alarms due to falling leaves or birds may be minimized by incorporating a signal-processing feature and a multibeam system that is able to distinguish object size.

These systems come in a variety of shapes, sizes, and enclosures depending upon the architectural requirements of the application. They range from indoor systems disguised as electrical receptacles to outdoor systems that may be installed in decorative lanterns mounted on a security wall.

Passive Infrared Detector   These systems operate on the principle that humans emit body heat in the form of infrared radiation. They consist of an infrared-sensitive detector that initiates an alarm upon sensing a sudden temperature differential within its field of view. These devices vary as to their sensitivity and detection patterns.

Vibration Detector   These devices consist of an electromechanical transducer and a control unit. The control unit contains an amplifier/accumulator circuit with variable sensitivity which acts as an alarm discriminator to minimize false alarms caused by random noise resulting from building or equipment vibrations. The final sensitivity adjustment will depend upon the mounting method of the transducer and the material to which it is attached. This type of control unit may be used in conjunction with many different kinds of transducers. This includes microphones for audio noise detection or linear transducers for fence or buried-line detection.

Capacitance Detector   This device depends on the electromagnetic principle that when a small electric charge is placed on a metal object, the latter acts as an antenna and a capacitive coupling exists between the antenna and an electrical ground. When a person or other large object enters the field of the antenna, the electrical capacitance of the connected circuit is changed, and an intrusion is detected. This type of device is typically used for the protection of safes or other metal objects. In applying such a system, the integrity of the electrical ground is very important.

Ultrasonic Motion Detector   This detector is a type of "space" detector. It consists of transmitter-receiver pairs, either in single or multiple configurations, that fill a space with standing waves of ultrasonic energy. When the standing-wave pattern is disturbed, an alarm condition is created. Ultrasonic waves are usually confined between partitions, and their intensity may be adjusted at their control box.

This type of device also has certain limitations. Ambient noises or noises created outside the protected area which also emit sound waves can upset the sound-wave pattern, causing a false alarm. Air conditioning or heating vents pouring air into a room protected by the ultrasonic device may also trigger a false alarm.

Microwave Motion Detector   This detector is similar in principle to the ultrasonic "space" detector in its operation except that it uses high-frequency electromagnetic microwaves as its standing-wave medium. Microwaves can penetrate building partitions and structural materials and may therefore be used for detection in multiple areas. This type of detector may be susceptible to false alarms caused by the electromagnetic emissions of fluorescent lights or electric motors. Resistance to these factors should be present in a well-designed system.

Pressure-sensitive Devices These detectors, which may be in the form of a strip or a mat, react to applied pressure. Mats are very thin and are very effective detection devices under carpeting.

Remote Control Most electronic security systems have the capability for remote control of an electrical contact or switch. This capability may be used to turn anything on or off. Typical applications include the remote control of door operators, door locks or releases, security lighting, audible alarms, public address system circuits, elevator controls, or central-station signaling devices.

Surveillance Cameras These are of two types: photographic or closed-circuit television.

Photographic cameras are similar to those used for home movies. They may take single frames on a timed basis, film continuously when triggered by an alarm device, or carry out a combination of both. The type of film used will depend upon ambient lighting conditions, in addition to the required resolution of the photographs. Lens selection is a very important part of the design process because this item will both determine the camera's field of view and affect the resolution of the resulting photographs.

Closed-circuit television systems are used where continuous surveillance of a remote area by a centrally located officer is required. Closed-circuit television cameras themselves are available in varying light sensitivities and scene resolutions. Lens selection will determine the field of view of the camera. Various sizes of fixed-focal lenses are available, in addition to remotely controlled zoom lenses. Nomographs relating lens sizes with their fields of view and depths of field are readily available from lens manufacturers. Camera accessories such as mounts, enclosures, and remote-controlled or automatic pan/tilt units are readily available. Pan/tilt units move the camera left or right or up or down on command, thereby increasing its field of view. The application of these devices is left to the imagination of the designer. It must be noted that closed-circuit television systems are very expensive and should be used sparingly, after first considering other less expensive detection devices. For further references see Chapter 16, "Surveillance Cameras."

Audio Sounding Devices These may be bells, intercoms, or public address system speakers. Typical applications include the commandeering of guards or the issuance of emergency instructions.

Access Control Technology A large amount of research and development effort is being expended in this field. Access control identification stations used in conjunction with turnstiles, intruder traps, and electric door-locking mechanisms are becoming a necessity in any security system and save costly labor. The simplest access control identification station utilizes an intercom and/or closed-circuit television camera for communication to a centrally located officer who decides whether or not access should be granted. The next step in access control eliminates interaction with the centrally located officer. Each individual requiring access is issued a uniquely coded electronic card. When this card is brought in proximity with a card reader, the electronic code is transmitted via a data collection system to a computer that searches its data file for the code. The computer then grants or rejects access. The computer can take into account the selected door and the time of day in addition to the individual's code in just a few seconds. These systems are available as packages with dedicated computers, or they may be part of an integrated system. New systems entering the commercial marketplace purport to use personal characteristics of the individual, such as fingerprints, voice characteristics, or even handwriting characteristics. Though these systems open new avenues of design for the security consultant, they should be carefully studied prior to their application because of the enormous technical problems they attempt to solve.

Security Guard Tour Reporting Stations These allow the guard at the security center to monitor the whereabouts of a roving guard during the course of his or her tour. Typically, these devices may be electrical keyswitches connected to package dedicated systems or to the data collection portion of an integrated system.

Radio Communication System This is a necessary tool of any security force. It enables security personnel to be mobile and minimizes response time to an emergency situation. Because all radio communications are licensed by the Federal Communications Commission, a thorough knowledge of their rules and regulations is required to design a system. In general, radio systems provide communication in the form of voice or signaling between a fixed location (the base station) and mobile units. These mobile units may include personal portable two-way radios, vehicular radios, pagers, or signaling devices. In most systems mobile-to-mobile communication is required, as well as base-to-mobile communication. When the base station is configured so that it automatically rebroadcasts weak mobile signals to other mobiles, it is called a repeater-type operation. Portable radios and vehicular radios are generally used for two-way voice communication. Paging and signaling systems are generally used for selective calling by use of a modulated tone. Pagers receive coded signals transmitted from a base station, while signaling systems transmit coded signals to a base station. All paging, signaling, and repeater systems require a base station. Two-way voice communication requires a base station only if the transmitted power of the mobile is not sufficient for coverage of the desired area. Power requirements and frequency allocation design are discussed later in this chapter.

THE SECURITY CENTER

The security center is the location at which all centralized functions may be performed and monitored. A well-designed system will be integrated from both a physical and an electronic viewpoint. Efficient design will make optimal use of the operator's physical as well as mental capabilities. The frequency of use of a device will determine its location.

Alarm Annunciation This is the term used to describe the equipment that monitors the alarm conditions sensed by the previously mentioned detection devices. The simplest annunciators have individual lights denoting the status of the secured circuit. The items monitored include the secure/access, alarm/normal, and trouble conditions of the circuit. In addition to the visual display, an audible alarm to draw the operator's attention is required. Therefore, an "Acknowledge" or "Silence" button is included to stop the noisy "attention getter." Most alarm annunciators are configured for multiple "points" or "zones." This means that each alarm device or set of devices grouped in a logical manner may be monitored individually. Some annunciators have a common acknowledge button for all zones.

Fig. 6 Single-zone alarm receiver/annunciator. *(Photograph courtesy Honeywell, Inc.)*

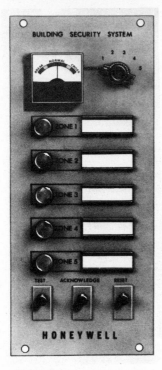

Fig. 7   Five-zone alarm receiver/annunciator. *(Photograph courtesy Honeywell, Inc.)*

Other annunciators are in the form of electronically driven displays. These may be in a digital format, where information is spelled out in coded English by lighting respective elements to form letters and numbers. The most sophisticated annunciators utilize a television-screen type of display called a cathode ray tube, which in conjunction with a typewriterlike keyboard and printers provides full English-language messages. Because of the extreme flexibility and variations available in initial system design, only an experienced electronics engineer should design such a system.

Secure/Access Switching All alarm systems should have the capability of enabling or disabling the alarm function on the annunciator according to variations in day or night operation. When an annunciator zone is placed in the secure condition, it monitors the alarm condition of the detection device. In the access condition, the alarm condition of the detection devices is ignored. These must be operator-controlled functions.

Remote Controls These controls may take the form of momentary or maintained pushbuttons, toggle switches, or coded keyboard entries (computerized system).

Video Monitors and Controls Every closed-circuit television camera must have an associated monitor in the security center on which its viewed scene will be displayed. Monitors come in various sizes, of which 9 in (diagonally measured) should be the smallest used in security surveillance. An important phenomenon to be considered is the concept of visual clutter. It means that an operator who has too much to watch will in reality watch very little. Therefore, the number of monitors should be kept to a minimum. A good rule of thumb is to keep the number below ten or twelve. Controls for pan/tilt/zoom should be located in the security center near their respective monitor.

Another type of video control is the video switcher. This enables the operator to (1) manually select a camera for output on a specific monitor, (2) sequentially display many camera scenes on a single monitor, or (3) have an alarm automatically switch a camera scene to a monitor. This piece of equipment is very important in a well-engineered video system. Video tape recorders of the real-time or time-lapse type are easily included. They may be manually or automatically activated.

Audio Systems Modern audio systems contain a large amount of zone control and switching. As with all remote controls, the switching feature may take many forms. Automatic gain control is becoming a very popular feature in well-engineered audio systems, but volume controls to compensate for ambient noise levels are still required. All modern audio systems for security and safety are fully electrically supervised. This means that alarm-monitoring points from the supervisory circuits must be provided on appropriate annunciators. Multiple system inputs in the form of tone generators, tape recorders, and microphones are common occurrences. System balance and preamplifier controls must, therefore, be provided.

Access System Controls Additions, deletions, and modifications to the access control system data file must be operator-controlled functions. This includes the voiding or entering of entrance codes and entrance time frames. Alarms occurring from invalid access attempts must also be monitored.

Security Guard Tour Programming   Various levels of programming exist, depending on the sophistication of the system. This may range from the setting of a manual timer in a simple system to the full programming afforded by a computer. Simple systems may require the setting of pins in a grid or the wiring of a patchboard for tour programming. Computerized systems will allow operator programming of random station-to-station tours with variable time allocations between stations. The two critical items to be specified in such a system are the number of tours to be programmed and the number of stations per tour.

Radio Communication Controls   The Federal Communications Commission requires that radio systems have a control point at which all communications may be monitored. This is usually located in the security center. In addition, encoders for paging systems and annunciators for signaling systems should also be located in the security center.

DATA PROCESSING AND DISTRIBUTION

After the decisions on remote equipment and security center capabilities have been made, the link between these two functional blocks must be designed.

Data Collection and Distribution   This portion of the system is critical because of its high cost in relation to the total system. Three major classifications exist:

- Hard-wired
- Hard-wired—central multiplex
- Remote multiplexing

A hard-wired system is one where dedicated wires exist for each control and monitoring point in the system. For small systems, this is the most economical method. For larger systems (over 200 zones) the material and installation costs become very high.

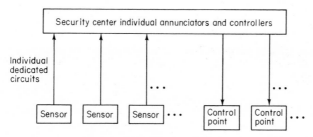

Fig. 8   The hard-wired system.

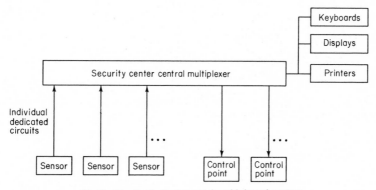

Fig. 9   The hard-wired central multiplexed system.

When a hard-wired system is connected to a central computer or processor-multiplexer, all advantages of computerization may be realized. This includes English-language displays and commands, printed summaries and logs, and the integration of the programmed subsystems such as access control and security guard's tour. It must be noted that the high installation costs of a noncomputerized hard-wired system still exist.

For large systems (over 200 points) remote multiplexing techniques become economically attractive. Each point of monitoring and control is given a unique electronic code which is transmitted via a single data trunk cable to the central computer. This eliminates the long hard-wire runs encountered in the two previously mentioned systems.

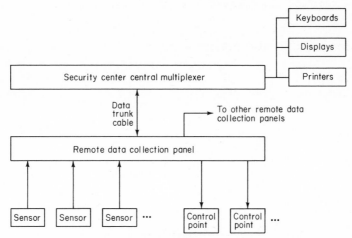

Fig. 10   The remote multiplexed system.

Fig. 11   Modern electronic multiplexed control and monitoring system. *(Photograph courtesy Honeywell, Inc.)*

The most important and costly portion of computerized-system design relates to system software or programming. This determines how the hardware will work and how the information will interact with the operator, whose capabilities are a prime consideration in a well-designed system; it should not be necessary for the operator to possess the skills of a programmer.

Line Supervision   This is a feature of an electrical circuit designed to monitor its operating condition (i.e., are the electrical lines in disrepair or being compromised?). There are many methods and many specifications for line supervision. Two of the most common references for definitions are the standard Federal Specifications and the codes of the National Fire Protection Association. In these two documents, however, identical terminology for different line supervision methods is used. Although the terminology is identical, the definitions are very different and result in different systems. Therefore, governing codes and specifications must be carefully defined in the development of system design criteria.

The most common method of line supervision used in commercial applications is a current-sensing technique. An end-of-line resistor is placed in the detection circuit, and a low supervisory current applied. Thresholds of sensed current corresponding to "alarm" and "circuit trouble" conditions are set in the annunciator or alarm receiver circuit. The setting of these thresholds will determine the system's sensitivity.

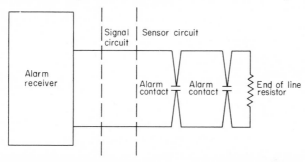

Fig. 12   Typical supervised line utilizing current-sensing techniques.

Video Distribution   Video distribution systems must be carefully designed because of the large bandwidth (high information content) of video signals. Coaxial cable and special connectors must be used, and signal attenuation in the cable must be compensated. These signal characteristics require complex circuitry in switching systems compared with audio or power-switching systems. Proper cable shielding must be provided to reduce the noise caused by external sources, such as large electric motors.

Audio Distribution   This consists of all transducers, amplifiers, switches, and cables required for quality audio reproduction. Modern systems incorporate self-supervision and equipment redundancy to ensure system reliability.

Radio Spectrum   Because of tight governmental control on the use of this transmission medium, efficient design is a necessity. A radio survey of the premises for transmission power requirements must be made. Most manufacturers will perform this survey for little or no cost. When power requirements are minimized, equipment cost will be minimized.

Another important characteristic in system design involves the number of required frequencies. At a minimum, separate frequencies should be specified for different functions (security, maintenance, etc.).

System Power Distribution   As previously mentioned, integrated security systems depend on electrical power to make them work. Therefore, a redundant or standby power source is a requirement for any security system. It may be in the form of local battery packs or a centrally distributed system. It may be uninterruptible, as is required for computers, or a transfer time may be permitted. The point to be emphasized is that power requirements of these systems may be large, and system designs may be complex. The design of the power source cannot be ignored.

CONCLUSION

Electronic security system design has become a highly complex, multidisciplinary application engineering field, and current trends indicate that its complexity will only increase. Before considering the installation of expensive equipment, those responsible for security in a given project should undertake a thorough examination of the contemplated security program.

Chapter **12**

Glass and Glazing

California Crime Prevention Institute

Edited by OSCAR S. GLASBERG, Publisher and Editor of *Glass Digest*

ORIGINS AND DEVELOPMENT

While exact details about the origin of glass are not known, there is some evidence that it existed in Egypt as early as 2000 B.C., and since that time its use has expanded to fit the needs of a changing society.

The need for glass in security applications is evident in the use of "bulletproof" glass in the banking industry, "security" glass for store windows and display cases, and "safety" glass for shower doors, sliding glass doors, commercial building entrances, and adjacent fixed glass panels. The riots in the mid-1960s stimulated a greater interest in security glazing materials, both glass and plastic.

CATEGORIES OF GLASS

From the standpoint of safety and security in buildings, there are four general categories of glazing materials: laminated glass, tempered glass, wired glass, and approved rigid plastic.

Laminated Glass

Laminated glass consists of a vinyl interlayer sandwiched between two layers of glass. Many local law enforcement agencies have enacted or intend to enact security ordinances. Most include definitions of "Burglary-resistant glazing material," which is generally described as $5/16$-in security laminated glass with an interlayer of 0.060-in vinyl or $1/4$-in polycarbonate. The use of this glass or plastic, required in many of the ordinances, applies to window lights in doors and all window lights less than 48 ft^2 in area.

Variations in laminated glass can include different types or grades of glass used in the various layers; color or tinting; different thicknesses of the vinyl interlayer; and different thicknesses of the glass layers themselves. The number of total layers is another variable.

"Bullet-resistant glass" is a form of heavy laminated glass. Underwriters' Laboratories tests for low-, medium-, and high-powered guns require thicknesses from $1^{13}/_{16}$ to 2 in. The spalling encountered on the inner side of bullet-resistant glass is a problem that can be solved by using plastic. Tables 1 and 2 show properties of both types of these laminated glasses for "Safelite," manufactured by Safelite Industries, Inc. Tables 3, 4, and 5 are for the bullet-resistant laminate "Lexgard," made by General Electric. Figure 1 shows a typical cross section of this material.

TABLE 1   Properties of Laminated Security Glass

Thickness, in	Type	Maximum size	STC rating	Approximate weight, lb/ft^2
$^5/_{16}$	Plate	84 × 128	36	3.60
$^7/_{16}$	Plate	84 × 128	38	5.10
$^9/_{16}$	Plate	84 × 128	40	6.50

TABLE 2   Properties of Bullet-Resistant Glass

Product	Thickness, in	Maximum size	Approximate weight, lb/ft^2
BRLG 34	$^3/_4$	84 × 128	9.71
BRLG 100	1	84 × 128	13.01
BRLG 136*	$1^3/_{16}$	84 × 128	14.9
BRLG 112*	$1^1/_2$	84 × 128	20.0
BRLG 134*	$1^3/_4$	84 × 128	23.0
BRLG 200*	2	84 × 128	26.0
BRLG 300	3	84 × 128	39.5

*UL listed.

TABLE 3   Lexgard® Light Transmission

Type of laminate		1-in %	1¼-in %
Clear	112	66	63
Bronze	5109	42	38
Gray	713	36	33
Green	31035	62	59

TABLE 4   Lexgard® Sound and Thermal Transmission

Sound transmission			
ASTM-E90-70	(36″ + 84″)	1″	1¼″
STC rating		39	42
U-factor winter design conditions			
1″	.55 Btu/hr/sq ft/°F		
1¼″	.62 Btu/hr/sq ft/°F		

Tempered Glass

Tempered glass is made by placing a piece of regular glass in an oven, bringing it almost to the melting point, and then chilling it rapidly. This causes a skin to form around the glass. Once this skin is pierced, the glass disintegrates into small cubes or crystals about the thickness of the tempered glass panel. Fully tempered glass is four to five times stronger than glass that has not been tempered. Once tempered, the glass cannot be cut or further processed. Tempered glass ranges from ⅛ in thick up to the maximum thickness of glass being manufactured. Almost any type of color of glass can be tempered, except for wired glass or obscure glass with a deep-patterned surface.

Wired Glass

Wired glass ¼ in thick is approved by Underwriters' Laboratories as fire-resistant; $7/32$ in is not approved by UL but is used in shower and tub enclosures. Both thicknesses can be cut to exact size.

TABLE 5   Lexgard® Bullet-Resistant and Laminate Data

Specifications		Weight		
Defeats	Weapon	B-R glass, lb/ft	Lexgard B-R laminate lb/ft²	Lexgard B-R laminate reduction, %
Med. power Small arms 475 ft/lb 1280 ft/s	.38 Super	14.9	6.5	56
High power Small arms 740 ft/lb 1450 ft/s	.357 Mag	20.0	8.0	60
Super power Small arms 1150 ft/lb 1470 ft/s	.44 Mag	23	8.0	65

Specifications		Thickness			
Defeats	Weapon	B-R glass, in	Tolerance, %	Lexgard B-R laminate, in	Tolerance, %
Med. power Small arms 475 ft/lb 1280 ft/s	.38 Super	1³⁄₁₆	+⅛ −0	1.05	±5
High power Small arms 740 ft/lb 1450 ft/s	.357 Mag	1⁹⁄₁₆	+⅛ −0	1.30	±5
Super power Small arms 1150 ft/lb 1470 ft/s	.44 Mag	1¾	+⅛ −0	1.30	±5

Plastics

Plastics are commonly used as safety glazing material and are divided into two types: acrylic and polycarbonate. The acrylics are available in clear and in many colors, both translucent and opaque, and in many thicknesses. They are more than ten times stronger than glass of the same thickness.

Polycarbonate sheets are superior to acrylics in their ability to stop bullets, although they have a relatively short life. Polycarbonate, such as General Electric's "Lexan," is advertised as 250 times more impact-resistant than safety glass and twenty times more so than other transparent plastic (see Table 6).

Using an acrylic or polycarbonate instead of glass generally costs twice as much. Over a long-range period, however, the application of plastics for security can become less expensive.

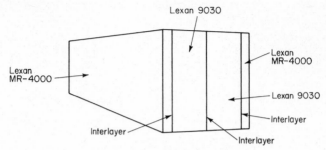

Fig. 1.   Cross section of Lexgard® bullet-resistant laminate.

TABLE 6   Design Stress of Lexan® Plastic Sheet

	Test ASTM	Average value
Tensile strength ultimate, lb/in²	D638	9,500
Elongation, %	D638	110
Compressive strength, lb/in²	D695	12,500
Flexural strength, lb/in²	D790	13,500
Modulus of elasticity, lb/in²	D638	345,000

CONSUMER SAFETY

Indirectly related to security is the subject of safety. The Consumer Product Safety Commission has published a consumer product architectural glazing standard (Federal Register, January 6, 1977, Part V) which requires architectural glazing materials to comply with this standard. The following are required to comply with this standard, which took effect on July 6, 1977: storm doors or combination doors, bathtub doors and enclosures, glazed panels, and sliding glass doors (patio type). Details of the requirements, testing procedures, and exceptions are listed in the referenced issue of the *Federal Register.*

SAFETY GLASS PRODUCTS
FROM MAJOR MANUFACTURERS:
LAMINATED, TEMPERED, WIRED

Safety glass products and functions	*For use as or in*

ASG Industries, Inc.
    Supratest (laminated)
      (breakage-resistant)
	Storefronts, jewelry stores, liquor stores, payroll windows, etc.

Wired—Nuweld Mesh, Hexagonal Mesh	Schools, industrial buildings, skylights
Securit	Bath and shower enclosures, sub-skylights, shelving, office doors and partitions

Safety glass products and functions	*For use as or in*
CE GLASS COMBUSTION ENGINEERING INC. Misco (wired glass) (resists impact, fire-resistant)	Partitions, doors in schools, office buildings
CHROMALLOY SAFETEE GLASS (all laminated) Riot-Glas (burglar-resistant)	Stores, banks, jails, liquor stores
Bullet-Resisting	Banks, armored cars, "drive-in" windows, military vehicles
Gemguard (breakage-resistant)	Same application as Riot-Glas to a lesser degree, display cases, museums, jewelry stores
Tranquilite (glare, sound reduction)	Factories, schools, offices, churches, hospitals, public buildings, airport terminals
CY/RO INDUSTRIES Acrylite (shatter-resistant cast acrylic sheet)	Schools, industrial buildings, areas with high degree of vandalism
FOURCO GLASS COMPANY Cleartemp (tempered)	Patio doors, shower and tub enclosures, large windows, etc.
GENERAL ELECTRIC COMPANY Lexan (breakage-resistant plastic sheet)	Schools, office buildings, switch centers for telephone companies, housing projects, warehouses, hospitals, museums, photographers' studios, police vans, riot shields, greenhouses
Lexgard bullet-resistant laminate	Banks, penal, and other institutions, computer rooms, outside modular units such as tollbooths
GLOBE-AMERADA GLASS COMPANY (all laminated) Secur-Lite, UL listed (burglar-resistant)	Warehouses, department stores, liquor stores, athletic areas such as school gyms, detention areas of penal and psychiatric institutions, banks, jewelry stores, TV and radio stores, fur shops, general offices, retail businesses susceptible to loss, patio doors
Bullet-Resistant (bullet-resisting, resists scattered shots, small arms to high-powered rifles)	Armored cars, bank teller windows
Acousta-Pane (sound reduction)	Airport terminals, nightclubs, offices, motels adjacent to airports, helicopter lounges
Glare-Gard (glare reduction)	Offices, other areas where glare poses a problem
Twi-Lite (heat, glare, safety control)	Schools, hospitals, office buildings
Fade-Safe (protects against fading caused by ultraviolet rays, available in Acousta-Pane and Secur-Lite glazing materials)	Department stores, areas where merchandise is exposed to sun
LAMINATED GLASS CORPORATION Riotshield (security glass)	Storefronts, show windows, interior display cases
Vista Safe, UL listed (bullet-resisting)	Bank teller cages, armored trucks, observation windows in pressure test chambers
Britelite (safety mirror)	Hospital observation windows, supermarkets, banks, post office, police departments

Safety glass products and functions	*For use as or in*
LIBBEY-OWENS-FORD COMPANY	
Vigil Pane	Storefronts, display windows, any store where
(burglar-resistant)	valuables are on display
Laminated Vari-Tran	Same uses as Vari-Tran insulating glass. Can
	be used in conjunction with Vigil Pane for
	protection of display articles
Heavy Laminated Glass	All places where strength is a factor
(high penetration resistance)	
Bullet-Resisting Glass	Banks, jails, stores, automobiles for maximum
	security
Tuf-flex (tempered)	All building and architectural applications
PILKINGTON BROTHERS LIMITED	Entranceways, patio doors, shower doors, tub
Armourfloat (tempered glass)	enclosures for strength and safety
Armoursheet (tempered glass)	
Armourclad	Spandrel glazing
(float and cast tempered colored	
glasses)	
Armourplate (suspended glazing	Entranceways, large glass areas (racetrack
assemblies)	grandstands, etc.) obviating need for glazing
	bars, etc., without the inherent dangers of
	annealed glass breakages
Triplex (sheet and float laminated	Doors, entranceways, etc.
glasses)	
Triplex Bandit Glass	Store windows, display cases, etc., protection of
	valuables
Diamond Mesh (polished wire and	Roof lights, doors, partitioning, etc.
cast glass)	
Georgian Mesh (polished wire and	
cast glass)	
(impact-resistant, fire-retardent)	
POLYCAST TECHNOLOGY	Schools, office buildings, industrial areas
CORPORATION	
Evr-Kleer	
(impact-resistant plastic sheet, cast	
acrylic plastic)	
PPG INDUSTRIES, INC.	
Herculite (tempered)	
Herculite K (tempered)	Schools, industrial areas, sliding patio doors,
	storm doors, tub enclosures
Duplate and H6 (laminated)	Storefronts, jewelry stores, liquor stores
Multiplate (laminated)	Banks, teller windows, armored cars, etc.
(bullet-resistant)	
Watchguard (glass and	Banks, teller windows, prisons, boilers
polycarbonate sandwich)	
ROHM and HAAS COMPANY	Safety glazing for schools, industrial plants,
Plexiglas (acrylic plastic)	hospitals, utilities, banks, motels, retail stores;
(breakage-resistant)	police, fire, and taxi vehicles: protection for
	spectators at hockey rinks, baseball parks, etc.
Tuffak (polycarbonate)	
SAFELITE INDUSTRIES, INC.	
Laminated security glass (sheet or	Computer rooms, financial institutions, jewelry
plate glass with plastic interlayer)	stores, fur shops, department stores, ware-
	houses, liquor stores, penal and psychiatric
	institutions
Bullet-resistant glass	Drive-in teller cages, cashier booths, currency
	exchanges, turnpike tollbooths, bank teller
	cages, ticket offices, banks, financial institu-

Safety glass products and functions	*For use as or in*
	tions, computer rooms, armored vehicles, taxicab partitions
SHATTERPROOF GLASS CORPORATION Tempered sheet (impact-resistant)	Storefronts, entrances, storm doors, sliding patio doors
Laminated sheets (impact-resistant, sound reduction)	Storm doors, sliding patio doors, airports and other areas of heavy noise, interior glazing to reduce sound
Tempered plate (impact-resistant)	Storefronts, entrances, sliding patio doors, schools, walls exposed to areas such as playgrounds, skylights (to resist snow load)
Laminated plate (impact-resistant, sound reduction)	Sliding patio doors, airports, other buildings in heavy noise areas
Laminated plate or sheet with 0.060 plastic interlayer (burglar-resistant)	Jewelry stores, storefronts
TEXAS TEMPERED GLASS COMPANY TTG Fast Glass (tempered and laminated glasses)	Storefronts, entrances, sidelights, storm doors, etc.
VIRGINIA GLASS PRODUCTS CORPORATION Transpan (breakage-resistant)	Entrance doors, sidelights, partitions, dividers
Tempar-Glas (breakage-resistant)	Spandrels for specific use in curtain walls, tempered to be used in shower and tub enclosures, sliding doors, furniture tops, storefronts, entranceways, sidelights

SOME MANUFACTURERS OF GLASS AND PLASTICS BY CATEGORY

Tempered Transparent Glass
ASG Industries, Inc., Greenland, Tennessee
Anglass Industries, Inc., San Fernando, California
Armour World Wide Glass Company, Inc. Santa Fe Springs, California
Artistic Glass Products Company, Trumbauersville, Pennsylvania
M.L. Burke Company, Cornwells Heights, Pennsylvania
C-E Glass, Cinnaminson, New Jersey
Cal Temp, Santa Fe Springs, California
Canadian Pittsburgh Industries, Ltd., Owen Sound, Ontario, Canada
Chromalloy-Safetee Glass Division, King of Prussia, Pennsylvania
Doulton Tempered Glass, Ltd., Bradford, England
Downey Glass Company, Downey, California
Falconer Glass Industries, Inc., Falconer, New York
Feather-lite Manufacturing Company, Malvern, Arkansas
Ford Motor Company, Detroit, Michigan
Fourco Glass Company, Bridgeport, West Virginia
General Glass Imports Corporation, Medias, Romania
Guardian Industries Corporation, Webster, Massachusetts
Hamilton of Indiana, Inc., Vincennes, Indiana
LOF Glass, Inc., Laurinburg, North Carolina
Libbey-Owens-Ford Company, Rossford, Ohio

Minex-Poland, Sandomierz, Poland
Northwestern Industries, Inc., Seattle, Washington
Ohio Plate Glass Company, Lewisburg, Ohio
PPG Industries, Inc., Carlisle, Pennsylvania
Safelite Industries, Wichita, Kansas
Sun Valley Tempered Glass Company, Oxnard, California
Taylor Products, Inc., Payne, Ohio
Tempered Glass Corporation, Tampa, Florida
Tempglass, Inc., Perrysburg, Ohio
Temp-Safe, Inc., Edmond, Oklahoma
Texas Tempered Glass Company, Houston, Texas
Tuf-flex Glass, Inc., Toledo, Ohio
Tyre Brothers Glass Company, Los Angeles, California
Vidrierias de Llodio, S.A., Alva, Spain
Vidrios Securit, S.A., Barranquilla, Colombia
Viracon, Inc., Owatonna, Minnesota
Virginia Glass Products Corporation, Martinsville, Virginia

Laminated Transparent Glass
ASG Industries, Inc., Kingsport, Tennessee
Armour Glass East Corp., Brooklyn, New York
Buchmin Industries, Reedley, California
Central Glass Company, Ltd., Tokyo, Japan
Chromalloy-Safetee Glass Division, King of Prussia, Pennsylvania
Downey Glass Company, Taipei, Taiwan
Globe-Amerada Glass Company, Elk Grove Village, Illinois
Guardian Industries Corporation, Carleton, Michigan
Laminated Glass Corporation, Detroit, Michigan
Libbey-Owens-Ford Company, East Toledo, Ohio
PPG Industries, Inc., Creighton, Pennsylvania
Safelite Industries, Denver, Colorado
Texas Tempered Glass Company, Houston, Texas
Viracon, Inc., Owatonna, Minnesota

Transparent Wired Glass
ASG Industries, Inc., Kingsport, Tennessee
C-E Glass, St. Louis, Missouri
Central Glass Company, Ltd., Tokyo, Japan

Safety Plastic Sheet, Polycarbonate
General Electric Company, Mount Vernon, Indiana
Rohm and Haas Company, Kensington, Connecticut
Sheffield Plastics, Inc., Sheffield, Massachusetts

Safety Plastic Sheet, Acrylic
Flex-O-Glass, Inc., Dixon, Illinois
K-S-H, Inc., Tustin, California
Manchester Products Company, Chatsworth, California
Mitsubishi Rayon Company, Ltd., Otake, Japan
Plaskolite, Inc., Columbus, Ohio
Rebeco Products, Inc., Tainan, Taiwan
Rohm and Haas Company, Knoxville, Tennessee
Rotuba Extruders, Inc., Linden, New Jersey
Sheffield Plastics, Inc., Sheffield, Massachusetts
Swedcast Corporation, Florence, Kentucky

Chapter **13**

Doors and Windows

Adapted from material prepared by
California Crime Technological Research Foundation

The subject of security criteria for the design, selection, and installation of doors and windows has, until recently, received scant attention. While doors have been labeled in terms of fire resistance for many years, no nationally accepted standard exists to determine resistance to forced or surreptitious entry.

The Law Enforcement Standards Program of the National Institute of Law Enforcement and Criminal Justice (Law Enforcement Assistance Administration of the U.S. Department of Justice) is completing three such standards at the time of this writing, and they are expected to be available to the public shortly. The standards deal with physical security of door assemblies and components, sliding glass door units, and window assemblies, and they are listed in the references at the end of this chapter. While these standards are quite technical in nature and deal principally with testing procedures, they will be accompanied by guideline documents which provide nontechnical information regarding the capabilities of equipment currently available and can be used to select equipment appropriate to the performance required.

The California Crime Technological Research Foundation (CCTRF) has undertaken a testing program to determine the security capabilities of door and window systems for private residences and light commercial structures. The results of these tests, given in the following sections, are extracted from CCTRF's preliminary report of May 1974.

SPECIFIC THREATS

Exterior Doors

The common threats to exterior doors posed by the "standard" intruder have been studied and tested in order to quantify them in engineering terms. The objective was to determine the forces or amounts of energy most likely to be deployed in each of the threats. During this phase of the program, the threats investigated were established as shown in Figs. 1 through 9.

Fig. 1   Threat 1: shoulder impact.

Fig. 2   Threat 2: foot impact.

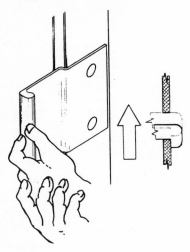

Fig. 3   Threat 3: lifting.

Fig. 4   Threat 4: prybar.

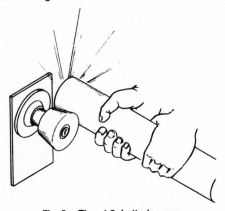

Fig. 5   Threat 5: battering ram.

Fig. 6   Threat 6: hammer.

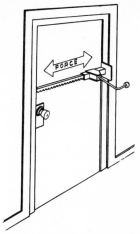

Fig. 7   Threat 7: bumper jack.

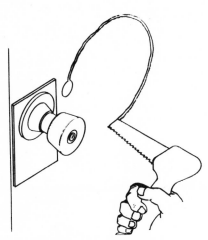

Fig. 8   Threat 8: sawing.

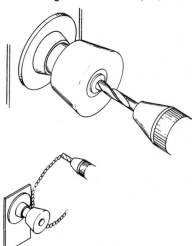

Fig. 9   Threat 9: drilling.

Glass Systems

The threats to the glass system of exterior doors and windows are shown in Figs. 10 through 13.

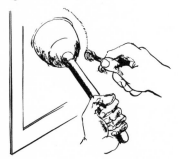

Fig. 10   Threat 10: glass cutter.

Fig. 11   Threat 11: spring-loaded punch.

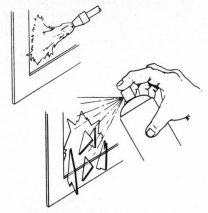

Fig. 12   Threat 12: thermal shock.   Fig. 13   Threat 13: thrown missile.

Lock Systems and Circumvention

The key- or combination-operated component in a locking system is vulnerable to attack in five fundamental ways: (1) trickery, (2) circumvention, (3) force, (4) manipulation, and (5) robbery. They may be used separately or in any combination by an attacker. Research on locks has indicated that there are at least fifty different ways to defeat common locking devices. Standards developed under this research program were directed toward what was considered to be the majority of common techniques that are employed under field situations by burglars, although any locking system can be defeated given time and proper circumstances. However, a great deal can be done to reduce the likelihood of attack on the locking system if the recommendations made in this report are implemented into the manufacturing process by the makers of security products.

Key-operated and combination locks vary greatly in their resistance to attack. This is true for individual locks with the same design specifications as well as locks employing the same basic design principles as high-security locks but using materials and manufacturing techniques that are recognized as detrimental. Many locks can be easily defeated by simple prying tools or with a few hammer blows; quickly opened with one or a very limited number of keys; or quickly opened with simple manipula-

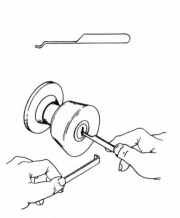

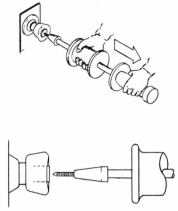

Fig. 14   Threat 14: lock picking.   Fig. 15   Threat 15: puller.

tion tools (lock picks, tryout keys, manipulation keys, etc.). Many combination locks have only two tumblers (wheels) that can be operated by running through a very few combinations. They are easily forced with simple prying and percussion tools, and can be manipulated with very little skill. The burglary threats most commonly applied to door locks are illustrated in Figs. 14 through 22.

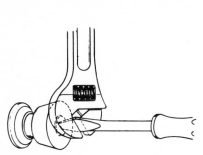

Fig. 16   Threat 16: screwdriver and wrench.

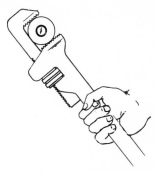

Fig. 17   Threat 17: pipe wrench.

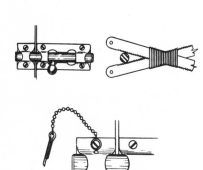

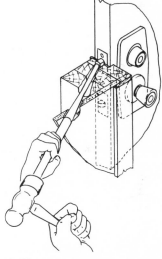

Fig. 18.   Threat 18: hacksaw or hacksaw blade.   Fig. 19   Threat 19: drift punch and hammer.

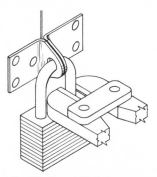

Fig. 20   Threat 20: bolt cutter.

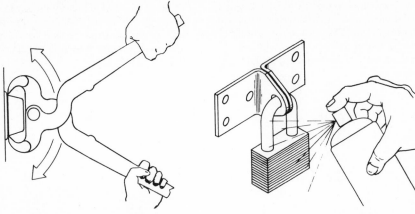

Fig. 21   Threat 21: bolt nipper.   Fig. 22   Threat 22: freezing.

EXTERIOR SINGLE-DOOR SYSTEMS

Static Load Failure Tests

The results of eight static load tests conducted on the doors are summarized in Table 3, which defines the test configurations, load application points, failure loads, and failure location. In the first three tests on the hollow doors with a conventional latch, loads were applied at the upper hinge, lower hinge, and doorknob. In each case, failure occurred in the wooden doorjamb at the screw holes. The lowest failure load was 353 lb in Test 3 at the striker plate screws, with the load applied at the doorknob. In Test 4, with the load applied at the doorknob and the latch system being both the knobset latch and a deadbolt, the failure load occurred at 724 lb when the deadbolt failed. In the next two tests, Nos. 5 and 6, the striker plate was modified to increase the edge distance on the screw holes. The design modification is shown on Fig. 25 (Striker Plate Design No. 1). Testing of this configuration, with a knobset latch only, showed that it did not appreciably increase the strength of the system. In Test 5, the latch portion of the lock rotated and caused the door edge to fail at 371 lb, while in Test 6, with the door latch reinforced against rotation, the latch failed at 372 lb. Therefore, in the next test (No. 7) a heavy steel bar was used to simulate the door latch to measure the strength of the striker plate redesign. In this design, the striker plate resisted an applied load of 1,042 lb before the doorframe itself rotated excessively due to lack of exterior and interior wall sheeting.

Test 8 was conducted using a solid-core (particleboard) door and both a redesigned striker plate and door edge stiffener. These redesigned components are shown in Figs. 25 and 26. Application of loads to this assembly at the doorknob location was successful up to 1,192 lb. At this load, excessive rotation and separation occurred in the FHA framing due to lack of inside and outside wall sheeting. Removal of the load showed no damage to any of the door components, and the lock system was completely functional.

Static Lateral-load Tests

Static load tests were conducted by applying lateral loads to the standard FHA door framing with exterior and interior sheeting. These tests simulated the load represented by threats 4 and 7. A door was not included in either of the test configurations. In a bumper-jack spreader threat, the bolt of a conventional door latch cannot provide resistance to the applied load. Only the doorframe resists the threat. In the case of the pry-bar threat, the door must be capable of a local resistance to the

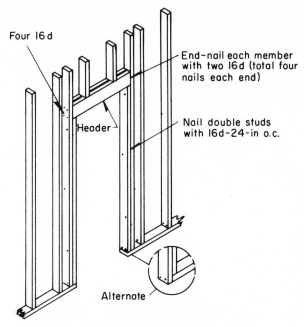

Four 16 d

End-nail each member
with two 16d (total four
nails each end)

Header

Nail double studs
with 16d-24-in o.c.

Alternate

Fig. 23   Typical FHA single-door framing.

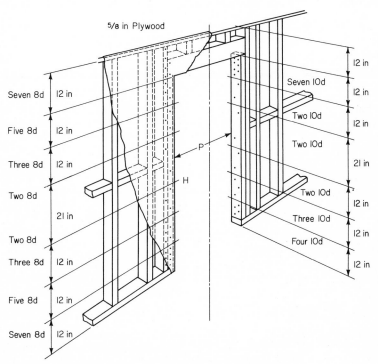

5/8 in Plywood

Seven 8d   12 in

Five 8d   12 in

Three 8d   12 in

Two 8d

21 in

Two 8d

Three 8d   12 in

Five 8d   12 in

Seven 8d   12 in

P

H

12 in

Seven 10d

12 in

Two 10d

12 in

Two 10d

21 in

Two 10d

12 in

Three 10d

12 in

Four 10d

12 in

Fig. 24   Nailing schedule to reduce spreading of door jambs under lateral loading (CCTRF). _H_ = one-half door height; _P_ = applied load = 2000 lb.

compressive bar load. In addition, the door and hinges must be capable of transferring the bar load to the frame. Again, the primary resistance factor is the framing system.

The results of the tests indicated that the 2,000-lb load provided by a bumper-jack spreader could produce a deflection of 0.5 in at the latch location, and a pry-bar

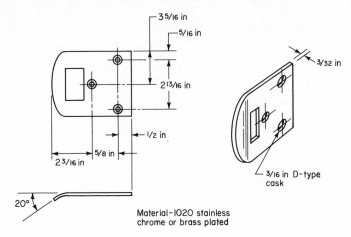

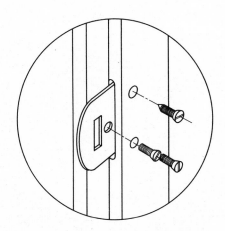

Fig. 25   CCTRF striker plate, Design No. 1.

attack of 6,000 in·lb also resulted in a 0.5-in deflection of the frame at the same location. These deflections establish the length of the throw bolt required in the lock system.

It should be noted that the fire struts placed between studs in the FHA framing are, from a structural point of view, very necessary to resist the spreading of the jambs by the "bumper jack" threat. For the same purpose, any shimming that may be required to fit the doorjamb facings to the 2 × 4 frames should be extended to the areas opposite the lock and the hinges.

If the nailing schedule shown in Fig. 24 is used in construction of the doorframe, a 2,000-lb static force of a bumper jack applied to the jambs would cause a deflection of only 0.3 in, which precludes the disengagement of any standard 1-in latch.

CCTRF Striker Plate and Exterior Door

CCTRF Striker Plate Design

The initial static load failure tests (Nos. 1 and 3) of the exterior doors determined that the standard lock striker plate installed in the doorjamb constituted the weakest area of the system. In each test, the wooden doorjamb split at the striker plate screw holes, with no damage occurring to the actual striker plate. Failure loads as low as one-third of an adult's impact capability were observed.

At this time, it was necessary to strengthen the striker plate installation before proceeding with the test program to determine the strength of other components in the door system. Various methods were considered and tested, including longer

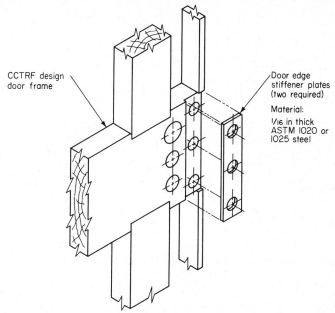

CCTRF design
door frame

Door edge
stiffener plates
(two required)

Material:

1/16 in thick
ASTM 1020 or
1025 steel

Fig. 26   CCTRF door edge stiffener plate, Design 1-A.

screws and bonding agents between the striker plate and the doorjamb. The most effective strengthening modification found was a simple increase in the distance from the screws to the edge of the doorjamb. The revised design (No. 1) that was adopted is depicted in Fig. 25. It was utilized in the subsequent static door-system testing without being failed.

The final static strength test incorporated a door edge reinforcement (design 1A), which is shown in Fig. 26. A more structurally adequate latch reinforcement, design 2, was developed for the dynamic load tests and is described in Fig. 27. In this design the jamb is held between two steel plates, with loads being transferred into the framing studs by both tensile and shear loads on the screw attachments. In order to fail this striker plate assembly, the applied load would have to shear the doorjamb and fail the attachment screws in the framing studs.

CCTRF Exterior Door Design*

The results of the static failure test program demonstrated that both the standard hollow and solid-core exterior doors had serious weaknesses in construction and

*Proprietary design.

ability to transfer loads to the remainder of the door system components. During these tests, the weaker component parts were strengthened in order to increase the overall strength of the door system. The modifications were all incorporated into a hollow-door design described in Fig. 28. This door design incorporates the following features not normally found in commercially available residence-type doors:

1. Expanded steel screen to prevent sawing
2. "Soft" edges to absorb pry-bar loads by deformation

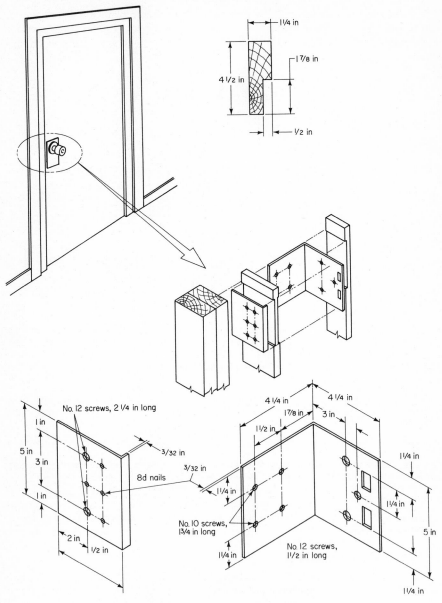

Fig. 27   CCTRF striker plate assembly, Design No. 2.

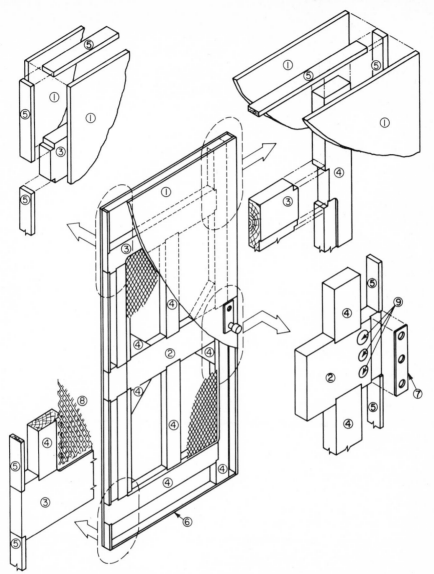

Fig. 28 CCTRF door design (proprietary design). (1) 1/4-in exterior grade plywood—glued to structure; (2) 2 × 8 Douglas fir—select structure; (3) 2 × 6 Douglas fir—select structure; (4) 2 × 4 Douglas fir—dense No. 1; (5) 1 × 2 clear pine; (6) 2 × 2 clear pine; (7) door edge stiffener plates (two)—1/16-in-thick ASTM 1020 or 1025 steel. Outside plate to be blank: the two plates secured by screws installed from inside. These may be incorporated in lock design; (8) carbon steel expanded metal screen—1/16-in-thick ASTM 1010 steel; secured by staples and epoxy resin glue; (9) lock installation holes.

3. Hardened attachment point for hinge screws

4. Hardened attachment point for knob/lockset

5. Efficient load-carrying structure connecting hinges and lock, assuring proper load distribution

A prototype door was constructed to this design and tested under dynamic loading as described below. The door successfully resisted all test loadings well in excess of the expected threat loads without damage.

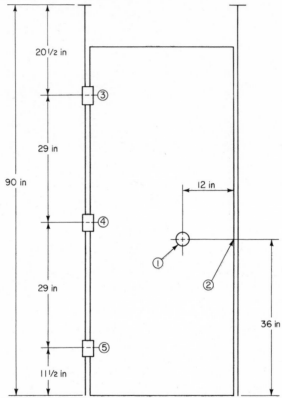

Fig. 29 Dynamic load door tests; location of extensiometers and load imput. (1) Load point; (2) latch; (3) upper hinge; (4) middle hinge; (5) lower hinge.

SLIDING GLASS DOOR AND WINDOW SYSTEMS

Sliding Glass Patio Door

The results of the sliding glass door tests are summarized in Table 7, which shows that the static test loads applied to the handle produced a failure of the latch at 660 lb, and of the handle fasteners at 870 lb.

Results of the tests for a pry-bar attack (threat 4) demonstrated the door system to have a low resistance. A force less than 50 lb on a 12-in level arm, or 600 in·lb, broke the latch and removed the rollers from the guide rail. The input threat is 6000 in·lb. In the spring-loaded centerpunch attack, the glass was severely damaged, and only a light touch was required to push out the glass and gain access to the latch.

TABLE 1   Exterior Single-door Dynamic Test Configurations* (FHA Framing)

Resistance parameters	Test No. 1	Test No. 2	Test No. 3	Test No. 4
1. Door material	Wood (D.F.)	Wood (D.F.)	Wood (D.F.)	Wood (D.F.)
2. Door aspect ratio	36″ wide	36″ wide	36″ wide	36″ wide
	80″ long	80″ long	80″ long	80″ long
3. Door thickness	1¾″	1¾″	1¾″	2″
4. Doorframe thickness†	1½″ wood	1½″wood	1½″ wood	1½″ wood
5. Type of door construction	Hollow core	Solid core	Solid core	Hollow core CCTRF‡
6. Boundary fasteners	Butt hinges	Butt hinges	Butt hinges	Butt hinges
7. Method of fastener attachment	#9 × ¾ screws	#9 × ¾ screws	#9 × ¾ screws	#9 × ¾ screws
8. Type of support structure	FHA	FHA	FHA	FHA
9. Striker plate reinforcement	None	None	CCTRF§ design	CCTRF§ design
10. Latch fastener	Deadlatch	Dead bolt and deadlatch	Dead bolt and deadlatch	Dead bolt and deadlatch

Notes:
*Load normal to door.
†Wood used—white pine.
‡Figure 28.
§CCTRF Design No. 2, Fig. 27.

TABLE 2   Summary of Maximum Static and Dynamic Resistance Capabilities of Single Exterior Door Systems (FHA Framing), Normal Load Threats*

Door system	Dynamic tests				Static tests	
	Test impactor input kinetic energy (in·lb)	Measured dynamic energy capability (in·lb)	Measured dynamic load capability (lb)	Failure location	Measured static load capability (lb)	Failure location
Group A— standard hollow core	1078	800	915	Jamb at latch	724	Latch and lock mechanism
Group B— standard solid core	1332	560	1130	Jamb at latch	None	None
Group C— solid core with CCTRF reinforced latch†	2620	2296	2068	Door at latch	>1192	None
Group D— CCTRF door‡ and latch	4602	>2020	>2070	No failure	None	None

*Maximum expected is shoulder impact (Threat No. 1) at 1800 in·lb.
†Figures 25, 26, 27.
‡Figure 28.

TABLE 3 Summary of Exterior Single Door Static Load Failure Tests, Loads Normal to Door (FHA Framing)

Resistance parameters	Test number 1	2	3	4	5	6	7	8
1. Type of construction	Hollow core	Hollow core	Hollow core	Hollow core	Hollow core	Hollow core	None*	Hollow core
2. Striker plate reinforcement	Standard	Standard	Standard	Standard	CCTRF Design #1	CCTRF Design #1	CCTRF Design #1	CCTRF Design #1A
3. Latch fastener	Deadlatch	Deadlatch	Deadlatch	Deadlatch and dead bolt	Deadlatch	Deadlatch with door stiffener	Simulated door latch	Deadlatch
4. Component tested	Lower hinge	Upper hinge	Lock	Knobset/ dead bolt	Striker plate	Striker plate	Striker plate	Door system
5. Load application point	Adjacent lower hinge	Adjacent upper hinge	Adjacent doorknob	Adjacent doorknob	Adjacent doorknob	Adjacent doorknob	Striker plate	Adjacent doorknob
6. Failure location	Doorjamb lower hinge screw hole	Doorjamb upper hinge screw hole	Doorjamb at latch	Latch and lock mechanism	Latch and door edge	Latch mechanism	None*	None
7. Measured failure load capability	627 lb	633 lb	353 lb	724 lb	371 lb	372 lb	>1042 lb	>1192 lb

*Door frame test structure only; door not in test setup.

TABLE 4 Summary of Single Exterior Door Dynamic Load Tests, Shoulder Impact Threat* (FHA Framing)

Resistance parameters	Test number			
		Single doors		
	1	2	3	4
1. Door material	Wood (D.F.)	Wood (D.F.)	Wood (D.F.)	Wood (D.F.)
2. Door aspect ratio configuration	36″ wide 80″ long	36″ wide 80″ long	36″ wide 80″ long	36″ wide 80″ long
3. Door thickness	1¾″	1¾″	1¾″	2″
4. Door frame thickness†	1½″ wood*	1½″ wood	1½″ wood	1½″ wood
5. Type of door construction	Hollow core	Solid core	Solid core	Hollow core CCTRF
6. Boundary fastener	Butt hinges	Butt hinges	Butt hinges	Butt hinges
7. Method of fastener attachment	#9 × ¾ screws	#9 × ¾ screws	#9 × ¾ screws	#9 × ¾ screws
8. Type of support structure	FHA	FHA	FHA	FHA
9. Striker plate reinforcement	None	None	CCTRF Design‡	CCTRF Design‡
10. Latch fastener	Deadlatch	Dead bolt and deadlatch	Dead bolt and deadlatch	Dead bolt and deadlatch
11. Threat energy input, U_i	1800 in·lb	1800 in·lb	1800 in·lb	1800 in·lb
12. Maximum applied test energy, U_a	1078 in·lb	1332 in·lb	2620 in·lb	4602 in·lb
13. Maximum energy absorption, U_R	800 in·lb	560 in·lb	2296 in·lb	>2019 in·lb
14. Maximum dynamic load capability	914 lb	1130 lb	2068 lb	>2069 lb
15. Failure and location	Jamb at latch	Jamb at latch	Door at latch	No failure
16. Security safety margin, E (%)§	−40	−26	+45	>+156

Notes:
*Load normal to door.
†Wood used—white pine.
‡CCTRF—Design No. 2 (Fig. 27).
§$E = (U_a/U_i − 1)\,100$.

13-15

TABLE 5   Summary of Single Exterior Door Dynamic Load Tests, Various Impact Threats (FHA Framing)

Door system	Threat No.	Threat energy input (in·lb)	Failure energy (in·lb)	Energy rec'd by assembly (in·lb)	Measured dynamic load (lbs)	Security safety margin,‡ %
Group A—standard hollow core	(1) Shoulder	1800	1078	800	915	−40
Group B—standard solid core	(1) Shoulder	1800	1332	560	1130	−26
Group C—solid core with CCTRF reinforced latch*	(6) Hammer	125		114	461	+High
	(5) Ram	1050		500	965	+150
	(2) Kick	775		1192	763	+238
	(1) Shoulder	1800	2620	2296	2068	+45
Group D—CCTRF door† and latch	(2) Kick	775		378	895	>+494
	(1) Shoulder	1800	>4602	2020	2070	>+156

*Figure 27.
†Figure 28.
‡$E = (R/M - 1)\ 100$, where R = resistance failure energy applied input and M = threat energy.

TABLE 6 Summary of Ultimate Strength Dynamic Tests, Single Exterior Doors*

Type of door assembly	Velocity of the 180-lb impactor, in/s	Input kinetic energy of impactor, in/lb	Energy absorbed by assembly, in·lb	Energy absorbed by assembly, % of input K.E.	Equivalent dynamic load reacted by assembly, lb	Failed member	Dynamic load on failed member at failure, lb
FHA standard framing hollow-core door, standard striker plate	68	1078	800	74.2	915	Jamb at striker plate	610
FHA standard framing solid-core door, standard striker plate	76	1332	560	42.0	1130	Jamb at latch	753
FHA standard framing solid-core door, CCTRF striker plate	103	2620	2296	93.3	2068	Door split at latch	1379
FHA standard framing CCTRF door, CCTRF striker plate	141	4602	2020	45.0	2070	No failure	

*Point of impact, 12-in from latch.

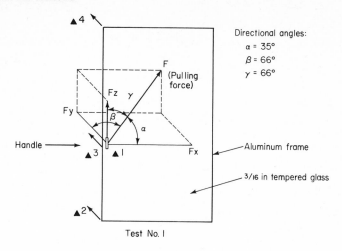

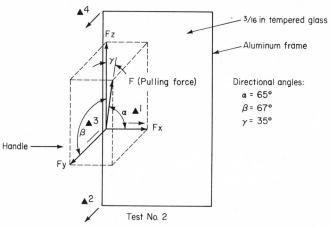

Fig. 30   Sliding-glass-door applied test loads, test No. 1 and test No. 2.

TABLE 7   Summary of Sliding Glass Door Tests

| Test No. | Threat | Threat load | Failure load | | | Failure location | Security safety margin* |
			Normal	Vertical	Lateral		
1†	Combined load handle pull	To be determined	269 lb	269 lb	538 lb	Latch	To be determined
2†	Combined load handle pull	To be determined	332 lb	712 lb	362 lb	Handle, Bolt	To be determined
3	(No. 4) Pry bar	6000 in·lb		600 in·lb		Latch	−90%
4	(No. 11) Spring-loaded punch	To be determined	To be determined			Glass	To be determined

*Margin of safety $E = (R/M - 1)\,100$, where R = resistance failure load (lb) and M = threat load (lb).
†See Fig. 30.

Sliding Glass Window

Several preliminary tests were completed on a standard aluminum sliding glass window (double-strength glass). These tests determined that a glass attack by threat 10 easily produced access to the latch.

LOCK SYSTEMS

Pertinent results of the tests on lock systems were as follows:

Body-Slam Puller

(Threat 15, Fig. 15)

1. Average number of slams to remove lock cylinder core was seven; to break slam puller screw, twenty.

2. Slam puller screw would not enter lock cylinder when hardness of cylinder was greater than 90 F Rockwell.

3. Slam puller screw stripped out of lock cylinder when hardness of cylinder was less than 75 F Rockwell.

Pipe Wrench

(Threat 17, Fig. 17)

1. Torque to fail knob was as low as 180 in· lb.

2. Torque to fail lock cylinder was as low as 480 in· lb.

Since the maximum expected threat is a torque of 3300 in· lb, these tests demonstrated the doorknob and lock cylinders to be greatly inadequate in resisting torsion loads.

REFERENCES

1. Attorney General's Building Security Commission, *Building Security Standards: A Final Report to the California State Legislature,* Office of the Attorney General, Los Angeles, 1974.
2. California Crime Technological Research Foundation, *Building Security Standards,* Sacramento, 1974.
3. U.S. Department of Justice, Law Enforcement Assistance Administration, *Physical Security of Door Assemblies and Door Components,* Washington, D.C., 1975.
4. ———, *Physical Security of Sliding Glass Door Units,* Washington, D.C., 1976.
5. ———, *Physical Security of Window Assemblies,* Washington, D.C., 1976.

Chapter **14**

Lighting

WILLIAM A. WEIBEL, P.E., F.I.E.S.

Lighting Consultant, Chicago, Illinois

Security lighting can be defined as illumination of sufficient quantity and adequate distribution so as to (1) deter or permit detection of unfriendly personnel as they approach, enter, or circulate within a security-sensitive area and (2) ensure the safety of friendly personnel as they approach, enter, or circulate within an area.

Most seeing tasks are accomplished by using subjective brightness (that detected by direct view and evaluation) of objects and areas and the interrelation of those areas of brightness. Such brightness is the result of light reaching the object or area and then being reflected or transmitted to the eye or a photosensitive device. For an object to be detected against its background, there must be sufficient difference in brightness and/or color.

In selecting light sources, luminaires, and systems to provide the recommended illumination of areas and the brightness of surfaces involved in security, the general zones of concern can be designated as:

- Zone I: Building exterior surfaces—entrances, walls, and roof
- Zone II: Exterior areas near buildings—parking lots, roadways, and walkways
- Zone III: Exterior, intermediate areas, between the buildings and the area perimeter—storage areas, parking lots, roadways, walkways, and open areas
- Zone IV: Exterior, perimeter areas—fence lines, water approaches, rail entrances, roadway entrances, pedestrian entrances, and open areas

Since most areas and objects in the field of view will be in a horizontal or vertical position, a basic technique is to cover these areas with the required illumination. Another technique is to locate and direct beams of light to provide a "barrage" or curtain of light which causes glare in the eyes of an intruder while at the same time acting as a shield behind which the security personnel can view the scene. Such a "glare barrier," even without physical barriers like fences, ditches, etc., can be very effective as a deterrent. Care must be taken, however, with the location and direction of light sources so that security patrols, or others approaching with legitimate purpose, will not be hampered by having to look toward such glare sources.

Another possible problem with this method is that "spill light" often reaches adjacent property. If there are likely to be any objections as to luminaire location, aiming, and resulting light patterns and brightnesses, this should be considered early in the design of the security lighting system. With careful forethought, lighting plans and goals for the facility under consideration can be coordinated with those for adjoining areas in order to give mutual help, make maximum use of "spill light," and reduce chances of complaints.

LIGHTING REQUIREMENTS

The following suggested levels of illumination, in minimum footcandles (fc), are based on the recommendations of available standards.[1,2,3] (For critical areas, these minima could be doubled for increased effectiveness.)

Zone I
- 2.0 fc for building entrances and exterior walls, to a minimum height of 8 ft, for vital locations or structures[2]
- 1.0 fc for roof surfaces requiring surveillance

Zone II
- 1.0 fc for parking lots[1]
- 0.4 fc for roadways[3]
- 0.2 fc for storage areas[1]
- 0.2 fc for walkways[3]

Zone III
- 1.0 fc for parking lots[1]
- 0.4 fc for roadways[3]
- 0.2 fc for walkways[3]
- 0.1 fc for storage areas[2]
- 0.05 fc for open areas

Zone IV
- 2.0 fc for pedestrian entrances[1]
- 1.0 fc for roadway entrances[1]
- 1.0 fc for rail entrances[1]
- 0.2 fc, on vertical plane, at points 3 ft above the ground plane, for "glare barrier"[1]
- 0.1 fc for fence line (nonisolated)[1]
- 0.1 fc for water approaches[1]
- 0.05 fc for open areas
- 0.05 fc for boundary line (isolated fence or no fence)[2]

LIGHT SOURCES

For many years incandescent lamps were the principal light source for security lighting. They have been and are being improved, in both design and application, and they are versatile, being available in a very wide range of wattages, voltages, shapes, and sizes. In general, their low first cost and small size makes practical the design of compact optical systems for very good light control with luminaires of relatively low first cost. Electrical circuitry and control are simple and of low cost, relative to other sources. The lamps suffer no delay or "restrike time" following an interruption of power, but resume their function, even on greatly reduced voltage. However, incandescent lamps have a limited rated life, low efficacy (lumens of light output per watt of power input), and high replacement cost over the life of the system. An incandescent system, because of the low efficacy of the lamps, usually requires more and/or higher-wattage lamps to provide the required illumination than a system utilizing lamps of higher efficacy.

The incandescent lamp is being supplemented, and in many applications replaced, by fluorescent, mercury, metal halide, high-pressure sodium (HPS), and low-pressure sodium (LPS) lamps. All of these nonincandescent lamps are classified as "arc discharge lamps," and the mercury, metal halide, and high-pressure sodium lamps, as a group, are often referred to as "HID" (high-intensity discharge) lamps. The arc discharge lamps have been and are being improved and are available in a very wide range of wattages, shapes, and sizes. Efficacies and rated life for these lamps are much greater than for the incandescent. The greater quantities (lumens) of light available per lamp of a given wattage can mean a reduction in luminaire quantities and electrical system requirements, as well as a lower owning cost per system for equal lighting performance.

As to their limitations, the arc discharge lamps are higher in first cost; their shape and size usually require larger, more complex optical systems for the required light control; and the luminaires are usually larger and of higher first cost than for the incandescent. The arc discharge lamps require an electrical control device (ballast) to provide the necessary voltage to start the arc and then to control the operating current. These ballasts add to the size, weight, and initial cost of the luminaires, contributing to the complexity, installation costs, and maintenance costs of the electrical system.

Lamp Types   Tables 1 to 6 include representative types, photometric sizes, and electrical sizes of lamps selected from lamp manufacturers' catalogs. This information should however be supplemented by referring to the latest available data because of continuing research, production, and application of improved sources.

Interchangeability   Lamp bases serve the dual purpose of positioning the lamp and providing the necessary electrical connection to the external circuit. Many lamps, of widely differing photometric, electrical, and physical size, have the same type and size of base. Some of these lamps can be electrically and physically interchanged in a given luminaire. In some cases, the lamp socket in the luminaire will effectively prevent an undesirable interchange. In other cases, the lamps can be physically interchanged but should not be because of possible ballast requirements or adverse effects on the electrical system. It is advisable to check very carefully before considering an inter-change of lamps other than those selected in the original design of the system. When in doubt, consult the manufacturers of the lamps and ballasts.

Temperature   Lamp operation and maintenance, depending on source type and size, may be influenced by the temperature of the filament, arc tube and/or bulb wall, base, socket, wiring, and ambient air. Incandescent lamps, by their very nature, are dependent on the temperature of the filament to produce the desired light output. Such temperatures are so high that they are not influenced, for all practical purposes, by the ambient temperature. Fluorescent lamps can, however, be very dependent on the ambient temperature unless appropriate ballasts, jacketing, or suitably enclosed luminaires are provided so that the lamp will start and operate at or near the design temperature and light output. This is a very important consideration if fluorescent is to be used for security lighting, especially outdoors.

The HID and LPS lamps are similar in their construction, which provides for some thermal insulation. However, for outdoor use in low ambient temperatures, appro-priate ballasts should be specified for satisfactory starting and operation of these lamps.

Temperatures of ambient air and of parts therefore frequently cause certain restrictions in the choice and application of lamps. Some of these restrictions include cautions such as "use only in enclosed luminaires," "protect from falling moisture," etc. These restrictive details are usually given in the footnotes of the lamp catalogs or similar references.

Warmup and Restrike   Arc discharge lamps are dependent on the voltage and current supplied and the resulting temperature and pressure of the gases and vapors in the arc tube. Once the lamp is started, the contents of the arc tube increase in temperature and pressure until the design requirements are met and the lamp attains full light output. The HID and LPS, by their construction, are somewhat insulated from the ambient temperature. If, however, such lamps experience an interruption of the supply voltage, the arc will extinguish and require a time for the arc tube contents to reduce in temperature and pressure so that the then-available voltage can restrike the arc. The insulation of these lamps can therefore slow the cooling and delay the restrike, even if the voltage interruption is of very short duration. This restrike time varies with lamp type, size, and age, but it should be a recognized factor when designing lighting for areas where security is critical. In such areas it may be advisable to use largely incandescent light or coordinate it with the arc discharge sources. Some luminaires for arc discharge lamps include a small incandescent (often a tungsten-halogen) lamp within the optical system which is wired to an emergency power circuit.

Dimming   In some areas and at certain times it is an advantage to be able to change the illumination level in fixed steps or continuously. Such a feature could be desirable at a change of work shift, when large numbers of employees would move to and from a parking lot area. In these cases, a change to a lower illumination level could result in substantial savings in electrical energy.

Incandescent lamps can be dimmed by inserting resistance into the electrical circuit—for example, with rheostats—for smooth control of the illumination but with little or no savings in energy. Today there are solid-state devices for incandescent, fluorescent, and HID lamps that permit smooth dimming and energy savings. Also, some ballasts are available which, simply switched, will provide a "high" and a "low" level of illumination from the lamps.

Bulb Finish   Fluorescent lamps are coated on the inside surface of the tube with selected phosphors which convert the invisible, ultraviolet radiation of the arc to visible radiation. This results in a diffuse light coming from the entire surface of the lamp. Also, phosphors are used on some mercury and on some metal halide lamps. Some HPS lamps have a diffuse finish on the inside surface of the outer bulb. LPS lamps have essentially clear, light-transmitting surfaces, with little diffusion of the light.

The phosphors are used to improve the efficacy and the color rendition and serve to increase the lighted area of the lamp, reducing the unit luminance (photometric brightness) of the arc discharge. A diffuse material or surface used on some incandescent and HPS lamps also acts to provide a larger-area, lower-brightness surface. However, such larger source areas require somewhat larger or more complex optical systems in order to provide the desired light control; alternatively, if used in a luminaire designed for use with a clear lamp, these lamps will provide a broader distribution of light.

This detail of bulb finish is an essential element in the initial selection of a lamp and luminaire and becomes of vital importance when the luminaire is to be relamped. The indiscriminate replacement of a clear with a diffuse finish or a phosphor lamp can do much to alter the light distribution of the original system.

Incandescent Lamps

The incandescent lamps in Table 1 generally have a rated life of from 750 to 2000 hours, but other lamps are available with a life beyond this range, depending on use, type, and voltage. The tungsten-halogen lamps, a major breakthrough in the development of incandescent lamps, represent greatly increased lamp life as well as improved efficacy and color rendition, and their small physical size is an important element in the design of compact optical systems for good beam control.

Beam spread of the lamps can be influenced, in addition to the choice of clear or diffuse-finish bulbs, by reflector surfaces or other light-control elements molded into the surface of the bulb. Such control is utilized in several of the PAR (parabolic aluminized reflector) and EAR (elliptical aluminized reflector) lamps.

Some of the incandescent lamps are available in a choice of voltages. If desired, lamps can then be chosen so that available system voltage will cause them to be operated over or under the lamp design voltage. Over-voltage operation will increase lamp efficacy, lumen output, and source brightness, but it will decrease lamp life and increase lamp replacement cost. Under-voltage operation will increase lamp life and

TABLE 1   Incandescent Lamps

Watts	Base	Code	Description	Life*	Lumens†
100	Medium	100R40/FL	Reflector floodlight	2000	1,160
100	Medium	100R40/SP	Reflector spotlight	2000	1,160
150	Medium	150A	Inside-frosted	750	2,865
150	Medium Skirted	150PAR38/FL	Projector floodlight	2000	1,735
150	Medium Skirted	150PAR38/SP	Projector spotlight	2000	1,735
150	Medium	150R40/FL	Reflector floodlight	2000	1,885
200	Medium	200A	Inside-frosted	750	3,975
200	Medium	200R40/FL	Reflector floodlight	2000	2,040
200	Medium	200R40/SP	Reflector spotlight	2000	2,040
250	Medium Skirted	K250PAR38/FL	Projector floodlight	4000	3,100
300	Medium	300M	Clear	750	6,330
300	Medium	300R40/FL	Reflector floodlight	2000	3,625
300	Medium	300R40/SP	Reflector spotlight	2000	3,625
500	Mogul	500	Clear	1000	10,650
500	Mogul	500R40/3FL	Reflector floodlight	2000	6,500
500	Mogul	500R40/3SP	Reflector spotlight	2000	6,500
750	Mogul	750	Clear	1000	16,800
750	Mogul	750R52	Reflector high bay	2000	12,800
1000	Mogul	1000	Clear	1000	23,300
1000	Mogul	1000R57	Narrow-beam reflector	2000	17,500
1000	Mogul	1000R60/FL	Reflector floodlight	2000	16,800
1500	Mogul	1500	Clear	1000	33,600

*Rated hours, approx.
†Rated initial light output, approx.

decrease lamp replacement cost, but it will decrease lamp efficacy, reduce lumen output, and decrease source brightness. Rated lamp voltage is usually understood to be 120 V unless otherwise stated.

In general, incandescent lamp efficacies range from 18 to 23 lm/W for the larger lamps.

Fluorescent Lamps

The fluorescent lamps in Table 2 are only a few of the many such lamps available. The designer should review lamp manufacturers' listings and other references for a more complete selection of lamp types, wattages, current (mA) loadings, lengths, etc.

Fluorescent lamps respond to the ambient temperature; the coolest spot on the surface of the lamp tube controls the temperature, pressure, and light output of the arc discharge. Ambient temperatures below or above the design temperature of the lamp will result in a light output lower than the lamp's rating.

For best results indoors, the fluorescent lamp luminaires should provide for natural or forced circulation of air about the lamps so they will operate at or near the design ambient temperature. For outdoor use, lamps should be suitably housed or protected when lower ambient temperatures are anticipated and provided with ballasts rated for those temperatures.

Fluorescent lamps usually have symmetrical distribution of light about the circular surface of the lamp, but some have asymmetric distribution. This is accomplished by reflectorizing part of the surface of the tube, with the directional light coming through a slot or "window" which runs the length of the lamp. These lamps, in appropriate luminaires, provide linear systems having closely controlled beams of light. However, the usual application of fluorescent lamps is in an enclosing luminaire having appropriate reflectors, refractors, diffusers, louvers, or shields external to the lamp to provide the desired light control.

In general, fluorescent lamp efficacies range from 68 to 86 lm/W for representative lamp types, with a rated life of 10,000 to 20,000 hours.

TABLE 2   Fluorescent Lamps

Watts	Base	Code	Description	Life*	Lumens†
40	Medium bipin	F40CW/430mA	Cool white	20,000	3,200
60	Recessed double contact	F48T12/CW/ 800mA	Cool white	12,000	4,300
110	Recessed double contact	F48T12/CW/ 1500mA	Cool white	12,000	6,500
110	Recessed double contact	F96T12/CW/ 800mA	Cool white	12,000	9,100
205	Recessed double contact	F96T10/CW/ 1500mA‡	Cool white	9,000	14,000
215	Recessed double contact	F96T12/CW/ 1500mA	Cool white	10,000	15,000

*Rated hours, approx.
†Rated initial light output, approx.
‡Lamp with clear glass outer jacket, for use in low ambient temperatures.

Mercury Lamps

Mercury lamps have gained acceptance over incandescent lamps for many applications because of increased efficacy and rated life. These advantages usually offset the higher first cost of mercury lamp, ballast, and luminaire and can result in a lower system cost when compared with an incandescent or fluorescent system of equal lighting performance. The early mercury lamps were available only as clear lamps, and the resulting light output, although of high efficacy, did not render colors accurately; it had a greenish-blue cast and lacked red, therefore distorting skin tones. Also, these early lamps were limited to a few higher-wattage sizes. Today there is a wide range of wattages and many are available either clear or with a suitable phosphor coating on the inside of the outer bulb to provide a choice in color rendition, efficacy, and diffusion.

The addition of phosphor to the mercury lamp and the availability of smaller-wattage sizes are widening its range of application, both indoors and outdoors.

Table 3 lists mercury lamps ranging up to 1,000 W, with a rated life of up to 24,000 hours and an initial output of up to 63,000 lm. In general, mercury lamp efficacies range from 42 to 63 lm/W for representative lamp types.

Metal Halide Lamps

The metal halide lamp is very similar to the mercury lamp in size, shape, and electrical operation and has improved efficacy and color rendition, but, at its present stage of development, it has a shorter rated life and is more limited in the choice of wattage sizes. The principal difference is that the inner arc tube contains small quantities of metals in their halide salt form, in addition to mercury, and a small amount of argon gas (as an aid in starting), as used in the mercury lamp. All metal halide lamps have a clear inner arc tube, as does the mercury, but they also have a choice of clear or phosphor-coated outer bulb to increase light output, improve color rendition somewhat, or provide a larger-area, lower-brightness source of light.

The designer of a lighting system, noting the increased efficacy of the lamp and the larger number of lumens available from a lamp of given wattage, and recognizing the

TABLE 3   Mercury Lamps

Watts	Base	Code	Description	Life*	Lumens†
100	Mogul	H38JA-100DX	Deluxe white	20,000	4,200
100	Medium	H38BP-100DX	Reflector floodlight	24,000	2,850
175	Mogul	H39KC-175DX	Deluxe white	24,000	8,600
175	Medium	H39BM-175	Reflector floodlight	24,000	5,700
250	Mogul	H37KC-250/DX	Deluxe white	24,000	12,800
400	Mogul	H33GL-400/DX	Deluxe white	24,000	22,750
400	Mogul	H33FS-400/DX	Reflector floodlight	24,000	15,500
700	Mogul	H35ND-700/DX	Deluxe white	24,000	42,500
1,000	Mogul	H36GW-1000/DX	Deluxe white	24,000	63,000

*Rated hours, approx.
†Rated initial light output, approx.

TABLE 4   Metal Halide Lamps

Watts	Base	Code	Description	Life*	Lumens†
175	Mogul	MH175	Clear	7,500	14,000
250	Mogul	MH250	Clear	7,500	20,500
400	Mogul	MH400	Clear	15,000	34,000
1,000	Mogul	MH1000	Clear	10,000	110,000
1,500	Mogul	MH1500	Clear	1,500	155,000

*Rated hours, approx.
†Rated initial light output, approx.

higher first cost of lamp and luminaire, will conclude that the metal halide offers advantages over the incandescent.

Table 4 includes metal halide lamps ranging from 175 to 1,500 W, with a rated life of from 1,500 to 15,000 h and an initial output of up to 155,000 lm. In general, metal halide lamp efficacies range from 84 to 115 lm/W.

High-Pressure Sodium Lamps

The high-pressure sodium (HPS) lamp is somewhat similar in size, shape, and electrical operation to the mercury and metal halide lamps but has significant differences. The inner arc tube is ceramic, developed to withstand the action of the hot sodium vapor. This tube, at the elevated operating temperature, becomes translucent, of high transmission, releasing the golden-colored light of the sodium-arc discharge. Phosphors are not used, but some lamps are available with a diffuse coating on the inner surface of the outer bulb.

The inner arc tube of the HPS lamp is smaller in diameter than those of the mercury and metal halide lamps. This aids in the design of optical systems for luminaires and their application for better light control. The diffuse-coated outer bulb (optional) is useful in providing a larger-area, lower-brightness source and for replacement in luminaire optical systems which were designed for a diffuse source, such as a phosphor-coated mercury or metal halide lamp.

The designer of a lighting system, noting the long life of this lamp, its high efficacy, and the larger number of lumens available from a lamp of given wattage, and recognizing the high first cost of lamp and luminaire, will conclude that the HPS lamp offers advantages over the other lamps.

The conventional ballast for the HPS lamp includes a provision for high peak voltage necessary to start the lamp. However, a recent development is an HPS lamp with a starting ring around one end of the inner arc tube and a rare gas mixture included within the arc tube for lamp start without the necessity for the high peak voltage. Such lamps operate on some ballasts that mercury lamps use, permitting ready replacement with the higher-output HPS lamp.

Table 5 includes HPS lamps ranging from 70 to 1,000 W, with a rated life of 20,000 to 24,000 h and an initial output of up to 140,000 lm. In general, HPS lamp efficacies range from 95 to 140 lm/W for representative lamp types.

TABLE 5 High-Pressure Sodium Lamps

Watts	Base	Code	Description	Life*	Lumens†
70	Mogul	HPS70	Clear	20,000	5,800
100	Mogul	HPS100	Clear	20,000	9,500
150	Mogul	HPS150	Clear	24,000	16,000
250	Mogul	HPS250	Clear	24,000	30,000
400	Mogul	HPS400	Clear	24,000	50,000
1,000	Mogul	HPS1000	Clear	24,000	140,000

*Rated hours, approx.
†Rated initial light output, approx.

Low-Pressure Sodium Lamps

The low-pressure sodium (LPS) lamp is somewhat similar in electrical operation to the HID lamps but differs in size and shape. It has an inner arc shaped like a long, narrow "U" and enclosed in an outer, tubular bulb; the base is at one end only, and the outer bulb is not as slender in proportion to length as the typical fluorescent lamp.

Low-pressure sodium lamps, in various shapes and sizes, have been available for many years, but with recent improvements in lamps and luminaires they are now finding wider application in this country. They have the highest efficacy of any of the commercially available light sources for general application, but they do not render colors strictly accurately. The LPS arc operates at a very low pressure, and the light emitted by the sodium is a monochromatic yellow which seems to impart a heightened clarity to the lighted scene, according to many viewers, but admittedly is limited for any seeing task requiring color discrimination. Because of this, the LPS lamp is used mostly for outdoor applications. It is also being used for some interior spaces, such as warehouses, when color rendition is not critical.

The inner arc tube of the LPS lamp contains sodium and a small amount of neon gas to facilitate starting. At the start, the light is the characteristic red of the neon, but as the arc increases in temperature, it quickly turns to the yellow of the sodium.

The lumen rating of the LPS lamp is sustained, with little or no decrease, through-out the long life of the lamp. This long life, sustained high light output, high efficacy, and larger number of lumens available from a lamp of given wattage (recognizing the high first cost of lamp and luminaire) add up to advantages for the LPS over other lamp types in comparisons of complete systems for equivalent lighting performance.

Table 6 includes LPS lamps now commercially available ranging from 35 to 180 W, with a rated life of 18,000 hours and an initial output of up to 33,000 lm. The LPS lamp efficacies range from 137 to 183 lm/W for these five wattages available.

Luminaires

A luminaire is basically a mechanical means of positioning a light source (or sources) in space and then controlling the intensity and direction of the light leaving it. Some luminaires include electrical controls such as switches, ballasts, or dimmers. A few lamps, such as the R (reflector) and PAR types, in some applications, act as a complete luminaire and require only positioning in space, since the light control is provided by the lamp itself.

Enclosure   In providing the positioning and protection of lamp and optical system, a luminaire can range from a very simple optical assembly to one of considerable complexity because of the photometric, electrical, mechanical, and thermal requirements. It might be of open, enclosed, or ventilated construction in order to anticipate any hazards of the application (certainly including environmental conditions) which would threaten the integrity and performance of the luminaire.

Luminaires for outdoor use are usually of the enclosed type for protection of the

TABLE 6   Low-Pressure Sodium Lamps

Watts	Base	Code	Description	Life*	Lumens†
35	D.C. Bay.‡	LPS35	Clear	18,000	4,800
55	D.C. Bay.	LPS55	Clear	18,000	8,000
90	D.C. Bay.	LPS90	Clear	18,000	13,500
135	D.C. Bay.	LPS135	Clear	18,000	22,500
180	D.C. Bay.	LPS180	Clear	18,000	33,000

*Rated hours, approx.
†Rated initial light output, approx.
‡Double contact, bayonet.

lamp and optical system. Enclosed, gasketed luminaires are usually designed to meet the requirements of the fixture standards of Underwriters' Laboratories, Inc., and are identified with "wet label," "damp label," "explosion-proof," "hazardous location," or other such listing.

Traditionally, the housings, reflectors, louvers, and shields have been of cast or sheet metal, with a suitable finish to protect the surfaces and to act as an element in the control of light. Glass is the usual material for refractors and clear covers to enclose luminaires, but plastic is often used where the resulting temperatures will not affect parts made of it. Some housings are available in materials such as fiberglass, often with savings in weight and in maintenance.

Lamp Position   In most luminaires, the lamp's position is fixed with respect to the luminaire optical system. In others, the lamp position may be adjusted one or more times, as required, at the application site in order to obtain the desired light distribution. When luminaires are cleaned and/or relamped, it is important to ensure that the resulting position of the lamp provides the light distribution that was intended.

It is possible for the replacement lamp to be interchangeable electrically and physically as far as the luminaire is concerned but to be unsatisfactory optically because of bulb finish.

Optical System   The principal means of controlling the light from the lamp are reflectors and refractors; the control of luminaire brightness is mainly accomplished by diffusers, shields, and louvers. In luminaire design, these means are utilized singly or in combination, as required, to produce the desired control of light distribution and brightness.

Altering the position of any elements of the optical system with respect to the design position and light center of the intended lamp(s) could result in a distinctly different light distribution of the luminaire and the entire lighting system.

The R and PAR type lamps (and some other sources) have reflecting, refracting, or diffusing surfaces as an integral part of the lamp, with the advantage that these control surfaces are replaced with each new lamp and will be only minimally affected by dirt and dust conditions. However, they need to be placed and aimed as originally intended.

Location and Mounting   Luminaire system design is basically that of selecting the light source and luminaire and then locating and positioning them so as to provide the desired control of light and brightness, all at an acceptable cost. The location and position of luminaires should not produce deep shadows which might provide concealment for an intruder.

Luminaire locations and mountings could include:

1. Roofs, for Zones I, II, III, or IV
2. Walls, for Zones I, II, III, or IV
3. Building interiors, for lighting walls and ceilings in order to provide areas of brightness that indicate occupancy and suggest security awareness
4. Ground, for Zones, I, II, or III
5. Poles, for Zones I, II, III, or IV

Until comparatively recently, pole mounting of luminaires was somewhat restricted to heights of 15 to 30 ft, primarily because of accessibility required for maintenance of lamps and luminaires. The growing use of mobile, boom-type service equipment and/ or lowering devices has been influential in the trend to higher mountings of luminaires on poles and masts.

In most systems the luminaires are at fixed locations, mounted on horizontal or vertical surfaces and having fixed or adjustable positioning, while occasionally they are mobile. The light distribution of each luminaire in the system and the distance to the surfaces to be lighted will determine the spacing, mounting, positioning, and numbers of the luminaires.

Light Distribution   Light sources and luminaires can provide a range of light distribution from that of a very narrow, closely controlled beam to that of a very widespread beam, and from a small area with high brightness to a large area with low brightness. Light sources and luminaires are classified in various ways with regard to their light distribution and utilization, as shown in Table 7.

A floodlight is a light source or luminaire designed to provide a controlled, directional beam or "cone" of light to illuminate an object or surface, usually outdoors, to a higher level of light than certain background or adjacent areas. A spotlight provides a light beam of smaller angular width than a floodlight. A searchlight provides a narrow, essentially parallel beam of light, usually larger in cross section than a spotlight; it is generally used outdoors and has readily adjustable aiming for search and identification.

Floodlights are classified as to beam spread, which is defined as the angular spread between beam limits where the candlepower has decreased to 10 percent of the maximum candlepower in the beam. Candlepower is the luminous intensity or "light-making ability" of a light source or luminaire expressed in candelas, usually indicated in a given direction.

The classification of floodlights, as established by the National Electrical Manufacturers' Association (NEMA), is as follows[1]:

Beam spread in degrees	NEMA type
10 up to 18	1
18 up to 29	2
29 up to 46	3
46 up to 70	4
70 up to 100	5
100 up to 130	6
130 and up	7

TABLE 7 Typical Equipment for Protective Lighting

Luminaire		Type	Photometric Designation	Open or enclosed	Typical distribution characteristics	
					Vertical	Lateral
Streetlight		I	Two–way Four–way	Enclosed	73 to 78°	30° Lobes parallel Parallel lobes at 90°
Streetlight		II	Narrow asymmetric Four–way	Enclosed	70 to 75°	25° (20 to 30°) Lobes approximately 25° from luminaire axis
Streetlight		III	Medium wide asymmetric	Enclosed	70 to 75°	40° 30 to 50° Lobes approxitmately 40° from luminaire axix
Streetlight		IV	Wide asymmetric	Enclosed	70 to 75°	60° 50 to 90° Lobes approxitmately 60° from luminaire axis
Streetlight		V	Symmetric	Enclosed	70 to 75°	Same through 360°
Reflector		Asymmetric Symmetric	Asymmetric or Symmetric	open		or
Fresnel lens		Glare projection	Asymmetric	Enclosed		180° flat beam
Searchlight		Pilot house control / Trunion	Extremely narrow beam	Enclosed	Less than 10°	Approxitmately circular * (with clear lens)
Floodlight		1	Very narrow beam	Enclosed	10° to less than 18°	Approxitmately circular * (with clear lens)
Floodlight		2	Narrow beam	Enclosed	18° to less than 29°	Approxitmately circular * (with clear lens)
Floodlight		3	Medium beam	Enclosed	29° to less than 46°	Approxitmately circular * (with clear lens)
Floodlight		4	Medium wide beam	Enclosed or open	46° to less than 70°	Approxitmately circular * (with clear lens or open)
Floodlight		5	Wide beam	Enclosed or open	70° to less than 100°	Approxitmately circular * (with clear lens or open)
Floodlight		6	Very wide beam	Enclosed or open	100° and up	Approxitmately circular * (with clear lens or open)

Note: If a spread lens is used, the vertical spread will remain approximately the same, while the horizontal beam will be widened considerably. A clear lens is without control media.
   Street lighting luminaires are typical according to ASA designation.
   Floodlighting luminaires are typical according to NEMA and IES designation.
   Reflectorized lamps fall into floodlight classifications according to their distribution characteristics.
   Table given by courtesy of the Illuminating Engineering Society.

Floodlights with asymmetric beams are often classified using a combination such as "7 × 6" for a horizontal beam spread of 143° and a vertical beam spread of 120°.

The spacing, mounting, and aiming of floodlights should be such that the overlapping patterns of the individual floodlights will provide, at all essential points on the lighted area and at all times, the minimum recommended level of illumination for that area and intended use.

If the area covered by a quantity of lumens is known, or can be estimated, the average illumination over that area can be computed using the beam-lumen method. "Beam lumens" refers to that stated quantity, or percentage of the lamp lumens, confined to the defined beam. A surface with an area of 1 ft² is said to be receiving illumination of 1 fc if there is a uniformly distributed quantity of 1 lumen over the 1-square-foot area. Floodlight beam lumens as stated (or as lamp lumens multiplied by beam efficiency), divided by area of work plane (in square feet), will indicate the average illumination over that area (in footcandles).

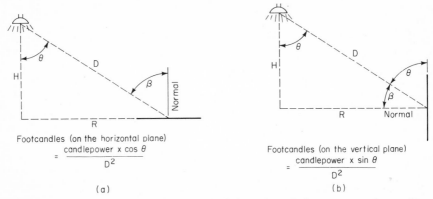

Footcandles (on the horizontal plane)

$$= \frac{\text{candlepower} \times \cos \theta}{D^2}$$

(a)

Footcandles (on the vertical plane)

$$= \frac{\text{candlepower} \times \sin \theta}{D^2}$$

(b)

Fig. 1   Fundamental relationships for point calculations where the inverse-square law applies. *(From "IES Lighting Handbook." Reproduced courtesy of Illuminating Engineering Society.)*

For determination of illumination at a point on a plane, the "inverse-square method" (sometimes referred to as the "point method") is used. (See Fig. 1.) For illumination (E) at the point (in footcandles), the candlepower I (in candelas) and the distance D (in feet) are as related in the figure.

Computations using either of these two methods are usually made with data for new lamps and luminaires and then adjusted by using an appropriate "combined light-loss factor" (LLF) in order to provide a depreciated value of illumination.

Because of the sometimes complex geometry involving the luminaire position and the point on the plane, computations have been made and data published in the form of isofootcandle curves or isolux curves (see Figs. 2 to 5).

Total illumination (in footcandles) at a point is the summation of all light from all lamps and/or luminaires directing light to that point. This summation can be of actual results of beam-lumen or inverse-square method computations and/or data from isofootcandle curves.

Most of the luminaires designed for roadway applications have an asymmetric distribution, which enables them to lay down a "ribbon" of light on the roadway surface, with the usual luminaire mounting at one side of the roadway. This light on the roadway is referred to as "street side" in contrast with the "house side" distribution. Luminaires are classified as to range (short, medium, or long) and type (I, II, III, IV, and V), as illustrated in Fig. 6.[3]

A given luminaire light distribution must then be coordinated with the spacing and

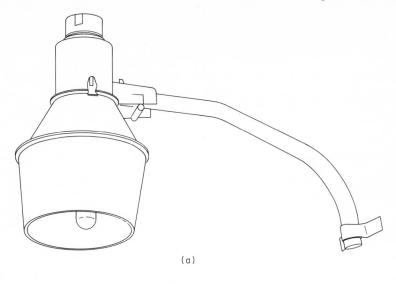

(a)

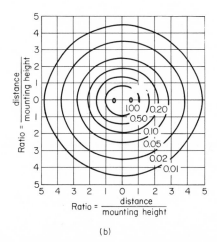

(b)

Fig. 2 (a) **Low-pressure sodium area luminaire.** (b) **ISO-footcandle curve (mounting height = 20 ft) for a 35-W (4800-lm) low-pressure sodium lamp. Mounting height conversion table:**

Mounting height, ft	10	15	20	25	30	40
Footcandle correction factor	4.00	1.78	1.00	0.64	0.44	0.25

(Reproduced courtesy North American Philips Lighting Corporation.)

mounting height of the intended luminaire system in order to provide roadway illumination of recommended levels[3] and acceptable uniformity (average-to-minimum illumination ratio should not exceed 3 to 1). In order to determine illumination at the points in question on the roadway, the point method is used with candlepower data for the given luminaire, or the isofootcandle data can be used.

In order to determine the average illumination E_{av} on the roadway, a sufficient number of points can be averaged, or the lumen method, with the appropriate coefficient of utilization CU, can be used (see Fig. 7). The CU is that percentage of the

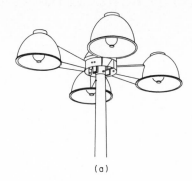

(a)

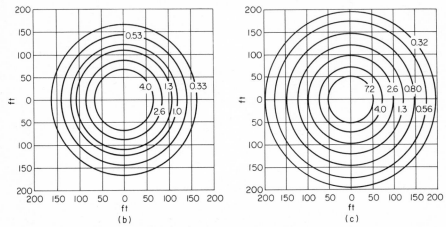

(b)   (c)

Fig. 3   (a) Hi-Mast luminaire. (b) Isolux curve showing horizontal footcandles for four 1000-W
mercury **luminaire (No. 5600) with deluxe white mercury lamp at a 50-ft mounting height (c)**
Isolux curve showing horizontal footcandles for four 1000-W *metallic vapor* **luminaire (No. 5600)**
with deluxe lamp at a 50-ft mounting height. Mounting height conversion table:

Mounting height, ft	35	40	45
Footcandle correction factor	2.04	1.56	1.23

(Reporduced courtesy QL Incorporated.)

total lamp lumens *LL* which reaches the width and length of the roadway for a given
type, distribution, and mounting of luminaires. Therefore:

$$E_{av} = \frac{LL \times CU}{\text{area of roadway}}$$

If data are for initial conditions, an appropriate LLF must then be used to provide
a depreciated value of illumination.

Roadway luminaires, because of their asymmetric types of light distribution (see
Fig. 7), were early choices for lighting off-roadway areas such as parking lots, filling
stations, shopping malls, etc. For many of these uses they are now being superseded
by downlights, usually with symmetrical light distributions, designed for area lighting
and mounted on high masts 50 to 100 ft or more above an area. Such high masts,
equipped with four to eight or more luminaires, each with a symmetrical light
pattern, provide overlapping cones of light for the area. Because of the overlap of
light, the resulting distribution is less affected by a single lamp outage. With the
multiple mounting of luminaires, fewer poles are required, simpler electrical circuitry

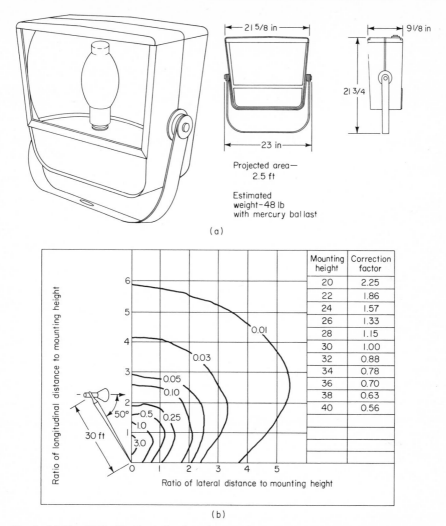

← 2 15/8 in →

← 91/8 in →

21 3/4

← 23 in →

Projected area—
2.5 ft

Estimated
weight—48 lb
with mercury ballast

(a)

Mounting height	Correction factor
20	2.25
22	1.86
24	1.57
26	1.33
28	1.15
30	1.00
32	0.88
34	0.78
36	0.70
38	0.63
40	0.56

(b)

**Fig. 4   (a) Floodlight. (b) Chart showing photometric performance of H33 GL-400/DX lamp.
Photometric data for various lamps:**

Lamp	Beam spread, H × V	Beam lumens	Candlepower	NEMA-IES beam
H33CD-400	148 × 112	13,792	10,535	7 × 6
H33GL-400/DX	150 × 122	11,886	6,518	7 × 6
MH400BD/4	147 × 109	17,824	15,466	7 × 6
C400	144 × 109	27,924	22,213	7 × 6

is needed, and fewer obstacles to vehicular traffic are presented in parking or storage lots (see Fig. 3).

SURVEILLANCE WITH CLOSED-CIRCUIT TELEVISION

The use of closed-circuit television has greatly increased the effectiveness of security systems. In choosing a TV system, whether the camera positions are to be fixed, adjustable, or mobile, a basic consideration is the amount of light available or to be provided for satisfactory functioning of the cameras. The available illumination might range from starlight on a clear, moonless night to full, direct daylight—a range of approximately 0.0001 to 10,000 fc.

Cameras to be used for surveillance during daylight hours only can usually be of lower sensitivity, and generally of lower cost, than those to be used at very low levels of light. A camera for 24-hour use needs to be designed so as not to experience "washout" of image as the light level increases.

The light available, or to be provided, will need to be matched to the requirements of available cameras or those to be supplied. In some cases, an economic compromise

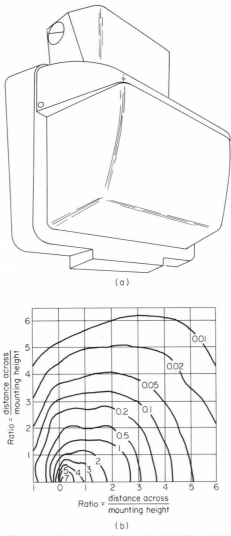

(a)

(b)

Fig. 5   (a) Wallpack. (b) Isolux chart for wallpack with 250-W, 11,000-lm clear mercury lamp. Illumination at mounting height of 15 ft. (*Reproduced courtesy of Johns-Manville, Holophane Division.*)

might be to supply somewhat more than the recommended minimum level of light in an area in order to utilize cameras of less than full sensitivity and of lower cost.

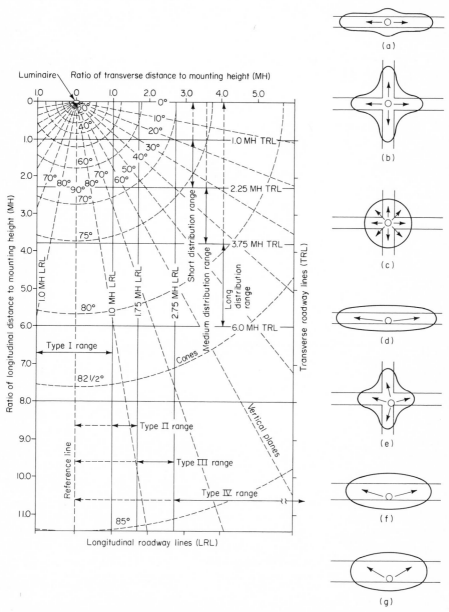

Fig. 6   Plan view of roadway coverage for different types of luminaries. (a) Type I; (b) Type I—four-way; (c) Type V; (d) Type II; (e) Type II—four-way; (f) Type III; (g) Type IV. *(From American National Standard "Practice for Roadway Lighting." Reproduced courtesy the Illuminating Engineering Society.)*

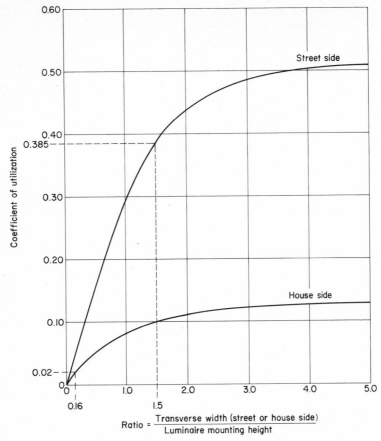

Fig. 7 Example of coefficient of utilization curves for luminaire providing Type III-M light distribution. *(From American National Standard "Practice for Roadway Lighting." Reproduced courtesy the Illuminating Engineering Society.)*

ELECTRICAL SYSTEMS FOR LIGHTING

An electrical system designed for incandescent lamps exclusively will require a higher current-carrying capacity (voltage and light output being the same) than a system of fluorescent, HID, or LPS lamps, because of the low efficacy of the incandescent lamps. In some cases, this higher capacity of an existing incandescent system has been helpful when part or all of the system was converted to fluorescent, HID, or LPS.

At one time many outdoor systems for roadway and area lighting were of the series-circuit variety, but today the multiple-circuit type is preferred.

Voltage The traditional 120-V multiple-circuit voltage is very popular, but other voltages are used, especially for large systems. Incandescent lamp design voltages (120, 130, 230, 250, etc.) should be selected so that the system voltage will result in desired lamp performance as regards light efficacy, wattage, and life. Arc discharge ballasts, for a given lamp wattage, are usually available in a range of line voltages (120, 208, 244, 277, 480, etc.), so that the lamp can be matched more effectively to a higher system voltage where such is available or can be supplied. Lamp arcs usually require starting and operating voltages well above 120 volts, so a ballast with a higher-input voltage will usually make the system more energy efficient.

Ballasts are designed and listed for various ambient temperatures (+105, +50, +40, +32, 0, −10, and −20°F). Low ambient temperatures can greatly slow or prevent the starting of an arc discharge lamp and prevent it from increasing in light output to the design level. Ballasts should be selected so as to provide the required starting and operating voltages in the expected ambient temperature.

Power Factor   Incandescent lamps operate at a "unity" power factor, but arc discharge lamps operate at a lower power factor (lag). The combined lamp-ballast power factor might range from 50 to 90 percent, depending on lamp and ballast type and design, and this directly affects the amount of energy used.

Current   The current required by an incandescent lamp either is published or can be estimated, using lamp wattage and voltage data $(I = W/V)$. The current required by a given lamp-ballast combination is usually included in published ballast or nameplate data. Ballasts are available for single or multiple lamps, and the input current of a ballast includes ballast and lamp(s).

Wattage   The usual listing of data for an incandescent lamp includes the wattage input to produce the rated lumen output. The usual listing for arc discharge lamps includes wattage for the lamp only. The total input of watts required for a lamp-ballast combination is usually included in listings of ballast data.

Switching   The electrical system for security lighting can be switched manually, by time clock, or by photocell control. The usual photocell control is designed and built on the fail-safe principle, so that in the event of a malfunction of the cell the lighting circuit will become energized.

Incandescent systems can use lamps of higher design voltage while operating on a lower voltage to provide the desired light for routine use. By simply switching to a higher voltage, much more light is produced for emergency security situations. Some ballasts are available for operation, with suitable switching, with two levels of light output of the lamp(s).

Dimming   Traditionally, incandescent lamps have been dimmed by inserting resistance in the electrical circuit, as by the use of rheostats. The dimming of fluorescent and HID lamps is accomplished by using special ballasts and/or solid-state devices.

The use of dimming can result in considerable savings of electrical energy and provide a choice of light levels for a given application. For example, the lighting system of a hospital parking lot can be equipped for dimming to suitable levels for most of the night hours, with a provision for increasing the lighting level when a change of personnel brings an increase of traffic to the lot.

Emergency Power   A major decision in designing electrical systems for security lighting is how to provide a backup system for emergency power. Some fluorescent lamps can be used with ballasts which will operate on a self-contained battery supply during the interruption of the primary voltage and will be recharged when regular service is resumed. However, a lighting system of other than modest size will probably best be supplied by a separate source of energy, such as a motor-generator set and/or batteries, with relays and switches to change from and to the available power sources as required.

In order to limit the size and cost of such a system for emergency power, the designer should carefully select the luminaire locations which are to be switched to the emergency system. In making such a selection, light source types must be kept in mind, and any anticipated delay in the restrike of an arc discharge lamp should be evaluated with regard to areas where the security lighting is critical.

MAINTENANCE OF LIGHTING SYSTEMS

The design of a security lighting system must include provision for the continued maintenance of all elements of the system if satisfactory performance is to be expected. Aging of lamps, dirt collecting on optical systems, incorrect luminaire positioning, and other similar factors can seriously diminish the original effectiveness of the system.

Lamps Major considerations in the selection of a light source type and size are the amount of light (lumens) initially available from the lamp and what decrease of light output can be expected during the life of the lamp. The "initial" lumen rating is usually stated or understood to be 0 for incandescent and LPS lamps and 100 hour for fluorescent, mercury, metal halide, and HPS lamps. The lumen output of the 100-hour-rated lamps decreases at a higher rate during those first hours of operation and then continues to decrease, but at a lower rate, during the remaining hours of life.

This decrease of light output is referred to as "lamp lumen depreciation" (LLD), and published figures are usually based on light output at 70 percent of rated life. Approximate figures, for various lamp types and operating situations, are: LPS, 100 percent; tungsten-halogen, 95+ percent; HPS, 90 percent; general-service incandescent, 85 percent; fluorescent (rapid start), 65 to 85 percent; mercury, 75 percent; and metal halide, 70 percent.

The published rated average life for a lamp is based on tests of large groups of lamps of that type and recognizes that lamp burnouts occur within and beyond rated life. A burnout in a single-lamp luminaire could be a mild inconvenience or could be vital in an area of critical security. To minimize such a situation, switching can be provided to change from an inoperative lamp to a new lamp, in the same or in a standby luminaire, although rapid spot replacement is generally used to restore system integrity as promptly as possible.

Lamps continuing to operate beyond rated life should be routinely replaced because of reduced light output and/or to avoid emergency replacement. Lamps should be marked and records kept so that they will be replaced as required by the LLD, lamp life, and the economics of the situation.

Luminaires A totally enclosed luminaire is required for some lamps and is desirable for most outdoor applications. Such luminaires "breathe" with changes of internal air temperature and pressure, and the amount of dirt brought into the luminaire enclosure will depend upon the amount and type of dirt in the surrounding atmosphere, interior volume, luminaire filtering action (if any), temperature and pressure differentials, and the time cycles of such differentials. Higher-wattage lamps can be expected to cause a luminaire to "breathe more deeply," and this should be taken into consideration in planning maintenance schedules.

The light-control surfaces of the luminaire optical system will collect dirt, and some will suffer deterioration as time passes. Then not only will the surfaces absorb more light, they will fail to control the light as originally intended. These surfaces require maintenance, preferably on a regularly scheduled basis. Some solutions good for cleaning glassware can damage the surface of an aluminum reflector, so caution is advisable in establishing maintenance procedures. Manufacturers' literature should be followed for recommended cleaning materials and procedures.

Dirt collection on luminaire light-control surfaces and the resulting loss of light are referred to as luminaire dirt depreciation (LDD), usually expressed as a percentage, with the standard being 100 percent for a new, clean luminaire. The LDD to be used in planning a given system will be that decreased performance which the luminaire will be permitted to reach before its surfaces will be cleaned or renewed. An actual LDD could be 90 or more for an open luminaire operating in a very clean environment and scheduled to be cleaned frequently, or it could be 50 or less for some enclosed luminaires operating in a very dirty environment and cleaned very infrequently. Appropriate LDD data are available from manufacturers and suppliers of luminaires and from suitable publications.

Light-Loss Factors The principal light-loss factors (LLF) are usually the LLD and LDD, but other light-loss factors (OLL) will need to be included in some cases (LLF = LLD × LDD × OLL). Other factors include voltage variations, luminaire ambient temperatures, burnouts, ballast factor, room surface depreciation (RSDD), and luminaire surface depreciation. The minimum recommended illumination at any point should then be the initial footcandles multiplied by the total LLF ($E_{min} = E_i \times LLF$).

Ballasts The various electrical components of a ballast are vulnerable to elevated temperatures. Ballasts can have an extended life if operated below the design temperature, so intended application and replacement conditions should be prime considerations.

Some interchangeability of lamp and ballast might be permitted (e.g., some metal halide lamps and some LPS lamps may be used on some mercury ballasts), but this should be done only after study of lamp and ballast information.

Luminaire Mountings The mounting and positioning of luminaires (fixed, adjustable, or mobile), as determined originally for the lighting system, should be reviewed periodically so that unplanned changes can be corrected or compensated for. An original mounting and bracketing of a luminaire may have become corroded or otherwise threatened in position or stability. A mounting intended to permit movement of the luminaire for search purposes and/or relamping may have become corroded or restricted from disuse. A new structure or reclassification of an area may require a different positioning of existing or new luminaires to provide the changed requirements for lighting the area.

Other Electrical Elements All elements of the electrical system should be suspect in that, at one time or another, they could fail without warning. A segregated, secure, inventoried stock of switches, circuit breakers, lamps, etc., should be set up to be used only for the security lighting system.

Switches, fuses, and circuit-breaker settings should be reviewed periodically, especially at the time of contemplated or actual changes in the system.

Motor-generator sets, batteries, relays, switches, etc., of a standby electrical system should be checked periodically and actually operated to ensure reliability in case of an emergency.

REFERENCES

1. *IES Lighting Handbook,* 5th ed., published by the Illuminating Engineering Society, 345 East 47th St., New York, N.Y. 10017.
2. *American National Standard Practice for Protective Lighting,* published by the above society.
3. *American National Standard Practice for Roadway Lighting,* published by the above society.

Chapter **15**

Locks and Keying

GEORGE E. WHEATLEY, D.A.H.C.

Campbell Hardware, Inc.

LOCK CONSIDERATIONS

Because of many code requirements, specifying locking requirements for a particular building is not a simple task. However, with the variety of locking functions available today, few situations arise that cannot be handled.

It must be kept in mind that a lock in itself does not necessarily provide adequate protection. The door to which it is attached must be properly fitted to the frame and durable in its construction, or else the protection provided by the lock is easily defeated.

Control of the keys for the lock is equally important. The most expensive lock offers little security if the keys which operate it are handled in a careless or haphazard manner so that they may be easily obtained or duplicated.

Another important consideration is that a lock or latch not only gives protection from the standpoint of security against entry, but also has a direct relationship to life safety. The investigation of numerous fires involving loss of life has brought to light that most of these fatalities occurred from the inhalation of smoke and fumes and not from the fire itself. This has resulted in the revision of building codes in many states; many now require that corridor doors opening into rooms must be self-closing and self-latching.

This chapter considers the various types of locks and other locking mechanisms available, the limitations within which they should be used, and the security they provide.

References are to products normally used in commercial construction for buildings such as schools, hospitals, office buildings, universities, industrial buildings, stores, and so on. Jails, mental institutions, and other similar buildings which have their own special requirements are not discussed here.

LOCKS AND LOCK FUNCTIONS

Locks generally fall into four basic classifications or types: mortise (Fig. 1), bored or cylindrical (Fig. 2), unit (Fig. 3), and rim (Fig. 4).

Mortise Locks

Mortise locks have been in use for nearly 150 years, are the oldest of the three types still being produced, and are predominant in usage for commercial construction.

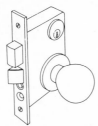

Fig. 1   Mortise lock.

Fig. 2   Bored or cylindrical lock.

Fig. 3   Unit lock.

They provide the widest range of function and trim designs. They also provide the maximum in security. While mortise locks were originally operated by bit keys (Fig. 5), this type of key is now obsolete. Today's mortise locks operate with a cylinder key, which provides greater keying flexibility and security.

There are four general functions for mortise locks. These are: latch, no key (Fig. 6); latch, locked with buttons in the face (Fig. 7); latch, locked by key (Fig. 8); and latch, with dead bolt (Fig. 9).

To provide proper security, the latch bolt should have a projection of at least $5/8$ in. Dead bolts normally project $1/2$ in but are also available with a 1-in projec-

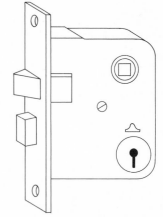

Fig. 5   Bit key mortise lock.

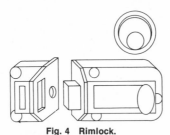

Fig. 4   Rimlock.

tion, and where maximum security is required, they can be furnished with two hardened steel inserts in the dead bolt. For the weights available, latch and dead-bolt projections, and other detailed information for each manufacturer's product, refer to ANSI A 156.2 (Locks and Lock Trim).

Bored or Cylindrical Locks

Locks of this type have been available for over fifty years, but did not come into general use for commercial work until after World War II. The heavy demand for buildings of all kinds created an even greater demand for items readily available and easy to install, which promoted the use of this type of lock.

These locks are only available with a latch bolt (see Fig. 2), but they can be obtained with a separate dead bolt (Fig. 10). Their functions are similar to those of the mortise lock, but instead of being in the face, the button is in the inside knob (Fig. 11). Key control corresponds to the mortise lock.

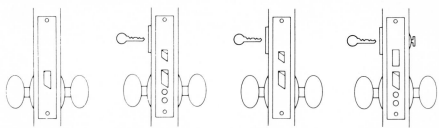

Fig. 6 Mortise latch, no key.

Fig. 7 Mortise latch, locked with buttons in face.

Fig. 8 Mortise latch, key-locked.

Fig. 9 Mortise latch with dead bolt.

Unit Locks

The unit lock first appeared in the early twentieth century. It was at the time (and still is today) the ultimate in lock construction. Being preassembled as a complete unit

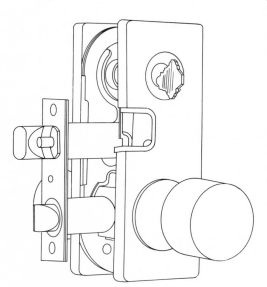

(Fig. 12), it eliminates all the problems associated with improper installation which frequently occur with the other types of locks. The other types require the assembly of the parts right on the door to make the installation, whereas the only requirement for a unit lock installation is a U-shaped cutout on the door (Fig. 13). The misalignment of holes and incorrect spacing which create real problems with hollow metal doors are completely eliminated. Unit locks provide the same range of functions as mortise locks.

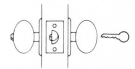

Fig. 10 Bored (or cylindrical) lock with separate dead bolt.

Fig. 11 Bored lock with button in inside knob.

Rim Locks

This type of lock is used for the most part as a supplemental lock after the initial installation. It requires no mortising in the door, merely a hole for the cylinder. For maximum security, the best type of lock is a rim lock with interlocking bolts (Fig. 14) or with an extra-long-throw dead bolt (Fig. 15).

Deadlocks

Many times locks are required for doors of the "push-pull" variety to provide security when these doors are not in general use. Deadlocks are available in both the mortise type (Fig. 16) and the cylindrical type (Fig. 17). Operation may be by cylinder on one side only, cylinder on the outside with thumb turn inside, or cylinders on both sides. For doors in schools, these locks are available with a thumb turn which will retract the bolt but not project it, which makes it impossible to lock anyone in a room.

Identification for Labeled Fire Doors

All locks for labeled fire doors that have been approved by Underwriters' Laboratories (or a similar rating agency) bear an identifying code mark stamped on the face of the lock (Fig. 18).

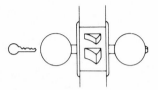

Fig. 12.   Pre-assembled unit lock.

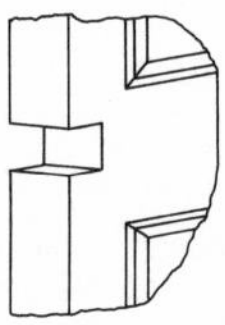

Fig. 13   Door stile cut for unit lock.

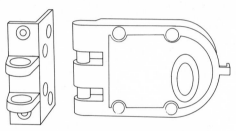

Fig. 14   Rim lock with interlocking bolts.

Mortise Lock Trim

Doorknobs or lever handles for mortise lock sets should have spindles with pinned attachment for the locked side of the door to provide adequate security (Fig. 19). Attachment for the inside knob is also recommended (as shown in Fig. 19).

Exit Devices

There are many openings in schools, hospitals, and other public buildings where code requirements demand the use of exit devices. These are available in rim-type (Fig. 20), mortise-type (Fig. 21), and vertical rod–type (Fig. 22). Either the rim type or the mortise type may be used for single doors; however, for security the rim type should have a deadlocking latch (Fig. 23).

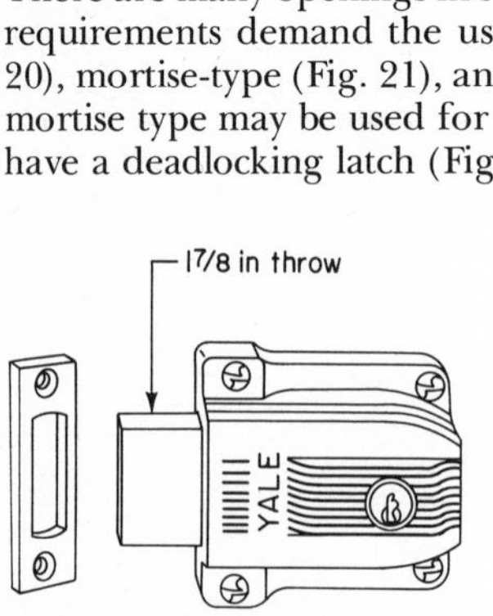

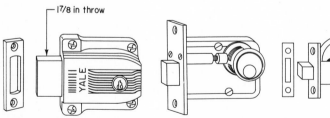

1 7/8 in throw

Fig. 15   Rim lock with extra-long-throw dead bolt.

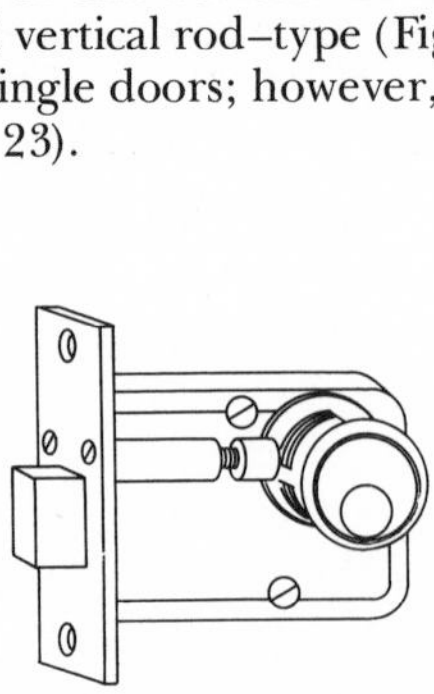

Fig. 16   Mortise-type deadlock.

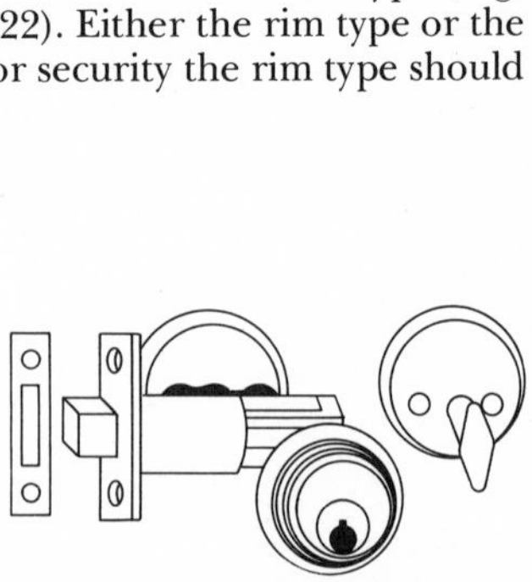

Fig. 17   Cylindrical-type deadlock.

Rim devices are not recommended for the active leaf of pairs of doors. Pairs of doors should be equipped with vertical rod devices (as in Fig. 22). These provide positive locking at the top and bottom of the door. The meeting stile should have spring-loaded astragals (Fig. 24), which would make it difficult to open the door by inserting a coat hanger (or similarly hooked wire) to engage the crossbar and pull it down, thus gaining entrance.

Exit devices can now be obtained with a horizontal-type movement of the crossbar (toward the door), which seems to eliminate completely problems such as the one mentioned above.

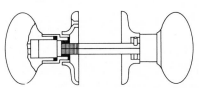

Fig. 18 Fire-labeled identification.

Fig. 19 Screwless shank for mortise lock.

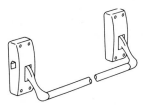

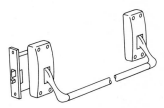

Fig. 20 Rim-type exit device.

Fig. 21 Mortise-type exit device.

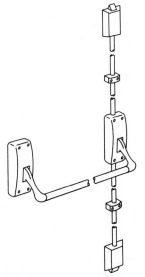

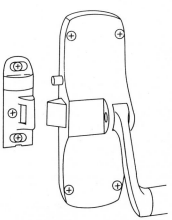

Fig. 22 Vertical-rod-type exit device.

Fig. 23 Deadlocking latch for rim-type exit device.

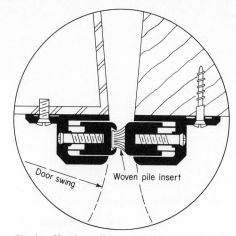

Fig. 24   Meeting rail for pair of doors equipped with exit device.

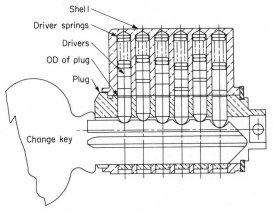

Fig. 25   Conventional keying arrangement.

KEYING

The heart of any lock or locking mechanism is the cylinder which activates the unit when the door is locked and, in many cases, also provides the means to lock the door.

Conventional cylinders consist of a round threaded shell which fits the threaded hole in a mortise lock or is incorporated into the knob in cylindrical or unit locks. Rim locks and certain exit devices use a cylinder with a tailpiece which is fitted to the unit. Into this shell is fitted a barrel or plug which is broached to accept the key. Corresponding holes are drilled in the barrel and in the shell. Pins and springs are loaded in the shell, and pins are loaded in the barrel. The length of the pins in the barrel corresponds with the cuts in the key. When the key is inserted in the barrel, the pins form a shear line, allowing the key to turn and activate the lock (Fig. 25).

The security of any key system is directly related to the number of levels of access required by the system. We refer to this as "levels of control in master keying." The levels are identified as follows:

One Level—Change Key   All locks are operated by change keys only and are keyed differently or alike as required. Examples: homes, stores, etc.

Two Levels—Master Key   All locks are operated by change keys and a master key. Examples: small schools, apartments, etc.

Three Levels—Grand Master Key   All locks are operated by change keys, master keys, and a grand master key. Examples: office buildings, large schools, small hospitals, etc.

Four Levels—Great Grand Master Key   All locks are operated by change keys, master keys, grand master keys, and a great grand master key. Examples: large hospitals, hotels, colleges, etc.

Five Levels—Great Great Grand Master Key   All locks are operated by change keys, master keys, grand master keys, great grand master keys, and a great great grand master key. Examples: large hospital complexes, large university complexes, and large industrial complexes.

As stated in the introduction to this section, the security of a lock is dependent on many factors. A few of these are:

Control of Keys   The failure of locking systems probably occurs more in this area than in any other. To maintain security it is imperative that keys be properly filed and identified, locked up at all times, and controlled, preferably, by one person thoroughly oriented to the system and armed with the authority to exercise complete control over the issuance of all keys.

Selection of Keyways or Key Sections   All cylinder manufacturers provide a range of key sections. Those produced for stock sales use common sections easily obtained by all locksmiths, and thus keys with these sections may be readily duplicated. However, all major manufacturers have many key sections available which are reserved for systems requiring high security. Keys and key blanks can be obtained stamped with the name of the using institution and the words "Do Not Duplicate," which acts as a deterrent against duplication.

Updating the System   As master keying is computed on a mathematical basis, any system, if it is to provide security, must be well planned, properly recorded, and kept up to date. Obviously, this should be done by the producer of the cylinders. All additions and extensions must be done by the original manufacturer, or the system will be violated. Under no circumstances should any cylinders be added to the system without code information from the manufacturer.

Construction Master Keying   To provide security and assure proper control of all keys, all locks should be furnished "Construction Master Keyed." This aids in preventing any keys getting into unauthorized hands during construction. Upon completion, all keys are sent directly to the owner of the structure. The general contractor is furnished with "construction master keys" to be used until the structure is accepted by the owner, at which time these keys are made inoperative.

Removable-Core Cylinders

Most major manufacturers offer, in addition to their conventional cylinder, a cylinder with a removable core (Fig. 26). This cylinder has several advantages:

1. The key for any individual cylinder can be made inoperative in less than a minute by removing the core with a control key and inserting a new one.

2. If a master key is lost or stolen, it can be made inoperative by changing the cores that are operated by that key. The cost for this change is considerably less than the cost for replacing or rekeying the existing cylinders.

3. In the case of dormitories or similar dwellings where the occupants are frequently changing, sets of spare cores can be kept on hand to replace those that must be changed when the occupants change. The cores which were removed would be re-used at a later date, but not in the same location in which they were previously used. It is also possible to change the key sections. Thus, if a previous occupant attempted to use his or her old key to gain entry to the location formerly occupied, the key could not be inserted into the cylinder.

Special High-Security Cylinders

There are several cylinders now available which provide a high degree of security against picking, drilling, and other known methods used to defeat the security of the cylinder. These can be master keyed, just as conventional cylinders, but, at the present time, they cannot be "construction master keyed" (Fig. 27).

Again, it must be emphasized that money spent for security in a lock or cylinder is a complete waste unless the door is properly fitted to the frame, the type of lock selected will give the security desired, and the control of all keys has been delegated to one person having absolute authority to control the issuance of all keys.

For more detailed information about keying, refer to the Door & Hardware Institute's handbook entitled *Keying Procedures, Systems and Nomenclature,* obtainable from the Door & Hardware Institute, 1815 N. Fort Myer Drive, Rosslyn, VA 22209.

ELECTRIC AND AIR-ACTIVATED LOCKING DEVICES

Within the past few years, the emphasis on security has led to the development of lock functions that are controlled either electrically or by air. Restrictions on the amount of voltage which may be transmitted into a door place certain limitations on some items (exit devices, for example) which can be controlled electrically. Air operation, on the other hand, has no restrictions and will function in practically all situations.

Control of these locks or other devices may be located at the door or at a remote station monitored by audible or visible observation—i.e., an annunciator system, visual detection, or closed-circuit television. Monitor panels provide individual observation of each opening, showing the door in open, closed, or locked positions.

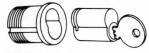

Fig. 26   Removable-core cylinder.

Locking devices may be automatically time controlled, that is, locked at a certain time and unlocked at a certain time. They can be made "fail-safe," so that if the electric current fails they will lock or unlock automatically, or they can be wired into the fire alarm or sprinkler systems so that the doors will lock or unlock automatically if these systems are activated in case of fire. It should be kept in mind that electric lock control must conform to all applicable life safety codes, which vary from state to state.

Let us now consider the various functions available for electric operation. Probably the most common is the electric strike, which is used with all types of locks (Fig. 28). Operation may be by card reader (Fig. 29) at the opening or by remote control. Regular key operation of the lock is usually also provided. Electric strikes are available

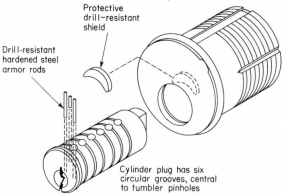

Protective drill-resistant shield

Drill-resistant hardened steel armor rods

Cylinder plug has six circular grooves, central to tumbler pinholes

Fig. 27   High-security cylinder.

in a wide price range. The inexpensive ones provide little security. Recently, an electric strike was introduced which can be used with a lock having a dead bolt, which should provide additional security.

All types of locks may be converted to electric operation, which is usually remotely controlled. These locks must be wired for operation. Hinges are available ready-wired for connection with the wires in the door and those in the frame. Locks of this type are built to custom specifications. Several voltages are available, but 24 V ac seems to be used most frequently for electrically operated locks and electric strikes.

In addition to the regular locks and electric strikes already described, the introduction of electricity into lock function has produced a new product, the magnetic lock (Fig. 30). This type of unit, which is usually operated by remote control, provides

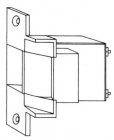

Fig. 28   Strike for electric operation.

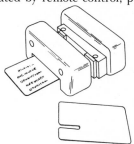

Fig. 29   Card-reading operator.

variables in the amount of force it takes to open the door when it is locked. This means that a door may be locked against normal force used for opening, but in the event of an emergency, abnormal force against the door will release the lock.

Magnetic locks or bolts are also available which will remain retracted while the door is open but will lock automatically when the door is closed. These may be operated at the opening by a key switch or card reader, or they may be remotely controlled. They may also be controlled by a time clock. Where friction is a strong factor, air operation may be more desirable.

Exit devices may also be electrically or air operated. This is accomplished by dogging the crossbars so that the devices are unlocked or by releasing the crossbars to lock the doors.

CONCLUSION

Locks alone, no matter how expensive or hard to defeat, cannot provide totally adequate security. It is a matter of record that instances of breaking and entering accomplished by picking locks or unlocking them in some illegal manner are relatively few. Carelessness, poor key control, and ignorance of a potential security problem all contribute to making an opening vulnerable.

This set of conditions, for example, allowed the famous Brinks robbery in Boston to take place with ease. During the day, one of the bandits removed the cylinder of a door which should never have been unlocked at any time, took it to a locksmith, had a key made, and had the cylinder back in the lock in less than an hour. This allowed the criminals access into the building during the night of the robbery, thus completely surprising those working inside.

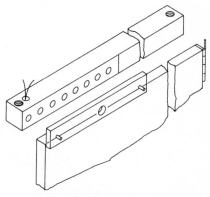

Fig. 30   Magnetic lock.

New techniques in security are developing rapidly, and it is quite possible that newer and more secure methods of locking have become available since this handbook was written. Nevertheless, while this chapter cannot guarantee the elimination of all door security problems, following the concepts expressed here will greatly increase building security.

CHECKLIST

The following checklist should always be used in approaching the security of an opening:

1. Make sure the door and frame are adequate.

2. Select a lock which provides the maximum in security, meets code requirements, and functions to the owner's requirements.

3. Plan the master keying to provide adequate security.

4. Use a key section which is not of the stock type that is easily duplicated by any locksmith.

5. Have one person in complete control of the system and responsible for the issuance of all keys.

6. Have all locks furnished as "construction master keyed," with all keys delivered directly to the owner.

7. Where extra security is required, use special security cylinders with all keys registered and available only from the lock manufacturer.

LIST OF ANSI STANDARDS

Butts and hinges .... ANSI A156.1 1970
Locks and door trim .... ANSI A156.2 1975
Exit devices .... ANSI A156.3 1972
Door control closers .... ANSI A156.4 1972
Architectural door trim .... ANSI A156.6 1972
Template hinge dimensions .... ANSI A156.7 1972
Door controls .... ANSI A156.8 1974

LOCKING GLOSSARY*

ACTIVE DOOR: When two doors are installed as a pair, the active door is the one which must be opened first.

ANTI-SHIM DEVICE: Some spring bolts have this added feature to prevent the spring bolt from being depressed when the door is closed by slipping or loiding (see definition). This device is normally adjacent to the bolt and is depressed by the strike when the door is closed.

BACK PLATE (used on rim locks): The metal plate which enables the rim cylinder to be clamped to the door by the cylinder retaining screws.

BARREL KEY: A key with a round post and having a hole in the end which fits over a pin in the lock; used often for trunks, cabinets, suitcases, and handcuffs.

BIT KEY: A key with a bit projecting from a round shank. This key is similar to the barrel key but has a solid rather than hollow shank. The call-box or old-type skeleton key is a bit key.

BLANK: An uncut key, or the unfinished key as it comes from the manufacturer before any cuts have been made.

BOLT: The fastening element of a lock. It is either manually or electrically operated.

BOTTOM PINS: These are usually made of brass and vary in length to create different combinations. They are tapered at one end to facilitate the "V" cut in the key. When the proper key raises the pin to the correct height, the bottom pins level off at the cylinder plug shear line, allowing the plug to turn and activate the lock or unlock function.

BOW: The handle or head of a key.

BOX STRIKE: A strike which provides a complete housing for the bolt, often giving better protection.

*Source: California Crime Prevention Institute.

CAM: The end piece on a mortise cylinder which is screwed to the plug. This part activates the bolt as the key is turned.

CHANGE KEY: A material or device planned and constructed to operate a specific lock having its own individual combination.

CLEVIS: A metal link for attaching a chain to a padlock.

CODE: An arrangement of numbers or letters by which a key can be cut so it can operate a lock without first having a pattern or the original key. The code can be for either the key or the lock.

COMBINATION:
  - This term denotes the grouping together of cuts on a key, especially when different arrangements are possible.
  - The arrangement of numbers to which a combination lock is set.

CONNECTING SCREW: This screw passes through the back plate to hold the cylinder in place on rim locks.

CORRUGATED KEY: A key made of sheet metal where corrugations are pressed longitudinally into the blade.

CUTS: The indentations made in a key to correspond to the tumblers of a lock, whether square or round.

CYLINDER GUARD: A protective device used to encompass the cylinder of a lock rendering it less vulnerable to wrenching and twisting attacks.

CYLINDER SET SCREW: The set screw prevents the cylinder from turning after installation. Found on mortise and narrow-stile locks.

DRIVER PINS: These are the upper set of pins in a pin tumbler cylinder which, when activated by the springs, project into the plug until raised by insertion of the key.

ESCUTCHEON PLATE: A plate, either protective or ornamental, containing openings for the controlling members of the lock, such as the knob, handle, cylinder, etc.

FACE PLATE (used on mortise locks, tubular locks, and narrow-stile locks):
  - The portion of a lock through which the bolt protrudes and the lock is fastened to the door.
  - The part of a rim lock through which the bolt protrudes.

FLAT KEY: A key made of steel and having no grooves or corrugations. This type of key is used for some safety deposit boxes, locker locks, and cabinets.

HASP: A fastening device consisting of a loop and a slotted, hinged plate.

HEEL: The end of the shackle on a padlock which is not removed from the case upon unlocking.

JIMMY-RESISTANT: This refers to a specific type of lock in common use today. A typical jimmy-resistant lock is a rim type with a vertical-throw dead bolt.

KEY: A material or device providing means for operating a mechanical lock. This usually is accomplished by arranging the barrier passageways into a straight line.

KEYING: Pin tumbler cylinders offer complex keying possibilities. Some of the basic terms are as follows:
  - Individual Key—A key for a specific individual cylinder.
  - Keyed A like—All cylinders may be operated by the same key (not the same as master keyed).
  - Keyed Different—A different key operates each cylinder or group of cylinders.
  - Master Keyed—All cylinders may be operated by a master key, but each cylinder has its own change key which will not operate other cylinders in the system.

KEYWAY: The longitudinal cut in the cylinder plug. These usually have millings in the sides to restrict unauthorized key sections.

LOCK—COMBINATION: In this type of lock, tumblers or barriers are generally made in the form of disks. These disks are rotated by a dial located on the face of the enclosure and having a series of numbers or symbols on its face. Rotation of the dial causes rotation of the control means, which is generally a pin (fly) or some other device on one of the tumblers, which in turn cooperates with another tumbler, and so on. Turing the dial will locate the tumblers, line up the passageways, and permit the traveler to pass through all the tumbler barriers.

LOCK—CHANGE KEY OPERATED: A device for fastening two or more members or objects together which in a locked or fastened condition limits their relative movement or separation. This lock is planned or constructed to be operated by a single change-key combination and includes means, operated by a change key having said individual combination, for operating the device into an unlocked condition, permitting relative movement or separation of the members or objects.

LOCKING DOG: The part of the padlock mechanism which engages the shackle and holds it in a locked position.

LOCK-IN-KNOB: This is a lockset containing the cylinder and lock mechanism in the knob.

LOCK—MASTER KEYED: A mechanical device for fastening two or more members or objects together which in a locked or fastened condition limits their relative movement or separation. This lock is planned and constructed as one of a series or group of mechanical key locks, all of which are operable by a key having the same master key combination, and each of which is operated by a key having a planned individual key combination and a master key having a planned master key combination.

LOCK—PERMUTATION: These locks are key operated. The function of the key is to arrange the barrier passageways into a straight line. The traveler, then, instead of following through a tortuous labyrinth, moves in a straight line through the barrier openings. Locks of this type include pin tumbler locks, lever locks, and disk tumbler locks.

LOCK PICKING (MANIPULATION): The process of operating a lock into a locked or unlocked condition by means other than the specifically planned method (key). This can be accomplished by using lock picks to raise the pins to the proper height while maintaining tension on the plug to overcome the spring tension on the drivers.

LOCK—TUMBLER: These are movable-labyrinth locks which may be divided into two classes—permutation locks and combination locks.

LOCK—WARDED: These are fixed-labyrinth locks. They are made of a housing with an opening (keyhole) to receive a key. The labyrinth may be created in two planes—by wards obstructing the keyway and by internal wards arranged normal to the center line of the key barrel.

LOIDING: The action of slipping or shimming a spring bolt with a piece of celluoid or other thin material, such as a credit card.

MANIPULATION: The process of operating a lock to a locked or unlocked condition by some means other than that planned for opening the said lock.

MANIPULATION KEY: A material or device which may be variably positioned or manipulated in a lock's keyway until such action develops a condition within the lock which enables the lock to be operated.

MASTER KEY: A material or device planned and constructed to operate all locks in a series or group of locks where each has its own individual combination and change key other than the master key for operating that combination only, and where each lock construction is a planned part of the series or group for operation with the master key.

MASTER PINS: Master pins or disks are inserted between the bottom and top drivers to allow for more shear lines and thus set the lock so it can accept more than one key.

MORTISE CYLINDER: A lock cylinder (usually pin tumbler) specifically made for use with mortise locks. They are usually fitted or screwed into the lock housing and held by a set screw.

MORTISE LOCK: A lock placed into a mortise cut in the edge of the door. "Mortise" is both a noun and a verb.

MUSHROOM PINS: These pins are installed in some cylinders in place of some or all of the driver pins to provide increased security against picking.

PADLOCK: This is a detachable lock with a hinged or sliding shackle to press or pass through an eye or staple.

PANIC BOLTS: This type of device provides top and bottom points of fastening connected to horizontal bars for the inside of buildings used for theaters, schools, etc.

PIN TUMBLERS: These are among the most important components of pin tumbler locks and are often referred to by different names depending upon the type of tumblers (bottom pins, master disks, drivers, etc.) involved. Pins are usually made of brass and vary in length. Bottom pins have one end tapered to fit into the "V" cut of a key. It is through the use of varying lengths that the combination of the lock is determined.

PLUG: The round core of a lock cylinder which rotates when the key is turned.

RESTRICTED KEYWAY: A special keyway restricted to such applications as telephone company locks, U.S. mailboxes, or others which are specially ordered by the user.

RIM CYLINDER: A lock cylinder (usually pin tumbler) specifically made for use with a rim lock. Because of the position of the lock, it must be long, have a narrow diameter, and have a tail piece long enough to extend through the door and activate the lock function.

RIM LOCK: A lock made for mounting on the surface of the door. The term "rim" refers to the method of mounting only.

ROSE: That portion of a lock used as an ornament or bearing surface for a knob. It is normally placed against the surface of the door.

SHACKLE: The hinged or sliding part of a padlock that fastens to the staple by passing through the eye or loop that is provided on a door or receptacle that is to be locked. The shackle is then closed and locked so that it cannot be released without using the proper key.

SHEAR LINE: The area between the housing and plug which is normally obstructed by the pins until the correct key is inserted.

SPINDLE: That part of the lock, usually square in shape, which is fitted in the handle or knob and passes through the hub to engage the locking mechanism in a mortise lock.

SPRING BOLT: This type of bolt is spring operated and retracts upon contact with the lip of the strike. It extends into the hole in the strike when the door is fully closed, thus securing the door. It can be withdrawn by turning the inside knob or through the use of a key on the outside when it is locked.

STAPLE: That part of the hasp that receives the shackle of the padlock.

STILE: The vertical members in a paneled door or narrow-stile door.

STRIKE PLATE: A metal plate installed on or in a doorjamb with screws; the bolt or spring bolt of a lock is extended into it.

TAIL PIECE: This part is fastened to the plug of the cylinder and activates the bolt in a rim lock.

TOE: The portion of the shackle that comes out of the padlock case upon unlocking.

TRYOUT KEY: A material or device which may or may not be one of a set of similar devices; each key is made to operate a series or group of locks of the total lock series or group, the key or keys being constructed to take advantage of unplanned construction similarities in the series or group operated thereby.

TUBULAR LOCK: This type has a simple tubular construction consisting of a bolt, a spring bolt with an anti-shim device, and a cylinder on one side with a thumb on the other side.

Chapter 16

Surveillance Cameras

Excerpted from "Selection and Application Guide to Fixed
Surveillance Cameras," published by the U.S. Department of Justice,
Law Enforcement Assistance Administration

THE SURVEILLANCE PROBLEM

When and Where Is Fixed Surveillance Photography Needed? In trying to decide
whether to install surveillance cameras, an individual or firm must first identify and
define the problem at hand. It may be that the problem is not significant enough to
warrant the expenditure required. It may also be that the problem cannot be solved
with photographic surveillance.

Photographic surveillance has only two purposes. The first tangible objective of the
installation is to obtain identifiable photographs of persons engaged in an illegal act.
Such a photograph is presumably used in the apprehension and prosecution of the
criminal, although company policy may limit itself to some other course of action.
The second objective is deterrence. This is more difficult to measure on a cost basis.
There is obviously no way of knowing how many crimes were not attempted because
of the presence of a camera. If one of these two is the objective, fixed surveillance
photography may be necessary.

The Bank Protection Act of 1968 provided for the establishment of security
measures for banks and other financial institutions for purposes of identification and
apprehension of those committing criminal acts. Although the act does not require
the installation of surveillance cameras, their use is encouraged. Retail establishments
of smaller size may find a similar incentive for the use of surveillance cameras, and
insurance rates may be lower.

Cost will usually be a significant consideration. Generally speaking, as with most
equipment, the more sophisticated and effective the system needs to be, the more it
will cost. Obviously, it is not cost-effective to spend more on a surveillance system than
it will save.

Based on loss history and the vulnerability of the situation, one can determine if
there is a realistic need for surveillance equipment.

Applications Each site considered for surveillance, whether it be a retail store,
bank, parking lot, warehouse, loading dock, or building entrance, has its own unique
and specific requirements which can vary according to the objectives established. The

type of site to some extent determines the application of fixed surveillance photography, although there can be an overlap of applications. For instance, a surveillance system set up in a retail store to thwart shoplifters may also record the events in a robbery, or a surveillance system protecting loading docks may uncover theft by employees.

THE EQUIPMENT

Types of Photography

Still Photography   A good photograph of a crime being committed can be of great value. Certainly such a photograph constitutes dramatic evidence in court. For this reason still photography is the standard method of surveillance for anticrime applications, since it produces the clearest photographs.

A large selection of equipment types, makes, and film sizes, from 8 mm to 70 mm, is available for still surveillance photography. Most can be set to operate on either a continuous or demand basis, and some have the capability of increasing the rate at which photographs are taken when signaled to do so. If security needs include protection against bad-check passers, cameras are available that automatically photograph a person as his or her check is stamped at the teller's window.

Motion-Picture Photography   Motion pictures capture more information than still photographs because more pictures are taken. However, any single frame of motion-picture photography will normally make a poorer print than a still photograph because of subject motion. Surveillance motion-picture cameras with higher shutter speeds, unfortunately, require higher light levels.

Operating costs are greater for motion-picture cameras than for still cameras of the same film size, since more pictures are taken. Initial equipment costs, too, can be higher.

Most experts in surveillance photography recommend still photography unless there is an unusual requirement—a highly talented shoplifter, for example, who cannot be convicted by other means. A still camera which normally operates at a slow rate but can be speeded up on demand, may be a better choice.

Television   Television provides a highly flexible method of surveillance. It can be adapted to almost any requirement, whether continuously attended or automatic. The output may be taped and studied later, and this tape may be erased and re-used for a cost saving. Through the use of remote-control devices, recorders, and still-photography adapters, television surveillance may be used to guard against pilferage, armed robbery, burglary, unauthorized entry—in short, nearly anything. Its output is immediately available, so that there is no uncertainty about whether the exposure was correct or whether the equipment worked. This type of surveillance has a significant advantage to offer over photography: for example, it can assist in apprehending a shoplifter in the act.

There are many variables involved in planning a television surveillance system, particularly from a cost standpoint. The versatility of the system and its final effectiveness depend upon how much is put into it. Some of these variables are:

1. If the output is not taped, equipment costs will be lowered, but the system will not provide any evidence for prosecution.

2. If one person is not specifically assigned to watch the monitor, personnel costs will not be a factor (the monitor, for example, can be placed in the manager's office and watched at random). Obviously, taking this cost shortcut means there will be a chance of missing a shoplifting or employee theft in progress.

3. Personnel costs will vary tremendously depending on how many guards are assigned to watch how many monitors. In large buildings with a full-time door guard

on duty anyway, costs may be insignificant, but the owner of a small store may not be in a position to hire someone just to watch one or two television screens all day.

One drawback to television surveillance which is taped but unattended is that someone has to play back the tape and watch it. Eight hours of tape recorded in the back room to pinpoint employee theft will have to be monitored intently for eight hours. In antirobbery installations, of course, this disadvantage does not occur—the investigator knows which part of the tape to replay. Still photographs can be checked in a hurry, and even motion pictures can be rapidly viewed (at three to five times the camera's filming speed).

Another major disadvantage to television surveillance is that although still photographs can be taken from the monitor, picture quality is not as good as that from still cameras. When a requirement of the surveillance system is to obtain evidence to support a prosecution, this drawback alone may be enough to rule out television.

If you believe that television offers the best solution to your surveillance requirements, it is worth investigating thoroughly. A complete discussion of these systems is outside the scope of this guide; the above brief treatment may help with the decision whether to pursue the subject further.

Continuous or Demand Operation

Basically, still cameras may be classified as operating either continuously or on demand, but the distinction is not a firm one. Many systems combine elements of both modes.

Cameras which operate continuously are known as sequence cameras. Once started, they continue to operate automatically, taking pictures at predetermined intervals until the film is expended.

Demand cameras, on the other hand, remain inactive until they are actuated by some means. Depending on the application, the camera may then function continuously or it may not. For example, protection against bad-check passers does not require more than a single frame per transaction. Cameras used for such a purpose take one picture at a time, upon demand only.

The basic distinction, however, is frequently blurred. Many makes of equipment can be actuated by a timing device. For example, a sequence camera can be rigged to operate only during business hours where the basic application requires it—robbery or shoplifting are examples. Cameras can be actuated by business alarms, motion detectors, sonic detectors, wireless tramsmitters carried by employees, switches mounted in strategic locations—the list is lengthy and growing. Finally, some sequence cameras have the capability of increasing the rate at which they take pictures upon a demand signal.

Demand cameras, of course, offer a substantial saving in film cost. However, there is a compensating disadvantage: personnel education. Often the camera is started too late, or not at all; even when the employees retain the presence of mind required to activate a demand camera, there may be a risk involved in doing this at gunpoint. The best results from demand cameras are obtained when the personnel are instructed to activate the camera when they first become suspicious rather than waiting until an overt act is committed. This is not only much safer, but photos taken when a criminal is less on guard are likely to be better for identification.

Sequence cameras, operating continuously over a period of time, offer more complete coverage at an obvious added film cost. When the intended use is against pilferage or shoplifting, this cost is fixed; it can, however, be reduced in antirobbery applications by processing only that film expended during the crime. The camera may be set to take pictures at a wide variety of film intervals—one every second, one every 30 seconds, one every minute. A sequence camera does not rely on employee awareness for operation.

Investigation of the various means available for actuating camera sytems or for changing their rate of operation is advisable. If switches for this purpose must be hidden for employee protection, many means can be used. There are also switches that, beyond being hidden, require no overt act for their operation—such as a switch inside the cash register that closes when a stack of currency is removed.

CAMERA FILM

Choosing a Film Size

Four sizes of film are generally used in surveillance cameras: 8, 16, 35, and 70 mm. The equipment using the smaller film sizes is generally less expensive.

Analysis of many bank robbery photographs has shown that 35- and 70-mm cameras generally produce the best pictures for use in subject identification; obviously, the larger the image on the film itself, the clearer an enlarged print will be. When properly installed and properly lighted and adjusted, however, 16- and 8-mm cameras can produce good photographs. For example, a 35-mm will record a subject's face on film roughly 2½ to 3 times larger than a 16-mm camera will, if both cameras are set to cover the same area. If the 16-mm camera is set to cover a proportionately smaller area, the image will then be the same size. Moreover, some types of 16-mm camera systems are designed to use film without sprocket holes, allowing an image area to be nearer the size offered by 35-mm film.

The major consideration is the size of the image on the film; it must be large enough to do the job intended. Small images yield very poor detail; if the end object of the surveillance system is convincing a jury that a photograph and a defendant possess the same face, detail is very important. Small details like eyes, ear shape, skin texture, or small scars require a film image large enough to capture them. If the subject is not a stranger, that is, if your problem is employee theft, and only the criminal's identity need be pinpointed, photographs of much less clarity will serve. However, studies have shown that for identification of total strangers, a photograph must show details approximately 3 mm (⅛ in) in size.

Assuming a resolving power of 80 lines per millimeter, a typical film resolution capability, it is possible to calculate the largest area of camera coverage that can be reduced to an image the same size as the film and still provide the necessary 3-mm detail. (See Fig. 1, with its accompanying tabular material, which presents this maximum area coverage for some of the more common film sizes.) If the image on a given film size is from a smaller area of coverage, the detail will be improved. These areas of coverage provide the upper limit of usefulness for a given film size if photographs for identification purposes are to be obtained. The actual field of view (the area "seen" by the camera) that will be included in the image on the film is totally dependent upon the distance to the subject and the focal length of the camera lens. The proper selection of a camera lens for specific surveillance applications will be discussed in detail later in this chapter. The calculated coverage represents high-quality camera systems that are capable of producing top-quality identification photographs. Many systems will not meet these specifications; very few will exceed them. Some will meet these performance levels only through the use of slow film requiring higher and more uniform light levels on the subject's face. Salespeople who claim substantially better performance for their company's products should be asked to produce pictures, taken on your premises, of people that you do not know. Such identification tests are the only true method you have of evaluating equipment manufacturers' claims. (See Fig. 2 for relative quality of images.)

If a photograph cannot be used, the camera system that took it is not usable. If it is essential to cover a counter 5 m (16 ft) wide, for example, it is simply not realistic to attempt it with a single 8-mm camera. As stated above, the smaller film sizes *can* produce good pictures, but only if they are used for covering a small area. If compensation for this small coverage must be made, it must be made by installing more cameras.

Types of Film Available

As indicated, types of film used in surveillance photography vary from 8- to 70-mm sizes. Some are available in instant-load cartridges and some are not. Some offer an

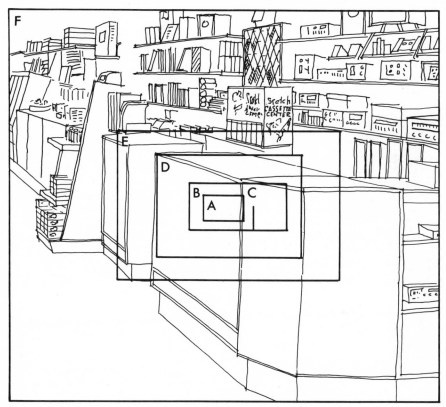

Fig. 1 Area coverage of common film sizes for ⅛-in (3.18-mm) subject detail:

Film size	Image size, mm	Height coverage		Width coverage	
		m	ft	m	ft
A—Super 8 mm	4.2 × 5.8	1.03	3.4	1.46	4.8
B—16 mm	7.4 × 10.3	1.89	6.2	2.62	8.6
C—16mm, unperforated	7.4 × 15.0	1.89	6.2	3.81	12.5
D—35 mm	17.0 × 24.0	4.33	14.2	6.09	20.0
E—35 mm, double frame	24.0 × 36.0	6.09	20.0	9.14	30.0
F—70 mm	60.0 × 70.0	15.24	50.0	17.77	58.3

enlarged image through elimination of the conventional sprocket holes. All these factors should be considered early, because film requirements may dictate equipment requirements if only one type of camera can be used with the type of film necessary.

It should also be noted that some films are compatible with the reader-printers used in some businesses for microfilm viewing. With a reader-printer, use of a film that can be quickly shown and copied on it may be a real time and money saver, particularly in employee theft cases.

Also, film is available for processing to either a positive or negative image. Negative processing is cheaper and requires less accurate exposure, making it better for installations where the light level varies. It is preferred where copies of the photograph are required.

In positive film, the film image is the same as in a photographic print (dark is dark, light is light). In applications such as employee theft, where the photograph is intended for the owner's use only and no copies will be made, positive (also called reversal) film may be a good choice.

The film used in surveillance photography is normally black and white. Color film is not widely used because of its higher cost, critical lighting requirements, and more expensive, complex, and time-consuming processing. These disadvantages are usually not offset by any greater ease of apprehension or conviction. Although there may occasionally be an application where color film could be of value, such applications are so rare that the discussion here is limited to black and white photography.

a   b   c

Fig. 2   Image quality. (a) Good; (b) poor; (c) unacceptable.

The film speed required for a specific camera should also be considered. Most of the cameras using the smaller film sizes have lenses which permit the use of relatively slow-speed film, which normally has small grain size and good resolution. Cameras using the larger film sizes, however, may have lenses that require the use of high-speed film, which is often more grainy and therefore lacks the resolution of the slower-speed film. Once again, potential users should have photographs taken on their premises in order to see the quality of pictures that can be expected from a given film.

Handling and Storage

The characteristics of any given film change with age. Aging effects include change in speed and fogging, both of which can be reduced through proper storage. Good storage conditions include temperature no higher than 21°C (70°F) and relative humidity below 50 percent. Most users of film who keep a great deal of it on hand store unused film in a refrigerator, with the precaution that film containers that have been refrigerated should remain at room temperature for at least 3 hours before being opened and used.

Needless to say, film storage areas should be free of dust, chemicals, fumes, radioactivity, and other pollutants. Whereas dust may not have any effect on a normally sealed container, chemical fumes, such as ammonia or sulfur dioxide, x-rays, or unnecessary heat can fog films even before the package is opened.

Processing

Exposed film should be processed as soon as practical. A certain amount of image is lost if the interval between exposure and processing becomes too long; in surveillance applications, this latent image loss may be critical to subject identification. Exposed film, like unexposed film, should be stored at low temperature and low humidity and in a clean environment.

Before deciding on a certain brand of film, it is important to determine who is going to process it. The answer may influence the choice of film. If processing is not available at a reasonable cost for a particular brand of film, it may be impractical to use that brand.

If a crime has occurred, law enforcement agencies usually prefer to process the film themselves because it simplifies courtroom procedure. If a federal crime has occurred or is suspected, the FBI will want to process the film. In any case, it is not wise to turn the film over to an independent processor until the authorities arrive.

In cases where a great deal of surveillance film is regularly used, it may be practical to consider the purchase of equipment to process one's own film. These cases are unusual, however, for equipment costs can represent a significant investment, and trained processing personnel are required. A decision to process one's own film can only be based upon careful analysis of all costs or other benefits relative to the expense of purchasing such services.

THE INSTALLATION

Camera Location Considerations

The location of a surveillance camera must be carefully planned so as not to waste funds spent on its purchase and installation. This chapter will discuss some things to be considered in determining camera location. The floor plan shown in Fig. 3 illustrates a possible camera layout.

In many installations a simple choice must be made at the beginning: Is it desired that the camera be visible or hidden? To put it another way, is the objective to convict or deter? As in many other areas, there is no clear line here; visible cameras can succeed and have succeeded in convicting felons, both those who did not notice the cameras and those who did. Generally, visible camera locations are selected for the deterrent value they offer, however difficult it is to measure. Shoplifters, holdup men, tempted employees are not likely to commit a crime in front of a camera they can see. A very visible camera installation is commonly used in routine check-cashing transactions; the equipment and various notices around it can cut bad-check losses significantly.

On the other hand, if the objective is to convict the unwary, a hidden camera location may be preferred. Hidden installations are used for combating burglary (a complex subject, as noted earlier, which this chapter does not cover) and in many situations involving employee theft. Hidden installations are not numerous, because most shopkeepers would prefer to prevent a crime rather than go to the effort of prosecuting someone who has committed one, particularly an employee. Another important factor is cost; in order to hide the camera, it is first necessary to buy something to hide the camera in. Furthermore, such an enclosure will probably have to be soundproof as well. Decorative fixtures, domes, and one-way mirrors are commonly used for this purpose.

Another consideration important to site selection is the sun. Beyond the characteristics of normal overall lighting, the sun presents a special problem: the light it provides is variable. A good light situation in the morning may deteriorate into an

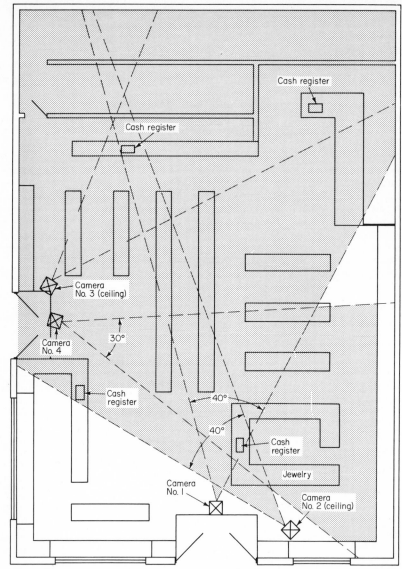

Fig. 3   Optimum camera locations.

impossible glare in the afternoon. Furthermore, if a camera's lens opening is set to depend on sunlight, the results obtained on a dark day may be worse than poor—they are likely to be useless. In many cases, it becomes necessary to screen out the sun all the time to permit good surveillance photographs to be exposed. In other cases, it may be necessary to obtain an automatic exposure-control device.

In some cases, particularly with the smaller film sizes, it has been found advantageous to place cameras over exits. This permits narrow-angle coverage of an area where a subject must approach the camera directly and at a time when he or she may be comparatively off guard, even in the process of removing a disguise before stepping out onto the street. In bank surveillance applications or other places where the likely crime is armed robbery, the victim does not have to activate the camera until the subject has left the counter. This approach, however, frequently does not produce better surveillance; it is generally used as a cost cutter (fewer cameras, intermittent expenditure of film). In what is becoming a well-told story, one defendant shrugged off such a photograph with the remark, "So? You have a picture of me leaving the bank." Where good surveillance is a major need, cost-cutting efforts may prove self-defeating. If the surveillance is needed, whatever is required to do a thorough job must be purchased, and sometimes continuous filming may be a necessary expense, particularly if it would be dangerous to have employees activate a demand camera.

And finally, although it would appear that a camera mounted at the highest possible location will see more, this is not the case. Persons photographed from this height may not be recognizable, and high camera locations sacrifice a great deal of floor area coverage. A good spot is one just high enough to see over the obstacles, as well as high enough to afford protection for the camera itself.

Lens Selection

For a given camera-to-subject distance, lens focal length determines image size—the longer the focal length, the larger the image. Experience with surveillance cameras has shown that a facial image on a photograph should be at least 1 in high for ready identification, and this dictates image size on the film. In order to get a film image which will produce the 1-in facial image print required, the lens focal length should be about $\frac{1}{300}$ of the distance from camera to subject. Another rule of thumb, a little easier to use, is that the subject distance in feet should not exceed the lens focal length in millimeters. Thus, if your subject distance is 12 m (40 ft), a lens of at least this length in millimeters should be used. In this case, a 50-mm lens is the next standard size available. Unfortunately, if a long focal length is required for good subject detail, the area covered in the picture will be reduced. This fact may force a compromise in image detail or the use of a larger film size than anticipated.

The nomographs on Figs. 4 and 5 provide a simple method for tailoring a lens choice to a particular width coverage. Using a straightedge, connect the subject width to the subject distance in Fig. 4. On the diagonal line in the center of the chart, the straightedge will intersect a particular coverage angle. Proceed to Fig. 5 and connect this angle with the film size being used; the straightedge will intersect a lens focal length along the right column. This is the size which can be used to achieve the desired objective; if the focal length indicated is not available, the next larger size of focal length can be used, but it should be remembered that a longer lens will result in less subject coverage.

Variable-focal-length lenses (zoom lenses) can be set to any desired focal length within their range. They are useful for testing camera locations and can be highly valuable when used with equipment which must be moved periodically. For most fixed installations, these zoom lenses are unnecessarily large, expensive, and limited in maximum aperture (f stop).

Lens Aiming and Focusing

Aim and focus of the camera lens are accomplished by methods varying with the camera manufacturer. In some, these factors can be checked from the floor without touching the camera. Other equipment can be aimed from the front. You should expend several rolls of film during the initial installation to ensure that aim and focus are correct.

Proper aim is critical. A 3° aiming error can, for example, result in a loss of 25 percent of the usable viewing area. The final setting depends on many factors such as camera height, film format, anticipated subject height, and required depth of focus.

Aim, once obtained, should not be disturbed unnecessarily. Some camera systems

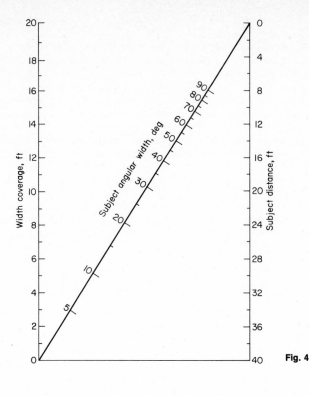

Fig. 4

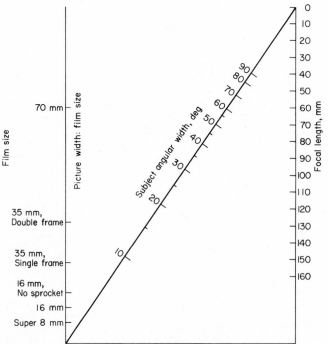

Fig. 5

Figs. 4 and 5   Lens selection charts.

may require that the camera be taken off its mount to reload film. In general, the simplest method of reloading (some types of film are available in quick-change cartridges) that results in the least camera disturbance is the best. If it is necessary to remove the camera frequently, special quick-release mounts are available that maintain camera aim very precisely.

The best method of setting and routinely checking the camera aim is to examine the photographs that result.

Remember to take depth of field into account when focusing. One cannot focus on very close objects and very distant objects at the same time; it may be necessary, for example, to sacrifice sharp focus at the end of the floor in order to obtain sharp focus directly in front of the door.

Similarly, it is important to consider the factor of image blur caused by movement of the person being photographed. If an individual moves from side to side in front of the lens, the image will also move during the exposure, resulting in a blurred photograph. However, if he or she moves toward or away from the lens, there is relatively little side-to-side motion of the image, resulting in a reasonably sharp image. When selecting the camera location and aiming it, one should try to pick viewing angles that look along the natural path of movement, rather than across it.

Lighting and Exposure

With today's high-speed films, particularly considering the high level of illumination commonly used in retail establishments, there is usually enough light to permit good photographs. But sufficient light is not the only consideration; identifiable photographs will depend more on variation in the light level and the direction from which the light comes.

Photographic equipment is adjusted for efficient operation at a specified light level. If this light level changes a great deal during the day, photograph quality deteriorates. This deterioration begins when the light level becomes double or half the level for which the camera was set. The usual culprit is the sun.

The human eye does not react in the same way to light changes as the surveillance camera, because the eye has an automatic exposure control, and cameras used in surveillance work generally do not. For this reason you cannot trust the eye to judge light-level variations; a light meter is required.

The direction of light must be considered too. Normal lighting in a retail store is primarily from the ceiling. In narrow aisles with dark floors, this may result in deep eye, chin, and cheek shadows. Such photographs may not bear any resemblance to the subject. Here again, the sun may create problems if it comes in a window in the afternoon and casts glare into the cameras.

Both difficulties—light variation and light direction—can be overcome, but it is possible that the entire lighting characteristics of the store may have to be changed. Sunlight can be blocked out or overpowered by artificial light. Lights placed high can be supplemented by showcase lighting below face level. Light-colored floor coverings, wide aisles, display counters not over waist height, and large-area luminous ceiling fixtures all tend to minimize shadows.

Normal background lighting can be supplemented in many other ways, even with infrared lighting. This may be a requirement where hidden cameras are used. Films and equipment are available which use invisible infrared light to good advantage, either constant light or infrared flash.

Maintenance

All the benefits of an expensive surveillance system are lost if the camera does not operate when it is needed, is improperly aimed or focused, or, worst of all, is out of film.

The very minimum periodic maintenance on a surveillance camera is an operational check to ensure that the camera mechanism is free and operative and that the aim and focus are still correct. Though carefully aimed upon installation, cameras can be accidentaly moved during cleaning and film changing. A shutter mechanism that stands unused for months is unlikely to operate satisfactorily when needed.

Film expended in testing operations should never be considered an unnecessary expense. It is a small but vital investment. Neither should false economy be allowed to let the film supply become too low. Three minutes' worth of film at the fastest camera rate is the minimum that most authorities consider prudent. When the camera film supply gets to this point, remove the film and reload. Some cameras are equipped with a means of warning when only a 3-min supply of film remains. If simply throwing unused film away seems wasteful, this film can be used to run any necessary tests. The company manafacturing the equipment will provide recommendations and requirements for periodic maintenance on its particular products, and these should be followed carefully.

HOW MUCH WILL IT COST?

The cost of surveillance camera systems depends on so many variables that this discussion can do little more than deal in generalities. Even when a firm price exists for one aspect of the surveillance market, economic factors, technological advances, and production economies can greatly change the picture within weeks.

If deterrence is the only requirement, easily the most economical product available is an imitation camera. These products, widely available and crafted to look exactly like the genuine article (complete with glowing lights), sell for less than $100. They can be used with scanners that move back and forth through a selected range, thus calling as much attention to them as possible. However, when a real camera is required, variables begin to enter the picture.

The **8-mm camera systems** are generally the least expensive, and they use the least expensive size of film. Most are priced in the $300 to $500 range. For the price of a single 16-mm system it is generally possible to buy three 8-mm cameras. Of course, area coverage must be kept in mind. The 16-mm camera should cover the same area as the three 8-mm installations, and it will then offer film economy.

16-mm camera systems generally run in the $600 to $1,200 range, 35-mm systems $1,000 and up. But again, there is no simple way to compare systems in this general treatment. This is because of differences in design. A system which costs much more initially for a one-camera installation may cost less for additional cameras, because some systems have built-in control boxes in the cameras while others can use one control box to operate as many as five cameras. Either system may be better for individual purposes.

Costs for a television system contain a similar variable. A single vidicon camera can be bought for under $800, but with control and viewing equipment a complete installation may run close to $2,000. With large systems containing several cameras and monitors, $10,000 is not an uncommon figure. Those who purchase very large systems (sixteen cameras, for example) for office and apartment building surveillance will pay around $40,000 for equipment alone.

Camera accessories also bring the equipment cost up. Swiveling scanners, video-tape recorders, check-passer identification units, remote-control switches, emergency speed-up equipment for sequence cameras, hidden "money clip" switches, or burglar alarm tie-in equipment all add value to your system, but all cost money. Depending on the situation and the problem, some will be worth the extra expense, and some will not.

Videotape is expensive, but note that it can be re-used almost indefinitely.

Film cost is a two-part question that involves initial purchase and processing:

Naturally, the smaller the **film size,** the less it costs. Super 8-mm film, for example, costs about one-third as much as 16-mm film, frame for frame—considering both purchase price and processing cost. A potential purchaser should disregard the cost per reel or per cartridge offered by the manfacturer and ask instead about the cost per frame. The figure will be small enough to be expressed more easily in cents per 100 frames. The cost per hour will be a variable, too, depending upon the rate at which the camera is operated. Assuming a system with a film cost of 11 cents per 100 frames, it will cost 26 cents per hour to run it at a sequence rate of once every 15 seconds, but only 9 cents per hour at 45-s intervals. If the camera is used on demand only, film costs become negligible.

Processing costs should be covered carefully with the salesperson before making any decisions. Some systems sold in the past have not lived up to expectations because of disappointment in this area alone. If one buys a system that uses film which can be obtained only from one source and can be processed only at one source, one should investigate carefully the reliability and cost of both the film and the processing arrangements. Some firms have been charged hundreds of dollars on a take-it-or-leave-it basis by surveillance film processors for handling a single roll of film late at night.

An estimate of **maintenance costs** will naturally start with a check of the warranty offered with the system, but the service policy must be examined too—assuming that there is one. Some policies are very good and offer routine maintenance at quite reasonable cost, even including free processing of a stated amount of film.

Finally, there are likely to be hidden costs involved in the installation of a surveillance system. Lighting changes, sunlight screening, installation of electrical outlets, structural changes to eliminate blind spots—all these will add to the initial outlay.

MAKING A SITE SURVEY

Once it has been determined that photographic surveillance may be beneficial, a necessary first step is to make a complete survey of the site. This can result in both time saved and a better final installation.

Floor Plan   A site survey is most easily evaluated if it is done on a scale drawing of the floor plan. The drawing should include blind spots, areas of high loss potential (with special emphasis on small items of high unit value), exits, windows, cash registers, electrical outlets, and any other data that may have significance to the particular situation.

Lighting   The next topic is the lighting in the surveillance area. As pointed out earlier, many situations do not require more lighting than exists normally. Using an illumination meter (or a photographic exposure meter of the "incident light" type), measure the light level at significant points on the floor and enter this information onto the site plan. The meter should show a light level of 50 to 75 fc at face level. A photographic exposure meter should be set for a film speed of ASA 250 and a lens opening of $f/2.8$; the light level is adequate if the meter calls for a shutter speed of $1/125$ second or faster. These settings duplicate typical surveillance camera settings.

If daylight enters the area, make meter tests during the brightest part of the day and during the darkest portion of the period when photographs are to be taken. If the light level does not go below 30 to 40 fc or above 150 fc, the variation in level can be tolerated by the film. If the variation falls outside this range, or if the light is constant but low, the system will probably require additional lighting, possibly combined with sunlight screening.

Television systems are more tolerant because compensations can be made electronically at all times by the viewer. In addition, illumination requirements are lower (approximately 20 fc).

If supplemental lighting is out of the question, the supplier can provide information on low-light-level camera systems.

Traffic Flow   Now study the traffic flow over the course of a typical day to discover where the greatest concentration of routes lies. Consider both vehicular and pedestrian traffic, employees, and outsiders—again, all according to the individual situation. If the installation is limited to just a few cameras, this traffic flow study will enable them to be placed more efficiently. The most important route to consider is usually the most likely exit path for the robber.

Surveillance Purpose   Finally, the basic problem for which the system is being considered must always be kept in mind. Shoplifting protection requires surveillance of high-value merchandise, particularly when it is small in size. Robbery protection will call for coverage of such places as tellers' cages, cash registers, or exits. Protection against employee theft usually means placing cameras in back areas where outsiders do not go. Thus, it is obvious that one type of installation cannot always solve every problem, particularly on a tight budget. Concentrate on the most pressing problems first.

After completing the site survey, the potential buyer should be ready to discuss his or her needs with several salespeople, then select and purchase specific equipment for installation. The *Catalog of Security Equipment* (DESP-RPT-0308.00) issued by the National Institute of Law Enforcement and Criminal Justice lists a number of manufacturers of fixed surveillance cameras who will provide product literature, prices, and distributor information upon request. In addition, banks and the police department may be able to suggest local sources of supply.

SOME QUESTIONS TO ASK BEFORE BUYING A SURVEILLANCE CAMERA SYSTEM

1. Has the salesperson demonstrated that the recommended system will produce recognizable pictures of the entire area that needs to be covered?
2. Can the system do double duty—using robbery cameras to photograph check cashers, for example?
3. Who will install it?
4. How can the aim be checked?
5. How is the camera tested for correct operation?
6. Can all adjustments be locked to prevent accidental changes during loading and testing?
7. How does one know that the camera is operating?
8. Is it easy to load film or videotape? Can regular personnel do it?
9. How can one tell that the film is properly loaded?
10. How is the speed of a continuous-acting camera varied if necessary?
11. How can one tell when the camera is almost out of film?
12. What indicates that the camera is out of film entirely?
13. Who is going to process the film? Can it be done round the clock?
14. How long does processing take?
15. How much does processing cost? What about emergency processing?
16. Is there a service contract? How much does it cost, and what does it provide?
17. Is the camera design such that repair must be done by a distant facility?

Chapter 17

Safes, Vaults, and Money Collection Areas

ROBERT A. WILGUS
Market Support Manager, Diebold, Inc.

FROM CAVES TO SAFES

Throughout the ages people have been plagued with the problem of protecting their personal possessions. Early humans availed themselves of the only solution they knew and buried their valuables in the ground or concealed them inside inaccessible caves. As intelligence grew, people came to recognize the need for more definitive security, and there emerged the first crude strongboxes, which afforded greater protection against the limited skills then in use. But such boxes, with their improved resistance to the tools and muscle of the day, served to stimulate the avarice of thieves and to encourage their efforts at overcoming the best among such containers. The development and addition of locks provided a limited deterrent. However, to this day, nothing has ever been invented that can offer absolute assurance that unlawful entry cannot be accomplished.

BURGLARY-RESISTANT MONEY SAFES

Today's chests or money safes have been developed using the experience of past failures and successes to provide very capable resistance against the tools and expertise of would-be criminals.

While a high degree of security is achieved in many of our present money safes, it cannot be assumed that all safes are equally well designed. Since all security is relative, it naturally follows that where the risk is limited, the degree of security will normally be limited too. It obviously is not practical to buy a $3000 money safe to protect $200 or $300. A burglar must make the decision whether to risk his or her continued freedom against (1) a money safe offering a lucrative reward but high resistance or (2) a unit of limited protective capabilities that offers a correspondingly limited return on the skill and time being invested. For this reason, there are money safes available today which will meet different levels of security requirements. Money safes fall into two major categories: those tested and classified by Underwriters' Laboratories, Inc. (UL), and those which have not been subjected to the UL testing standards.

Safes Not Tested by UL

The untested safes, as a general rule, can be expected to afford a lower degree of security against physical attack than the UL-rated safes. The former are usually smaller and quite frequently are designed to be mounted into the floor. (See Fig. 1.)

The walls of floor-installed safes will range in thickness from ¼ in up to 1 in, and the door is usually from under 1 in to 1½ in thick.

Although most of the floor-installed units are unrated, they will for the most part afford a surprisingly good degree of protection in relationship to their cost. This type of safe is used frequently by gasoline service stations, convenience food stores, and similar retail establishments where frequent small cash transactions occur.

Since the safes are mounted in the floor and usually have concrete completely surrounding the body, they become a rather difficult target for would-be burglars; the body of the safe is not exposed and cannot be reached with most attacking tools. Because there is usually limited cash available from this type of store, these safes do not attract the expert safecrackers. There are, however, some practical drawbacks to the use of floor safes. Because they are installed having the door level with the floor, working accessibility may become rather difficult. It also becomes a problem to keep cleaning water and dirt, which may have an adverse effect on the locking mechanism, from getting into the safe. Most unrated money safes are classified for burglary insurance purposes by the Insurance Services Office, with the classification based entirely upon material specifications.

Fig. 1 Money safe designed for mounting in floor. The top of the safe would be flush with the floor level and is machined to accept a protective cover. This type of safe may be equipped with a solid steel door or one having a deposit slot, as this one, which permits putting money into the safe without opening the door.

The lowest classification is "B" (which would result in the highest premium for the insured); safes in this group have a steel door less than 1 in thick and a body of steel or iron less than ½ in thick. Safes one step up the ladder would be classified as "C" and would have a steel door at least 1 in thick and a body made of steel at least ½ in thick. At the top of the unrated classifications would be the "E" safe, which has a door made of steel at least 1½ in thick and a body of steel at least 1 in thick. Each of the foregoing must be equipped with a combination lock.

The Insurance Services Office provides additional classifications for burglary insurance, with all the remaining classifications requiring the safes to be labeled by Underwriters' Laboratories.

Safes Tested by UL

Underwriters' Laboratories, Inc., is the testing source for burglary-resistant safes generally recognized by the industry. Underwriters' is an independent laboratory operating as a nonprofit organization. Among its objectives are those of investigating and testing various types of safes according to the published UL standards covering requirements for construction and performance.

While Underwriters' Laboratories maintains sound basic requirements for materials used in the construction of safes, the organization's greatest significance lies in the performance testing of the units. Here, actual tests using common burglar tools are carried out by experts intimately familiar with the product being tested to determine whether it can withstand attack.

The material requirements for Underwriters' Laboratories specify steel bodies at least 1 in thick, with an ultimate tensile strength of 50,000 lb/in^2. However, if it can be shown that other material is as good, or better, it may be listed. Some safe manufacturers are now using high-tensile steel in the bodies of safes and are actually providing a better unit with metal of lesser thickness.

The UL classifications take into consideration two basic elements—a time limit, which extends from 15 min to a maximum of 1 hr, and methods of attack, which consist of tools alone, tools in combination with cutting torches, or tools with torches and explosives.

Underwriters' Laboratories works closely with any manufacturer desiring to test money safes for listing under its standards. The group's involvement is, however, confined to the testing and evaluation of the safe. The design, special drill- or torch-resisting materials, and actual fabrication procedures are left to the imagination and ingenuity of the manufacturer.

Fig. 2 Unencased TL-15 money safe equipped with a key-locking dial.

The time element involved in the testing is worthy of some additional explanation, since the testing is actually much more severe than the listed time might indicate. The time for each test is actual test time and does not include such time-consuming activities as moving the necessary test tools to the test site, setup, and other miscellaneous activities incidental to the testing. During the actual test, timing is stopped if the operators stop the testing to examine the progress of their activities. In addition, those conducting the tests have been given a complete opportunity to examine the safe under test, including all drawings of the unit which would indicate the materials used in construction and their position within the safe. The time element is further complicated by the fact that quite a few different tests may be conducted on the same safe. In other words, a safe being tested for a tool-resistant classification may have one test conducted to drive out the lock spindle, another to drill through the locking bolt, another to force the bolt handle, etc. As long as none of the tests exceed the time classification limitations, all of these and more, at the discretion of the testing personnel, may be made.

It is only logical that users of the higher classes of UL-marked money safes benefit by receiving lower rates for their burglary insurance. And while the higher classes of safes cost more, it is an expense that is only borne once, while the reduced insurance premiums continue year after year.

At the lower end of the scale of UL-marked burglary-resistant safes would be a tool-resistant safe with a time limitation of 15 min. This classification is commonly referred to as a "TL-15." (See Fig. 2.) This safe must be equipped with a combination lock of at least a Group II classification, must have a relocking device, and must weigh

TABLE 1 SMNA Burglary and Robbery-Resistive Labeled Equipment

SMNA Spec.	Group	UL label	Door	Wall	Lock	Mercantile Safe Policy	Broad Form
UB-1	U1	TXTL60	1½″S ⊙	1″S, P	C	I	G
UB-1	U2	TRTL60	1½″S ⊙	1″S, P	C	I	G
UB-1	U4	TRTL30	1½″S ⊙	1″S, P	C	H	G
UB-1	U5	TL30	1½″E ⊙ ▭	1″E, P	C	F	F
UB-1	U6	TL15	1½″E ⊙ ▭	1″E, P	C	ER	ER
B-1	1	TX60*	1½″S ⊙	1½″S, SC	C	H	G
B-1	1	TR60*	1½″S ⊙	1½″S, SC	C	H	G
B-1	1	X60*	1½″S ⊙	1½″S, SC	C	F	F
B-1	2	**	1½″S ⊙	1″S, SC, CH	C	E	E
B-1	3	**	1½″S ⊙	1″S, SC	C	E	E
B-1	3	TR30*	1½″S ⊙	1″S, SC	C	F	F
B-1	4	**	1½″S ⊙	1″S, P	C	E	E
B-1	4	TR30*	1½″S ⊙	1″S	C	F	F
B-1	5	**	1½″S ▭	1″S, P	C	E	E
B-1	6		1″S ⊙ ▭	½″S, SC, or P	C	C	C
R-1	6		1″S ▭	½″S, SC, or P	C	C	C
R-1	8		1″S ⊙ ▭	½″S	KL	***	—
R-1	9		½″S ⊙ ▭	¼″S	KL	***	—
R-1	9		½″S ⊙ ▭	¼″S	C	B	B
R-1	10		NMT		C	B	B
R-1	10		NMT		KL	None	—
M-1	12	Deposit slot accessible from exterior of container, steel construction					

CODE:

B—Burglary-resistive
R—Robbery-resistive
C—Combination lock
KL—Key lock
P—Plate
E—Steel or equivalent material
▭—Rectangular door
⊙—Round door
UL No.'s—Minutes (TX60, for example indicates Tool and Explosive Resistant for 60 min)
S—Steel
SC—Steel casting
CH—Case hardened

TL—Tool-resistive
TR—Torch- and tool-resistive
NMT—No minimum thickness
†—Insurance Services Office and Mutual Insurance Rating Bureau
TX—Explosive- and tool-resistive
U—Underwriters' Laboratories
UL—Underwriters' Laboratories
UL—Burglary
*—No longer manufactured
**—UL Label for relocking device only; SMNA label for unit
***—Coverage available if SMNA-labeled

NOTE: Burglary-resistive equipment is designed of laminated or solid steel. "Laminated steel" is defined as two or more sheets of steel, with the facing surface bonded together with no other material between the sheets. It is designed to prevent burglaries, which are defined as forcible entry after premises are closed.

Robbery-resistive equipment is designed to protect property in the possession of the custodian. Such equipment includes robbery-resistive safes, cages, alarms, bullet-proof glass, and others. Robbery is defined as violence or the threat of violence used against an individual with the intent of taking property or other valuables.

SOURCE: Safe Manufacturers National Association.

at least 750 lb or be equipped with anchoring devices and instructions for securely anchoring in larger safes, in concrete blocks, or in the building where it will be used. This safe must withstand, during its testing, attacks using common hand, mechanical, and portable electric tools. Grinding points and carbide drills are also used, but not devices used to apply additional pressure, rotary saws, or abrasive wheels. The attacks are confined to the door. The TL-15 safe will qualify for the Insurance Services Office rating of "ER" under both Broad Form and Mercantile Safe insurance.

The next higher classification is the "TL-30" (tool-resistant safe, 30 min). All the requirements used for the TL-15 must also be met by the TL-30, and in addition magnetic drill presses, abrasive wheels, and rotating saws may be used during the testing. A TL-30–marked safe will entitle the user to a class "F" insurance rate for either Broad Form or Mercantile Safe insurance.

During the testing of TL-15 and TL-30, the safe is considered to have met UL

TABLE 2   SMNA Fire-Resistive Labeled Equipment

Product classification	SMNA spec.	SMNA class.	UL rating	Test feature
Fire-resistant safe	F 1-D	A	Class 350—4-hr	Impact
Fire-resistive safe	F 1-D	B	Class 350—2-hr	Impact
Fire-resistive safe	F 1-D	C	Class 350—1-hr	Impact
Insulated filing device	F 2-ND	D	Class 350—1-hr	No-impact
Insulated filing device	F 2-ND	E	Class 350—½-hr	No-impact
Insulated record container (ledger file)	F 1-D	C	Class 350—1-hr	Impact
Insulated record container	F 2-D	C	Class 350—1-hr	Impact
Insulated record container	F 2-D*	Class 150	Class 150—4-hr	Impact
Insulated record container	F 2-D*	Class 150	Class 150—2-hr	Impact
Insulated record container	F 2-D*	Class 150	Class 150—1-hr	Impact
Fire-insulated vault door	F 3	6-hr	Class 350—6-hr	—
Fire-insulated vault door	F 3	4-hr	Class 350—4-hr	—
Fire-insulated vault door	F 3	2-hr	Class 350—2-hr	—
Fire-insulated file room door	F 4	1-hr	Class 350—1-hr	—

NOTE:

Class A	protects paper records from damage by fire (2000°F) up to 4 hr.
Class B	protects paper records from damage by fire (1850°F) up to 2 hr.
Class C and D	protects paper records from damage by fire (1700°F) up to 1 hr.
Class E	protects paper records from damage by fire (1550°F) up to ½ hr.
Class 150	protects EDP records from damage by fire and humidity for rated period.
The Drop (or Impact) Test	The Drop (or Impact) Test is used to determine whether or not the fire resistance of a product would be impaired by being dropped 30 ft while still hot. Fire-resistant equipment is designed specifically to resist fire and consists of a metal shell filled with a fire-resistant insulation.

*Impact tested unloaded.
SOURCE: Safe Manufacturers National Association.

requirements if the door cannot be opened or a hand hole of not more than 6 in^2 cannot be made through the door. From the tool-resistant safes, the UL classifications move on to encompass additional attacks using oxy-fuel gas cutting or welding torches. The torch- and tool-resistant safe with a 30-min time element is the next higher classification. This classification is identified by the "TRTL-30" mark (torch- and tool-resistant, 30 min). Any of the test methods previously covered may be used in attacks on the TRTL-30, plus oxy-fuel gas torches. Tool attacks are limited to the door of the safe, and the torch attacks are confined to the door and front surface. A successful attack would be one which opened the door of the safe or which created an opening in the door or front surface of at least 2 in^2.

A safe that is marked TRTL-30 would qualify for an "H" classification in Mercantile Safe insurance and a "G" classification in Broad Form insurance.

In addition to the aforementioned units, Underwriters' Laboratories has established standards for two other classifications of money safes; however, neither of these classifications is in production at the present time for the general public. The two classifications are the torch- and tool-resistant safe for 60 min ("TRTL-60") and the torch-, explosive-, and tool-resistant safe for 60 min ("TXTL-60"). On either of these classifications, the mechanical tools, except carbide drills and abrasive cutting wheels, may be used anywhere on the safe during the testing. Carbide drills and abrasive cutting wheels may be used on the door, locking components, and front face of the safe only. Torches may be used on any part of the safe during testing for TRTL-60, and torches and explosives likewise may be used anywhere during the TXTL-60 testing. In order to be marked by UL, the safe must not have had its door opened during the test period of 1 hr, nor may a hole of 2 in^2 or more be made anywhere in the body which would permit "fishing out" of part of the contents after introducing water into the body of the safe.

Safes marked TRTL-60 and TXTL-60 both qualify for class "G" Broad Form insurance and for class "I" Mercantile Safe insurance.

FURTHER SUGGESTIONS FOR IMPROVING PROTECTION

While the actual design and construction are of great importance in selecting a proper money safe, there are other significant considerations with regard to providing better security for cash and other negotiable valuables. Here are some suggestions for achieving better burglary protection.

1. The first recommendation is to use a safe specifically designed for the protection of money. The unit should preferably be encased in steel-clad block of reinforced concrete and should have the UL mark (label). Obsolete varieties of money safes or record safes should be avoided. Record safes, even those with UL labels, are for fire protection only and will not afford adequate security against a competent burglar.

2. If the type of business and the building design permit, the safe should be positioned where it is easily seen by passers-by from the street. The front window of a store is very desirable, since most burglars find working conditions in this area rather unsatisfactory. Hiding a safe in the back of the store or in a secluded area creates ideal conditions for burglars and invites their attacks.

3. The safe must be properly installed by having it anchored securely to the floor so it cannot be easily moved. Some burglars are quite ingenious, so adequate steps should be taken to prevent them from moving the safe to an area where it can be worked on in secluded safety.

4. Always try to provide an unobstructed view of the safe through the window. A store that plasters the window in front of the safe with posters and signs is inviting attack. A store with its window covered might just as well have the safe in a storage room.

5. When the sun goes down, lights must come on. There should always be at least one, and preferably two, bright lights trained on the money safe all night long. Burglars do not like to work under these conditions, so the lights must stay on all night.

6. Another essential is a good alarm system which includes protection of the safe. There are only a few things that burglars can do to a safe. They can move it, pound on it, drill it, or burn it. The preceding four attacks encompass the use of explosives, inasmuch as it is necessary to either drill or use a torch before introducing the explosives. The alarm should provide protection against any of the preceding and should also be one that cannot be turned off without proper authority.

7. Local law enforcement officials should be taken into one's confidence. They are there for one purpose only—to help, so there is no point in trying to be a lone wolf. The owner of a safe must show them where it is, let them know it is anchored to the floor, and explain that a light should always be on after sundown. Officers should be asked to investigate if these conditions are not maintained or if the windows are suddenly covered.

8. One last suggestion: avoid the old-timer. Most of the old safes look like real fortresses; they are usually built with massive doors and walls, but they offer little challenge to the modern well-equipped, well-trained burglar.

ARMED ROBBERY

So far, we have confined our discussion to protection against burglary. Of equal or greater significance is the hold-up or armed robbery. Before investing in a money safe that will provide only burglary protection, consider seriously the few simple steps that can add security against the armed robber. This protection is accomplished by making the money in your safe inaccessible to robbers.

In many of our larger retail establishments, two distinct categories of money may be on hand in sufficient magnitude to encourage armed robbery attempts. The first category obviously is the receipts that are taken in during the normal course of business. These will consist of both cash and checks. Most safe manufacturers provide safes equipped with inner compartments in which money may be deposited but cannot be removed except under conditions which are favorable to the user. This is accomplished by having a depository slot (equipped with an inner baffle to prevent fishing) cut in the upper section of the inner compartment. (See Fig. 3.) The receipts may be removed from the compartment only by opening a door controlled by two keys, only one of which is kept on the premises. The other key remains in the custody of an armored car service. Only when both keys are present can the door be unlocked and the receipts removed. If an armored car service is not used, a delayed-action time lock may be installed on the door which requires a waiting period of usually 15 min to elapse before access can be gained to the compartment. Once the time-delay period has elapsed, the lock will provide a permission period of, usually, 3 to 5 min, during which time the door may be opened. At the expiration of the permission period, the timer automatically relocks the lock. This prevents the compartment being inadvertently left unlocked by a forgetful user.

The second category of cash that may be on hand is money delivered to the store for use in their normal transaction of business. This must also be protected against robbery but should be kept in a separate compartment where the establishment may have access to it on demand. This can also be accomplished by using another delayed-action time lock on the door.

Both the delayed-action time lock and the dual keylock provide security against robbery by denying access to the area where money is stored for a period of time during which the robber cannot afford to wait.

Using safes equipped with inner compartments utilizing dual-control locks or delayed-action time locks requires some basic precautions by the user of the equipment. First, these devices are of no value if cash is allowed to accumulate in cash registers where it becomes readily available to the robber. Limits should be established restricting the cash which may be maintained in the register and a program instituted whereby the registers are regularly stripped of the excess.

Second, it is always a good idea to have some cash available in the safe that can be given to a robber. In this way the criminal can satisfy his or her objective and still not be frustrated to the point of violence. Safes using inner compartments requiring two

Fig. 3.   TL-30 money safe encased in reinforced concrete block. Inner compartment at right-hand side equipped with lock requiring two keys for opening. Next compartment to left has delayed control timelock.

keys or delayed-action time locks should always be equipped with a sign prominently mounted on the safe and clearly pointing out that these devices are in use and that access cannot be gained to the inner depository area of the safe.

Safes can also be equipped with key-locking dials or key-locking handles for additional security or convenience.

The key-locking dial can be used in areas where dual responsibility is desired. Since the combination of the safe cannot be dialed until the dial is unlocked, one person may be entrusted with the dial key and another with the combination. Under these conditions, both must be present before the safe can be opened.

The key-locking handle is primarily a convenience to permit access to a safe during working hours. The combination lock is unlocked at the start of the day, then during the remainder of the work period access can be gained by using the key to unlock the handle. At the conclusion of the working period, the safe should always be locked with the combination lock.

BULLET-RESISTING ENCLOSURES

The sharp upward trend in armed robberies has led to increased usage of bullet-resisting enclosures by many operations where large amounts of cash or other negotiables are on hand. These specially constructed rooms or enclosures are effective in operations where the safe cannot be positioned in the front of the building in full view from the street. And, even in areas where this is possible, there may be good reasons to install this equipment.

Basically, a bullet-resisting enclosure consists of an area which is separated from the rest of the business-transacting floor but still permits person-to-person contact with customers. The secured area protects the working staff engaged in handling cash from outside assault by using bullet-resistant glazing to separate the employees and money from the public. Voice contact is maintained by utilizing properly designed speaking apertures that prevent the insertion of firearms which could be aimed at the persons inside the enclosure. (See Fig. 4.)

Documents and money may be readily passed between customer and employee by deal trays, and larger devices permit passage of money bags and packages without introducing an opening through which firearms could be used. The wall area

Fig. 4   Bullet-resistent enclosure provides security for employees and permits personal contact with customers. Small cash transactions are handled through deal trays, large packages are moved through the package passers.

surrounding the bullet-resisting glazing should be made of bullet-resisting metal. Access into the enclosure by intruders is denied by utilizing an entrance compartment equipped with two interlocking doors controlled from within the enclosure.

While the glazing material and steel should be UL listed, it is also desirable to have the various assemblies themselves properly designed by companies experienced in dealing with security problems and to have these components UL listed. The bullet-resisting material is of little value if the assembled components can be entered from the outside or even dismantled from without.

Bullet-resisting enclosures are normally utilized where numerous cash transactions are conducted or where traffic in drugs or similar commodities is transacted. Some good examples are department stores, supermarkets, gasoline stations, drugstores, motels, and credit unions.

PROTECTION OF RECORDS

Our entire discussion so far has been confined to the protection of money from the attacks of burglars and robbers. However, of equal importance to any business is the safeguarding of valuable records. Without the preservation of records, our business world would come to a complete standstill. The kinds of records and recommended retention periods are far too numerous to list here. However, since fire is probably the greatest cause of lost records, a good rule of thumb is the "after-the-fire need." Every business person should ask the simple question, "If we have a fire today, what records will we need to be in business tomorrow?" After this determination has been made, steps should be immediately taken to place these records in properly rated insulated containers. As with burglary-resistant equipment, Underwriters' Laboratories is the primary source for testing this equipment.

UL Categories and Ratings

For paper records, Underwriters' Laboratories has established the following categories:

    Insulated Record Containers
        Class 350—4 hr (A)
        Class 350—2 hr (B)
        Class 350—1 hr (C)
    Insulated Filing Devices
        Class 350—1 hr (D)
        Class 350—½ hr (E)
    Fire-Resistant Safes
        Class 350—4 hr (A)
        Class 350—2 hr (B)
        Class 350—1 hr (C)

The most commonly used product in the insulated record container category is the 1-hr-rated "C" insulated file. An insulated file bearing this "mark" will have been tested for fire endurance, explosion, and impact. (See Fig. 5.) The most widely recognized example of the insulated filing device category is the Class 350 1-hr "D" file, which has been tested for fire endurance and explosion but not for impact.

In the category of fire-resistant safes, all hourly ratings are readily available. The safe bearing the appropriate UL mark will have been tested for fire endurance, explosion, and impact. (See Fig. 6.)

The testing conducted by Underwriters' Laboratories is very demanding, and the

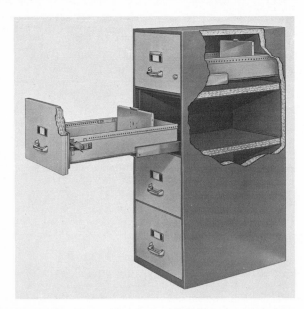

Fig. 5   Insulated file (Insulated Record Container Class 350–1 hour, "C") illustrating insulation in body and drawer head of file.

UL mark attached to the product is the user's assurance that a prototype has been subjected to testing and that during the test period the interior temperature of the unit did not exceed 350°F, the point beyond which paper records may char or burn (See Fig. 7).

The UL fire endurance test involves placing the unit in a furnace with contents consisting of newsprint and coated or uncoated magazine, letter, file, and record-form paper. The test consists of raising the temperature in the furnace, in accordance with the "standard time-temperature curve" from the ambient temperature to the level prescribed for the classification desired (Fig. 8). For 1-hr units, this is 1700°F, for 2-hr units 1850°F, and for 4-hr units 2000°F. Thermocouples placed at critical points inside the safe record the temperature during the test. At the conclusion of the time period for which the unit is being tested, the furnace is turned off. However, the furnace doors are not opened, nor is anything done to alter the natural cooling of the test product. If the temperature does not reach 350°F during the testing period, which includes the cooling time, and the contents are usable, the unit has passed the fire endurance portion of the testing.

In testing for the explosion hazard, the furnace is preheated to 2000°F and the unit being tested is put into it, remaining there for 30 min. If no explosion occurs during this period (20 min for ½-hr-rated units), the unit is allowed to cool and is considered to have passed if examination reveals no other damage.

Fig. 6   Fire-resistant safe Class 350—2 hours, "B." This type of safe is recommended for protection of records from fire only. Only very limited security is provided against a forced entry.

The fire and impact test is conducted by using a new sample which is prepared for testing as in the fire endurance test, except that no temperature-measuring thermocouples are used. With the unit under test in the furnace, the furnace is left on for 60 min in the case of a 4-hr test. The furnace is then shut off, and the test unit is removed and hoisted so that its bottom is 30 ft above a riprap of brick; the unit is then dropped. An elapsed time is permitted, not exceeding 2 min, between extinguishing the furnace and the drop. After cooling, the unit is inverted and returned to the furnace, where it is again subjected to 60 min of fire endurance. After the 60 min, the fire is extinguished and the furnace allowed to cool without opening. After cooling, the safe is opened and the contents examined. If the contents are usable and there is no evidence of undue heat transmission, the test is successful.

Tests for 2-hr and 1-hr units are similar, except that the time element is 45 min for 2-hr units and 30 min for 1-hr units.

It is important to recognize that a fire occurring in one type of building can be more severe and burn for a greater duration than a fire in a building of another type of construction. Most manufacturers of record-protection equipment provide their representatives with devices that enable them to measure this potential hazard for prospective users. Using a safe rated for 1 hr in a building with a potential for a 4-hr fire could result in destruction of the safe's contents during a fire.

Time and temperature, °F

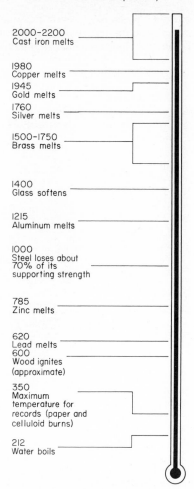

2000–2200
Cast iron melts

1980
Copper melts

1945
Gold melts

1760
Silver melts

1500–1750
Brass melts

1400
Glass softens

1215
Aluminum melts

1000
Steel loses about
70% of its
supporting strength

785
Zinc melts

620
Lead melts
600
Wood ignites
(approximate)

350
Maximum
temperature for
records (paper and
celluloid burns)

212
Water boils

Fig. 7   Melting temperatures of various substances, including paper and celluloid products. *(Source: Safe Manufacturers National Association.)*

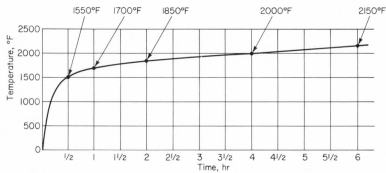

Fig. 8   The standard "measuring stick" for fire endurance. *(Source: Safe Manufacturers National Association.)*

Protecting Computerized Records

The proper protection of records has been made more complicated since the advent of the computer age. Paper records and documents that were formerly protected by a fire-resistive safe may now be on tape, disk packs, or similar storage devices. None of the previously discussed containers can be relied upon to provide any protection for computerized records during a fire. Paper records can withstand temperatures up to 350°F, whereas tapes have a normal limit of around 150°F. A safe or file used to protect paper records will have an interior relative humidity approaching 100 percent during a fire, while the relative humidity should not exceed 85 percent for computerized records.

The problems of providing adequate protection for tapes have been solved by the UL-marked insulated record containers designated Class 150. These units are currently available in 4-, 2-, and 1-hr ratings, with interior components designed to accommodate all the various record forms and microfilm records. (See Fig. 9.)

Record vaults should be considered no better than record safes for protecting computer tapes (a vault is really nothing more than a built-in safe), so if computerized records are maintained in a standard fire-resistive safe or vault, the results could be disastrous in the case of a fire. Since computerized records tend to be more concentrated into a central working area, the peril can be compounded if adequate security steps are not taken.

Dual-Purpose Safes

The various containers considered here have been designed to protect either records or money. One will not do the job of the other. A money safe has very limited capability for protecting paper records during a fire, and a record safe, even though equipped with a combination lock, can withstand only briefly the efforts of a competent safecracker.

New safes have recently been introduced that have successfully passed UL testing for burglary-resistant TL-30 markings as well as UL testing for fire-resistant safes marked Class 350—1 hr. This new breakthrough makes available a single unit that will perform both functions. With the growing concern of business about corporate

Fig. 9 Insulated Record Container Class 150—4 hours. Illustrates the various types of data-recording devices that may be protected. Both inner and outer doors are insulated and sealed with gaskets to reduce penetration of heat and humidity.

espionage, this offers an excellent solution. Those who operate small businesses should also find it a welcome economy measure, since a dual-purpose safe makes it no longer necessary to invest in two separate pieces of equipment. (See Fig. 10.)

Fig. 10   Insulated money safe affords protection against physical burglary attack and also against damage from fire. This particular safe is UL marked as a TL-30 as well as Fire Resistant Safe Class 350—2 hours, "B." Additional holdup protection could be added by using other interior components.

COMBINATION LOCKS

Since most devices involved in physical security are equipped with combination locks, a few tips may be in order.

It is always good security procedure for the owner to change the combination of a new safe to one of his or her own choosing. This is perfectly feasible when the safe is equipped with a key-changing combination lock, which makes it easy to change to a new combination by following the instructions accompanying the safe. It should then become a policy to set a new combination periodically—perhaps once every quarter, or at the very least once annually. In choosing numbers for a combination, easily recognized combinations of numbers, such as license numbers, etc., should be avoided, as should all numbers ending in 5 or 0 and combinations in rising or falling sequence, such as 17 - 34 - 51. After setting a new combination, it should be tried at least three times *with the door open.* If a mistake has been made, it can be corrected. If the door is closed and a mistake has been made, the wisdom of trying it with the door open will be recognized.

After selecting the new combination, the owner should not write it down and leave it in the desk or tape it under the desk, a chair, or some other readily available article. Finally, combinations should be kept secret. The fewer people who are told, the less chance there is of someone else discovering a combination.

Chapter **18**

Security Personnel

TIMOTHY J. WALSH
President, Harris & Walsh Management Consultants, Inc.,
New Rochelle, New York

RICHARD J. HEALY
Head, Security and Safety Department, The Aerospace Corporation

THE MODERN CONCEPT OF A SECURITY GUARD

The building designer seldom thinks of the security guard as an integral part of building design. Frequently, for facilities which require special security, the architect simply suggests to the client that it will be necessary to consider hiring guards when the building is ready to be occupied.

Security guards *are* an essential part of the building's security if the designer considers them as an element in a systems approach to security. A guard can be the *sole* security element or an integrated part of a *total* security system. Finally, there may be occasions when a guard is *not* the most appropriate solution to a security problem. In order to make rational decisions, the building designer must understand the security guard's role as it relates to the whole area of building security.

More money spent on security countermeasures is paid out for the salaries and related payroll costs of guard personnel than for any other single class of security resource. This has historically been true, and even today, despite the change in emphasis on security expenditures caused by the "systems" approach, guard costs remain the chief expense item in most security budgets. Chapter 10, titled "Site Protection," briefly discusses an example of the average cost of one guard post. As guards remain the major focus of security investment, it is important to understand what should be expected from them and what should not.

DUTIES OF A TYPICAL GUARD

The duties and functions of a guard include the discharge of any protection function for which discretion, discriminatory ability, initiative, improvisation, or variability is a requirement. In brief, a guard should be able to perform, and can be trained to perform, all those security tasks for which there is no equivalent substitute for the human being. The following is a suggested summary of tasks which require the services of a guard:

- Judgment and intellect
- Nonmachine types of tasks
- Physical force
  Apprehend
  Direct
  Restrain

Such tasks include interior and exterior patrol; staffing control points for pedestrian and vehicular traffic; monitoring processes; conducting inquiries and preliminary investigations; watching over activities and places; preparing reports and commentaries; restraining and apprehending persons; administering emergency life sustenance and support services; performing rescue and relief functions; transporting persons and materials; and providing information, direction, and general assistance.

Many of the listed functions can also be performed, at least in part, by mechanical equipment rather than human beings. Process monitoring, surveillance, and restraint are among them. At some point, however, with the functions that can be performed in part by equipment, and almost continuously with the other functions, one of the qualities noted earlier as being appropriate for guards will be required.

The first key principle in employment of guards is based upon the distinction between functions which require a human quality and those which do not. *Guard use is indicated in those situations which require one of the enumerated qualities; it is generally not indicated in other situations.*

Traditionally in the protection field, the guard (actually the "watchman," whose stereotype is the tired old man, often with a serious physical disability, nodding sleepily at some gatehouse) has been the standard resource in any protection scheme. It is this indiscriminate use of often inappropriate resources which has led to criticism of and dissatisfaction with security performance. When a guard is used in the incorrect application, three events generally follow: (1) There is no way to demonstrate any relationship between the expense of the security measure and its benefit; (2) the guard does not do the task well, because it does not engage him or her as a human being, and thus grows inattentive (as at an inactive traffic control post)—perhaps missing the very thing for which he or she was assigned; (3) guard morale is lowered, leading to worsened relationships with other elements of the company organization and ultimately to generally lowered performance quality in other guard operations.

DETERMINING QUALIFICATIONS

Because the applications of guard use have so often been wrong in the past, the qualifications required of security personnel have also been wrong. Individuals with serious physical impediments, of advanced age, or with unsuccessful job histories in other work have been hired as guards because such jobs were not attractive and had pay rates that were not usually an inducement to more qualified persons. It was not uncommon (and is still the case in too many places) to find a guard being paid at less than one-half the rate of the lowest-paid nonprotection wage earner in the facility. At such scales it is not really possible to insist upon any specific qualifications because the labor market or pool is not adequate to provide them.

If the rule suggested earlier is followed and guards are employed *only* where the noted qualities are required, fewer guards will be used in most cases, and the real tasks required will be of a higher order of skill. For these reasons better qualified persons will be needed, higher compensation will be paid, and the available labor pool will change. Because of the basic emphasis upon cost-effectiveness in security system design, the increased expense for individual guard personnel will not lead to increased expense for the system as a whole. It is this feature which makes possible the use of appropriately qualified personnel in guard tasks within a properly designed security system.

To identify exactly which qualities and skills are required of guards, it is necessary to compile a very detailed function description of each guard task. This can be regarded as a function or position specification, and it will catalog the particular skills, physical and mental, and the particular qualities, emotional and temperamental, which are necessary to accomplish the assigned tasks.

Specific Rather Than General Job Descriptions

The following four functions are taken from a typical guard job description. They identify, in general terms, the first three of a rather long list of guard tasks:

1. Enforce the system of personnel identification and control at entrances, exits, and gates throughout the premises.

2. Patrol and observe assigned areas for activities of security interest.

3. Check persons and vehicles entering and leaving the premises or other established security areas.

While these statements describe the tasks in general terms, they do not indicate what specific things the guard will do to accomplish them, and hence they do not indicate the required skills. To make employee selection as effective as possible, each of the listed tasks should be broken down into its components, and from each of these should be extracted the ability, skill, qualification, or quality required for its performance.

For example, taking the first listed task, the activity can be broken down into the following components:

Component Tasks

1. Examine identity documents which are in several colors and contain photographs and written descriptions of the holders.

2. Stop inbound and outbound persons until presentation and verification of the correct identity document are completed.

3. Know the varying schedules under which certain classes of persons (as shown by their identity documents) are admitted through certain gates and doors at certain times.

4. Know the appropriate identity document and area coding for all locations on the premises.

5. Observe all persons within visual range at all times on the premises to ensure that they are authorized (as indicated by the identity document displayed) to be where they are.

6. Detain and exercise all lawful control over persons found entering or leaving or upon the premises not in possession or not displaying properly the appropriate identity document.

From the foregoing list of tasks, it is apparent that the following skills and abilities and qualifications will be needed:

Skills and Qualifications

1. Normal visual acuity.

2. Normal color vision.

3. Literacy in the language used on the identification media.

4. Ability to compare and recognize persons and their photographs and physical descriptions.

5. Knowledge of and ability to recall the access control scheme and area authorization codes.

6. Physical capability to use that amount of force legally permissible and required to stop or detain persons.

7. Knowledge of the legally permissible extent to which persons can be detained or restrained when in apparent noncompliance with the identity and control requirements.

A further analysis of the derived qualities and skills suggests that some are physiological in nature (visual acuity and color vision); some are the result of prior general cultural development (literacy, discriminating recall); some are physical or involve physical prowess (the ability to use force); and some require specific training or education in the assigned task (knowledge of the identification scheme, interior facility locations, legal principles governing use of force).

Upon reflection it will be clear that no amount of training will compensate for lack of the physiological or physical prerequisites. It will also be clear that the nature of the training expected to provide the special program knowledge would not be suitable to provide basic literacy.

For most security systems requiring guards, the only practicable training that can be provided is in the specialized job content knowledge. Since the other skills and abilities are required, guards must already possess these when they are assigned.

The breaking down into components thus accomplishes three purposes: (1) It identifies the skills and abilities which guards must possess before they are assigned, (2) it indicates the special job content knowledge they must possess to function after they are assigned, and (3) it identifies the activities relating to the assignment which must be specified in a guard's orders or mission documents and used as the basis for specific training.

GUARD ORDERS AND MISSION DOCUMENTS

Next to inappropriate use or assignment of guards, the most serious problem has been the lack of proper orders or mission statements. A guard, unlike the often higher-paid production worker, is expected to work alone, make independent decisions, improvise, deal on a regular basis with unprecedented or emergency situations, observe everything in the surrounding area rather than concentrate on a limited job task, and assume responsibility for the safety and well-being of other persons and the physical assets of the enterprise. Examined in this light, the true task of the guard is formidable. To make it possible for security personnel to carry out such assignments, every effort should be made by the security system designer or manager to limit discretion, anticipate the unprecendented, and provide at least general rules for guidance in novel circumstances. This can best be done by the preparation and maintenance on a current basis of adequate orders. It is particularly important when the turnover of guard personnel hinders familiarization through actual on-the-job experience.

An adequate order will do the following: (1) Identify and deal with a single subject, (2) distinguish clearly between what is required and what is discretionary for the guard, (3) list every required action in sufficient detail to permit its performance, (4) suggest the areas of discretion and give some guide as to its use, and (5) provide guidance for situations apparently included in the order but not resolvable from its specific content (exception situations).

Writing the Orders

Rather than hurried memos, the guard orders should be carefully considered and skillfully drawn documents. The compilation of tasks and skills will suggest the beginning. A flowchart or sequenced procedural analysis of the task will then suggest what the guard must do and in what priority. Visualizing the anticipated task and even stepping through it or simulating the transaction will help point up aspects of content that might otherwise be missed. When planning the inclusion of a guard in the system, the security system manager or designer should have a concept of the guard's function that is clear enough to serve as the basis of a written order for each task. If the concept is not sufficiently clear, there is not adequate justification for the guard in the design plan. If the order is not written, there will not be adequate performance, even if the design is sound.

PREPARING GUARD SCHEDULES

When the purpose and content of each guard function are clear and the nature of the guard force is evident, the next task is to devise a working schedule of the numbers and distribution of guards. This is often called a *schedule of posts and hours.* It is a matrix which lists on one axis the posts or locations where guards are needed, and on the other axis the days, hours, and numbers required. Table 1 is a representative

TABLE 1   Specimen Schedule of Posts and Hours
The following two schedules are for the same guard assignments. Schedule A is based on the use of an employed force of seven persons with each working five consecutive 8-hr days. Schedule B is cast in terms of hours, not employees.

Schedule A				Day shift*				
Post	Sun	Mon	Tue	Wed	Thu	Fri	Sat	
Supervisor†‡	—	1	1	1	1	1	—	
Main gate	2	2	2	2	2	3	3	
South gate	—	4	3	3	3	5	—	
Reception	—	5	4	4	5	6	—	
Vehicle patrol	5	6	6	6	6	7	5	
Foot patrol	7	7	7	O/T§	4	4	7	

Schedule B	7			Day shift*				Total hours
Supervisor¶	—	8	8	8	8	8	—	40
Main gate	8	8	8	8	8	8	8	56
South gate	—	8	8	8	8	8	—	40
Reception	—	8	8	8	8	8	—	40
Vehicle patrol	8	8	8	8	8	8	8	56
Foot patrol	8	8	8	8	8	8	8	56
	24	48	48	48	48	48	24	288

*Same schedule needed for other two shifts.
†Dash (—) means no scheduled requirement.
‡Numeral represents individual guard employee.
§O/T means overtime by scheduled guards.
¶Numeral means clock hours per post.

schedule of posts and hours. From it will come recruitment levels and labor cost calculations. Note that the material has been prepared in two ways: In Schedule A, for each 8-hr single-tour post, a numeral has been inserted to represent one of the seven employees making up a proprietary or employed guard force. This is necessary because of the 7-day, 24-hr nature of security work and the typical 5-day, 40-hr work week limitation. Schedule B merely shows the total number of worker hours required by each post. This will be useful when planning a guard force to be provided by a contract agency or through the mixed use of full- and part-time personnel.

The proper sequence in the development of guard schedules is:
1. Identify the system functions which require a guard.
2. Develop a comprehensive statement of individual post duties and functions.
3. Determine the days and hours during which those functions must be performed at specific locations.
4. List the specific locations in the vertical axis of the schedule matrix.
5. List days of the week (once for each shift) in the horizontal axis.
6. Insert the required hours or personnel codes for each post under each day during each shift.

HUMAN RELATIONSHIPS

In the previous discussion there has been no indication that police-type duties and qualifications are required. The reason is that security guards are not police officers, and it is a mistake to attempt to have them assume such a role, even though many security operations in the past were organized and operated much like police departments. Typically, such organizations tended to depend on an authoritarian, enforcement-type fear-producing approach for results. This was the attitude of the House of Krupp in Germany in 1872, which was defined as follows: "Whatever the cost, workers must at all times be watched by energetic and thoroughly experienced men, who will receive a bonus whenever they arrest anyone guilty of sabotage, laziness, or spying."*

Security in organizations which were patterened after law enforcement agencies normally consisted mostly of guards, who were the focal point of the protection program. As a result, any protection problem was usually solved through the use of guard personnel. The effectiveness of the operation depended to a great extent on the psychological impact of the guards, and so uniforms, badges, guns, and other accouterments of this type were utilized to give the impression that the guards had authority. Guard personnel in these situations were also often busily engaged in performing police-type duties such as issuing traffic tickets and concentrating on other enforcement-type duties.

Personnel in such organizations usually reacted to problems only after they occurred, depending on the threat of apprehension or the use of force to discourage workers and others involved with the organization from violating the rules of the enterprise. Further, they had a tendency to view everyone with suspicion and distrust, often reacting to problems they encountered by attempting to take disciplinary or corrective action on the spot. The natural result was that troublesome confrontations would develop between the guards and individuals from time to time.

With such an approach to security, employees reacted in a negative fashion to protection personnel, and so they had a tendency not to cooperate with or accept the guard function. Management had a tendency to relegate the guard function to a minor role in the management structure and not give it support, with the result that it operated in what might be described as a vacuum, insulated from the remainder of the enterprise. Because of the negative human relations factors already discussed, as well as the lack of proper qualifications mentioned earlier, an unfavorable public image of the security guard has developed over the years. This was also highlighted in the 1971 five-volume study conducted by the Rand Corporation.‡

*Jacques Bergier, "Secret Armies," Bobbs-Merrill, New York, 1975, p. 19.
‡James S. Kakalik and Sorrel Wildhorn, "Private Police in the United States," 5 vols., report of a study by the Rand Corporation, Santa Monica, Calif.; U.S. Government Printing Office, Washington, DC.

Although an enforcement approach and scare-producing tactics at one time might have had some effect on a work force, management authorities now tend to agree that fear is no longer effective in the motivation of present-day workers.† In spite of the fact that some enterprises still have a tendency to operate the type of guard-oriented enforcement programs already discussed, over the years senior management in progressive enterprises has insisted that the authoritarian, fear-producing approach to protection be abandoned in favor of a program stressing service and the prevention or avoidance of loss as the objective of the protection organization.

The comments already made about the guard function are not intended to indicate that guards are a liability or are not required. Instead, it should be stressed that they are an essential and vital element in any effective protection program if properly utilized and trained. If the systems approach as mentioned in Chapter 9, "An Overview of Protection Systems," is followed in the planning of a protection program, this should ensure that the guards required are being properly utilized. Next, it is essential that the guards found to be necessary are properly trained. This should include emphasis on the need for a service attitude, courtesy, and an appreciation for good human relationships. The resulting guard operation should become an extension of the management of the enterprise, whose responsibility it is to protect and conserve the firm's assets, including the workers.

Better cooperation and a good relationship between guards and workers, which is necessary if any protection program is to be successful, will result if workers understand that the guards are not in an adversary position but are there in order to protect and assist them. Well-trained guards who are courteous, act with restraint, and use good judgment and common sense are the key to the development of a good relationship between employees and the protection organization.

On the other hand, employees must also understand that such an attitude is not a sign of weakness and that they cannot assume that a permissive protection program free from all restraint has been implemented. Instead, they must be made to understand by management of the enterprise that guards will exercise appropriate controls, i.e., those which are reasonable and not oppressive, for the protection of the enterprise as well as those associated with it. Employees can also be made to understand by management that they will be expected to follow the direction of the guard, since the latter are there to ensure that company rules and regulations are followed, and that furthermore any violations will not be handled by the guards, but instead such problems will be referred to the appropriate level of supervision for corrective or disciplinary action.

As a guard is often the first contact a visitor has with an organization, the value of guards as public relations representatives should not be overlooked. The initial treatment a visitor receives and the way the visit is handled can have a lasting effect— good or bad—on the impression the visitor forms of the enterprise. A guard who is officious, careless in the performance of his or her duties, or slovenly in appearance will give a bad impression not only of the protection organization but of the enterprise as a whole. As a result, it should be stressed during guard training that the human needs of visitors must be given particular attention, that visitors must be treated with courtesy, and that guards must display an attitude of service.

Some organizations have demonstrated that they are changing from an enforcement image to a more service-oriented approach by eliminating the traditional uniform worn by guards. The police- or military-type uniform has been replaced in some facilities with a blazer-type jacket and contrasting slacks for both male and

---

†Peter F. Drucker, "Management: Tasks, Responsibilities, Practices," Harper and Row, New York, 1974, p. 176.

female uniformed personnel (see Fig. 1). All outward appearances of authority, such as guns, badges, or insignia of rank, have been eliminated.

The employees and others who normally come in contact with the security organization usually accept the concept immediately. The "new look" is generally recog-

Fig. 1   The "new look" in uniforms.

nized as an outward indication of the elimination of the authoritarian approach. The usual result is an immediate indication of cooperation with guards in this type of uniform and a more friendly approach toward them. Of course, along with the uniform change the guards must be motivated and trained to adopt a service-oriented, nonthreatening type of approach to individuals.

ARMED OR UNARMED GUARDS?

Although the question whether guards should be armed or unarmed is frequently debated by experienced executives in the protection field, the viewpoint seem to be generally equally divided. Some argue convincingly that it is essential for guards to be armed if they are to be effective, while others are adamant in adopting the opposite position. The following quotation from the previously mentioned Rand report seems to confirm this divided viewpoint: "Over half of all contract personnel and over half of all in-house personnel carry a firearm on the job at least 25 percent of the time."[*]
As a result, it must be concluded that there is no one answer to the question.

---

*Kakalik and Wildhorn, vol. 2, p. 211.

Some who favor the use of firearms for guards are oriented to the police or enforcement type of protection approach mentioned earlier and therefore feel that a guard, like a policeman, must be armed to adequately perform enforcement- or police-type functions. They also feel that possession of a weapon creates a psychological advantage which is of value in the performance of guard duties.

Those who do not favor arming guards argue that a weapon does not represent a psychological advantage, but will encourage resentment against the guard. Further, since a basic reason for a having a firearm is to combat deadly force, and such force does not ordinarily exist in the typical enterprise utilizing guards, there is no need to have weapons. It is further argued that if a threat of deadly force should develop, local law enforcement should be called to handle the problem.

If firearms are to be issued to guards, management must clearly recognize the responsibility which has to be assumed for the proper instruction of those so equipped. Training must include not only the care and use of the weapon but also clear instructions as to when a weapon may be used. Such training is essential because the improper use of a weapon by an untrained guard could result in both criminal and civil actions against the enterprise and the guard involved. Also, if it were shown that management had been wantonly or grossly negligent in not providing adequate training, insurance coverage for damages assessed might be refused because it is impossible to indemnify against one's own gross negligence. In addition to the legal liability, the potential of the unfavorable public image that might be created must also be considered.

An effort has been made to adopt legislation in most states specifying standards for guards to include training with respect to firearms. A group designated the "Private Security Task Force to the National Advisory Committee on Criminal Justice Standards and Goals" was organized in 1975, with the encouragement of the Law Enforcement Assistance Administration, to develop and recommend common standards which would assist state legislatures and other executive bodies in the adoption of local regulations.* However, it cannot always be assumed that because guards have met state or other standards with regard to firearm handling and training, they are in fact proficient. In the final analysis, the management of an enterprise must ensure that guards employed are properly trained.

In deciding whether guards should be armed, some basic criteria might be mentioned for general guidance in determining under what conditions firearms could be considered. Two of the conditions are: (1) The guard or personnel being protected will be exposed to probable attack by individuals using deadly force; (2) the guard must perform the duties of a police officer as well as the normal duties of a guard. However, other situations will be encountered which may indicate that a guard should be armed. For example, a guard inside an industrial building in a high-crime area at night would probably not require a firearm. However, if the guard were also required at times to patrol exterior areas, such as parking lots, the use of a weapon could be considered.

CONTRACT OR IN-HOUSE GUARDS?

As with the previous question—armed or unarmed guards—there is no positive answer to the question whether contract or in-house guards should be utilized. This is a management decision that should be based on an understanding of the advantages and disadvantages of each type of operation.

Probably the most eloquent argument for the use of contract guards—the one most

---

*National Advisory Committee on Criminal Justice Standards and Goals, "Private Security: Report of the Task Force on Private Security," U. S. Government Printing Office, Washington, D. C., 1976.

often used by companies supplying this type of service—is cost. It is generally stated that contract companies can provide guards at about 20 percent less than the cost of in-house guards.* This savings is usually based on the fact that contract guards will be paid less than in-house guards and that the contract company has less overhead than the enterprise utilizing the service. With regard to overhead, contract service companies usually offer fewer fringe benefits to their personnel, such as insurance, vacations, and sick leave. Also, their other administrative costs (training, supervision, etc.) are less.

The fact that a contract guard may be paid less than an in-house guard should not be overlooked, because if the pay is too low the quality of personnel supplied may be adversely affected. This may be particularly true if a contract is let on a low-bid basis, as the low bidder might have based the contract price on the minimum wage, with the result that this company is more limited in its selection of personnel than if it had based the bid on a higher wage rate.

Generally, contract guard companies base their contract price on the following formula:

- 70%   Paid to the guard
- 20%   Administrative costs
- 10%   Profit

A comparison of the total cost of an in-house and contract guard paid at the rate of $3/hr is as shown in Table 2. Knowing the formula used by a contractor, a user can check to ensure that the guards being furnished are being properly paid.

TABLE 2   Cost Comparisons: Company Guards vs. Contract Guards

Company guards	Contract guards
Pay rate X	Direct labor at 70% X
Benefits at 20% . . . . B	G & A at 20% . . . . B
Overhead at $1/hr . . . . . . O	Profit at 10% . . . . O
X = 3.00	X = 3.00
B = 0.60	B = 0.86
O = 1.00	O = 0.43
$4.60 per hour	$4.29 = contract price

Another persuasive reason advanced by contract representatives for the use of their company's guards is that the contractor will take full responsibility for the training and supervision of the personnel supplied. As a result, the using organization will usually be assured that there is no need to be concerned about such time-consuming details. However, management of a using organization should not assume that the contract company will perform as promised, and so arrangements should be made to check periodically on the performance of personnel being furnished by the contract company. In this connection, it should be kept in mind that all the assets of the enterprise will be entrusted to the contract company for protection when their guards are on duty. A random inspection from time to time during the hours when the facility is not in regular operation will serve to alert the contract organization that the effectiveness of their personnel is being checked. In addition, the management of the using organization can be assured that the level of service contracted for is actually being furnished.

Proponents of in-house guards will generally agree that contract guards are less expensive when all the costs to the using enterprise are considered. However, their usual argument is that any cost benefit is outweighed by a number of disadvantages;

*Kakalik and Wildhorn, vol. 2, p. 96.

for example, the quality of personnel may be poorer than in-house personnel because contract guards are paid less and are not as well trained as in-house guards. Also cited is the fact that there is less stability of personnel because there is more turnover of guards, and that contract personnel have their loyalty divided between the guard company and the enterprise they have a duty to serve. It is often maintained that since guards employed by a contract service have a tendency to be shifted from facility to facility as the need arises, they do not remain in any one organization long enough to develop a feeling of loyalty to any client. Whether valuable proprietary information is being protected is one concern that might result from fears about divided loyalty. Contract guards, for example, might be in an excellent position to steal valuable information from an enterprise they are assigned to protect.

Some organizations desiring to utilize contract guards have made an effort to overcome some of the disadvantages mentioned here by writing detailed personnel and performance specifications which must be met by the contract company. Also, in some cases the pay range for contract personnel has been controlled by the using company and set high enough to ensure that personnel of adequate quality are provided. It is also expected that this arrangement will discourage turnover. In some instances, using companies have made arrangements to take full responsibility for the training and supervision of personnel supplied by the contracting company. Under such an arrangement, the contract company assumes the responsibility only for providing personnel and for paying them. The using company, then, assumes all the other administrative and operational responsibilities for the performance of the guards furnished by the contract guard company.

COMMUNICATIONS

Effective communications are essential in a guard organization for two reasons—to transmit information between security guards and to assist with their supervision. Radios and telephones are usually utilized for communications between guards. Communication of information under a system of fixed posts can be accomplished with either telephones or radios. With respect to mobile patrols, radio is particularly effective. Both vehicular sets and portable sets for use by foot patrols can be incorporated into the network. Also, two types of radios can be used—two-way sets or sets that only receive. A combination of both types may also be indicated.

In utilizing communications to assist in the supervision of personnel on patrol, a series of key reporting stations might be installed throughout the facility being protected. Each key station could be wired into a light and a printing device at a control point staffed by a supervisor. On passing a key station, the guard would insert a key and turn it, and a light would be activated at the control point indicating the guard's location. The printer would also be activated and would print out the location and the time the key was activated. With this type of system, the supervisor would know the general location of all personnel on patrol at all times. If the guards were equipped with portable radios, the supervisor could contact a guard or any number of guards at any time, enabling them to respond quickly to handle any problem developing in the facility.

Chapter 19

Fire Alarm Communications

RICHARD W. BUKOWSKI
RICHARD L. P. CUSTER
RICHARD G. BRIGHT
National Bureau of Standards Center for Fire Research

A good fire alarm system is a key part of the overall fire protection designed into any building. Whether it be residential, office, manufacturing, or any other type of occupancy, a properly designed and installed fire alarm system can do much to limit both life and property loss in the event of a fire. Since approximately 80 percent of the fatalities caused by fire occur in buildings, the use of early-warning fire alarm systems in buildings can have a profound effect on the reduction of this figure.

The systems themselves can take many forms, ranging from one single-station smoke detector in a small single-family detached dwelling to a complicated computerized high-rise building system handling incoming data from numerous sources and performing a number of independent actions as a function of the input data. Emergency communication systems in high-rise buildings can be very effective in preventing panic and allowing orderly evacuation of the endangered portions of the building as well as direction of the fire-fighting operation within the building.

This chapter will give a general overview of the fire alarm and communication equipment normally used in buildings in order to provide a better understanding of the function of this equipment on the part of the architect or specifying engineer.

CONTROL UNITS

Common Features　The "brain" of any fire alarm system is referred to as the control unit. This is the central equipment cabinet to which all other subsystems of the fire alarm system are connected. The control unit provides power to all active devices and contains all the switching functions controlled by the initiating devices which perform all the intended operations of the system. The control unit also contains lights which indicate the status of the system and switches for silencing audible signals, resetting alarm conditions, etc.; other switches function as test or drill switches, for example.

There are some basic common features of all control units regardless of type. Each has a primary power supply (usually the commercial light and power service), and most have some sort of emergency power supply, such as engine-driven generators or battery supplies. They have one or more initiating-device circuits, to which the detectors and manual boxes are connected, and one or more indicating-device circuits, to which the evacuation signals such as bells, horns, sirens, etc., are connected.

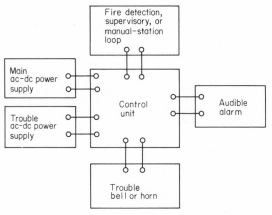

Fig. 1   Local fire alarm system (NFPA 72A). Typical features: (1) No alarm transmission to outside agency. (2) Minimum cost. (3) Minimum insurance credit. (4) All equipment is usually purchased. (5) The system is ineffective when the building is vacant or unattended. *(This diagram and accompanying legend material is reproduced through the courtesy of the NFPA.)*

For larger buildings most control units have more than one initiating-device circuit, so that the fire location can be indicated on an annunciator panel by floor, wing, or subsection. This annunciator panel may be built into the control unit or may be a separate cabinet located near the control unit or in a lobby or maintenance area.

Control units have three distinct types of audible signals. These are **alarm signals, trouble signals,** and **sprinkler supervisory signals.**

An **alarm signal** is given when a fire is detected either manually or automatically by an initiating device. Alarm signals generally involve the ringing of bells or horns throughout the building, but in large buildings alarms may initially be sounded only in the areas in immediate jeopardy. In some newer high-rise building systems the alarm signal may be a taped or live voice message over a special speaker system.

Trouble signals are given when a malfunction occurs in any critical circuit of the control unit. These critical circuits are referred to as being "supervised." Circuits which are normally supervised include main power, initiating (detector) circuits, and indicating (alarm bell) circuits. The trouble signal is usually sounded only in areas where maintenance personnel are normally present.

Sprinkler supervisory signals are given when a critical component in the sprinkler system is in other than its normal position. This would include low water service pressure, loss of power to a fire pump, closing of a water supply valve, or low water level or near-freezing temperature in an outdoor water supply tank.

Like trouble signals, sprinkler supervisory signals are usually sounded only in maintenance areas.

Local Control Units   The local control unit, as its name implies, is intended only to sound the local evacuation signal in the protected building (see Fig. 1). It generally contains little more than the basic features indicated above and is not required to have emergency standby power, since a power failure in an occupied building should be known to the occupants. The local control unit is generally of limited value other than in protection of the occupants, since the alarm is not automatically relayed to a fire department, and no action by the fire department would be possible unless someone

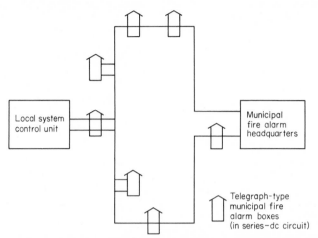

Fig. 2   Auxiliary fire alarm system (NFPA 72B). Typical features: (1) System alarm transmission is only as good as the city auxiliary loop and receiving equipment. (2) Alarm transmission is a coded signal directly to the Fire Dept. (3) Equipment in the building is usually the property of the building owner, but the coded transmitter, though bought by the building owner, usually becomes the property of the city. (4) The city is usually responsible for maintaining the loop up to and including the transmitter. Interior maintenance is the owner's responsibility. (5) The interface of these responsibilities is sometimes a problem. (6) Auxiliary loop connections may be unavailable or reserved for city property and schools. (7) Maintenance is often a problem. To be considered standard, a system should have periodic maintenance, inspection, and tests. If the system is installed for insurance credits, most rating bureaus require that this be a contract for monthly maintenance by an authorized installer. Auxiliary loops are usually maintained by city personnel and, as a consequence, may not be acceptable for insurance credits. The arrangement and requirement of the city auxiliary loop are shown in NFPA Standard 73. *(The above diagram and legend material reproduced with the permission of the NFPA.)*

remembers to call them if the alarm occurs while the building is occupied. If unoccupied, they would rely on a passerby hearing the alarm and calling the fire department.

Auxiliary Control Units   An auxiliary control unit is a local control unit which has an additional circuit electrically connecting it to the municipal fire alarm station on the street corner (see Fig. 2). Thus the auxiliary control unit not only rings the evacuation signals, it also automatically informs the fire department through the municipal fire alarm circuit that a fire has occurred on that particular city block. The signal received by the fire department is the same as if someone had manually tripped the street corner box, so they would have to locate the fire among the buildings on that block when they arrive at the scene. Since only alarm signals are automatically transmitted to the fire department, auxiliary control units are required to have a 60-hr minimum emergency power supply capacity to operate the system in case of a power failure over a weekend.

Remote-station Control Unit   A remote-station control unit is similar to an auxiliary control unit except that it transmits its signal to a compatible remote-station receiving unit at a location which is normally staffed round the clock (see Fig. 3). This may be a police station, all-night garage, restaurant, or even a funeral parlor. The signal is transmitted over a leased telephone line and is announced audibly and visually at the receiving station, from which the fire department is notified. Again, since only alarm signals are automatically transmitted to the remote receiving station, remote-station control units are required to have a 60-hr emergency power supply capability.

Proprietary Control Units   The most widely used type of control unit in large commercial occupancies is the proprietary system (see Fig. 4).

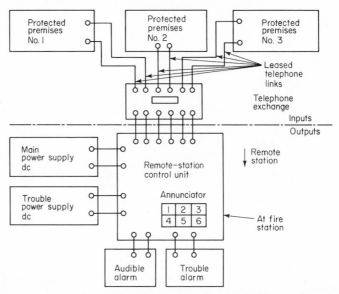

Fig. 3   Remote station fire alarm system (NFPA 72C). Typical features: (1) Usually a direct connection (uncoded) between the transmitter and the receiver. (2) Equipment may be bought or leased. Leased systems usually incorporate design, installation, testing, and maintenance. (3) The fire department may be unwilling or unable to receive trouble or supervisory alarms. This will require a separate transmitter, transmission lines, and receiver. (4) Multiple-alarm transmissions require separate circuits. (5) Number of automatic detection devices in a single circuit should not exceed 100. *(The above diagram and legend material reproduced with the permission of the NFPA.)*

Proprietary and central-station systems are identical except that the station receiving the fire alarm signal in a proprietary system is operated by someone who has a proprietary interest in the protected buildings. This is generally a guard office within the building, or group of buildings, protected by the system. The difference is that a central-station receiving station is manned by operators who have no proprietary interest in the protected buildings. This is, in effect, "protection for hire."

In the past, most proprietary systems have had separate initiating-device circuits for each zone or subsection within the building. This would be similar to the local, auxiliary, and remote-station systems.

Because of the increasing use of electronics, newer proprietary systems for larger buildings are now using signal multiplexing and built-in minicomputer systems which receive all signals from the building over a single pair of wires and determine the exact location of the fire by use of different frequencies or digitally coded information transmitted over the pair. Figure 5 shows the complexity and interrelationships between the many facets of a modern computer-controlled, proprietary high-rise communication system. This system is being used in the new Federal Office Building in Seattle, Washington. While a proprietary transmitting unit is similar to the other types of control units, the receiving console is quite different. A proprietary receiving console has individual lights or a digital visual display indicating the exact alarm point, an audible alarm to alert the console operator, and some type of visual indication on a permanent printer such as a teletype or line printer and, in some cases, a CRT display. These large proprietary multiplex and computer control systems do much more than just indicate to the operator and ring evacuation bells. These systems are used for controlling smoke by automatically closing and opening

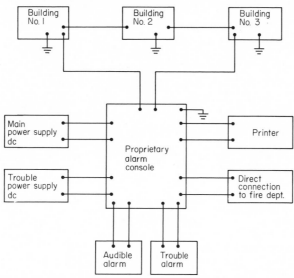

Fig. 4   Proprietary fire alarm system (NFPA 72D). Typical features: (1) It is practical only for large facilities because it requires constant attendance by two trained workers plus runners. Normally a "Class A" circuit is required. (2) All alarm signals must be recorded at the alarm office, preferably automatically. (3) Alarm office should be in a separate detached fire-resistive building or in a fire-resistive portion of a building with outside access. (4) Two means of alarm transmission are usually required, the one being a direct supervised line and the other either a municipal fire alarm box within 50 ft or a telephone that does not go through the plant switchboard. (5) Can be used for nonfire alarm service such as burglar alarm, building monitoring, or energy management systems. *(The above diagram and legend material are reproduced with the permission of the NFPA.)*

dampers in the HVAC systems, turning on exhaust fans, adjusting elevator controls so elevators cannot stop on fire floors, automatically routing all elevators to the lobby floor for use by the fire department, and almost any other automatic functions which one would wish.

In addition to the increased flexibility of these proprietary systems, the use of multiplexing signals has greatly reduced the installation cost by minimizing the amount of wire used in the building. A very new concept which is now being explored is the method of multiplexing the fire alarm signals over the existing power wiring within the building by a line carrier technique not very different from that used in the wireless intercom units sold for home use.

Proprietary systems are required to transmit all signals to the remote receiving station, so the standby power requirements are 24 hours for these systems.

Central-station Control Units   As was stated earlier, the central-station system is almost identical to the proprietary system (see Fig. 6). While the main difference is in the type of personnel staffing the receiving station, there are some additional differences in the means of signal transmission between the protected building and the receiving station.

Since the proprietary receiving station is generally within the protected building or very close to it, proprietary systems transmit signals between the two points by means of single or multiple pairs of wires. This would be impractical, however, in the central-station systems since the central-station receiving point is generally a long distance from the protected building. Thus, two means of transmitting the signals in a central-station system are used.

The oldest transmitting means in central-station use is called the **"McCulloh" circuit.** A McCulloh is one that normally transmits over two wires but can be switched, manually or automatically, to transmit over one wire and ground. With this capability, a break or ground fault of a single wire will not render the system inoperative. In addition, a single McCulloh circuit may have as many as twenty-five protected buildings on it. Each building transmits a coded signal which generates an audible tone at the receiving station, which follows the code. In addition, some type of

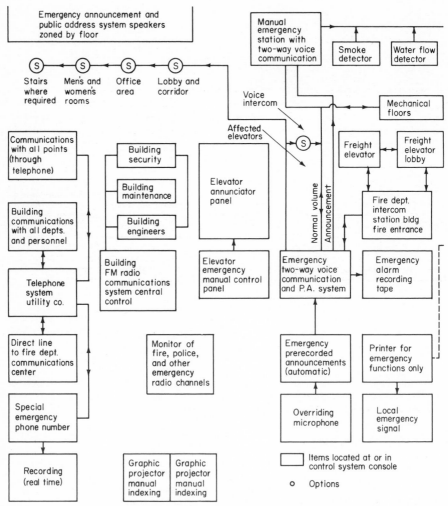

Fig. 5 High-rise proprietary fire alarm system.

automatic printing means, such as a punch or pen register, is provided to give a permanent record of the code transmitted.

The second means of signal transmission in central-station systems is called the **direct wire circuit.** This is, as its name implies, a direct dedicated pair of leased telephone lines running between the building and the central-station panel. In this case codes are not necessary, since each building is on its own separate circuit.

When a signal is received at a central station, the appropriate authorities are informed, and the central-station operator dispatches a "runner" (usually an armed guard) to the protected building. This runner acts as an agent of the property owner at the scene and attempts to minimize loss.

As with proprietary systems, central-station systems transmit all signals to the central station, so the standby power requirements are 24 hours.

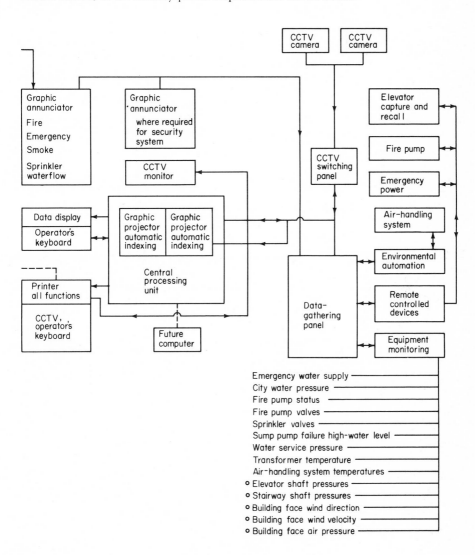

INITIATING DEVICES

An initiating device is defined as any device which informs the control unit of the presence of a fire. This can be done in the following ways:

Manual   A manual initiating device is nothing more than a fire alarm pull station located on the wall of a building. Most manual stations are noncoded and provide a simple contact closure to the control unit indicating the presence of a fire. In order to

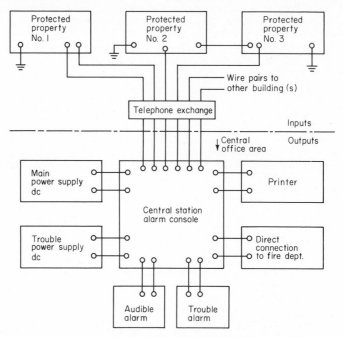

Fig. 6   Central station fire alarm system (NFPA 71). Typical features: (1) Leased equipment, no capital investment. (2) System design, installation, maintenance, and test by the central station. (3) If an Underwriters' Laboratories listed central station office, insurance credits are possible. (4) Automatically recorded coded signals. (5) Essential transmission circuits arranged so that a single break or ground fault does not cause a false alarm and will not prevent transmission of a true alarm (McCulloh circuit or other alternate path). (6) Runner, usually armed, sent to take action to protect occupant property. (7) It can detect and alarm for other, nonfire conditions—burglar, building temperature, water pressure, loss of electrical power, condition of automatic extinguishing system features. (8) Direct-line voice communication with the proper fire department to explain in detail the fire or other emergency. This is usually done by direct-wired telephone, with a requirement for an alternate means of contacting the fire department. (9) Direct wire circuit not currently acceptable for fire alarm service since it cannot transmit signals under single open fault conditions. It is used for burglar alarm service only. *(The above diagram and legend material reproduced with the permission of the NFPA.)*

get floor or zone discrimination with a noncoded system, the control unit must have multiple initiating circuits.

The other type of manual station is a coded station where each individual manual station generates a specific impulse code to the control unit, which, in turn, rings the building fire alarm bells in the coded pattern. Anyone in the building can then determine the location of the fire from the code sounded on the fire alarm bells.

Obviously, manual initiating devices are only effective when the protected area is occupied, and so they are usually employed only in public buildings in areas which are normally occupied or where the primary fire hazard is present only during the time the area is occupied. Another reason for using a manual system is its very low false-alarm rate. Occupancies such as hospitals and schools are good examples of manual system use areas, since false alarms in these areas are highly undesirable.

Frequently, schools which have high false-alarm incidence from manual stations will use what is known as a "presignal" alarm system. In a presignal system, pulling of the manual station does nothing more than ring an alarm bell in the principal's office and/or any other areas where people in authority would normally be present. When this occurs, someone in authority proceeds to the point of alarm and verifies the problem. If it is determined that a fire is present, the person must then operate a key switch on the manual station, which then sounds the evacuation signals and automatically notifies the fire department (in other than a local system).

Automatic   Automatic fire alarm initiating devices are actuated by heat, smoke, flame radiation, or other aspects of a fire. The following discusses the aspects of each type of detection mode.

CLASSIFICATION OF DETECTORS

Fire detectors may be classified in several ways. Classification can be made on the basis of placement by functional characteristics of detectors or by operating principle. Classification by placement and functional characteristics is described in this section, and classification by operating principle is described in subsequent sections.

Geometric Classification   Detectors may be classified by the geometry of the area they cover. **Spot detectors** are devices whose detecting element responds to conditions at a single point. A **line detector** senses conditions along a continuous linear path. **Volume detectors** are those which monitor conditions within a specified volume and will respond to signals anywhere within that volume.

Restoration Classification   Detectors may also be classified by the way in which they are placed in service following operation. Restorable detectors are those which can be restored to operative condition following a fire. Those may be either of the **self-restoring** or the **manually restoring type.** Nonrestorable detectors have sensing elements which are destroyed by the fire.

Alarm Contact Circuit Classification   The type of alarm contact circuit can also be used to classify detectors. An **open-circuit** detector has contacts which are normally opened and closed on alarm, while a **closed-circuit** type opens the contacts or breaks a circuit on alarm. A **transfer-circuit** type opens one circuit and closes another when the alarm conditions are reached.

HEAT DETECTION

Heat detectors are the oldest type of automatic fire detection device. They began with the development of automatic sprinkler heads in the 1860s and have continued to the present with a proliferation of different types of devices. A sprinkler can be considered a heat-actuated fire detector when the sprinkler system is provided with water flow indicators tied into the fire alarm control unit system. These water flow indicators detect either the flow of water through the pipes or the subsequent pressure drop upon actuation of the system and automatically sound the alarm as the water is being put on the fire.

Electrical heat detectors, which only sound the alarm and have no extinguishing function, are also used. Heat detectors are the least expensive fire detectors, have the lowest false-alarm rate of all fire detectors, but are also the slowest in detecting fires. Heat detectors are best suited for fire detection in small confined spaces where rapid fires with high heat output are expected and in other areas where ambient conditions would not allow the use of other fire detection devices or where speed of detection or life safety are not a consideration. One example of this would be low-value protection where fire could cause minimum damage to the structure or contents. Heat detectors may be thought of as detecting fires within minutes of ignition.

Convected-Energy Heat Detectors

Heat detectors respond to the convected thermal energy of a fire. They may respond either at a predetermined or fixed temperature or at a specified rate of temperature change. In general, heat detectors utilize some physical or electrical change which occurs in a material when exposed to heat.

Fixed-Temperature Detectors   Fixed-temperature detectors are designed to alarm when the temperature of the operating element reaches a specified point. The air temperature at the time of operation may be higher than the rated temperature due to the thermal inertia of the operating elements. Fixed-temperature heat detectors are available to cover a wide range of operating temperatures. This is necessary so that detection can be provided in areas which are normally subjected to high ambient (nonfire) temperatures.

Eutectic Metal Type.   Eutectic metals, alloys of bismuth, lead, tin, and cadmium which melt rapidly at a predetermined temperature, can be used as operating elements for heat detection. The most common such use is the fusible element in an automatic sprinkler head. Fusing of the element allows water to flow in the system, which triggers an alarm by various electrical or mechanical means.

A eutectic metal may be used in one of two ways to actuate an electrical alarm circuit. The simplest method is to place the eutectic element in series with a normally closed circuit. Fusing of the metal opens the circuit, which triggers an alarm. The second method employs a eutectic metal as a solder to secure a spring under tension. When the element fuses, the spring action is used to close contacts and sound the alarm. Devices using eutectic metals cannot be restored; either the device or its operating element must be replaced following operation.

Glass Bulb Type.   Frangible glass bulbs similar to those used for sprinkler heads have been used to actuate alarm circuits. The bulb, which contains a high-vapor-pressure liquid and a small air bubble, is used as a strut to maintain a normally open switching circuit. When exposed to heat the liquid expands, compressing the air bubble. When the bubble is completely absorbed, there is a rapid increase in pressure, shattering the bulb and allowing the contacts to close. The desired temperature rating is obtained by controlling the size of the air bubble relative to the amount of liquid in the bulb.

Continuous-Line Type.   As an alternative to spot-type fixed-temperature detection, various methods of continuous-line detection have been developed. One type of line detector uses a pair of steel wires in a normally open circuit. The conductors are insulated from each other by a thermoplastic of known fusing temperature. The wires are under tension and held together by a braided sheath to form a single cable assembly (see Fig. 7). When the design temperature is reached, the insulation melts, contact is made, and an alarm is generated. Following an alarm, the fused section of the cable can be replaced to restore the system.

A similar alarm device utilizing a semiconductor material and a stainless steel capillary tube has been developed for use where mechanical stability is a factor (see Fig. 8). The capillary tube contains a coaxial center conductor separated from the tube wall by a temperature-sensitive glass semiconductor material. Under normal conditions, a small current (i.e., below alarm threshold) flows in the circuit. As temperature rises, the resistance of the semiconductor decreases, allowing more current flow, triggering the alarm.

Bimetal Type.   When a sandwich of two metals having different coefficients of thermal expansion is heated, differential expansion causes stresses in the assembly which are resolved by bending or flexing toward the metal having the lower expansion rate. The low-expansion metal commonly used is Invar, an alloy of 36 percent nickel and 64 percent iron. Several alloys of manganese-copper-nickel, nickel-chromium-iron, or stainless steel may be used for the high-expansion component of a bimetal assembly. Bimetals are used for the operating elements of several types of fixed-temperature detectors. These detectors are generally of two types, the bimetal strip and the bimetal snap disk. Bimetal detectors actuate when the element is heated and flexing action closes a normally open circuit.

BIMETAL STRIP: Devices using bimetal strips place the strip directly in the alarm

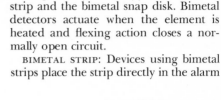

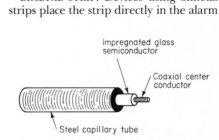

Fig. 7   Line-type fire detection cable, using insulated parallel wires.

Fig. 8   Line-type fire detection cable using a glass semiconductor.

circuit. As the strip is heated, it deforms in the direction of its contact point. The width of the gap between the contacts determines the operating temperature. The wider the gap, the higher the operating point. One drawback to this type of device is its lack of rapid positive action. The gradual bending of the element as it is heated may result in false alarms from vibration or jarring as the rated temperature is approached—for example, during periods of transient high ambient temperatures which are below the alarm point.

SNAP DISK: The operating element of a snap-disk device is a bimetal disk formed into a concave shape in its unstressed condition (see Fig. 9). As the disk is heated, the stresses developed cause it to reverse curvature and become convex. This provides an instantaneous positive action which allows the alarm contacts to close. The disk itself is not usually part of the electrical circuit. Snap-disk devices are not as sensitive to false or intermittent alarms as the bimetal strips described above.

A different application of the thermal expansion properties of metals is found in rate-compensation detectors, which use metals of different thermal expansion rates to compensate for slow changes in temperature while responding with an alarm for rapid rates of temperature rise and at a fixed maximum temperature as well. For a

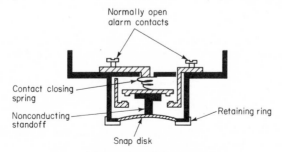

Fig. 9   Bimetal snap-disk heat detector.

further discussion of this device, see the later section on combination rate-of-rise and fixed-temperature detectors.

All thermal detectors using bimetal or expanding metal elements have the desirable feature of automatic restoration after operation when the ambient temperature drops below the operating point.

Rate-of-Rise Detectors   One effect which a fire has on the surrounding environment is to generate a rapid increase in air temperature in the area above the fire. While fixed-temperature heat detectors must wait until the room ceiling temperature reaches at least the designed operating point before sounding the alarm, the rate-of-rise detector will function when the rate of temperature change exceeds approximately 15°F (8.33°C)/min. Detectors of the rate-of-rise type are designed to compensate either mechanically or electrically for normal changes in ambient temperature which are expected under nonfire conditions. The various types of rate-of-rise heat detectors are discussed below.

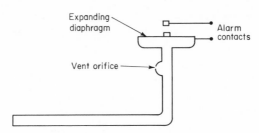

Fig. 10   Pneumatic-type heat detector.

Pneumatic Type.   The expansion of gas when heated in a closed system can be used to generate the mechanical forces needed to operate alarm contacts in a pneumatic fire-detection device. A completely closed system presents problems in that false alarms can occur strictly from slow changes in ambient temperature, since the pressure exerted on the operating mechanism is related only to the absolute change in temperature, regardless of the rate of temperature change. The pneumatic detectors is use today avoid this problem by venting the pressure which builds up during slow changes in temperature. The vents are sized so that when the temperature changes rapidly, such as in a fire situation, the pressure change exceeds the venting rate, and the system is pressurized. These systems are generally sensitive to rates of temperature rise exceeding 15°F (8.33°C)/min. The pressure is converted to mechanical action by a flexible diaphragm. A generalized schematic of a pneumatic heat-detection system is shown in Fig. 10.

Pneumatic heat detectors are available for both line and spot applications. The line systems consist of metal tubing in a loop configuration attached to the ceiling of the area to be protected. Except where specifically approved, Underwriters' Laboratories requires that lines of tubing be spaced not more than 30 ft (9.1 m) apart and that no single circuit exceed 1000 ft (304.8 m) in length. Zoning can be achieved by insulating those portions of a circuit which pass through areas from which a signal is not desired.

For spot applications and in small areas where line systems might not be able to generate sufficient pressures to actuate the alarm contacts, heat-collecting air chambers or rosettes are often used. These units act like a spot-type detector head by providing a large volume of air to be expanded at a single location.

The pneumatic principle is also used to close contacts within spot detectors of the rate-of-rise fixed-temperature type. These devices are discussed below.

Combination Detectors   Several devices are available which use more than one operating mechanism and will respond to multiple fire signals with a single unit. The combination detectors may be designed to alarm either from any one of the fire signals or only when all the signals are present at predetermined levels.

Rate-of-Rise Fixed-Temperature Type. Several heat-detection devices are available which operate on both the rate-of-rise and fixed-temperature principles. The advantages of these is that the rate-of-rise elements will respond quickly to rapidly developing fires while the fixed-temperature elements will respond to slowly developing smoldering fires when the design alarm temperature is reached.

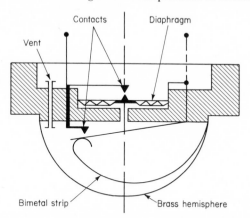

Fig. 11   Rate of rise-fixed temperature detector using a bimetal element.

The most common type uses a vented hemispherical air chamber and a flexible diaphragm for the rate-of-rise function. The fixed-temperature element may be either a bimetal strip (see Fig. 11) or a leaf spring restrained by a eutectic metal (see Fig. 12). When the designed operating temperature is reached, either the bimetal strip has flexed to the contact point or the eutectic metal has fused, releasing the spring which closes the contacts.

A second device which can be classified as a combination type is the rate-compensation detector. This detector uses a metal cylinder containing two metal struts. These struts act as the alarm contacts and are under compression in a normally open position (see Fig. 13). The outer shell is made of a material with a high coefficient of thermal expansion, usually aluminum, while the struts, usually copper, have a low coefficient. When exposed to a rapid change in temperature, the shell expands

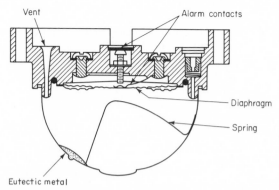

Fig. 12   Rate of rise-fixed temperature detector using an eutectic metal.

rapidly, relieving the stress on the struts and pulling them closed. Under slowly increasing temperature conditions both the shell and struts expand. The contacts remain open until the cylinder, which expands at a greater rate, has elongated sufficiently to pull them closed. This closure occurs at the device's fixed-temperature rating.

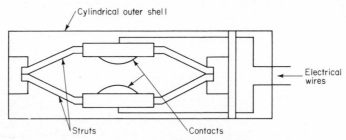

Fig. 13   Rate-compensation detector.

Thermoelectric Detectors   Various thermoelectric properties of metals have been successfully applied in devices for heat detection. The properties used are the generation of a voltage between bimetallic junctions (thermocouples) at different temperatures and variations in rates of resistivity change with temperature.

Spot Type.   Spot-type devices, which operate in the voltage-generating mode, use two sets of thermocouples. One set is exposed to changes in the atmospheric temperature and the other is not. During periods of rapid temperature change associated with a fire, the temperature of the exposed set increases faster than the unexposed set, and a potential is generated. The voltage increase associated with this potential is used to operate the alarm circuit.

SMOKE DETECTION

Smoke detectors are more costly than heat detectors but provide considerably faster detection times and subsequently higher false-alarm rates due to their increased sensitivity. Smoke detectors are very effective for life safety applications but are also more difficult to locate, in that air currents which might affect the direction of smoke flow must be taken into consideration.

Smoke detectors operating on the *photoelectric principle* give somewhat faster response to low-energy (smoldering) fires, as these produce large quantities of visible smoke. Smoke detectors using the *ionization principle* provide somewhat faster detection times on high-energy fires (open flaming), as these produce smoke particles which are smaller in diameter and are more easily detected by this type of detector.

Smoke detectors should be used in areas where the value of protection is high and

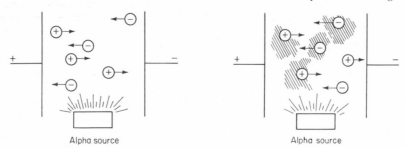

Fig. 14   Ionization of chamber air space.   **Fig. 15   Effect of aerosol in ionized chamber.**

in areas where life safety and fast response times are desired. Smoke detectors can operate within seconds of fire ignition.

Smoke detectors are installed in the return air ducts of the HVAC systems in large buildings to prevent recirculation of smoke through the HVAC systems from a fire within the building. Upon detection, the smoke detector automatically shuts down the circulating blowers or changes them over to a smoke exhaust mode.

Smoke detectors are also used to automatically close smoke doors in large buildings to limit the spread of smoke in case of fire. This may be done with individual smoke detectors near the doors or with smoke detectors that are built into the door closure units themselves.

Ionization Chamber Type The ionization chamber detector reacts both to the visible and the invisible components of the products of combustion. It responds best to particle sizes between 0.01 and 1.0 μm. The ionization chamber has been used for many years as a laboratory instrument for detecting microscopic particles. In 1939 Dr. Ernst Meili, a Swiss physicist, developed an ionization chamber device for the detection of combustible gases in mines. The major breakthrough in the field resulted from Dr. Meili's invention of a cold-cathode tube which would amplify the small signal produced by the detection chamber sufficiently to trigger an alarm circuit. This reduced the electronics required and resulted in a practical detector. In most models today, the cold-cathode tube has been replaced with solid state circuitry, which further reduces the size and cost.

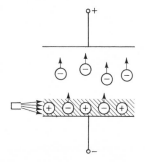

Fig. 16   Unipolar ion chamber.

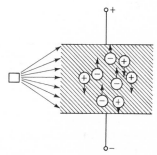

Fig. 17   Bipolar ion chamber.

The basic detection mechanism of an ionization detector consists of an alpha or beta radiation source in a chamber containing positive and negative electrodes. Radiation sources are commonly American 241 or Radium 226. The strength of the sources ranges from 0.05 to 80 μCi. The alpha radiation in the chamber ionizes the oxygen and nitrogen molecules in the air between the electrodes, causing a small current (10^{-11} A) to flow when voltage is applied (see Fig. 14).

When smoke aerosols enter the chamber, they reduce the mobility of the ions, reducing the current flow between the electrodes (see Fig. 15). The resulting change in the balance of the electronic circuit is used to trigger an alarm at a predetermined level of aerosol in the chamber.

By proper placement of the alpha source, two types of chambers may be produced. These are unipolar and bipolar chambers. A unipolar chamber is created by using a tightly collimated alpha source placed close to the negative electrode, thus ionizing only a small part of the chamber space (see Fig. 16). With this configuration, most of the positive ions are collected on the cathode, leaving a predominance of negative ions flowing through the chamber to the anode. The bipolar chamber has the alpha source centrally located so that the entire chamber space is subject to ionization (see Fig. 17). The unipolar chamber is theoretically a unipolar and a bipolar chamber in series (see Fig. 18).

A comparison of the relative merits of the two types of chamber design indicates that the unipolar chamber has approximately three times the sensitivity of the bipolar configuration. It has been proposed that this is due to the fact that there is less loss of ion carriers by recombination or neutralization of ions of opposite signs which occurs in the bipolar chamber. This results in a higher signal-to-noise ratio and a stronger alarm signal to the amplifier circuit.

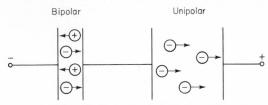

Fig. 18   Unipolar and bipolar ion chambers in series.

The alarm signal in an ion chamber detector is generated by a voltage shift at the junction between a reference circuit and the measuring chamber. The voltage shift results from a current decrease in the measuring chamber when products of combustion are present. The reference circuit may be either electronic, which compensates for power supply variations and component aging, or a second ion chamber only partially open to the atmosphere (see Fig. 19). These circuits are referred to as single-chamber and dual-chamber, respectively. The dual chamber has an advantage in the reduction of false alarms resulting from changes in ambient conditions. The reference chamber will tend to compensate for slow changes in temperature and humidity.

It should be noted that some ion chamber detector designs are subject to changes in sensitivity with varying velocity of air entering the sampling chamber. Some designs will lose sensitivity as velocity increases, and others will shift sufficiently in the more sensitive direction to trigger a false alarm. Care must be taken to choose the appropriate design for the area to be supervised.

Tests have indicated that ion chamber detectors are not suitable for use in applications where high ambient radioactivity levels are to be expected. The effect of radiation is to reduce the sensitivity. Tests also indicate that false alarms can be triggered by the presence of ozone.

Ion chamber detectors are available for both industrial and domestic use. Models

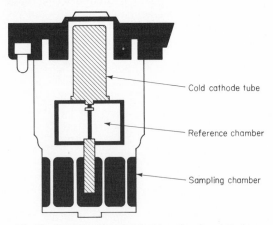

Fig. 19   Configuration of a dual ion chamber detector.

are produced for both single-station and system applications. Power supply requirements vary from 240 and 120 V ac to battery units using 9 to 12.5 V dc.

Photoelectric Type The presence of aerosols generated during the combustion process affects the propagation of light as it passes through the air. Two effects of the aerosol/air mixture can be utilized to detect the presence of a fire. These are (1) attenuation of the light intensity integrated over the beam path length and (2) scattering of the light both in the forward direction and at various angles to the beam path.

Light Attenuation Operation.   The theory of light attenuation by aerosols dispersed in a medium is described by the Lambert-Beer Law. It states that the attenuation of light is an exponential function of the beam path length (l), the concentration of particles (c), and the extinction coefficient of the particles (k). This relationship is expressed as follows:

$$I = I_0 e^{-kcl}$$

where I is the final intensity at length l and I_0 is the initial intensity at the light source.

Smoke detectors which utilize attenuation consist of a light source, a collimating lens system, and a photosensitive cell (see Fig. 20). In most applications, the light source is an incandescent bulb. A new light source is currently being used in newer photoelectric aerosol detectors. Light-emitting diodes (LEDs) are a reliable long-life source of illumination with low current requirements. Pulsed LEDs can generate sufficient light intensity for use in detection equipment.

Fig. 20   Beam-type light attenuation smoke detector.

The photosensitive device may be either a photovoltaic or photoresistive cell. The photovoltaic cells are usually selenium or silicon cells, which produce a voltage when exposed to light. These have the advantage that no bias voltage is needed, but in most cases the output signal is low and an amplification circuit is required. These units alarm when the photocell output is reduced by attenuation of the light as it passes through the smoke in the atmosphere between the light source and the photocell. Photoresistive cells change resistance as the intensity of the incident light varies. Cadmium sulfide cells are most commonly employed. These cells are often used as one leg of a Wheatstone bridge, and an alarm is triggered when the bias voltage shift in the bridge circuit reaches a predetermined level related to the designed light attenuation desired for alarm.

In practice, most light-attenuation or projected-beam smoke detection systems are used to protect large open areas and are installed with the light source at one end of the area to be protected and the receiver (photocell/relay assembly) at the other end. In some applications, the effective beam path length is increased by the use of mirrors. Projected-beam detectors are generally installed close to the ceiling, where the earliest detection is possible and where false alarms resulting from inadvertent breaking of the beam are minimized.

Although most systems employ a long path length and separation of the light source and the receiver, there are spot-type detectors which operate by light attenuation. One such unit uses a 7.8-in (0.19-m) light path with a sealed reference chamber and an open sampling chamber. Presence of smoke in the sampling chamber results in a voltage reduction from the selenium photocell which is measured by a bridge circuit containing the photocell from the reference chamber (see Fig. 21).

There are several problems associated with projected-beam detection. Since these devices are essentially line detectors, smoke must travel from the point of generation into the path of the light beam. This may take time and allow the fire to develop headway before the alarm is sounded. In addition, owing to the long path lengths often used, considerable smoke must be generated in order for sufficient attenuation to be achieved. This problem can be reduced somewhat by the use of multiple beams or reflecting mirrors. Finally, continuous exposure to light can damage or accelerate the aging of photocells, resulting in increased maintenance and possible system failure.

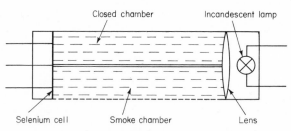

Fig. 21   Spot-type light attenuation smoke detector.

Light-scattering Operation.   Scattering results when light strikes aerosol particles in suspension. Scattered light reaches its maximum intensity at about 27° from the path of the beam in both the forward and backward directions, and the intensity is at a minimum in the direction perpendicular to the beam path. The intensity of scattered light is also related to particle size and the wavelength of the incident light. This intensity, as described by Rayleigh's theory for particles up to 0.1 times the wavelength of the incident light, is directly proportional to the square of the particle volume and inversely proportional to the fourth power of the wavelength. The theory of scattering for larger particles (0.1 to 4 times the wavelength of light) has been defined by Mie. These theories of light scattering are valid only for isotropic spherical particles and are very complex. Aerosol from a fire is a nonhomogeneous mixture of particles which are often neither spherical nor isotropic, and scattering intensities must be determined empirically for each aerosol mixture.

Smoke detectors utilizing the scattering principle operate on the forward scattering of light which occurs when smoke particles enter a normally dark chamber or labyrinth. The presence of smoke will increase the forward scattering of light from 10 to 12 times, but the intensity of the scattered light will decrease as the angle between the beam path and the photocell increases. The photocells used in these detectors may be either photovoltaic or photoresistive. Typical component configurations are shown in Fig. 22. These units are of the spot type and may be used as single-station devices with self-contained power supply and alarm or as part of an integrated system with remote power supply and alarm- and zone-indicating hardware.

Flame Detectors   Flame detectors optically sense either the ultraviolet or infrared radiation given off by flames or glowing embers. Flame detectors have the highest false-alarm rate and the fastest detection times of any type of fire detector. Detection times for flame detectors are generally measured in milliseconds from fire ignition.

Flame detectors are generally used only in high-hazard situations such as fuel loading platforms and hyperbaric chambers, high-ceiling areas, and any other places with hazardous atmospheres in which explosions or very rapid fires may occur. Flame detectors are "line of sight" devices, as they must be able to "see" the fire, and they are subject to being blocked by objects placed in front of them. The infrared types of flame detectors do have some capability for detecting radiation reflected off walls. In general the use of flame detectors is restricted to no-smoking areas or places where highly flammable materials are stored or used.

Infrared Type. Infrared detectors basically consist of a filter and lens system to screen out unwanted wavelengths and focus the incoming energy on a photovoltaic or photoresistive cell sensitive to the infrared. Infrared radiation can be detected by any one of several photocells, such as silicon, lead sulfide, indium arsenide, and lead selenide. The most commonly used are silicon and lead sulfide. These detectors can

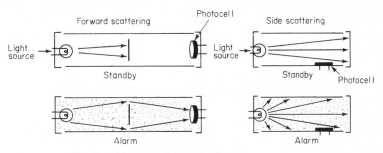

Fig. 22   Light-scattering smoke detectors.

respond to either the total IR component of the flame or flame flicker in the frequency ranges of 5 to 30 Hz.

Interference from solar radiation in the infrared region can be a major problem in the use of infrared detectors receiving total IR radiation, in that the solar background can be twice that of a flame signal from a fire of 500 cm^2. This problem can be partially resolved by choosing filters which exclude all IR but that in the ranges of 2.5 to 2.8 μm and /or 4.2 to 4.5 μm. These represent absorption peaks for solar radiation owing to the presence of CO_2 and water in the atmosphere. In cases where the detectors are to be used in normally dark applications, such as in vaults, this filtering is not necessary. Another approach to the solar interference problem is to employ two detection circuits. One circuit is sensitive to solar radiation between 0.6 and 1.0 μm and is used to indicate the presence of sunlight. The second circuit is filtered to respond to wavelengths between 2 and 5 μm. A signal from the solar sensor circuit can be used to block the output from the fire-sensing cell, giving the detection unit the ability to discriminate against false alarms from solar sources. This is often referred to as a "two-color" system. For most applications, flame-flicker sensors are preferred in that the flicker or modulation characteristic of flaming combustion is not a component of either solar or human interference sources. This results in an excellent signal-to-noise ratio. These detectors use frequency-sensitive amplifiers whose inputs are tuned to respond to an alternating current signal in the flame-flicker range (5 to 30 Hz).

Flame-flicker detectors are designed for volume supervision and may use either a fixed or scanning mode. The fixed units continuously observe a conical volume limited by the viewing angle of the lens system and the alarm threshold. The viewing angles range from 15 to 170° for units from various manufacturers. One scanning device has a 400-ft (122-m) range and uses a mirror rotating at 6 r/min through 360° horizontally, with a 100° viewing angle. The mirror stops when a signal is received and alarms after a 15-second delay to screen out transients.

Infrared detectors provide volume surveillance by rapidly responding to the designed alarm level anywhere within their range of vision. In addition, they will respond to reflected or reradiated infrared signals originating in areas which might be shielded from direct observation. There are also detectors of this type designed to respond to passing sparks or flame fronts in piping.

Ultraviolet Type.   The ultraviolet component of flame radiation is also used for fire detection. The sensing elements may be solid state, such as silicon carbide or aluminum nitride, or gas-filled tubes in which the gas is ionized by UV radiation and becomes conductive, thus sounding the alarm. The operating range of UV detectors is in the region of 0.17 to 0.30 μm, and in that region they are insensitive to both sunlight and artificial light. The UV detectors are also volume detectors and have viewing angles from 90° or less to 180°.

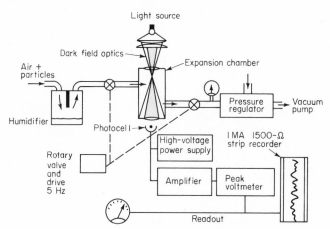

Fig. 23   Schematic of condensation nuclei particle detector.

Combination Ultraviolet-Infrared Type.   The combination of UV-IR sensing has been applied to applications in aircraft and in hyperbaric-chamber fire protection. These devices alarm when there is a predetermined deviation from the prescribed ambient UV-IR discrimination for fire warning in conjunction with a continuous-wire overheat detector, the analysis being performed by an on-board minicomputer.

DETECTORS COUNTING SUBMICROMETER-SIZE PARTICLES

During the earliest stages of combustion, in the pyrolysis or precombustion stage, large numbers of submicrometer-size particles are produced. These particles fall largely in the size range between 0.005 and 0.02 μm. Although ambient conditions normally find such particles in concentrations from several thousand per cubic centimeter in a rural area to several hundred thousand per cubic centimeter in an industrial area, the presence of an incipient fire can raise the submicrometer-particle concentration sufficiently above the background levels to be used as a fire signal. In the area of its flame, for example, a match can produce 10^{11} particles per cubic foot (10^7 particles per cubic centimeter). Production of these particles can fill a volume 10^{12} times the volume of the material lost in producing them to a concentration 10 times a normal ambient of 3×10^8 to 2×10^9 particles per cubic foot (2×10^4 to 10^5 particles per cubic centimeter).

Condensation Nuclei Type   Condensation nuclei are liquid or solid submicrometer (0.001 to 0.01 μm) particles which can act as the nucleus for the formation of a water droplet. By use of an appropriate technique, submicrometer particles can be made to act as condensation nuclei on a one particle–one droplet basis, and the concentration of particles is measured by photoelectric methods. A mechanism for performing this function is shown schematically in Fig. 23. An air sample is drawn through a humidifier, where it is brought to 100 percent relative humidity. The sample then passes to an expansion chamber, where the pressure is reduced with a vacuum pump. This causes the relative humidity to rise above 100 percent, resulting in condensation of water on the particles. The droplets quickly reach a size where they can scatter light. The dark-field optical system in the chamber will allow light to reach the photomultiplier tube only when the water droplets are present to scatter light. The output of the photomultiplier tube is directly proportional to the number of droplets (i.e., the number of condensation nuclei) present.

The system uses a mechanical valve and switching arrangement to allow sampling from up to four detection zones with as many as ten sampling heads per zone. Each zone is sampled once per minute for 15 seconds. All four zones are sampled each minute.

The system is nominally set to alarm at concentrations exceeding 2.2×10^{10} particles per cubic foot (8×10^5 particles per cubic centimeter), although it is possible to select different thresholds for each zone, depending on the background noise and the sensitivity required. It is also possible to have the sensitivity vary for different conditions with time of day. The system design is such that with the maximum sample travel distance from the most remote sampling head, fire will be detected within 2 minutes of the time the products of combustion first reach the head.

AMBIENT CONDITIONS AFFECTING DETECTOR RESPONSE

Ambient conditions have a strong influence on the choice, placement, and response of detectors. Improper choice of detection mode or improper placement can lead to problems ranging from no alarm to delayed alarm, when a fire occurs, to excessive false alarms.

Background Levels of Fire Signals When choosing a detector for a specific location, consideration must be given to the background levels of the signals to which the detector might be exposed under nonfire conditions. For example, the use of a UV or IR detector in a location where gas or arc welding is commonplace will generate false alarms. This is not a failure of the detector but rather a response to the presence of the signal for which the unit was designed. Detectors responding to invisible aerosols are especially prone to false signals from such sources as cooking fumes, cigarette smoke, and automobile exhaust fumes. A survey of false calls from automatic detection systems in Great Britain revealed an overall ratio of eleven false calls to one real call for all types of detection, including sprinkler alarms. The same survey showed that ambient conditions such as extraneous heat and smoke, extremes in ambient temperature, moisture (snow, rain, and steam), and high-velocity air movement were responsible for 25.9 percent of the false calls.

It is unlikely that false alarms caused by localized and transient changes in the ambient levels of fire signals can be completely eliminated. However, with sufficient information about ambient variations in different occupancies, the number could be considerably reduced. A program to establish a data base for variations in ambient conditions is presently under way in Great Britain. This study will include data on aerosols, temperature, humidity, radiation, air velocity, and vibration. It is possible that raising the threshold of alarm for certain fire signals in specific occupancies could reduce the incidence of false alarms without sacrificing the design goal of the installation. Difficulties arising from transient false signals might also be reduced through the use of multiple signal detectors and integration of the signals such that an alarm will sound either at a high threshold of any one signal or a lower threshold with multiple signals.

HEATING AND AIR-CONDITIONING EFFECTS

Heating and air-conditioning systems in buildings can exert several effects on the placement and operation of detection devices. These effects result from forced or convected air movement and the development of thermal inversions. Detectors sensing radiant-energy signatures are not affected by these factors. Devices responding to the convected energy are only slightly affected, since the convected energy of a fire large enough to actuate these units easily overpowers ambient circulation patterns. The most important effects of heating and air-conditioning are on the movement of the products of combustion which make up the aerosol and gas signals. Detectors sited without regard to air flow and thermal effects may be slow to respond or, in extreme cases, may miss the fire signal completely.

Forced-air systems are widely used for heating in many occupancies. Air-flow patterns must be considered in placing detectors; these patterns are related to the overall air flow in the building between the supply registers and the cold-air return. In a two-story dwelling, for example, each room can have its own supply register, and the cold-air returns may all be on the first floor or in the basement. Under these conditions, cool air descending from above and warm air rising from below create air currents in the stairwell which move products of combustion to the upper floors. Detectors placed at the top of a stairwell can sense the aerosols originating in the areas below. Air flow up the stairwell is not always uniform. Changes in direction such as that at the ceiling of the second floor can produce a stagnant area where there is little or no movement. Aerosol or gas detectors placed in this area may be slow to respond owing to lack of sufficient air velocity to carry products through the detector housing to the sensing element.

It is not uncommon with forced-air systems to find detectors placed too close to the air stream issuing from a supply register, with the result that the units are actually being continuously purged when the system is in operation. Often detectors are placed in the return air ducts in order to detect aerosol drawn into the system. They may be used to shut down circulating fans or convert the system to an exhaust mode. Consideration must be given to the effects of dilution of aerosols by air drawn from areas unaffected by the fire. Often intolerable conditions can exist elsewhere in the building long before a strong signal can reach the detector.

Apartment and office buildings often utilize heating systems which serve as a single unit. In apartments, the building corridors may serve as a make-up air supply through undercut or louvered doors with exhaust through kitchen and bathroom ventilators. Noxious products of combustion originating in other areas of the building are often drawn into apartments by this means. Detectors placed appropriately in the corridors can be used to sound a general alarm. The air flow to kitchen and bathroom exhausts should be considered when siting detectors within an apartment. In offices where make-up air is drawn from outside the building, corridors often function as a return air plenum. Air flow within rooms in such cases may tend to be toward the corridor doors.

Gravity hot-air systems are often found in older buildings. When in use, they depend largely on vertical supply ducts and natural openings between floors for circulation. Usually the air-flow patterns are from supply registers at floor level to the ceiling and down natural openings to the lowest level. Lacking the impetus of fans for diffusion of the supply air, the paths of air flow are often restricted, leading to "dead" spaces and eddy effects. Detailed siting surveys should be conducted prior to installation of detectors where these systems are used. Hot water–steam radiator systems are also common in older buildings. These systems are gravity dependent and have less effect on the transport of aerosols than forced-air systems. Movement will be confined to two general regions: the convection cell developed around the radiator itself and the vertical circulation from floor to floor by natural openings in the structure. As in the case of gravity hot air, care must be taken to seek out the eddy areas and dead spots and to avoid them. Radiant heating using electric coils in the ceiling, which is common in certain areas, can produce a problem. When the system is in operation, a layer of hot gases at the ceiling can prevent the combustion products from reaching ceiling-mounted detectors. In such cases, detectors may have to be wall-mounted perhaps 12 in below the ceiling.

Complete building air-conditioning systems will generate air-flow patterns which are, in general, similar to those of the forced-hot-air system. Two additional problem areas can be found with the use of cooling systems. In the dry areas of the country, air cooling is accomplished using evaporation techniques. Air cooled by this method has a high relative humidity. The effects here are to enhance the agglomeration of smoke particles and trap them in the moist air. The warm dry air rises to the ceiling, and a sharp boundary condition is created. Cool moist smoke rising to the ceiling can be trapped at this interface. Unless the air is agitated by a rapidly burning fire, ceiling-mounted detectors, even in the fire area, may not respond to the aerosol signal at all.

Although some specific detector-siting information is available in the National Fire Protection Association (NFPA) Standards 72E and 74 and in various manufacturers' application guides, few design data are available to assist in understanding the effects of comfort heating and cooling systems on detector location. Optimization of detector location for heat-on, heat-off and cooling-on, cooling-off conditions should be based on studies of air-flow conditions in buildings and existing heating and air-conditioning technology.

RELIABILITY OF DETECTION DEVICES

Although detailed reliability data are lacking for most detection devices, some general statements can be made regarding certain critical components based on field or laboratory experience and manufacturers' literature.

Heat Detectors   Heat-sensing detectors are generally the most reliable types in terms of component failure, since these devices respond directly to the presence of heat by a physical change in the detector's operating elements. Heat detectors may fail as a result of mechanical damage or abuse after installation or through malfunction of components or circuitry in peripheral equipment such as power supplies or alarm-indicating equipment.

Detection devices for fire signals other than heat employ electronic circuitry of varying complexity to sense the presence of a fire signal and to monitor the output of the sensing element. The reliability of the device is related to the reliability of its components as they are used in each type of circuit.

Light Sources and Photocells   The lamps used in photoelectric-type smoke detectors are critical to detector operation. The operational lifetime of incandescent bulbs used in photoelectric detectors ranges from about 1 month to about 37 months. Lamp life can be increased by operation at reduced dc voltages. Lowering the operating voltage reduces filament evaporation, one of the causes of failure. Vibration and shock, particularly with fragile, aged filaments, often lead to lamp failure. Power surges and power failures are also significant factors. It appears that an average life of 3 years in continuous service can be expected with present bulbs. The problem of bulb life might be solved through the use of light-emitting diodes (LED). Manufacturers' data on LEDs indicates a possible life span on the order of 10^6 hr, approximately 100 years. At this time, barring traumatic damage, the light intensity would be reduced by one-half. These light sources are mechanically stable and should be less prone to damage from vibration.

The sensitivity of photocells used in detectors may have a tendency to drift somewhat with aging. The usual method of compensation for such changes is through the use of compensation photocells in various configurations. These cells act as a reference to maintain balance in the circuit.

Batteries The use of batteries as the primary power supply for single-station smoke detectors has several problems which can affect detector reliability. The present requirements for battery-operated devices call for a 1-year lifetime and an audible trouble signal lasting 7 days when some critical voltage is reached. The type of battery being used can affect the operation of the detector. Alkaline batteries have a constantly decreasing voltage curve as they wear out. Some detectors using these batteries require periodic sensitivity readjustments to maintain the designed alarm threshold. A homeowner's failure to readjust the detector could result in delayed detection or render the unit inoperative. Mercury batteries have a constant voltage throughout most of their life and can be used to control the sensitivity-drift problem. At the end of their life, however, mercury batteries undergo a rapid drop in voltage. This will present two problems. First, the sensitivity will decline rapidly, and second, it is possible that the reduced power available may shorten the operating time of the alarm horn or, in some cases, prevent its operation.

MAINTENANCE OF DETECTORS

Maintenance problems also affect detector reliability, particularly in photoelectric and ionization types. Accumulations of dust, along with film on the bulbs, lenses, and photocells, will reduce the intensity of light within the detection element. The effect of this varies with the type of detector. Projected-beam–type photoelectric detectors will become more sensitive with contamination, increasing the possibility of false alarms. Light-scattering detectors, on the other hand, will become less sensitive as light intensity is decreased. Ionization detectors are also affected by contamination. Deposition of dust and film inside the ion chamber will decrease the current flow across the chamber and raise the sensitivity. This can result in an increase in the false-alarm rate. Collections of dust, particles of lint, and other large airborne contaminants can often be trapped in the protective screens or light shields or delay an alarm. This can block the entry of smoke and prevent or delay an alarm. Proper cleaning and maintenance are important to retain the designed operating characteristics of these detectors.

SELECTION OF DETECTORS

When laying out a fire detection system the design engineer must keep in mind the operating characteristics of the individual detector type as they relate to the area protected. Such factors as type and quantity of fuel, possible ignition sources, ranges of ambient conditions, and value of the protected property are critical in the proper design of the system. Intelligent application of detection devices using such factors will result in the maximization of system performance.

Heat detectors have the lowest cost and false alarm rate but are the slowest in response. Since heat tends to dissipate fairly rapidly (for small fires), heat detectors are best applied to the protection of confined spaces, or directly over hazards where flaming fires could be expected.

Heat detectors are generally installed on a grid pattern at their recommended spacing schedule, or at reduced spacing for faster response, or where beams or joists may slow the spread of the hot gas layer.

The operating temperature of a heat detector is usually selected at least 25°F above the maximun expected ambient temperature in the area protected. Pneumatic heat detection systems have a device known as a "blower heater compensator" which is used to prevent false alarms caused by the sharp initial heat rise from ceiling-mounted unit heaters.

Smoke detectors are higher in cost than heat detectors but are faster responding to fires. Because of their greater sensitivity, false alarms can be more frequent, especially if they are not properly located.

Smoke detectors do not have a specific space rating except for a 30-ft maximum guide derived from the UL full-scale approval tests which they must pass. Grid-type installation layouts usually are not used since smoke travel is greatly affected by air currents in the protected area. Thus, smoke detectors are usually placed by engineering judgment based on prevailing conditions.

TABLE 1   Summary of Detector Application Considerations

Detector type	Response speed	False alarm rate	Cost	Application
Heat	Slow	Low	Low	Confined spaces
Smoke	Fast	Medium	Medium	Open or confined spaces
Flame	Very fast	High	High	Flammable material storage
Particle counter	Fast	Medium	High	Open spaces— high value

Since smoke does not dissipate as rapidly as heat, smoke detectors are better suited to the protection of large open spaces than heat detectors. Also, they are less appropriate for small spaces because cost can be prohibitive.

Smoke detectors are more subject to damage by corrosion, dust, and environmental extremes than the simpler heat detectors since smoke detectors contain electronic circuitry. They also consume power, so the number of smoke detectors which can be connected to a control unit is limited by the power supply capability. The number of heat detectors used, however, usually depends only on the limitation of resistance of the detection circuit. Where very long runs are necessary, this can be handled by using heavier gage wire.

Photoelectric smoke detectors are particularly suitable where smoldering fires or fires involving PVC wire insulation may be expected. Ionization smoke detectors are particularly suitable where flaming fires involving any other materials would be the case. The particle counter detector responds to all particle sizes equally, so they may be used without regard to the type of fire expected. These systems, however, are fairly expensive and complex to install and maintain. The design and layout of the sampling tubes is very critical and must be done by someone very familiar with the equipment.

Flame detectors are extremely fast responding but will alarm to any source of radiation in their sensitivity range, so false alarm rates are high if improperly applied. Flame detectors are usually used in hyperbaric chambers and flammable material storage areas where no flames of any sort are allowable.

Flame detectors are "line of sight" devices, so care must be taken to ensure that they can "see" the entire protected area and that they will not be accidentally blocked by stacked material or equipment. Their sensitivity is a function of flame size and distance from the detector, and some can be adjusted to ignore a small flame at floor level. Their cost is relatively high but they are well suited for areas where explosive or flammable vapors or dusts are encountered as they are usually available in "explosion-proof" housings.

Table 1 contains a summary of the information contained in this section. The reader is also referred to NFPA 72E, *Automatic Fire Detectors*, for more specific information on the installation of the various types of detectors.

SPRINKLER SUPERVISORY DEVICES

Sprinkler systems are usually electrically connected into the control unit in more ways than just the water-flow indications described previously. Since the integrity of the sprinkler system's water supply is vital to its operation, the position of critical water supply valves, operation of electric fire pumps, and factors such as the temperature or level of water within a water supply tank outside the building are all monitored. Signals from these monitoring devices are called "sprinkler supervisory signals" and are used to generate separate signals at the control unit distinctive from the fire alarm signals and the trouble signals indicating malfunction of the fire alarm equipment.

INDICATING DEVICES

The indicating devices connected to a control unit are those audible devices used to indicate the signals. These can be bells, horns, sirens, etc., and there may be as many as three different audible signals associated with the control unit. These would be a fire alarm (evacuate the building), a trouble signal (indicating a malfunction in one of the control unit's detection or other critical circuits), or sprinkler supervisory signals (indicating closure or malfunction of a critical feature of the sprinkler system). In general these three audible signals must be different, but there are no national standards concerning them. Thus, in one area one might find bells for fire alarm, horns for trouble, and electronic tone signals for sprinkler supervisory, with another combination in an adjacent building. In some of the newer high-rise systems, live or taped voice messages are used which give specific instructions on what to do in case of fire. These systems operate from a computer-controlled proprietary system and in many cases give different messages depending on the listener's location with respect to the fire. There will be one message for the floor on which the fire occurred and the next above it, a different message for people in the elevators, and a third message for the rest of the building. Not only does this eliminate confusion as to what the signal means, it also provides the beneficial effect of hearing a calm voice giving explicit instructions during the crisis situation.

COMMUNICATION SYSTEMS

Voice communication systems have been outlined earlier. In addition to their use as indicating devices in the automatic systems, they can also be used by the fire department at the scene for overriding the automatic messages and giving manual instructions, as well as for communications with their own people inside the building. Many high-rise communication systems have fire warden stations on each floor which contain a telephone directly connected to the fire command center. A designated occupant of each floor goes to the fire warden station in case of fire and directs the evacuation operations on that floor. This individual can be questioned by the fire command center and used to quickly evaluate the situation.

Whether one feels the high-rise building fire problem is large or small, there is one thing that all experts agree upon—it is impossible to evacuate a high-rise building in a reasonable time. Therefore, occupants must be moved to an area of safety within the building and may have to be moved more than once before the fire is out. This means that an effective and reliable method of communication with the building occupants is imperative.

The high-rise communication system also serves other purposes. Fire department radios may not operate properly in a modern steel structure, so an internal means of directing the fire-fighting operations is necessary. The communication system serves this purpose through the two-way capabilities of the fire warden stations on each floor. Of course, the third important purpose is the calming effect of a voice message on persons who realize that they must stay in a building on fire.

RESIDENTIAL FIRE ALARM SYSTEMS

Automatic fire alarm systems for residential occupanies can vary from the minimum to the maximum. In a high-rise residential occupancy one might find a complete sprinkler system as well as a proprietary computerized control unit fully equipped with systems for elevator capture, smoke control, and high-rise communication. At the other end of the scale, the single-family detached dwelling will involve the use of one or more self-contained fire detectors. All four of the national model building codes have adopted the requirement, by their 1975 editions, for at least one single-station smoke detector to be installed in every living unit. Thus the architect and building designer of residential occupancies will now specify single-station smoke detectors in all such units. "Single-station smoke detectors" means a self-contained unit containing detection device, power supply, and indicating device.

In residential units requiring more than one detector, the building designer may specify what is known as a multiple-station detector, which is nothing more than single-station detectors which can be interconnected so that when one unit alarms, all interconnected units alarm. This is highly desirable in larger living units where detectors remote from the sleeping areas may not be audible there.

In general, all living units should have a smoke detector located in the hallway outside the bedrooms and at least one detector on each level of the home. The location within a given level is not tremendously critical, although the unit is generally located near the base of the stairway to the next level.

REFERENCES

Codes and Standards

Every building must be designed to meet the building and fire codes of the area in which it is located. In many cases these local codes are based wholly or in part on the standards of the National Fire Protection Association (NFPA). Even if they are not, these standards contain a great deal of excellent information with which the architect should be familiar.

NFPA Standards 72A, 72B, 72C, and 72D cover the installation of *Local, Auxiliary, Remote Station,* and *Proprietary Alarm Systems,* respectively. NFPA 71 covers *Central Station Alarm Systems,* and NFPA 74 covers *Household Fire Warning Equipment.*

NFPA 72E gives excellent guidance on the proper installation of automatic fire detectors, and NFPA 101 specifies the types of alarm systems required for various occupancies.

While the installation standards of the NFPA are probably familiar to most architects, the performance standards of the approval laboratories may not. Underwriters' Laboratories or Factory Mutual approval of all components of the fire alarm and communication equipment is an important indication that the equipment is properly designed and reliable.

Additional Readings

1. Bright, Richard G., "Recent Advances in Residential Smoke Detection," *Fire Journal,* vol. 68, no. 6, pp. 69–77, November 1974.
2. Custer, Richard L.P., and Richard G. Bright, *Fire Detection: The State-of-the-Art,* TN 839, National Bureau of Standards, Washington, D.C., June 1974.
3. Factory Mutual Engineering Corp., Norwood, Mass., *Handbook of Industrial Loss Prevention,* 2d ed., *McGraw-Hill, New York, 1967.*
4. Harrison, Gregory A., "The High-Rise Fire Problem," *CRC Critical Reviews in Environmental Control,* vol. 4, no. 4, pp. 483–505, October 1974.
5. Langdon-Thomas, G. J., *Fire Safety in Buildings: Principles and Practice,* A. & C. Block Ltd., London, England, 1972.
6. Marchant, Eric W. (ed.), *A Complete Guide to Fire and Buildings,* Medical and Technical Publishing Co., Ltd., Lancaster, England.
7. National Fire Protection Association, Boston, Mass., *Fire Protection Handbook,* 14th ed., January 1976.

Chapter 20

Sprinkler Systems

RAYMOND J. GEORGES

**Fire Protection and Life Safety Consultant; President,
Lancaster Sprinkler Company, Lancaster, Pennsylvania**

FUNCTIONS OF A TYPICAL SYSTEM

Automatic sprinkler systems are provided inside buildings to control and extinguish fires. They have proved to be very successful, and in fact the sprinkler system is still the most economical single means of performing all the immediately required functions that a fire emergency requires. Without the hesitation involved in human decision, a sprinkler system combines fire detection, suppression, containment, the initial alarm of fire, and extinguishing. The excellent record of the automatic sprinkler is due to its simplicity and the reliability of its design and component parts. Few industries can match the strict test criteria and installation standards applied to the sprinkler industry. After its initial installation, it may be forgotten, poorly maintained, blocked by closed valves, rendered obsolete by building changes, frozen, painted over, obstructed, clogged with debris, corroded, maligned as unaesthetic, and blamed as a source of water damage, yet the sprinkler system has maintained a record of 96 percent effectiveness since its introduction over a hundred years ago. When properly installed and maintained it is among the most faithful of the mechanical devices in the service of humanity.

The System Defined

As it remains today, water has been for centuries the most widely used fire-extinguishing agent because of its low cost and its cooling, smothering, diluting, and emulsifying characteristics. Various other (or additional) extinguishing agents such as carbon dioxide, dry chemicals, wetting-agent foams, halogens, and combustible-metal extinguishing agents may be more appropriate for certain specialized purposes. These employ design principles different from those of water-supplied systems. However, when the term "sprinkler system" is used, it usually describes a system which uses water as the extinguishing agent, and this chapter is written in that context.

The sprinkler system is an engineered arrangement of underground and overhead piping, fitted with sealed valves that open automatically to discharge water on a newly started fire and its immediate vicinity and to signal an alarm. This infers a water supply constantly available to the sealed valves, which can be either individual sealed sprinkler heads or remote-system control pipe valves. The degree of reliability of the water supply depends upon the degree of hazard, local code requirements, and the insured value of the property.

Components

A typical system includes:
1. A reliable and adequate water supply
2. A secondary supply—usually a fire department connection with check valves on both supply and pumper inlet
3. Protection from freezing
4. Alarm-signaling devices
5. Control valves
6. Sprinkler heads
7. Piping to deliver water density at the rate of application required by hazard and occupancy
8. System drains
9. Inspector's testing connection
10. Extra sprinkler heads
11. Exclusive use of approved equipment
12. Detailed layout drawings indicating conformance to standards

Partially sprinklered buildings can be fed from domestic water lines if these are sufficient to deliver the required flow and pressure for sprinkler heads to function. These minisystems must completely cover the areas served but do not require the secondary water supply of the basic system. They can be used in low-hazard occupancies or on partially sprinklered floors of high-rise buildings supplied from fire standpipes. Each of these lines should have test, drain, and control valves and flow alarms that are protected from surges of water use.

SOURCES OF WATER

Public Water Systems

The availability of water for fire protection is a prime concern in the selection of building sites. The cost of a sprinkler system can be quadrupled if on-site fire-protection water supplies are required. Public water supplies are the most economical sources of water, and if gridded or fed from two directions, they can provide both primary and secondary sources of water. This holds true despite the fact that public water connections are frequently made expensive in some localities where back-flow prevention devices must be installed to isolate sprinkler piping from potable water supplies. Most water departments require single detector check valves with bypass meters, underground fittings, and concrete vaults to detect water hijacking on fire service connections. This is often considered an unnecessary addition to the cost of fire protection, since the standby charges of most water suppliers more than cover any water that may be wrongfully used. The latter expense can be minimized by installing the detector check inside the building rather than in an outdoor pit. Water meters on sprinkler supplies must be the low-friction-loss type for high-volume flows, since ordinary water meters can throttle sprinkler operation.

Adequacy of Supply The adequacy of the public water supply in terms of volume and pressure available is the key to its use in sprinkler systems. Adequacy is determined by flow tests of hydrants on water mains near the site. Standard flow-test procedures are outlined in waterworks manuals and insurance test guidelines. The static pressure is the usual gauge reading on a water system which indicates the pounds per square inch of pressure charging the water supply. When water is flowed for testing, it simulates the flow required during a fire at the location tested. By reading a pitot gauge held into the stream, the pressure reading can be converted into

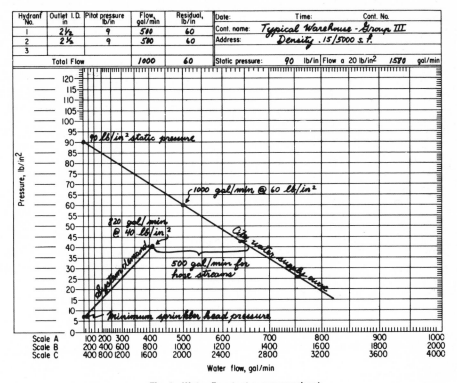

Hydrant No.	Outlet I.D. in	Pitot pressure lb/in	Flow, gal/min	Residual, lb/in
1	2½	9	500	60
2	2½	9	500	60
3				
Total Flow			1000	60

Date: Time: Cont. No.
Cont. name: *Typical Warehouse - Group III*
Address: *Density .15/5000 s.f.*
Static pressure: 90 lb/in Flow a 20 lb/in² 1580 gal/min

Fig. 1   Water flow test summary sheet.

gallons per minute flowing and can be related to the static pressure drop. Also during the testing, the residual pressure is related graphically to the total flow in gallons per minute and the static pressure with no flow in order to establish a supply curve for the site. This curve is plotted against the demand curve to determine the adequacy of the supply. The test flow should exceed the anticipated demand. (See Fig. 1.)

Demand is determined by the density of application required applied over the largest area in which a single fire might spread, plus an allowance for protecting exposures with hose streams. Accuracy in the determination of demand is more critical today since the advent of the hydraulically calculated system in which pressure and volume are considered as dollars and cents by system designers. The proper establishment of demand is by considered judgment of a fire protection engineer after evaluating all the conditions surrounding each installation.

Reliability of the supply is based on insurance acceptance as well as local codes and the degree of hazard involved. For low-hazard, low-value properties the fire department connection can serve as a secondary supply source for the system. As the hazards and values increase, an automatic secondary or third source of water is required. While a partially sprinklered low-hazard building can have a single connection to domestic water if the sizing is adequate, a $25 million plant will require three automatic sources of supply for insurance acceptance. The reliability then is related to the size, value, and hazard of the property protected, and this should be explored with insurance carriers and code enforcement agencies *before* design begins.

Improving the supply may be necessary to provide for sprinkler system requirements. When the supply curve falls short of the demand, the difference should be considered in terms of a booster pump on the public supply. The reliability of this pump is determined in the same manner as the supply. If the public water mains need extensions, this should be pursued with water authorities prior to site acquisition, if possible. An adequate fire-protection water supply is considered the responsibility of local public protection agencies. If the site is remote, the cost of extending a public system should be carefully weighed against the cost of going into the water business. The standards for an on-site fire-protection water system are more restrictive than those for a public water system. In addition to the original cost, the costs of continuing maintenance and inspection programs should be seriously investigated.

On-Site Water Supplies

Storage   The amount of storage is related to the duration of an anticipated fire and the requirements of reliability of supply based on local codes and insurance requirements for the system. In seismic areas, all high-rise buildings are now required by building codes to have at least 15,000 gal of on-site storage. For most buildings a duration of 2 hours is the minimum for supplying the full system demand. This duration can vary from $\frac{1}{2}$ to 6 hours, depending upon the hazard and imposed requirements. The means of storing on-site water can be by gravity tanks, suction tanks, nonpotable natural bodies of water, or pressure tanks.

Gravity Tanks   These can be employed as primary supplies when the bottom of the tank is at least 35 ft above the top line of sprinklers. This would allow for 15 lb/in² available at the top of the riser nipple on branch lines and for small demands could provide the most economical on-site protection. Tanks are commonly manufactured in the following shapes and capacities:

Oblatoid	250,000–1,500,000 gal
Double ellipsoidal	20,000–500,000 gal
Spherical	50,000–200,000 gal
Flat-bottom	5,000–50,000 gal

A cylindrical standpipe could be employed as a primary supply in its top portion, with a fire pump taking suction from the storage below the required height as a secondary supply.

Suction Tanks   Along with diesel-driven fire pumps, these form the most commonly employed sprinkler system supply in areas where public water is insufficient to meet demand and reliability requirements. The most popular tank in new installations is the steel cylindrical tank resting on a concrete foundation at ground level. These tanks are available in all sizes and are approved by all interested agencies.

Wood tanks are available up to a 300,000-gal capacity. Fabric tanks, such as those manufactured by the Firestone Corporation, can be used as in-ground storage reservoirs. The latter are probably the least expensive. Concrete basins and cooling-tower reservoirs have also been utilized as water sources for sprinkler systems.

Protection from Freezing   This is another function of the reliability of the system. Normally the standards for tank heaters apply, with all the controls necessary for these devices. However, an unheated, open-roofed steel tank would be acceptable to underwriters, if the values protected were low, with only a vacuum breaker floating on the tank water's surface.

Pressure Tanks   Systems with a small demand that do not have a public water supply can utilize the hydropneumatic storage tank. Since these tanks are generally built for 150 lb working pressure, they should preferably be in an elevated location to avoid the excessive pressures required to supply tall buildings. The tank capacity depends upon maximum demand and duration of flow. The cost of supporting these tanks may exceed the cost of a heavier tank at ground level in buildings of moderate height. Water usually occupies no more than two-thirds of the tank. The pressure is maintained by automatic regulation or nitrogen.

Fire Pumps   The diesel-driven centrifugal, horizontal-shaft, split case fire pump is the usual installation. Where electrically powered fire pumps function in a primary supply, their power must be completely reliable. Regardless of the drive provided, all pumps should be supervised by a reliable electrical controller complete with standby power.

The sizing of the fire pump should be carefully considered, allowing for pressures available to the pump. Sprinkler system components are rated at 175 lb/in^2 working pressure, and hand-held hose lines exceeding 100 lb/in^2 can be dangerous to personnel. Approved pumps have rated capacities from 500 to 2500 gal/min and net head pressures of from 100 to 200 lb/in^2. The standard for fire pump installations is NFPA Standard 20—*Centrifugal Fire Pumps*.

Natural Bodies of Water

Ponds, lakes, rivers, and oceans can all be considered as sources of sprinkler system supply. These supplies may not be as economical as they seem, since clogging and corroding of the system is possible. Strainers are required on suctions, and fluctuating water levels and freezing pose problems. The vertical turbine pump required for these sources is more expensive than the common horizontal-shaft fire pump. In addition, the back-flow preventer would be required by most health authorities if such storage were utilized in conjuction with a public water system.

SYSTEM COMPONENTS

Underground

Sprinkler system lead-ins and connections to public water or on-site storage are made in the standard pipe sizes of 4, 6, 8, and 10 in, with 12- and 16-in mains. Fittings for these sizes are readily available, while 14-in pipe is relatively rare. A loop formed by smaller sizes is more reliable than single large mains. These lines should be valved to allow repairs without shutting down the complete system, thus losing protection. The smallest allowable lead-in for sprinkler systems is a 4-in main, and the largest single sprinkler zone allowed is, by present standards, 52,000 ft^2 fed from an 8-in riser. While more than one riser is commonly placed on a lead-in, the reliability required for the system dictates how many risers can be fed from a single main. Runs of underground piping below building floor slabs should be avoided because of access problems for maintenance or repairs.

Approved materials for underground use are cement-lined ductile iron, cast iron, steel with cast-iron fittings, cement asbestos, fiberglass-reinforced plastic, and polyethylene pipe. Since the major cost of underground piping is not in the material, it is prudent to specify the one with the better properties. Based on the experience of sprinkler fitters installing underground piping, Class 2 ductile iron is frequently preferred. It is least likely to be damaged in handling and comes with snap-on joints or mechanical joints.

Control Valves

The post indicator valve (PIV) is the standard means of providing sprinkler system control. It should be located so that it can operate during a fire. The use of underground valves in valve boxes requiring the use of valve keys is not recommended since the possibility of their being parked on, paved over, or covered with ice and snow is obviously a problem. If the PIV is not practical for the installation, a wall indicator valve against a wall that offers some protection from fire is an acceptable alternative. An open-screw-and-yoke gate valve on the riser inside the building can also be provided as an alternative to outside control; it should be located against an outside wall with fire separation from the rest of the building, and direct access to it from outdoors should be identified.

In connections to public water mains, a tapping sleeve and valve are usually provided. This valve can be utilized economically together with an open-screw-and-yoke gate valve on the riser for system control if its reliability is accepted by the governing authorities.

Check Valves

The sprinkler rules require a check valve to pressurize the system from the fire department connection. Local water authorities may require a detector check valve or a back-flow preventer assembly composed of two detector check valves.

Pipe and Fittings

The sprinkler rules are explicit as to allowed materials, but they provide latitude for new materials that have been approved by nationally recognized testing and inspection agencies.

Welded Systems   These can use seamless steel pipe with a minimum wall thickness of 0.188 in for pressures to 300 lb/in² in sizes 4 in and larger. For $3\frac{1}{2}$-in and smaller sizes in welded systems, Schedule 10S pipe is allowed, with 0.120 in thickness. For new installations this can mean a material savings of half the cost of standard-wall pipe (Schedule 40). It should be understood that thin-wall pipe is not threadable, and later welding on existing systems in occupied buildings is not generally allowed. The advantage of thin-wall in sizes above $2\frac{1}{2}$ in is its increased flow capability due to a larger internal diameter. Welding allows greater prefabrication savings, and grooved fittings allow for speedier installations. Schedule 40 or 30 is best for supporting the alarm check valve assembly and for branch lines, since the latter allows for ease of modifications. Grooved pipe with mechanical couplings provides greater system flexibility than an all-screwed pipe system with occasional flanged unions. Slugs and tailings should be removed from piping to avoid blockages.

Copper Systems   The functioning of copper under fire conditions indicates many advantages, including uses where weight and size are critical. On the negative side, unsoldered joints in piping are not always immediately obvious; sometimes they hold temporarily under test conditions but develop failure at a later time. Plumbers argue that copper sprinkler systems are within their province, and this tempts some novices in sprinkler installations to bid such jobs. Materials costs are higher for copper, which is susceptible to pilferage problems.

Galvanized Pipe   This should be specified for all above-ground exterior pipe and connections passing through walls, with emphasis on areas where aesthetics are a consideration.

Fittings   Fittings of the cast-iron screwed type are the most economical for steel pipe which is 2 in or less in diameter. In these sizes, couplings should be the beaded malleable-iron type. Cast-iron flanged fittings provide necessary riser support under alarm check and dry pipe valves. Welded fittings can be cut into pipe lengths in a fabrication shop, allowing for single-piece installation of many fittings previously attached in the air. New fittings have been introduced which meet all approvals utilizing grooved-pipe mechanical joints or plain end couplings with side outlets for sprinkler heads or drops, allowing the use of thinwall in the 1- to 2-in pipe sizes. Another fitting allows the exterior application of a single head to a pipe run by drilling a hole in the pipe and attaching an outlet clamp.

Sprinkler Heads—General

The general public's main indication that sprinkler protection is provided—the visible aspect of the sprinkler head—is also the key to the system's success. As a sealed valve, the head restrains the discharge of water with a heat-actuated element that keeps a cap on the head's orifice until the preset thermal limit is reached. The size of

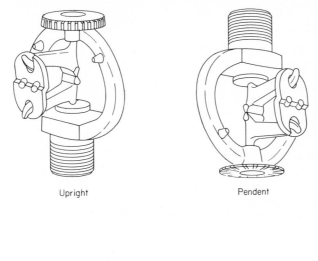

Upright   Pendent

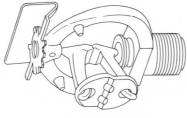

Side-wall sprinkler

Fig. 2   Upright, pendent, and side-wall heads shown in position as mounted.

the orifice and the short tube formed by the threaded connection for attachment to the piping system represents a discharge coefficient that is used as the constant K in hydraulic calculations; K increases proportionately with the orifice. The heat-actuated elements in commonly used heads are a fusible link in the link and lever type, a glass bulb that shatters, or a meltable pellet in a small sliding cylinder.

Deflectors control the direction of spray, which is distributed by standard heads in a hemispherical pattern below the plane of the deflector, the latter being supported by the frame arms of the head. In a wet system the only difference between upright pendent heads of the same manufacture is the deflector detail (see Fig. 2). Heads are marked SSU and SSP, Standard Sprinkler Upright or Pendent. The sidewall sprinkler has a deflector that directs the water one way in a half-hemispherical pattern.

Temperature ratings are critical in the selection of sprinkler heads near heat sources, since overheating is a main cause of sprinkler failure. The choice of rating is also subject to the characteristics of the fire area and the hazard protected against. Common ratings are listed below in degrees Fahrenheit:

Common ratings, °F	Maximum ceiling temperatures, °F	Manufacturer's settings, °F	Frame color code
165 Ordinary	100	135 to 170	None
212 Intermediate	150	175 to 225	White
286 High	225	250 to 300	Blue

Other temperature heads with higher ratings are manufactured for special equipment applications, such as ovens and dryers.

Tests of heads are constantly made by the manufacturers to maintain the mechanical qualities required for FM (Factory Mutual) or UL approval. Designed to operate at a working pressure of 175 lb/in^2, they are subjected to 1000 lb/in^2 at the factory. Their initial approval is also based on their function in the designed use, their ability to discharge and distribute water uniformly, and their performance effectiveness under fire conditions.

Types of Heads

Standard Spray Sprinklers These are the most common and are available with $\frac{3}{8}$-, $\frac{1}{2}$-, and $\frac{17}{32}$-in orifices. The latter are called large-orifice heads and have either the common $\frac{1}{2}$-in IPT (iron pipe thread) or a $\frac{3}{4}$-in IPT. Upright types are bronze, and pendents can be bronze, chrome-finished, or lead-coated and waxed for corrosion protection. All heads are normally sealed, but they can be supplied unsealed for deluge use.

Dry Pendent Sprinkler Heads These are the most expensive, since they incorporate an extension nipple valved at the inlet end to prevent water from freezing while trapped in the drop. (See Fig. 3.)

Sidewall Sprinkler Heads This type is designed with a special throw to allow single-head coverage in areas which otherwise might require more heads. They are not approved for all uses but are excellent for aesthetics in light-hazard areas.

Special Heads These include the recycling type that shuts off when the initial thermal limit is reduced, the flush type for pendent concealment in ceilings, the window and cornice type for outdoor exposures, the cooling-tower type, foam water sprinklers, and water spray nozzles for protecting flammable liquid hazards. Quick-actuating devices are now available for standard head types. The recently developed threshold-pressure-type head will help systems to reduce their water demands, since such systems will never operate with insufficient pressure. Larger orifices such as 1 in allow for better densities and will become more commonly accepted, since they improve initial fire control and decrease extraneous head operation.

WET SYSTEMS

The wet-pipe sprinkler system is the most economical and represents about 75 percent of all sprinkler protection. It is employed only where no danger of freezing exists and is usually provided with an alarm check valve. A system with only an electric-vane-type flow alarm switch is known in the trade as a "gutless" riser. The equipment on wet systems includes:

Alarm Check Valves These are designed for a standard water working pressure of 175 lb/in^2. Figures 4, 5, and 6 show typical risers and a cross section of a typical alarm valve, which is basically a check valve with a pilot valve sealing off the alarm line. When small surges occur, the clapper can move a short distance without unseating the pilot valve. A correctly sealed clapper has a slightly higher pressure on the system side than on the supply side of the valve because of entrapped air. The distance the clapper must travel to lift the pilot valve can be raised to discourage false alarms or lowered for greater sensitivity.

Retard Chambers A retard chamber is provided on all variable-pressure systems and, except for gravity-supplied systems, is the normal installation. This device is a cylindrical cast-iron chamber mounted on the alarm line adjacent to the alarm check

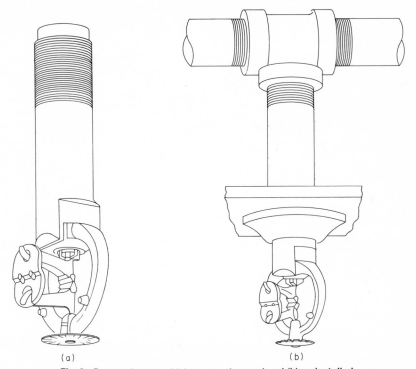

(a)   (b)

Fig. 3   Dry pendent head (a) as manufactured and (b) as installed.

valve, with a drain for bleeding off surges which is held closed on sustained water flow to operate the water motor gong and/or the alarm pressure switch.

Water Motor Gong The water motor alarm is a mechanical means of operating a gong (mounted outdoors) by the force of water pressure. Spent water must be provided with a drain, and the water motor should not be more than 75 ft nor less than 20 ft above the alarm valve. Piping should not be less than ¾ in and must be galvanized. The alarm line should be increased to 1 in if pressure is low. One to three systems protecting the same fire area can be connected to one gong. If the discharge line is directed outdoors, a galvanized angle elbow facing down will inhibit the formation of rust and ice at the end of the drain.

Alarm Pressure Switch This is a switch operated by water pressure that actuates an electric circuit to a local and/or a remote alarm on a pressure rise of 4 to 7 lb/in². When pressure is relieved, the switch is automatically reset. For systems with a limited water supply, a manual reset switch is available.

Excess-Pressure Pump An excess-pressure pump is installed on wet systems only when the water supply is subject to extreme pressure variations or when retards on alarm check valves are omitted. It is a low-capacity, high-gear, self-lubricating, electric-driven pump requiring an inlet strainer. The water pressure above the alarm valve is increased from 20 to 30 lb/in² above the normal supply pressure to the system.

The excess pressure should not be set too high, since alarms on system activation may be delayed. Fill time after system maintenance should not exceed about 20 min. Pressure switches should be set about 5 lb/in² above and 5 lb/in² below the desired excess-pressure level.

DRY SYSTEMS

Dry systems for suspended ceiling areas are the most expensive, since they require dry pendent heads which are costly in material and labor. They are designed for areas normally below 40°F and are slower to operate and more expensive to maintain than a wet system. The restraint of water flow is by the dry pipe valve rather than the sprinkler heads. Piping to the sprinkler head is filled with air or nitrogen, and its discharge causes a reduction in air pressure sufficient to trip the valve. These systems require electric air compressors if plant air is not available or, alternatively, nitrogen cylinders in outdoor locations. Accelerators must be provided for larger systems. By triggering the dry valve with a heat detector the speed of the system's response is improved. (See Fig. 7.)

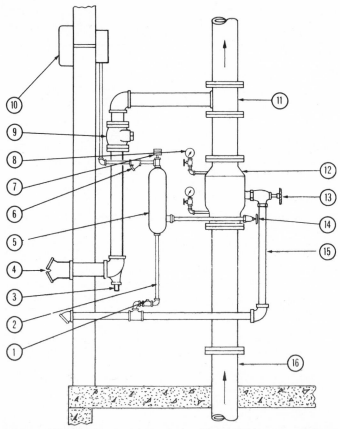

Fig. 4   Typical riser with alarm valve. (1) Check valve; (2) retarding chamber drain; (3) ball drip; (4) fire department connection; (5) retarding chamber; (6) alarm line strainer; (7) pressure switch; (8) water guage (two required); (9) check valve; (10) water motor alarm; (11) tee connection; (12) wet pipe alarm valve; (13) main drain valve; (14) alarm test valve; (15) main drain; (16) riser from main water supply.

DELUGE SYSTEM

A deluge system is a series of open heads providing total flooding when a deluge valve trips upon activation by hydraulic, penumatic, electric, or manual release. These are commonly used to deliver foam water in aircraft hangars or in other rapid-spread potential fire situations.

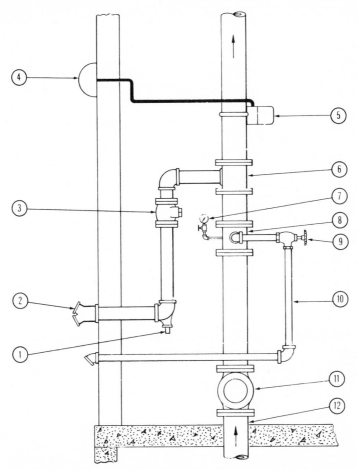

Fig. 5   Typical riser with water indicator only. (1) Ball drip; (2) fire department connection; (3) check valve; (4) electric alarm bell; (5) water flow indicator; (6) tee connection; (7) water gauge; (8) tee connection; (9) main drain valve; (10) main drain (flow test line); (11) check valve; (12) riser from main water supply.

DESIGN CONSIDERATIONS

Required Information for Bidders

1. Availability of water—city supply or well water on-site
2. Site plan
3. Property insurance underwriting firm's requirements
4. Occupancy layout, with anticipated hazards
5. Type of construction

6. Ceiling plans and partition plans
7. Location and dimensions of floor and roof supports
8. Roof slope
9. Elevations: final grade, finished floor, height of ceiling, and top of steel
10. Sprinkler head locations, if required by aesthetics.

Architectural drawings and specifications, including required finishes, are often omitted from sprinkler contractors' bid sets but should be provided to ensure a coordinated project.

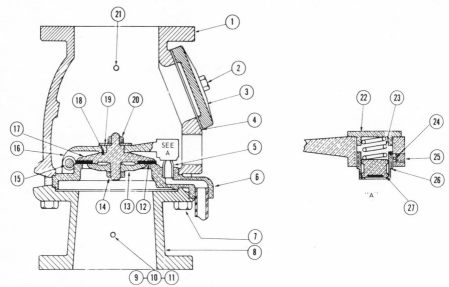

Fig. 6   Alarm check valve cross section. (1) Housing; (2) hexagonal head screw; (3) hand hole cover; (4) hand hole gasket; (5) auxiliary valve seat; (6) seat; (7) hexagonal head cap screws; (8) base; (9) pipe bushing; (10) pipe plug; (11) pipe plug; (12) water seat rubber; (13) clamp plate; (14) clamp plate nut; (15) hinge pin; (16) clapper arm; (17) clapper; (18) locating pin; (19) washer; (20) clapper arm nut; (21) pipe plug; (22) auxiliary valve cap; (23) auxiliary valve spring; (24) lead ball; (25) set screw; (26) auxiliary valve sleeve; (27) auxiliary valve clapper.

Piping Layout Drawings

Unless proposed systems are sized for future expansion, or in cases where dimensions are extremely critical or exceptional design elements must be considered, it is usually unnecessary to show piping to head locations. The practice of showing piping employed by many architectural firms may remove the potential of providing the most economical and functional design for many projects, since the sprinkler contractor's engineers must prepare detailed shop drawings for fabrication and approvals no matter what may be shown on the bid drawings. While space must be left available for piping runs and hangers, the advent of computerized hydraulic design by contractors can achieve economies that may not be feasible with a manual piping layout. The pipe schedule of the Sprinkler Rules is no longer the only valid design reference for large projects.

Hydraulic Design

Computerized programs now allow for precision in water supply analysis, branch line balancing, multiple loops, and the use of the Hardy-Cross formula in a network analysis that includes velocity pressures. The effect on sprinkler installations has been a reduction in labor and material costs. It has become vital for the density and rate-of-application specifications to be as professional as possible, since demand is the cost basis of the installation. In addition, water supply data must be accurately evaluated and must include projections of future consumption.

SPRINKLER INSTALLERS

The **sprinkler contractor** is prepared to quote on a complete sprinkler installation, including underground piping, tanks, pumps, controls, and the interior sprinklers. Many mechanical contractors have been able to lower their overall job bids by maintaining an in-house sprinkler installation capability. This enables them to reduce their overall selling prices based on the volume involved in a combined bid. Sprinkler-installing contractors are represented by the National Automatic Sprinkler and Fire Control Association, 45 Kensico Drive, Mount Kisco, NY 10549.

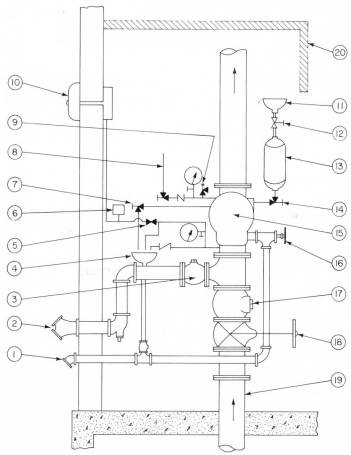

Fig. 7 Dry pipe valve riser. (1) Main drain; **(2)** fire department connection; **(3)** check valve; **(4)** drip cup; **(5)** alarm control valve; **(6)** priming water level test valve; **(7)** alarm pressure switch; **(8)** air supply line; **(9)** air relief valve; **(10)** water motor alarm; **(11)** priming funnel; **(12)** upper priming valve; **(13)** priming chamber; **(14)** lower priming valve; **(15)** dry pipe valve; **(16)** main drain valve; **(17)** check valve; **(18)** OS&Y gate valve; **(19)** riser from supply; **(20)** heated enclosure.

Sprinkler fitters are members of the Sprinkler Fitters locals, which represent about 5 percent of the membership of the United Association of Journeymen and Apprentices of the plumbing and pipe-fitting industry of the United States and Canada. Each apprentice must pass a series of courses devised by the University of Pennyslvania for each step in the 5 years required to become a journeyman. All major sprinkler contractors utilize their services, and sprinkler installation supervisors normally rise from their ranks. The bulk of sprinkler work today is performed by union members.

SPRINKLER STANDARDS

Prerequisite to the design of sprinkler systems is an understanding of the NFPA standards governing them. These include the latest editions of Standard 13, *Installation of Sprinkler Systems;* Standard 14, *Installation of Standpipes and Hose Systems;* and Standard 24, for yard water mains, called *Outside Protection.* In addition, Standard 20 applies to the *Installation of Centrifugal Fire Pumps,* and Standard 22 covers *Water Tanks for Private Protection.* Standard 26 relates to the *Supervision fo Valves,* and the generally overlooked Standard 92M covers *Waterproofing and Draining of Floors.* These and other standards pertinent to sprinkler installations are listed in the Sprinkler Rules, and all are available at a nominal charge from the National Fire Protection Association, 470 Atlantic Avenue, Boston, MA 02210.

The codes outline the basics but can leave the serious designer with many questions. The mystique of sprinklers is the simplicity of concept that is too often misunderstood, resulting in greater costs for the purchasers of sprinkler installations. While many systems are approved, all sprinkler equipment is not alike in function, aesthetics, or cost. The savings possible by utilizing the talents of a fire protection engineer should not be overlooked, especially in the conceptual stages of design where sprinkler ramifications have a wide effect on building materials, locations of exits, height and areas of buildings, water supply, and overall costs of protection. Large corporations have often expended hundreds of thousands of dollars to meet the requirements of building codes, fire prevention codes, and insurance regulations that could have been satisfied with previously obtained professional design advice. Smaller companies and building owners have also paid for the lack of this expertise in high insurance rates and often overly expensive sprinkler systems.

THE APPROVAL PROCESS

The Sprinkler Rules

The sprinkler system as it is known today was originated by Henry F. Parmalee of New Haven, who demonstrated his "automatic sprinkler" to a group of manufacturers and insurance underwriters in 1874. The sprinkler industry began its growth soon after in 1882 and was then regulated by the individual standards of fire underwriting companies. By 1895 the standards for sprinkler systems were as numerous as the insurers of sprinklered risks. The need for uniformity in fire protection standards prompted the formation of the National Fire Protection Association, which developed the first edition of NFPA Standard 13, *Standard for the Installation of Sprinkler Systems.* It was the first of two standards developed by the NFPA in 1897, the second being NFPA Standard 70, *The National Electrical Code* (NEC). Of these two, the NEC has enjoyed wider universal acceptance, since underwriters have been in general accord and its local enforcement is well provided for. The "sprinkler rules" are the minimum acceptable standards, since property underwriter groups still add their own requirements. For a sprinkler system to be acceptable to approving agencies, it must conform with all aspects of Chapters 1 through 8 of those sprinkler rules. The entire sprinkler industry is geared to produce this conformance automatically, so that paraphrasing of these basics is considered unprofessional.

Sprinkler contractors must receive approvals of their designs and layouts from insurance agencies as well as the local authority having jurisdiction. This approval process has built-in quality control, since experienced sprinkler contractors are cited in the sprinkler rules as being qualified to install systems; such contractors constantly deal with these agencies and avoid a reputation for violating the standards.

Sprinkler Equipment Approval

All sprinkler manufacturers have to obtain Factory Mutual, Underwriters' Laboratories, and other agency approval of their equipment in order to remain in the business. In addition, the larger corporations obtain the approvals of foreign testing agencies.

Inclusion in both the UL's *Fire Protection List* and the FM System's *Approval Guide,* both published annually, is the best assurance that the equipment is suitable for general application, subject to the limitations in the listing. Current copies of both lists should be part of every designer's library. They may be obtained at a nominal charge from the Director of Public Information, Factory Mutual System, 1151 Boston Providence Turnpike, Norwood, MA 02062, or from Underwriters' Laboratories, Inc., 207 East Ohio Street, Chicago, IL 60611.

Design Approval

Insurance-sponsored agencies provide the bulk of sprinkler system design reviews. The foremost of these is the Insurance Services Office (ISO), a merger of all rating bureaus sponsored by capital-stock insurance companies. In the states of Hawaii, Idaho, Louisiana, Mississippi, North Carolina, Texas, Virginia, and Washington, the individual state sponsors the rating bureaus for this purpose. Other sprinkler review desks are maintained by the local offices of the Factory Mutual Engineering Association, the Industrial Risk Insurers (a recent merger of the Factory and Oil Insurance Associations), the Kemper Group, and the Improved Risk Mutuals. These organizations all review designs for conformance with the basics of the sprinkler rules plus the requirements for risks underwritten by their member companies.

The **local authority having jurisdiction** is cited by the sprinkler rules as the deciding factor in code enforcement and interpretation. These authorities may be governmental agencies, such as state and local building inspection departments, fire marshals' offices, or state labor and industry bureaus. Where these agencies do not have the capability for detailed sprinkler review, the design review stamp by the ISO or similar insurance group has been accepted as evidence of compliance with the standards. In cities and towns with a fire protection design review staff, the authority having jurisdiction reviews and approves the drawings, which must also bear an insurance stamp for underwriting purposes.

Sprinkler layout shop drawings are prepared by the sprinkler contractor after detailed engineering surveys of an existing building or reviews of structural and architectural detail drawings of a project. These drawings are made as accurately as possible to facilitate an exact listing of the fittings and length of piping required, so that as much of the work as possible can be fabricated in a shop. These are the drawings that give full details of sprinkler head locations, branch lines, feed and cross mains, and equipment to be used. For systems based on hydraulic calculations, the details of the calculations used are presented with the drawings for approval in a format specified in Chapter 7 of the sprinkler rules. Architectural and engineering drawings are never sufficiently detailed to replace the required sprinkler shop drawings. It is less confusing if bid drawings only locate risers, specify the density and spacing required, and plot head locations where desired in suspended ceiling plans. To include the piping dimensions and sizes is to increase the costs not only of the drawings but of the project itself.

Sprinkler system acceptance is made by both the owner or owner's representative and the property insurance underwriting company or its designated agency.

At the completion of each sprinkler installation, the contractor completes a contractor's material and test certificate. Tests required by the sprinkler rules are witnessed by the owner's representative and signed by both parties, with copies to the approving authorities.

On occasions the underwriting insurance company may have more requirements than those provided in the sprinkler rules. In these cases it would be beneficial to have their representative review the design drawings and be on hand for the final tests on the system.

At the time of acceptance, the owner should be presented with operating and maintenance instructions for the system, which should include the location of control valves and instructions for the care of equipment.

Part Four

Building Types—Special Security Provisions

Chapter 21

Banks

ROBERT BARRY

A.M. MARZANO

RONALD MOWATT

RONALD SILVERS

Product Managers, The Mosler Safe Company, Hamilton, Ohio

BUILDING SECURITY FOR FINANCIAL INSTITUTIONS

There are many types of financial institutions—for example, commercial banks, savings and loan associations, mutual savings banks, and credit unions. The distinctions between these institutions are important for the owners and customers. For the purpose of this chapter, however, they have one common feature: Each must store considerable amounts of cash (and perhaps other valuables in safe deposit boxes) which must be protected by physical and electronic means. Therefore, these institutions will be considered without distinguishing among the various types and, for convenience, will be called "banks." These banks have another shared characteristic: The vast majority of them are regulated and/or have their deposits insured by one or more of several federal government agencies and thus must comply with the Bank Protection Act of 1968.

The Bank Protection Act of 1968, Revised 1973

This act was initiated and supported by federal agencies when it was discovered that many banks, particularly in rural areas, did not have even basic protection against robbery and burglary. All federally regulated or insured banks now must have security equal to or better than that required by the act. Critics of the act point out that the regulations are strictly minimal and that most banks should have a much higher degree of security. Therefore, they strongly support strengthened regulations and the closing of what they consider to be gaping loopholes. The act was revised in 1973, and, as of this writing, further revisions are being proposed. The insurance industry tacitly supports these critics by insisting on considerably higher standards of security, in most cases, before bonds will be issued.

The Insurance Services Office (ISO)

The Insurance Services Office is supported by insurance companies to provide a consistent basis for setting standards and rates. As these standards, in most instances, are higher than the Bank Protection Act (BPA) requirements, architects should first consider ISO recommendations when preparing building plans.

There is, however, a considerable range between the lowest acceptable rating and the highest. Selection of equipment and systems thus becomes a series of trade-offs between the following basic factors:

1. Compliance with BPA and ISO regulations
2. Loss potential
3. Loss experience
4. Cost of insurance bond premiums
5. Cost of security equipment

Banker's Blanket Bond premiums are first determined on the basis of loss potential (how much cash the bank has in its vault on the average weekend, for example). Discounts are then applied for higher-than-average security equipment ratings. Further discounts (or additional premiums) are applied in accordance with the bank's loss experience. For instance, a large city bank may have a base premium of $100,000. Loss experience greater than average may result in actually *doubling* this premium. On the other hand, lower-than-average loss experience may decrease the bond premium as much as 50 percent or more.

Therefore, it is to the bank's advantage to install higher-rated security equipment to earn discounts and discourage burglaries and robberies, since the latter would increase their loss experience. The savings in premiums could quickly offset increased security equipment costs.

Underwriters' Laboratories Classifications

Underwriters' Laboratories, Inc., tests and classifies most security equipment and systems used in a bank, *except* bank vaults. Safes, alarms, vault ventilators and similar devices usually must be UL approved to meet ISO recommendations.

PROTECTION AGAINST BURGLARY

The Vault

The familiar walk-in bank vault is the heart of the bank's security system as well as its symbol of trustworthiness. Figure 1 is a page from the ISO Burglary Manual listing its

	Bank (Revised)			Mercantile	
Class	Door thick.	Vault wall (optional) construction	Class	Door thick.	Vault wall construction
1	None; iron or steel	Brick, concrete, stone, iron or steel; no thickness given	B	Less than 1″	Brick, concrete, stone, tile, or iron or steel; no thickness given
2		Eliminated	C	At least 1″	½″ Steel lining or 9″ Reinf. conc. or stone; Non-reinf. conc. or stone 12″ thick

3	At least 1½"	(a) ¼" Steel lining* or (b) 9" Reinf. concrete		**E**	At least 1½"	½" Steel lining or 9" reinf. conc. or stone;Non-reinf. conc. or stone 12" thick
4	At least 2½"	(a) ½" Steel lining* (b) ¼" S.L.& 9" Reinf. conc. (c) 12" Reinf. conc.		**E**	At least 1½"	½" Steel lining or 9" reinf. conc. or stone; Non-reinf. conc. or stone 12" thick
5R	3½"	(a) ½" Steel lining* (b) 12" Reinf. conc.				
6R	3½"	(a) 1" Steel lining* (b) ½" S.L. & 12" Reinf. conc. (c) 18" Reinf. conc.				
9R	7"	(a) 1" Steel lining* (b) ½" S.L. & 12" Reinf. conc. (c) 18" Reinf. conc.				
10R	9½"	(a) 1½" Steel lining* (b) 1" S.L. & 12" Reinf. conc. (c) ½" S.L. & 18" Reinf. conc. (d) 27" Reinf. Conc. or 18" listed reinf. conc.				
11	16"	Classifications 11, 12, & 13 are recommended by the Bank Vault Industry for construction of security vaults requiring additional protection. Details are available from your Mosler representative upon request.		**G**	At least 3"	½" Steel lining or 12" reinf. conc. or stone; non-reinf. conc. or stone 18" thick
12	20"					
13	25"					

*With fire resistant materials to meet local building codes.

Explanation

Bank classifications 1, 3, 4, 5R, 6R, 9R, & 10R above represent the latest specifications for construction of security vaults as specified by the Insurance Services Office, formerly known as the National Insurance Rating Board.

Bank classifications 1 thru 4, which are comparable to Mercantile classifications B thru E, should not be used for bank vault construction because they do not meet minimum requirements of the Bank Act. This also pertains to classification "G" which does not compare with any of the Bank classifications, but is shown for reference purposes. For Mercantile vault applications requiring better protection than class "G," use the 5R thru 10R Bank Vault classifications.

In accordance with the Bank Protection Act of 1968 and revisions of 1973, classifications 5R thru 10R are acceptable for bank vault construction provided that

the vault walls, floor, and ceiling are constructed of reinforced concrete at least 12" thick. Any alternative using less than 12" of reinforced concrete should comply with the Bank Act Procedure as set forth by the appropriate governing agency.

Classifications 11, 12, & 13, not listed by the Insurance Service Office, are vault industry accepted standards for construction of security vaults requiring protection that exceeds the 10R classification.

The old bank vault classifications 5, 6, 9, & 10, which are listed in the Burglary Insurance Manual for insuring existing vaults, are not shown and should not be used for constructing new vaults because they have been replaced by the new revised classifications 5R thru 10R. When constructing new vaults, follow the requirements of the Bank Act revisions of 1973 and the 1968 revised classifications of the Insurance Services Office.

Fig. 1   Comparative classifications for security vaults published by the Insurance Services Office.

comparative classifications for security vaults. Vaults classified 5R to 10R are acceptable as bank vaults. Classifications 11 through 13 refer to special high-security installations not normally found in an average bank. They are, of course, also acceptable as bank vaults. In addition, ISO recognizes equivalent classifications up to 6R in *non-walk-in* vaults. The Bank Protection Act differs from these requirements in that at least 12 in of reinforced concrete must be placed in vault sides, ceiling, and floor. BPA restricts the use of equivalents and *non-walk-in* vaults, and at the same time it requires only 5R classification (12 in of reinforced concrete) to meet federal requirements for vault construction when, in fact, exposure demands higher and more secure classifications as recommended by the ISO for risk premium calculation. Figure 2 provides construction details required by the ISO and, with the exception mentioned above, by the BPA as amended in 1973 for 5R (12 in of reinforced concrete) only. If, for some reason, these requirements cannot be complied with, the BPA has procedures for reviewing and approving acceptable alternatives. Architects must remember that all six "sides" of a vault must be of the required "classification" thickness and construction, or equivalent, and that the massive weight of the vault structure requires special attention to floor loadings early in the building design stage. Equivalents are available; see Fig. 1 for those specified as acceptable by the ISO if floor loading is a problem, or if portability of the vault is a requirement (leased bank space, for example).

Vault Doors

The weak points in the vault structure are, of course, the necessary openings for access and services. Obviously the vault door is the largest of these weak points. Figures 1 and 2 list door thicknesses required for each vault classification. This rating refers to the thickness of solid steel incorporated into the door's construction. The door itself will be thicker to accommodate the locking mechanism and boltwork. Vault doors manufactured by reputable firms meet or exceed both BPA and ISO specifications for various classifications. Over the past hundred years or so, manufacturers have upgraded vault door materials and design to such a high level that modern doors are, for all practical purposes, impenetrable. It is less difficult to break through reinforced concrete walls than it is to force a vault door. Therefore, instances of burglary by means of compromising a vault door are rare indeed.

Configuration of a typical modern vault door would consist of a 7-in rated door with dual combination bank-type locks and a three-movement, 120-hour time lock. This door, attached to 18 in of reinforced concrete, or equivalent, would yield a vault classification of 9R (see Fig. 1). Special torch- and drill-resistant material protects the locking mechanism.

Door selection is based primarily on three major considerations:

1. Rating requirements (vault classification).
2. Cost.
3. Appearance (if the vault door can be seen from public areas, a massive, secure appearance lends weight to the bank's solid, trustworthy image).

Heating, Air Conditioning, Emergency Air, and Electrical Services

Other openings for heating, air conditioning, emergency air, and electrical and telephone services are also covered by ISO and BPA regulations. In general, conduits for wiring cannot have a diameter larger than $1\frac{1}{2}$ in and must make one and preferably two right-angle bends before entering the vault. Security products for emergency air, heating, and air-conditioning services must be listed by Underwriters' Laboratories, as specified by ISO. Figure 3 gives a typical design of heating and air-conditioning devices for vault wall installation. (Similar devices are available for installation in vault ceilings.)

Safe Deposit Boxes, Lockers, and Other Vault Equipment

Vault equipment and lockers of various sizes (where tellers' cash trays are stored and reserves of cash are kept) are available in many configurations to suit the application. Most are modular in dimension, so that various combinations can be assembled without wasting wall space. Figure 4 shows typical equipment available. Safe deposit boxes are installed in the same vault. These vaults must meet ISO and BPA vault classifications, as previously mentioned.

Vault Alarm Systems

According to BPA regulations, bank vaults must be protected by burglary alarm systems which (1) can detect attacks on vault walls, floor, and ceiling and transmit this alarm to the proper authorities; (2) sound a loud bell outside the bank (optional); (3) are safeguarded against accidental transmission of an alarm; (4) are equipped with visual and audible signals capable of indicating improper functioning; and (5) have an independent source of power in case the line power fails.

To accomplish the above, manufacturers have used primarily two types of detection sensors: audio microphones which can be set at wall, floor, or ceiling attack sound levels and within attack frequency bands, and thermostats and door contacts to sense vault door attacks. These devices have one common purpose: to detect a burglary attempt and send a signal to the proper authorities. Selection of these devices is usually the prerogative of the bank's security officer. The architect, however, must plan for conduit to contain alarm sensor electrical connections with the junction boxes and main control cabinet. Figure 5 illustrates details of typical conduit requirements for the vault as well as for other alarmed equipment and initiating switches. Note that the alarm control is installed inside the vault. This device receives signals from the various detectors and, in turn, transmits a signal, usually in coded form, to the proper authorities. (A later section on Outside Alarm Connections contains a further discussion of outside alarm connections and types of secured lines.)

Night Depositories

Figure 6 shows a typical "letter and bag" night depository unit that is UL listed. Most banks offer night depository service because it allows customers, usually commercial customers, the means to safeguard and deposit cash that is accumulated after banking hours. Figure 7 illustrates the operation of a night depository device and shows construction details of how these units are installed in wall masonry. Detail on Figure 5 illustrates the method of alarming the unit and the receiving safe.

Automatic Tellers

Automatic teller machines are relatively new, but most experts agree that they will be as common as night depositories in a few years. Briefly, automatic tellers permit various transactions by customers of financial institutions at any hour of the day or night, seven days a week. Typically, customers can make deposits, withdraw cash, transfer money from one account to another, and in some cases pay utility bills (see Fig. 8). Automatic tellers require masonry openings of a type shown in Fig. 9 and are, of course, alarmed. The trend seems to be to install automatic tellers anywhere people congregate (law permitting), such as in railroad stations, airline terminals, shopping centers, and store interiors. The console of these machines is exposed to the public, but deposits, cash storage receptacles, and cash-dispensing mechanisms are usually enclosed in a UL-rated money safe appropriately alarmed.

Auxiliary Safes

A bank may elect to forgo the construction of a vault in a very small branch office or in temporary bank quarters. In its place, a "portable vault" may be used. These are

Bank Vault Classifications (5R thru 10R)

description

1. Reinforcing rods in walls, floor, and ceiling. Refer to specifications below for details.
2. Concrete walls, floor, and ceiling. Refer to specifications below for details.
3. Steel lining on walls, floor, and ceiling by Mosler as required.
4. Wall opening for bank vault door. Refer to appropriate masonry opening drawing for details.
5. Pit area for setting and leveling vault door. It is important that the full width of the pit have a solid foundation for support of door. Refer to vault door M.O. drawing for details.
6. Wall opening for emergency vault ventilator. Refer to appropriate M.O. drawing for details.
7. Wall opening for air-guard ventilation port. Refer to appropriate M.O. drawing for details.
8. Outlet box for vault door alarm contacts. Refer to alarm conduit drawing for details.
9. Outlet box for alarm microphones as required. Refer to alarm conduit drawing for details.
10. Outlet boxes for vault lighting as required.
11. Conduit for alarm system and vault lighting as required. All conduit for the alarm lights, telephone, etc., to be furnished by others in accordance with the National Electrical Code. It is recommended that all conduit shall not exceed 1½'' dia., exit from vault floor with drainage to exterior, and all outlet boxes be installed after at least two consecutive 90° bends.

specifications

Reinforcing Rods: No. 5 (5/8'' dia.) deformed steel reinforcing bars are to be located in vertical and horizontal rows in each direction to form a grid not more than 4'' on centers and weighing at least 6 lbs. per sq. ft. Grids are to be located not less than 4'' apart and staggered in each direction. Number of grids required for reinforced walls, floor, and ceiling of bank vaults is as follows:

12'' thickness requires 3 grids

18'' thickness requires 4 grids

27'' thick or greater requires 5 grids

Note: Grids of expanded steel bank vault mesh weighing at least 6 lbs. per sq. ft. with an open area not to exceed 4'' on centers can be substituted in place of No. 5 deformed steel reinforcing rods.

12'' thickness requires 2 grids

18'' thickness requires 3 grids

27'' thickness requires 4 grids

Concrete: The concrete used in walls, floor, and ceiling of bank vaults shall develop an ultimate compressive strength of at least 3,000 lbs. per sq. inch in accordance with the American Concrete Institute standards. While 3,000 lbs./sq. in. is required, 4,500 lbs./sq. in. is recommended for 5R, 6R, 9R, & 10R bank vault classifications.

weights

No. 5 steel reinforcing rods equal 6.26 lbs. per sq. ft. for each grid.

3000 p.s.i. concrete equals approximately 144 lbs. per cubic foot.

12'' thick reinforced concrete equals approximately 156.62 lbs. per sq. ft. of wall, floor, & ceiling area.

18'' thick reinforced concrete equals approximately 234.78 lbs. per sq. ft. of wall, floor & ceiling area.

27'' thick reinforced concrete equals approximately 349.04 lbs. per sq. ft. of wall, floor & ceiling area.

Steel Reinforcing

Front elevation of single steel reinforcing grid showing maximum space requirements of No. 5 (5/8'' dia.) deformed steel reinforcing bars.

Refer to "vault sections" for spacing details of two or more steel reinforcing grids.

Source: Insurance Services Office
160 Water Street
New York, New York 10038

including revisions of October 30, 1974 also Bank Protection Act of 1968 Amended 11-1-73.

BANK PROTECTION ACT REQUIREMENTS	INSURANCE SERVICE OFFICES REQUIREMENTS (FORMERLY KNOWN AS INSURANCE RATING BOARD)
Bank Vault Classifications 5R thru 10R as illustrated below meet or exceed minimum requirements of the Bank Protection Act of 1968 and revisions of 1973 for the construction of new bank vaults which require at least a 3-1/2'' bank vault door with 12'' of specified reinforced concrete walls, floor and ceiling.	All of the types of bank vault construction, including steel lining and special reinforced concrete equivalences, illustrated below under Bank Vault Classification 5R thru 10R and as listed in the Burglary Insurance Manual are acceptable by the Insurance Services Offices for construction of new vaults.
Under certain conditions, as set forth under "Equivalent burglary-resistant materials for vaults", and under "implementation" in the Bank Act, alternatives are possible. Any alternative using less than 12'' of reinforced concrete should comply with the Bank Act procedure of the appropriate governing agency.	Bank vault classifications 11, 12 & 13 not listed below or in the Burglary Insurance Manual, are Bank Vault Industry accepted standards for 16'', 20'' & 25'' bank vault doors. Details for these classifications are available from Mosler upon request.

Minimum Bank Vault Door, Wall, Floor & Ceiling Requirements Complying with Specifications

Vault Door Class.	Minimum Door Thickness
NO. 5R	3½''
NO. 6R	3½''
NO. 9R	7''
NO. 10R	9½''

Vault Wall, Floor, and Ceiling Class. and Constr.

5R — Construction No. 1 / No. 2
½'' Steel Lining — Adequate Fire Protection — 12'' Reinforced Concrete

6R — Construction No. 1 / No. 2 / No. 3
1'' Steel Lining — Adequate Fire Protection — ½'' Steel Lining — 12'' Reinforced Concrete — 18'' Reinforced Concrete

Equivalent: 2 Grid expanded bank vault mesh

Equivalent: 3 Grid expanded bank vault mesh

Fig. 2   Bank vault construction required in order to earn Insurance Services Office classification.

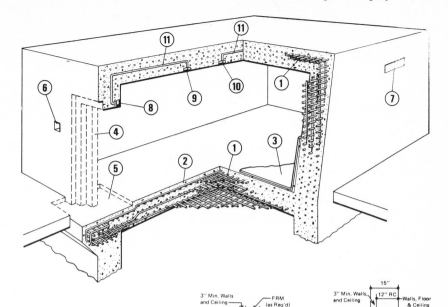

Cutaway Perspective of Typical Bank Vault

SR (12" Reinforced Concrete with 1" Steel Lining Shown)
EXP (2 Grids of Expanded Steel Mesh can be substituted for 3 Grids of Reinforced Steel)

VAULT SECTIONS ILLUSTRATING OPTIONAL MINIMUM WALL, FLOOR, AND CEILING CONSTRUCTION.

Legend

FRM = Fire-resistive material
SR = Steel reinforcing
C = Concrete
RC = Reinforced concrete
WF = Wall finish
FFI = Finished floor inside vault
FFO = Finished floor outside vault
EXP = Expanded Steel Mesh

Note: If additional information is required, contact your local Mosler representative.

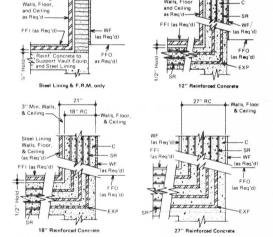

Steel Lining & F.R.M. only

12" Reinforced Concrete

18" Reinforced Concrete

27" Reinforced Concrete

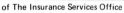

of The Insurance Services Office

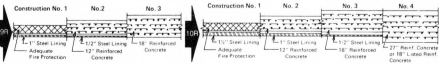

Equivalent: 3 Grid expanded bank vault mesh

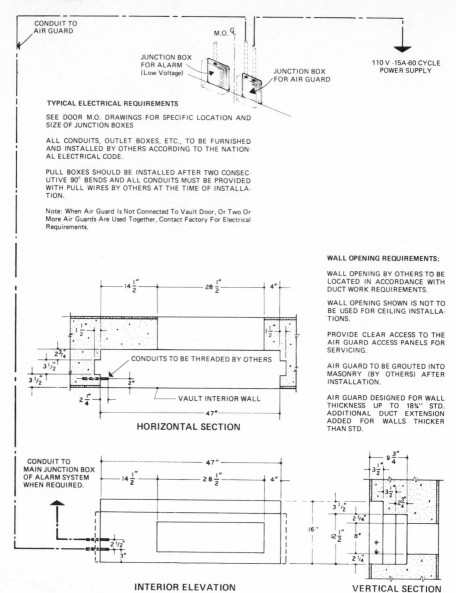

Fig. 3   Wall opening details for a vault ventilation unit.

highly rated money safes equipped with a teller drawer compartment and cash storage lockers. Similar safes may be used for safe deposit boxes. Alarm protection can be of the proximity type, as the safe is free-standing. Portable vaults built into a wall can be laced with conductors or equipped with an audio microphone backup. The architect should be aware that these units may require the support of floor loadings totaling 5000 lb or more.

Internal Line Security

Alarm lines (usually telephone wires) that lead from the bank control cabinet to the police station or other alarm supervisory authority are usually protected (supervised) in some way against attempts to compromise their integrity. However, much less attention is often paid to the security of internal alarm lines, i.e., the connecting wires leading from, say, the night depository to the control cabinet. Thus, a burglar who manages to enter a bank undetected (not an impossible maneuver) can simply "jump"

Fig. 4 Boxes for storage of bulk cash and tellers' cash drawers in the bank's main vault. An alarm panel is visible in the upper right corner.

the internal alarm wires and loot the night depository, the automatic teller, or the auxiliary safes without activating an alarm.

Systems are available now to code the electric characteristics of internal alarm lines to make them much more difficult to compromise. As discussed in the first part of this chapter, one burglary can increase a bank's loss experience factor sufficiently to cause a substantial increase in insurance bond premiums—at times more than an internal line security system would have cost.

BUILDING SECURITY

Building security is usually thought of in three categories:

1. *Point or object protection,* of which the alarming of a vault or safe is an example.

2. *Area or space protection,* of which the detection of movement within the room in which the safe is located is an example. This may be accomplished by radiating space alarms, such as a radar unit, or by a passive sensor, such as an infrared detector. Devices which, in effect, break the room into segments or traps are also included in this category.

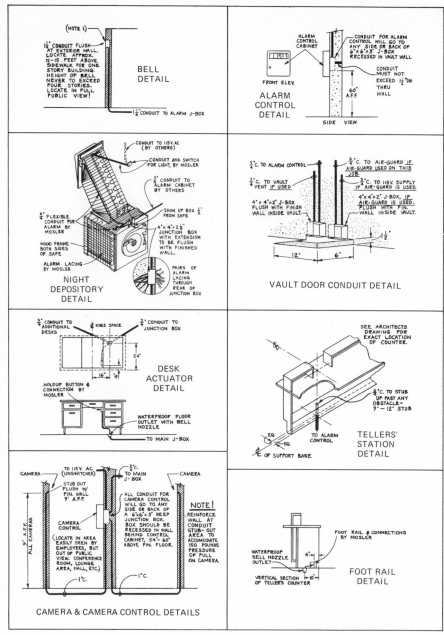

Fig. 5 Typical conduit requirements for alarm and security camera wiring.

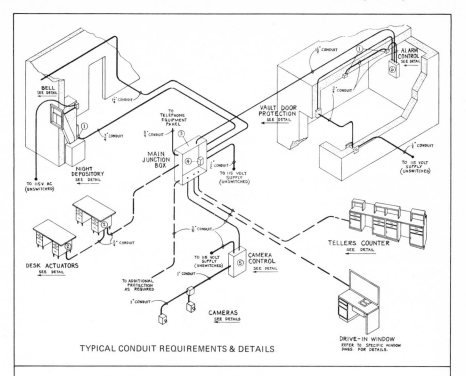

TYPICAL CONDUIT REQUIREMENTS & DETAILS

SPECIFICATIONS

1. <u>OUTLET BOX</u> (4" SQUARE $\times$ 2$\frac{1}{8}$" DEEP) TO BE FLUSH WITH FINISHED WALL OR CEILING.

2. <u>WATERPROOF FLOOR OUTLET</u> WITH BELL NOZZLE.

3. <u>MAIN JUNCTION BOX</u> (12" $\times$ 8" $\times$ 4") COMPLETE WITH COVER AND LOCATED IN AN ACCESSIBLE PLACE IN EQUIPMENT ROOM OR WORK AREA.

4. <u>OUTLET BOX</u> (2" W. $\times$ 3" H. $\times$ 2$\frac{1}{4}$" D.) WITH DUPLEX RECEPTACLE COVER FOR TRANSFORMER BY MOSLER. MOUNT AS ILLUSTRATED IN MAIN JUNCTION BOX.

5. <u>CAMERA CONTROL</u>. LOCATE OUT OF PUBLIC VIEW, ACCESS AND HEARING, PREFERABLY IN LOUNGE OR VAULT AREA. ALL CONDUIT TO TERMINATE IN A 6" $\times$ 6" $\times$ 3" D. J-BOX BEHIND OR UNDER CAMERA CONTROL. 115V AC MUST BE BROUGHT DIRECTLY INTO UPPER LEFT OF CAMERA CONTROL PER DETAIL.

6. <u>ALARM CONTROL CABINET</u>. MUST BE IN VAULT WHENEVER POSSIBLE.

GENERAL NOTES

A. ALL CONDUIT, OUTLET BOXES, AND COVERS TO BE SUPPLIED AND INSTALLED BY OTHERS IN ACCORDANCE WITH NATIONAL ELECTRICAL CODE AND OR LOCAL CODES WITHOUT EXPENSE TO THE MOSLER SAFE CO.

B. NO MORE THAN (2) 90° BENDS IN A CONDUIT RUN.

C. CONDUIT MUST HAVE PULL WIRES IN PLACE AT TIME OF INSTALLATION.

———————————— MUST BE SEPARATE CONDUIT RUN!

— — — — — — THESE CONDUITS MAY BE COMBINED WITH EACH OTHER WHEREVER PRACTICAL TO ELIMINATE AND/OR SHORTEN CONDUIT RUNS. INCREASE SIZE AS REQUIRED.

3. *Perimeter protection,* of which the securing of doors, windows, and other building openings is a form.

Security experts follow the principle of "security in depth" when planning a system. If a bank is located in a high-crime area, they may use all three lines of defense: point, area, and perimeter. On the other hand, banks in well-lighted, well-policed areas may simply alarm their vault, night depository, and automatic teller and either insure or self-insure the office furniture and equipment. Economics and level of threat dictate to what extent protection is extended.

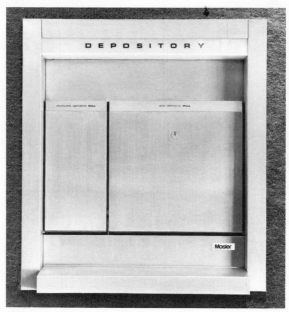

Fig. 6   Many different types of night depositories are available. This model is designed to accept both envelope and bag depositories.

Typical bank security falls within these two extremes and is worked out with the help of local and federal law enforcement agencies and representatives from security equipment manufacturing firms.

Point Security Systems

Point security refers to the protection of a particular storage unit in a facility, a unit with a high value. Usually this is either a safe or a vault, which can be protected by:

Proximity Sensors   The body to be protected, typically a safe, is isolated from its surroundings by mounting it on electrically insulated blocks. The approach of an intruder results in an electrical resistance change which the sensor circuit detects.

Audio Systems   Essentially microphone pickups with associated electronic equipment that can be set to activate an alarm when a certain sound level is reached. They will detect attacks on vault walls, ceilings, and floors with great effectiveness. However, they must be restricted to areas with very low ambient sound levels (such as the inside of a vault), which limits their usefulness.

Area Security Systems

Area systems detect the presence of a person within a room or lobby. Theoretically, these systems are ideal, for they need only one or two installations and can secure a large area. As a practical matter, however, they have limitations and require great care in application and selection if they are to be reliable. They are best used as part of a comprehensive system planned by experts. Area systems include:

Ultrasonic Systems   These systems, like the microwave system discussed below, use the doppler shift principle to detect intruders. Ultrasonic systems generate sound

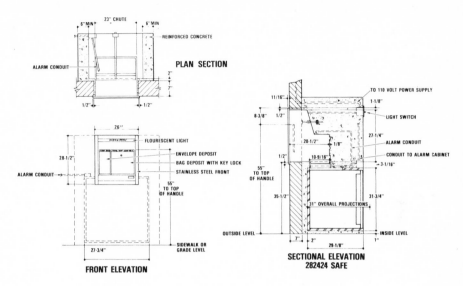

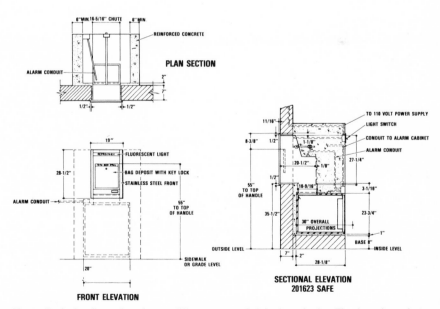

Fig. 7   Typical wall openings for two different types of night depositories. The depository chute and receiving safe are alarmed by "lacing" the unit walls with electrical conductors, as shown in Fig. 5.

waves (inaudible to the human ear) that fill the space to be secured. An intruder in motion changes the frequency of the reflected ultrasonic waves. This "shift" is detected, and an alarm is activated. The very sensitivity of this type of system is its disadvantage. It can be set off by external sounds, moving columns of air, or the motion of a flag or banner. Also, it will not detect a very slow-moving person, and some people with very sensitive ears can "hear" the ultrasonic sound and find it very irritating.

Fig. 8   Typical automatic teller machine. Deposits, cash supply, and dispensing mechanism are protected by a UL-approved safe, appropriately alarmed.

Microwave Systems   Electronic microwave systems flood an area with electromagnetic radio waves. They are not sensitive to air currents, noise, or light. However, it is difficult to contain the radio waves inside a room. Therefore, movement outside the building and radio transmitters may cause false alarms.

Passive Infrared Systems   Infrared systems measure the amount of thermal energy in a patterned array. If that thermal energy changes and moves from one section of the room to another, an alarm is activated. Air turbulence, noise, vibration, or radio transmissions will not adversely affect this system (see Fig. 10).

Photoelectric Cells   Photoelectric cells are generally used as an area-securing system by having them criss-cross a room with light beams. The major disadvantage in this application is the narrowness of the light beam, which may be avoided easily once the light source is discovered.

Mat Switches   These are strips of contact material within an insulating mat. Pressure on the mat will squeeze the contacts together and cause an alarm signal.

Perimeter Security Systems

As the title suggests, perimeter security refers to alarm detectors installed against the interior of the outside building structure. Some of the devices commonly used for banks are:

Foil Tape   This tape is bonded to windows (or walls) and glass doors. If the glass is broken, the electric current potential in the tape system is interrupted, and an alarm signal is generated.

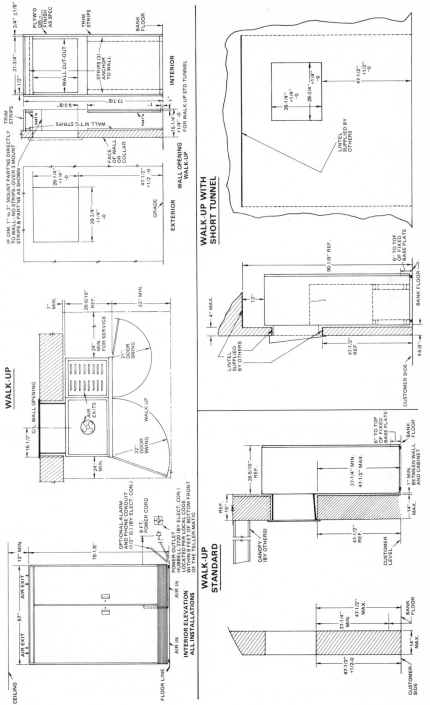

Fig. 9 Details of typical automatic teller machines for walk-up and walk-up with a short tunnel.

21-17

Magnetic Switches These are similar to microswitches. The magnet half is mounted on the moving portion of a door or window and the switch half on the frame. When the two parts are adjacent, the magnet holds the switch closed. When pulled apart, the switch opens and causes an alarm. There are many variations in types of actuating devices available in the security market. They also vary widely in quality and reliability. Needless to say, a bank should not entrust the security of many thousands of dollars to substandard equipment or to substandard services. Underwriters' Laboratories provides standards which are used for testing alarm components submitted by manufacturers. UL also approves the installation and service capability of the companies who wish to install these products. The Insurance Services Office requires that all banks have UL-approved security equipment.

Architects should be aware of perimeter protection plans so that provisions can be made for the concealment of necessary wiring.

Fig. 10 A passive infrared detection unit. Because air turbulence, noise, vibration, or radio transmission will not adversely affect systems of this type, they function very effectively as space alarms.

PROTECTION AGAINST ROBBERY

Robbery, by definition, involves the threat of injury to bank personnel. Also, many robberies take place during business hours and involve the safety of customers as well. Therefore, an entirely different set of defense systems must be employed to secure the bank's assets as well as to decrease the risk of personal injury as much as possible.

Modern vault construction and electronic alarms have kept bank *burglary* rates stable over the past ten years. Bank *robbery* rates, however, have increased steadily. For example, the number of bank robberies increased 34 percent in one year from 1974 to 1975. It is no wonder that robbery has become a major concern in the banking industry.

Most authorities agree that there are four basic methods to combat robberies:

The Silent Alarm Various devices (see below) are available to tellers and other bank personnel for initiating a silent alarm in the event of a robbery. As the name implies, there is no obvious indication inside the bank that the alarm has been activated. The alarm signal is transmitted to the police, a central security station, or the bank's own security center, depending upon the type of security system the bank employs. Ideally, police response will be rapid enough to intercept the bandits as they emerge from the bank. At the very least, this system severely restricts the time robbers have to complete their crime.

Surveillance Cameras Automatic cameras designed to take photographs of a robbery in progress have been very effective in the apprehension and conviction of bank robbers. Apprehension rates of 70 to 80 percent are not uncommon where surveillance cameras are involved. The high arrest rate, it is hoped, will discourage robberies.

Bandit Barriers In many high-crime areas, banks are now installing bullet-resistant glass and counters to protect tellers and to deter holdups. Indications are that these barriers are successful in doing just that (as well as improving employee morale). Although bank managements do not like to reduce the degree of person-to-person contact between customers and tellers, high risk of injury or even death is sometimes an overriding consideration. In these instances bullet-resistant enclosures are strongly recommended.

Remote Transaction Systems   Some banks are going one step further by locating tellers in a remote, secure room and employing two-way closed-circuit television to communicate with customers. Such systems are ideal for after-hours banking convenience, since stations can be installed in public building lobbies, bank vestibules, etc.

The ultimate in security against robbery is the automatic teller machine. No one has ever "robbed" an automatic teller, although ATM "burglaries" are sure to show up in crime statistics as these units become more common. Fortunately, it is easier to defend

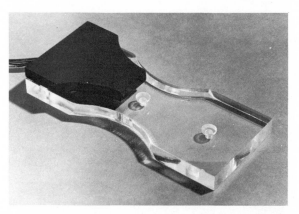

Fig. 11   Moneyclip alarm activator. It is usually mounted in a teller's cash drawer and holds the last bill in a baitmoney bundle. When the last bill is pulled out of the clip and given to a robber, a silent alarm is activated.

against such burglaries. Thus, automatic tellers should prove to be as secure as well-protected night depositories.

The various types of equipment available for protection against robbery and appropriate installation details are described below. Although this security equipment will be selected by the bank's security officer, the architect must be aware of the need for and location of wiring conduit and masonry openings for drive-up windows, automatic tellers, and the like.

Alarm-Activating Devices

There are many activating devices on the market. Figures 11 to 13 show three of the more common types. (Figure 5 illustrates necessary wiring connections and construction detail.) These devices are employed as follows:

Money Clip   The last bills in one of the tellers cash drawer compartments are held in a special clip. During a robbery, the teller is instructed to pull the bills free (a natural action in response to a robber's demand for cash), which will complete an electrical circuit and activate the silent alarm.

Pull Button   Tellers' stations and the desks of supervisors and managers are usually equipped with buttons that will also activate the silent alarm. These buttons are pulled, rather than pushed, an action less likely to cause accidental alarms.

Toe Switch   This device is located under the teller's counter. To operate it, the teller places his or her toe under the switch and lifts up, a natural movement as the teller backs away from the counter.

Suspicious-Person Camera Activator   This device is designed not to activate the alarm but to operate holdup cameras only. Tellers are trained to use this switch when they observe a suspicious character in the bank. It is operated by squeezing the buttons on either side of the switch box.

Fig. 12   Pull-button alarm activator. Pulling the knob sends a silent alarm to police. Usually installed at every teller station and appropriate bank officer and supervisor desks.

Fig. 13   Footrail alarm activator. Raising the toe under the rail activates the bank's silent alarm. It is employed at teller stations and other suitable locations.

Bandit Barriers

Figure 14 shows a typical bank counter with "protected work stations"; Figure 15 illustrates a cross section of such an installation. The counter is protected by bullet-resistant steel plate, and bullet-resistant glass or plastic is installed to completely span the distance from counter top to ceiling or soffit. It is important to understand that bandit barriers are not bullet*proof*. Repeated fire from handguns or shots from a high-powered rifle will penetrate the best material in use today. (See Fig. 16 for details of Underwriters' Laboratories test procedures and classifications.)

Drive-up and walk-up windows (see Figs. 17 and 18) are also constructed of bullet-resistive material. Details of construction and masonry openings required for a typical window are shown in Fig. 19. Bullet-resistant doors, vision windows, and package and deposit pickup devices are also available from security equipment manufacturers.

Figures 20 and 21 give details of installation requirements for doors and deposit pickup models

The deterrent against robbery that these bandit barriers provide is only partly physical. Perhaps more important is the psychological advantage bank employees enjoy by being protected against injury, at least to some degree. Whatever the reason, banks equipped with bullet-resistant enclosures experience substantially fewer robberies. These banks also seem to have less employee turnover, higher efficiency, and an improved public image.

Fig. 14   An attractive, but secure, "protected work station" installation. Bullet-resistant glass above and steel plate behind the lower panels provide protection against weapons specified by the UL rating. Note the bullet-resistant door at left.

Television-Equipped Transaction Stations

Figure 22 shows a television-teller installation employed by many banks throughout the country. Objects such as passbooks and cash are carried by a reversible pneumatic tube. Two-way TV and intercom maintain visual and voice communication. Figure 23 has typical construction details. Banks employ this equipment for both drive-up and walk-up applications. Because the teller is secure in another location, attempts to rob this system are misguided.

Remote Transaction Systems

Drive-in bank facilities also include remote transaction units such as that shown in Figs. 24 and 25. Objects are carried by a reversible pneumatic tube system, and voice communication is by an intercom. Because this transaction system requires visual control by a teller, usually located in a drive-up window enclosure, it is not as secure as a television-equipped installation. However, there have been relatively few instances of drive-up window robberies in comparison with crimes that occur inside the bank itself where personal contact between customer and teller is maintained.

PROTECTING SENSITIVE AREAS

Computer, counting, and proofing rooms require special attention to security. Certainly doors and windows, if any, should be constructed of bullet-resistant material, and if guards are not stationed at the door, some means of controlling access should be provided. Some such facilities employ "man traps," a bullet-resistant door at each end of a short corridor. Electrically operated door locks are interconnected so that only one door can be opened at a time. This design prevents bandits from taking

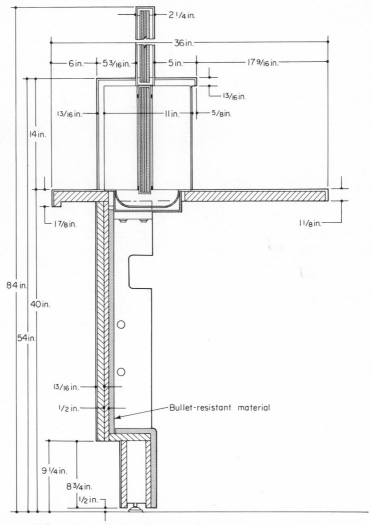

Fig. 15   Cross-sectional view of a bullet-resistant teller station. Heavy lines indicate bullet-resistant material: a sandwich of glass above the counter, steel plate beneath. Note that the deal tray is also bullet-resistant and designed to deflect bullets upwards.

guards by surprise and also provides the means of trapping suspicious persons between the doors until police arrive.

Usually, only a few areas require such tight security. In a large bank building there are many other areas (such as executive offices, accounting departments, employee lounges and locker rooms, and utility service locations) where access must be

All ballistics tests shall be conducted under laboratory conditions at close range (15 feet) using weapons for specific ratings.

Each device for small arms ratings shall resist three shots spaced 4 inches apart in a triangular pattern with no indication of spalling on an indicator 18 inches behind the tested device. The device should also resist penetration of two shots spaced 1½ inches apart. For high power rifle rating each device shall resist one shot without penetration.

Teller window units shall be designed in such a manner that components, i.e., deal trays, voice apertures, glazing material, framing methods, etc., shall be shot at with the rated firearms and a shot gun and there shall be no visable marks on nor material imbedding in an indicator 18 inches behind unit when hit with a direct or ricocheted shot.

All these tests shall be conducted under laboratory conditions with the use of electronic equipment to record the velocity of the projectile. Each test shall not exceed 105% nor be less than 90% of rated velocity.

All units or devices shall have Underwriters' Laboratories listing tag permanently affixed on inside showing:
Type of unit or device
Model
UL rating
Manufacturer's number

| UL Ballistic level | Specifications | | Weight | | | | Thickness | | | | | |
	Defeats	Weapons	B-R glass lb/ft²	Lexgard B-R sheet lb/ft²	Lexgard B-R sheet reduction	Plex. G. lb/ft²	B-R glass	Tolerance	Lexgard B-R sheet	Tolerance	Plex. G.	Tolerance
Class I	Med. power Small arms 475 ft/lb 1280 ft/sec	.38 Super	14.9	6.5	56%	7.70	1³⁄₁₆"	+⅛ −0	1"	+¹⁄₁₆ −0	1¼"	+.052 −.044
Class II	High power Small arms 740 ft/lb 1450 ft/sec	.357 Mag.	20.0	8.0	60%	12.32	1⁹⁄₁₆"	+⅛ −0	1¼"	+¹⁄₁₆ −0	2"	+.058 −.152
Class III	Super power Small arms 1150 ft/lb 1470 ft/sec	.44 Mag.	23	8.0	65%	24.64	1¾"	+⅛ −0	1¼"	+¹⁄₁₆ −0	4"	+.142 −.268

NOTES: These are currently three U.L. approved Bullet Resistant glazing materials:
1. B.R. Glass . . . . Laminated Glass
2. Lexgard . . . . Laminated Polycarbonate
3. Plexiglas G. . . . . Acrylic

Fig. 16 Underwriters' Laboratories testing procedures for bullet-resistant enclosures.

Fig. 17   Walk-up windows are constructed of bullet-resistant glass and steel plate.

Fig. 18   Drive-in windows are made of bullet-resistant materials.

restricted to assure the security of the bank as a whole. Some banks use card access control systems for this purpose. (See Figs. 26 and 27.) In this type of system, all employees are issued plastic cards magnetically encoded with their personal identification number and special numbers which restrict access to certain areas at certain times of the day. In other words, an individual's card may permit access to the loan

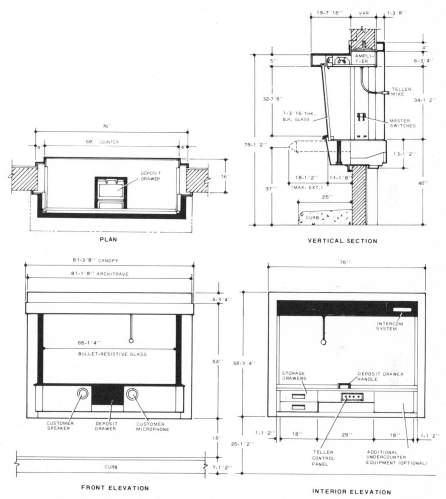

Fig. 19 Construction details of a drive-in window. Manufacturers offer many models to meet budget and usage requirements.

department record room and employee lounge area only from 8:30 in the morning to 5:30 in the evening. If the employee inserts the card into the card reader at the lounge door at 8:00 P.M., the door will not unlock. Each time a card is used, the centrally located control console records the number, location, and time in order to provide an audit trail in case suspicious circumstances occur. The control console can also be used to change card assignments or "block" certain cards if, for example, an employee leaves the bank and takes his or her card along.

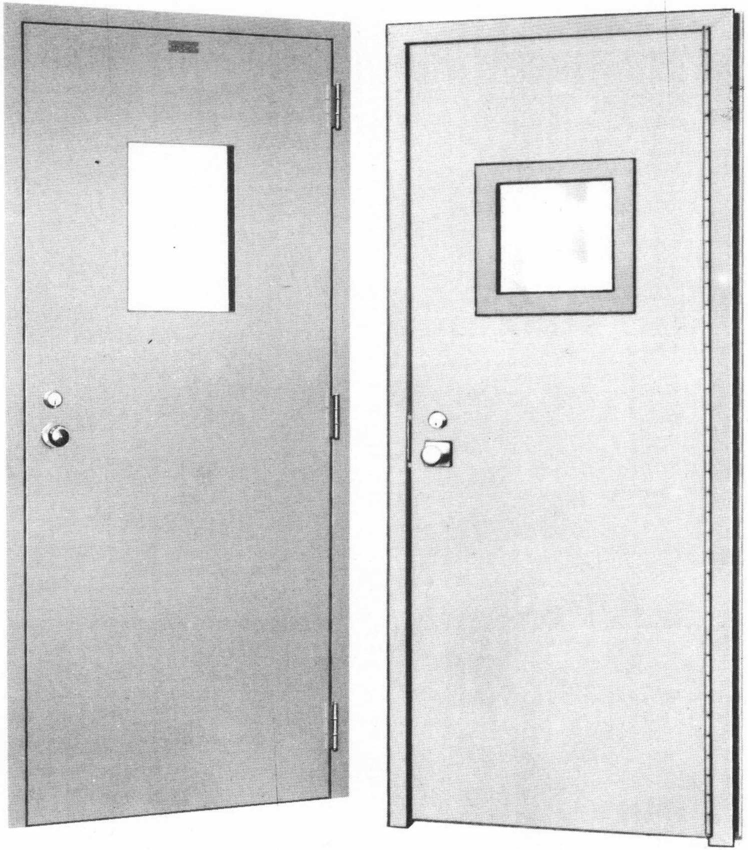

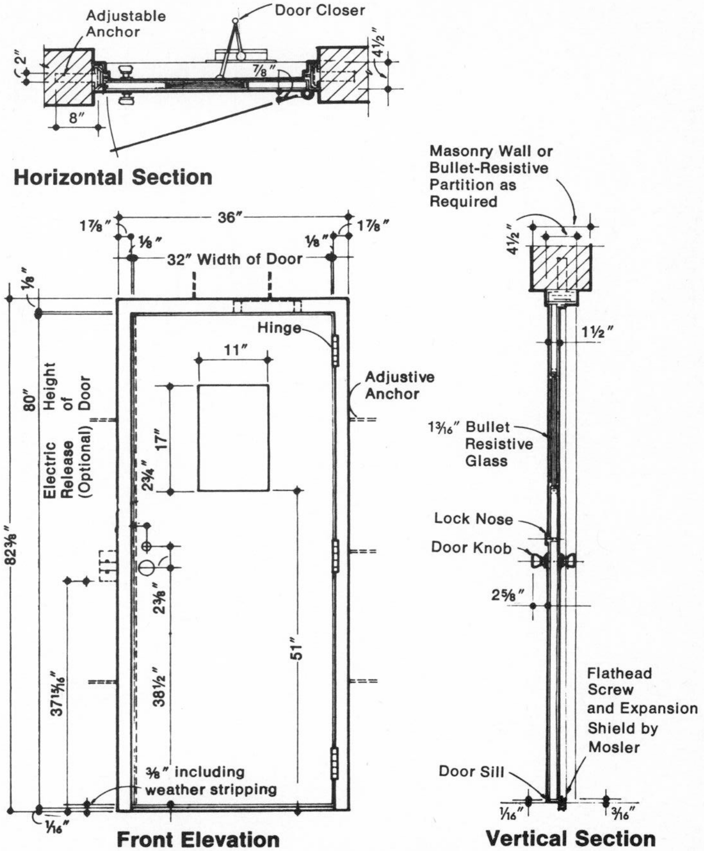

Adjustable Anchor
Door Closer
2″
8″
7/8″
4½″
Horizontal Section
36″
1⅞″
1⅞″
⅛″
⅛″
32″ Width of Door
Hinge
11″
17″
2¾″
51″
Adjustive Anchor
80″
Height of Door
Electric Release (Optional)
82⅜″
⅛″
37 13/16″
2⅜″
38½″
⅜″ including weather stripping
1/16″
Front Elevation
Masonry Wall or Bullet-Resistive Partition as Required
4½″
1½″
1 3/16″ Bullet Resistive Glass
Lock Nose
Door Knob
2⅝″
Flathead Screw and Expansion Shield by Mosler
Door Sill
1/16″
3/16″
Vertical Section

Fig. 20 Details of bullet-resistant door installation. Lintels and partitions into which these doors are set must also be bullet-resistant.

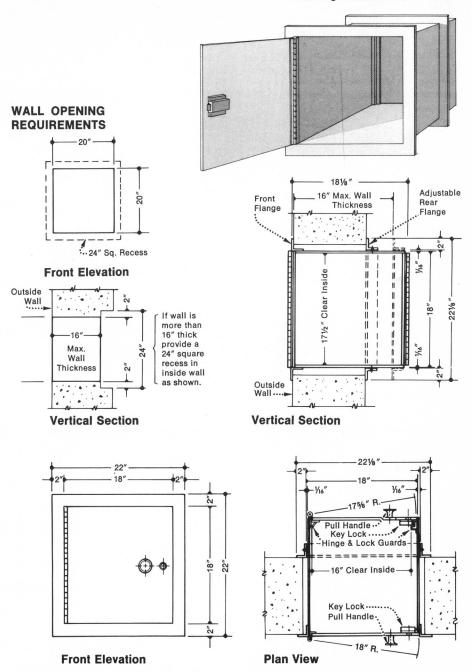

WALL OPENING REQUIREMENTS

20″

20″

24″ Sq. Recess

Front Elevation

Outside Wall

2″

16″ Max. Wall Thickness

24″

2″

If wall is more than 16″ thick provide a 24″ square recess in inside wall as shown.

Vertical Section

18⅛″

Front Flange

16″ Max. Wall Thickness

Adjustable Rear Flange

2″

1/16″

17½″ Clear Inside

18″

22⅛″

1/16″

2″

Outside Wall

Vertical Section

22″

2″   18″   2″

2″

18″

22″

2″

Front Elevation

22⅛″

2″   18″   2″

1/16″   1/16″

17⅝″ R.

Pull Handle
Key Lock
Hinge & Lock Guards

16″ Clear Inside

Key Lock
Pull Handle

18″ R.

Plan View

Fig. 21   Deposit pick-up box used for bulk transfer of checks and records. This unit is made of bullet-resistant steel.

Access control systems have their weaknesses. For instance, if the cardholder allows it, any number of people can follow him or her through an unlocked door unless turnstiles are employed. But this requires a conspiracy, and the access record reveals the conspirator's identity. There is no way of knowing how many crimes have been prevented in access-controlled banks. However, it must be assumed that any effective

Fig. 22   Some remote teller stations are equipped with CCTV communications. Tellers are located in a secure room within the bank building.

obstacle put in the path of a potential robber or thief must have a degree of deterrent value.

It should be noted also that magnetic computer tapes require environmental protection as well as security against burglary and misuse. Tapes can be damaged or even destroyed in temperatures above 140°F, in high-humidity environments, and in situations where a magnetic device (like a security guard's flashlight equipped with a magnet holder) is placed in close proximity. Such conditions can arise easily if the air conditioning should fail on a very hot, humid day or if a disgruntled employee should place a small magnet on the steel back of an unprotected data tape cabinet. Security equipment manufacturers have available safes and vaults which will resist magnetic attack and maintain proper humidity and temperature levels until building services can be restored.

SURVEILLANCE CAMERAS

Automatic Holdup Camera Systems

These camera systems are installed in banks at strategic locations primarily to photograph holdups and aid in the identification and apprehension of robbers. As previously mentioned, 70 to 80 percent of bank robbers identified by holdup cameras are apprehended. Thus, holdup cameras are considered excellent anticrime systems and are highly recommended by local and federal police authorities. Generally speaking, these cameras are activated when the bank robbery alarm is triggered. If they are properly placed and maintained, a number of clear photographs of the bandits should result. Figure 5 illustrates typical conduit requirements for holdup cameras and mounting detail. There are several types of holdup camera systems available today.

16-mm Motion-picture Cameras These cameras are activated by the holdup alarm and take motion pictures at, usually, 24 frames a second until film is exhausted. The advantage of 16-mm film is that it takes true motion pictures. Any peculiarities in a robber's walk or mannerism will be recorded and aid in identification. However, the small image area of 16-mm film, which limits the size and clarity of enlargements, is a major disadvantage. Therefore, new film-camera installations employ the larger 35-mm models.

35-mm Holdup Cameras 35-mm film has eight times the area of 16-mm film, comparing image size. Therefore, enlargements of greater resolution and identification value can be obtained. Typical 35-mm cameras (see Fig. 28) take photographs at 2 to 4 frames per second when activated by the holdup alarm. They will operate until the film supply has been exhausted. Figure 29 shows an actual holdup scene taken by a 35-mm camera.

These cameras can also be operated in a "suspicion" mode. A teller who suspects that a person might be "casing" the bank for a future robbery attempt can squeeze a suspicion switch without activating the robbery alarm. The cameras will then take a burst of four frames in one second and stop. Cameras of any type must be correctly located for best results and should be positioned over the main entranceway. (For further information, refer to the chapter entitled "Surveillance Cameras.")

16-mm Programmed Sequence Cameras Programmed sequence cameras (see Fig. 30) take photographs at preset intervals ranging from one frame per second to one frame each 45 seconds. Their primary use is identification of bad-check passers. Thus, they are located behind the teller counter, as shown in Fig. 31. Usually, these cameras are set for 20- to 30-seconds intervals to conserve film and still record every customer. A calendar and clock are deliberately located within view of the camera to record date and time. By comparing the date/time stamp on the check with a film frame taken at the same instant, an identifying picture of the check-passer can be obtained.

These cameras will also take holdup photos when the alarm is activated—at a faster rate, usually one frame per second. It is strongly recommended that 35-mm holdup cameras be employed in addition to the sequence cameras for adequate protection. Although the 16-mm sequence cameras usually take satisfactory photographs of customers at the counter, their value at greater distance is limited.

CCTV Sequence Cameras The newest sequence camera system employs closed-circuit television (CCTV) equipment. (See Fig. 32.) A typical system utilizes several cameras, some located behind the tellers for identification of bad-check passers. Others are positioned over the main exits and serve as "backup" holdup cameras. The output of each camera is fed into a sequence switcher and from there to a time/date generator and, finally, to a time-lapse videotape recorder. (See Fig. 33.) The video recorder records a field view from each camera in sequence on the tape. A TV monitor provides continuous display of the camera "frames." Photographic prints of any scene on the tape are easily obtained by photographing the screen with a Polaroid camera.

The advantages of a CCTV system compared with sequence camera systems using film are:

1. Videotape can be used repeatedly.
2. Protected areas can be monitored continuously.

21-30

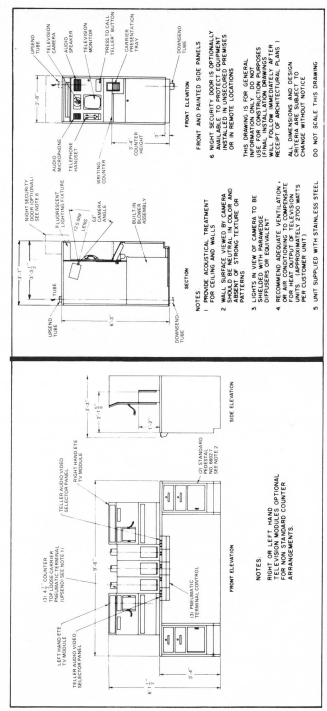

Fig. 23 Typical remote teller station employing CCTV for communication. Passbooks, cash, and other transaction materials are transported between customer and teller via reversible pneumatic tubing.

Fig. 24   Most suburban banks have drive-in facilities similar to these.

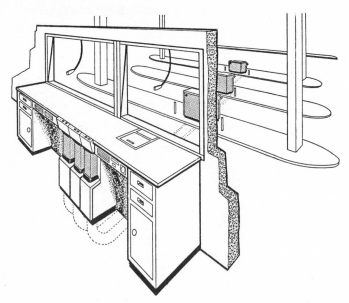

Fig. 25   Multiple-lane drive-in facilities rely on sight and intercom communication. Units on islands are staggered so that tellers can see drivers in all lanes even if facilities are fully utilized.

3. Hard copies of scenes can be obtained immediately with a Polaroid camera.

4. By properly positioning a number of cameras, the system can be used for several purposes:

(*a*) Identification of holdup suspects

(*b*) Identification of bad-check passers

(*c*) Monitoring of many areas (e.g., hallways, remote-transaction systems, nonpublic entrances) in addition to the public bank lobby

(*d*) Monitoring of counting and proofing rooms and the actions of employee suspects

The disadvantages of CCTV sequence-recording systems compared with film cameras are:

1. Playback from video records results in resolution that is lower than 16-mm and much lower than 35-mm film. CCTV is therefore not recommended as a primary holdup system.

2. The sequential switcher skips from camera to camera in the system. One picture is recorded every second. Although more than adequate for check cashing, this can be marginal for holdups if more than two cameras are involved.

Continuous-Surveillance CCTV Cameras The CCTV system described above is a time-lapse system which permits the fields seen from several cameras to be viewed on one monitor screen sequentially and recorded on one videotape. The full-time CCTV monitor system is perhaps more widely known. These systems can selectively display a single camera scene on a TV monitor and selectively video record that which is of interest. Sequential switching systems can also be used to reduce the number of monitors required, but this can be tiring to the duty guard.

In a large bank building, however, CCTV is economical because it reduces the cost of guard service. Several sensitive areas such as corridors, elevator banks, money delivery docks, etc., can be surveyed at one time by one guard at a control console.

OUTSIDE ALARM CONNECTIONS

The Bank Protection Act requires that a bank be provided with a robbery and burglary alarm system that is designed to transmit to police, either directly or through an intermediary, a signal indicating that a crime is taking place or has occurred. Security experts generally divide such "reporting" systems into three basic categories.

Local Bell or Siren

An alarm system that sounds a bell or siren outside the protected building is termed a local alarm. This type of system is meant to unsettle burglars and scare them away. It also attracts attention so that the police may be notified. However, because it is not designed primarily as a method to notify police for apprehen-

Fig. 26 One type of access control system employing magnetically encoded plastic cards. To unlock a door, the person inserts his or her card into the card reader and enters a personal identification number on the keyboard.

sion purposes, it does not satisfy BPA requirements unless the police are over 5 minutes away.

Central Station

A central station is defined as a continuously staffed reporting office. It is usually thought of as the central station of a commercial security company where alarms

Fig. 27   Control console of a card access control system. This unit keeps a printed record of card usage and provides the means to encode and change coding on the card's magnetic strip. Operator can also "block" cards that are in the hands of unauthorized personnel.

from many customers—for example, stores, factories, banks—are connected. A central station complies with the BPA because the guards, receiving an alarm signal from the bank, will immediately notify the police as well as respond themselves. A proprietary security system can be envisioned as a central station except that it is located on the premises to be protected (or in the headquarters building of a bank with branches) and owned by the bank itself.

Direct Police Connection

Most police departments permit alarms to be directly connected to their headquarters or precinct building. The terminals are continuously monitored. When an alarm is activated, an audible signal will be generated and a light will flash on a particular terminal so that the establishment under attack can be identified. Figure 34 shows a typical police alarm terminal setup.

The most serious problem faced by police authorities, security equipment manufacturers, and protected businesses is false alarms. Electric alarm systems can be misapplied so that the slightest abnormality in a protected establishment will set off an alarm. In addition, improperly trained or new bank personnel can cause an alarm during opening, closing, or operating procedures. Police and central stations will respond rapidly to the first or second false-alarm occurrence, but it is only human nature to take repeated false alarms less seriously and respond less quickly, if at all. At this stage the concept of protection by means of alarm systems is negated.

To reduce this problem, alarm sensors are adjusted so that their sensitivity is lessened, but not, it is hoped, to a point where they become ineffective. Also, security equipment manufacturers are constantly trying to develop the perfect system that is both economical and foolproof. That stage has not been reached as yet, and thus security experts generally agree that the proprietary security system provides the highest level of security.

Security of the Alarm Line

The weak link in any remote-reporting alarm system is the leased signal-grade telephone line over which alarm signals are transmitted to a central station or police department. Obviously, if a burglar can defeat the telephone line at any point, the best bank security system in the world will be rendered ineffective.

When alarm systems were first introduced in the 1800s, a simple two-conductor line was used to transmit the alarm signal. It worked like a doorbell circuit. The thief would inadvertently close a contact switch while breaking in, which would complete a battery-powered electrical circuit, and this in turn would ring a bell in the police department.

Burglars quickly learned that if they cut the wire, the police would not only not receive an alarm, they would not

Fig. 28 35-mm hold-up cameras are usually mounted over lobby entrances where robbers must pass on their way out. This camera takes photos at two to four frames a second when activated by the bank's silent hold-up alarm.

even know the wire had been cut. Security equipment manufacturers countered with the closed-circuit alarm system design, which sets off the alarm when the circuit is broken. Thieves then "jumped" the line. Ever since, criminals and security engineers have countered one another with ever more sophisticated line security and defeat techniques.

Underwriters' Laboratories classifies alarm-line security systems with an "AA" rating, designating "high quality." Within that classification, however, are systems that most security experts would consider woefully inadequate for financial institutions. Therefore it is strongly recommended that banks not only investigate systems in the Grade AA category, but consider seriously the highest-quality system within that classification which is known as the *random, digitally coded, interrogate-response line security system.*

This system employs a complex digitally coded sequential which is transmitted between police or central-station monitor and the bank being protected. Each end of the system recognizes the coded transmission from the other end. It is extremely sensitive to attempts at signal substitution or duplication.

PROPRIETARY SYSTEMS

Security systems owned and operated by the bank itself are termed "proprietary systems." Normally, such systems are economically feasible only for medium- to large-size banks with a number of branch offices. Once the breakeven point is reached,

Fig. 29 An actual hold-up scene taken by a 35-mm surveillance camera. Other frames in this sequence showing the robber's face were used by police for identification purposes.

however, the proprietary system's economic advantages become increasingly attractive.

The heart of a proprietary system is the central control room, usually located in the

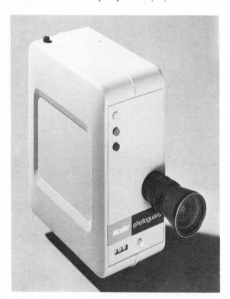

Fig. 30 This 16-mm sequence camera can be preset to take photographs at intervals ranging from 1 s to 45 s. It is used primarily for identifying bad check passers and is not recommended as a holdup camera.

bank's headquarters building. Because all alarm and auxiliary systems report to this center, it must be very secure. Windows and doors of bullet-resistant glass, interconnected locking systems, "man traps," and other security devices and alarms are used to secure this room. If armored cars unload at this facility, it is common to locate the control center so that it overlooks the loading dock through bullet-resistant windows. Figure 35 shows a typical bank control center. It incorporates the following:

1. Terminals for all alarms originating from banking offices in the building and all branch offices

2. Terminals for all fire alarms in the building

3. Guard tour panel indicating guard tour progress from station to station

4. Security control panel displaying access/secure condition of all protected entranceways, such as doors, gates, and elevators

5. CCTV surveillance monitor screens

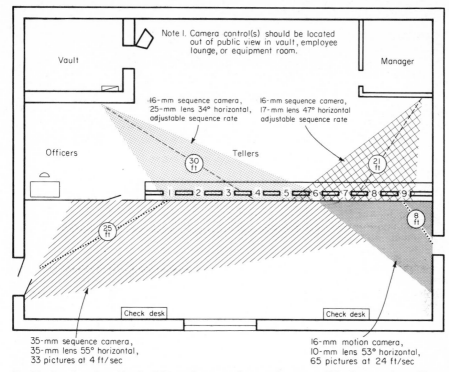

Note I. Camera control(s) should be located out of public view in vault, employee lounge, or equipment room.

Vault

Manager

16-mm sequence camera, 25-mm lens 34° horizontal, adjustable sequence rate

16-mm sequence camera, 17-mm lens 47° horizontal adjustable sequence rate

Officers

Tellers

30 ft

21 ft

25 ft

1 2 3 4 5 6 7 8 9

8 ft

Check desk

Check desk

35-mm sequence camera,
35-mm lens 55° horizontal,
33 pictures at 4 ft/sec

16-mm motion camera,
10-mm lens 53° horizontal,
65 pictures at 24 ft/sec

Fig. 31 A well-equipped bank might employ several types of cameras. This diagram shows 16-mm cameras (upper cone areas) to photograph possible bad check passers, and a 35-mm sequence camera over the main entrance (lower left) as the primary hold-up camera which is backed-up by a 16-mm motion picture camera over the side entrance (lower right).

Fig. 32 CCTV time-lapse camera systems are employed primarily for fraudulent check passer identification. They find secondary use as a back-up for the main 35-mm camera system and, to a lesser extent, for live monitoring of secured areas.

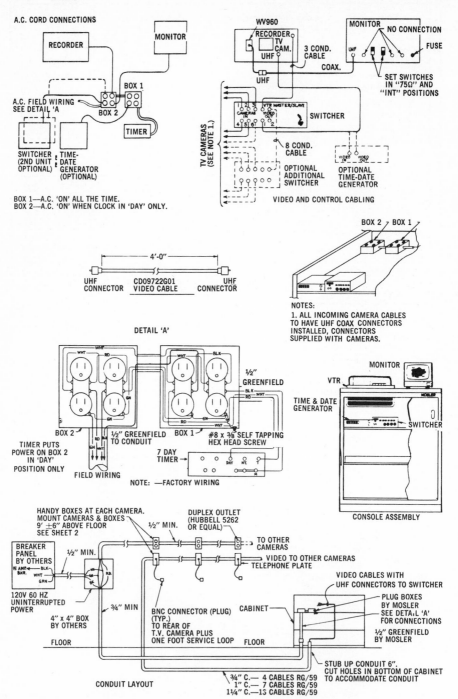

Fig. 33   Conduit requirements for a typical CCTV security system. Because of poor picture quality compared to images produced by 35-mm cameras, CCTV is not recommended for primary hold-up protection.

6. CCTV videotape recorder unit

7. Teleprinter to keep records of all security activities, such as alarms, resets, opening and closing of vaults, guard actions, etc.

8. Communications console including radio contact with walkie-talkie-equipped guards and security cars, intercom system within the building, and direct telephone lines to city police and fire departments

9. Card access control console

Each proprietary system is custom-designed to fit the needs of the customer bank, using standard components wherever possible. Other available equipment, not part of the illustrated system includes:

1. A computerized printer which keeps an activity record and also prints preprogrammed instructions for guards when emergencies arise.

2. A display panel which shows, in large type, procedures to follow in alarm situations

3. Systems for monitoring building services such as heating, air conditioning, steam pressure, etc.

When burglary/robbery alarms are received in this control center, guards are instructed to call the police or fire department first and then to ascertain whether it is a real or false alarm and how serious the emergency is. They will

Fig. 34 A typical police alarm terminal. This unit will accept five connections.

then advise city authorities and take appropriate action themselves. Proper procedures are fully as important as proper equipment if maximum security is to be maintained.

CONCLUSION AND RECOMMENDATIONS

The material in this chapter will provide the reader with basic information concerning the theory behind bank building security and some of the equipment needed to do the job. Applying this theory and selecting security equipment properly requires a great deal more information, training, and experience. Therefore, we strongly suggest that designers faced with their first bank building project take the following steps:

1. Obtain copies of the Bank Protection Act of 1968; Insurance Services Office manuals on burglary and robbery; and literature available on security equipment from Underwriters' Laboratories.

2. Confer with the bank security officer as early as possible, and work closely with this individual thereafter.

3. Consult with representatives of the local police department and the Federal Bureau of Investigation.

4. Discuss the level of security required for the most cost-effective insurance coverage with bank insurance executives and representatives of the underwriter.

5. Ask security equipment manufacturers for advice and recommendations.

Fig. 35   The control center for a proprietary security system. CCTV monitors, communications controls, and terminals for fire and security alarms are grouped for efficient monitoring.

SOURCES FOR FURTHER INFORMATION

Bank Protection Act of 1968, Revised 1973

The act's provisions are listed in the Federal Register, vol. 38, no. 194, Oct. 9, 1973. For copies write to the appropriate Washington, DC agency listed below:

  (*a*) Bureau of the Comptroller of the Currency, Department of the Treasury
  (*b*) Federal Reserve System, Board of Governors
  (*c*) Federal Deposit Insurance Corporation
  (*d*) Federal Home Loan Bank Board

Insurance Services Office

Copies of Burglary and Robbery Insurance Manuals may be obtained by writing to Insurance Services Office, 160 Water Street, New York, NY 10038.

Underwriters' Laboratories, Inc.

Literature concerning classification of security equipment may be obtained by writing to Underwriters' Laboratories, Inc., 207 East Ohio Street, Chicago, IL 60611.

Chapter 22

Cargo Storage

Adapted from "Guidelines for the Physical Security of Cargo,"
Department of Transportation, Office of the Secretary, Washington, D.C.,
May 1972

There are no universal one-time solutions to the problem of cargo security. Each mode of transportation, every terminal, and each transfer point is unique, with its own individual strengths and weaknesses. There are, however, certain basic principles of cargo security which should be considered in the design of all facilities to enhance their security potential. The general principles can be adapted by management to almost any mode of transportation, or to any facility—large or small.

Other chapters in this book address the more generalized elements of a comprehensive security plan. Other considerations include employment screening, identification systems for employees and visitors, service and maintenance crews, and package control—all of which must be dealt with in establishing a comprehensive security plan. This chapter addresses the physical security elements that should be incorporated into the design of cargo-handling facilities.

PHYSICAL SECURITY

Physical security measures cannot interfere with the operating requirements of the facility. The receipt, sorting, processing, and moving of cargo must be able to proceed unimpeded by security measures.

To determine the type and extent of physical protection required, the following factors should be considered:

1. The volume of cargo moved through the facility
2. The value of cargo in the facility at normal peak periods
3. The amount of time required for cargo to move through the facility
4. The area to be protected, the kind of activity within it, and the number of personnel working there
5. The vulnerability of the type of cargo to loss, damage, or theft
6. Maintenance and custodial services needed in the facility
7. Environmental factors affecting the operation of the facility

8. Current labor-management relations

9. Cost to purchase, operate, and maintain physical protection for critical areas and activities

10. The possible expansion, relocation, or retrenchment of the facility

11. Alternative methods of providing protection

The plan must provide that all security measures employed complement and supplement each other. In large facilities, where a number of companies operate, individual security plans must be integrated. Failure to do this can waste resources and jeopardize the security of all.

CONTROLLED AREAS

A controlled area is any area whose access is governed by special restrictions and controls. The transportation industry provides a public service, and thus some of its operations must be open to the general public. In the design of a cargo facility, recognition must be given to the fact that general offices, the personnel office, and freight receiving offices need to be outside the controlled area.

Access points to any controlled area, regardless of the degree of security involved, should be locked at all times when they are not under physical or electronic surveillance. Strict control of keys and combinations to locks is essential. Management should make periodic checks, in addition to security checks made by security representatives, to determine the integrity of controlled areas.

A controlled area can extend over many acres and include vehicle marshaling yards, docks, warehouses, and service or supply buildings. Such an area is a first line of defense for the protection of cargo in the transportation system.

Limited Area   Within the controlled area, a limited area can be established. This will provide a higher degree of security. A different pass, issued to fewer people, should be necessary for entry to a limited area. Sorting, recoopering of crates, and storage may be accomplished here.

Exclusion Area   An exclusion area can be located inside the limited area. Again, a different pass should be required, and the number of people granted access should be strictly limited. The exclusion area is used only for handling high-value, low-volume cargo. The crib, vault, or cage that comprises the exclusion area should be kept locked or under surveillance at all times.

Vehicle Control   Only bona fide cargo-carrying or cargo-handling vehicles should be allowed inside a controlled area. Employee and visitor parking lots should be located outside the controlled area. This is an especially important principle; if the controlled area is not fenced, private vehicles should be required to park behind a clearly defined line well removed from cargo or storage buildings.

Generally, there are three types of vehicles that operate within a controlled area: (1) the facility work vehicles, primarily small trucks, cargo-handling vehicles, and cargo-loading vehicles; (2) the freight pickup and delivery and freight forwarder vehicles; and (3) the cargo carrier vehicles.

Facility vehicles usually remain in a controlled area, but if it is necessary for them to leave, their departure should be recorded. The freight pickup and delivery vehicles and the freight forwarder vehicles should be checked in and checked out, with records maintained to ensure that each one is the authorized vehicle for that particular cargo. Cargo carrier vehicles should be inspected and manifested upon arrival at or departure from the facility.

All vehicles entering or departing a controlled area should pass through a service gate controlled by physical or electronic means. The size of the facility will determine the complexity of the gate procedures used.

BARRIERS

The most basic protection for cargo is a barrier which prevents would-be thieves from approaching their cargo target. Physical and mechanical barriers are the subject of this chapter, along with a discussion of recommended procedures to be followed outside the terminal facility.

Types of Barriers

Barriers can be used to create physical and psychological deterrents to accidental entry; to prevent deliberate unauthorized entry; to delay intrusion, making detection and apprehension by guards more likely; to make guards more effective; and to direct the flow of pedestrian and vehicular traffic.

There are two kinds of physical barriers: natural or structural. Natural barriers include rivers, marshes, or terrain difficult to negotiate by vehicle. Structural barriers include fences, walls, buildings, grilles, bars, and gates. A barrier should be under physical or electronic surveillance to be fully effective.

A body of water, whether it is a river, a lake, or an ocean, does not in itself constitute an adequate barrier. Additional measures such as a fence, frequent security patrol, and floodlighting are necessary.

To be effective, barriers have to be well maintained. Breaks or damage to the structure should be repaired as soon as they are discovered. Frequent inspections of the barriers must be made by the guard force to locate defects. In addition, the security officer should periodically tour the barriers, giving particular attention to cuts or openings in the barrier which may have been camouflaged.

If the barrier encloses a large area, an interior all-weather road should be provided for guard force vehicles. The road should be in the clear zone and as close to the barrier as possible. Its use should be limited to guard and emergency vehicles.

The kind of barrier to be used depends on the size of the controlled area, the flow of traffic during the busiest and least busy periods, and the most prevalent local hazards.

The perimeter of a large controlled area may be a combination of natural and structural barriers. A limited area, however, must generally be bounded by a structural barrier.

Fencing Fences should be the chain-link type, made of 9-gauge or heavier wire; they should be no less than 8 ft high, with mesh openings no larger than 2 in per side, and with a twisted-barb selvage at the top. They should be stretched taut and securely fastened to metal posts set in concrete. The bottom should be within 2 in of hard ground or paving. On soft ground, they should extend below the surface to compensate for shifting soil or sand. Culverts, troughs, or other openings with an area larger than 96 in^2 should be protected by fencing or iron grilles to prevent unauthorized entry, yet allow proper drainage.

A top guard should be attached to perimeter fences and interior enclosures for greater security. A top guard is an overhang of barbed wire along the top of a barrier facing outward and upward at an angle of 45°. The supporting arms, at least 2 ft long, are attached to the top of the fence posts. Four strands of standard barbed wire are tightly stretched between the supporting arms. Some fences have a double overhang, facing both outward and inward, which makes it more difficult to enter the facility by scaling the fence.

The top guard can be firmly fixed or mounted on springs. The spring-type guard further increases the difficulty of scaling the fence. If a building less than three stories high forms a part of the perimeter, a top guard should be used along the coping to deny access to the roof.

The fence should be as straight as possible to provide ease of observation by the guard force. If practicable, fences should be located no closer than 50 ft to buildings or cargo in a controlled area, and 20 ft of clearance should be allowed between the perimeter barrier and exterior features, such as buildings or parking areas, which might offer concealment to a thief.

Fencing for limited areas should conform to the same specifications as for controlled areas, although it is recommended that the height be increased to 10 ft and that a top guard be used.

Entrances The number of gates and entrances should be limited to the minimum required for safe and efficient operation of the facility. A top guard, equal to that on the adjoining fence, should be attached to each gate. The bottom of the gate should be within 2 in of hard ground or paving. Adequate lighting should be provided for fast and efficient inspection.

When gates or doors are not provided with guards, so that all those entering will be challenged, they should be securely locked, illuminated during hours of darkness, and periodically inspected by a roving guard.

Semiactive entrances, such as railroad siding gates or gates and doors used only during periods of peak traffic flow, should be locked except when actually in use. Keys to these entrances should be in the custody of the security officer or the chief of the guard force and should be strictly controlled. These entrances should be inspected periodically.

Inactive entrances, which are used only occasionally, should also be kept locked. They are subject to the same key control and inspection as semiactive entrances. Emergency exits should have alarmed breakout hardware installed on the inside. Sidewalk elevators and other unusual entrances that provide access within controlled-area barriers should be locked and patrolled.

Control signs stating the conditions of entry to a facility or controlled area should be erected at all entrances. They should inform entrants that they are subject to personal search and that all vehicles or packages may be searched; they should state any prohibitions against packages, matches, smoking, or entry for other than business. The signs should be legible at least 50 ft from the point of entry under normal conditions.

To maintain the integrity of the barriers to controlled areas, guard control stations should be established at all entrances in service.

Locks Locks are an essential and integral part of the barriers and the security they provide. To be effective, however, keys and combinations to locks must be strictly controlled. If they are compromised, the security of the entire facility is compromised.

Regardless of their quality or cost, locks can only be considered as delay devices. They are not positive bars to entry. Many ingenious locks have been developed, but equally ingenious means have been devised to open them surreptitiously. Some locks require considerable time and expert manipulation to open but will eventually succumb to force and the proper tools. The protection afforded by a well-constructed lock can be measured in terms of how long the locking mechanism will resist picking, manipulation, or drilling.

To determine a facility's lock requirements demands specialized knowledge. Few security officers and fewer transportation managers have the necessary expertise. It is advisable when selecting the equipment to be used to consult a professional locksmith.

The following list describes locks commonly used in the transportation system (see also Chapter 15 for more information on the subject of locks).

1. *Key locks* can be opened by an expert in a few minutes. The ease with which (*a*) a key can be lost and compromised or (*b*) an impression can be made should be considered in determining the security value of a key lock.

2. *Conventional combination locks* may be opened by a skillful manipulator able to

determine the settings of the tumblers of a common three-position dial-type lock through a keen sense of touch or hearing. Although some combination locks may require several hours to open, a skillful individual can open the conventional combination lock in a few minutes.

3. *Manipulation-resistant combination locks* are designed so that the opening lever does not come in contact with the tumblers until the combination has been set. This provides a higher degree of protection for important material.

4. *Other combination locks* with four or more tumblers afford still greater protection for very important items.

5. *Relocking devices* furnish an added degree of safety against forcible entry to a safe or vault door. This type increases the difficulty of opening a combination lock by punching, drilling, or blocking. It is recommended for heavy safes and vaults.

6. *Interchangeable-core locks* have a core that can be removed and be replaced by another using a different key. The cores can be replaced quickly, instantly changing the matching of locks and keys if their security is compromised. Other advantages are that all the locks in a facility can be keyed into an overall master-keyed system.

Interchangeable-core locks are economical, involving lower cost for maintenance and for provision of new locks. The system simplifies recordkeeping, is flexible, and can be engineered to the needs of the facility.

7. *Kingpin locks* are placed on the kingpin of a trailer or container chassis to make it impossible to connect a tractor. They provide a medium to high degree of security, depending on the type of lock. Although they are expensive, one lock can protect a number of trailers simultaneously if the locked trailer is parked in a blocking position. As the lock can provide positive security, it is recommended for use in an area where only periodic surveillance rather than constant observation is possible.

For effective control of locks, keys, and combinations, accurate records must be maintained and periodic physical inventories made. Combinations and keys should be issued only to those whose official duties require them.

The facility key and combination control should be exercised by the security officer. Records containing combinations and keys should be securely stored, with only limited and controlled access allowed. Lists of persons authorized to draw keys to controlled areas should be kept in the key storage container, which should be inventoried at the end of each shift; all keys should be accounted for at that time. Above all, keys should not be issued for permanent retention or removal from the facility. Keys should be logged out at the beginning of each shift and logged in at the end.

Combinations to safe locks and padlocks securing containers should be changed once during each twelve-month period, but in any case they should be changed immediately following the loss or possible compromise of a combination or key; after the discharge, suspension, or reassignment of anyone who knows the combination; or upon receipt of a new container with a built-in combination lock.

Each facility will have requirements for key and lock control systems peculiar to itself. A survey should be conducted to determine the actual need for additional protection afforded by locking devices. When this determination has been made, an annex to the security plan can be drafted which will show:

1. The location of key depositories
2. The keys (by building, area, or cabinet number) to be held in each depository
3. The method of marking or tagging keys for easy identification
4. The method of control for issue and receipt of keys, including register maintenance and identification of personnel authorized to receive keys
5. The action required if keys are lost, stolen, or damaged
6. The frequency and method of lock rotation
7. The assignment of responsibility and accountability by job or position title

8. The availibility of emergency keys to the guard supervisor
9. A list of persons to whom this plan is made available

LIGHTING

A protective lighting system enables the guard force to maintain a level of security at night approaching that observed during the day. Adequate lighting is relatively inexpensive, but if it cannot be provided, management must consider more costly alternatives, such as additional guards, sentry dog patrols, or extended alarm systems.

Protective lighting will permit guards to observe activities around or inside a facility. It is achieved by providing even light on areas bordering the facility, directing glaring light into the eyes of a potential intruder, and maintaining a low level of light on guard patrol routes.

When planning a protective lighting system, the creation of high contrast on an intruder and the background is a primary consideration. The ability of a guard to distinguish a darkly clothed person against a dark background improves significantly as the level of illumination is increased. Predominantly dark, dirty surfaces require more light to facilitate observation than those consisting of clean concrete or light-colored paint. This is also true inside buildings, where ceilings and walls redirect and diffuse light.

Generally, lighting should be directed downward and away from the area or structure to be protected, and away from the guards assigned to patrol the facility. It should create as few shadows as possible.

Units for lighting perimeter-fences of controlled areas should be located within the protected area and above the fence. The light pattern on the ground should include an area both inside and outside the fence. Adjacent highways, waterways, railroads, or residences may limit the depth of the light pattern. Similarly, piers and docks forming part of the facility perimeter should be safeguarded by illuminating both the pier area and the water approaches. The area beneath the pier flooring should be lit with low-wattage floodlights arranged to dispel shadows.

Movable lighting that can be controlled by guards is recommended as part of the protective system for piers and docks, but lighting in these areas may not violate marine rules. The U.S. Coast Guard should be consulted to ensure that proposed lighting systems adjacent to navigable waters do not interfere with aids to navigation.

The lighting of open areas within a perimeter should be the same as that required at the perimeter. Lighting units in outdoor storage areas should be so placed as to provide even distribution of light in aisles and recesses to eliminate shadows where intruders may conceal themselves.

Special Terms Special terms used in describing lighting must be understood to discuss and develop a protective lighting system.

One **candlepower** is the amount of light emitted by 1 international candle (candela).

One **footcandle** is the amount of light on a surface 1 ft from the source of 1 cd. The amount of light varies inversely as the square of the distance between the source and the surface, so the foot-candles decrease rapidly as the distance is increased.

Horizontal illumination is the amount of light expressed in footcandles on a horizontal surface.

Vertical illumination is the amount of light expressed in footcandles on a vertical surface.

Continuous lighting *(stationary luminaires)* is the most common protective lighting system. It consists of a series of fixed luminaires arranged to flood a given area continuously with overlapping cones of light.

Glare projection lighting provides a band of light with great angular dispersal. It directs the glare at an intruder while restricting the downward beam. It is a strong deterrent to a potential intruder and protects security personnel by keeping them in comparative darkness. It should not be used if it would interfere with adjacent facilities.

Controlled lighting allows adjustment of the lighted strip to fit a particular need. If a highway, railroad, or airport adjoins the perimeter, this method will permit illumination of a narrow strip outside the fence and a wide strip inside the fence. The weakness of this method of lighting is that it often illuminates or silhouettes guards as they patrol their routes.

Standby lighting *(stationary luminaires)* is similar to continuous lighting, described above. The luminaires, however, are not continuously lit but are activated manually by the guard force or automatically by the alarm system only when required.

Movable lighting *(stationary or portable)* consists of manually operated movable searchlights that can be lighted during hours of darkness or only as needed. The system is a supplement to those described above.

Emergency lighting can duplicate any or all of the above systems. Its use is limited to emergencies which render the normal system inoperative. It needs an alternate power source, such as installed or portable generators.

Incandescent lamps are common glass light bulbs which produce light by the resistance of a filament to an electric current. Special-purpose bulbs are manufactured with interior coatings to reflect the light or with a built-in lens to direct or diffuse the light. A regular bulb can be mounted in a shade or fixture to secure similar results.

Gaseous discharge lamps are of two kinds—mercury vapor and sodium vapor. They are limited in their use as protective lighting, since they require a 2- to 5-min period to light when cold and a slightly longer period to relight, when hot, after a power interruption.

Mercury-vapor lamps emit a blue-green light caused by an electric current passing through a tube of conducting, luminous gas. They are more efficient than incandescent lamps of comparable wattage. They are used widely for interior or exterior lighting where people are working.

Sodium-vapor lamps are made on the same general principle as mercury-vapor lamps but emit a golden-yellow glow. They are more efficient than mercury-vapor or incandescent lamps and are used where the color is acceptable, such as on streets, roads, or bridges.

Power Sources   Normally, the primary power source for a transportation facility is the local public utility. The concern of the security force begins at the point where the power feeder lines enter the facility. Feeder lines should be located underground or, in the case of overhead wiring, inside the perimeter, to minimize the possibility of vandalism damaging the lines.

An alternate source of power should be available to supply the system in the event of interruptions or failure. Standby gasoline-driven generators that start automatically upon the failure of the primary source will ensure continuous light. They may, however, be inadequate for sustained operation. Generator- or battery-powered portable or stationary lights should be available at key control points for use by the guards in case of a complete power failure that makes the secondary power supply inoperative.

Circuit Design   Both parallel and series circuits can be used to advantage in protective lighting systems. However, circuits should be arranged so that the failure of one lamp will not leave a large portion of the perimeter or a segment of the critical area in darkness.

The design should be simple and economical to maintain. It should require a minimum number of shutdowns for routine inspections, repair, cleaning, and lamp replacement. Specific design criteria are included in Chapter 14, "Lighting."

PHYSICAL SECURITY STANDARDS

The following "Standards for Cargo Security"* were drafted by the U.S. Customs Service for the guidance of terminal operators. The *General Standards* should achieve an acceptable degree of security. The *Recommended Specifications* suggest means by which these standards can be met.

All cargo-handling and storage facilities should provide a physical barrier against unauthorized access to cargo. Usually, this requires a covered structure with walls and apertures which can be securely locked. In addition, fencing may be needed for the following purposes:

1. As supplementary protection to prevent unauthorized persons and vehicles from entering cargo areas.

2. As sole protection for open storage of bulk cargo or large articles which do not require covered storage because they cannot be easily pilfered or removed without mechanical handling equipment or which have their own inherent security.

Buildings

General Standard

All buildings used to house cargo and associated support buildings should be constructed of materials which resist unlawful entry. The integrity of the structure must be maintained by periodic inspection and repair. Security protection should be provided for all doors and windows.

Recommended Specifications

1. Equip all exterior doors and windows with locks.

2. Protect all windows through which entry can be made from ground level by safety glass, wire mesh, or bars.

3. Similarly safeguard all glassed-in areas where shipping documents are processed.

4. Construct all delivery and receiving doors of steel or other material that will prevent or deter unlawful entry, and keep them closed and locked when not in use.

5. Where fencing is impractical or guards insufficient, equip the building with an intrusion detection or alarm system.

6. Inspectors must particularly ensure that there are no avenues for surreptitious entry through floors, roofs, or adjacent buildings.

Fencing

General Standard

Where fencing is required, it should enclose an area around cargo storage structures, support buildings, and exterior stored cargo sufficient to provide maneuvering space for pickup and delivery vehicles and to prevent use of buildings or cargo to surmount the fence. The fence line must be inspected regularly for integrity and any damage promptly repaired.

Recommended Specifications

1. Install chain-link fencing at least 8 ft high (not including a barbed-wire extension) and with at least 9-gauge, 2-in mesh. If the level on which the fence is constructed is lower than the area outside the fence line, increase the height of the fence to provide an effective 8-ft fence at all points.

Standards for Cargo Security, Department of the Treasury, U.S. Customs Service, Washington, D.C., 1973.

2. Top the fence with a 2-ft barbed-wire extension, consisting of three strands of barbed wire properly spaced and at a 45° angle to the vertical.

3. Place fence posts on the inside of the fence, and secure them in a concrete foundation at least 2 ft deep.

4. Ensure that objects or persons cannot pass beneath the fencing by providing at least one of the following:

    a. Concrete aprons not less than 6 in thick

    b. Frame piping

    c. U-shaped stakes driven approximately 2 ft into the ground

5. Avoid any condition which compromises the fence line. Prohibit the placing of objects (containers, dunnage, cargo, vehicles, or any other item that may facilitate unlawful entry) adjacent to the fence line.

6. Where necessary, install bumpers or fence guards to prevent damage by vehicles.

Gates

General Standard

The number of gates in fences should be the minimum necessary for access. All fence gates should be at least as substantial as the fence. Gates through which vehicles or personnel enter or exit should be staffed or under observation by management or security personnel.

Recommended Specifications

1. Equip gates with a deadlocking bolt or a substantially equivalent lock which does not require use of a chain. All hardware connecting the lock to the gate should be strong enough to withstand constant use and attempts to defeat the locking device.

2. Construct swing-type gates so that they may be secured to the ground when closed.

3. Separate gates for personnel and vehicle traffic are desirable.

Gatehouses

General Standard

Operators of facilities handling a substantial volume of cargo should maintain a gatehouse, with security personnel in attendance, at all vehicle entrances and exits during business hours.

Recommended Specifications

1. Set the gatehouse back from the gate so that vehicles can be stopped and examined on terminal property.

2. Equip the gatehouse with a telephone or other communication system.

4. Post prominently on the exterior of all gatehouses signs advising drivers and visitors of the conditions of entry. Include in conditions of entry a notice that all vehicles and personnel entering the area are subject to search.

Parking

General Standard

Private passenger vehicles should be prohibited from parking in cargo areas or immediately adjacent to cargo storage buildings. Access to employee parking areas should be subject to security controls.

Recommended Specifications

1. Locate parking areas outside fenced operational areas, or at least a substantial distance from cargo handling and storage areas or buildings and support buildings.

2. Require employees exiting to the parking area from the cargo area to pass through an area under the supervision of management or security personnel.

Require employees desiring to return to their private vehicles during hours of employment to notify management and/or security personnel.

3. Allow parking in employee parking areas by permit only. Maintain a record of each issued permit, listing the vehicle registration number, model, color, and year. The permit should consist of a numbered decal, tag, sticker, or sign placed in a uniform location on the vehicle.

4. Issue to vendors and other visitors temporary parking permits which allow parking in a designated area under security controls.

Lighting

General Standard

Adequate lighting should be provided for the following areas:
- Entrances, exits, and around gatehouses
- Cargo areas, including container, trailer, aircraft, and rail-car holding areas
- Along fence lines and stringpieces
- Parking areas

Recommended Specifications

1. The Society of Illuminating Engineers recommends the following light intensities at ground level:

Vehicle and pedestrian areas ....2.0 fc
Vital structures and other sensitive areas ....2.0 fc
Unattended outdoor parking areas ....1.0 fc

2. Illuminate all vehicle and pedestrian gates, perimeter fence lines, and other outer areas with mercury-vapor, sodium-vapor, or power-quartz lamps or substantially similar high-intensity lighting, employing a minimum of 400 W per fixture. Locate lights 30 ft above ground level and have them properly spaced to provide the appropriate light intensity for the area to be illuminated.

3. Establish a system of planned maintenance.

4. Protect lighting subject to vandalism by wire screening or other substantially equivalent means.

Locks, Locking Devices, and Key Control

General Standard

Locks or locking devices used on buildings, gates, and equipment should be so constructed as to provide positive protection against unauthorized entry. The issue of all locks and keys should be controlled by management or security personnel.

Recommended Specifications

1. Use only locks having (a) multiple-pin tumblers, (b) deadlocking bolts, (c) interchangeable cores and (d) serial numbers.

2. To facilitate detection of unauthorized locks, use only locks of standard manufacture, displaying the owner's company name.

3. Number all keys and obtain a signature from the recipient when issued. Maintain a control file for all keys. Restrict the distribution of master keys to persons whose responsibilities require them to have one.

4. Safeguard all unissued or duplicate keys.

5. Remove and secure keys from cargo-handling equipment and vehicles when not in actual use.

High-risk Cargo

General Standard

In each cargo-handling building there must be adequate space capable of being locked, sealed, or otherwise secured for storage of high-value cargo and packages which have been broken prior to or during the course of unloading. When such cargo must be transported a substantial distance from the point of unloading to the special security area, vehicles capable of being locked or otherwise secured must be used. (These standards are required by Customs Regulations, 19 CFR 4.30.)

Recommended Specifications

1. Construct special security rooms, cribs, or vaults that can resist forcible entry on all sides and from underneath and overhead.

2. Locate these special security areas, where possible, in such a way that management and/or security personnel may keep them under continuous observation. Otherwise, install an alarm system or provide for inspection at frequent intervals.

3. Release merchandise from such an area only in the presence of authorized supervisors and/or security personnel.

4. Log all movement of merchandise in or out of the special security area, showing date, time, condition of cargo upon receipt, name of trucker and company making pickup, and registration number of equipment being used.

CARGO SECURITY CHECKLIST

The checklist below may be used for many different types of facilities. Individual facility managers may select the elements that pertain to their particular establishment and location when making a security survey.

1. Barriers

a. Is the perimeter of the facility or activity defined by a fence or other type of physical barrier?

b. If a fence or gate is used, does it meet the minimum specifications?
  (1) Is the top guard strung with barbed wire and angled outward and upward at a 45° angle?
  (2) Is its total height at least 10 ft?
  (3) Is it located so that it is not adjacent to mounds, piers, docks, or any other aid to surmounting it?

c. If building walls, floors, and roofs form a part of the perimeter barrier, do they provide security equivalent to that provided by chain link fence? Are all openings properly secured?

d. If a masonry wall or building forms a part of the perimeter barrier, does it meet minimum specifications or perimeter fencing?

e. If a river, lake, or other body of water forms any part of the perimeter barrier, are security measures equal to the deterrence of the 10-ft fence provided?

f. Are openings which permit access to the facility—such as culverts, tunnels, manholes for sewers and utility access, and sidewalk elevators—properly secured?

g. List number, location, and physical characteristics of perimeter entrances.

h. Are all portals in perimeter barriers guarded, secured, or under constant surveillance?

i. Are all perimeter entrances equipped with secure locking devices, and are they always locked when not in active use?

j. Are gates and/or other perimeter entrances which are not in active use frequently inspected by guards or management personnel?

k. Is the security officer responsible for security keys to perimeter entrances? If not, which individual is responsible?

l. Are keys to perimeter entrances issued to other than security personnel, such as those engaged in cleaning, trash removal, or vending machine service?

m. Are all normally used pedestrian and vehicle gates effectively and adequately lighted so as to ensure:

      (1) Proper identification of individuals and examination of credentials?

      (2) A clear view into interiors of vehicles?

      (3) That glare from luminaires does not shine in the guards' eyes?

n. Are appropriate signs setting forth the provisions for entry conspicuously posted at all principal entrances?

o. Are clear zones maintained for the largest vehicles on both sides of the perimeter barrier? If clear-zone requirements cannot be met, what additional security measures can be implemented?

p. Are automobiles permitted to park against or too close to the perimeter barrier?

q. What is the frequency of checks made by maintenance crews regarding the condition of perimeter barriers?

r. Do guards patrol perimeter barriers?

s. Are reports of inadequate perimeter security immediately acted upon and the necessary repairs effected?

t. Are perimeters protected by intrusion alarm devices?

u. Does any new construction require installation of additional perimeter barriers or additional perimeter lighting?

2. Lighting

a. Is the perimeter of the installation protected by adequate lighting?

b. Are the cones of illumination from lamps directed downward and away from the facility proper and away from guard personnel?

c. Are lights mounted to provide a strip of light both inside and outside the fence?

d. Are lights checked periodically for proper orientation, and are inoperative lamps replaced immediately?

e. Do light beams overlap to provide coverage in case a bulb burns out?

f. Is additional lighting provided at vulnerable or sensitive areas?

g. Are security gatehouses provided with proper illumination?

h. Are light finishes or stripes used on lower parts of buildings and structures to aid guard observation?

i. Does the facility have a dependable auxiliary source of power?

j. Is there alternate power for the lighting system independent of the plant lighting or power system?

k. Is the power supply for lights adequately protected? How?

l. Is the standby or emergency equipment periodically tested?

m. Is emergency equipment designed to go into operation automatically when needed?

n. Is wiring tested and inspected periodically to ensure proper operation?

o. Are multiple circuits used? If so, are proper switching arrangements provided?

p. Is wiring for protective lighting securely mounted?

      (1) Is it in tamper-resistant conduits?

      (2) Is it mounted underground?

      (3) If above ground, is it high enough to reduce the possibility of tampering?

q. Are switches and controls properly located, controlled, and protected?

      (1) Are they weatherproof and tamper-resistant?

      (2) Are they readily accessible to security personnel?

      (3) Are they located so that they are inaccessible from outside the perimeter barrier?

      (4) Is there a centrally located switch to control protective lighting? Is it vulnerable?

r. Is the lighting designed and locations recorded so that repairs can be made rapidly in an emergency?
s. Is adequate lighting for guard use provided on indoor routes?
t. Are materials and equipment in shipping and storage areas properly arranged to permit adequate lighting?
u. If bodies of water form a part of the perimeter, does the lighting conform to other perimeter lighting standards?

3. Alarms

a. Is an alarm system used in the facility?
   (1) Does the system indicate an alert only within the facility?
   (2) Does it signal in a central station outside the facility?
   (3) Is it connected to facility guard headquarters?
   (4) Is it connected directly to an enforcement headquarters outside the facility proper? Is it a private protection service? Police station? Fire station?
b. Is there any inherent weakness in the system itself?
c. Is the system supported by properly trained, alert guards?
d. Is the alarm system for operating areas turned off during working hours?
e. Is the system tested prior to activating it for nonoperational periods?
f. Is the alarm system inspected regularly?
g. Is the system tamper-resistant? Weatherproof?
h. Is an alternate alarm system provided for use in the event of failure of the primary system?
i. Is an alternate or independent source of power designed to cut in and operate automatically?
k. Is the alarm system properly maintained by trained personnel?
l. Are periodic tests conducted frequently to determine the adequacy of response to alarm signals?
m. Are records kept of all alarm signals received to include time, date, location, action taken, and cause for alarm?

4. Communications

a. Is the security communications system adequate?
b. What means of communications are used?
   (1) *Telephone*
      (a) Is it a commercial switchboard system? Independent switchboard?
      (b) Is it restricted for guard use only?
      (c) Are switchboards adequately guarded?
      (d) Are there enough call boxes, and are they conveniently located?
      (e) Are open wires, terminal boxes, and cables frequently inspected for damage, wear, sabotage, and wiretapping?
      (f) Are personnel cautioned about discussing cargo movements over the telephone?
   (2) *Radio*
      (a) Is proper radio procedure practiced?
      (b) Is an effective routine code being used?
      (c) Is proper authentication required?
      (d) Is the equipment maintained properly?
   (3) *Messenger*
      (a) Is the messenger always available?
   (4) *Teletype*
      (a) Is an operator available at all times?

    (5) *Public address*
        (a) Does it work?
        (b) Can it be heard?
    (6) *Visual signals*
        (a) Do all guards know the signals?
        (b) Can they be seen?

c. Is security communications equipment in use capable of transmitting instructions to all key posts simultaneously?

d. Does the equipment in use allow a guard to communicate to guard headquarters with minimum delay?

e. Is there more than one system of security communications available for exclusive use of security personnel?

f. Does one of these systems have an alternate or independent source of power?

g. Has the communications center been provided with adequate physical security safeguards?

Chapter **23**

Computer Power Security

JAMES M. DALEY, P. E.
Product Manager, Switch Department, Automatic Switch Company

INTRODUCTION

The computer represents the most widely used tool in the conduct of business today across the whole spectrum of commerce—from manufacturing to environmental protection, including such industries as finance, banking, health care, transportation, and communications. Yet, with this wide usage, it is perhaps one of the least understood aids to business because of its virtually unlimited possibilities for application.

In terms of the design of computer facilities, so many factors enter into the computer's requirements that at first the task seems monumental. One aspect of the challenge is the fact that a firm's computer is such an essential part of daily operations.

This chapter is intended to reduce the apparent complexity by outlining the basic considerations in designing a computer center and by recommending some ways of reducing computer vulnerability in view of the serious consequences when needed computer services are lost.

Categories of Computers

Regardless of the ultimate application of the computer, it can be viewed as fitting into one of two classifications.

Real-Time Processing A computer which computes and processes new data received from remote terminals and initiates actions as a function of that new data can be considered a real-time computer.

Batch Processing A computer which is preprogrammed to repeat functions based upon continuous input of known data and which can easily be programmed to automatically and periodically check computer data or results for correctness can be considered a batch-process computer.

It is obvious, then, that computers in the first classification will require a more careful consideration of design criteria than those in the second category. Yet there will be instances where the latter, too, will require equally careful consideration regarding design.

Electricity Requirements

If the service rendered by the computer is essential to the successful, efficient, economical, and/or safe continuation of the overall operation of a business, then it must be viewed as a critical and essential electrical load. It should therefore be treated as such in the design of the electrical distribution system.

The electrical distribution system should be capable of protecting the computer load from natural and man-made disturbances, either accidental or intentional. The degree to which the design should include these means will be a function of the criticality of the computer operation and the economics of providing such means. This determination will be a function of the application under consideration.

Factors Affecting Operation

Some of the factors which will affect operation of a computer are:

1. Natural disturbances—lightning storms, severe snow- rainstorms, icing, floods
2. Accidental—traffic accidents knocking down utility poles, accidental tripping of power switches, cutting of buried cables, fire
3. Vandalism—intentional interference with power feed, destruction of equipment
4. Normal disturbances—power transients caused by network switching, internal building load fluctuations, brownouts

The above list is not complete, but it shows that there are three conditions to guard against in the power system design:

1. Transients
2. Power blackouts—complete loss of power
3. Power brownouts—cutbacks in transmission voltage to conserve energy

Any other factor which can be added to these will affect the computer in one or more of the three conditions stated.

RATIONALE OF DISCUSSION

Designing the power system to account for the three conditions stated will be a function of the relative size of the computer center as well as of previously stated factors. It seems natural, then, that an analysis of design considerations and recommendations be divided in a manner that will more clearly reveal all the subtleties of design features. Accordingly, this discussion will proceed on the basis of a division in computer center size with respect to the overall project. For want of better terminology, the size discrimination will be:

1. Small computer center
   a. Computer power demand 100 kVA or less
   b. HVAC included with building supply
   c. Power fed from common service with remainder of building
   d. Most often a batch-process operation

2. Medium computer center
   a. Computer power demand 100 to 500 kVA
   b. HVAC partially integrated with building system or separate
   c. Power fed from same service, but may be a separate substation
   d. Usually a real-time operation
3. Large computer center
   a. Computer power demand over 500 kVA
   b. HVAC is separate and distinct
   c. Power fed from isolated service and substation
   d. Real-time operation

Experience has shown the most frequently used category to be the medium-sized computer center. The large computer center is most likely to be found in the financial industry—in insurance companies, large banks, stock brokerage houses, etc. Surprisingly, the large computer center is the simplest of the three sizes to protect adequately from the design standpoint.

THE SMALL COMPUTER CENTER

The small computer center is usually found in manufacturing plants, regional banking and financial institutions, communication centers, and some hospitals. It often uses the batch-process operation. This implies that lost or erroneous data due to power disturbances are usually recoverable, but not without lost productivity or reduced efficiency.

Any disturbance or discontinuity in electric service to the computer is likely to cause degradation in computer data. Consultation with a specific computer manufacturer will reveal the permissible limits of power fluctuations within which computer operation is reliable. As a general rule, the system cannot tolerate excursions in voltage beyond +10 percent and −8 percent steady state of nominal or excursions of ±0.5 Hz frequency from 60 Hz nominal. Transients exceeding 15 to 18 percent for 30 cycles or more are also not tolerable.

The Uninterruptible Power System (UPS)

Since the small computer center is likely to be installed in a facility which will have random load switching and fluctuations, it is often necessary to filter and isolate the computer from the electrical power distribution system. There are several means to achieve this isolation. One such means (and perhaps the most popular) is an uninterruptible power system (UPS). This system is available in many mechanical configurations, all of which include a flywheel of some type. It is also available in a solid-state electronic configuration. Since the latter is the more popular, the ensuing material will assume the use of the solid-state UPS.

A brief explanation is needed of what a UPS is, what it does, and how it does it. As this device is a filter of sorts, it protects its load or output from line disturbances at its input side. In short, the UPS maintains a constant and well-regulated power output regardless of the condition of the power input. Of course, there are limits to the UPS's ability to correct. These limits apply to time more than they do to power input limits. For a better grasp of the UPS concept, refer to Fig. 1. Notice that the system is composed of four identical units in parallel. Because of limitations in current-carrying and -switching abilities of solid-state devices (diodes, SCRs, etc.), the UPS is made up of several paralleled units. Usually, UPS systems of 15 kVA or higher will require this configuration. Each parallel unit is comprised of a rectifier to convert the ac input to dc. This dc then feeds a common dc power bus as well as individual inverters which reconvert the dc to ac. The inverter outputs then feed a common ac output power bus. The dc bus feeds battery banks which, under normal operating conditions, are on a float charge basis. In this configuration, the batteries serve to clamp the dc bus to a fixed potential, thus filtering voltage transients and consequently maintaining a constant dc input to the inverters. The inverters are synchronized together through control by a master oscillator, which controls the firing of SCRs for the purpose of reconstructing an approximation of a sine wave. To produce a harmonic-free output, this reconstructed wave is fed into a ferro-resonant tank circuit whose output is sinusoidal. Since the inverters are all in synchronism, their outputs are fed to a common-output power bus to make up the total output capability of the UPS.

The UPS is self-protecting in most cases and is usually well monitored. If a malfunction occurs in any one module, that module is automatically removed from

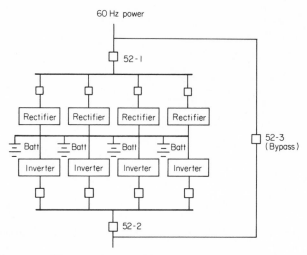

Fig. 1   Block diagram—solid state uninterruptable power system.

service. Under normal conditions, the UPS can remain in operation with no degradation of output on loss of one module. There is usually sufficient overload capacity in the remaining units to pick up the slack. When the malfunction is serious enough to require shutdown of the UPS system, internal circuitry will cause the UPS to bypass itself prior to shutdown. To be ready for such an eventuality, the master oscillator synchronizes the output of the UPS with the ac input in a manner that causes the phase angle difference between input and output ac sine waves to be approximately 2° (electrical). The output lags the input by this angle. Upon initiation of a bypass operation, the UPS signals circuit breaker 52-3 to close. When it is closed, the UPS then signals circuit breaker 52-2 to open. The UPS can then cause circuit breaker 52-1 to be opened.

Under normal operating conditions, when the ac input voltage is reduced or lost altogether, the batteries will support the output through the inverter with no noticeable transients on the output bus. Upon return of the ac input to acceptable limits, either from the commercial source or from an on-site emergency power source, the rectifier output will reassume the feed to the inverter and recharge the batteries. Most UPS systems can be furnished with control circuitry to limit the initial inrush to the rectifier upon restoration of ac power input. This circuit serves to reduce power requirements on restart after battery charge has been reduced. It can be used to good advantage when the UPS input comes from an on-site emergency power source. In such a circumstance, the load requirements can be reduced, thus allowing more loads to be fed from the emergency source or allowing the use of smaller engine generator sets. As a rough rule of thumb, it can be assumed that the power requirements of a UPS system with fully discharged batteries will be approximately 125 percent of that same system with fully charged batteries. This number will vary with the charge state of the batteries as well as the relative size of the battery bank. It will be necessary to ascertain the exact requirements and configuration for the UPS in any specific application to ensure adequacy of design of the distribution system. In addition to this consideration, efficency of the UPS must also be considered. Again as a rough rule of thumb, efficiencies of UPS systems average around 80 percent, conservatively. This also must be considered in the design of the power distribution system.

The UPS serves to produce the highest degree of reliability and quantity of operation of the computer and other critical loads. When considering these other loads, it is essential to keep in mind that the UPS has little ability to start high-inrush loads without losing regulation of its output. Accordingly, where the computer system requires 400 Hz of power derived from motor generator sets, the electrical distribution system should be designed to permit starting of these 400-Hz sets on the unprotected ac power bus. Once started, it should then permit transfer of these motors to the UPS output bus. Figure 2 is a typical switching scheme for such a subsystem. It should be remembered that the output of the UPS is phase-locked to the input. Consequently, out-of-phase transfer of the motor can be avoided by utilizing a transfer switch with a minimum off time during transfer. In this instance, overlap or closed-transition transfer must be avoided. The output of the 400-Hz generator is closed to, and paralleled with, the other 400-Hz generators only when the motor is powered from the UPS output bus.

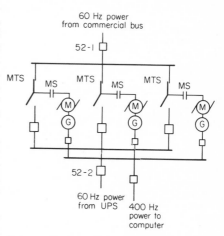

Fig. 2 One-line power diagram for 400-Hz motor-generator start–transfer–run power scheme.

The final load for consideration of operation on the UPS output bus is the security system. Since the computer is the key to the successful, economical, and efficient operation of the business, those subsystems responsible for its security should also be afforded the same degree of reliability as the computer and should also be fed from the UPS output. Examples of security subsystems are closed-circuit television for controlling access; personnel identification systems; and smoke or fire detection, alarm, and extinguishing systems. Since the power requirements of such systems are relatively small in comparison to the computer systems, little if any additional expense will be incurred by their inclusion in the UPS output load content.

Support Loads: Air Conditioning and Lighting

At this point, "support loads" should be examined, since without them the computer is rendered inoperable. Essentially, there are two: air conditioning and lighting. The modern computer is a neatly packaged electronic system composed of millions of circuits. It is usually packaged in a manner that will take advantage of all usable internal space. Since the device must be capable of performing innumerable operations with remarkable speed, it is principally made up of densely packaged integrated circuits, as well as discrete components. All of these components perform the various operations by control of current flow, and current flow in a conductor produces heat. Because of this density of packaging and amount of current flow, cooling by convection to normal outside air is totally inadequate to produce sufficient cooling. Since heat is an arch enemy of solid-state devices, it is essential to air-condition the equipment to maintain adequate cooling. Not only must the air be cooled, its humidity must be controlled as well. Too high humidity causes condensation in the equipment, with resulting insulation breakdown and short circuiting. Too low humidity causes static electric charge buildup, resulting in potential semiconductor junction breakdown due to arc-over. It is therefore essential that the HVAC (heating, ventilation, air conditioning) system be designed to protect the computer. It is not economically feasible or physically desirable to place the computer HVAC equipment on the UPS output bus for two reasons. First, the eletrical power requirement for a computer HVAC system is approximately equal to the electrical power requirements of the computer system itself. If the cooling requirements of the UPS were added to the power requirements of the computer, the installation would require approximately double the UPS capacity. Second, HVAC loads are mostly motors of considerable size and have automatic controls which start and stop at random as a function of the cooling load. Such starting and stopping would introduce voltage transients on the UPS output bus beyond the level of tolerance of the computer; consequently the benefits gained by the installation of the UPS would be negated. It is therefore obvious that the HVAC must be isolated from the computer.

Since a computer center is normally located inside a building and away from outside walls for security, there is no access to natural light. This creates the need to ensure adequate artificial lighting.

A Typical Electrical Power System

A typical electrical power distribution system for a building with a small computer center can now be examined. Figure 3 depicts a one-line diagram for such an example. Since the building is defined as a small system, a single service entrance is shown. From the diagram, it can be seen that feeder circuits are broken out in accordance with the types of loads they are designated to feed. This design approach is taken so that a failure in a lighting branch circuit will not affect the computer UPS input or HVAC branch. In addition, starting currents of mechanical loads will cause voltage drops in distribution systems. These voltage drops will have the minimum effect on other loads if the mechanical loads are not fed from the same branch feeders as the others. This design practice should be followed in any type of distribution system, whether or not computers are involved.

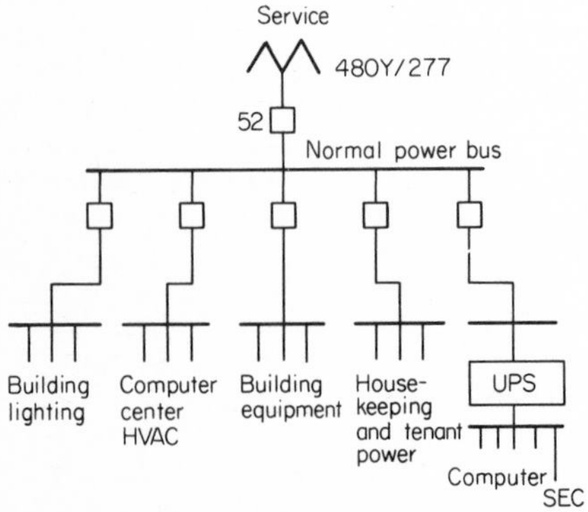

Downstream circuit isolation should also be applied to those circuits which feed the computer center. This is demonstrated in Fig. 4, where the emergency power provisions have been added to the distribution system of Fig. 3. A multiplicity of automatic transfer switches (ATS) has been selected to provide maximum protection to the essential loads. It is good design practice to place the automatic transfer switch as close to the load it serves in the distribution system as is practical. This practice affords the highest level of protection, because it not only protects against loss of commercial power feed to the building; it also protects against malfunc-

Fig. 3   **Typical one-line power distribution diagram for a small computer center.**

tions and failures in the distribution system inside the building as well. Surveys reveal that more than 50 percent of power outages to loads are due to accidents, operating errors, and line failures within the perimeter of a building.

To grasp the subtleties of the system shown, a typical operation will be examined. First, let us assume that the power loss has been caused by a failure outside the building. In such a case, each automatic transfer switch would sense the loss of power and initiate the start of the emergency engine generator set. If this set operates on

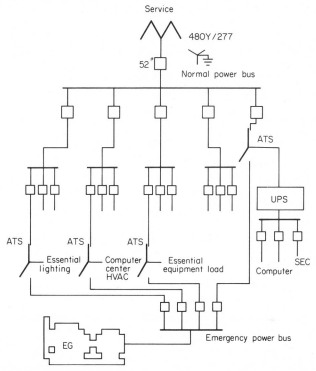

Fig. 4 Typical one-line power distribution diagram including emergency power system for a small computer center.

diesel fuel, natural gas, or gasoline, it can be expected to come up to operating conditions ready to load within 10 seconds. If it is a turbine, it will require about 40 to 60 seconds to be ready to load. In either case, since the computer is powered through the UPS, it will continue to run from the battery bank. There is usually sufficient cooled air in the HVAC duct system to sustain computer operation within allowable temperature limits, so in either case the starting time is acceptable.

While the engine generator set is capable of assuming the full load in a single-step application, it would be good practice to sequence the transfer of loads, beginning with the lighting load, followed by the computer-center HVAC, then the essential equipment, and finally the UPS. A delay of approximately 5 seconds is sufficient between the transfer of each load.

The nature of the restoration of commercial power feed after an outage is such that it comes on and off a few times before it is back to stay. Accordingly, the ATSs should be equipped with delay functions which will require constant voltage for a period of time; this ensures that premature retransfer is avoided. This delay function should be included on each ATS so that load buildup on the commercial feed can also be staggered.

A note of caution is offered here with regard to the operation of ATSs whose loads consist of large motors. If these motors drive mechanical loads with high inertia, retransfer to the commercial feed should be arranged to occur only when the emergency and commercial sources are approaching synchronism. This operation will protect the mechanical loads from abnormally high torque impulses. Such features are readily available for ATSs and should be considered for mechanical loads driven by motors of 25 hp or more. As an alternate to synchronous retransfer, ATS circuitry can signal the momentary disconnect of the motor until transfer is completed, and then initiate reconnect of the motor when the residual motor terminal voltage has reduced to a safe value (approximately 25 percent of nominal).

When the power loss is caused by a malfunction in the building distribution system, only those loads affected will initiate the start of the emergency source and load transfer. Restoration will be the same as in the case of a complete commercial power loss.

In either type of power loss, the emergency system should be arranged to run the emergency engine generator set for a period of 5 min after all loads are retransferred to the commercial power feed. Since most diesel and gas engines are turbo-charged through blowers driven from exhaust gases, this unloaded running will evenly cool the blower turbine drive blades with the lower exhaust gas temperature. This precaution will prolong the life of the blowers and help to maintain optimum power performance of the engine. This reasoning is applicable to turbine engines as well.

THE MEDIUM-SIZED COMPUTER CENTER

It is safe to say that the load considerations applicable to small computer centers are applicable to medium-sized computer centers. However, since the latter draws more power, it will require more emergency power. In addition, factors imposed by the National Electrical Code will require additional design consideration. To demonstrate these additional requirements, Fig. 5 is presented. As before, the basic design

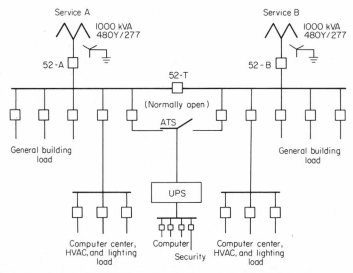

Fig. 5 Typical one-line power distribution diagram for a medium computer center.

philosophy is to produce a system which maximizes reliability and efficiency; with this in mind, the figure depicts a commercial power distribution system consisting of a double-ended unit substation configuration for the incoming service to the building.

For symmetry of design, two equal-size service transformers are chosen which have sufficient capacity to carry the connected load, with the inclusion of a provision to feed the computer UPS from either transformer. Without emergency power available, this design configuration will permit feeding the UPS from either service, depending on which transformer is less loaded. Furthermore, if either transformer should fail, the UPS can automatically transfer to the surviving transformer. In the interim, building operations personnel can set about reducing the connected load by dispensing with nonessential building loads. Having accomplished this, the normally open tie breaker (52-T) can then be closed after the appropriate service breaker (52-A or 52-B) is opened. This configuration will permit the pickup of the remaining half of the computer center's lighting and HVAC load.

Where emergency power is installed and available, full building operation can be restored by causing the computer center's lighting and HVAC load and essential building loads to be transferred to the emergency power system. If so desired, the computer UPS can also be transferred to the emergency power system. Notice that this design approach facilitates the full operation of the complete building when only one of the commercial services is available. (See Fig. 6.)

Ground-Fault Detection

In this system, the size of 1000-kVA service transformers was chosen for a demonstrative purpose to point out an additional design consideration. For the service shown, the National Electric Code requires ground-fault protection to be included in the protective scheme of the main service entrance. Notice that each service is in

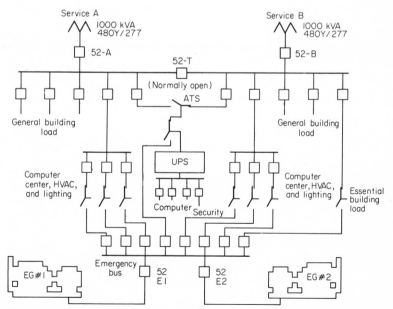

Fig. 6   Typical one-line power diagram including emergency power system for a medium computer center.

excess of 1200 A and that the voltage to ground is greater than 150 V. Consequently, to protect against fires resulting from arcing ground faults, ground-fault detection is required. There are several schemes for accommodating ground-fault protection. The most commonly used is "zero sequence detection." In this scheme, it is critically important to its proper operation to ensure the integrity of the ground and neutral conductor circuits so as to eliminate the multiplicity of return paths for ground currents. This must be maintained in a way that will also avoid the system transients and voltage imbalances which occur whenever the neutral conductor is switched in a 3-phase, 4-wire system. The best means of limiting the ground return paths while avoiding transients and voltage imbalances is to transfer the neutral conductor with the three main conductors at the automatic transfer switch in such a manner that the neutral transfer contact momentarily overlaps both neutrals (normal source and emergency source) for a brief period during the actual transfer of the main power poles. Such an operation will ensure the highest integrity in the neutral and ground conductors by avoiding contact wear on the neutral switching contact.

Automatic Synchronization

Because of the likelihood that the emergency power system will be relatively large, it will more likely than not require two or more emergency engine generator sets to carry the total emergency load. This introduces the need to automatically synchronize and parallel these emergency-power engine generator sets. The technology to perform this operation is in widespread use today and continues to expand in its application. Because of the ready availability of such systems, one can indeed specify and fully expect to get a fully automatic emergency power system capable of automatic synchronization and paralleling. These systems will produce closely regulated voltage and frequency and indeed can be operated at constant frequency regardless of load from 0 to 100 percent load (i.e., isochronous operation). The designer should be careful to specify isochronous operation if the UPS is to operate satisfactorily on the emergency source. It must be remembered that the UPS phase locks its output to its input so as to be ready to bypass itself automatically upon detection of an internal UPS malfunction. In achieving phase lock, the UPS output frequency will track the input frequency. If isochronous operation of the emergency power system is *not* specified, the designer can fully expect to lose the computer on a frequency-out-of-tolerance condition resulting from dynamic load fluctuation on the emergency power system.

Random-Access Emergency Power System

Of primary concern in the overall application is the continuity of power. All reasonable design efforts should be exercised to minimize power outages. One way to achieve this operation is to make the system a random-access emergency power system. Simply put, such a system would cause simultaneous starting of all emergency-power engine generator sets. The system would select the first set available at normal voltage and frequency and connect it to the emergency bus. This connection would permit the transfer of the most vital load (not exceeding the set rating) immediately upon sensing power available at the emergency bus. While all of this is occurring, the system would randomly and independently select the remaining sets as they achieved nominal voltage and frequency, automatically and independently synchronizing and paralleling these sets to the emergency power bus. Where diesel engines are the prime movers, it is not unreasonable to expect all sets to be on line within 10 seconds of the initiation of the starting sequence, even where the emergency power system requires six generator sets.

THE LARGE COMPUTER CENTER

The same concepts found applicable to small and medium computer centers are applicable to large computer centers. Additional considerations are discussed here mainly because of the amount of power required by the computer and its support equipment. Figure 7 is a typical power distribution diagram for a large computer center. Not shown in this diagram is the additional distribution system for the remainder of the building. It is not unreasonable to expect computer centers to reach the size indicated in this diagram. Indeed, the writer has encountered computer centers requiring from 5 to 12 MW of emergency power to back up the computer and its support HVAC. The trend is definitely toward larger computer installations, particularly in the financial industry.

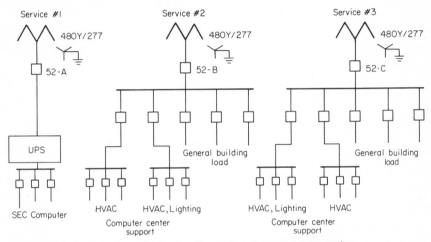

Fig. 7 Typical one-line power distribution diagram for a large computer center.

Figure 8 is a diagram of the power distribution for this system, including the emergency power provisions. (This particular system requires four emergency generator sets.) In addition to the topics outlined in the previous discussion, such as synchronous motor load transfer, random-access paralleling, ground-fault protection, and sequencing load transfer, some other considerations must enter into the design of larger systems. Typically, these larger systems will have generator-set ratings exceeding 750 kW. To produce higher kilovoltampere starting capacities, such generators will incorporate excitation support systems which will result in generator X"d of 8 to 10 percent. Simply stated, this excitation support will enable the the generator to produce 10 to 12.5 times its full-load current rating for up to 10 cycles. This being the case, it becomes necessary to apply the same careful short-circuit consideration to the emergency power distribution system as is applied to the normal power distribution system. An illustrative example will show the impact of this statement.

EXAMPLE: *Assumptions*
1. Four (4) engine generator sets
2. X"d Gen = 10 percent
3. Generator rating 900 kW, 480Y/277
4. All engines on line
5. 50 percent motor load
6. Ignore limiting impedance of conductors

Short-circuit considerations
Generator contribution:

$$\frac{I_{FL}}{X''d} = \frac{1,350}{0.1} = 13,500 \text{ A rms}$$

4 generators on line, therefore $13,500 \times 4 = 54,000$ A rms

Motor contribution:

Total bus $5,400 \times 4 \times 0.5 = 10,800$
Short circuit available at bus $= 54,000 + 10,800 = 64,800$ A rms

This calculation shows that unless the protective devices are 2,000 A or above in frame size, special consideration must be given to the overcurrent protective device. In most cases, this will lead to the use of integrally fused circuit breakers or fused switches. By contrast, if the Service 2 distribution system is analyzed for maximum short circuit available, it is seen that only 33,600 A rms are available. (This presupposes the above assumptions and a transformer impedance of 6 percent, with an unlimited primary kilovoltampere supply.) From this example, it is seen that the available short-circuit current from the emergency supply is almost twice that of the normal feed to any given load on the system. Consequently, extreme care is essential if the system is to survive accidental or deliberate faults.

Not previously introduced, a bypass and isolation switch (BP/IS) is shown in the UPS ATS distribution system. The function of this BP/IS is to permit periodic inspection and preventive maintenance procedures on the UPS ATS without requir-

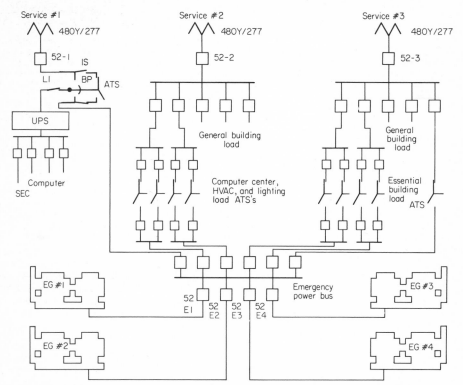

Fig. 8 Typical one-line power distribution diagram including emergency power system for a large computer center.

ing shutdown of the UPS and computer. It is introduced here because it is usually these large computer systems which operate round the clock, 7 days a week.

Scheduling maintenance for large systems has become a major problem. This is not normally the case with the small computer center and seldom the case with the medium computer center. When it does pose problems, however, consideration for its inclusion into the distribution system should be made. For optimum performance and reliability, preventive maintenance is essential. The systems shown here facilitate such maintenance through load division and segregation.

Parallel paths and redundancy are two of the essentials with regard to overall system integrity. A review of the system discussed above will show that preventive maintenance can easily be performed on any part of the overall system without major system shutdown. While in some cases this may add a little to the initial cost of installation, the protection these design approaches afford and the resulting flexibility will greatly outweigh the consequences of a fault or malfunction resulting from a less thorough design.

Chapter 24

Educational Facilities

JOHN W. POWELL

President, John W. Powell Consultants, Inc., Hamden, Connecticut

LUCIUS W. BURTON

Security Advisor, City Public Schools, Alexandria, Virginia

THE CASE FOR CAMPUS SECURITY

The need for seriously considering security in the design of new facilities being planned for universities, colleges, and schools is relatively new. The spotlight was first focused on this need in the late 1960s during the era of student dissent, when violent campus demonstrations involving "takeovers," "sit-ins," destruction, and arson were relatively commonplace. The intensity of this spotlight increased in the 1970s because, although student disorders have become somewhat more sporadic, a new and ever-increasing challenge has emerged—crime!

This chapter deals with the entire range of educational facilities. It is recognized that schools for grades K through 8 utilize different planning principles from those of institutions of higher learning, and therefore somewhat varying approaches to security planning will apply to each. The major distinctions are in the layout of the physical plants. Schools for the lower grades are usually more compact, and control of access and circulation is more centralized, while secondary schools and institutions of higher learning normally tend to be more spread out and to have a lower density of land use.

Colleges and universities also differ from most elementary and secondary schools in that the former are frequently self-contained communities with many on-site residents. Finally, an urban setting for an educational structure will undoubtedly require security provisions different from those needed in a rural or suburban setting. The reader must therefore apply the security considerations that best fit the particular institution's setting.

Magnitude of the Problem

There are few meaningful statistics on campus or school crime, but administrators have testified to its seriousness by elevating it to the top of the list of problems they must cope with. A brief look at the crime problem is therefore worthwhile.

In our schools, vandalism is a major problem. For example, in 1973 New York City spent $4 million to restore vandalism-caused damage, and this expense continues to rise. The problem has reached such a magnitude that, at this writing, federal legislation is being seriously considered to aid school systems in coping with vandalism, assaults on teachers (70,000 physically assaulted annually), burglaries, and other crimes. The Subcommittee to Investigate Juvenile Delinquency, chaired by Senator Birch Bayh, issued a report in April 1975 entitled "Our Nation's Schools—A Report Card: 'A' in School Violence and Vandalism." This report gave an accounting of the problem which the committee hoped would stimulate the development of federal legislation.

The subcommittee's report included some revealing facts: In a survey of over 750 school districts, the statistics gathered indicated that violence in the schools affected every section of the nation and, in fact, continued to escalate to even more serious levels. The survey found that in the years between 1970 and 1973:

1. Homicides increased by 18.5 percent.
2. Rapes and attempted rapes increased by 40.1 percent.
3. Robberies increased by 36.7 percent.
4. Assaults on students increased by 85.3 percent.
5. Assaults on teachers increased by 77.4 percent.
6. Burglaries of school buildings increased by 11.8 percent.
7. Drug and alcohol offenses on school property increased by 37.5 percent.
8. Dropouts increased by 11.7 percent.

A 1970 survey conducted by *School Product News* found that damages from vandalism cost an average of $55,000 for every school district in the country. By the end of the 1973 school year the average cost per district had risen to $63,031. Although these figures indicate that the incidents of vandalism are certainly widespread, it is in the larger urban districts with upwards of 25,000 students that the most costly destruction occurs. Almost 60 percent of all vandalism takes place in these larger districts, with an average cost per district in 1973 of $135,297.

The source of this destruction ranges from broken windows, found in over 90 percent of our districts, to fires, reported by 35 percent of the districts. Significant incidents of theft and malicious destruction of educational equipment occur in 80 percent of the school districts in the country.

Staggering as these figures are, they undoubtedly represent a very conservative estimate of economic loss attributable to school vandalism. A study of school vandalism by Bernard Greenberg of the SRI states:

> It should be noted that the cost figure is grossly understated because it does not include in all instances losses attributable to burglary, theft and property damage repaired by resident maintenance staffs. Nor does it take into account costs to equip and maintain special security forces, which are considerable for the larger school districts, and law enforcement costs to patrol and respond to calls reporting school incidents. Many school districts carry theft insurance, but the costs are exceedingly high.

Spiraling insurance rates are a significant but often overlooked factor in the overall cost of vandalism. The Greenberg study found a West Coast state which underwent a 40 percent rise in fire insurance costs within one year. Another survey reported:

> Many school administrators point out that only a few years ago schools were wooed by the insurance industry as good risks. Now this has changed. And school districts all over the country are reporting difficulty in obtaining insurance. Half the districts answering the Education U.S.A. survey said rates have increased. Many are either paying higher premiums, higher deductibles, or, in all too many instances, having policies cancelled or flatly rejected.

In addition to higher insurance rates, school districts are facing increasing costs for security guards, fencing, intrusion and fire detectors, special lighting, emergency communications equipment, and vandalism-resistant windows. In 1965, for instance, the Los Angeles school system had a total of 15 security guards, but in six years that force was compelled to increase to over 100 members at a cost of over $1 million per year. During the 1972–1973 school year, Los Angeles spent over $2 million for security agents. A report of the Panel on School Safety for New York City found that in 1971 the taxpayers had paid $1,300,000 for security guards and over $3,500,000 for police stationed in schools, and in spite of such efforts had incurred at least $3,700,000 worth of vandalism damage. It was estimated that New York City schools had over 248,000 window panes broken at a replacement cost of $1.25 million. Over 65 percent of the urban districts polled in the 1973 *School Product News* survey reported that they were using vandalism-resistant windows, and 62 percent had at least one security guard assigned to their schools.

The overall impact of violence and vandalism on our educational system cannot, of course, be adequately conveyed by a recitation of the numbers of assaults and the dollars expended. Every dollar spent on replacing a broken window or installing an alarm system cannot be used on the education of students.

In 1973, Florida became the first state to pass the "Safe Schools Act." This act allocated $1.85 million in 1973 and 1974 to school districts for programs to combat vandalism and crime. Some of these funds have been used to program effective security design and provide security systems for new school facilities.

Crime has also become the major problem on the nation's college campuses. Campus security programs have experienced rapid progress toward professionalism since the student dissent era, but crime continues to grow. Although the threat of vandalism and arson is not as great as in our school systems, other crimes have reached new highs. Thefts of student and college property continue to escalate, with many of these thefts involving burglaries from student rooms and college facilities. Crimes against the person such as rape, armed robbery, assault, and molestations are increasing at an alarming pace. These serious crimes can cause a campus community to exert intense pressure on administrators to provide better protection and security. For example, on some campuses women residents refuse or are most reluctant to occupy accessible ground-level dormitory rooms.

The advent of the "open campus," although excellent for campus community relations, has contributed to the security problem by making our campuses and practically all facilities easily accessible to thieves, rapists, and other undesirables. The days of controlling access to a campus by having fencing and guard posts at access roads are gone, for in most cases these measures are neither practical nor acceptable. Therefore, campus facilities must be designed with the full recognition that outsiders, including criminals, will probably have easy access to the campus. This calls for facilities to be designed and equipped so that residents and employees will feel safe, and their property, as well as college property, will have at least a reasonable degree of protection.

The question often arises as to who perpetrates campus crime. Although no accurate figures exist, it can be estimated that at least 70 percent of the thefts are committed by outsiders, some of whom live like parasites off the campus, and about 30 percent by students and employees. Crimes of violence such as rape and assault are practically all committed by outsiders, and these are the people we are seeking to control and keep out of student rooms and other campus areas.

PLANNING FOR NEW FACILITIES

At the outset, it is important to know the proper approach, from a security standpoint, to planning and designing a new school or campus building. After a new building is completed, a frequent comment from security administrators and others is, "Those architects never even considered security." There is some validity to these remarks in that, for too long, there has been a wide gulf and practically no communication between architects and security professionals. Fortunately, however, this gulf is narrowing as architects and security professionals realize that they need each other to ensure safe structures at a time of increasing crime.

Security planning *must start at the inception* of the project and not become an expensive afterthought when the building is completed. Time and time again, consulting firms are called in *after* the completion of a large facility because little or no thought was given to security prior to construction. At that time, problems arise concerning aesthetics when outside wiring and moldings must be used, or when various alarms and other electronic intrusion devices need to be surface-mounted rather than recessed and an integral part of the structure.

The Security Consultant

Architectural firms are increasingly realizing the need for using security consultants in the same way that they use consultants for mechanical services, landscaping, and other specialized functions.

Security today is big business, with many sophisticated electronic and other devices flooding the marketplace, and the time is rapidly approaching when architects and engineers can no longer rely entirely on manufacturers, dealers, and contractors to handle the security aspects of new facilities. While much of the available equipment is excellent, some of it is virtually worthless. Even security consultants, who live with security every day, find it increasingly difficult to keep up with the "state of the art" and recommend the best equipment to do the job at the lowest cost. Too often, those responsible for security are persuaded by some convincing salesperson to purchase expensive equipment which is not the most cost-effective or the most suitable for a particular application.

What are the criteria for selecting a security consultant for an educational facility, or, for that matter, any type of installation? The most important is that the consulting firm be completely impartial, objective, and capable of performing in a professional manner—just as with consultants for the other building trades. Consultants cannot be objective if they sell equipment, make installations, or are obligated in any way to a supplier, manufacturer, or installer. Their concern must be strictly for their clients and the owners of the buildings involved.

Another factor to be considered is the security consultant's ability to relate and work with the owner, the architect, the engineers, and all segments of the large team involved in the design and construction of a facility. Today, the public and private owner of new facilities is becoming increasingly involved as a relatively new member of the building team during the planning process; in the past, by contrast, much of the actual planning process was handled entirely by the architect. Since security will be one of the owner's major concerns, the security consultant must work closely with the owner to design an effective and acceptable program.

In selecting a security consultant, it is also important for the owner to decide whether the firm will be concerned only with designing a security system and locking hardware, or whether they will be responsible for setting up the complete security package, involving a security force that will provide intelligent and effective response to problems. For additional information on selecting a security consultant, refer to Chapter 5, "Selecting a Security Consultant."

The Step-by-Step Security Planning Process

Phase I—Concept This phase involves considerable research and communication with all concerned. At this stage the consultant should meet not only with the architects, engineers, and others directly concerned in the planning and building, but also with the owners.

Consultants should meet with those who will be directly concerned and who will have to "live with" the completed building and security system. These meetings will explore items such as any security problems that have been encountered in the past, security staffing, concerns and philosophy regarding security, etc. Basic information such as hours of operation, key control, and present security procedures and their effectiveness should also be discussed. This type of approach gives the owner and those who will occupy the premises a "voice" in security planning from the outset and avoids the after-completion complaint of "nobody ever asked me about security." A report should be submitted describing the proposed security system and program. This report should be nontechnical and should clearly describe, in everyday language, the system, equipment, and, possibly, personnel to be utilized. Estimated budget figures should also be included.

Phase II—Specifications   After everyone has been given an opportunity to read the concept report, comments should be solicited. Eventually, meetings are held to answer questions and narrow the list of security recommendations to those on which the majority agree.

The next step is the writing of specifications for the system (central monitoring console, various alarms, CCTV, access control systems, etc.). They should be designed to ensure the best possible system at the lowest cost. If possible, they should be directed at writing a complete package so that one supplier would be responsible for the entire system. Otherwise, certain equipment may not be compatible, and suppliers are inclined to blame "the other firm's" equipment for problems, not their own.

These specifications then go out for competitive bidding to responsible, qualified security contractors.

Phase III—Review and Selection of Contractor   The consultant should be involved in reviewing the bids and selecting the successful bidder, taking great care to ensure that any equivalent equipment is of high quality and truly "equivalent" as far as the specifications are concerned.

A key factor to be considered in choosing the contractor should be the company's ability to provide prompt and efficient service after installation.

Phase IV—Inspection During Installation   The consultant should perform several inspections during installation to make sure that the specified equipment is being utilized and that it is correctly installed and wired. For example, in one large new facility, the author's firm once discovered that all television cameras were installed upside down.

Phase V—Final Check-Out   In this final phase, the consultant must check out the entire system to ensure that it meets specifications and is working properly.

PREVENTION OF VANDALISM, ARSON, AND BURGLARY

As stated above, the architect holds a vital key in security design for new construction and building additions. Proper and early coordination with school security officials is a requirement of the first order. This, when coupled with the architect's own special fund of knowledge in the security area, can result in a design for the school and its grounds that possesses the greatest natural and built-in safety and security.

American School and University magazine, in its March 1976 issue, reported on a conference of school officials and architects to discuss design approaches which might mitigate school vandalism. A number of important factors were pointed out:

1. *Schools with relatively small enrollments,* say under 500, are less susceptible to vandalism than large, impersonal facilities. The students' personal sense of scale in relation to their environment can be helpful in making them feel that this is "their" place—one that they would be disinclined to destroy. For larger facilities, this sense of scale can be simulated by providing broken-up spaces and clustering of facilities, and by creating a feeling of individual small campuses. Similarly, large spaces, such as cafeterias, should be broken into smaller, more personal areas.

2. *Security consciousness should be evident* to school occupants, but not to the point of creating a prison-type environment which could cause them to feel "I'm a prisoner. Treat me as one"—a statement that can become a self-fulfilling prophecy.

3. *In selecting a school site,* as well as in determining the site's use, the community should have a sense that the facility is a *part of the community,* not a new kind of ghetto. If the facility is used on a round-the-clock basis, it will become an integral part of the community and provide less incentive to vandalism because of its constantly being occupied. An isolated, deserted building can be most attractive to vandals.

4. *The school's administration should expect the architect (or security consultant) to provide life-cycle cost data* which will provide trade-offs on replacement and repairs as opposed to increased initial costs. Higher original costs for better and more vandal-resistant materials can be one of the wisest investments a school board can make.

5. *Plain common sense* in detailed design should be exercised by the architect. This may seem obvious, but it is frequently overlooked. Glass near play areas and accessible to street frontage should be minimized; exterior hardware for doors used primarily for exit purposes should be eliminated; screws for removable panels, doors, and windows should be avoided.

Site Selection

The school site selected should be generally open and must include a perimeter road planned with easy access for security or police patrol surveillance. The provision of exterior functional security lighting in addition to the ordinary parking and decorative lighting is most important. Security lighting should be vandal-proof, high off the ground, and not subject to destruction with bricks or guns.

Special Facilities

The architect may find it necessary to design certain schools with special teaching requirements which may provide more difficult security problems. The open schools and "pod" arrangements are examples.

Vocational structures, workshops, physical education buildings, structures with kitchens and expensive food-handling equipment, and the sophisticated music and theater rooms of a modern school all require a great deal of extra money and cause considerable trouble when security provisions are *not* designed into the building in proper fashion by the architect prior to construction.

Protection of special facilities with present-day electronic anti-intrusion equipment (closed-circuit TV, microwave, ultrasonic, audio, infrared, etc.) requires preplanning. It makes a great difference and saves much time and effort when the conduits and various support systems are installed as an integral part of the design. See Fig. 1 for a conceptual illustration of such built-in elements.

Security Elements

Items which merit consideration are vandal-resistant window panes; burglar-resistant windows, doors, and hardware; and barricading of any other points of entry into the building. Very secure locks and sophisticated keying systems and control are needed from the outset. In many situations, mechanical security systems, guard booths, and "no-access" roofs are needed. A complete fire- and smoke-reporting system should be designed into the structure at the same time.

In some cases, sprinkler systems are needed, as well as reporting devices to indicate heating failures, boiler trouble, refrigerator failures, loss of water pressure, and power failures; these must be made known to the school's security control system in order to prevent major damage or loss without delay. Anti-intrusion systems are fast becoming a requirement in new school buildings. Wherever possible, these should be accomplished on a *school district–wide* basis and be handled by a *systems development approach.*

After-Hours Protection

School buildings, unlike many on college campuses, are more vulnerable to vandalism, arson, and burglary because they are usually completely unoccupied and unprotected during hours when classes are not in session or the premises are not being used. Nevertheless, all educational facilities share similar problems in security.

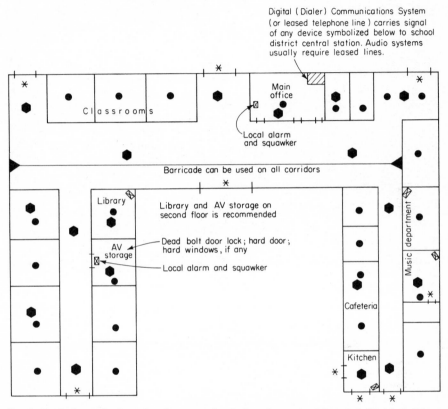

Digital (Dialer) Communications System (or leased telephone line) carries signal of any device symbolized below to school district central station. Audio systems usually require leased lines.

Fig. 1 Symbolic application of various security devices in a school layout. * All exterior door switches; ⬤ sound system (e.g., Mk.V, multraguard, sonotrol, etc.; locate strategically, maximum of 16 to 20 sensors); ● school intercom speakers—can be used as sensors with audio alarm discriminator (e.g., Bogen); ▶ infrared long corridor beam (e.g., microwave long-range unit or corridor ultrasonic); ⊠ local alarm (e.g., ultrasonic, microwave, passive infrared, etc.). Sound sensors can be used to transmit alarms to a central station. Other units require a control device to send alarms. (The illustration is not intended to indicate that all of the devices must be used—rather that the architect or security director may select and employ such units where the characteristics fit the particular local environment.)

The best after-hours protection against intrusion in a school building is an effective electronic detection system which will signal intrusion to the local police department, or a central monitoring station that will immediately notify the police. Other sections of this handbook provide specific selection criteria for protective alarm systems, but any system utilized for school buildings should be able to detect not only physical entry and fire, but also the smashing of windows from the outside by rocks or other objects—a major vandalism problem.

Figure 2 shows what can be termed "the ultimate in vandalism." Though juveniles from the community were found to be responsible for the fire which destroyed two

Fig. 2 The ultimate vandalism—a northern California school. (*Photo courtesy the San Jose Mercury-News.*)

wings of this northern California school, it was a devastating lack of security which made it possible. Damage was estimated at half a million dollars. During the two months prior to the result shown in the picture, the schools had been vandalized on almost every weekend. Classrooms, cafeteria, library, and resource rooms had been vandalized and defaced. The administrative offices had been entered, and a set of master keys were stolen. These keys, it was reported, were being offered for sale on community streets. When the fire occurred, classroom locks were still in the process of being changed, but such minimal security protection proved to be inadequate. Even after the fire, security for the rest of the building that was not burned was spotty.

Access Control

Educational facilities are frequently used for community affairs as well as for students. Therefore, entrances should be designed so as to maintain security when community affairs are held (usually in the evening hours). For example, a school auditorium is probably the area most frequently used by outside groups. The entrances should be designed to permit access to the auditorium, lobby, restrooms, and coat rooms without requiring visitors to enter other doors or other areas of the school.

Channeling of outside groups to the area which they will utilize can also be accomplished by the use of keyed, electronically operated, flexible built-in corridor gates that can selectively close off other sections of the school.

School offices and information facilities should be located at main entrances and designed so as to permit a view of who is entering and leaving. If a security department exists, its office, which should be designed to permit clear visibility, should also be located at the main entrance.

A common practice has been to design school entrances with glass doors permitting a clear view of the interior. This approach, although desirable from a community relations standpoint, presents some security hazards, particularly when there is no means of differentiating between when the school is open and when it is closed. Therefore, the thief, vandal, or arsonist is attracted to the unoccupied building and often finds it easy to enter by breaking a glass panel, reaching in, and using the panic hardware to enter. In many facilities entry can also easily be obtained merely by inserting a properly bent coat hanger through the opening at the edge of the door and pulling down the panic bar (Fig. 3). This leads to custodians and school security forces chaining or otherwise immobilizing panic hardware and doors when the building is closed—and sometimes even certain problem doors when it is open (Fig. 4). Occasionally, on less frequently used doors, the chains are kept in place all the time, an illegal and hazardous action since, in an emergency, the occupants will find themselves trapped at the door while in the process of trying to exit from the building.

The following are some steps that can be considered in design to promote better security.

- Building entrances should be designed so as to clearly indicate whether the building is open or closed. This can be accomplished by pull-down or sliding grilles, shades, or other means to cover the glass doors and not permit a view of the interior.
- The use of unnecessary glass areas should be avoided as much as possible at all entrances.
- Secondary doors which are used for fire exit purposes only should be solid and have no exterior hardware.
- Glass panels which, if broken, permit easy access to the panic bar should be avoided.
- Metal astragals or flanges should be specified on all doors with panic hardware to prevent inserting a piece of wire through the crack and pulling down the panic bar.

The use of electronics, which eliminates unsightly and unwieldy panic bars, might also be explored. Although fire regulations and, particularly, fire marshals' interpretation of them will vary from state to state, the author's firm was able to convince the fire marshals in one state and city to *eliminate panic hardware entirely* on the multiple

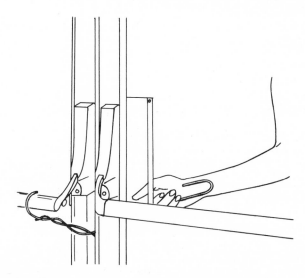

Fig. 3   Inserting a bent coathanger to enter a locked door equipped with panic hardware.

doors of a large civic center and control after-hours egress by using an infrared beam. The only people in the complex during these hours were service and security personnel, who were channeled through one monitored entrance and exit.

In this case, the electronic system involved the use of electromagnet-type locking forces mounted on the header of the door which could be locked at a specified time by activating an energized key-controlled circuit. (If a central console is installed, control can be managed at that point.) Each door automatically unlocks when the infrared beam aimed across the entire width of the door is broken by a person approaching from the inside. All doors would also be wired to unlock automatically in case of a fire alarm or power failure.

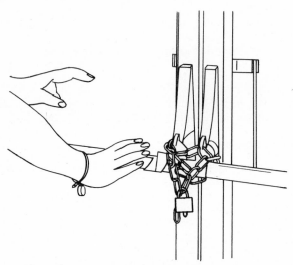

Fig. 4   A door equipped with panic hardware locked with a chain and padlock is illegal since it prevents door operation from the inside during an emergency.

Control of Roof Access

School roofs are often used not only for clandestine entry through skylights or by actually chopping through the roof, but also as unauthorized and sometimes dangerous play areas for children.

Access to roofs can be controlled to some extent by the design of the building and landscaping. Some of the steps that can be taken to discourage and prevent easy access are:

- Eliminate the installation of permanent-type service ladders from ground to roof or from roof to roof. Specify a secure storage space for portable ladders.
- Limit footholds on exterior surfaces, such as indented areas, lamps, and other exterior hardware.
- Avoid planting trees and bushes close to the building which might be climbed to gain access to the roof.
- Roofs should be as high from the ground as possible, and differences in roof heights should make it difficult to climb from one level to the other.

Glazing

Window vandalism constitutes one of the major expenses experienced by schools. Statistics reveal that 25 cents of every dollar expended on school vandalism in 1974–1975 was spent to replace broken glass. The average urban school district spent $1.38

per pupil on glass breakage, while the average suburban school district spent 81 cents per pupil.

Breakage-resistant window glazing should be considered for schools. However, different window areas will require different degrees of breakage resistance. For example, ground floor and basement windows would need stronger materials, such as a high-impact polycarbonate, while upper windows could be glazed with a medium-high-impact acrylic.

COLLEGES AND UNIVERSITIES

Many of the previous suggestions regarding school security can be applied to campus buildings. This is particularly true of community colleges, which for the most part have no residents on campus and whose buildings can be locked and secured when college is not in session.

Residence Halls

The most critical buildings on any campus today are the residence halls, where a high percentage of crime takes place. Unfortunately, with students demanding complete freedom and round-the-clock visiting privileges for both sexes, serious security problems have resulted. Undesirables have been attracted to these locations because of the ease of access and the slight chance of being detected (particularly if they are young and blend with the students).

Crime in the residence halls has caused the pendulum to swing somewhat away from the open-door policy, and some students, particularly women, are demanding a return to tight access control systems, security personnel on the premises, and other measures reminiscent of the past.

High-Rise Versus Low-Rise

A comparison of high-rise versus low-rise residence halls as far as crime and other problems are concerned deserves examination. There is probably no campus security director in the country who will not state (and usually prove the statement by statistics) *that crime is considerably more frequent in the high-rise complexes.* For example, at the University of Massachusetts at Amherst, where excellent computerized crime statistics exist, crime has been *at least 50 percent greater* during 1974 and 1975 in the four 22-story high-rise dormitories than in the thirty-five 4-story low-rise dormitories.

David L. Johnston, former Director of Public Safety at the University of Massachusetts, states that four high-rise dormitories, each housing approximately 2000 students, are "breeders of crime and other problems." Living in these large complexes becomes very impersonal, with students not even getting to know their neighbors, which makes it easy for outsiders to trespass freely and commit crimes without detection.

Johnston also states that studies by the University have revealed that students do not like to live in these high-rise buildings and voice their unhappiness and displeasure by committing acts of vandalism, particularly on the elevators, which have become the symbol of the high-rise. Willful damage to elevators has been so great that the University now offers a $50 reward to anyone reporting a person committing these acts. The elevator problem is so bad that service employees are often harassed by students when they attempt to fix student-caused damage. On several occasions, students forced open elevator shaft doors, threw down objects, and even urinated on elevator servicemen as they worked at the bottom of the shaft to restore service.

The clustering of four high-rises and approximately 8000 students in one relatively small area has, according to Johnston, caused a "horrendous parking and traffic problem." Because of limited vehicle access to the high-rise units, a public safety hazard has also been created when fire lanes become clogged with illegal parkers and traffic.

As a result of the University of Massachusetts experience and that of other campuses, one is forced to conclude that high-rise buildings, from a security standpoint, are not necessarily the best answer and, furthermore, are normally unacceptable to students.

Entrances

One of the major problems in residence halls is how to provide ready access to students at all hours while still keeping out thieves, rapists, and other undesirables. Colleges and universities have tried various means of access control, such as card key systems, remote-controlled locking devices, and simply issuing students keys to the main entrance. These systems are only as good as the resident students desire them to be. If they use and prop open fire doors, duplicate keys or lend them to outsiders, and otherwise circumvent the system, it is of no value. That is why so many campuses have given up on various alternative schemes and use an expensive guard or monitor to supposedly screen those entering and to admit students when all doors are locked.

As few ground-floor doors as possible should be specified in the design of residence halls. If possible, there should be one main entrance which can be controlled rather than several; fire doors should be alarmed and clearly marked as such and should have no hardware on the outside.

Locking Hardware

A cylinder requiring a key that can be duplicated only at the factory or by an authorized locksmith using specialized equipment should be utilized for entrance doors—particularly if students are issued keys. This same key can also be programmed to admit the student to his or her room.

Interchangeable-core locking cylinders have also been successfully used where tight key control procedures exist. This enables the keying system for an entire dormitory or certain floors to be changed periodically at very little expense.

In terms of key control, the author has yet to see a campus where key control is really effective. The main problem is the wholesale, careless dispersal of keys, including master keys, and the subsequent duplication of them. The usual procedure is that keys are *furnished to anyone* on campus upon written or telephoned authority *by practically anyone.* For example, some faculty member will authorize all of his or her students to have master keys to all doors in that department and building. There is almost a complete lack of administrative backing on most campuses regarding tight key control.

Landscaping

The use of shrubs, bushy trees, and other plantings outside the first-floor rooms and adjacent to entrance walks often contributes to crime by furnishing hiding places for peeping Toms, muggers, rapists, and thieves. Such plantings should be avoided, or low-growing shrubs should be selected.

Campus Lighting

It is recognized that the approach to lighting from a security point of view may be at odds with that of lighting consultants and architects, who are largely concerned with aesthetics. However, as a security professional, and knowing what a deterrent to crime and reassurance to the community lighting is, the author must recommend proper lighting, particularly in certain areas.

When conducting a security analysis for a campus, planners should not feel obliged to use measured footcandles or the usual scientifically oriented lighting studies as the determinant factor in lighting design. The beginning of an effective lighting design should involve students and other members of the campus community, who should be asked to state where they feel insecure after dark because of a lack of lighting. Almost without fail, when these areas are checked as to existing installations, such feelings of insecurity will be borne out by fact and will provide the basis of an improved lighting design.

With the advent of the need for energy conservation, a careful balancing must be made of security needs vis-à-vis energy consumption. A designer should not confuse *better lighting* with *more intense lighting.* Often, low-level uniform lighting can provide better overall security than "hot spots" of intense lights which, by contrast, will leave adjacent areas virtually totally dark.

The designer should not assume that bright lighting alone is necessarily a deterrent to crime. While there is some evidence supporting the view that high-intensity lighting reduces crime, there are few statistics proving that high lighting levels *alone* are barriers to crime. Of much greater importance is the *quality* of the lighting system, and this includes considerations such as the location of fixtures, elimination of shadows, reliability of the system, and, in general, a thorough consideration of what is to be protected. Some of the areas of greatest concern regarding lighting are:

Parking Lots Although most faculty and staff cars are removed after dark, student cars remain, often in dead storage for long periods. Student parking areas are also usually the farthest removed from the campus and are sometimes in rather isolated areas. One of the major problems on most campuses is the stealing of stereos, tires, batteries, and other equipment from student vehicles and an increasing number of thefts of these vehicles from campus parking areas.

Saturating all parking areas with light is recommended. High-mast clustered reflector-type lighting has proved very effective. Some parking areas can be well illuminated by six 1000-W mercury or metal-halide reflectorized lamps mounted on a single mast 100 ft high. It is estimated that such lighting would illuminate an area as large as four football fields.

Advantages of this type of lighting are that it cuts down on the need for a great many lampposts or masts, and the lamps can be easily replaced and serviced by means of a secure control that allows them to be raised and lowered.

Residence Halls The exterior of residence halls should be illuminated so as to produce a moat of light around the dormitory building. Naturally, lighting has to be positioned so it will not shine directly into bedroom windows and, possibly, interfere with sleep. Lights should also be positioned so that security officers or others inside will not be blinded by the light when they observe the outside area and entrance walks.

Other Areas Campus sidewalks and paths, particularly those that are heavily used by students, should be well illuminated. Students are for the most part "night people," and sometimes there is more pedestrian traffic after dark than during the day.

Another often forgotten area where good lighting is usually necessary is the football stadium or other outdoor athletic facility, which can be the target of high jinks on the part of students from rival campuses, as well as other forms of vandalism. For example, many campuses have suffered expensive damage to Astroturf by fire or chemicals.

Location and Design of Security Department

The proper location and design for a security department office is an element that deserves serious consideration.

The initial location for these departments reflected the fact that they were considered part of the plant operation, and they were usually buried out of sight in a basement or boiler house (because they had to be staffed at all times).

The crime problem dictates that the department be located at the core of the campus, on a first-floor level where it is visible and easily accessible to students and the campus community. Many colleges are building separate one-story buildings to house their security and sometimes their fire and safety departments.

Figure 5 depicts a typical security department office. The size and number of rooms will naturally vary with the size and scope of the department's operations.

PLANNING A COMPLETE SECURITY SYSTEM

Frequently, a local sales representative attempts to sell to a school what is actually only one component of a security system, even while making extravagant promises that all their problems will be solved with the device under consideration.

School districts vary so much in size and character that the type of anti-intrusion system needed should be determined by an exceptionally qualified person or firm. There are only a limited number of qualified school security consultants in the country. There are a fair number of architectural and engineering firms developing this talent, and all should attempt to do so, as the demand for school security is rapidly growing. Some of the major national security firms and manufacturers can put together a comprehensive and capable system. Others, erroneously recommend *only* their component device as a system.

A primary system can be achieved with a simple audio system that makes fine economic use of the school's existing intercommunication or public address system. However, with an audio system, a security monitor is required—someone with exceptional audio analytical capability. Such a controller is not to be found ordinarily

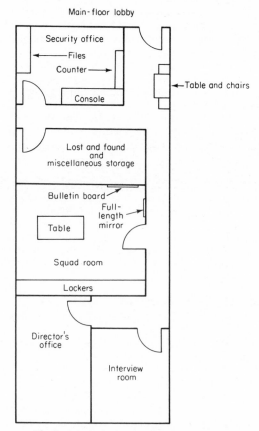

Fig. 5 A typical security department layout.

in the local police station, for example. A capable monitor has to be trained long enough to develop a high degree of skill in sound analysis.

For the more complex school districts, and even for the not-so-complex ones covered by audio, the number of components in a system will increase. For example, special areas must be protected in special ways; kitchens, music departments, audiovisual storage areas, main office suites, food storage units, and computer complexes need to be protected with specially capable techniques and devices for each environment.

The Central Control Station

If a school district has a central control station, this houses the electronic reporting devices from all the schools (including video, wire and radio communications, master data and plot plans) and, of course, the school security monitor or controller. The central station would include, desirably, a simple computer to organize data, accurately report alarms, and identify the school from which the alarm came, where in the school the alarm took place, and what it was caused by. Using the school security computer, several of which are now produced in the United States, the security controller or monitor in the central station is provided with a simple report to be given directly to school security personnel, the police, the fire department, or the school maintenance engineer, as may be appropriate; a written permanent record is obtained of what occurred and when. (See Fig. 6.)

The various school buildings should employ a number of intrusion-reporting devices, using the operating technique that is most suitable for the particular environment. For school corridors, these could include microwave, capable of covering very long "barricade" corridors; infrared long-distance beam; or corridor ultrasonic units. (See Fig. 7.) Whichever is chosen will depend on the characteristics of the corridor to be covered. The band room or musical instrument storage area might well have spread-area microwave or ultrasonic coverage, or even, in the case of closed-circuit TV coverage, a video camera.

Fig. 6 A school security central station is shown in operation. Security Director Lucius W. Burton, the author, is shown on the police direct line.

An audiovisual storage room, which is usually completely enclosed, might use a small ultrasonic unit mounted over the single door or beaming across two doors to report burglar intrusion here. A major building, such as a large high school where activities go on day and night, will require closed-circuit TV in high-value corridors and in the lobby or cafeteria areas.

Where the use of TV is planned, exterior cameras can be placed for both parking area surveillance and the protection of visually obstructed areas around the school. In this case the newest of low-light-level cameras will produce excellent results.

Full employment of mechanical devices to supplement the various electronic or sonic units should be encouraged as an excellent backup and or as primary intrusion detectors. These include magnetic switches, vibration detectors, pressure devices, and many others now on the market.

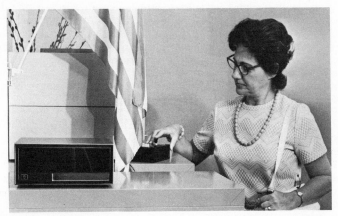

Fig. 7   The principal's secretary at a large high school is shown activating the infrared alarm device in the main office suite before leaving for the day.

The various schools in a district can be connected to the district central station by leased telephone line, digital communicators, or even radio. The protective security described herein must have a VHF or UHF radio network in order to connect the central station controller with any of the school security personnel. Desirably, the police and fire departments would also be a part of this network. The leased telephone line is effective, but sometimes it can be expensive and hard to get.

A school central station is most often developed and managed within the school district itself because of its special requirements. Alternatively, school buildings can also be successfully monitored by commercially operated central-station proprietors.

Chapter 25

Health Care Facilities

JAMES L. BRODIE, M.P.A.

Director of Public Safety, Oak Forest Hospital, Oak Forest, Illinois

Security in a health care facility, obviously an extremely complex organization, is a topic of such endless variety that it could fill a separate book. It is not possible within one chapter to cover all the vulnerable areas in a health care facility, so we shall concentrate primarily here on hospital access controls, pharmacy protection, cashier protection, and protection in the receiving, storeroom, and laundry areas.*

HOSPITAL ACCESS CONTROLS

One of the major problems in most hospitals, from a security standpoint, is the easy, undetectable, unchallenged access. As a general rule, people who act as if they belong and appear to know where they are going are seldom stopped and questioned.

Because of the nature of the facility, a hospital should be as secure as possible. Access to the premises should be controlled at all times. Every door into the hospital, day or night, should have some means of control of ingress and egress.

Main Entrance and Lobby

Control of access to hospital buildings must begin at the main entrance, where most nonemployees, authorized or unauthorized, enter the building. The following measures should be considered when designing the main entrance and lobby:

Visitor Control Desk The visitor control desk should be a counter-type desk equipped with a rolodex or similar system listing all patients. It should have telephone and intercom communications to the administrative suite, admitting office, outpatient clinic, security department, and any other office with which direct communication is necessary. The control desk should be equipped with an alarm button which notifies

---

*The author wishes to take this opportunity to acknowledge the illustrations by architectural engineer, Richard T. Maryonovich, the technical advice of Richard W. Prendergast., Jr., Associate Administrator of Physical Plant at Oak Forest Hospital, and his secretary, Sharon Ryan, for the preparation of the manuscript.

the security department in case of trouble at the desk or in the lobby. If there is no security department or attended complaint room, the alarm should sound in an attended telephone switchboard room.

The visitor control desk should be located as close to the main entrance as possible in order to provide the clerks with complete physical and visual control of all persons entering the hospital. If there is not a separate entrance to the outpatient clinic, outpatients should enter through the lobby and be required to check in at the visitor control desk, where the appointment can be verified.

Visitor control desks should also be established for special units as desired, such as the maternity, psychiatric, intensive care, or any other unit where tight visitor controls may be indicated.

Lobby   The lobby should be designed to provide visual observation of waiting areas by visitor control personnel. If this is not feasible, a television camera and monitor should be used for this purpose.

After visiting hours, the main entrance should be secured, and a silent door alarm that reports to security or the switchboard should be activated. In the late evening and midnight hours, the lobby ceases to be the hub of activity and suddenly becomes deserted and unattended. This area becomes an ideal place for visitors who may have lingered after hours—or dishonest employees—to take hospital property from the premises. In most instances, the doors are equipped with panic hardware to meet fire exit requirements. A television camera armed with video tape may be utilized to observe this area. If pilfering is taking place, a carpet alarm triggers the camera, and even if the thieves escape, the tape will provide identification evidence for prosecution.

Elevators

Visitor Elevators   Certain elevators should be designated primarily for visitors. Ideally these should be located in the lobby, where entry can be under the scrutiny of the visitor control desk. These elevators should be programmed not to go below the lobby level, except by key control, in order to prevent visitor access to maintenance or storage areas in the basement and sub-basement.

If the elevators are located out of sight of the visitor control desk, closed-circuit television can be utilized to provide observation. A bell should be installed at the control desk that will ring when the elevator returns to the lobby, thus calling attention to the monitor for observation of ingress and egress from the elevator.

Restricted Elevators   When feasible, specific elevators should be installed for patient care or maintenance purposes. A maintenance elevator would be utilized for transporting maintenance personnel, laundry, food, garbage, supplies, etc.

Operating Room Elevator   A specific elevator or elevators should be designated for use in transporting patients and surgical staff to the operating rooms.

Clinical Elevator   In most hospitals, during the daytime hours, there is a constant flow of patients to various clinics and laboratories for tests and therapy. If possible, there should be a separate elevator for this purpose.

Elevator Controls   Access to maintenance, operating room, and/or clinical elevators should be by coded dialing or key control systems in order to eliminate the use of elevators by unauthorized persons.

All elevators should be equipped with telephones for use in emergencies. Alarm bells have a tendency to muffle communications with persons in a stuck elevator. A silent alarm to security and/or the switchboard room for trouble in the elevator has been found to be most effective.

Provisions should be made to return elevators to the main floor automatically in case of fire. Elevators should be equipped with manual control for use in fires and other disasters, and provisions should be made for designated personnel to operate the elevators under emergency circumstances. An intercom from the disaster control center or other appointed place to the elevators is a helpful tool for directing fire fighters to proper areas, for organizing patient evacuation, and for relaying warnings about floors that should be bypassed because of dangerous conditions.

A purchase contract for elevators should include training of maintenance and security personnel in emergency procedures involving elevators that are stuck, fire in the shaft or motor room, and any other type of anticipated emergency common to elevators.

Outpatient Clinic

If the outpatient clinic has separate ingress and egress from the outside, a patient registration desk should be provided to control persons entering this area. This desk should be similar to the visitor control desk in the lobby and should be placed where control of access to the clinics can be provided. Some hospitals with a large outpatient involvement may desire an electrically controlled door into the clinic/examining areas from the waiting room, with panic hardware on the inside to provide fire egress from the clinics.

If the outpatient clinic is on the ground floor, provisions should be made to provide protection from illegal entry. Wire-mesh window guards with padlocks may be utilized. Windows and doors should also be equipped with silent alarms reporting illegal entry to security and/or the local public police department (Fig. 1).

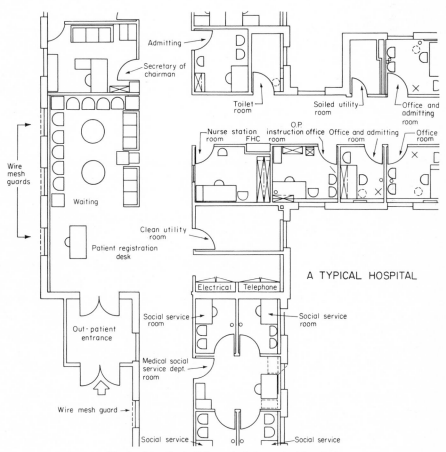

Fig. 1   Outpatient clinic control at a typical hospital.

It is not uncommon for robberies, rapes, and other crimes to occur in outpatient treatment rooms, especially in metropolitan areas. Foot or hand alarms should be installed at the patient control desk as well as in all examining and treatment areas.

Stairwell Ingress and Egress

It is the author's opinion that stairwells should be utilized *only* in case of emergency and not for floor-to-floor access. On this basis, all stairwell doors should be marked for fire and emergency use only and should be equipped with audio door alarms that ring when violated.

All stairwell doors on the main floor should be locked to prevent ingress and equipped with panic hardware for egress from the stairwell so as to eliminate easy access by unauthorized persons, including thieves, robbers, and rapists.

Fire Exits

All ground-level fire exits should be utilized for emergencies only, with the doors alarmed and marked accordingly. Panic hardware should be provided for emergency egress, with the doors kept locked from the outside to prevent ingress. Preferably, all ground-level doors leading to the outside should be equipped with silent alarm devices reporting to a central console which would identify the door being opened. Certain doors could be deactivated during business hours, if desired.

Emergency-Room Entrance

Ideally, the emergency-room entrance should be utilized solely for receiving emergency patients. In many hospitals, however, the emergency entrance is also the employees' entrance and provides uncontrolled access to the hospital for visitors. If at all possible, only the admission of emergency patients should be allowed at the emergency-room entrance. An emergency-room control desk should be designed, similar to the visitor control desk, for the admitting clerk at the emergency entrance. If a clerk is not utilized, the emergency-room nurses' station should become the access control desk.

Ingress and egress should be controlled at all times by automatically locking doors that can be opened by designated persons only.

A television monitor with two-way intercom should be placed at the emergency entrance, with a doorbell at the point of ingress which would alert emergency-room staff to observe the monitor and determine through the intercom whether admission to the emergency room is indicated.

An intercom or direct-ring phone link with security personnel can be most helpful. Emergency call buttons should be placed strategically throughout the emergency area in order to alert the security department in cases of patients threatening staff or other disturbances in the emergency room.

Employees' Entrance

It is no secret that most thefts of property in a hospital are perpetrated by employees. Employees' ingress and egress usually are not controlled, and any door into the institution may be utilized.

Plans should be made to control employees' ingress and egress by designating a specific entrance for this purpose. The employees' entrance should be planned in close proximity to employee parking areas. If possible, the security department headquarters should be included in this area. The security department radio and alarm room should be planned in conjunction with this entrance so as to make it possible for one security officer to receive telephone complaints; operate two-way radio as dispatcher; monitor alarms and closed-circuit television; control ingress; and conduct package inspection of employees entering and leaving the premises. If time clocks are utilized by various departments, they should be placed in this area so that the officer may supervise "clock punching" in an effort to eliminate theft of services by employees (Fig. 2).

Security quarters should be planned to meet both present and long-range needs. They should include space for lock and key equipment and storage, a squad room for roll call, report writing, and on-the-job training, a locker room, a toilet facility, supervisors' offices, an interrogation room, and a place to conduct ID processing of

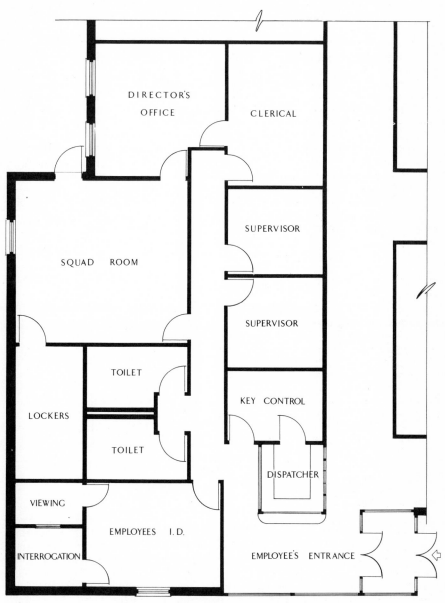

Fig. 2 Security quarters and employee entry.

employees. The security director's office may be located near the employees' entrance or in the administrative office area.

PHARMACY

The pharmacy should be planned with certain divisions of space, for example:

Pharmacy Counter and Prescription Preparation Area   This room should have tight access control. The counter should be constructed with complete protective measures to safeguard the pharmacist from armed robbers. A holdup/burglar alarm system should be installed with foot and hand controls, ingress and egress being controlled electrically.

Pharmaceutical Storeroom   This room should be planned in an area where fire and smoke can be contained. Because of the great amount of flammable and combustible materials stored in this area, a sprinkler system along with a smoke- and heat-detection system are essential. Special provisions should be made for the storage of alcohol and other flammable liquids used in the pharmacy. The room should be ventilated and on an outside wall.

Shelves and bins should be limited in depth to provide for easy audit and inventory and to prevent overstocking, which creates great internal theft opportunity.

Controlled drugs should be stored in a room with a burglar alarm, temperature control, and provisions for refrigeration of drugs that require it. Windows, especially at ground level, should be protected by alarms and mesh screens.

A central silent alarm system which notifies the security department and/or police department should protect all possible routes of entry into the pharmacy, including windows. Proper visibility and lighting are necessary to provide easy observation by officers on patrol.

Although the use of vacuum tubes in delivering drugs to a nursing station may be more expedient, it creates an opportunity for theft. In one hospital, the author observed this sort of system in operation. The nursing clerk was assigned a floor identification card, which was used for ordering medications from the pharmacy by tube. Anyone in possession of this card could order any amount of drugs and charge it to any number of patients.

A more practical system, and less costly, is a drug delivery cart equipped with individual boxes similar to post office boxes. Each box is cored to a specific nursing unit, where the medicine nurse is issued a key to open that unit's box. The delivery person does not have a key or access to this cart. The cart may be cored to the hospital's master key system or an independent master key with the systems control keyway for removal of cores. The pharmacist has a master key for this cart so that he or she may place the ordered medications in the respective boxes for delivery. This keeps the responsibility for handling medications limited to the pharmacist preparing the order and the nurse responsible for medication in a given unit (Fig. 3).

CASHIER

Hospital Cashier's Office

With the huge volume of business conducted by a hospital each day, the cashier's office becomes a hub of activity, especially in large metropolitan hospitals. Many hospitals throughout the United States have been victimized by burglars and armed robbers, who become aware of the large amounts of currency handled there, sometimes with great carelessness, by the cashiers.

In most hospitals, the cashier's function is integrated into the general business office, where protective measures are usually not provided. Often, metal money boxes may be observed sitting unprotected on desk tops or in an open drawer. These offices generally have a constant flow of traffic through them, making it quite simple for someone to commit theft.

To overcome the vulnerability of the cashier to crime, the first step should be to provide separate quarters for the cashiers, with access to this area limited to them alone. A currency-exchange type of enclosure should be considered, with bullet-resistant glass and service windows which eliminate physical contact with the cashier. (For further information, see Chapter 12, "Glass and Glazing," and Chapter 21,

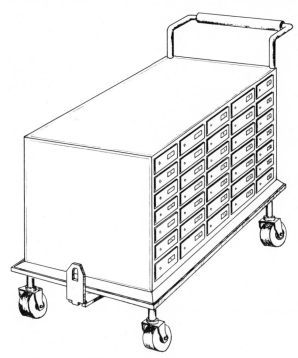

Fig. 3   Drug delivery cart with lockable sections.

"Banks.") If feasible, a toilet should be provided to minimize the need for the cashiers to leave the office; this cuts down the opportunity for thieves to gain access. Electrical control devices should be installed on the door to provide access control by the cashier (Fig. 4).

A safe or walk-in vault with an entry alarm should be installed in this area. The counter and each desk should be equipped with holdup alarm buttons or foot devices, and all windows and doors should be equipped with a silent alarm reporting to the security department and/or the local police department. Bank deposits should be picked up by an armored money carrier.

Mirrors should be placed strategically to provide cashiers with a complete view of the area before admitting persons to the cashier's office or allowing them to leave.

Restaurant, Cafeteria, Snack Shop, and Gift Shop Cashiers

Protective measures should also be provided in hospital restaurants, cafeterias, snack shops, and gift shops. Usually the cashiers in these operations handle large amounts of currency. Yet in most hospitals, little, if any, thought is given to protecting these vulnerable areas from robbery or burglary.

All cashier positions should be equipped with hand or foot holdup alarm buttons which report silently to the security department and/or the local police department. The alarm system should be versatile and capable of providing burglar-alarm protection of safes, doors, and windows.

Drop safes should be provided at all cashier positions. Only the necessary amount of currency to make adequate change should be kept in the cash register drawer, with all other currency placed in deposit envelopes and then into the safe. An armored service should be employed to make pickups from the safe for delivery to the bank, and the money carriers should have the only access to the safe. Signs should be posted at entrances and at the cashier's position advising that the cashier does not have a key to the safe and that the currency is picked up by an armed money carrier.

When designing these functions, consideration should be given to visibility and night lighting. Ideally, a security or police officer on patrol should be able to make visual checks of these premises without entering. The availability of a television monitor station may indicate the desirability of a closed-circuit television camera to monitor cashiers in order to provide additional protection.

RECEIVING AND STORAGE

Since they are highly vulnerable activities, the receiving and storage of supplies in a hospital warrant close planning and design in order to minimize theft.

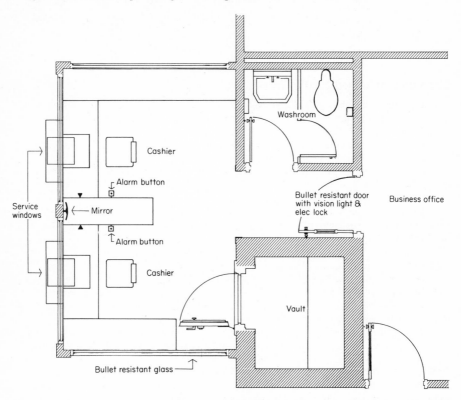

CASHIER'S OFFICE
Fig. 4   Cashier's office.

Storage

Plans should call for a minimal distance between the receiving area and supply storage areas. Food storage should be planned in direct relationship to the food-processing areas. Storage areas should be designed to provide easy access for ongoing inventory.

Storage in food-production areas should be limited to daily needs to prevent pilferage from overstocking. Visibility and lights should be considered in order to provide visual inspection of storage areas by security personnel.

All storerooms should be equipped with window and door alarms that report to the security department and/or police department. Closed-circuit television may also be utilized for storage areas, especially production storerooms where continual access is made by several persons.

Receiving

The receiving dock should be located in an area where easy vehicle access is possible without causing traffic congestion, and it should be built with a partial enclosure to protect the receiving platform from inclement weather.

An office or receiving booth should be provided for the receiving clerk located in an area that provides a constant view of the receiving dock. A commercial floor scale should be installed, as well as an overhead scale (with a track to storage), to verify weights of merchandise. Conveyors should be installed with the capability of being directed to various storage areas; this is especially desirable for food items.

Receiving-room doors should be alarmed. Closed-circuit television may also be utilized on a 24-hr basis at the receiving area. This would deter theft during working hours and serve as burglar protection at night.

The receiving area should be well lighted for patrol observation.

LAUNDRY AND LINEN STORAGE

Theft of linen supplies from hospitals seems to be a costly and universal problem, whether the hospital has its own laundry or utilizes a linen supply company.

If a laundry is being planned, several things should be considered:

1. Isolation from the main hospital area in case of lint or equipment fires, which are common in a busy hospital laundry.

2. Control of access from the outside. Window and door alarms are a must, and, where fire codes permit, other measures such as metal screens and iron bars should be considered.

3. A storage area, preferably in the form of a completely enclosed wire-mesh cage, should be designed for storage of clean linens; it should be connected to the alarm system.

4. Ingress to and egress from the laundry should be limited to laundry personnel.

5. The laundry should be designed to provide visual observation by officers on patrol. Adequate night lighting should be provided inside and out.

6. Linen-room doors should be equipped with automatic locking devices and windows protected by metal screens.

7. Designated smoking areas should be provided for laundry employees.

PARKING FACILITIES

A thorough study should be made of the parking needs of the hospital, with future expansion in mind. The cost of land in some areas necessitates the building of parking structures. In metropolitan areas, this type of facility is becoming more common in health care settings.

Whether a parking area is on the ground level or several stories high, there are certain basic protective measures that should be considered. Parking lots usually attract two types of criminals: those who commit crimes against persons and those who only commit crimes against property. The criminal who preys on persons in parking lots depends on easy access and low visibility. This individual can lurk between cars and choose a victim according to whim. These crimes usually include rape, murder, and robbery. The other type of criminal usually takes advantage of the easy access to motor vehicles and their parts and contents.

In either case, the greatest advantage to these criminals is that their presence is difficult to detect and that commission of a crime can be easily concealed. With this in mind, the planning of parking facilities should include the following measures:

1. Whether on the surface or in a structure, parking facilities should be fenced in at ground level to prevent foot access.

2. All parking facilities should be well lighted, with no dark areas. Emergency generators should be included to provide continuous lighting in the event of a power failure.

3. All parking lots or structures should have control gates, with card or coin control.

4. Closed-circuit television cameras should be mounted to provide constant visual surveillance by the security radio/desk personnel. If high-rise parking is utilized, each tier should have television surveillance on a rotating basis. Cameras should be mounted where there is little access to them and be enclosed in weather-protective covers (Fig. 5).

5. In an enclosed structure, emergency buttons should be placed strategically for potential victims to use in reporting suspects or attacks to security.

6. Parking facilities should be in close proximity to the hospital, for if a long walk is required between the two, patrons may be vulnerable to street crimes.

7. An attendant booth should be located at the entrance of a structural lot or strategically for ground-level lots, to provide control and observation by a security officer during visiting hours and change of shifts in order to provide added protection during these peak hours of use.

As with parking facilities elsewhere, everyone wants to be close to the hospital entrance. One approach to solving this problem in ground-level parking lots is to designate specific parking areas for particular departments, i.e., volunteers, medical staff, executives, sales representatives, visitors, and so on, with separate access to each section. Entry cards would be issued for the authorized section to employees, medical staff, executives, etc., and parking in each designated section would be on a first-come, first-served basis. Visitors' lots could be arranged to permit entrance but to require a token, coin, or ticket for exit. In structure parking, floors or portions of floors may be designated by color code or number coding for specific authorized parking, but this requires strict enforcement by the hospital in order to be effective.

LOCK AND KEY CONTROL

Lock and key control in a hospital may not stop a professional burglar from entering the premises. It has been proved, however, that this type of crime against hospitals is minimal compared with the everyday internal theft of expensive hospital equipment and provisions. One might simply say that lock and key control helps keep employees honest by eliminating access to vulnerable areas.

In order to be functional, a lock and key system must be planned to conform with the hospital organization. There should be a grandmaster and control key from which each department has its own submaster system, permitting the department head to narrow down responsibility for certain rooms and areas by limiting key access to as few persons as possible.

There should be only one key system. In some older institutions, a variety of locks can be found. These systems should be updated under one lock and key system in order to provide proper control and to allow such exchange of cores as may be required without changing the entire locking mechanism.

If the hospital has an effective security department, the administration of the lock and key system should be placed there. A separate space should be set aside as a shop where keys and cores can be made, and to provide storage for key blanks and the keeping of comprehensive records on each key and core issued. A member of the security department may be designated as the "protective measures officer" and trained to handle the entire function. There is no conflict of trade unions in using a security officer for making keys, recoring, and locking cores into a door-locking mechanism. All installation of permanent lock jewelry can be made by a member of the appropriate skilled trades.

In developing a lock and key system as well as other protective measures, the architect should involve the hospital's security department in planning to ensure that the system will meet existing and future needs of the institution.

Self-closing and self-locking devices should be considered for linen and medicine rooms in patient care units. A great portion of the loss of linens and pharmaceuticals is attributed to the poor locking habits of nursing personnel; this carelessness leaves linens and pharmaceuticals vulnerable to theft.

Security locking systems for desks, metal filing cabinets, and narcotics lockers

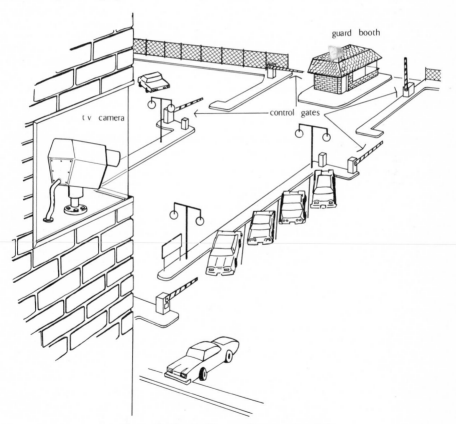

Fig. 5 Parking facility surveillance and control.

should also be controlled by security. All keys should be turned over to security for issuing and recording.

In new construction or renovation, designers should ensure that the lock and key system conforms with the system selected by the hospital security department. Arrangements should be made for the security department to deal directly with the key company in planning the system for installation of cores and distribution of keys.

Security of a health care facility goes far beyond the points covered in this chapter, and many hospital security departments are also charged with the responsibility for fire protection and occupational safety. This chapter is limited to theft control, however, and the reader is directed to other chapters in this volume for information on related topics.

HEALTH CARE SECURITY CHECKLIST

Access Controls

- Visitor control desk with communications capability, alarm buttons, visual contact with entry and egress
  - Control desks for special units
  - Silent door alarm for after-hours
  - Closed-circuit TV monitoring of access points
  - Elevators for specific purposes
  - Elevator communications to control center
  - Patient registration desk for outpatient clinic
  - Electric door controls for outpatient clinic
  - Ground-floor window protection
  - Audio alarms for stairwell and emergency doors
  - Panic hardware on exits, locked from outside
  - Separate employee entrance
  - Emergency-room control desk
  - Monitored emergency-room entry
  - Security department location and design

Pharmacy

- Tight access control
- Protection from armed robbers
- Burglar-alarm system
- Sprinklers, smoke- and heat-detection systems in storeroom
- Special storage for flammable liquids
- Limited shelf and bin depth for easy audit
- Special storage for controlled drugs
- Physical and alarm protection for windows
- Lighting and visibility for easy patrol observation
- Close monitoring of drug delivery system

Cashier

- Separate quarters for hospital cashier
- Restricted access
- Bullet-resistant glass enclosure
- Electric door controls
- Safe or walk-in vault with entry alarm
- Holdup buttons at desk
- Protected miscellaneous cashier stations
- Drop safes at cashier stations
- Armored carrier for cash pickups

Receiving and Storage

- Minimum distance from receiving area to storage
- Visibility and lights for visual inspection
- Closed-circuit TV monitoring
- Office or booth near receiving area with good visibility
- Commercial scales to verify weights
- Alarmed doors at receiving area
- Well-lighted receiving area with easy observation

Laundry and Linen

- Isolated from main hospital due to fire hazard
- Door and window alarms
- Control of outside access
- Completely closed and alarmed mesh cage for clean linens
- Adequate night lighting, both inside and outside
- Automatic locks on doors
- Physical window protection
- Special employee smoking areas

Parking Facilities

- Fenced at ground level
- Well-lighted, no dark areas
- Emergency power generators
- Control gates
- Closed-circuit TV surveillance
- Emergency alarm buttons
- Location close to hospital
- Attendant booth

Lock and Key Control

- Plan with hospital organization
- Grandmaster and departmental submasters
- Limit to one key system
- Security department to administer key system
- Self-closing and -locking devices on linen and medicine rooms

Chapter **26**

High-rise Office Buildings

CHARLES E. GAYLORD
Life Safety Systems, Johnson Controls, Inc.

JERRY W. HICKLIN
President, Hicklin Security Service, Inc.

(The following section was prepared by C. E. Gaylord, Johnson Controls, Inc.)

Modern high-rises such as the Watertower Place in Chicago, the Peachtree Plaza Hotel in Atlanta, and the World Trade Center in New York are in reality vertical cities with offices, stores, shops, restaurants, etc. As in any city, people must be free to come and go as they please. The high-rise must, however, provide for certain environmental functions such as temperature, security, and fire safety consistent with its inhabitants' needs.

Many of the solutions which have been used by the owners of small multiple or single-story dwellings are not practical in a high-rise building, and the special procedures to meet the needs of the tenants and the various businesses operating in the high-rise building require careful planning.

As costs of electronic equipment come down and the cost of energy goes up, operators of the large high-rises recognize that a computer control center for building engineers and security personnel is necessary if the structure is to be run successfully and economically. Consequently, an increasingly large percentage of high-rise buildings are being constructed with computer centers which provide the building engineer with the tools to operate more efficiently. These centers are now available from companies like Johnson Controls, Robertshaw, Powers, or Honeywell.

In any discussion of automated systems covering fire, burglary, protection from assault, emergency communication, or HVAC, there are two key areas to be considered:

1. What do the codes require?
2. Which solution provides an adequate safe environment?

Codes generally specify the minimum required by the city to meet applicable standards. However, the automated system can achieve a higher level of performance and provide ongoing economies with the ability to extend and integrate a multitude of building services. Decisions on system design should therefore also consider the owner's personal principles, insurance company requirements, and the tenants' needs for the type of risk.

Within high-rise buildings there are several categories of locations, each with differing requirements. Mechanical equipment rooms, computer rooms, money-handling areas, legal and financial record rooms, elevators, stairwells, parking lots, parking structures, and general office areas are all examples of such categories.

After this brief introduction to the problems of providing security for a highly complex structure, a more detailed plan for each major system will be provided.

FIRE PROTECTION

The most important building security requirement is the fire safety system. At the turn of the century, a great fear of fire existed, especially in large cities, where the threat of destruction was always present.

Better methods of providing fire safety were gradually developed, and the goals of protection gradually changed; from 1900 to 1920 the need was to "save the city," from 1920 to 1950 it was "save the building," from 1950 to 1970 "save the floor," and from 1970 it has become "save the person."

With the concept of "save the person" came the awareness of the need to contend with smoke, which is deadly because it prevents escape by reducing visibility and dulling the senses, in addition to eliminating oxygen. In fact, recent studies indicate that 85 percent of all fire deaths result from smoke—more than are caused by burns, falls, explosions, heart attacks, and all other causes combined related to fire!

Firemen are hampered in their rescue attempts by smoke, which makes it difficult to locate and effectively fight fire. The deadly toxic gases that are released during a fire migrate to upper floors in the building, thereby endangering other lives and aiding the spread of fire. Many passages exist in buildings for smoke migration—stairways, elevator shafts, vertical pipe chases, communications and wiring riser spaces, mail chutes, trash chutes, etc.

Further, explosions can result if the gases are not promptly vented, a reason why firemen arriving at the scene of a fire will break out windows and, if necessary, chop a hole in the roof to vent the smoke. There are many factors to consider when exploring the potential for fire safety in a structure. Some of the major elements are shown in Fig. 1. The ability to integrate HVAC, fire safety, and security capabilities into a total system allows the designer to provide maximum protection for the individual in a high-rise building. The sections which follow elaborate on how these component areas can be integrated into the total systems approach. They are:

- Fire-detection systems
- Personnel movement and protection
- Smoke control, pressurization, smoke barriers
- Safe areas of refuge
- Emergency communication and controls

Fire Detection Systems

The NFPA presently classifies fire-detection systems into four areas, indicated in the codes commonly known as 72A, 72B, 72C, and 72D. The 72A provisions cover local protective signal systems. The word "local" is the key factor, as the initiating and signaling are done at the local level. They are not transmitted to any other area within the city. In a system with an initiator circuit that utilizes manual pull stations or smoke detectors, and one of these devices goes into alarm, the signal would be sent to the control panel. The control panel, in turn, signals the alarm only on the premises that are being protected. In other words, it would signal the fire condition locally.

NFPA 72B is an auxiliary system and essentially the same as a local system, except it sends the signal to the city fire department via municipal fire boxes.

72C occurs when a local system connects the alarm signal to a central station via a communication line (normally a telephone pair). This central communication station is not located on the premises. The difference between 72B and 72C is the method of transmission of the signal to an area outside the fire station. The 72B connection usually goes to the fire department, whereas 72C goes to a central station via a pair of telephone lines.

A 72D fire alarm system is owned and operated by the user, with a control center

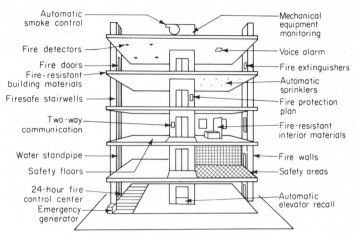

Fig. 1   Major fire safety components.

located on the premises and staffed round the clock. The ability to have a municipal hookup on a 72D system is an option, so that it can actually meet the requirements for 72A or 72B.

Thus, if an automation system is already contemplated for other operational control systems, such as the building's air conditioning or heating, it is usually economical to incorporate the fire-alarm system. This total systems approach can provide a fire-alarm system with a great deal of flexibility in its operation, and all the codes and requirements placed on a high-rise building can be met.

Some of the detection devices that can be monitored and powered by an automation system are water-flow switches, ionization or obscuration detectors, infrared or ultraviolet detectors, and duct detectors. The actual location of these devices will be dictated by considering the personnel involved, methods of egress from the building and individual areas, the fire fuel load, floor plans for efficient zoning of the detection system, air flow for smoke control, and sprinkler zoning. The ability to control all these areas by using a hard-wired system with switching networks can be cumbersome and expensive, and a computer system based on multiplex communication between the control console and the area being protected can provide an economical solution.

The following list of additional fire considerations will be useful as a checklist of key elements:

- Fire department response time
- Point of entrance into the building by the fire department
- Time needed for total evacuation of the building
- Location of maintenance office
- Location of security office
- Training of personnel

- Does the building have a fire brigade?
- Does the building have a watch tour?
- Type of building occupants
- Floor-to-floor construction
- Location of plumbing and electrical wiring
- Fire rating on structural barriers such as walls
- Elevator-bank zoning
- Quantity of people inhabiting during peak hours
- Type of inhabitants—transient or nontransient
- Who will be informed that an alarm condition exists?
- How will the alarm information be transmitted to the municipal fire department?
- What are the ambient environmental conditions of the area to be protected?
- What is the monetary value of the area to be protected?
- What type of fire-suppression equipment is available, and is it manual or automatic?

Personnel Movement and Protection

The ability of people to move quickly out of the fire zone during a fire condition is directly proportional to how much they know about egressing from the area. Therefore, employee training on what to do when a fire condition exists becomes a very important factor in the fire protection plan. Floor wardens or fire brigade personnel maintain stability among people egressing from the fire area. Whatever method is chosen, employees should know what to do in case of a fire to avoid panic. Preplanning to ensure that everybody listens to instructions is essential, so that egress will be quick and efficient.

Another important reason for egress, other than life safety, is to clear the area so that firemen may have a free hand in dealing with the fire.

One of the methods of moving personnel out of a fire area is through the stairwell, with personnel always moving away from the fire—never into a fire zone. This means that people on and below the fire floor should move down. But what happens to the people above the fire floor? Several methods are used, but the key consideration should be that people above the fire floor must move up and away from the fire, to a safe area of refuge or to a safe means of exit. In larger buildings lateral movement may be possible.

All high-rise building codes require more than one fire exit located on opposite sides of the building. The areas of refuge and method of movement should also be part of employee training. If there are separate building sections, such as crossover floors to elevator banks that do not serve the fire area, this information should be emphasized in the training sessions.

More buildings are now being constructed with a section of the roof designed to support a helicopter; this section is not used during normal operation of the building but is usable as a landing pad during emergencies. This concept of life safety and egress from a building was very evident in the disastrous Andraus fire in Sao Paulo, Brazil, in which several hundred people were saved by helicopter transportation. (See Fig. 2.)

It is very important to ensure that the elevators left operating do *not* service the fire zone. Most codes call for immediate capture of the elevators servicing the fire zone in the event of a detection and their immediate return to the first floor or lobby, unless that is the fire floor. This capture is to fulfill two requirements: First, it will ensure that personnel in the elevator will not be able to get off on the fire floor. Second, the firemen arriving on the scene will have a method, upon the elevator's conversion to manual control, of reaching the fire floor. Without this immediate capture, elevators can prove to be unreliable and hazardous during fires.

In 1970, two guards died in a fire at 1 New York Plaza when their elevator stopped on the fire floor. During the same fire, firemen had to chop their way out of an elevator. Four months later, three more elevator deaths occurred in a fire at 919 Third Avenue, New York. In the same fire, firemen had to rescue elevator passengers after their descending elevator stopped on the fire floor and would not move beyond it. Five died when an elevator stopped on the fire floor of a New Orleans motor hotel ... and so on.

Fig. 2   São Paulo, Brazil—a "towering inferno."

The Safety to Life Code (NFPA 101) at one time included elevators as a means of fire egress. Four reasons were given for a subsequent change:

1. People can be overcome by smoke while passively waiting for elevators to arrive.

2. Power loss may prevent elevator operation and/or cause people to be trapped.

3. Elevators can be caused to stop on a fire floor, exposing passengers to the hazard.

4. An elevator is unable to depart from a floor if panicked people rush to get in, not allowing the doors to close.

Some existing codes do provide for continued use of some elevators in a fire, requiring smoke detectors in the elevator lobbies of all floors. Activation of any smoke detector would then bring all elevators of that bank to the ground floor. Other elevator banks would still be in service.

Another method is "locking out" the elevator to prevent stopping on the fire floor when smoke has been sensed on that floor, but continuing to service other floors. Subsequent activation of a thermal detector would remove the elevator bank from service and return the elevators to a predetermined floor.

Safe use of elevators is enhanced by placing elevator banks on opposite sides of fire walls or enclosing elevator shafts within pressurized vestibules.

Though elevators provide quick vertical transportation, their use during a fire is increasingly being prohibited by modern life safety guidelines. It is unfortunate that the vehicle used daily by high-rise occupants cannot be relied upon when needed most. Until elevators are made more fire-safe, the admonition will continue to be: *"In case of fire do not use the elevator. Use the stairs."*

Smoke Control

Using the stairwells as a means of egress presents what could be a very difficult problem if it were not for the flexibility and capabilities of a building automation system. This problem comes in the form of smoke propagation and the many passages in a building through which smoke may spread. Fans are not necessary to cause smoke movement, since differences in density of outside air and the building air create a stack effect, providing the upward movement of the lethal thermal gases created by a fire.

The most effective way to keep smoke out of the stairwells and other unaffected areas is to positively pressurize the unaffected area. Pressurization is one of the most effective methods of smoke control. If it were not for the computerized building automation system with flexible software features, this concept would be next to impossible as a life safety means.

To achieve integration of the HVAC and the fire-detection system, the control equipment should be able to develop a large number of interlock sequences based on the area and number of devices to be controlled. Manufacturers now integrate these functions into a computer-based program to ensure the flexibility required. A typical smoke-control block diagram is shown in Fig. 3.

In many high-rise buildings, the return-air system is designed to exhaust the smoke from the fire area to the outside. Simultaneously, it provides full outside supply air to adjacent areas, creating a positive pressure differential between the uninvolved areas and the fire zone. (See Figs. 4 and 5.)

The HVAC system plays a significant role in the handling of smoke. By locating thermostatic devices and/or duct smoke detectors throughout the HVAC system, supply and return fans can be shut down, preventing distribution of smoke throughout the building by the air-duct system. By creating a negative pressure in the zone of the fire with respect to the pressure in the surrounding areas, an exhaust of the fire atmosphere from the fire zone occurs.

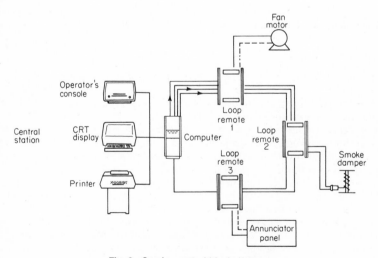

Fig. 3 Smoke control block diagram.

Figures 4 and 5 illustrate the concept of pressurization. The illustrations are purely conceptual, but they do relate to many contemporary design ideas found in the industry.

The first figure shows a portion of a high-rise building during normal operating conditions. The supply-air dampers and the return-air dampers are open on all

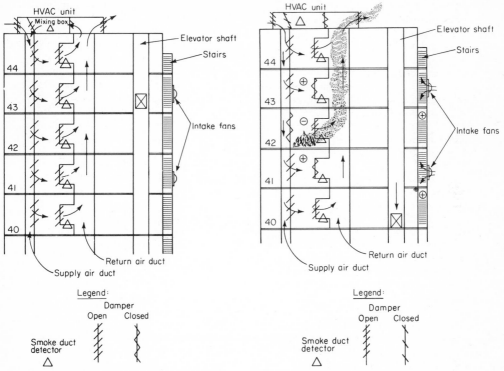

Fig. 4   Air supply and return systems under normal operation.

Fig. 5   Air supply and return systems under alarm conditions.

floors. The normal air flow is the outside air mixed with the return air and distributed into the space to be conditioned. From the conditioned space, the air goes through the return-air dampers into the return-air duct and is then vented to the outside or partially remixed with the supply air. (Note the location of detectors in the return-air ducts on each floor.)

In this example, each floor is considered as a fire zone, with the understanding that a fire zone can be further compartmentalized on the individual floor or expanded to encompass several floors in one fire zone. (Note the duct detectors located at the supply-air intakes of the system. These detectors are shown in the mixing box of the HVAC unit. Many, however, are located in the supply to prevent HVAC short circuiting if the wind is blowing the wrong way.)

During normal operating conditions there is little or no pressure differential between any of the floors. Whatever differential exists would be by virtue of the environmental conditions desired by those persons inhabiting each floor. Note that the elevator shafts and the stairwell shafts have normal ventilation.

In this example, a fire is assumed to occur on the forty-second floor of a high-rise building. After detecting the condition on the fire-floor, dampers, both supply air and return air, change: supply air closes, return air opens. In Fig. 5 can be seen the difference in return-air and supply-air dampers on each adjacent floor above and below the fire zone: the supply air is open, the return-air damper closed. Under these conditions, a positive pressure differential will develop between the adjaçent floors and the fire floor, preventing the smoke from spreading into either of the adjacent areas provided the fans are left running.

The duct detectors on floors other than the adjacent floors will prevent smoke propagation into those uninvolved floors. If smoke *does* become a threat to them, however, the duct detector will go into alarm, indicating to both the control center and the associated dampers that smoke is trying to enter that particular area (the forty-fourth floor, for instance). Subsequently this area is considered as an adjacent area, and also goes into the adjacent-fire-zone condition, along with the forty-third and forty-first floors.

The purpose of the duct detectors in the supply-air entrance ports is to prevent the smoke from being recycled into the outside vent of the return-air damper and drawn back into the supply-air section of the building; this also prevents HVAC short-circuiting.

Pressurization alone cannot do the job of complete smoke control. It must be possible to control the smoke via smoke dampers, smoke doors, and partitions throughout the involved areas. The method most normally used to create this pressure differential in the area surrounding the fire zone is for the return-air smoke damper ducts to be closed and the supply-air dampers to be open. In the fire zone just the opposite occurs—the return-air damper is open and the supply-air dampers closed. This demonstrates that smoke propagation is controlled not only by air supply but also by the method of dampering.

Aside from the ducting system, hallways and passageways are good avenues for smoke propagation. The method of controlling smoke here is with pressurization, as described above. The fire can be confined with smoke partitions placed in a zoned manner, as well as smoke barrier doors with self-closing devices. The self-closing device may be a door holder/closer, or a magnetic contact associated with a door closer. Any of these devices can be controlled electrically through the building automation system by removing the voltage associated with that device, thus permitting the door to close. By using these three methods, i.e. pressurization, damper control, and smoke doors with partition enclosures, a fire can be confined within a specific location.

Safe Areas of Refuge

Good fire-safety design provides "safe" areas or areas of refuge in large structures so that people have somewhere to go in the event that smoke does penetrate other areas in a building. Sometimes an entire floor is designed to be a safe area, the difference between this area and other parts of the building being the type of construction. Many buildings have more than one safe area. Typically, a safe area is designed with fire partitions that have a much higher rating than those in other parts of the building. For example, doors, walls, and ceilings might have a 2- or 4-hr fire-barrier rating. Normally this area is sprinklered and has been designed so that evacuation as directed by the fire department can be accomplished.

The safe area or area of refuge is often the cafeteria or a large conference room or auditorium. It is generally a place where people can congregate during an emergency situation and where there are satisfactory atmospheric conditions supplied by a dedicated HVAC system for that particular area. If no other area in a building has smoke control, this area of refuge should be pressurized and have smoke control, along with a reliable communication and detection system.

Emergency Communication and Controls

When the building control center receives a warning from an alarm system that a fire has occurred, many interrelated events must take place with accuracy and speed. Some are:

1. Calling the fire department
2. Elevator capture
3. Isolating the fire
4. Changing the air-flow patterns and pressurizing
5. Establishment of emergency communication

The last item has developed into major systems for many high-rise buildings. Loudspeakers meeting UL and insurance requirements are located throughout the building and provide sound levels of sufficient volume and clarity to be heard in all areas.

While there are differing views on the best type of sound for a fire alarm, several accepted sounds are used:

- Bells
- Vibrating horns
- Slow whoop
- Temporal pattern
- Voice, both live and tape

Most often used is a combination of sounds, i.e., a slow whoop followed by a taped or live voice message.

In a high-rise building, not all floors are necessarily warned of the fire. The following is one of many possible alarm combinations:

1. The affected area receives the fire warning—followed by a message asking people to move calmly to a safe area.

2. The uninvolved area or areas nearby are then given a warning sound indicating the presence of a fire alarm on an adjacent floor—followed by a voice message advising that people from these affected zones will be coming into their areas.

3. Speakers in the elevators broadcast a message advising occupants of the emergency and stating that the elevators will move to the ground floor.

4. The remaining areas of the building may or may not be aware of the fire alarm. This will be determined by local codes and insurance requirements.

The design of these emergency communication systems will involve options such as all call and zone selection for voice communication. (The term "all call" refers to calling a portion of a building, or the entire building itself. "Zone selection" refers to calling a specific zone of the building normally not involved in the fire sequence. An example of the latter might be a high-risk security area in some other part of the building because the fire may be a diversion to gain entry to this area.) Figures 6 and 7 show a typical voice alarm communication system.

These optional floors can be controlled by the building automation system control console and/or the firemen's communication panel.

An integral part of the emergency communication system is the firemen's communication panel, located at the entrance to the building for use by the fire fighters. This panel will include a display of the fire zones, indicating where the alarm has occurred. It will also include the ability to control the exhaust fans by inputs at the control center. A voice communication system will allow the fire fighters both to communicate with each other and, if necessary, to broadcast directions via the loudspeakers located on the various floors.

Some codes require the provision of a floor warden station where a trained supervisor is permanently located. During an emergency, the warden will coordinate the movement of people from the affected floor and assist in transferring people to safe areas. From the building control center, voice messages can be directed to the floors through the computer-controlled software program.

One of the codes for the type of system being discussed requires a minimum of two types of display equipment. One display must be a printer to provide a hard-copy record of all the events as they occur. The other type of display could be a visual television monitor (CRT), a graphic annunciator using a slide projector, or a hard-wired annunciator that would be back-lighted, providing a graphic description of the area in which the detection has occurred. Existing codes still contain the standard fire-alarm-zone annunciation panel aside from these other two types.

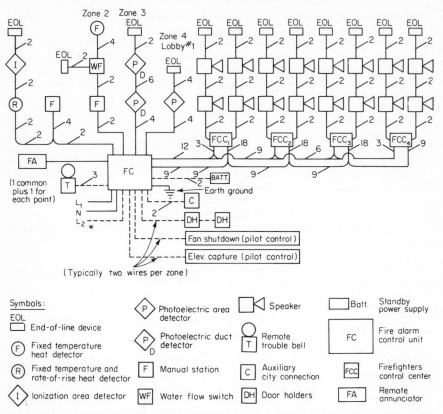

Fig. 6 Emergency voice alarm communication system riser diagram. This system incorporates Johnson Controls System #7000 initiating system and system #7100 two-way communication system with remote supervised annunciator. *Notes:* **(1) Asterisk indicates devices to be deleted if standby power or power failure indicator is required; (2) two wires required for photoelectric detector power (included as shown); (3) dashed lines denote optional equipment.**

To visualize the total system in operation, assume a fire on the sixtieth floor in a building with more than sixty floors. Assume that the fire occurs in a remote location of the building where occupants cannot readily detect the fire by either seeing or smelling smoke.

As the fire starts, smoke begins to develop, and a smoke detector goes into alarm. A printout will occur on the control console telling the operator there is a fire in a zone on the sixtieth floor. At the same time visual and audible annunciation will occur. It may be a temporal pattern beginning on the sixtieth floor and in the zone where the fire occurred. This warns the occupants of that zone that a fire condition exists in their area. Upon completion of the time duration for the temporal zone, a pre-recorded taped message will be broadcast requesting all personnel in the fire zone to proceed to a safe area of refuge as indicated during prior training. At the same time, the elevator banks associated with the fire zone will be overridden and sent to the first floor. An elevator message will be broadcast automatically, indicating to the occupants of the elevator that a fire condition exists on a floor served by these elevators.

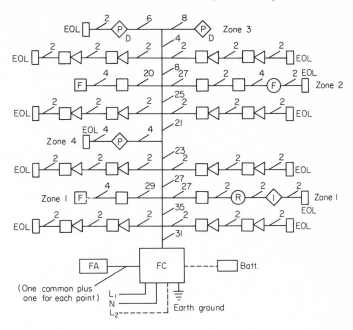

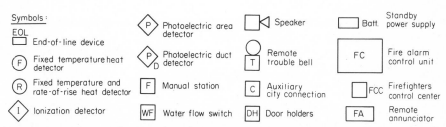

Fig. 7   Emergency voice alarm communication system showing typical conduit wiring. _Notes:_ (1) All circuit wiring No. 14 AWG minimum except where distances indicate excessive voltage drop; (2) initiation circuit wiring may utilize approved cable for power-limited circuit (see Art. 760, National Electrical Code).

Occupants will be advised that they are being transported to the first floor for safe evacuation.

On the floors immediately below and above the fire floor, warning messages are generated via a taped message. The message indicates that a fire condition exists on an adjacent floor but that there is no need to worry, as the building personnel have everything under control. (The fire department has already been notified, automatically by the computer or manually by the operator, at the very outset.) The pressurization system is now placed automatically into operation.

All of the supply-air fans for the adjacent areas around the fire zone have been opened, and the return-air fans for the adjacent areas around the fire zone have been closed. The supply-air damper for the fire zone has been closed, and return-air damper for the fire zone has been opened. The smoke travel pattern is now through the return-air damper out of the building. The other parts of the building are pressurized so that smoke cannot move into them. A printed record of these events occurs as they happen.

The fire department arrives on the scene; they immediately see that the fire is in a zone on the sixtieth floor, as indicated by the firemen's communication panel or graphic annunciator. They take command of the elevators sent down to the lobby for their use and arrive on the sixtieth floor. Via the emergency communication system provided, the fire commander on the sixtieth floor plugs into his communication loop and has direct communication with the battalion chief. Since he is on the fire floor, he is able to discuss the situation and describe the area to the battalion chief. At this time the firemen begin suppressing the fire.

By the time firemen arrive at the fire area, a sprinkler system has been activated and has controlled the fire within a specific area. They are able to put out the remaining fire with a minimum of effort.

People above the sixty-first floor and below the fifty-ninth floor have no knowledge that a fire condition existed. Panic has not been created, and the situation has been dealt with quickly and effectively.

This is *not* an unreal situation. It is a factual account of how building automation systems in high-rise buildings can, and do, contain and control fires today.

PROTECTION OF PERSONNEL AND PROPERTY FROM BURGLARY

As mentioned earlier, a high-rise building can be compared to a small city. One of the things the two have in common is the need for burglary protection, and here their needs are similar if not identical. Of course, the police are the primary source of protection of both personnel and property in a city, but police departments in a high-rise are not economically feasible. A combination of guards and security devices is therefore frequently employed.

In cities, a central-station company acts as a monitoring arm for protection of large and small businesses along with residential homes. As its name implies, this station is normally located in the center of the city; it can monitor several types of alarm systems, and when an alarm is received, guards are dispatched to the area. This ensures that the individual receiving the protection gets the earliest possible response in case of an intrusion. The requirements for central control equipment in a high-rise are virtually the same as those of a central-station alarm company in a city.

The type of security in a high-rise can be as complex (if not more so) as the type of security for the different businesses within a city. Adding to the problems of security are (1) the close proximity to each other of the businesses or areas to be protected and (2) the different levels of protection that an area might require.

When designing a security system for a high-rise building, the most important concept that must be kept in mind is what is to be protected. This will provide the best guide as to the type of equipment and the complexity of the system to be used.

For example, a jewelry store has a higher risk factor than a dry-cleaning establishment, and a prescription drug store might have an even higher risk factor than a jewelry store. Nevertheless, the "risk factor" is affected by other conditions, such as construction, location, ease of access, ease with which material is disposed of by a criminal, and the profit margin it would realize. The profit margin is a major factor, as this determines to what length and risk the criminal will go to to acquire this product. Jewelry and fur coats bring about half the retail market value, whereas drugs can bring as much as 200 or 300 percent of the retail value. And, of course, money is always a prime target, as this has a 100 percent conversion rate.

After determining what is to be protected, a protection system must be designed.

There are several basic systems available, and most incorporate more than one of the following concepts. Some of the most widely used are watch-tour systems by patrolling guards, adequate lighting, closed-circuit TV (CCTV) cameras located both externally and internally in the protected area, perimeter protection systems, access control systems, area protection, object protection, and (a very important feature) a reliable communication system.

Prevention of unauthorized entry into a secured area is the most common type of protection system. However, other features must be included in a high-rise building, such as protection against assault in remote locations or elevators. Normally a detection system is specifically designed for an individual building. It takes into account such factors as business location, structural strength, and various methods of entry to the high-risk area. A full understanding of how detection devices work is necessary to design an effective security system. Using a combination of detection devices as parts of an integrated system is the best method of designing a security program. It should be understood that a singular "off-the-shelf" system may not necessarily meet the total security needs of a high-rise building.

Access Control

The term "access control" is one of the more identifiable terms in the security industry. It means exactly what the words indicate: controlling access into a secured area.

Certain types of buildings, such as factories and high-rise buildings, have a considerable number of people entering and leaving on a regular basis, and it is therefore desirable to establish a means of identifying those who should be inside the building.

Access control can be accomplished in many ways. One of the methods is simply visual recognition by a guard. While this is effective, it is one of the most costly methods, especially if there are several areas to be secured under the access-control concept. One of the most commonly used methods of access control is the use of card readers. (See Fig. 8.) A card reader is a device which electronically identifies a card or badge—usually made of plastic—with some sort of electronic coding imbedded in the plastic. This badge can be coded in such a manner that access during prescribed hours can occur only if the badge is recorded in the memory of the building control center's computer. It will tell a computer that the bearer of this card has access to a given secured area.

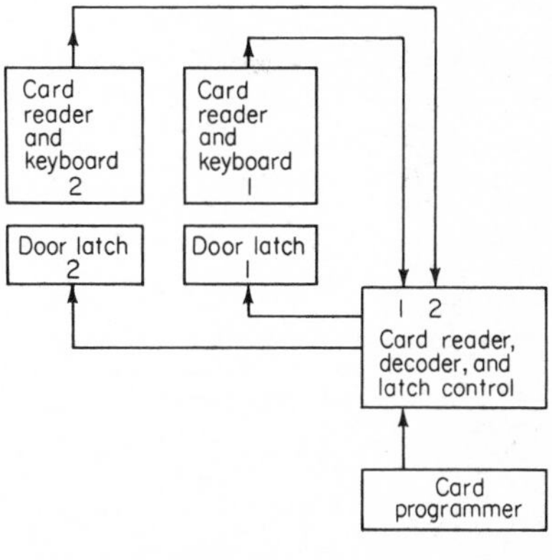

Such badge readers are located in entrances to the building, in the parking areas, in the elevators, and at the entrance to individual high-risk locations, such as computer centers. While the card reader can be an effective access-control tool, one must bear in mind that the equipment only reads the card and has no control over who in fact is using the card.

At the opposite end of the spectrum, access-control equipment can become extremely sophisticated to the point where it reads an individual's palm prints—i.e., scanning the palm and reading the actual prints. As accurate as this is, it is also extremely expensive.

Fig. 8   Card access control subsystem for high-level security.

In most instances the badge reader method is sufficient for proper access control. If higher security is required for a specific area, visual identification by either a CCTV system or a guard at the entrance may suffice.

A badge reader system can be programmed in terms of time or days, or a combination of both. Examples would be an engineering firm where the worker can arrive an hour before normal starting time and gain access to the building during the normal work week. However, a first-shift worker would not gain access to the building during the second shift. Subsequently, the same worker would not gain access to the building during weekends or one hour after his or her shift ended, if the computer were not so programmed. Summaries of the times people enter and of all invalid attempts to enter are available on printed reports at the building security center.

This concept, when used for a firm, may lead to difficulties in cases when, say, a particular department wishes to have several employees work overtime. If the specific date on which these employees are to come into the building is not entered into the computer, they will not be permitted access into the area unless they contact the security control center. Although such complications can develop from use of an access-control system, the benefits more than outweigh the disadvantages.

A good access-control system, when accompanied by a watch-tour system or any of the other systems described, provides an excellent means of first-line deterrence to intruders.

Perimeter, Area, and Object Protection

Even though each one of these approaches is a system in its own right, the systematic approach toward a given building will often include more than one of these systems. Perimeter protection can be applied in a relatively thin "layer," whereas area protection can cover a sizable space. Object protection, however, is just what the term states: a specific object such as a safe, an art object, a diamond, or a rack of furs is the item being protected.

All three of these—perimeter, area, and object protection—are part of a normal and logical sequence of security: (1) protect the perimeter of a building; (2) if the intruder gets inside the perimeter, protect the area in which the object is contained; (3) protect the object itself.

Adequate Lighting

As everyone knows, vandals or criminals prefer to do their work in situations where they cannot easily be recognized. Therefore, parking lots and high-risk places such as jewelry stores, fur storage spaces, and similar areas should be adequately lighted so that criminals are discouraged and so that roving guard personnel or surveillance systems (CCTV) have sufficient light to determine who is in these areas. Specifics are more thoroughly discussed in Chapter 14, "Lighting."

Closed-Circuit Television

Closed-circuit television (CCTV) can be used to protect either exterior or interior areas. In an exterior application, unless surveillance is directed specifically at one point (such as a gate), many closed-circuit television systems have the ability to move the camera and zoom in on a specific object. When used internally the pan/tilt features are not as common, since the areas being viewed are usually more restrictive. Passageways, elevator entrances, stairwells, front entrances, and doors are examples of places where stationary cameras may be used.

The physical placement of the camera becomes critical. It must be determined whether or not the intruder is to see the camera—i.e., will it be used not only to provide the means of identification, but also as a visual deterrent? If it is used for its deterrent value, the intruder's ability to stay out of camera range must be considered. This will involve the selection of lens types, sizes, viewing area, magnification factor, light levels, cameras, etc. In any case, the use of the CCTV equipment is, in most areas, a required feature for security systems. The most obvious reason is in the case where an intruder sets off an alarm—a CCTV system permits immediate viewing of who and where the intruder is. An added feature of a CCTV system comes into play when a fire condition occurs in an area where there is a camera. The fire area can be viewed by security personnel, who can then direct a guard dispatched to the fire zone, or by the fire department immediately upon arriving at the scene.

It is not necessary to have a monitor for every TV camera in the building. Monitor-switching devices and slave monitors allow the operator to view certain sections of the building as required. CCTV monitors, in conjunction with a watch-tour system, provide good visual and personal security. These subjects are discussed in greater detail in other chapters.

Security Personnel Tour Stations

Inspection of a high-rise building on a regular basis is an important part of the security program. Trained personnel familiar with the various risks throughout the building and aware of the locations where equipment or tenants may require assistance should regularly inspect each area. The watch-tour system provides a report to the building control center, which is always aware of the times a guard should be at a certain location. The control center responds with a warning if, for any reason, the guard does not reach the desired point at the predetermined time.

The flexibility of computer programs today allows many independent tours to be operated concurrently. Building security officers, should an emergency occur, know that the central control area will respond to assist them.

A guard may be injured, accosted, or involved with other emergencies that prevent the completion of his or her tour. The programs are able to react to these emergencies. If the central building security officer determines that the emergency is not major, and a guard can respond and correct the problem without further assistance, the computer program keeps the sequence for that station on "hold." After the problem is corrected, the program will continue in its normal sequence.

A watch-tour program used with a central control system has many advantages. There is a means of monitoring the tour of a security guard; and furthermore, the watch-tour program not only adds to the security of a building, it aids in providing fire detection. In fact, the NFPA codes reference watch-tour systems as a method of fire detection to complement the automatic devices.

For example, when an alarm condition is turned in to the central control station in a high-rise complex and a watch-tour system is in effect, the personnel operating the central station can dispatch the guard to the area indicated in the alarm. In this manner, assuming the guard is trained in the use of fire extinguishers, an extremely early response to the fire—prior to that of the fire department—is available. If the guard feels unable to combat the fire for whatever reason, he or she is an important link to the central station. When the fire department arrives, the guard will be able to pinpoint the source of the fire.

With regard to security, the watch-tour adds a high degree of deterrent value in the area being toured. In most watch-tour systems, the routing of any tour can be changed at the central station to meet the needs of the building. In other words, a guard will not be traveling the same route day in and day out, and the time he or she passes any given point will vary from day to day.

Many watch-tour systems have a reporting device at various points throughout the building. These devices can be activated with a card system or a watch-tour key. Each time the device is actuated, it causes a printout at the central station, which tells the operators that everything is secure up to that point. Capability for verbal communication is also desirable, so that the guard can communicate with the central station via the intercom system, or vice versa, for further instructions during the tour.

There are many watch-tour configurations. Some systems provide a printout of tour information, noting each time a guard reaches a guard tour station, for example.

Other types are those giving a time frame in which the guard should arrive at a station. These give an alarm only if the guard arrives either too early or too late at this station, i.e., outside the time frame provided by the central control station.

* * * *

(The following section was prepared by J. W. Hicklin, Hicklin Security Service,, Inc.)

SPECIAL OFFICE BUILDING CONSIDERATIONS

Because high-rise office buildings must readily permit access to the general public, security concepts should be incorporated in their design. The data presented in the preceding sections of this chapter relate largely to the "do's" necessary to provide positive security design. Equally important are the "don'ts" frequently found in inadequately conceived structures. Some advance knowledge of these pitfalls can help avoid such problems as the addition of security hardware after occupancy, the changing of doors and walls, traffic pattern alterations, or the creation of an armed camp after-the-fact. This section, therefore, addresses the "don'ts" to be avoided in designing office buildings for security.

The Building Control Center

Control centers for buildings require careful planning, since they are likely to include at least several of the accepted systems of security and surveillance: closed-circuit TV, alarms (fire, smoke, and intrusion), radio and intercom links, stairwell phone connections, paging systems, elevator controls, and tenant-notification systems.

In one major office building, the center has been located on a main entrance level adjacent to the elevators which take patrons to the cocktail lounge and restaurant. It is not uncommon for these patrons to seek entry into the control center accidentally, or to press the buzzer outside with some unusual, and sometimes humorous, requests. The center operator is seldom inclined to enjoy the festive occasion, and certainly does not care to mix "one for the road."

It would not be difficult for someone to follow an authorized person into this center by force and thus gain control of the center, negating the effect of all the security controls for the building. A more appropriate location would have been adjacent to, or as part of, the engineering console located in the basement. However, relocation after-the-fact in this case is likely to be quite expensive.

In an effort to economize, control centers are often located in the lobby area, with the building directory in front and the CCTV, intercom, alarm, radio, paging and notification equipment, and elevator controls facing the lobby attendant or guard. In an emergency situation, this person would be expected to control access, direct emergency personnel, handle alarms, notify tenants, and maintain building security and safety, all under stressful conditions. A better idea would be a separate, locked room nearby housing the elevator controls, emergency notification equipment, and communications systems used only in emergency conditions. This room could become the command post for fire fighters or building management in case of emergency. Trained building or security personnel would then operate the emergency systems in a controlled environment.

In one instance in an existing building, "planning" provided emergency power backup with storage batteries and generators for maintaining computers, stairwell lights, etc., but did not include emergency power to the control center. Frequent power failures have rendered the control center inoperable. This center houses the alarm annunciators for branch banks throughout the state, as well as local alarms, CCTV, radios, etc., thus creating the potential for serious problems related to law enforcement in the event of an emergency.

An even more incomprehensible situation is the control center in a modern office building which uses the most up-to-date computerized life-safety monitoring equipment. Realizing that problems can occur, the planners for this building provided a complete backup unit consisting of another computer, another set of storage batteries, and a separate additional generator. With all of this far-sighted thinking, the backup equipment was located in the same room, side by side with the primary equipment. It is not difficult to imagine the results if this room were damaged by fire, flood, earthquake, or a bomb. This particular control center has another unique capability: access can be gained only when the operator inside depresses an electric lock release. Should the operator be overcome by smoke, experience a heart attack, or inadvertently allow the door to close while standing outside, the only method of regaining entry would be with the old reliable "key" at the end of the fire fighter's ax handle!

The control center for a modern office building should be considered the most important operational element within the structure. Within its walls pumps the lifeblood of the entire building, whether during an emergency or while performing routine monitoring of the life-safety and security systems. Access to the area should be through a "man trap" which allows visual identification. The personnel and equipment therein should be protected like cash and must be immune to all outside interference, whether human or environmental. The building itself may be burning or falling down, but if control of the situation is to be maintained, it will be emanating from this center.

Personnel Emergency Exits

Because of fire code requirements, thieves may find it easy in many buildings to gain access to the stairwell area, walk down a few floors with their ill-gotten gains, and exit to the street without ever being challenged. To prevent this, many exit doors are alarmed to notify security that the door has been opened. Some are even equipped with CCTV. The inherent deficiency in this concept is that it frequently permits escape of the thief by failing to allow for challenge and possible detainment. At the time of this writing, in a building under construction an attempt was being made to provide a remote, electrically controlled locking of exit doors for nonemergency situations to detain individuals until security personnel could reach the location. Computer software was to ensure that these doors would unlock during emergency conditions. A basic question to be answered here is whether a lock manufacturer can provide this type of mechanism and whether fire codes will permit such an installation. A successful design would, however, increase protection capability considerably. Alarms located further from the exit and CCTV with an intercom would permit detection of an individual with sufficient time to decide on an appropriate course of action.

Even with alarms and CCTV, strange situations often come into existence when there has been inadequate planning. One facility has the CCTV pointing from an alarm-equipped interior passageway toward the street door. When someone opens the door, an alarm sounds at the central control station, and the operator looks at the CCTV monitor—which shows the top of the head and the rear of the departing person. It is thus impossible to see what the person may be carrying in front, and identifying him or her is, of course, virtually impossible. Ten steps later, the culprit is out of the front door, on a public street, and lost in a crowd!

In the case of CCTV installations at exit areas, the camera wiring is often exposed. Certain fun-loving individuals apparently cannot resist the temptation to try chinning themselves on these wires, thus pulling them out of the camera and disabling it for several days until repairs are made. Such cameras are often examples of equipment added after occupancy, rather than planned units with the wiring secured within conduits.

Evacuation Stairwells

A recommendation seems appropriate in light of recent experiences with terrorist bombings. Studies of the placement of bombs reveal that the most popular location is in restrooms, which afford sufficient privacy for the bomb installer to place and activate the device. With such privacy, the bomber is able to booby-trap the package and thus create the near certainty that the device will explode, possibly while being removed from its hiding place by bomb-squad personnel. Many bombs are secreted so well that retrieval is impossible in the short time often available after a warning call is received. While police and security personnel are searching, building occupants are being evacuated down the stairwells. Those modern buildings which provide service facilities in the central core pose a great risk to persons in the stairwell when it passes behind or adjacent to restrooms. Service facilities such as telephone equipment rooms, janitor closets, or engineering areas, all of which are normally locked, should also be located away from restrooms.

Public Access Areas

Building lobbies, hallways, public restrooms, service elevator lobbies, fire equipment closets, mechanical spaces, even mail slots at office doors are prime locations for criminal activity and bomb placement. A compromise is necessary between aesthetics and security to deter this kind of activity as much as possible. Acts of vandalism in office buildings—such as cutting fire hoses, discharging fire extinguishers, ripping out wiring, turning lights on or off—are not uncommon.

Many mysterious instances of theft have been made possible by locating the mail slot near or in the door. Placing mail slots near door handles permits insertion of a belt or towel through the slot to the inside door knob. The door is easily opened, allowing the individual to enter, close the door, and spend as much time inside as the criminal activity requires. It will usually be easy enough to find the file-cabinet keys in the bookkeeper's desk drawer, along with the petty cash, stamps, and other items of value or proprietary interest.

Public restrooms should be constructed with a minimum of potential for placement of explosives or disposing of stolen property. Purse and wallet thefts occur relatively often in office buildings. After extracting the cash and credit cards, the criminal will often discard the remainder in the restroom area. If security thinking were the sole consideration, all restrooms would be locked and the interiors designed like jail cell toilets. Some compromise between design and security is therefore recommended.

Fluorescent lights with removable panels and removable ceiling panels should not be located directly over water closets or lavatories. These fixtures often function as steps up to the ceiling area for placement of explosives or concealment of stolen goods.

Exterior Lighting

Placement of ornamental or protective lighting should be considered in relation to its effect upon the vision of security personnel inside. Often, the lobby guard inside cannot observe beyond the glass because the lighting is directed to illuminate the exterior of the building, thus shining into the guard's eyes. As with protective lighting at the fenceline of a factory, building illumination should shine into the eyes of the intruder, not the protector.

Loading Docks

Loading-dock ramps for delivery and service trucks should be designed with several security factors in mind. After hours, these areas must have the same level of security as other outside doors. Sliding metal screen doors with controls out of the weather usually suffice. Large office buildings often require tenants to move furniture in or out after normal office hours. The inability to close off access to the loading-dock area while the truck is inside and being loaded results in adding a guard or breaching security during this time. Tenants occupying more than one floor may require several trucks or several trips, opening the building to unauthorized visitors via the loading-dock ramp for an extended period of time.

Ramp ceiling height should be increased to accommodate today's higher vehicles. One particular building experienced a "fire alarm," with the resultant arrival of the fire department, the news media, and interested spectators en masse, only to discover that a truck driver had been unaware of the height of his truck and had knocked off a sprinkler head. Such difficulties can be avoided by providing the proper height for loading docks and the proper location of sprinkler heads.

Protection of Electronic Equipment

Electronic equipment is increasingly being utilized to provide cost-effective security in high-rise buildings. Sometimes, in the process of focusing on the degree of sophistication desired for this equipment, elemental security precautions can be overlooked. The following reminders may be helpful:

1. Cabling for security control centers should not pass through public areas.
2. CCTV wiring should not be exposed to vandals.
3. Alarm control panels must not be installed in unprotected areas.
4. Card access readers need a special wall for recessing the controls.
5. Card readers require special wiring. (In one location which uses an optic-type card reader, the building's electrician decided to replace some wires between the reader and the control panel. The new wires could not carry adequate current to the bulb, so that any credit card inserted was able to open the door. The manufacturer's recommendations for such special security equipment should be strictly followed.)
6. Certain electronic transmission lines require special protection. (The author is familiar with a monetary-transfer data line handling credit-card charges for a data center where the transmission lines are above grade outside the facility and thus easily accessible to the public.)

Executive Protection

In recent years, the kidnaping of executives or government leaders has been on the increase. If this trend continues, planners will need to consider constructing barriers to such threats. The seriousness of the problem is already causing add-on construction for security, which creates major problems. One such activity on the drawing boards at the time of this writing is the provision of secure reception areas (including bullet-resistant glass), intercoms, remotely controlled doors, etc. The weight of the glass alone necessitated the strengthening of the floors below, which disrupted normal office activity and required a great deal of after-hours construction work, with its related overtime pay.

For security planning to be complete, consideration needs to be given to proposed occupants and their potential as targets for threats. Not only must executives of multinational corporations be protected, but many of the personnel closely associated with senior executives may require varying levels of protection. In designing interior space, even the receptionist should be afforded sufficient security so that the job can be done without fear. Even small companies and their executives are finding themselves on threat lists. Sometimes, these lists seem to be passed on from group to unrelated group. Long-range planning for major office buildings must concern itself with future tenants and the possibility that any downtown tenant may need more protection than is commonly being provided for today.

To provide security for personnel, tiers of observation are helpful. The receptionist's space should be visible from two other desk locations, without the personnel at these second-line desks being observed by visitors to the primary contact point. Alternate routes of ingress and egress should be provided for emergency evacuation in case it becomes necessary to allow personnel to escape unobserved. If assassination should become as commonplace in this country as in some foreign countries, electric door-locking hardware and more secure areas for senior-level executives will need to be considered more seriously than in the past.

* * * *

CONCLUSION

In today's high-rise buildings, the owner/operator faces a changing environment. Cities and code-writing organizations are introducing new requirements to improve the safety and quality of life for building occupants. This provides a challenge to the designer and the owner as they face a changing set of design standards.

While the opportunity exists today for management to use computer-based systems to integrate various security-oriented services and thus bring about significant savings in the building's costs of operation, it will remain important to select a system that is flexible—one which can change without major modifications to meet new requirements and which will allow the addition of further features that may not be available at the time of its original installation.

Finally, the selected system must, of course, meet the standards of the insurance companies and city officials to ensure that it has the reliability necessary for long-term performance. If it fulfills these considerations, the possibility of a future "Towering Inferno," or some other disaster occurring in a high-rise building, will be left only to the imagination of the movie world. (*C.E.G.*)

Chapter **27**

Industrial Plants

RONALD S. WOODRUFF
Chief of Security, Mentor-Towmotor Corporation

THE ARCHITECT'S RESPONSIBILITIES

To a great extent, the architect will be responsible for the success of an industrial security program long before the plant is in operation. The architect's consideration of the plant's security needs during the design phases can contribute to both the efficiency and the costs of operating the protection functions.

Many of the security factors that are applicable to other types of facilities and have been discussed elsewhere in this volume are, of course, also applicable to the design of industrial plants. The reader is referred to such specific subjects as "Site Protection" (Chapter 10), "Electronic Security Systems" (Chapter 11), "Locks and Keying" (Chapter 15), "Surveillance Cameras" (Chapter 16), "Security Personnel" (Chapter 18), and "Fire Alarm Communications" (Chapter 19) for additional material.

This chapter will present some of the factors which are specifically applicable to the protection of an industrial complex, both from the viewpoint of maximum effectiveness as well as in consideration of the cost factors of operating the plant's security department.

EXTERNAL PERIMETER BARRIERS

There is a growing need to establish perimeter barriers for industrial plants in order to improve access to and from the area, to control the movement of personnel and vehicles, to define the limits of the site, and to create a psychological deterrent to those who might otherwise enter the private property of the company.

External perimeter barriers not only help in deterring illegal entry by criminals, terrorists, and industrial saboteurs, they also discourage the innocent trespassing of children and others who might become injured and subsequently initiate civil damage suits against the owner.

Needs Analysis Prior to the selection of those external barriers which will form the first line of defense for the industrial site, the architect should consider the following factors:

1. Owner requirements
2. Insurance company recommendations
3. Location of the plant
4. State and local building and zoning codes
5. Exposure to other facilities in the area
6. Type of neighborhood
7. Possibility of future industrial or commercial neighbors
8. Type of manufacturing processes
9. Locations and types of site storage
10. Site orientation
11. Present and proposed roadways and railways
12. Future expansion
13. Perimeter maintenance requirements

Natural Barriers

Wherever possible, natural barriers such as bodies of water, valleys, and cliffs should be utilized. These natural formations can be expanded to provide more complete perimeter coverage where necessary. For example, if a large pond covered all but a few hundred feet of a property line, the possibility of increasing the length of the pond to cover the entire side should be considered.

Structural Barriers

After utilizing all natural barriers, the architect should consider the type of structural barrier best suited to the needs of the facility in terms of appearance as well as utility. Structural barriers consist of fences or walls. The most common of these available to the architect are as follows:

1. *Brick or block walls* constructed either as independent structures or as a functional part of the building proper serve as excellent protection against intrusion. If these walls are an integral part of the building and contain windows or other openings, consideration should be given to providing metal grilles or protective screens along the exterior property line.

2. *Stone walls* can be quite effective in controlling a perimeter as well as architecturally beautiful. They are, of course, relatively expensive.

3. *Concrete slab walls* are as effective in controlling access as brick and block, assuming that similar precautions are taken with regard to exterior openings.

4. *Hedges* such as boxwood, fuchsia, and locust can be planted to provide at least minimum-security barriers along property lines.

5. *Wooden barriers* such as stockade and woven fencing also serve as minimum deterrents against improper entry.

6. *Chain-link fencing* is probably the most popular type of perimeter barrier in use for industrial protection.

Fencing Classifications

One system of selecting suitable chain-link fences has been developed with three fence classifications:

Class A—Maximum Security
Class B—Medium Security
Class C—Minimum Security

The specifications for each class are given in Tables 27-1, 27-2, and 27-3.

An additional consideration as to external perimeter protection is the need for an adequate clear zone to encompass the whole site. An exterior clear zone consists of approximately 20 ft between the property line and all walls and fences on the site. This area should be kept free of cover vegetation and any structures which might serve to conceal a potential intruder. Such an area also allows maintenance activity to be conducted without the need to trespass on another's property. An interior clear zone of 50 ft should be allowed between walls or fencing and structures on the site.

If the perimeter of the facility covers a very large area, a roadway should be provided around the barrier for use by security patrols and maintenance employees to ensure its constant integrity.

A final step in planning exterior barrier protection should be a careful vulnerability survey of the proposed perimeter to be certain that no openings from the outside are left unprotected. This survey by the architect might reveal unprotected drainage tiles, utility pits, or low surface grading which could cause security problems when construction is completed.

TABLE 27-1   Class A: Maximum Security

A.1	Height	Minimum 10 ft above grade
A.2	Top guard	"V" arms to accommodate minimum of 12 strands of barbed wire plus concertina or other design as applicable
A.3	Rails	Three rails: top, middle, bottom
A.4	Mesh	Chain-link fabric to be 4-gauge galvanized 2-in mesh
A.5	Intermediate post	Spacing maximum 8-ft centers of a design to meet minimum bending moment of _____
A.6	Terminal posts	4-in O.D. galvanized pipe, 9.1 P.L.F., set in 16-in diameter × 52-in depth footing, 3000-lb/in² concrete
A.7	Grade security	a. Normal ground—bury fabric minimum 36 in below grade with minimum 6-in lap above grade, to be securely fastened to mesh and rail b. With curb—curbing should be 10 in wide × 18 in deep with 12 in below grade; mesh 6 in into curb; four ⅜-in rods
A.8	Fittings	All post bands to be minimum ⅛ in thick and to accommodate ⅜-in carriage bolts, peened; rail ties to be 9-gauge steel spaced on 12-in centers, line posts to have 6-gauge steel ties spaced on 12-in centers
A.9	Gates	Must be 2-in O.D. pipe, 2.72 P.L.F. with welded corners; details of hardware, bracing, or slide gates as applicable
A.10	Protective coating	Minimum 2-oz zinc P.S.F. on all materials
A.11	Submittals	Mill certificates and shop drawings to be submitted for approval prior to field construction

TABLE 27-2   Class B: Medium Security

B.1	Height	Minimum 8 ft above grade
B.2	Top guard	"V" arms to accommodate minimum of 12 strands of barbed wire plus other design as applicable
B.3	Rails	Two rails: top and bottom
B.4	Mesh	Chain-link fabric to be 6-gauge galvanized 2-in mesh
B.5	Intermediate posts	Spacing maximum of 10-ft centers to meet minimum bending moment of _____
B.6	Terminal posts	4-in O.D. galvanized pipe, 9.1 P.L.F., set 48-in below grade in 16-in diameter × 52-in depth footing, 3000-lb/in² concrete
B.7	Grade security	Mesh secured to bottom rail on 12-in centers using 9-gauge steel tie wires; curb or mesh below grade to be optional
B.8	Fittings	All post bands to be minimum ⅛-in thick and to accommodate ⅜-in carriage bolts, peened; rail ties to be 9-gauge steel spaced on 12-in centers; line posts to have 6-gauge steel ties spaced on 12-in centers.
B.9	Gates	Must be 2-in O.D. pipe, 2.72 P.L.F., with welded corners; details of hardware, bracing, or slide gates as applicable
B.10	Protective coating	Minimum 2-oz zinc P.S.F. on all materials
B.11	Submittal	Mill certificates and shop drawings to be submitted for approval prior to field construction

TABLE 27-3 Class C: Minimum Security

C.1	Height	Minimum 7 ft above grade
C.2	Top guard	Single arm to accommodate 3 strands of barbed wire
C.3	Rail	A top rail and bottom tension wire required
C.4	Mesh	Chain-link fabric to be 9-gauge, 2-in mesh
C.5	Intermediate posts	Spacing maximum of 10-ft centers to be 2⅜-in O.D., 3.65 P.L.F., or H second of equal bending strength
C.6	Terminals	3-in O.D. galvanized pipe, 5.79 P.L.F., or roll-form section of equal strength: set 36 in below grade in 12-in diameter × 40-in depth footing, 3000-lb/in² concrete
C.7	Grade security	Mesh secured to bottom tension wire, hog-ringed on 24-in centers
C.8	Fittings	All post bands to be minimum ⅛-in thick and to accommodate ⅜-in carriage bolts; rail ties to be 11-gauge steel or 9-gauge aluminum spaced 24 in on centers; line posts to have 6-gauge steel ties spaced on 14-in centers
C.9	Gates	Must be 2-in O.D. pipe, 2.72 P.L.F., with welded corners; details of hardware, bracing, or slide gates as applicable
C.10	Protective coating	Minimum 2-oz zinc P.S.F. on frame and fittings; fabric to have 40-ALM coating or 2-oz zinc P.S.F.
C.11	Submittals	Mill certificates and shop drawings to be submitted for approval prior to field construction

ELECTRONIC BACKUP SYSTEMS

Recent barrier penetration tests conducted by the federal government have revealed that even the best chain-link fences and other types of exterior barriers can be penetrated. With this in mind, the architect should consider the possible use of backup electronic support devices for natural and structural barriers.

Several types of electronic point-of-entry systems which detect an intruder approaching or attempting to compromise a barrier are available. They are as follows:

1. *Audio monitoring:* Listening devices are used to transmit unusual sounds.

2. *Proximity devices:* An alarm is sounded when an intruder trips the device.

3. *Photoelectric eye:* An infrared beam covers an area and transmits an alarm if broken.

4. *Closed-circuit TV:* Cameras are set up in fixed patterns or with scanning ability to watch an area.

These electronic support devices can be installed so that monitoring is conducted at some point on the site, such as the security office, or at some distant point, such as an alarm company office. With the exception of the CCTV units, they can be equipped to activate a local alarm bell or siren on the site in cases where it is not possible to have the system constantly being monitored. Specific criteria for these systems are discussed in other chapters of this volume.

DOOR LOCKS

Most facilities will require locks on doors even though barrier perimeter protection is provided. This will serve as additional backup protection from outsiders, as well as making it possible to restrict certain buildings and areas from entry by unauthorized persons who are legitimately on other portions of the site.

Usually, a plant security chief is responsible for controlling entrance into and egress from a plant site. The number of and location of doors and gates, as well as flow patterns of pedestrain and vehicle traffic, will have an effect on the security operation's costs and efficiency once the plant goes into production.

Whenever possible, the plant security chief should be consulted during the planning stages, particularly with reference to locations of doors and gates and with regard to the type of locks to be utilized.

An architect should make every effort to limit the number of entry points for personnel and vehicles, as each of those will require later control by the security department. (Auxiliary exit points required by codes for egress should be alarmed and accessible only from the interior.) For example, each entrance which must be controlled by security guards on all three shifts requires the following allocation of time and labor:

Gate A: Open three shifts, 7 days per week
           3 shifts = 24 h × 7 days = 168 h per week
           168 h ÷ 40 h per officer = 4.2 officers

Thus each opening which must be covered necessitates hiring more than four security officers.

Types of Access-control Systems

Several types of access-control systems are available which can replace mechanical key locks in certain situations. Examples of these are:

1. Card-key systems
2. Mechanical pushbutton
3. Electronic pushbutton
4. Fingerprint analysis
5. Hand geometry systems
6. Signature analysis
7. Voice grade systems

GATEHOUSES AND SECURITY STATIONS

Areas which have been designated as security officer stations—whether for gate duty, for fixed-post assignments, or as central security headquarters—have certain special requirements:

1. *Observation:* When parking lots or other areas are to be kept under surveillance, the structure should be designed to give maximum observation with minimum exposure for the officer assigned. Windows should be installed at an angle to reduce glare from inside lights.

2. *Lighting:* The ability to control the amount of inside lighting at the security station is important. Controls should be established to enable the officer to illuminate the entire room or a small area.

3. *Location of signal panel:* If the station is to be equipped with a console or signal panel, the location of the instruments should allow viewing of the outside area simultaneously.

4. *Protection from elements:* Since security stations must be occupied in all types of weather, doors and windows should be arranged to provide maximum protection for the officers on duty.

5. *Restroom facilities:* Whenever possible security stations and gatehouses should be equipped with restroom facilities to eliminate the need for relief assignments.

6. *Combining functions:* A gatehouse should be located so that multiple functions can be performed whenever possible—for example, the protection of a parking lot along with control of a truck and pedestrian entrance.

MARKING AND NUMBERING CONSIDERATIONS

When the plant is in operation, security personnel are expected to respond quickly to emergency situations occurring within and to report hazardous situations with accurate locations. Architects should always consider the future ability of plant occupants to use the room and space numbering systems and the column grid lines which they indicate on the construction drawings.

Large areas such as shops and warehouses should always be laid out using the letter and numeral grid system, and these symbols should be marked on columns and walls after painting is completed. Door numbers assigned by the architect can also be used effectively if care has been exercised to number all doors sequentially.

CONTROL OF LOCK SYSTEM

An industrial complex should adopt a master-keyed lock system for all exterior and interior doors, as well as for padlocks and other miscellaneous locks. This system should be controlled and maintained by the security department.

A recommended breakdown as to categories is as follows:

GRANDMASTER   Controls the entire plant lock series. Keys issued on approval of the plant manager.

SERIES "A"   Outside doors and gate entrances to company premises. Locks installed by approval of plant security. Keys issued on approval of plant manager.

SERIES "B"   Inside offices and factory doors. Submasters BA through BD. Submaster keys will be issued on request of the department head in charge of the area.

SERIES "C"   Maintenance—janitor closets, pipe space, fan rooms, substations, and transformer enclosures. Master and submaster keys issued and locks installed on written request of the supervisor, approved by the plant engineer.

SERIES "D"   Company tool boxes and cabinets, submasters as follows: DA through DN, DP and DR. Submaster keys issued and locks installed on request of the superintendent of the area to which the particular "D" series locks are assigned.

SERIES "E"   Master and disbursing cribs. Master keys issued and locks installed on written request of the tools and supplies superintendent.

SERIES "F"   Cafeteria and vending service areas. Master keys issued and locks installed on written request of the personnel services manager.

SERIES "S"   Safety lockout—locking out of electric current, as a safety measure, from areas in which maintenance work is being conducted. Padlocks and keys issued on written request from electrician supervisor.

Chapter 28

Libraries

RAYMOND M. HOLT

Library Consultant, Del Mar, California

Although library buildings are susceptible to the same range of security risks as other public structures, scant attention has been given to this problem in the library press or elsewhere. The chief sources of information include a book edited by Edward M. Johnson for the American Library Association in 1963, entitled *Protecting the Library and Its Resources: A Guide to Physical Protection and Insurance.* A bimonthly periodical, *Library Security Newsletter,* began publication in January 1975 as a product of the Haworth Press in New York.

Part of this lack of attention may stem from the attitudes of many who work in libraries. As a group, professional librarians are very much concerned with personal freedom and shun those things which may appear to impinge on personal privacy. Security systems, with their emphasis upon observing and regulating individual activities, seem to contravene the rights of the individual. Add to this the long-term budget reductions experienced by most libraries, and one can begin to understand the lack of interest in giving consideration to security systems which may be expensive to install and operate, as well as possibly violating basic individual freedoms.

Nonetheless, library-building security is a real and legitimate concern which *is* demanding increased attention. Fortunately, solutions to security problems in other types of buildings are often applicable to libraries. However, before becoming involved in the details of library security, it is perhaps worthwhile to distinguish between the various types of libraries, since such differences determine to some degree the nature and extent of security problems and the techniques required to deal with them.

TYPES OF LIBRARIES

While the various types of libraries have much in common, they also have essential differences which make it difficult, if not impossible, to seek and/or apply universal solutions to security problems. Libraries differ as to the materials they house, the publics they serve, and their relationship to the community in which they find themselves. These factors, in turn, are strong determinants in the kinds of structures used to house libraries and thereby influence security risks as well as control responses.

The Academic Library

Academic libraries include those associated with colleges, universities, community colleges, and derivations thereof, such as vocational trade schools, business colleges, etc. Collections and services of academic libraries are molded around the supporting institution's objectives and curricula. While academic libraries in larger institutions tend to be housed in one or more separate facilities, it is not uncommon for those serving smaller colleges to be part of another structure. At one time the combination of library and administrative building was fairly common. Now there is a trend toward combining library functions with classrooms, "learning resource centers," and related facilities. Joint tenancy brings with it many unique problems peculiar to each such facility. Since academic libraries tend to be open for long hours each day—some even have areas which never close—the separation and security of the library, as distinguished from the other elements in the building, becomes crucial.

Academic libraries often pride themselves on their "rare book" collections. These are frequently housed in a special room or area of the building. The contents and value of the rare-book collection vary widely from library to library. Because many such items lose much of their value if they are marked with any kind of property identification, they become prime targets of biblio thievery. In addition, rare-book rooms and collections require special security measures against fire and invasion by natural elements. Fragile paper containing irreplaceable printed matter can be reduced to worthless dust or pulp in the course of a very short period if control is not exercised over heat, moisture, direct sunlight, and vermin.

While many academic libraries maintain exhibit cases displaying treasures from their rare-book collections, access to these materials is normally limited to the few who have a demonstrated need for research purposes. Monitoring those admitted for research purposes constitutes a special security problem, since mutilation and loss by theft occur even under the most stringent screening regulations for researchers.

Theft, vandalism, and personal security are problems to be contended with throughout the library. The large university or college campus located in a congested metropolitan area obviously is more susceptible to security problems involving staff and users than a suburban or rural campus somewhat remote from urban violence.

Public Libraries

Public libraries, at first glance, would appear to vary only in size. This is deceptive. Like their academic counterparts, public libraries differ too in the materials they collect, preserve, and make available to the public. Some have only very general collections with few specialized materials, others accumulate rare books and other unique materials which rival those in academic libraries. Public library collections have usually been considered too general and too easily replaced to merit protection. However, soaring book prices have forced public library administrators and officials to look at the loss of materials many libraries sustain each year. As a result, some are joining their academic counterparts in installing electronic surveillance devices to guard their collections—or at least the items most susceptible to theft.

The very "public" nature of public libraries has posed even greater problems in personal security and protection against vandalism. In most instances, public libraries are located in highly congested downtown business areas. Frequently, they are in, or on the fringe of, civic centers or urban redevelopment projects, thus placing them closer to potential sources of trouble than other institutions. Physical crimes against staff and library users are reported with increasing frequency, not only in the large central libraries but also in suburban libraries and branches. Shielded by rows of bookshelving, the would-be attacker has ample opportunity to stalk an intended victim—whether the purpose be purse snatching, rape, or worse. Budget cuts in recent years have resulted in drastic reductions of library personnel, further limiting supervision. Additionally, public libraries are usually open several hours during the evening, making them an even greater attraction for would-be offenders. Particularly vulnerable are the staff members themselves, who must close the building and then find their way out to transportation, which may be a bus at a distant corner or a vehicle parked in an unsupervised lot.

Special and Institutional Libraries

Special libraries are usually private in nature and serve a particular commercial or industrial firm. As such, they are customarily housed within the corporate plant and utilized primarily, if not exclusively, by employees of the individual company; they generally have fairly small collections. Occasionally, the special library will be given the responsibility for maintaining corporate records.

Besides the special libraries serving business and industry, others are maintained by such diverse agencies as museums, art galleries, historical societies, governmental departments, hospitals, or prisons. Each is constructed around the particular interests of the sponsoring body, and the clientele is limited to those associated therewith. Security here must relate to the individual situation.

School Libraries, Media Centers, Learning Resource Centers

Responding to changing concepts in curricula and utilization of instructional materials, the traditional school library serving elementary and secondary schools has changed drastically in the past few years. In many schools terms such as "media center," "learning resource center," or "instructional materials resource center" are used instead of the more formal title of school library.

With the change in name, school libraries have also been relocated to suit the functional layout of the particular school. Currently they are apt to be closer to the center of things, whether housed separately or incorporated as an integral part of an "open"-classroom building. The open character of the library and the emphasis upon ready admittance have removed the controls which existed when the library occupied a well-defined area or separate building on the campus.

Today's permissive attitudinal climate and relative disregard for public property by many persons have multiplied the incidence of vandalism and theft. Even though school library collections seldom contain truly valuable materials, the losses sustained are still sizable. School librarians and school authorities find the mutilation of encyclopedias, dictionaries, and other standard works, as well as nonprint materials, expensive in terms of replacement and exasperating in terms of depleting collection resources.

After-hours vandalism, theft, and arson center on the school library, which offers a better and more immediate and attractive target for destruction than perhaps almost anything other than school records. Perhaps, too, there is something symbolic about attacks on school libraries, which contain the materials necessary for both the preservation of our society and the transference of knowledge from one generation to the next.

THE SYSTEMS APPROACH

As in the case of any other type of building, library security should be conceived as a total system combining necessary protective devices and conditions in an effective and complete package. It is worth repeating here that libraries are particularly vulnerable to both natural and human security threats because of the nature of their contents, the customary freedom of access, and the hours of opening, which tend to be longer than for other types of buildings. These factors must be borne in mind whether a library project involves remodeling, an addition, or an entirely new structure.

At the same time, libraries of all types and sizes are almost universally experiencing reductions in budgets and personnel which appear to have no end in the foreseeable future. Therefore, a security system must be proved cost-effective to merit serious consideration. Elaborate systems, no matter how well they might protect, are less apt to receive approval than those which incorporate relatively simple devices, require a limited amount of equipment, and make few demands on staff time. Further, the system's components must be reasonably compatible with library objectives and scale. For instance, barriers such as turnstiles, though used increasingly, are still frowned upon by many as unsightly obstacles which impede the easy accessibility traditionally associated with libraries of nearly every type.

The systems approach must also take into account the relatively large areas of public space supervised by staff members who cannot normally be confined to a particular spot where video monitors, for instance, might be placed. Most of the staff must be free to move about the building to assist users in finding materials, using reference tools, etc. In most libraries, the circulation desk is the only place which may be staffed during all the hours that the library is open. Yet, circulation staff are often much too involved in circulation routines to be effective in a security role. In fact, it is the failure of the circulation staff to be good door monitors that has been used to justify security systems in some libraries.

Where possible, security systems should be tied into those for other buildings, thereby eliminating the relative isolation of libraries. For instance, on school and college campuses controls should terminate in the campus security headquarters, providing it is adequately staffed on a round-the-clock basis. Public and other libraries should be incorporated into existing security systems monitored by local police and fire departments; direct notification to responsible emergency agencies is essential for prompt and certain response.

Since the trend is toward the remodeling and expansion of existing library structures in many places, the design of security systems may frequently be conditioned by structures which are a number of years old. As might be expected, older library buildings designed with little concern for security measures offer a particular challenge.

GENERAL BUILDING PROTECTION

The exterior walls of most free-standing libraries constitute their first line of defense. Therefore, the same defensive mechanisms available to other types of structures should be employed with libraries insofar as they are compatible with library usage. This includes such architectural design considerations as (1) elimination of unnecessary offsets which screen building areas from easy surveillance, (2) keeping openings in the "skin" to the absolute minimum consistent with library needs, (3) placement of windows and other openings above the height of easy reach wherever possible, (4) providing carefully designed exterior lighting of not less than 2 fc at ground level which fully illuminates the exterior and is controlled by a time clock, (5) undergrounding electrical and telephone wires to make them inaccessible to sabotage, (6) placement of fresh-air intake ducts where they cannot be used to spread noxious or other fumes throughout the building, (7) use of impact-resistant glazing materials on all windows which are susceptible to breakage by anyone armed with a weapon or glass cutter, (8) screening of all exterior light fixtures so that bulbs cannot be removed or broken by thrown objects, (9) assuring that all openings on the roof are intruder-resistant in design, (10) providing reasonably high light levels at all entrances to the structure, (11) specifying landscaping materials which give protection, such as thorny species near and against the structure, and are kept low enough (2 ft or less) to deny shelter to a would-be intruder, (12) providing adequate supplementary lighting along all walkways connecting the building with sidewalks, driveways, and parking, (13) specifying sturdy doors with heavy-duty intruder-resistant hardware, locks, etc., and (14) incorporating an appropriate alarm system into the building's design.

The selection of an appropriate security system to be incorporated in the design of the library building should come at a very early stage in planning. A security consultant, one whose practice is not connected with the sales, distribution, or promotion of any particular brand(s), should be retained by the time the planning has entered the schematic phase. The size and nature of the library's operations, site, and orientation, the location of structures on adjacent properties, and a variety of other matters will be of deep concern. Wiring for security devices should, of course, be incorporated into the general electrical plan. The need for a "security control room" or its equivalent in a smaller building should be an essential part of the program. Unless the security devices are considered on a system basis, the library may find itself with more than enough devices in some areas and insufficient, or nonexistent, protection elsewhere. Adding other equipment after the structure has been completed is always more expensive and seldom as satisfactory.

LIBRARY AREAS WITH SPECIAL SECURITY REQUIREMENTS

Perimeter barriers and exterior defenses for library buildings vary little from those appropriate for other public buildings. Inside, however, the differences are many, some obvious, others subtle. Perhaps the most apparent distinction is the fact that a sizable portion of every library's space is given over to collections of books and other materials, many of which must normally be readily available to the public. There are some similarities here with retail department stores, which must exercise control over their stock in trade. Libraries must depend upon a small number of personnel to cover a minimum of work stations. Although much of the library's space must be given to collections and public services, most buildings include offices and work areas which require freedom from public intrusion. Public meeting rooms add still another facet to the complexities of library security.

The Entrance

The entrance to each and every library, regardless of type or size, is almost invariably the most critical point for normal security. For this reason, the number of entrances should be kept to an absolute minimum and preferably to a single public entrance and one freight/staff entrance. Other emergency exits from the building may, of course, be required by building codes. The location of the library's main entrance, the placement of the staff desks located here, and the configuration of doors, counter work, etc., must all be given very serious attention from the standpoint of security. Lighting will play a role, as well as the location of possible user facilities such as lockers, restrooms, etc. The entry doors should be at grade to meet requirements for the handicapped. In the contemporary library, the entrance doors are usually glass and may be part of a sizable section of store front. Vulnerability of the entrance can be reduced through the use of break-resistant glazing materials. With increasing frequency, library doors are opened automatically, either swinging in an arc or sliding to one side. The designer must choose the type of door and the activating device that best suit library requirements while presenting a minimum of problems for security.

The location and configuration of desks in the entrance area vary with volume of traffic, type of circulation system used, requirements of any book theft detection system employed, number of staff available for duty at peak hours, and methods for handling routines—e.g., registration, payment of overdue fines, checkout of materials, or return of borrowed materials. These tasks can be divided into two groups, those associated with entering the library and those associated with leaving. In libraries with relatively limited patronage, a central desk may be provided at which all of these services are combined and, perhaps, performed by the same staff member. In the larger library, these functions can be split into a number of segments, keeping related services together. For example, the following are primarily associated with entering the library: (1) book return, (2) payment of fines, (3) registration. The checking out of materials stands alone as a major activity for those leaving the library. Since many people may enter simply to return books, pay fines, or register for future service, these activities are usually placed near the entrance; checkout, by the same token, should be related to the exit.

Since the vulnerability of the library's collections does not occur until a visitor penetrates beyond these desks, the latter can be considered as the first line of internal protection. Further, such desks are staffed at all hours during which the library is open to the public. Although the design of circulation areas must relate to the building of which they are a part, the solutions usually have much in common. Several of the most frequently encountered configurations are shown in Figs. 1 to 7, and their implications for security control are discussed in the following paragraphs.

Figure 1 illustrates the kind of response typical of those very much concerned with keeping tight control over both the incoming and outgoing users of the library. The entrance is opposite the book-return area, and passage into the library is controlled by restricting the opening between the circulation desk and the wall, which is equipped with a turnstile. The exit narrows to a single lane, compressing the users between the registration desk and the book checkout desk on the opposite side. While considerable surveillance may be indicated by this design, there is always a great deal of inconvenience to the user who has nothing to check out but must cope with the long queue which inevitably extends from the checkout desk during the busier hours. But it is still possible for a user who is determined to steal materials to slip through unobserved.

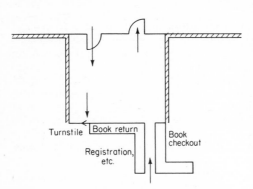

Fig. 1   Control desk with tight, restricted control.

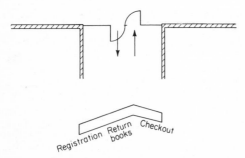

Fig. 2   Control desk showing "classic" configuration.

The layout seen in Fig. 2 is probably found oftener than any other configuration. Control is dependent upon alert staff and the degree to which passage is naturally reduced between the desk and adjacent walls. The desk, of course, may assume any of a number of shapes and sizes and still fit this general pattern. In this and other situations where control is limited, extra personnel in the form of guards or monitors are placed near the exit during the busiest hours. They are supposed to verify the fact that the books have been checked out. In addition, they may require people to open briefcases, bags, etc., for inspection. While this increases control somewhat, it is expensive and still dependent upon the human factor of observation. Libraries using monitors find their losses may be reduced—but far from eliminated.

In Fig. 3, all the circulation elements have been pulled to one side of the entrance. Those entering the library must cross the exiting line of traffic to deposit books, pay fines, register, etc. During busier hours, the staff will have little visual contact with those coming into the building. Supervision over those exiting is dependent upon the fact that the exit doors are on the same side as the circulation counter. Security is obviously very limited so far as staff supervision is concerned.

Figure 4 illustrates a layout aimed at improved supervision, though at considerable additional staff expense. The circulation desk has been divided so that the functions

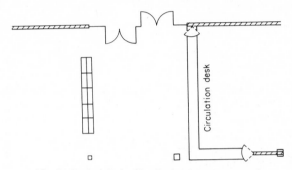

Fig. 3 Control desk with offset entry arrangement.

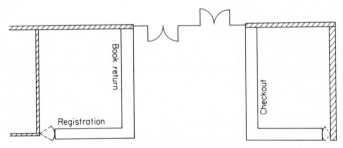

Fig. 4 Exit and entry arrangement with separation of functions.

related to the incoming library user are located near the entrance door, while the checkout procedures are situated adjacent to the exit. Depending upon the distance between the two desks, the size of the lobby area, and the emphasis given supervision by the circulation staff, this can be a reasonably effective solution—at least until the busier hours of the day and evening. However, for the person determined to leave the building without notice there is plenty of opportunity, especially when this area, which must double as a lobby, is congested. Some libraries with this pattern of desks have gone another step and set up barriers of one sort or another to keep entering and exiting users from mingling until they are beyond the lobby, thereby improving the effectiveness of control somewhat.

The library in Fig. 5 uses a rather different principle to gain at least a semblance of control while retaining the concept of a centralized circulation desk. The counter area is placed between the entrance and the exit doors; users entering the library pass close to the book return area, while those departing must walk by the checkout portion of the desk. Avoiding the division of circulation routines results in personnel savings.

The degree of security is determined by the use of automatic doors, which swing inward on the entrance side of the desk and outward on the exit side. The proximity of the entry and exit doors and adjacent walls or other barriers constricting traffic play a major role in control.

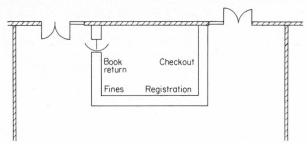

Fig. 5   Control desk with segregated entry and exit.

In Fig. 6, an attempt has been made to modify the typical supermarket counter for library use. Additional control is sought through the use of turnstiles, which also give the library user an alternative to walking through the aisle next to the circulation counter. This does relieve the pressure which builds up at this critical point during peak traffic hours, but it also dilutes the control exercised by the staff. Another criticism of this particular configuration is that the staff must unavoidably turn its back to traffic just entering the building. Various modifications might be made of this scheme, though it seems seriously flawed.

When a library building must have two or more public entrances on the same floor, the problem of security control is much more complicated. Either of two responses is possible: (1) Duplicate the same circulation counters at both entrances, using whatever configuration may be chosen, or (2) use a central desk situated at some point between the two entrances, and through the arrangement of furnishings, etc., guide people to it. Central circulation desks under such conditions take on all manner of shapes—squares, rectangles, ovals, circles, diamonds—or can even be divided into two elements, with each backed up to a work area or other walled-off space. Figure 7 shows one such arrangement. Security under these conditions, again, is marginal at best, and control suffers increasingly as the distance between the two entrances grows and as the space widens between the circulation counter and walls, fixtures, etc., which confine and direct people. Architects often use various design devices to enhance the psychological dominance of this central desk. Two of the more common techniques include changing the ceiling height and floor materials for the space between the two entrances, including the area covered by the circulation desk.

So far as entrance control is concerned, then, the above examples should make clear the limitations inherent in some of the typical configurations. Those hired for

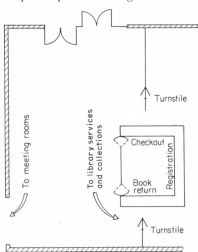

Fig. 6   Control desk using modified supermarket concept.

duty as circulation personnel usually find themselves too busy serving library users to have much time for supervising control of the entrance. Even if they wished to do so, any surveillance over the entrance at the busier times would be most impractical for staff, whose primary job is taking care of users, rather than overseeing the security of the entrance. Failure of both the circulation desk and the special guard to be effective

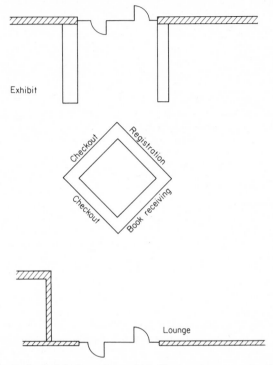

Fig. 7   Control desk serving multiple library entrances and exits.

security agents means that the problem of security at the library's entrance and exit doors is unresolved. The need for security is underplayed by those who feel the public prefers a more open and inviting entry area. In designing a library building, the resolution of this problem demands high priority and, perhaps, the use of some of the more sophisticated equipment and techniques in the security field.

Public Service Areas and Book Stacks

Beyond the circulation counter in most libraries are one or more stations manned by professional librarians or other staff. The objective of such personnel is to provide reference and advisory service to the user. Pursuit of this goal requires the librarian to move freely about the library to aid people at the card catalogs, assist with bibliographic and reference tools, search for answers to reference questions, and assist others in finding materials of a particular kind. Unfortunately and unrealistically, there is a general assumption that these individuals should perform an essential security function as well. They are therefore cautioned to watch for people whose actions or demeanor may make them suspect of possible antisocial behavior. Usually, they are expected either to take care of the situation by asking the offender to leave or to pass a warning to someone else who may contact authorities, and so on.

Among the people librarians must frequently cope with are the "peekers," who find refuge in the book stacks and practice their voyeuristic tactics with little fear of detection or interruption. Sometimes, such socially repulsive conduct ceases to remain passive and results in exposure, attempted rape—or worse. Libraries provide few security precautions against this constant threat other than such supervision as can be exercised by the staff in their normal rounds.

The answer, in part, lies in reducing visually unsupervisable areas to an absolute minimum. Sometimes this can be done by changing the position of service desks or by moving taller pieces of furniture against walls, where they will not form a barrier. In other instances, ranges of bookshelving can be turned at angles to the desks to permit easy visual supervision. What often appears to be a large, open, and easily supervised space on an architectural drawing becomes an almost impenetrable maze of shelving, file cabinets, card catalogs, etc., when it is converted to three dimensions. A good precaution is to draw simple sketches which show what the librarian will see from each desk. These, if done accurately, along with sight lines constructed as an overlay on floor plans, will help determine location of furnishings where they will least impair the kind and degree of supervision inherent in the various staff desks.

Since blind spots are almost inevitable, especially in larger libraries, other forms of security control are needed. Devices such as mirrors and closed-circuit television cameras seem particularly appropriate. TV monitors may be located near the reference desks as well as in the security control area. The effectiveness of TV will, of course, be partially determined by the height of the mount, the panning mechanism, and the layout of shelving. The advice of an expert in the use, deployment, and installation of TV equipment is essential. Further data on surveillance cameras are included in Chapter 16 of this volume.

Public Restrooms

As in many buildings, public restrooms in a library can be a focal point for security risks. Besides vandalism and assault, this is a favorite area for planting incendiary devices, etc. The location of the restrooms becomes a prime consideration in terms of supervision. Where restrooms have a continuing record as a source for mischief, there is often no choice but to keep the doors locked and issue keys upon request. This is a nuisance in any library and a major inconvenience in larger buildings, where restrooms are in almost constant use. A possible alternative to this is the use of a remote-control locking device which can be operated by the staff.

Restrooms should be constructed of materials which will resist vandalism. This includes floor-to-ceiling ceramic tile and tile floors. Toilet partitions should be sturdy and well mounted, with surfaces resistant to defacement. Floor drains are a "must," since one of the most common acts of vandalism is to stop plumbing drains and open faucets to create water damage. Waste receptacles should have tight-fitting lids to snuff out fires set in them. Plumbing fixtures should be chosen which feature vandal-resistant faucets, etc. Towel dispensers should be inserted into the wall and properly secured against attempts to remove them.

Card Catalogs and Shelf Lists

The loss of a library's card catalog and/or shelf list is about the most severe deprivation a library can suffer. The card catalog is the index to the library's collections, without which much of the material on the shelf is useless; the shelf list is the library's record of inventory. The 3 × 5 cards in these files are easily destroyed by fire or defaced in any of a number of ways—vandals have used spray paint, fast-drying glue, ink, acid, and a host of other materials with dire effect.

To avoid this potential loss, libraries have resorted to a variety of methods. Some have had their shelf-list cabinets, for instance, designed into recessed waterproof compartments, which can be closed off by fire-resistant doors and locked against vandals. More prevalent, of course, is the practice of systematically microfilming the entries and then storing the microfilm in a vault in a building elsewhere that is judged to be reasonably safe. As increasing numbers of libraries replace card catalogs with other catalog forms, such as microfilm, book catalogs, and computer-based catalogs, the card catalog is being replaced by tools less susceptible to security risks. Even the shelf list can be recaptured for libraries on many of these systems, if need be. This sort of protection seems more valid than attempts to isolate and secure the physical card catalogs and shelf lists.

Staff Work Areas

Most library buildings provide special work areas and offices for library staff involved in library operations and management. Sometimes these spaces are grouped together, while in other buildings they may be divided and associated with related public areas. In either case, they should be secured as "off limits" for other than authorized personnel. Little has been done about this in most libraries. Moreover, the layout of most work areas precludes much more than the visual supervision which may occur from one station or another.

One method of securing these nonpublic spaces is the use of electronic entry-control ID card systems on doors leading into office and work areas. In the large library, these could be coded by department, further restricting access by any employee bent on mischief.

The Delivery Entrance

While no statistics are available, many of the typical library's security problems are known to involve the delivery entrance. Unlike many other types of buildings where personnel are in or near the delivery entrance whenever the building is open, 25 to 30 percent of a library's hours of opening may occur when staff areas, including the delivery entrance, are vacated. This fact does not go unnoticed by the individual intent on victimizing the library.

As in many other buildings, library delivery entrances tend to be at the rear of the structure or in some other relatively secluded location. Many are guarded by a single light fixture adjacent to or immediately over the door—easily reached by the would-be intruder. Common practice is for a member of the staff to make a final check of the delivery entrance as the day shift leaves the building and the night shift begins its duties. After that, for a period of three or more hours, the door and its surroundings are left unguarded. In fact, unless the staff uses the delivery entrance as its exit after closing the building later that evening, the door may go unobserved until the first member of the staff enters the library the next morning.

Unfortunately for the purposes of security, the delivery door is most often equipped with the same lock used on other doors in the library. Unless protected by additional devices, such a door lock becomes easy prey.

The delivery entrance is part of the security picture in still another way for many libraries. It is a natural and easy avenue of escape, during and after hours. Because it often serves as a staff entrance, a certain amount of traffic is admitted through the door each day. Usually the delivery door opens onto an unattended and unguarded vestibule or corridor, so that a person entering here can quickly make his or her way elsewhere in the building. Nearly every librarian will admit to having found more than one "poor soul" who has gotten "lost" in the building and wandered into areas restricted to library personnel. Often, such occasions precede an unexplained loss of one kind or another. In one library, a very personable young man was bold enough to approach a librarian and admit that he had apparently wandered into the wrong part of the library—by mistake, of course—having assumed that the delivery entrance was a public entrance because he saw other (staff) using it as they returned from lunch. Hours later, staff lockers had been rifled, money had been taken from purses, and the custodian, who had vainly attempted to pursue the same youngster through the same delivery entrance, breathlessly related his story of having surprised the youth in the midst of the act.

Again, a comprehensive security system must safeguard the delivery entrance, using the full range of tactics: lights located out of reach, sophisticated locking devices, an alarm tied to the local police station as well as to the library's own security center, and perhaps a closed-circuit television camera trained on the door and its immediate surroundings.

In some libraries, procedures require that shipments of books and other library materials remain near the delivery entrance until they can be unpacked, invoiced, etc. A shipment received late in the day, or when the clerk responsible is otherwise engaged, may wait exposed for quite some time. Therefore, precautions should be taken to insulate this area and its contents from intrusion. Many a library shipment suffers loss at the hands of staff as well as unauthorized visitors to the delivery area. The vulnerability of the area can be reduced by enclosing the actual delivery room with either partitions or sliding screens, which can be locked when responsible staff are not present.

Finally, as in any building, the library's delivery entrance quite often serves as a staff entrance, as well as a required exit. The latter designation, of course, requires the use of panic hardware, which can be connected with an alarm system. However, because this entrance is used by the staff, the alarm mechanism on the doors is frequently disarmed during the day, rendering it useless. Even though a conscientious staff may remember to reset the device at closing time, it is all too often a local alarm, which may wail through the lonesome night hours without attracting attention. It is therefore essential that such alarm devices be tied to a central response agency.

The Book-return Slot—An Achilles' Heel

Long conscious of the need for "customer convenience," libraries have been concerned with supplying methods by which users may easily return library materials after hours. Devices vary from large slots opening into the building to curbside book returns. Some of the newer buildings have designed rather sophisticated book-return systems with materials being dropped into chutes which lead by gravity conveyor into lower-level recesses; there the items accumulate until they can be discharged and placed back on the shelves again. In recent years, a number of library buildings have suffered damage ranging from minor to total destruction resulting from the use of such openings by vandals and arsonists.

While there is an undeniable factor of convenience and efficiency attached to the traditional book slot located somewhere in the periphery of the structure, there is also increasing danger that it will be used for malevolent purposes. Therefore, designers of libraries are strongly encouraged to resist requests for this type of book return, substituting instead the free-standing curbside book-return unit, even though on busy weekends and holidays library personnel may have to be assigned to empty the container one or more times. Should the curbside book-return container be vandalized, the damage will at least be local in character, whereas the internal book return provides ready access to the library's interior for anyone using Molotov cocktails, bombs, or even water hoses.

As of this writing, one manufacturer of book-return equipment has sensed the potential danger of the internal book-return slot and has incorporated a "snuffing-out" device, which will prevent fires from most nonexplosive-type burning materials. When equipped with the proper chemical extinguisher, this book return has an even greater fire-extinguishing capacity. However, the "hole in the wall" still continues to be an opportunity for the planting of explosives and/or firebombs too powerful for such a device to extinguish.

If it becomes necessary to maintain an internal book-return slot, care should be taken to select hardware which can be secured during the hours of library operation. Failure to do so not only means that some of the people returning materials will continue to use the slot even though the library is open, it also creates a potential source of danger all the time people are in library. Since many of these slots are placed near the entrance, a fire initiated through the book slot will almost immediately involve the library's chief entrance, causing possible confusion and panic for those in the area.

Further, the area around the internal book drop should be isolated by fireproofed walls and equipped with smoke- and heat-sensing alarms and extinguishers. (See Fig. 8.) A floor drain will eliminate the problem of water and other liquids running into

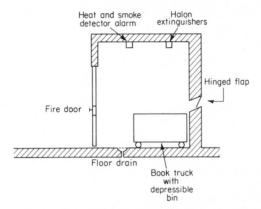

Fig. 8   Book return enclosure. It should be designed with 3-hour fire-resistive construction.

the library. When the cost of such a protective enclosure is excessive, serious consideration should be given to the aforementioned free-standing book-return units along the curb or walk, which maximize convenience for the borrower while eliminating the library's Achilles' heel.

Vaults and Safes

All but the smallest libraries should be equipped with some kind of safe, and larger libraries will require vaults varying in size with the amount and nature of the materials to be stored therein. In the smaller libraries, a standard safe capable of receiving the change drawer(s) from one or more cash registers, plus a few small cash receptacles, should be sufficient. The safe should be located in an area which can be reached by staff personnel at closing time without walking through public areas of the library and without entering spaces in which a would-be assailant might hide; often the person handling the money at the close of day is alone. Since library safes are frequent targets for attack by petty thieves, standard precautions should be taken regarding their location and protection against being forced open, etc. Interestingly enough, ingenious librarians who do not trust the obvious nature of a safe as the repository of cash receipts have long had considerable success in hiding funds in such secret places as hollowed-out books, between the pages of bound newspapers, etc. One librarian posted a record of never having lost a penny with such procedures over a long period of years, during which time the library's safe was repeatedly attacked!

Walk-in vaults are used in larger libraries to secure their valuable collections and display items. The size of such spaces should be determined by the nature and amount of materials to be protected. Librarians should be discouraged from using vaults, however, in lieu of safes, since doing so places the contents under double jeopardy. Unless otherwise required, vaults should be of 3-hr fire-resistant constructin, and the opening should have a suitable vault door with a combination lock. Sometimes the vault door is recessed behind an ordinary door to screen it from sight. Library vaults should be well lighted, with separate humidity and ventilation controls to keep the optimum humidity at about 45 to 55 percent and the temperature in the 65 to 75°F range. Where more valuable collections are concerned, this independent system should automatically be switched onto the library's emergency power service. The integrity of the vault should be carefully maintained by free-standing walls which, if possible, should be surrounded by a well-lighted corridor no wider than 3 ft to further deter vandals. Heat- and smoke-detection alarms should be installed in the ceiling, along with halon or some other fire-repressant chemical, which will be harmless to the vault's contents if released. Special attention should be made to avoid dampness and seepage if the vault is below grade. A greater quantity of rare library material succumbs to water than ever perishes by fire.

Custodial Rooms

Custodians are frequently relegated to spaces which are not useful for other purposes. Poorly planned and poorly located, these rooms can become overcrowded with supplies and cleaning equipment—some of it flammable. Often, custodians also operate and maintain the building's mechanical equipment, which results in accumulations of lubricants, refrigerants, and sometimes a pile of soiled, combustible rags. While librarians may monitor other staff work areas, all too few make any effort to regularly inspect custodial quarters. Storage and work areas for custodians should therefore include fire alarms and suppressant devices. Here again, chemical rather than water extinguishers should be used because of the likelihood that combustible materials will include petroleum and other products not susceptible to water extinguishment. One helpful preventative is to separate the janitorial storage area from the office/workshop room. If only supplies in current use are kept in the custodians' work area, fires are less apt to occur and will be confined to much smaller amounts of materials.

Strong emphasis should be given to the importance of a floor drain in the custodial area. Wherever custodians have access to mop sinks, basins, etc., floor drains should be mandatory, since without them negligence or faulty plumbing may well engulf the library during hours when the building is closed, possibly damaging or destroying large portions of the collections.

Coin-Operated Equipment

To satisfy library users' growing needs, coin-operated equipment is finding its way into libraries with increasing frequency; copy machines, pencil and pen dispensers, typewriters, and vending machines of various sorts are now commonplace. These are often the target of petty thieves who pilfer the change receptacles. Any safeguarding devices which are found useful elsewhere will probably serve the library. Location of this equipment will, of course, be a factor. Rental typewriters, often partially or totally secluded in study carrels or typing rooms, most often fall prey to the thief. Moving these to easily supervised sites can be a deterrent. Where librarians control the collection of receipts, the change boxes should be emptied each evening after business hours, leaving the coin box open. A sign on each machine stating that this procedure is followed will advise a potential thief that an after-hours raid on the vending-machine boxes will be useless.

The proliferation of coin-operated equipment and machines in libraries has increased the need for making change for customers. As a result, there is more money kept in various desks and counter drawers for the convenience of staff and public. Each of these is a temptation. Librarians should be persuaded to centralize all change-making operations where cash register control can be maintained, thereby avoiding additional caches of money. Where volume permits, the installation of change-making vending machines will alleviate this facet of the problem.

Mobile and Branch Libraries

Library branches, bookmobiles, and other extension agencies encounter many of the same problems as a main library. Because many such units serve neighborhoods with a high incidence of crime, problems are even more likely. In general, the same security precautions should be taken, tailored to the special nature of extension units. Of utmost importance is a suitable communications system. Perhaps the best is a short-wave radio network that encompasses the main library, all branches, and all mobile units. Emergency calls can then be made without hindrance from overloaded switchboards, busy lines, etc. Equally useful, the main library can broadcast emergency announcements simultaneously to all units. Such procedures are necessary when some type of disaster is imminent. The short-wave radio also gives the library system a communications network which can continue operating when telephone lines are incapacitated for any reason.

Elevators

In library buildings that have more than one floor, elevators of one kind or another become essential. At least one of these should be large enough to accept a person lying prone on a stretcher. While the dimensions of such an elevator cab may be greater than normally thought of for libraries, it is essential to provide adequate vertical transportation for swift evacuation of a person or persons from any floor in the building. All too often stretcher bearers or ambulance crews attempting to remove a stricken person from the building must resort to narrow stairwells in a life-or-death situation when every second counts.

Fire Extinguishers

Fire extinguishers can actually present a problem in many libraries. Often they are too large and heavy for women, who make up the majority of most staffs. Fear of using the wrong extinguisher (where more than one type is supplied) causes further concern and confusion. Therefore, selecting smaller extinguishers which can be used safely on any kind of fire, regardless of origin, should bring better results. These should be mounted on convenient brackets in places where fires are most apt to break out.

Emergency Light and Power

All libraries should have access to emergency power for essential lighting and other functions. When emergencies occur after dark, safe evacuation of the building is dependent upon at least a minimal level of illumination. In addition, alarm systems, sump pumps, communications systems, data-processing equipment, temperature and humidity machinery for vaults, and security control centers all require auxiliary power.

In libraries where auxiliary power equipment is not available, battery-operated emergency lighting should be supplied and circuited to turn on automatically whenever lights fail.

SECURITY OF LIBRARY COLLECTIONS

The security of library collections can be discussed in terms of the several major risks involved: (1) damage by water, (2) destruction by fire, (3) loss by theft and mutilation, and (4) damage by vermin. The degree of the risk will depend upon the type and size of the library, the nature of the collections, the characteristics of the community served, and the physical plant in which the collections are housed. Security measures found effective in one library will be apt to hold promise for any library facing similar problems.

Damage by Water

Water damage is a major threat to many library collections. The source may be a leaky roof, porous walls, stopped drains, inadequate plumbing, floods, vandalism, and so on. Extra care should be taken to waterproof library buildings in their entirety. Below-grade areas need special attention, since they are often used for book storage. Any evidence of a high water table must be taken as a warning that added precautions are needed. Floor drains should be required in every restroom, custodian's service area, and kitchen, or wherever other plumbing exists.

The salvage of water-damaged library materials was once almost impossible. In recent years, several major incidents have resulted in new methods which hold some promise for at least partial recovery, providing immediate efforts are made and the proper facilities are close at hand. These new procedures involve freezing water-damaged materials and storing them at temperatures of around 20°F. This stabilizes the damaged materials but does not, in itself, dry the paper or kill mold spores. However, it does provide time to assemble personnel for the laborious effort of reclaiming the materials and determining what method will be used. The problem and the new technique have been investigated by the Restoration Office of the Library of Congress, and a definitive monograph produced in 1975 may be used as the text on this subject.*

Destruction by Fire

Fire is another of the historic enemies of libraries. Although relatively few libraries are burned each year, the incidence is increasing—largely as a result of vandalism, overloaded electrical circuitry, and the use of aging structures with inadequate fire protection and alarm devices. While book collections are relatively slow to ignite under most circumstances, once on fire they may prove difficult to extinguish. Smoke damage from a smoldering fire can be almost as destructive as an open fire. Fires often begin elsewhere in a library, such as in equipment rooms, storage areas, or garages housing bookmobiles, vans, etc., which indicates the need for additional fire-suppressant measures in such areas.

All reasonable precautions should be taken in installing heat- and smoke-detection sensors and fire-extinguishing devices. On the whole, librarians have resisted the use of sprinkler systems over collection areas, arguing that the accidental discharge of a sprinkler, or a broken water line, is a greater threat to the collections than fire itself. New and more sophisticated designs, which tend to isolate the damage which can be done by any accidental discharge, may partially overcome this reticence. Wherever particularly valuable materials are housed which would be irreparably damaged or destroyed by water, other extinguishing agents such as halogen, carbon dioxide, dry chemicals, and high-expansion foam may be used.

In 1970, the National Fire Protection Association issued a special report from its Committee on Libraries, Museums, and Historic Buildings, which has much to offer in the way of advice on protecting libraries. Case histories of fires in libraries are cited, and numerous specific recommendations are made. This report, known as NFPA No. 910, is entitled *Protection of Library Collections* (1970) and can be procured from the National Fire Protection Association in Boston.

One of the observations made by the committee concerned the design of older library buildings, which often use multitiered stacks that create a natural flue, thereby making fire fighting an almost impossible task. While the chances of any contempo-

---

*Peter Waters, *Procedures for Salvage of Water-damaged Library Materials.* This pamphlet can be secured from the Library of Congress, Washington, D.C.

rary and well-designed library structure falling victim to fire may seem remote, precautions should nevertheless be taken in building design to facilitate fire fighting if necessary. Fire fighters should encounter no unnecessary obstacles in entering the library during an emergency. All standpipes should be readily available to provide reliable and effective streams in the shortest possible time. Above all, the fire alarm system, equipped with both heat and smoke detectors, should be wired directly to the responsible fire station's control board, eliminating any human delay or failure to report a fire. Frequent inspection and testing of all fire alarm and suppressant systems should be done routinely by qualified individuals to ensure that all is in readiness. Hand extinguishers should be recharged annually, all hose lines checked, and water pressure in the standpipes monitored. Above all, library staff should be trained in emergency procedures required to combat a small blaze, evacuate the premises, and otherwise follow procedures established by the local fire department in conformance with good practice.

Loss by Theft and Mutilation

There is little doubt that library collections have always been susceptible to pilferage and mutilation. Today, libraries are suffering greater losses than most care to admit; these seem to be at least partly attributable to the decline in respect for public and personal property.

Theft The materials most prone to loss are almost entirely determined by the purpose of the thief. Some seek first editions or other rare books to add to their own collections. Others steal items which they can convert to cash. Some take books which they want to use in their vocations or avocations, such as car repair manuals (almost always a high-loss item), expensive recipe books, music scores, dictionaries, and other reference books. By stealing the library's copy, others seek to avoid the cost and inconvenience of purchasing a book. Students, driven to the library by assignments and a host of other circumstances, may be tempted to steal materials and thereby have them readily available in their studies for as long as they wish without incurring overdue fines. No doubt some people steal from the library because it seems like an easy target and a symbol of "the establishment."

Detection of people pilfering the library collections was noted in the discussion about circulation desk control earlier in this chapter. Historically, it has been assumed that sharp-eyed personnel at the circulation desk would readily detect and apprehend anyone attempting to leave the library with materials not properly signed for. Numerous studies have proved otherwise. The location of circulation desks, the preoccupation of personnel with other duties, and a reticence to confront suspicious-looking individuals seriously limit this "first line of defense."

Fortunately, in response to this need and as an outgrowth of other related applications of technology, several manufacturers have introduced detection systems within the past decade or so. These systems utilize a sensitized material, imbedded in the book by one means or another, which activates a warning system if an attempt is made to remove the book without going through proper checkout procedures, which reverse the sensitivity of the sensor. Most libraries find the system practical, but extremely expensive to retro-fit, except on those volumes which are presumed to be the most frequent candidates for theft. In normal practice, cost-effectiveness of such detective systems dictates their use only when operational costs do not exceed a realistic estimate of annual loss through theft. Since these systems continue to be modified, it would be useless to describe them in detail here. However, a consumer-type analysis of the various systems is available as a result of a study undertaken in 1974 and published as a part of *Library Technology Reports* by the American Library Association; its title is "Theft Detection Systems for Libraries: A Survey."

While there is some variation among the manufacturers, these theft detection systems all have about the same impact on the design of the circulation desk area.

Each requires the user to pass between the desk and a screen, which may be disguised as a low partition between desks. Depending on the system, certain equipment of fairly minimal size must be accommodated at the circulation desk. Technological changes have already introduced modifications of equipment, so that anything other than these general details would be misleading. Obviously, the design for any given library's circulation desk must be worked out in accordance with the requirements of the particular detection system employed. The detection systems are sometimes used in conjunction with turnstiles or gates of some sort to further regulate traffic.

For all of their value in reducing normal thievery, book detection systems are of no help in apprehending those who avoid the circulation desk by illegally using other exits from the building. Libraries have been known to lose significant runs of material from secluded areas of the library which happened to have a nearby emergency exit, a window, or some other convenient opening. To prevent such losses, all openings in the library's perimeter walls through which materials and/or people can pass must be secured by appropriate means. Doors on required exits should be equipped with alarm-sounding panic hardware and monitored by closed-circuit television. Motion-sensing devices can be used in areas such as vaults for rare books.

Mutilation   None of the collection safeguards mentioned to this point deal with another serious library problem, namely, the mutilation of materials by users in the library. The extent of the loss sustained by libraries through mutilation is unknown, but it is sizable. Ingenious but simple devices incorporating bits of razor blades make it relatively simple to cut pictures, tables, even entire pages from books and other printed materials. More than one library has found sections missing from microfilm, audio tapes, motion pictures, and other materials—all cut out in the same manner. While art books, with their numerous illustrations, seem the most logical candidates for such treatment, nothing seems exempt. Colorful passages from books of fiction, extensive tables from technical texts, recipes in books and magazines, contest blanks and other reply forms in newspapers and periodicals, and pictures from every source are cut, torn, or otherwise taken from their source.

Since it is doubtful that any economically feasible solution will be forthcoming in the next few years, the prevention of mutilation boils down to visual detection by library personnel. Although they are usually vigilant, library staff members are necessarily preoccupied with their normal duties. Besides, visibility is frequently impaired by the structural elements or ranges of shelving. Therefore, the layout of the furnishings within the library building should conform to the necessity for good visual control from each staff desk. Where blind spots are unavoidable, mirrors or closed-circuit video cameras should be used. The location of staff desks should not require personnel to turn their backs on readers using library materials. These measures, though seemingly elementary, remain the best available at this time.

Destruction by Vermin

The bookworm is not a mythological being; it lives, and in all too many libraries. So do other pests and vermin, which feed on books and/or make their homes in them. Especially susceptible are library collections of less frequently used materials. Often located in dark areas of the library, such portions of the collections sometimes remain relatively undisturbed over fairly long spans of time, providing plenty of opportunity for all sorts of vermin to wreak their havoc.

The bookworm, itself, is any of several species of moths or beetles that feed on book bindings, paste, etc. Where termites are prevalent, they can be even more of a problem, tunneling their way through volume after closely packed volume with little noticeable evidence. Rodents love to make nests in dark bookshelving, while finding newspapers, magazines, and open books an ideal source for nesting materials.

Designing structures which inhibit such pests is not easy. Obviously, every precaution reasonably possible should be taken. These include tight joints between floors and walls and tight-fitting closures around all openings in the building. Since light is one of the natural enemies of most of these pests, illumination by windows or artificial light is essential. Where termites are a known threat, shelving should have an open base and be elevated 4 in or more from the floor to provide a maximum amount of air circulation. The natural inclination of librarians to place shelving along walls should be avoided. This will also help with moisture seepage problems occurring along walls by enabling quick detection. Dehumidification equipment should be installed in the ventilation system where mold is a problem.

To these measures, of course, must be added the continuing surveillance by personnel acquainted with the tell-tale signs left by the various pests. Early detection and the use of appropriate pesticides, etc., should keep destruction of the book collection by vermin to a minimum.

PERSONAL SECURITY OF LIBRARY STAFF AND USERS

The security of staff and library users against possible attack has been mentioned a number of times in this chapter. The dangers inherent in a library building are somewhat greater, perhaps, than in some public and commercial buildings because of the very nature of the library atmosphere. Library staff are, on the whole, trained to be responsive to users. Therefore, the public is encouraged to roam at will through the reading rooms and the book stacks. Busy at their assigned duties, staff members seldom take more than passing note of most who enter and leave the building, unless they indicate some need for assistance. Library users often stay for extended periods of time within the stack areas and/or reading areas as they pursue their searches. Therefore, what might be considered as "loitering" elsewhere may be quite normal behavior in a library. The library provides a "neutral" atmosphere with a minimum of surveillance, making few demands on individuals to identify themselves or otherwise breach the cloak of anonymity. Unless people disrupt the library in some manner, they are usually welcome for as many hours as they care to stay. Those intent on covert activities find the maze of shelving both a shelter and a convenient shield for escape. Having completed their business, such individuals can avert suspicion by quickly becoming one of the readers intent on some research at a nearby reading table—or can escape down an unguarded exit, if walking past staff desks and the circulation counter seems risky.

The remedies that suggest themselves have already been described elsewhere in this chapter. They include (1) careful arrangement of stacks and other furnishings to maximize visual supervision and (2) the use of mirrors, CCTV, and other aids to eliminate blind spots. Silent-alarm buttons should be installed where staff can use them quickly and safely.

A major security problem for library staff involves the closing of the building at the end of the evening. In many cases, substantial portions of the building which have been vacated by the day shift hours before must be entered. Since such areas may be susceptible to entry by intruders, staff must be particularly cautious. Light switches which can be turned on outside the room—perhaps at a panel—offer good protection. If doors to staff workrooms are equipped with small windows, a staff member can see into much of the area before entering.

Finally, staff security is very much involved when personnel leave the building at night. The path taken to a corner bus stop or to a parking area should be fully illuminated. Shrubbery, etc., which could conceal a possible assailant should be eliminated, and planting adjacent to bus stops, passenger delivery and pickup zones, and parking lots should be kept low—no higher than 2 ft or so. Such shrubbery should include abundant specimens of thorny plants to further discourage hiding.

Any exterior lighting which is intended to be turned off after the library is vacated should be placed on a time clock to provide the staff ample time to leave the building and the grounds—a half hour's delay will mean little in extra energy consumption, but everything to security of personnel.

THE SECURITY OFFICE OR CONTROL CENTER

As libraries increase their security equipment to cope with the multifaceted security threats they face, it becomes important to provide appropriate space for centralizing the security systems. In the smaller library, the necessary security and communications equipment can probably be accommodated in a relatively small area, perhaps combined with some compatible use. Larger libraries will probably find it important to centralize their security and communications systems in a separate office or control center.

This space should be toward the interior of the building, preferably below grade in a multilevel building. Protected by reinforced concrete walls, floors, and ceiling, this room can become the command post in time of emergency as well as an efficient routine operations center. This office should house a full range of communications equipment, including two or more means of communication, such as telephone, public address, and short-wave radio. Obviously, it must have access to adequate power from an auxiliary generator. If the room is staffed regularly, a lavatory and toilet should be included. Direct lines must be provided to key emergency stations, such as control centers for police, fire, hospitals, and civil defense offices.

In designing the security office, the concept of its being the "nerve and command" center for the library in times of crisis should be borne in mind. Larger libraries will want to staff these stations on a 24-hr/day basis. While no specific threshold of size can be named, libraries larger than 50,000 to 75,000 ft² in area should consider providing a separate security room of this sort.

CONCLUSION

The security of library buildings is a complex problem worthy of full attention of security experts. Because of the nature and extent of security risks which seem inherent in libraries, the adaptation of sophisticated security tools provided by today's technology should be welcome. However, certain basic and relatively simple safeguards are available now, such as well-designed buildings, use of vandal-resistant materials, careful layout of furnishings to maximize visual supervisory control by staff, and thorough staff training. When combined in the proper proportions, these elements should produce an effective security defense posture for most libraries.

Chapter 29

Multiple Housing: Security through Environmental Design

GEORGE RAND, Ph.D.*

University of California at Los Angeles, School of Architecture and Urban Planning

Nothing has proved quite as important in the development of multiple housing, and yet has been as overlooked, as the provision of security for residents. Despite increasing crime rates and new motivating concern about added economic risks of new housing ventures stemming from potential disruption by crime, basic lessons continue to be ignored. We continue to build new residential facilities in ways that discount the importance of social development objectives. We fail to deal seriously with the issues of anonymity that cuts residents off from natural social control mechanisms which would otherwise be at their disposal. All around the country, we have inherited a legacy of large apartment developments, especially in the public housing area, in which the level of anonymity and social instability equals that intended for transient hotel facilities.

Over the past few years we have come to recognize that these large-scale facilities are severe social and economic risks. In an increasing number of instances, otherwise physically sound multiple-housing developments (notably Pruitt-Igoe in St. Louis) have turned into virtual armed camps under siege of anarchy. Less dramatic evidence exists everywhere that multiple-housing developments on the urban fringe or in transitional communities fail to provide residents with a sufficient sense of order and stability to survive as settlements.

*Professor Rand was co-principal investigator with Oscar Newman on grants received from the Institute of Law Enforcement and Criminal Justice, LEAA, and the New York State Office of Crime Control Planning in 1969–1970 for early studies of crime prevention and environmental design. Assistance with illustrations by Gary Swift is gratefully acknowledged.

FOUR THEORIES OF CRIME PREVENTION THROUGH ENVIRONMENTAL DESIGN

What seems evident to all those concerned with the development of multiple housing is that industrially conceived solutions have produced some secondary side effects which are undesirable. Crimes among strangers are, in part, a simple by-product of the numbers of unacquainted people who come in close physical contact with one another in these industrially conceived structures. Appropriate guidelines can be developed to avoid the negative secondary consequences in the future, and existing communities can be redesigned to achieve relief in the present.

Indeed, the provision of residences for mass populations is intimately tied to the development of factories. The earliest prototype worker residences were built by industries to provide simple and efficient flats in which workers could live when not on the job. Likewise, introduction of time schedules and of work days (the nine-to-five job) was part of an integrated conception of life in a mass society. This concept did not include time at home for pastoral tasks like gardening or for efforts to expand earnings through cottage industries.

It should be apparent that it is not housing per se which produces the negative side effects, but the principles of social order that housing designs reflect. Likewise, in mounting a strategy for attacking crime in the streets one cannot approach every aspect of society at once. We begin with housing because it offers a place to begin. Obviously, the impact of redesigned residental communities will eventually be felt in the workplace, in the school, on the transportation system, etc., all of which will eventually undergo like transformations. Several key theories of multiple-housing design to provide security will be briefly reviewed.

Social Control Theory   The "social control" model is suggested by Jane Jacobs's well-known portrayal of New York's Greenwich Village. She pointed out that a city street is populated with strangers. Nonetheless, streets remain under a form of functional surveillance which results from the diversity of uses one finds in truly urban settings. Business establishments provide persons with a proprietary interest in the street directly in front of them. In addition, stores give people a reason for using the streets, that is, they create a flow of pedestrians. Jacobs's view of the role of commercial facilities reversed the notion that these intensely public areas attracted crime. Indeed, a proprietor accustomed to handling all types of abnormal situations acts, on balance, as a security asset rather than providing an incentive for prospective criminals. Elderly people and marginal "street characters" may, indeed, turn out to be beneficial in reducing crime simply by their presence on the street or their ability to respond to strange behavior. This reverses the traditional image of a person who inhabits the street from vagrant to street watcher.

Enclave–Access-Control Theory   This theory suggests that the environment can be designed to discourage the access of prospective criminals to potential victims or items of value. Airports provide total security with respect to the unauthorized carrying of weapons or dangerous materials. Large suburban shopping plazas employ this approach by performing implicit checks on the behavior of pedestrians prior to entry. While these centers are treated as if they are in the public domain, their physical organization actually limits entrance of undesirable pedestrians and acts as a closed street. Lobby attendants in large apartment complexes and guards monitoring walled-in communities serve the role of gatekeepers. Residential applications of this system are numerous, varying as they do from simple door buzzers and intercom systems to complex alarm and intrusion-detection systems. Once good security is provided at the perimeter of a community or a multi-occupancy residence, the potential for positive social interaction within the community is multiplied. The problems are (1) that this can only be done effectively within a homogeneous community, otherwise the potential perpetrators of crime would already be inside the community, and (2) the formation of enclaves leaves the streets outside the community devoid of positive activity and social life. For these reasons, enclave approaches are only partial solutions. While these create safe zones under the sponsorship and control of a local group, they leave large sections of the city as undeclared wastelands.

Criminal Justice Theory   This approach focuses on the presence of police as a primary deterrent to crime. It suggests a form of environmental design in which standards of lighting and access are maintained so as to provide optimal conditions for police patrols. In essence the approach focuses on crime prevention through making prospective criminals aware of the presence of public authority.

For example, a number of police departments around the country are involved in the review of multi-occupancy housing plans at an early stage of their formation. This is typical of a police-oriented evaluation, with questions being asked such as: "Will police be able to achieve access by car or foot patrol to the area?"

All entrances to residential buildings are clearly marked and lighted. Streets are simplified and street angles symmetrized in order to provide clear, unambiguous access. Where possible, emergency lanes do not end in cul-de-sacs; they provide an opportunity for patrol cars to pass through all areas casually, to maintain informal surveillance over an area as well as responding to actual calls for help. If possible, stair halls and elevators should be well lit and exposed to view from the street, especially from passing patrol cars.

The criminal justice model is based on the professional skill of the policeman at briefly yet thoroughly scanning a large area that he passes through very quickly.

Defensible-Space Theory   This approach suggests that crime is less likely when potential antisocial acts are framed in a physical space that is under observation by others. The effect of simple observation as a mechanism of social control is greatly increased when observers know one another, or when they are linked together by means of some common territorial marker. The theory goes on to suggest that would-be criminals are more reluctant to commit crimes in the areas which are perceived to be under the territorial influences of a surrounding community.*

Implicitly the theory suggests that a large number of crimes among the unacquainted are spontaneous crimes in response to opportunities that present themselves in anonymous settings. Like enclave–access-control approaches, denfensible-space theory suggests that bounding of an area near residences allows people who live in those residences to feel more of a sense of properietorship over that space. This is the most psychological of the four approaches to crime prevention through environmental design. It suggests that within our culture there are rules of territoriality that reflect a code through which we give individual and collective meaning to the environment.

Whereas security achieved under the enclave-access model is literal (the elimination of hand guns at the airport, for example), the security achieved as a result of defensible-space theory is symbolic. By creating multiple opportunities for surveillance and for the development of patterns of mutual accountability, the defensibly designed environment discourages crime by making people feel that they are known to others and will be held to account for their behavior.

THE SEARCH FOR NEW MULTIPLE-HOUSING PROTOTYPES

Tailormade for Crime: Brownsville/Van Dyke

In the early 1970s the results of a 3-year effort were published which were initiated by Oscar Newman and the author with the New York City Housing Authority to study

*Cf. Oscar Newman, *Defensible Space,* Macmillan, New York, 1971.

TABLE 1   Place of Occurrence of Crimes in Buildings of Different Heights

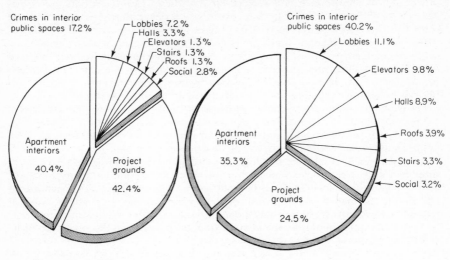

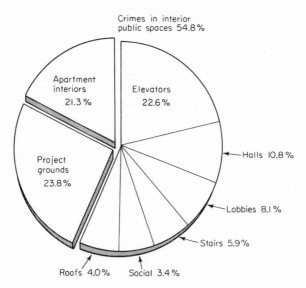

SOURCE: New York City Housing Authority Police, 1969 data (felonies).

the impact of housing design on crime and vandalism.* At the time crime had already become a problem of great magnitude. Perhaps the most convincing evidence, in that it provided the incentive for massive studies on the New York Housing Authority projects, was a comparison made of two public housing facilities directly across the street from one another in Brooklyn's Ocean Hill–Brownsville section.

One project, Brownsville Homes, was comprised of twenty-seven six-story buildings with three-story wings. It occupied 19 acres of land and was built at a design density of 287 persons per acre. In this project there happened to be many areas suitable for shared relaxation or recreation which had been included at times intentionally, often by accident. These convivial areas recalled older, more traditional styles of residences. Floor halls were organized so that three families shared a landing. Residents were encouraged by the small scale to leave their doors ajar while children played in the halls. These three-apartment subunits were then connected vertically to the rest of the building by open stairwells. Building entrances were under surveillance from windows above, and they in turn were used to frame informal outer courts along the street edge. Dotting the interior zones of the project were small courtyards, separated and sheltered from the public sidewalk by the buildings. A relatively small number of families and their guests used each entrance because outside areas were sheltered from passersby and under the surveillance and control of tenants in the building.

Van Dyke Houses, directly across the street, was a project consisting of twenty-three buildings, thirteen of which were high-rise (fourteen stories with seven units on each floor). Each hall had its apartment units lined up in a marching geometric progression with no apparent concern for establishing a congenial atmosphere in these larger, more public hall zones. At the ground level, buildings were sited largely on the basis of the geometry of the total area plan and not in an effort to create "friendly" outdoor spaces which would promote a sense of safety and territorial sanctity among the users.

Otherwise these two projects were almost identical. For example, they occupied equal total acreage; they were built at equal design density. (Van Dyke and Brownsville both have 288 persons per acre.) Discovering these projects side by side provided an opportunity that would ordinarily be present only in a prearranged laboratory experiment. Both projects serve persons with very low incomes, mainly black families with comparable profiles of family instability, broken homes, and extensive support by public assistance. The two building styles—Brownsville's *clustered, traditional,* and *convivial* style on the one hand versus Van Dyke's *linear, modern,* and *formal* style on the other—provided a simple theoretical contrast and allowed for a careful dissection of the behavioral implications of these very specific features of the environments.

Detailed investigation of these projects by Oscar Newman and his team revealed over and over that design differences had a predictable impact on the behaviors which occur in the contrasting environments. Everyone who had contact with the projects (for example, police, managers, maintenance personnel, and the tenants themselves) agreed that Brownsville "felt better to be in" than Van Dyke. The reduced scale of contact, intimately framed entrances, and convivial halls make people feel that they are known by their neighbors and heighten their awareness of the presence of strangers. These intuitive judgments are supported in detail by objective measures: Van Dyke turnover rates are higher, maintenance costs for Van Dyke are considerably greater, and the rates of crime in Van Dyke are greater than in Brownsville in almost all crime categories that are pertinent to differences in design (e.g., crimes outside apartment units).

The meaning of these results is plain: Van Dyke is chosen more frequently as the site for criminal activity when choice is possible; the environment shapes the opportunities which people have or do not have for developing a sense of shared purpose

*Ibid.

and for exhibiting their will to collectively secure their common living environment. The design of Van Dyke Houses drives people further into isolation by diminishing the number of opportunities they have for exchanging news, trading courtesies, or sharing responsibilities for child care, shopping, etc. While these designs do not cause crime per se, they set in motion a vicious cycle of indifference and alienation which results in crime-proneness.

Outside his apartment door, a typical Van Dyke tenant finds individuals or groups of people he does not recognize. If he has seen their faces before, he does not know what their relationship is to the apartments they enter or to other people in his world. This sets in motion a self-fulfilling prophecy. On her arrival home, another tenant finds a stranger standing in the hall or emerging inexplicably from the stairwell. Apartment units have small viewers so they may look out, but doors are placed on opposite sides along the length of long corridors. At best, residents can see only the door across the way.

As a result, one is likely to know only a few residents by name even over an eight- or ten-year period. Interchanges are relatively formal and infrequent, and they provide few opportunities for those casual remarks which lead to serendipitous discoveries and a sense of belonging to a peer group or a community.

In Brownsville Houses, the situation is very different. Strangers immediately feel a need to explain their presence. More tenants habituate floor landings and the outside courts; they maintain casual surveillance over the areas through apartment windows placed close to the entrances. The fact that one encounters fewer people, but the same people over and over, leads people to recognize others more readily and to develop more extensive forms of mutual dependence.

These diverse trends in the low-rise Brownsville project versus the high-rise Van Dyke project are reinforced by the administration and the project management. They immediately conclude that the high-rise project needs externally dictated and centralized management, planning, and control. The imposition of centralized planning further narrows the range of motivations tenants have to be active "shapers of their own community." In turn, this reduces trust and loyalty, increases the sense of arbitrariness concerning directions made from above, and produces a profound sense of alienation. Alienated tenants at this point appear to management to be poorly motivated, incompetent, restive, and recalcitrant. This further reinforces management's notion of the need for centralized planning and control. Once again a vicious cycle of negative feedback is set in motion.

Environments which intend to build a positive consensus discover within their midst a variety of opportunities to make people feel safe. For example, feedback systems are needed to communicate to people exactly where crimes have occurred and under what circumstances, so that a contagion of fear does not spread all over the neighborhood. Under such a system, professional knowledge currently held by police would be passed on freely, as a matter of course, to the people in the community. Also, information on emergency life-saving procedures and principles of self-defense would be made widely available.

In other countries diverse conventions have evolved to fulfill these needs. In France, for example, the role of the concierge remains well established as a kind of hotel clerk for apartment dwellers. In Spain, the serreño or gatekeeper is the guardian of residential streets—not unlike our colonial "town crier." Traditionally he carried keys for all the people who lived on the street and opened their gate when they entered their court.

New Responsibilities of Developers

The upshot of this approach to crime control suggests important developmental objectives to people who would invest in the building of new multi-occupancy communities. First, it is important to recognize that the provision of security hardware by itself or personnel devoted to security control may not be sufficient to reduce crime. In fact, there are many reasons to believe that this type of "target hardening" may make buildings or projects more desirable to criminals. Once a reasonably large housing development (say 200 to 400 families) begins to deteriorate, no matter what provisions have been made for security control, it is prone to a rapid decline, a downward spiraling of community consciousness and collective concern.

In addition to providing adequately for the traditional concerns of multiple housing, the new developer has to consider a number of subtle variables which will determine, to a considerable degree, whether the community develops a sense of local identity and a willingness to participate in the security of their shared environment. These criteria are vague and hard to measure. For each building type there is a set of critical design features which have to be addressed with special care and with recognition of the social consequences of these design elements. The remainder of this chapter will be concerned with the identification of those architectural or design elements which enhance or retard positive social communication.

It is not being claimed that these design elements directly determine the character and stability of the community, or that there are not other ways of achieving stability—for example, new management practices, clubs and associations, and so on. Architectural design features reflect the ordinary, everyday assumptions which people have about one another. They must be observed with special care as potential sources of either threats to the continued equilibrium of the community or critical opportunities for the community to realize important aspirations.

These critical features of each building type constitute the regular, conventional, everyday world which residents experience themselves to be sharing. Conceivably, under highly extraordinary conditions, security could be achieved through general participation of the public in patrols or parapolice actions to combat crime. These efforts transcend environmental design approaches and would be effective across a wide range of settings in the community. Crime prevention through environmental design communicates and specifies the degree to which a community needs to be aware of and concerned about crime as part of the everyday world. Target-hardening approaches are typically introduced when a community has reached the point where it is willing to give up a large measure of the complexity and spontaneity of the everyday urban world in order to achieve security alone.

What the author would suggest is that a certain amount of positive security, using locks and basic anti-intrusion systems, serves very important social-communication functions. It makes clear existing rules of access and egress and eliminates doubt as to the identification of ownership and proprietorship. Beyond these largely symbolic functions, the use of locks and other electronic surveillance and detection devices does not guarantee success, especially against the professional criminal.

Where these critical symbolic features of design have been ignored, a crime problem has often appeared unnecessarily. For example, some projects with underground parking garages provide only indirect access to halls at grade level. In one building several women were raped on their way home from the parking garage. This led to a massive exodus from an otherwise effective project for families with children, since the building had a preponderance of women living alone (with their children) who depended on one another for social and functional support in raising their families. The error could easily have been avoided through design analysis, by realizing that women would be vulnerable along these darkened paths at night. Parking could have been divided into smaller areas, only partially underground and within view of some of the residences.

As another example, simply turning a door 45° away from the street for decorative reasons makes a lobby a fearsome place to enter, since intruders who may be lying in wait cannot be seen on approach. A small, optional design feature like this can have significant long-term effects.

Spontaneous Anonymous Groups

It is no longer possible to view the control of crime through environmental design as a simple mechanical matter to be carried out by formula and prescription. While some alleviation is possible through target-hardening approaches, this is frequently at the expense of personal freedom for users of a development and at the sacrifice of the positive supervision which residents might have exercised over other parts of the city beyond the housing development's boudaries. Displaced crimes are those which have been moved from enclave–access-controlled areas to the city beyond these controlled zones. The more the city is divided into enclave–access-controlled zones, the less safe are the dwindling areas beyond these zones of protection. Eventually, this process eats into the fabric of the city and reaches a limit in its applicability. The problem with enclave–access-control theory is that it is fashioned out of functional reasons for buildings communities. It neglects the symbolic capacity of residents and the symbolic organization of the city. It is this system of symbolism to which we will now turn.

The eye of the criminal searches for inconsistency and ambiguity. As surely and stealthily as an animal searches for its prey, the would-be criminal scans the environment for any sign of defect or vulnerability. It is a constant search. Every element of the environment, each door, each lock, each walkway, is tested visually or manually, at some time or other. In multi-occupancy housing developments, these informal inspections take place all the time. Where a poor lock on the door, a removable hinge, or a window near a front-door lock for easy break-in is a serious error in a single home, in an apartment development it can be the cause of twenty or more burglaries.

Simply assuming that the environment is being tested for its vulnerability all the time can produce a radical change in perspective. In the past, many housing developments were designed from a twofold perspective. First, the building or project was viewed as a bearer of marketing imagery, as a secondary advertisement for itself—what life-style or income category did it suggest? Second, the building or project was assayed in terms of the attractive features it offered the consumer once inside the apartment.

Now one must add to these considerations (1) the sense of vulnerability which the building and its residents display to prospective criminals, (2) the role of the project in enhancing security in the surrounding area, and (3) the access which the building provides to other concerned neighbors, to police, and to formal authorities.

As well as a sensitivity to the physical vulnerability of a particular environment experienced criminals understand the stages in the development of an individual or group sense of emergency—they are sensitive to the psychological aspect of environmental vulnerability. They know that people first have to notice the event, then interpret its meaning, then begin to examine their personal responsibility for interceding in the event, and finally implement some course of action. They also know, as studies of bystander behavior have indicated, that few people who clearly witness a crime (e.g., stealing a case of beer from a liquor store) will report the crime, even with prompting by officials. A classic demonstration of this sort of situation occurred with the looting that took place during New York City's 1977 blackout.

In all these instances, the criminal is trading on anonymity and the inability for group consciousness to evolve. Group consciousness does not require any preknowledge in order to occur. It is as natural to people as the functions of language or art. Each of us has a built-in capacity to sense and respond to this kind of group consciousness.

The security of housing communities is highly correlated with the number of social and spatial settings in the community in which the formation of "spontaneous anonymous groups" is possible. Group formation in traditional terms (based on kinship or formal organizations) is far less complex and can be easily explained, but the spontaneous form of social agreement described here is difficult to predict and impossible to create by intentional design. Nonetheless, "groups" are formed all the time by people who fully intend to remain strangers to one another. They come into being in response to an intrusion or threat and tend to last only as long as an emergency or shared opportunity exists. While we may not be able to design or manage these groups systematically, it is possible to identify ways to create environmental conditions under which their probability of occurrence is heightened:

1. *Reduce the scale of housing developments to allow perception of residents based on "appearance."* Encourage "recognition" of others, as opposed to social relationships. The effective size of a functional unit (e.g., a hall or building) should be maintained below that point at which people respond to "typifications" of others rather than vaguely recognized but distinctive features of other individuals.

2. *Create opportunities for leaving, "opting out," or expressing discomfort with the setting.* "Spontaneous anonymous groups" cannot be subscribed to or joined, as can a club or organization. Nonetheless, neighbors in an apartment building indicate by their daily demeanor, their attitude, or their posture what they expect their future role to be should some "troubles" occur.

When troubles do occur, it is important to have had the opportunity to declare intentions in advance. Being friendly or accessible to others brings with it the expectation that you can be relied upon in the normal course as troubles of one kind or another erupt. People also need the opportunity to declare their unwillingness to participate, rather than encouraging others to believe their fates are intertwined when, in fact, they are not.

3. *Employ unambiguous spatial boundaries.* Crimes serve as an occasion for the temporary formation of *spatial boundaries, zones of use, and paths of exclusive access.* As the danger recedes, these distinctions become less critical and are violated more and more. Just as "spontaneous anonymous groups" need to be able to form and unform themselves in response to "troubles," environments require this flexibility. Well-designed environments "indicate" in advance of "troubles" their capability for responding to these unusual events. They are also capable of dissolving these boundaries once the threat has disappeared.

CRITICAL CRIME ENVIRONMENT FEATURES

Environmental design is an advance statement of social intentions. The structure and appearance of the setting frames the will of a community or group. The visual nature of the physical setting is taken by strangers, passersby, and would-be criminals as a sign of the willingness of residents as a group to respond to "troubles," to monitor and control strange or unusual happenings in and around their buildings. These advance messages are carried by a wide variety of building features, architectural elements, and administrative practices and policies. There is no single prototype multiple-housing development which communicates beyond doubt the willingness of a group to respond to "troubles." Crime deterrence results from environmental communication—everything from almost invisible window locks to high fences and controlled perimeters. The aggregate effect of these small messages which follow is an overall responsivity of the environment to perturbation by crime.

These subsystems will be classified according to the following categories:

1. Sociotechnical security and perimeter control
2. Positive exterior areas
3. Semipublic areas
4. Large-scale organizational features
5. Social communications systems
6. Multiple-use project plans
7. Management innovation

These are not intended to be presented as a catalog of tested techniques for alleviating problems resulting from crime. Rather, they are offered as a symbolic language, a way of using architecture and project planning to communicate to members of a multi-occupancy development regarding the type of setting in which they live, to suggest the openness of the setting to change and transformation, despite the lack of commitment by residents to become "members" of formal organizations. At a different level, however, this catalog of environmental recommendations suggests informal, spontaneous settings to achieve social control without the burden of permanent affiliation. These categories with suggested preventive measures, are illustrated in Figs. 1 through 39, which follow.

REFERENCES

1. Angel, Shlomo, "Discouraging Crime Through City Planning," Institute of Urban and Regional Development, University of California, 1968 (Working Paper No. 75).
2. California Council on Criminal Justice, Crime Specific Burglary Program, *Residential Burglary and What to Do About It,* CCCJ Bulletin, 1972.
3. Jacobs, Jane, *The Death and Life of Great American Cities,* Random House, New York, 1961.
4. Jeffry, C. Ray, *Crime Prevention Through Environmental Design,* Sage Publications, Beverly Hills, 1971.
5. Malt, Harold Lewis, "Tactical Analysis of Street Crime," Final Report, LEAA Grant No. NI-71-091-G, 1973 (available in the LEAA Library). Also by the smae author, *Furnishing the City,* McGraw-Hill, New York, 1970.
6. National Clearinghouse for Criminal Justice Planning and Architecture, University of Illinois, Urbana, Ill. (Frederic Moyer, Project Director), "Guidelines for the Planning and Design of Regional and Community Correctional Centers for Adults," 1971; "Guidelines for the Planning and Design of Police Programs and Facilities," 1973.
7. Newman, Oscar, *Defensible Space,* Macmillan, New York, 1972; "Architectural Design for Crime Prevention," U.S. Government Printing Office, Washington, D.C., 1973 (Stock No. 027-000-00161-1); *Improving Residential Security, A Design Guide* (HUD paper under a LEAA grant), U.S. Government Printing Office, Washington, D.C., 1973 (Stock No. 2300-00251); *Design Guidelines for Achieving Defensible Space* (LEAA grant paper), U.S. Government Printing Office, Washington, D.C., 1976 (Stock No. 027-000-00395-8).
8. Rainwater, Lee, "Fear and the House-as-Haven in the Lower Class," *Journal of the American Institute of Planning,* 1966; also by the same author, *Behind Ghetto Walls: Black Family Life in a Federal Slum,* Aldine-Atherton, Chicago, 1970.
9. Reppetto, Thomas A., *Residential Crime,* Ballinger, Cambridge, MA, 1974.
10. Tien and T. A. Reppetto, *CPTED Annotated Bibliography* (LEAA grant paper, 1975, to be published).
11. ———, *Crime/Enforcement Targets* (LEAA grant paper, 1974, to be published).
12. Wood, Elizabeth, "Housing Design, A Social Theory," in G. Bell and J. Tyrwhitt (eds.), *Human Identity in Urban Environments,* Penguin Books, New York, 1973; also by the same author, *Social Aspects of Housing and Urban Development,* United Nations, New York, 1967.

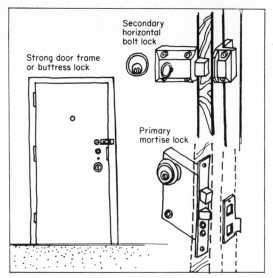

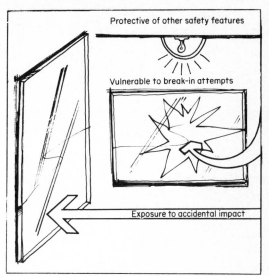

Fig. 1 Positive Locks. An optimum-performance lock apparatus should always be employed. Many states are now mandating more stringent codes and require deadbolt locks and/or prohibit poorly constructed jambs or hollow-core doors. In addition to providing easier access for burglars or would-be trespassers, inadequate locks and poorly constructed door systems decrease the sense of security of residents and make it less likely for them, because of their own sense of vulnerability, to respond in ways which inhibit crime.

Fig. 2 Durable Glass. Broken glass acts as a catalyst for crime where, by implication, it signifies neglect on the part of residents. Much vandalism has been demonstrated to have been induced in this manner; one cracked pane induces users to litter, leave windows dirty, etc., setting in motion a spiral of carelessness. Poor design often creates normal opportunities for glass breakage which are not intentional. Where extensive glass is used, it is important to be aware of these social and symbolic consequences.

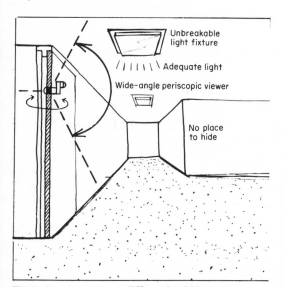

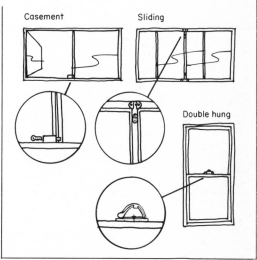

Fig. 3 Door Interviewers. Efforts should be made to provide visual access to as large an area as is plausible close to the apartment door. Periscopic viewers might be developed for this purpose to allow residents to look to one or the other end of a hall. These mechanisms serve as interior windows, allowing residents on the same floor to get needed information about one another's lives, family members, etc., so as to separate strangers from residents and their guests.

Fig. 4 Window Locks. Appropriate locking devices are available for all window types and are a necessity. While their primary value is as a deterrent, rather than a physical obstacle to entry (e.g., bars, gates), they are extremely effective.

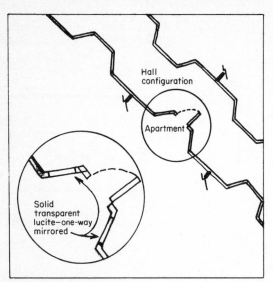

Fig. 5 Turreted Doors. A new idea involves creating apartment clusters in halls by designing apartment doors which jut out into the hall, with reinforced glass window panels facing up and down the corridor. This can act as a "front porch" to the apartment, providing information as to whether residents are at home, but no visual access to the interior. Panels can be made of half-mirrored glass to provide visual access to hall from apartment but no view into the apartment from the more brightly lit corridor.

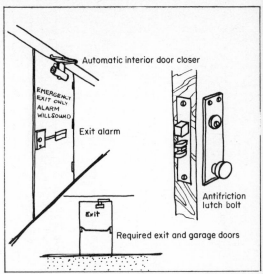

Fig. 6 Self-Locking Secondary Exits. There are often conflicts between fire-safety laws of access and egress and regulations required to reduce the risk of crime. If possible, secondary exits should terminate in a public zone (for example, in a building lobby or as a public path). It is best if these exits are self-locking and fitted with alarms to prevent use for ordinary traffic. Builders should, however, be aware of the need for multiple modes of access, especially in elevator buildings, and plan public, visible, primary stairways as part of the original design.

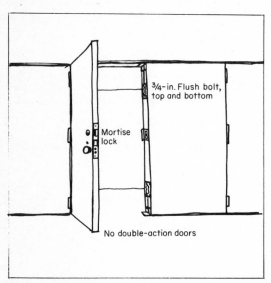

Fig. 7 Positive Closure for Interior Doors. The doors inside semipublic areas of a building are the basic elements of building security. They suggest the degree of vulnerability of the building as a whole. While there is need for a wide berth for access to meeting rooms, recreation rooms, laundry rooms, etc., each of these doors should be secured with a mortise lock and bolts.

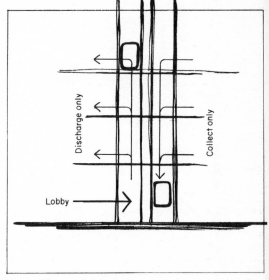

Fig. 8 Elevator Safety Systems (Discharge-Collect). Systems have been designed to prevent elevator crimes. The program allows discharge only on the way up, making it impossible for an assailant to press a call button at an intermediate floor to surprise a rider. One must return to the ground level in order to go "up."

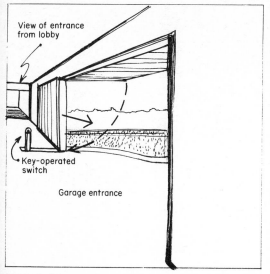

Fig. 9 Self-Closing Garage Doors. Garage entrances offer unsupervised access to buildings from the street. Gates should prevent entry by pedestrians and where possible be within view of a lobby window or resident window.

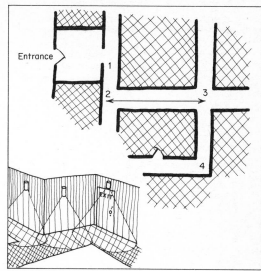

Fig. 10 Lighted Way. At night, the project paths and lanes should be bathed in warm light, avoiding shadows where possible and providing an opportunity to "telegraph" from one safe area to another. That is, once residents or guests enter a project, they should be able to achieve their final destination with a maximum of three or four separate path-components. Each of these decision points should be marked in a clear fashion, bathed in light, and maintained under surveillance either informally or formally. They should experience this transition as a smooth movement from one safe zone to another where they can project ahead of them the entire path. If necessary, safe zones may have to be provided by means of maintaining a small store in the interior of the project, subsidized to stay open all night, or by maintaining an all-night lobby under professional supervision. It is important to remember that it is not the length of the path that matters but rather the number of decision points and the ease with which path links may be telegraphed. No portion of a single link on a path should be unbroken for a distance of more than 200 ft. A break in the path requires that an entrance or surveillance point is present along the path to provide the residents or guests with a sense of safe access.

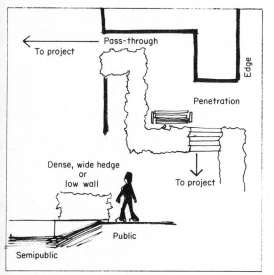

Fig. 11 Public Zones. Where public areas adjoin or pass through a project, very clear demarcations between these zones and semipublic areas should be encouraged. Where possible, a positive language of public life should be employed to highlight these pass-through areas, such as the use of public street furniture, fixtures, curb heights and configurations, and other common street features. Separation between these zones and more semipublic or semiprivate zones of the project should be reinforced by the use of fences (avoiding Cyclone fencing), low walls, bushes, steps, stoops, ramps, etc. It is important not to impair visual access across these zones to allow for police surveillance from the public street to the interior of the residential complex.

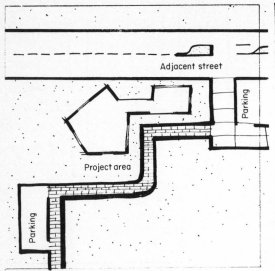

Fig. 12 Slow Traffic. Numerous studies have been performed on the effect of movement of traffic on the sense of community and on the interpretation of responsibility for maintaining surveillance on conduct in adjacent areas of the street. Optimum arrangement is to have some auto traffic brought into the body of a project or passing through a project. This provides the residents with the sense that there is direct access for both passers-by and cars and police. The traffic pattern must be sufficiently regulated, however, so that rapidly moving cars cannot negotiate the route readily. This can be done by a combination of curb extensions, barriers, or a simple change in materials to a brick surface.

Fig. 13 Distinctive Entrances. Allow a series of entrances to subportions of a project complex to be distinctive. A building form may include twenty apartments per floor, but it can be served either by a single internal double-loaded corridor or by a series of small entrances to the complex. Where possible, a series of entrances should be given distinctive qualities: for example, in the way it is decorated or the kind of entrance configuration through which passage is achieved. This design diversity will in turn encourage groupings of residents to find ways of augmenting it in small ways and encourage them to identify with particular design features, thereby discouraging vandalism and littering or loitering. Small variations in design of these spaces can be accommodated without structural-architectural changes in the design.

Fig. 14 Shared Interior Courts. Where possible, divide semipublic areas into courts, plazas, or gardens which are shared by three to eight groupings of units. These spaces may vary in size depending on the scale of a project and the quality of the design density within the project and in the surrounding community, that is, upon the conventional standards of density and open space which prevail. Some visual expression should be given on the ground for each distinctive architectural unit. For example, if a building complex includes four groupings of twenty-five families, there should be some clear indication of a common zone, space, green, or facility which reflects the common fate of these groupings. More importantly, designations on the ground should not be arbitrary or socially anomalous.

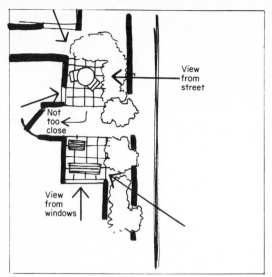

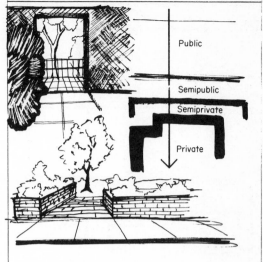

Fig. 15 Embellished Outdoor Spaces near Entrances.
Seating areas outside apartment entrances can be fashioned in a way which will attract adults and provide the sense of being under supervision for adolescents. This is done by putting them in view of windows of residences nearby, and by providing visual access to them from the public street. It is important not to put outdoor seating areas too close to the entrance itself, lest people who are sitting in these areas begin to perform an implicit gatekeeper function on the entrance and discourage residents from using the building. On the other hand, the facilities have to be clearly marked so that they are experienced as belonging to the building and not part of the public way.

Fig. 16 Unambiguous Boundaries. It is a fact of urban life that small jurisdictional differences as to who is responsible for a given piece of urban space cannot be left to chance. All available jurisdictional distinctions should be expressed in a two-dimensional visual boundary or a three-dimensional architectural form. The vocabulary of these gradations and jurisdictions from public to private can include elements like textured brick, changing color of the sidewalk, or the inclusion of a low wall between zones of use. All too often architects, in the effort to create general aesthetic statements like "entrance" or "amphitheatre," have placed these elements in the middle of large expanses of residential buildings without sufficient attention to jurisdictional concerns. Thus, they have either failed to tie these facilities to existing buildings by bringing them under their jurisdiction and/or they have created "no-man's lands" between existing buildings and these new facilities. A typical example of this concerns the space underneath ramped entrances into buildings.

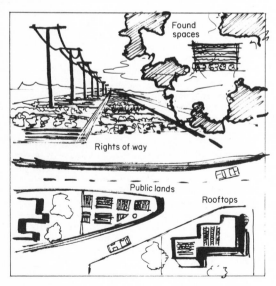

Fig. 17 Urban Gardens. In addition to planting flowers and other decorative items, urban gardens of limited foodstuffs in found spaces and on rooftops or along rights-of-way of electric and other utilities have become a moderately serious venture. Many communities (even resort communities for second homes in highly desirable areas) have begun to seek some integrating theme which can involve residents. Such themes might be very limited farming of specialized crops, hydroponic gardening, or trout farming on a limited scale to supply needs of the community. The securing function of these undertakings would be inestimable since they would place people on the street and provide a strong sense of vigilance about the presence of others in the area.

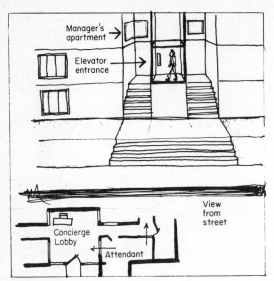

Fig. 18 Entry Visibility. Provide natural or artificial means of surveillance over the entrances to buildings. This may be performed through small windows and doors which enter into a hall, by having a concierge's desk in the lobby, or by means of a full-time attendant in the lobby area. Alternatively, some experiments have been made using video surveillance of entry lobbies which are connected to unused channels on resident's television receivers. These are very inexpensive arrangements and in most configurations can be attached to telephone lines or any double-wire system, for example, a television antenna. Where possible, it is always a good idea to have direct human contact with the hall or elevator lobby and to provide direct visibility of this area from the street through reinforced or unbreakable transparent glass areas.

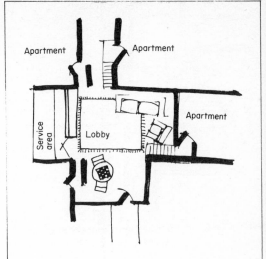

Fig. 19 Building Lobby Seats and Activities. Current conventions discourage the placing of seating areas inside building lobbies. These are often taken over by adolescents and/or vandalized. Seats inside the lobbies are, however, a good idea if the lobby area is under constant surveillance (for example, by a mail room) and if there are apartment doors which enter directly into the lobby. In the past, we have been all too unwilling to utilize differences among residents in their natural social proclivities in order to secure facilities against crime and to promote positive social atmospheres. In this age of "mixologists" in bars, and shipboard social directors, there is no reason why a small group of especially sociable tenants should not be recruited to occupy apartments next to busy lobby areas, to tend to bulletin boards, make announcements, and maintain active surveillance of these areas. These tenants could be induced to perform these special services with a small rebate in rent, just as dormitory proctors perform this role on college campuses.

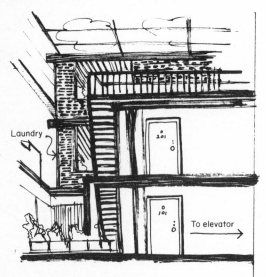

Fig. 20 Open Stairwells. The open stairwell is of some community significance. Where possible, this design should be employed in order to encourage casual interaction and because it is an architectural feature which encourages a wide range of discovered uses. Because of contemporary fire codes, these stairwells are less and less easy to employ and typically involve great expense. If, however, they are included early in the conception of a project, they may be employed without additional expense and with very positive social consequences. For example, a simple open stairwell going one story up to the second floor of a two-story lobby with a balcony internal to the structure including apartments above would be a favorable way to frame an entrance. Completely open external stairways must be used with great care so that they enter and exit or ascend and descend from strategically selected points on a path or within visual access of the building entrance. All too often external stairs exit into cul-de-sacs, and result in dangerous hidden spaces beneath themselves as well.

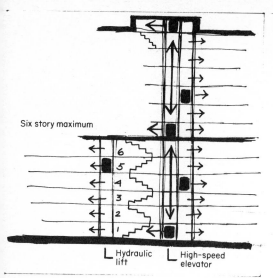

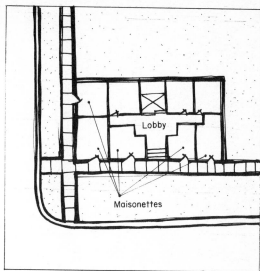

Fig. 21 Six-Story Maximum. Less expensive, low-speed hydraulic elevators should be employed where possible, and the "six-story maximum" should be set in force. This maximum is the feasible walking height when elevators do not work or when residents choose not to use them. If higher complexes are mandated by land requirements, they can be serviced by a combination of high-speed elevators and six-story hydraulic lifts, the distance an elevator covers again, wherever possible, not exceeding the number of floors to which people can ascend comfortably by walking. New design patterns should be sought which allow for dense stacking of six-story units on top of one another. These can be linked by a high-speed elevator which travels only from six-story block to six-story block, units within a six-story block being linked, where possible, by the slower and less expensive hydraulic elevators. Through this configuration, high-speed elevators can serve a large portion of the population of a vertical project. Perhaps they can each be run by an elevator operator serving as the equivalent of a gatekeeper for the small six-story units.

Fig. 22 Maisonettes. These are apartments which enter directly from the public street and serve to supervise an entryway or a building lobby. Their entrance being directly onto the street, separated from it only by a threshold, they thus provide an outside surveillance function as well. These units can also be placed around the periphery of a building which otherwise would provide only a brick or concrete wall to an otherwise unsupervised street. The design of maisonette apartments is important. They can have their windows guarded with decorative but sturdy grilles at the ground level, or they can be made into two-story townhouses with a second-level entrance, utilizing private stairs to get to the street.

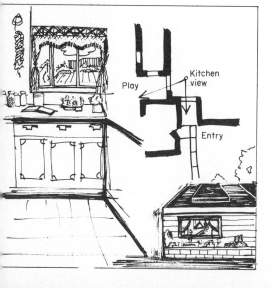

Fig. 23 Kitchen Views. Previous research has demonstrated the importance of using kitchen windows near building entrances to overlook and passively supervise children's play areas. Kitchen windows, because of their "unique size, shape, and decoration, have a softening effect on, and provide a sense of conviviality in the appearance of, a multi-occupancy building. They imply that someone is watching.

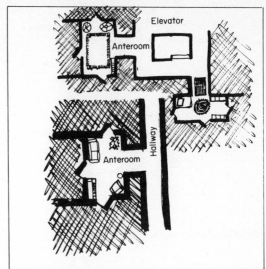

Fig. 24 Small Corridors. Where possible, corridors should be shared by a small number of families (three to eight). This is sufficiently small to allow people to get to know and accommodate themselves to one another's life styles, and to identify typical sounds, patterns of entrance and leaving, and friends and relations. Beyond that number, a dramatic shift seems to occur in the types of expectations people have of one another. First, they adopt rules of public demeanor, that is, they do not engage in patterns of greeting common to most neighborhood situations. Eyes are cast to the ground and people become indifferent to one another. When a small number of people share the corridor, they are forced to acknowledge one another when meeting, and in this way build a network of recognizability that acts as a strong deterrent to crime. It also provides people with positive psychological benefits by making them feel less isolated and alone. Oscar Newman and his colleagues found that, in dormitory life at Sarah Lawrence, greater stress among occupants was produced by large-cluster room groupings along double-loaded corridors than by small-cluster arrangements.

Fig. 25 Shared Anterooms. Small spaces can be created around an elevator lobby or a small entranceway separated from a larger hall by one or two steps. These vestibules, shared by two or three apartments, can be enclosed or open. They are very intimate transitional spaces which can be decorated by residents, and they function in a variety of ways. These small anterooms are important in several ways. First, symbolically, they suggest a hierarchy of spaces outside the residences and extend the residents' sense of territory outside the apartment door. Second, they encourage people to communicate with one another, if only to negotiate the type of painting which should be hung in a shared space, or its position.

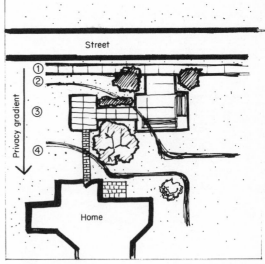

Fig. 26 Orderly Progression. The route from street to home should have the character of a differentiated landscape with clearly marked node points signifying progress from place to place. Geometry should be used to provide a sense of locale at all times with increasing spheres of privacy being achieved.

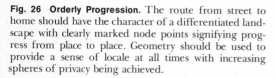

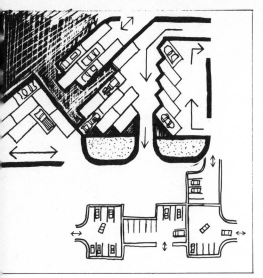

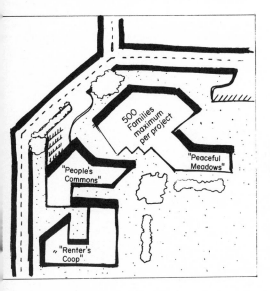

Fig. 27 Subdivided Parking Garages. Where possible, to avoid the phenomenon of long underground passages with many pedestrian entrances and exits, large underground garages should be broken into smaller sections served by separate entrances. This effectively eliminates the risk of strangers moving freely among vehicles, or preying upon residents far from exits or access to help. Above-grade parking should also be subdivided to provide the same benefits, and stalls should be located near residences, to help provide informal surveillance over them.

Fig. 28 Fewer than Fifty Apartments. A maximum size should be set for architectural units comprising the project. In a six-story facility, for example, there might be a maximum of fifty families allowed for a single elevator. Psychological studies suggest this figure as a limit above which elementary face-knowledge of people (i.e., knowing names, locations, or pertinent facts about neighbors) becomes difficult in a community of strangers. At greater numbers, to maintain a level of acquaintance where members of the same community are perceived as such, a distinctive social bond must be added.

Fig. 29 Limited Size under a Single Name. In any prospective project, no more than 500 families should be permitted to be housed under a single project name. Plans should be modified for each 500-family unit to provide these large groupings with a distinctive physical design and image and a unique nominal identifier. While master planning of large communities in regard to common services and other urban concerns should not be discouraged, these systems or frameworks can remain implicit and need not surface as primary design considerations.

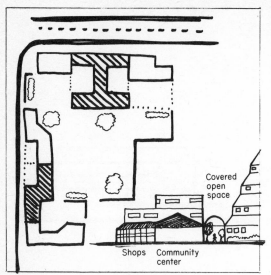

Fig. 30 Infill High-Rise Buildings. If high-rise buildings are mandated either by special needs of a population group or through land costs, they should be introduced in a way that maximizes their benefit to the community in which they are going to be placed and to the people who will reside in them. First, no more than three high-rise buildings should be located on the same uninterrupted site, and where possible individual buildings should be sited independently as infill between existing housing. High-rise buildings should be developed with awareness of the population group that is to occupy them. They require the presence of differentiated, intense activities on the ground level, as one would need in a hotel or a service facility such as a hospital. The ground-level activities can be justified when the occupants are single people or families who use the facility as if it were a hotel, or alternatively they can be justified if the occupants constitute a particular population group, such as the elderly, whose pooled social services create a need for ground-level activities.

Fig. 31 Shared Facades. Much of the final appearance of a multiple-occupancy building is not visible at the stages in which a designer is concerned with a project. After occupancy, people use plants, curtains, lights, and color in a personal and distinctive fashion. We note these accessory signs from the street and deduce from them something about the people who live in the building and the character of its environment. The charm of many brownstone streets is attributable in part to the fact that they provide an orderly context or a grammar for these displays. This allows people in a community to respond to one another's efforts and to build a collective image of the community. Too often in the design of large block buildings this tool of community design is all but eliminated.

Fig. 32 Vertical Streets. If high buildings are employed, opportunities should be created for protected circulation within each building proper other than at the street level. For example, the Atrium is a redesigned apartment hotel in New York City, in which the center of the building has been removed to provide a large multistoried open space. Apartments are linked by exposed internal corridors with balconies circling the "atrium." This provides a very safe atmosphere because residents coming from and going to their apartments can be seen across the open space. Other configurations which produce the same effect are possible. For example, Newman proposes an internal expanded elevator lobby area on each floor of buildings for the elderly.

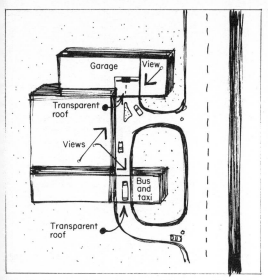

Fig. 33 Transportation Linkages. Where possible, allow buses and taxis to enter the development. Provide transit waiting areas under transparent roof tops in view of residents. Place all entries to garage areas within the configuration so that they are visible from apartment units.

Fig. 34 Communications with Guests. Video and audio monitoring systems for guests can be very productive in multi-occupancy communities. Operated at very low cost and on residents' own television sets, these interviewing systems can be introduced in a way that allows people to think of them as positive aids to communication, making possible more and safer interactions with guests and strangers and allowing for both less inhibited dropping-in behavior and more spontaneous interchanges among neighbors. In practice, it allows people to call into the body of a project and be seen by their prospective companions, to ask residents to come out, or to be invited upstairs. Mothers can communicate easily with their children, asking them, for example, to return from play areas. With more advanced systems, video advertisements or audio messages can be prerecorded to be sampled by residents later as a kind of electronic bulletin board. Of course this latter use immediately brings to mind the risk faced by the community at large of the possible *misuse* of these devices for propagandistic purposes or the purveying of illegal goods and services. However, it is important to recognize the difference between the use of these media on a scale of, say, a city, and the use of them on the scale of one to five hundred families. In the smaller multi-occupancy buildings, sanctions against abberant use of these systems are provided on a person-to-person basis, and not necessarily through mediation by the law. People become identified with their requests and the reputation lingers, so that ultimately users are subject to the benefits, or the unkindness, of a small community. In larger complexes, the problem of crime is obviously enhanced by the breakdown of the local web or network of relations possible where the number of residents is fewer. But in either instance, some balance clearly must be maintained between responsibility to the local community and access to and by the world outside.

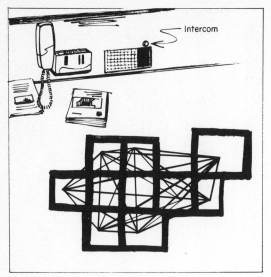

Fig. 35 Intercoms between Apartments. One of the advantages of living in apartment communities is the opportunity which people have to build up networks of friends and associates who are close enough at hand so that spontaneous informal contact is possible. In fact, it really does not matter whether the linkages are spatially contiguous or not. Functionally in a dense multi-occupancy unit, all apartments are spatially contiguous. What *does* matter is that there is no need for telephone-level technology (either the hardware, or the "software" such as dialing a seven-digit number to central exchange) in order to maintain relations among small clusters of people in a community. Intercoms can be used in a variety of ways: for example, as an emergency system by working mothers who share responsibility for one another's children, or as a small community-meeting device for circles of families who wish to keep in touch with one another. The new interest in CB radios may mark the beginnings of a revolutionary new use of electronic equipment, responding in main to the constraints of the telephone as a single-purpose instrument.

Fig. 36 Elevator Sounds. Modern elevators, unlike their early open-grille counterparts, are completely closed systems. While some elevators are employed which are essentially glass cages, having the elevator glazed either on the exterior of the building facing a street or suspended within an open interior space, as in the Bradbury Building in Los Angeles or Portland's Regency Hyatt House buildings in Atlanta and San Francisco, such instances are the exception rather than the rule, and even they are soundproof and lose contact with floor halls when in motion. Experiments have been contemplated with audio-amplifiers which would operate so as to project the sound inside elevators out into hall areas closest to the elevators' paths of ascent and descent. This would give the system an open-grille quality, simulated by the use of electronics. People could talk back and forth from the hall to the elevator, even if the door to the cab were closed, and this would make riders aware that screams or other loud sounds in the elevator could be heard by people in the adjacent hallways.

Fig. 37 Communal Phones. Provide seating areas in parks or in public areas under surveillance of nearby buildings. To enhance the sense of security for people who might use these spaces, include communal phone outlets which can be used to provide limited information and to make calls in case of emergency. These phones should be like call boxes in elevators, that is, activated by simply flipping a toggle switch or pressing a button. Care should be taken that these listening devices are obvious to anyone who might choose to sit in these areas. They might ordinarily be used for broadcasting music or informational programs.

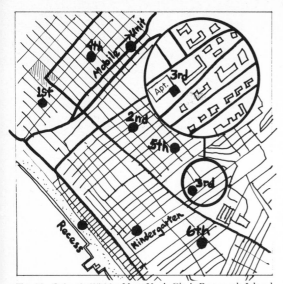

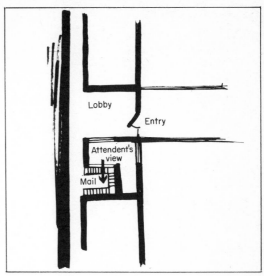

Fig. 38 Schools Within. New York City's Roosevelt Island Plan includes a network of semiautonomous school rooms, each in the lower floor of an apartment building. While the programming and curriculum requirements for this kind of system are immense and baffling, it nevertheless provides simultaneously for the legitimate needs of children inside the facility and on the street outside, and also for competent adult supervision both within the classroom and in the immediate surrounding area. These schools are designed to be used in the evenings by the community for adult educational purposes as well.

Fig. 39 Community Mailboxes. In many communities mailbox break-ins and fires have become a symbol as well as a fact of the presence of criminals. In one instance in New York, the Postal Service went to great pains in a public housing project to install bells on each floor so that the mailman could be protected on "check day" by the presence of the many elderly citizens who would come down to pick up their social security checks. Many projects have now gone over to designing special enclosed mail rooms which require a separate key. It may be that we should be thinking about providing less mail service rather than first-class door-to-door mail service. Like the rural post office which serves other social functions as well (for example, acting as a community bulletin board), a post office box arrangement might be attempted in a community for, say, 1000 families. Again, as in rural post offices, this would merit the employment of several people, perhaps during evening hours, and it would provide an implicit security function for the community.

Chapter **30**

Public Buildings

REX M. BALL, F.A.I.A., A.I.P.

President, HTB, Inc.

RALPH M. BALL, A.I.A.

Chairman of the Board, HTB, Inc.

ED HUDGINS, A.I.A.

Secretary, HTB, Inc.

THE NEED FOR SECURITY

The need for security systems in all types of buildings becomes an absolute necessity with crime increasing at the currently alarming rate. The changing attitude of ordinary citizens toward governmental and institutional units, added to general frustration with a rapidly changing society, has led to many new headaches for occupants of public buildings and consequently their architects.

A new generation of urban guerrillas has attacked public buildings in the last few years in highly destructive ways: airports have been bombed, museum artifacts mutilated, and courthouses raided. Embassy buildings have been stormed and their occupants held hostage, and even the Olympic Games were the target of a terrorist attack.

Architects and designers are devising new methods of construction and sophisticated hardware to thwart attacks that have not yet even been committed. They have entered into defensive, preventive security planning.

SECURITY PROBLEMS FOR PUBLIC BUILDINGS

Security problems involving public buildings may be divided into two separate categories: criminal and noncriminal. While the criminal security problems far outweigh the noncriminal problems, many of the measures taken for one are applicable for the other.

Those criminal acts which might actually affect the building are burglary, theft, vandalism, arson, rioting, and terrorism. Those affecting the building's occupants would be assault and battery, embezzlement, espionage, rioting, and terrorism. In the noncriminal category are threats which might be termed "acts of God"—fire, flooding, high winds, earthquakes, lightning, etc.

PLANNING FOR SECURITY IN PUBLIC BUILDINGS

No standard set of security measures can be realistically prescribed for all public buildings throughout the nation. In each instance, the security programs must be tailored to the circumstances of the particular project. This process is what security planning is all about.

Coordination of Planning   Planning must be a coordinated effort of the owner or governmental regulating body, the architect, the building manager, occupants or lessees, the police, and the security service agencies.

Defining the Public Building   Public buildings are those open to public activities where large or fairly large groups of people may congregate for different kinds of activities. These include federal, state, county, and city administrative, legal, and maintenance buildings; museums; libraries; fire stations; churches; post offices; and others similar in nature.

Surveying the Need   In existing buildings, a quick survey to determine what kinds of security problems actually exist can be carried out by examining past security records. This survey will usually determine what can feasibly be done with the building in terms of the strengths and weaknesses in the building's physical design and equipment.

Older Buildings.   Problems associated with older buildings are often more difficult to solve because of existing fire escapes, operable windows, older and worn locks, common walls, unused and forgotten connecting doors and windows, improperly secured shafts and accessways, and windows at the street and basement levels.

In reviewing potentials for improved security, the designer must constantly bear in mind the need for fire safety. For example, if bars are to be provided for windows, the designer must first determine that such security measures conform with the building's exit needs.

Among the more easily rectified security gaps in older buildings are windows with air-conditioning units that are easily removed for access. Such windows can be alarmed at lower floors; they should also be alarmed if accessible from trees, retaining walls, ledges, etc.

New Buildings.   In surveying the security needs for a new building, many factors should be taken into consideration.

■ What facts relate to the nature and degree of the threat of crime and vandalism which might affect the building?

■ What types of defensive measures and other factors might tend to encourage or prohibit each type of offensive behavior?

■ What are the relevant characteristics and trends in the immediate neighborhood and community?

■ How effective are the existing policing services for the area?

■ What are the possible options for new design, for hardware and software measures, and for costs?

■ What budget has been (or should be) allowed for the security program?

■ What other resources would be available for additional security measures?

■ What are the relevant characteristics of the building's users and daily visitors?

DRAWING UP THE PLAN

A key phrase in public building security is "freedom of access." This applies to both internal and external security problems and all public buildings to varying degrees.

External Security

Neighborhoods When considering the security of a public building, it is necessary to look at the area in which it is located in relation to the adjoining buildings. A higher crime rate in the adjoining areas may point to a need for securing additional measures for the building.

Site Placement of the building on its site is important. Traffic patterns and the building's relation to adjacent streets should be considered. Zones of transition from the street to the sidewalk and from the grounds to the building must be weighed.

Sidewalks and Access Pathways These public paths should be positioned to provide as much direct access as possible. The number of paths should be limited to ensure that they are well peopled during normal hours; they should be well lighted during off hours. Pathways should be positioned so that they can be scanned before use, should have no turns, and should be located so that users may see the point of destination from the point of origin.

Landscaping All planting along pathways and around the perimeter of the building should be selected, located, and maintained in a manner which would not provide concealing cover.

Fencing Fencing is a very effective means of limiting access, especially to areas containing storage and maintenance facilities. The designer should bear in mind that the principal purpose of fences is to prevent people from straying onto the property. To deter someone who is intent on climbing over it, the fence would need perimeter alarms and increased lighting, and even then it would be effective only if the fence were properly maintained.

Boundaries Government installations can be protected by one or more of a variety of intrusion-detecting systems. These include ultrasonic, infrared, seismic, photoelectric, microwave, magnetic, and acoustic-based systems, as well as television and other more familiar alarm systems.

Lighting Parking areas and all entrance points should be well lighted, especially rear and side doors.

Internal Security

Main entrance Glass should be used to maintain high visibility. Although glass is easily broken, it is rarely attacked, since main entrances and lobbies are usually well lighted and face well-traveled streets and sidewalks. It is possible to use UL-listed burglar-resistant glass or plastic glazing materials for street-level windows. This type of glass resists heat, flame, extreme cold, hammers, picks, and axes. These materials are more specifically described in Chapter 12, "Glass and Glazing." Because of their high cost, they are normally used only where attack seems likely.

Another alternate to the use of glass is UL-listed burglar-resistant polycarbonate or acrylic plastic glass. These materials can resist blows but are easily scratched. They are good for above-street-level windows and protect against rock-throwing vandalism.

Lobby Security Traffic may be monitored by a security guard/receptionist from a central point in the lobby, with mirrors installed to give the guard better visibility at all times. For highly sensitive buildings, the central control point may be equipped with a control board for monitoring activities throughout the building. This board, however, should be backed up by a concealed second control point.

For casual traffic, a simple sign in–sign out log may be sufficient. Additional security may be gained by a closing-hour check of the entire building.

Front Door The traffic through the front door may be monitored by the lobby guard through the use of a specially magnetized card inserted in a door-opening device. In case of high security, a guard may be stationed at the door and given the card to be inserted in the mechanism.

These cards can be monitored by a computer, which reads them, allows entry through the door, sets the elevator into motion (monitoring movement of the elevator to certain floors), and unlocks the user's office door. One advantage of this system is that the cards may be easily erased from the computer if desired—for example, when an employee is dismissed or a card is lost.

Elevators Elevators may be programmed to lock out all but authorized personnel during closed hours either through computer control or by requiring special keys to unlock the elevator at certain floors. If elevators cannot be secured from operating, a second door requiring a key should be installed to prevent easy access.

Another form of control for the elevator is a badge or card inserted into a reader at the lobby level. This method is only as secure as the degree of control exercised over the badges, unless a further check is added, such as computer verification.

Interior Doors For maximum security, access doors in high-security areas should have computer-controlled locks operated from a central point, either from the computer control panel in the front lobby or another security area.

For lesser security levels, various locks may be utilized. These are described in greater detail in Chapter 15, "Locks and Keying." It should be recognized that locks are nothing more than delaying devices, however; even so-called pick-resistant locks and longer bolts should only be considered as buying additional time.

Doorways offer more protection against forced entry if steel doors or solid-core wooden doors are used. If hollow-core doors are used, they should be lined with sheet metal. Doors with glass panels should not be used in any high-security area unless the additional visibility afforded by the glass is sufficient justification. When doorframes are weak, special pry-resistant locks with long bolts and special cylinder guards should be used. In addition, wall construction should be reinforced around this type of lock.

Exterior Doors Doors with glass panels should not be used in building entrances out of public or controlled view; but if they are used, the doors should be fitted with locks that are keyed to both sides.

Exterior door hinges on steel exit doors should be of the nonremovable type and should not yield when sawn.

Overhead doors should be solid and interior bolts secured with padlocks. Padlocks should be of hardened steel to deter forcing. Locking bars should have no external rivets and should be bolted through the door to the inside and through a backing plate, with the bolt ends burred over.

Restroom Doors Restroom doors should be locked at all times, with the restrooms intended for public use located on the lobby floor, unlocked, clearly marked, and in public view.

Equipment-Room Doors These doors should be locked at all times, day or night, to keep them from becoming hiding places for muggers or concealment places for bombs. Such rooms should also be separately master-keyed.

Walls In high-security areas, special care must be taken with wall construction. Many of the newer buildings have a relatively solid door hung in a steel frame with a concrete floor and an open ceiling. Tiles lying loose on suspended runners at the top of the partition walls for power and telephone lines and air-conditioning ducts can be easily pushed up, allowing access from room to room. Such walls next to securely locked doors often become the weak link in the security chain, and they should be reinforced for additional security.

Exterior Fire Doors These doors should be fitted with panic bars and alarms which can be wired into the main control to flash a signal and/or sound an alarm when opened.

Emergency Stairwells These should be locked against entry from the stairways, making elevators the only means of access to upper floors. Careful coordination with local building codes and ordinances is needed so that access to emergency exits is not restricted.

Signs Signs should be installed giving notice to the public that a security system is in operation.

COMPUTER SECURITY

An **adequate power source** must be provided that will be dependable and available at all times. The computer may be isolated from its primary power source by batteries which in turn supply the computer through alternators. For further details refer to Chapter 23, "Computer Power Security."

Adequate air conditioning must be provided for the computer equipment in addition to any that is being provided for the computer work area. Additional precautions would be to include sensitive fire indicators and suppressors, humidity monitors, fresh-air intakes, sensors to detect air pollutants, filters to eliminate internal and external dust, and vibration alarms.

Strict access control is an important factor for computer areas. The designer should consider the provision of magnetic detection equipment for personnel and packages entering the computer area, much like the magnetometers used at airports.

Area planning to strengthen access control should focus on a single two-way entrance/exit for the facility consisting of a riot door, a corridor, and a second riot door, both doors electrically controlled and under guard. These corridors should also be kept under protective surveillance by closed-circuit television.

A shield may be constructed around the computer rooms to screen against possible disruption of radio waves. While physical security controls are most important, computer security cannot be considered complete without the necessary management security controls. These include specifying different levels of the various programs to which personnel are permitted access. Only a limited number of people should be permitted full access to an entire program, and even fewer should be able to read the computer's basic instructions. Untrained personnel, through accidental manipulation, and disgruntled (or even discharged) employees can easily compromise a computer system that lacks carefully planned preventive measures.

BOMBS

Public buildings have recently become targets for bombs and bomb threats. The most important security measure is careful surveillance by all employees and occupants of the building. It is essential to have in advance (1) a security plan that relays information concerning any objects out of place to a central security point and (2) an evacuation plan of the building.

Evacuation plans must include routes which do not take occupants past elevators, restrooms, equipment rooms, etc., because most bomb explosions occur in or near the service core of the building.

Careful screening of packages and materials brought into the building is a must.

Places where bombs are usually planted include elevator shafts, access points, ceiling areas, restrooms, access doors, crawl spaces, unsecured points of access to plumbing or electrical fixtures, utility closets, stairwells, boiler and air-conditioning rooms, flammable storage areas, main switches and valves, indoor trash receptacles, record storage areas, mail rooms, ceiling lights with removable panels, and fire hose racks. Careful planning of building design can minimize the danger by preventing unauthorized access to these areas.

CHECKLIST FOR SECURITY PROBLEM AREAS

The following checklist incorporates the various areas of risk discussed in this chapter, as related to security problems which may arise. The design professional is encouraged to use it for both new buildings and existing buildings which are to be modified. Included are options for pinpointing locations where security needs must generally be considered, specialized types of existing security problems, and space for projecting measures to be taken in order to correct these existing problems. The spaces are intentionally left blank to permit the making of those notations which are most relevant to a particular building's design.

SECURITY CHECKLIST FOR PUBLIC BUILDINGS

Type of building:
Nature of surrounding community:
Community crime statistics:
Site placement:
Anticipated user population statistics:

Location	Existing conditions				Security measures to be taken
	Ease of access	Ease of egress	Monitoring devices	V—Vulnerability: th—theft; t—terrorism; a—arson; k—kidnaping; c—crowd potential	
1. Sidewalks and access pathways					
2. Landscaping					
3. Fencing					
4. Boundaries					
5. Lighting					
6. Main entrance					
7. Lobby security					
8. Front door					
9. Elevators					
10. Interior doors					
11. Exterior doors					
12. Restroom doors					
13. Equipment room doors					
14. Operable windows					
15. Inoperable windows					
16. Locks					

17. Walls					
18. Exterior fire doors					
19. Emergency stairwells and fire escapes					
20. Computer power source					
21. Computer access control					
22. Computer air conditioning					
23. Mass evacuation routes					
24. Roof and exterior wall openings					
25. Other					

Chapter 31

Single-Family Homes

RAY A. BRAY, M.P.A.

Senior Consultant, California Commission on Peace Officer
Standards and Training

CHARLES M. GIRARD, Ph.D.

Partner, Koepsell-Girard and Associates

The most urgent considerations in the process of buying a home—mortgage, insurance, structural soundness, building codes, clear title, and so forth—create such pressures on a buyer that the question of adequate physical security is most frequently overlooked. Despite the fact that, nationwide, burglary accounts for over one-half the major offenses* reported to the police, little attention is given to whether the structure is equipped with security hardware, locks, and doors, or is designed in a manner which will protect it against one of the greatest hazards facing homeowners today—the uninvited intruder.

Regardless of the cost of the home, the architect and builder will normally have specified and constructed it using a key-in-knob spring-latch lock costing no more than $5.00 and providing a commensurate amount of security. In short, the physical security of a home needs to be considered from the time it is on the drawing board; and builders need to know what they can do to provide consumers with safer residences for the least cost. Only in this way can criminal opportunity in our communities be reduced.

Unfortunately, few security experts have taken the time to provide adequate details to professionals involved in the construction industry. Architects, engineers, and builders have had to rely on standardized guidebooks, aesthetic considerations, and habit when designing and constructing homes. They have not been provided with the facts concerning steps they could take to design and construct more secure homes. Thus, the purposes of this chapter are to provide a few perspectives concerning the

---

Crime in the United States, Uniform Crime Report, 1974, U.S. Government Printing Office, Washington, D.C., 1975 (Stock No. 027-001-0013-1).

crime of burglary; to show what steps can be taken by members of the construction industry to counteract this crime; and to describe the equipment and materials available for use against the burglar. The provision of better security can be a key "selling" feature of a home, and the cost of security, when built into a new residence, is far less than one might think. Moreover, by providing secure homes the architect, engineer, and builder can play an important role in helping to curb this country's most rampant crime.

THE CRIME OF BURGLARY AND THE PERPETRATOR

First, it is necessary to examine who the burglar is, when burglaries are committed, and how the criminal enters a home. As pictured by many of us, the burglar is an experienced masked bandit with graying temples and a criminal mind. In actuality, the profile is quite different. Among those apprehended for burglary in 1973, 84 percent were 25 years of age or younger; and surprisingly, of this total, neary 65 percent were younger than 18. In short, the vast majority of burglars are *amateurs* looking for easy targets, often within their own neighborhoods. People generally think of the burglar as working at night, creeping quietly through the house. In reality, more than half of all reported burglaries occur during daylight hours. The burglar is often depicted as picking locks, scaling walls, and so on to enter a residence. However, in real life, most burglars are neither skilled nor daring. They enter quickly through insecure doors and windows so they will not make much noise or attract attention. Commonly, their tools include a screwdriver, a "jimmy" or pry bar, a pair of channel lock-type pliers, and a hammer.

Moreover, criminologists and police officials firmly agree that if homes are equipped with adequate security hardware (e.g., good locks and strong doors) and residents remember to use such devices to secure their doors and windows, a burglar ordinarily will not spend the time or make the noise required to gain entry. There is no need to, when so many homes have been built with locks, doors, and other hardware that can be easily defeated.

PHYSICAL SECURITY: THEORIES AND APPROACHES

There are two major aspects to physical security, One focuses on design concepts which have an impact on environmental security, and the other deals with security hardware such as locks, lighting, alarm systems, safes, doors, and security glazing. Each of these is discussed below.

Physical Security through Environmental Design

A group of architects and planners have recently substantiated what social psychologists have been saying for years—there is a relationship between environment and behavior. More importantly, they found that this relationship is directly correlated with crime. In fact, by studying housing projects with differing crime rates but comparable in terms of density, size, and the income of their tenants, it was discovered that those with less criminal activity had uniquely different building designs and areas surrounding the projects (e.g., lawns and parks), which were laid out to facilitate surveillance by the inhabitants. These design aspects resulted in "defensible space" through the creation of zones of "territorial influence"—where tenants acted as their own policing agents simply because they identified with the space and could easily monitor what was going on.*

*Oscar Newman, *Defensible Space,* Mamillan, New York, 1972, p. 60. Also refer to Chapter 29 in this Handbook, "Multiple Housing."

In short, it was found that the basic elements of environmental design that relate to security provide for the following:

- Opportunities for surveillance
- Differentiation of space
- The assumption of territoriality
- Separation of conflicting uses
- Community aesthetics
- Provision of more acceptable outlets for potential delinquent and criminal energies

These points should be kept in mind when a professional builder or architect deals with a specific site or plan. By including them in the design, a positive step can be taken toward a more secure environment.

Security Hardware and Building Materials

The nature of hardware and various building materials may also add to the security status of a home. In fact, such standard items as locks, doors, and windows can be the basic elements in the effort to discourage unwanted intruders. However, as mentioned earlier, when a home is being designed and built, all too often little thought is given to these potential invitation points for the burglar. Thus, the remainder of this discussion focuses on these common components of every residential structure.

Doorframes One of the weakest structural areas of a home is the door assembly. As a result, one common method of forcible entry used by home burglars is to impact a door, causing it or the frame to give way. Because of this fact, the California Crime Technology Research Foundation (CCTRF) tested a variety of door systems and established that a man weighting 180 lb can easily hit a door with his shoulder at 88 in/s, which produces an impact of 1800 lb on the door assembly.* Few doors or frames currently in use can withstand such force.

Another common method of attack used by burglars is spreading doorjambs with a common auto bumper jack. Standard bumper jacks are rated to 2000 lb. The force of the jack can be applied between the two jambs of a door to spread them and overcome the length of the latch-bolt throw.

As a result of the research, the CCTRF found that both of these attack methods can be overcome by a modified nailing schedule based on the Federal Housing Authority's standard single-door framing method (see Fig. 1). In fact, as Fig. 2 indicates, this can be accomplished by utilizing the standard FHA scheme with the addition of strategically nailed ⅝-in plywood.† This, of course, can be accomplished with little additional time and expense.

Doors Disregarding the locking and hinge mechanisms for the moment, the door itself may also be a vulnerable point in a home's security. Doors are of two common designs: panel and flush. Panel doors consist of vertical and horizontal members framing rectangular areas in which opaque panels of glass or wood or louvers are placed. Flush doors consist of flat panels running the full height and width of the door (see Fig. 3). Often, in an effort to save a few dollars when a new home is being built, hollow-core wood doors or doors with thin wood panels, glass, or louvers are installed. As the above tests indicated, a burglar can easily put a shoulder through such items, and they should therefore be avoided.

Wood doors, however, can be secure. Preferably, all exterior wooden doors should be of solid-core construction, with a minimum thickness of 1¾ in (see Fig. 4). Although flush doors provide better security, aesthetics may call for the use of panel doors; if so, glass panels should have a minimum thickness of ½ in. Some styles call for the use of glass on or next to doors, but this should be avoided if possible. However, if

---

*California Crime Technology Research Foundation "Building Security Standards Report to the Legislature," January 1974, p. 22.
†Ibid.

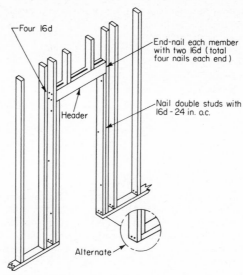

Fig. 1 Typical FHA single-door framing. *(From California Crime Technologucal Research Foundation.)*

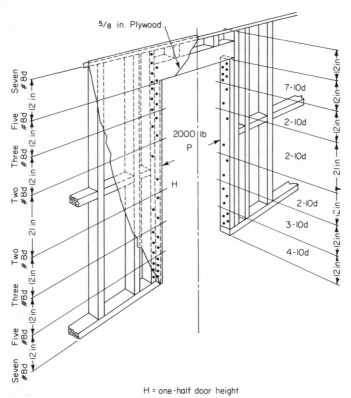

H = one-half door height

Fig. 2 Nailing schedule to reduce spreading of door jambs under lateral loading (under a force of 2000 lb, each jamb deflected 0.3 in).

design requirements dictate, or a customer is adamant about having glass on or around the door, special caution should be used. In fact, where small decorative windows are installed within 40 in of a door-locking device, some form of steel mesh or grillwork should be used to cover the glass. This will prohibit an intruder from breaking the glass, reaching in, and unlocking the door from the inside. Alternatively, polycarbonate or other types of burglary-resistant glazing material may be used in such windows.

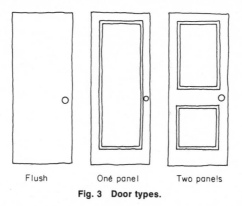

Flush   Oné panel   Two panels

Fig. 3   Door types.

Hinges   A very important and frequently ignored part of a door system is the hinge. Hinges on outswinging doors are especially vulnerable, thanks to the ease with which hinge pins can be pried upward and removed, thereby permitting the door to be opened from the hinge side. In addition, most hinges used in residential door systems are attached to the jamb with ½- to ¾-in wood screws. Considering jambs are usually of ¾-in fir or pine, little force is required to tear the screws from the jamb and open the door.

A number of steps can be taken to counteract this condition. Specifically, door

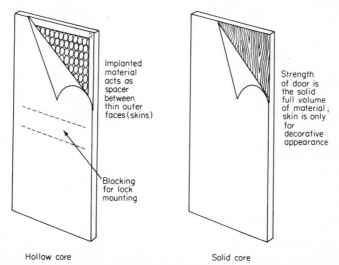

Implanted
material
acts as
spacer
between
thin outer
faces (skins)

Blocking
for lock
mounting

Strength
of door is
the solid
full volume
of material;
skin is only
for
decorative
appearance

Hollow core   Solid core

Fig. 4   Door construction. A solid cored door offers the best base for applying all hardware components, hinges, locks, closers, bolts, etc.

hinges with a nonremovable pin feature can be utilized, or at least one hinge of the two or three holding the door can be specially "pinned." Pinning can be accomplished by removing the center one or two opposing screws on both leaves of the hinge after it is installed and inserting a pin or concrete nail in one hole, leaving ½ to ¾ in exposed and drilling out the opposite hole to receive the protruding pin (see Fig. 5). This will, of course, prevent the door from being opened even if the hinge pins are removed by a burglar.

Another security precaution that can be taken at little cost is to install all hinges with no less than No. 9 screws, which are 1 in long. Generally, 1-in screws will grip into the stud behind the jamb for additional security.

Door Viewers   An additional security item in the total door system (see Fig. 6) is an optical interviewer or door viewer. Many types of interviewers are available, ranging in diameter from ¼ to 3 in. Viewer optics include one-way glass, plastic, and wide-angle glass. Viewers with a diameter over ¼ in are not recommended, in that they can be punched out to allow insertion of tools to open the door from inside. Wide-angle glass permits maximum visibility. Such viewers should be installed approximately 58 in from the floor and center in the door, and they should be a standard item on every exterior door.

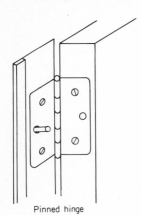

Pinned hinge

Fig. 5 Hinge protection. To prevent lifting of door from hinges: (1) remove two screws, opposite each other from both leaves of the hinge; (2) insert screw or concrete nail into jamb, protruding 1/2 in; (3) drill out opposing screw hole in door. Follow steps for top and bottom hinge of door. When the door is closed, the hinge pins can be pulled out, but the door will remain firmly in place.

Overhead Garage Doors   These doors are also frequently entered by intruders and should be equipped with additional security devices. Although the single sliding hasp and barrel bolt commonly used on garages is usually adequate, one should be affixed to each side of the door. In addition, good-quality padlocks should be used to secure the door. A good padlock is one with an extruded-metal case of laminated steel with a case-hardened shackle which locks both the heel and toe of the shackle into the case. A padlock should have a five-pin-tumbler key cylinder and a key-retaining feature.

Sliding Glass Doors and Windows   Various types of sliding glass doors and windows are also a potential security hazard. Such items generally have inferior locking systems, and/or they can be lifted from the slide track and removed completely from the frame.

Several preventive steps can be taken to upgrade the security of a sliding glass door. One—and the most valuable—is the installation of an auxiliary lock designed for such doors. These locking devices come in a variety of styles and are relatively inexpensive. The type with a key lock is generally considered most secure. The main function of such a lock is to tie the active and inactive leaf of the door together, prohibiting lifting out and/or prying the door open. An additional precautionary measure is to install two pan-head sheet-metal screws in the upper track of the active slider approximately 1 ft from each end and then adjust them downward until the sliding door just clears the track. This will aid in preventing someone from lifting the door out of the frame.

Windows vary in vulnerability based on their size and distance from the ground and on whether they are fixed or can be opened.

All windows can be broken unless they are made of burglary-resistant glazing material. Such material is available, but it generally requires replacement of the frame or sash, which is cost-prohibitive for most residential use. Notably, tempered glass is now required by many states—especially in sliding doors. Unfortunately, the security value of tempered glass is relatively low. Fully tempered glass is four or five times stronger than glass that has not been tempered, and in many cases it will resist a rock or stick, but it will break into small cubes or crystals when pierced with a spring punch or ice pick. When attacked with a sharp instrument and broken, the small cubes crumble easily and fall quietly, with less danger to an intruder because there are no sharp edges. Fortunately, this is a little-known fact, and intruders still go to great lengths to avoid breaking glass, at least because of the anticipated noise factor.

Several techniques can be employed to increase the security of windows with movable sashes. Unfortunately, the standard "clam locks" which are generally utilized provide almost no security. The simplest method, which works equally well with single- or double-hung windows and horizontally sliding windows of all types, is to

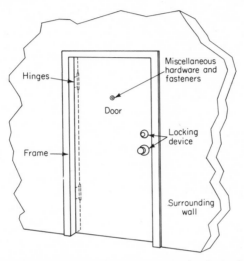

Fig. 6   Door system. The strength of a system is as good as its weakest component.

drill one or more holes through the sash or frame and insert a pin or nail to prevent the window from being opened. Many auxiliary locking devices are also available; some are key-operated, but these pose a potential safety hazard in the event of fire (when a window may be needed for escape). The principal alternative available for protecting vulnerable windows is steel bars, mesh, or grillwork. This method is commonly used in high-crime areas, but unless a quick-release mechanism is used, it is discouraged for obvious safety reasons.

Louvered windows tend to be particularly vulnerable, as there is no practical method to prevent them from being pried open. These windows should be avoided at ground level and at any height that is easily accessible to the potential burglar. If this type of window is required, one security method which has been tried in several areas is the use of epoxy resin to glue the window panes to the metal keepers. This method will, however, cause severe problems if it becomes necessary to replace an individual pane.

Security Lighting   Lighting is of extreme importance in residential security. Used properly, it discourages criminal attacks, increases observability, and reduces fear. Residential lighting for security has only recently become commonplace and has been derived from long-accepted commercial security lighting standards.

Good coverage is the most important aspect of protective lighting in residential outdoor use, where landscaping or structural barriers can create large shadows if light is coming from a single direction. In short, evenness is more important than the absolute level of light.

A simple, but handy, measure of adequate light is the ability to clearly see a 4-in-high street address number on the house from the center of the street.

In emergencies, the numbering of apartments can be an important factor for both security and safety. All entrances to apartment complexes should have an illuminated podium-type numbering system, using a simple method with clockwise numbering starting at the main entrance. In addition, if there are 100 or less units on a given level, the numbering for all apartments on the first floor should commence with 101, on the second floor with 201, etc. In this way, emergency personnel can easily find their intended location.

Locks   Security hardware for residential structures is also important. Although security devices for the home have been used since cave dwellers rolled a large rock in front of the entrance to their cave, increasing concern on the part of police and citizens has prompted lock manufacturers to produce more secure devices of excellent quality that are within the financial reach of most residents.

Locks are of many types and are used for many purposes. They are described in detail in Chapter 15, entitled "Locks and Keying." However, the five major categories that can be used in residences are:

1. Cylinder (key-in-knob) lock
2. Cylinder lock sets with deadlocking function
3. Cylinder deadbolt locks
4. Rim locks
5. Cylindrical lock sets with deadbolt functions

Cylindrical (Key-in-Knob) Locks.   Cylindrical locks, or key-in-knob locks as they are more commonly known, are the most widely used type of locking hardware. This is primarily because they are inexpensive and relatively simple to re-key. Figure 7 illustrates this type of locking system. There are generally two versions of the cylindrical lock. Both versions contain the lock cylinder in the knob and use a spring-activated bolt. The bolt automatically retracts, so the door can be closed. The spring-activated bolt then engages in the frame, securing the door.

One variation of this system relies solely on the spring bolt as the major locking device. This type of mechanism has numerous shortcomings from a security standpoint. For example, since the cylinder is located inside the knob, there is virtually no way of protecting against simple attack (such as breaking off the knob, which eliminates the locking capability of the system). Further, the spring bolt can be "slipped" open with a credit card, celluloid strip, screwdriver, etc.

In the second variation of this system, the spring bolt is augmented with an "anti-shim" device (see the example in Fig. 8). This lock works in the same manner, but the anti-shim device, which is adjacent to the spring bolt, prevents the bolt from being depressed or "loided" when the door is closed and the lock is engaged. Unfortunately, the security offered by this variation is also minimal, since the locking mechanism is still contained in the knob.

Cylinder Deadbolt Locks.   Deadbolt locks are rapidly becoming the most popular type of auxiliary security device in residences and commercial facilities.* There are two primary versions of the deadbolt lock: the single-cylinder (see Fig. 9) and the double-cylinder type (see Fig. 10). The bolt on both versions has no automatic spring action. Rather, it must be operated manually by a key cylinder, thumb turn, or lever and is therefore held fast when in a projected position.

The single-cylinder version is activated from the outside of the door by a key and

*U.S. Department of Justice, *Residental Security,* U.S. Government Printing Office, Washington, D.C., 1973, p. 24.

from the inside by a knob, thumb turn, lever, or similar mechanism. The second version, or double-cylinder type, has two cylinders, one on the outside of the door and one on the inside, both of which require key activation.

The best-designed locks of this type have hardened-steel cores and cylinder guards that can withstand most physical attacks (e.g., twisting, prying, hammering). In

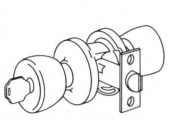

Fig. 7   Cylinder, or key-in-knob lock.

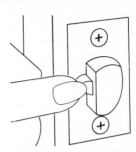

Fig. 8   Anti-shim device on deadlocking latch is a basic security requirement. It consists of a latch with adjoining small plunger that is held depressed—or that "deadlocks"—when the door is closed, making it impossible to release or push back the latch with the insertion of a "shim" such as a plastic credit card between latch and door frame.

addition, they are available with bolts having a 1-in throw, which makes it difficult for an intruder to gain entry by spreading the door frame (say, with a tire jack) and disengaging the bolt from the jamb.

From a strict security standpoint, the double-cylinder deadbolt is preferable to the single-cylinder type, since it effectively provides two separately operated locks. Thus, even if someone can reach inside by breaking a window, the door still cannot be unlocked without a key.

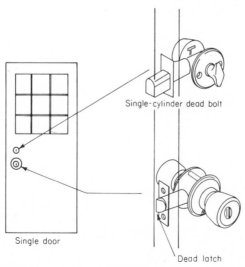

Single-cylinder dead bolt

Single door

Dead latch

Fig. 9   Auxiliary deadlock. Use 1-in deadbolt, single cylinder with hardened cylinder guard and thumb turn. (Bottom shows deadlatch).

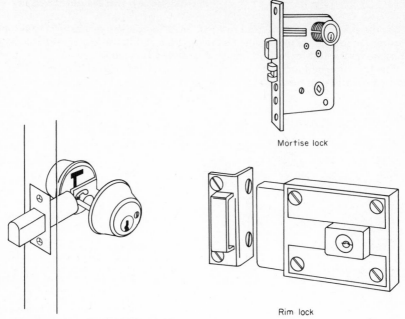

Mortise lock

Rim lock

Fig. 11 Mortise lock and rim Lock.

Fig. 10 Auxiliary deadlock, double cylinder. Use 1-in deadbolt with hardened cylinder guards. If cylinder is locked when house is occupied, leave key in inside keyhole as a means of fast exit in case of fire.

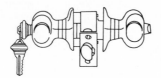

Cylindrical (key-in-knob) lock
with antishim device

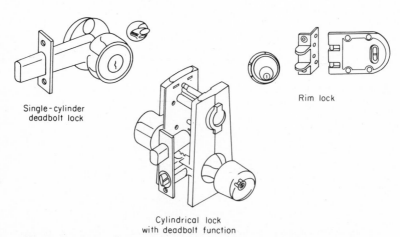

Single-cylinder
deadbolt lock

Rim lock

Cylindrical lock
with deadbolt function

Fig. 12 Types of locking devices. *(Koepsell-Girard and Associates, Falls Church, Virginia.)*

Rim Locks.   These are available in most hardware stores. A rim lock is installed on the inside of the door and may be equipped with either horizontal or vertical deadbolts or a horizontal spring latch. The example shown in Fig. 11 is the vertical-deadbolt variety, which is generally preferable to the horizontal-deadbolt type since it resists spreading attacks more effectively. Assuming the lock is properly installed,

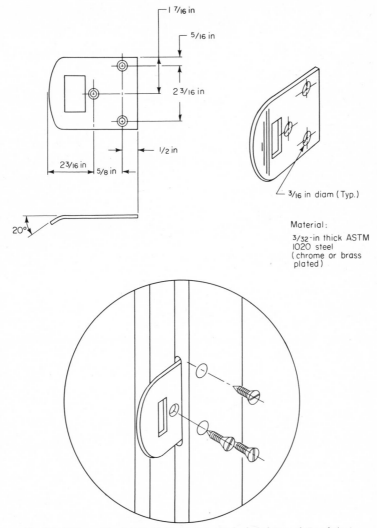

Material:
3/32-in thick ASTM 1020 steel (chrome or brass plated)

Fig. 13   Striker plate design. *(California Crime Technological Research Foundation.)*

with extra-long mounting screws being used, this type of rim lock may offer an acceptable and less expensive level of security.

Cylindrical Lock Sets with Deadbolt Functions.   Some cylindrical lock sets are designed to incorporate an auxiliary deadbolt locking function. Such lock sets combine the automatic locking features of the key-in-knob system with the security characteristics of the cylinder deadbolt. The better-designed systems of this type have a hardened-steel core, a 1-in-throw deadbolt, a recessed cylinder to make forcible removal difficult, a concealed armorplate to protect the locking mechanisms from defeat by drilling, and a cylinder guard that spins freely when the deadbolt is in a locked position. In addition, such systems include a panic feature which permits the knob on the inside to turn freely in case an emergency exit is necessary. The example shown in Fig. 12 incorporates several of these features. Although these lock sets provide good security, they are generally the most expensive of the alternatives discussed.

Lock Strikes   The lock strike is the metal receiver for the lock bolt (not used on rim locks), and it should also be a security consideration (see Fig. 13). The strike is normally installed around a drilled ¾-in hole in the doorjamb and held in place with ½-in screws, which provide little security due to the soft wood jamb. Screws of 1¼ to 1½ in, if used, will traverse the jamb and penetrate the stud, providing sufficient added strength. Several types of protective strikes are available on the market and should be considered in high-risk applications.

CONCLUSION

In this brief chapter only the basic physical considerations of residential security have been discussed. It should be a matter of deep concern for everyone to ensure that architects, engineers, planners, and builders are encouraged to seek additional information about security and crime prevention to make our communities safer. Only through advanced knowledge and conern on their part can we hope to overcome the existing deficiencies in the design and construction of our residential communities.

Clearly, any building design cannot, and should not, be thought of purely in security terms, and there will always be tradeoffs for priority consideration. Yet the importance of security to society has never been greater. Further, the authors know of no greater challenge facing any profession than that of effectively maintaining a system of building which places boundaries upon the freedom of individuals in order to permit them to enjoy their freedom.

Security Product Directory

J. E. THORSEN
Editor-in-Chief, Security World Magazine

This Security Product Directory has been reprinted from the pages of *Security World* Magazine, a recognized authority in the security field. Published annually, the list provides a creditable directory of manufacturers and distributors of security and safety equipment in a format not available elsewhere, and it provides a valuable resource for individuals responsible for specifying such equipment. Copies of current listings can be purchased from Security World Publishing Co., 2639 S. La Cienega Blvd., Los Angeles, CA 90034.

The directory has three components:

CROSS INDEX: Products are shown with reference to a numerical listing in the product directory.

PRODUCT DIRECTORY: Individual products are listed in alphabetical order and numerical sequence.

DIRECTORY OF MANUFACTURERS AND DISTRIBUTORS: Provides names, addresses, and telephone numbers of individual manufacturers and distributors.

CROSS INDEX

A

Access control . . . . . 1.a to 1.b.8, 12
Alarm components, fire 2.b.1
Alarm components,
  fire/intrusion 2.g
Alarm detectors, fire . . 2.a to 2.a.7
Alarm detectors, fire,
  combustion products 2.a.1
Alarm detectors, fire,

fixed temperature 2.a.2
Alarm detectors, fire,
  rate-of-rise 2.a.3
Alarm detectors, fire,
  smoke obscuration 2.a.4
Alarm detectors, fire,
  water flow 2.a.5
Alarm devices, intrusion . . . . 2.c to
  2.c.13, 17.a.1, 17.b, 17.k, 23.a
Alarm equipment distributors 23.a
Alarm installers' tools 24.b

Alarm power packs 2.i
Alarm reporting
  equipment, fire . . . . .2.b to
  2.b.1, 2.e to 2.e.2
Alarm reporting/annunciating
  systems . . . . 2.1 to 2.f.3
Alarm reporting systems, fire . 2.b
Alarm reporting systems,
  fire/intrusion . . . . 2.e to 2.e.2
Alarm reporting systems,
  hardwire 2.e.1

Alarm reporting systems,
intrusion . . . . 2.e to 2.e.2
Alarm reporting systems,
line carrier 2.e.2
Alarm reporting systems,
multiplex 2.e.1
Alarm reporting systems,
personal emergency 2.1.3
Alarm reporting systems,
power failure 2.f.3
Alarm reporting systems,
radio signaling 2.e.2
Alarm reporting systems,
special purpose 2.f.3
Alarm reporting systems,
telephone dialing 2.f.2
Alarm reporting systems,
wireless 2.e.2
Alarm services 22.a
Alarm stations, central
receiving 2.f.1
Alarm system components 2.g to 2.i
Alarms . . . . 2.a to 2.i, 17.a.1, 17.b,
17.k, 20.g, 20.h
Alarms, automobile 2.d.1
Alarms, components . . . . 2.g to 2.i
Alarms, fence 17.a.1
Alarms, intrusion . . . . 2.c to
2.c.13, 17.a.1, 17.b, 17.k, 23.a
Alarms, motor home 2.d.1
Alarms, portable 2.d.2
Alarms, recreational vehicle . 2.d.1
Alarms, reporting
equipment . . . . . . 2.b, 2.e to 2.f.3
Alarms, shoplifting 2.d.5, 20.g
Alarms, special purpose . . . 2.d to
2.d.6, 17.a.1, 17.b, 17.k, 20.g, 20.h
Alarms, telephone dialing . . . 2.f.2
Alarms, truck 2.d.1
Alarms, vehicle 2.d.1
Alerting systems, RF 6.a.6.a
Alternators 6.a.9
Ambulances 25.a
Ammunition 21.b.1.a
Amplifiers 6.a.7
Annunciators 2.g, 2.g.4
Antennas 6.a.8
Anti-shoplifting devices 2.d.5,
20.g, 20.h
Anti-tap devices 6.h.2
Area, passage and remote
entrance control equipment . .1.b
to 1.b.8
Armor, personnel protective .16.a
Armored vehicles 25.b
Assembly components 26.b
Associations 7.b
Audio alarms, sound actuated 2.c.3
Audio amplifiers 6.c
Audio recorders 18
Audio recorders, accessories . .18.g
Audio recorders, general
purpose 18.a
Audio recorders, miniature . .18.c
Audio recorders, portable 18.b

Audio recording/playback
components 18.g
Audio/visual training
materials 7.d.4
Auto insurance 13.a
Automatic/backup lighting . . 8.b.1
Automatic closures 17.c
Automobile alarms 2.d.1

B

Backup alarms, vehicle 10.f
Badge & ID equipment
(laminated) 12.b
Badge holders 21.a.6
Badges, identification (plastic) 12.a
Badges, metal 21.a.4
Ballistic vests 16.a
Batons & nightsticks 21.b.4
Batteries, primary 3.c
Batteries, rechargeable 3.a
Battery & battery chargers 3.a to 3.c
Battery rechargers 3.b
Battery systems,
emergency power 8.a.2
Bells, alarm signaling . . . 2.g, 2.g.1
Binoculars 14.a
Black light equipment 14.b
Boat alarms 2.d.1
Body armor 16.a
Body injury liability insurance 13.m
Bomb blankets 16.b
Bomb, explosives detectors . . .14.c
Bomb handling equipment . . .16.b
Books, reference sources 7.a
Booth equipment 1.b.1.a
Booths, cashiers' 20.b
Booths: guards, traffic, etc. . . 1.b.1
Break glass fire alarm stations 2.b.1
Breath testing equipment . . . 14.d
'Bugging' countermeasures . . 6.h.2
Bulletproof vests 16.a
Bullet resistive doors, walls,
partitions 17.l.1
Bullet resistive glazing
materials 17.l
Burglary insurance 13.b
Burglary resistive doors,
walls, partitions 17.l.1
Burglary resistive glazing
materials 17.l
Burglary resistive safes 20.e
Business interruption
insurance 13.c
Buzzers 2.g, 2.g.1

C

Cable 26.a
Camera equipment and supplies 4.a
to 4.g.6, 19.a, 20.f, 23.b
Camera equipment,
CCTV 19.a, 19.a.1
Camera equipment, film 4.a to 4.g.6
Camera equipment

distributors 23.b
Camera housings, CCTV 19.d
Camera mounts 19.d
Cameras, check cashing 4.a
Cameras, closed circuit
television 19.a, 19.a.1
Cameras, dummy (CCTV) . . . 20.f
Cameras, holdup, film 4.f
Cameras, identification 4.b
Cameras, low-light-level
(CCTV) 19.a.1
Cameras, miniature 4.c
Cameras, motion picture 4.d
Cameras, still 4.e
Cameras, surveillance (film only) 4.f
Cameras, television . . . 19.a, 19.a.1
Caps & hats 21.a.3
Cases tools/instruments 24.c
Cashiers' booths 20.b
Central clock station
reporting systems 17.j.1
Central credit verification . 5.a, 5.b
Central station equipment
components 2.f.1.a
Central station systems 2.f.1
Check authorization systems . .5.a
Check cashing cameras 4.a
Check/document and credit card
protection . . . . 5.a to 5.c, 4.a
Check verification & signature
authentication systems 5.a
Clandestine transmitter
detectors 6.h.2
Cleaners 24.d
Cleared temporary personnel 22.c
Clocks, watchmen's 17.j
Closed circuit television
cameras 19.a
Closed circuit television cameras,
low-light-level 19.a.1
Closed circuit television
dummy cameras 20.f
Closed circuit television
equipment . . . . 19.a to 19.f
Closed circuit television,
related equipment 19.d
Closed circuit television
surveillance systems 19.f
Closed circuit television
tape recorders 19.c
Clothing, protective 9.e, 10.c
Coats, uniform 21.a.1
Code card systems 1.a.1
Code operated locks
(pushbutton) 1.a.2, 17.f
Combination locks 17.f
Combustion products fire
detectors 2.a.1
Commercial multiple peril
insurance 13.d
Communications . . . . .6.a to 6.h.3
Communications, radio 6.a
to 6.a.11
Communications security
equipment . . . . 6.h to 6.h.3

Components, alarm system . . . .2.g to 2.i
Components, audio recording/ playback 18.g
Components, fire alarm 2.b.1
Conferences, security 7.c
Consultant services 22.b
Contacts 2.g, 2.g.2
Contraband walk-through detectors for control 14.g
Control panels . . . 2.b.1, 2.g, 2.g.3
Counterfeit money detectors 14.m
Countermeasures, electronic 6.h.2
Credit card verification systems 5.b
Cylinder guards, anti-pick, anti-pull 17.e.1

D

Data badge systems 1.a.3
Decals 12.e, 20.c
Detectors, fire . . . . .2.a to 2.a.6
Detectors, intrusion . 2.c to 2.c.13, 17.a.1, 17.b, 17.k
Detectors, special purpose . . . .2.d to 2.d.6
Dialers, digital 2.f.2
Dialers, tape 2.f.2
Dialers, telephone 2.f.2
Dictation equipment 18.d
Digital communicators 2.f.2
Digital counter 2.g.7
Digital dialers 2.f.2
Discriminators, sound 2.c.3
Distributors & importers 23
Document destruction equipment 15.d
Dog transporting equipment .16.b
Doors, security 17.a
Doors, burglary/bullet resistive 17.l.1
Door viewers 17.p
Doorway announcers 17.p
Dummy surveillance cameras, CCTV 20.f

E

Educational aids . . . . .7.a to 7.f
Electronic measures and countermeasures 6.h.2
Electronic/mechanical personnel ID systems . . . . .1.a to 1.a.7
Electronic parts 2.h, 26.b
Electronic release locks 1.a.4
Emblems, metal 21.a.4
Emblems, uniform (woven, embroidered) 21.a.5
Emergency & disaster equipment . . . . .8.a to 8.b.5
Emergency lighting . . .8.b to 8.b.3
Emergency power battery systems 8.a.2
Emergency power generators 8.a.3
Emergency power inverters . 8.a.4
Emergency power

transformers 8.a.5
Emergency rescue equipment 8.b.5
Employment services 22.c
Entrance control systems, remote 1.b.6
Equipment locks 15.b, 17.d.2
Errors & omissions insurance .13.e
Exit alarms 2.c.8
Exit hardware, fire 9.d.1
Exit signs 8.b.4, 9.d.1
Explosives detectors 14.c
Extended coverage insurance 13.f

F

Face protection 10.c
Facsimile transmitters/receivers 6.b
False arrest insurance 13.g
Fasteners, tamper resistive . .20.d
Fence alarms 17.a.1
Fencing 17.a
Fidelity bond insurance 13.h
Files, fire resistive 9.c
Film and film processing equipment 4.g.5
Films, training . . . . 7.d to 7.d.3
Fingerprinting equipment . . .14.e
Fire alarm reporting systems . 2.b, 2.e
Fire alarm components 2.b.1
Fire detectors . . . . .2.a to 2.a.6
Fire doors 9.d
Fire exit hardware 9.d.1
Fire extinguishers, portable . . .9.a
Fire extinguishing systems 9.b
Fire insurance 13.i
Fire prevention & protection training films . . . 7.d.1
Fire protection . . . . .9.a to 9.g, 2.a to 2.b.1
Fire resistive files, safes, vaults .9.c
Fire retardant doors/partitions . 9.f
Fire trucks 25.c
Firearms and parts 21.b
First aid kits & supplies 10.a
First aid & safety 10.a to 10.f, 7.d.2, 8.c.1, 9.e, 16, 25.a, 25.c
First aid & safety training films 7.d.2
Fixed temperature fire detectors 2.a.2
Flashers & signs 11.a
Flashlights 8.b.3
Forms, classified security 15.f

G

Garage door openers 17.p
Gate operating equipment . . 1.b.2
Gates 17.a
Generators, emergency power 8.a.3
Glass breakage alarms 2.c.11
Glass, unbreakable 17.l
Glazing materials, burglary/bullet resistive 17.l
Grilles .17.a

Guard booth equipment . . .1.b.1.a
Guard insurance 13.j
Guard patrol equipment 6, 11, 16, 21, 23.c, 25
Guard services 22.d
Guard shelters 1.b.1
Guardrails 1.b.3

H

Hand lamps 8.b.3
Handcuffs 21.a.7
Handguns 21.b.1
Handheld lights 8.b.3
Handheld microphones . . .6.a.10.a
Hangers, garment locking . . .20.h
Hardwire alarm reporting systems 2.e.1
Hats 21.a.3
Helmets, safety 9.e, 10.c
Highway safety training films 7.d.2
Hinges, electric 2.g.7
Holdup cameras 4.f, 19.a
Holsters 21.a.6
Honesty testing aids 14.j
Horns, alarm signaling . 2.g, 2.g.1

I

Identification 12
Identification badges (laminated) 12.a
Identification cameras 4.b
Identification card supplies . . .12.c
Identification, misc. . . .12.g, 12.h
Identification, nameplates & tags 12.e
Identification, suspect 14.i
Identification systems, access control . . . . 1.a to 1.a.7
Infrared intrusion detectors . 2.c.4
Inland marine insurance 13.k
Instrument cases 24.c
Instruments 24.a
Insurance 13
Insurance, auto, physical damage 13.a
Insurance, burglary & theft . .13.b
Insurance, business interruption 13.c
Insurance, commercial multiple peril 13.d
Insurance, errors & omissions 13.e
Insurance, extended coverage 13.f
Insurance, false arrest 13.g
Insurance, fidelity bonds 13.h
Insurance, fire 13.i
Insurance, guard industry . . . 13.j
Insurance, inland marine 13.k
Insurance, kidnap 13.l
Insurance, misc. body injury liability 13.m
Insurance, misc. property damage liability 13.n
Insurance, other 13.q
Insurance, surety bond 13.o

Insurance, workmen's
   compensation 13.p
Intercom systems 6.e.1
Intrusion alarm reporting
   systems ....2.e to 2.e.2
Intrusion detectors .. 2.c to 2.c.13,
   17.a.1, 17.b, 17.k
Inverters, emergency power . 8.a.4
Investigative aids ... 14.a to 14.m
Investigative services 22.e

J

Jackets, uniform 21.a.1

K

Key cabinets & carriers 17.i.1
Key control systems 17.i
Key devices, special 1.a.5
Key holders 21.a.8
Key making equipment 17.d.1
Keyless locks, combination ..1.a.2,
   17.f
Keyless locks, pushbutton 1.a.2, 17.f
Kidnap insurance 13.l

L

Ladders, escape 8.b.5, 10.f
Ladders, maintenance 24.d
Ladders, safety 10.f
Laminating equipment 12.d
Lavaliere microphones ...6.a.10.a
Law enforcement
   training media 7.e
Leather goods 21.a.6
Lenses, camera (film) 4.g.1
Lenses, closed circuit television 19.d
Letter bomb detectors . 14.c, l14.k,
   15.f
Lighting, automatic/backup . 8.b.1
Lighting controls, remote ...17.m
Lighting, emergency ..8.b.1, 8.b.2
Lighting, portable &
   vehicle mounted 8.b.2
Line carrier alarm
   reporting systems 2.e.2
Local control panels 2.b.1, 2.g, 2.g.3
Lock cylinders 17.e
Lock cylinders, anti-pick, anti-
   pull 17.e.1
Lock & key control systems .. 17.i
Lock working equipment ..17.d.1
Lockbars 20.d
Locks 17.d
Locks, combination 17.f
Locks, electric 1.a.4, 17.d
Locks, equipment 15.b, 17.d.2
Locks, pushbutton 1.a.2, 17.f
Locks, recording 17.g
Locks: typewriters, office/portable
   equipment 15.b, 17.d.2
Lockswitches 2.g, 2.g.7
Logging recorders 18.e
Loudspeakers 6.c
Loudspeakers, mobile 6.c.1

Loudspeakers, portable 6.c.2
Lubricants 24.d

M

Magnetic contacts 2.g, 2.g.2
Magnetic tape recorders,
   television 19.c
Magnifiers 14.f
Maintenance supplies 24.d
Mats, pressure sensing .. 2.g, 2.g.5
'Medical alert' equipment .. 2.f.3
Metal detecting equipment ...14.g
Microphones 6.a.10
Microphones, handheld,
   lavaliere, standing 6.a.10.a
Microphones, miniature,
   wired/wireless 6.a.10.b
Microwave intrusion detectors 2.c.2
Miniature cameras 4.c
Minature tape recorders 18.c
Miniature transmitters 6.a.5
Miniature wired/wireless
   microphones 6.a.10.b
Mirrors, convex, anti-theft ...20.a
Mirrors, traffic 10.b
Mirrors, two-way 20.a
Mobile loudspeakers 6.c.1
Mobile radio 6.a.3
Mobile radio telephone 6.a.3.a
Monitor panels 2.g, 2.g.3
Monitors, television 19.b
Motion detectors, video .2.c.7, 19.e
Motion picture cameras 4.d
Motion picture projectors .. 4.g.3
Motor home alarms 2.d.1
Multiplex alarms reporting
   systems 2.e.1

N

Nameplates & tags 12.f, 12.g, 20.c
Night viewing devices 14.h
Nightsticks 21.b.4

O

Office equipment 15
Office equipment locks 15.b, 17.d.2
Organizations 7.b
Outdoor, ground space
   protection 17.k
Outdoor intrusion detectors ..17.k
Overhead projectors 4.g.2
Oxygen equipment 10.d

P

Padlocks 17.h
Paging systems, portable ...6.a.6.b
Pan and tilt CCTV camera
   mountings 19.d
Panic buttons 2.g, 2.g.6
Paper shredders 15.d
Parking control equipment .. 1.b.4
Patrol vehicles 25.d
Perimeter barriers 17.a
Permanent records

storage 9.c, 15.a, 20.e
Personal emergency alarms . 2.d.3
Personal emergency
   alarm reporting systems ... 2.f.3
Personal protective
   body armor 16.a
Personnel protection
   equipment 16, 21.b
Photoelectric beam,
   intrusion detection 2.c.5
Plant patrol vehicles 25.d
Police equipment 6, 11, 16, 21, 25
Police equipment distributors 23.c
Polygraph instruments 14.j
Polygraph schools 7.c
Polygraph services 22.f
Portable alarms 2.d.2
Portable equipment locks ... 15.b,
   17.d.2
Portable fire extinguishers 9.a
Portable lighting 8.b.2
Portable loudspeakers 6.c.2
Portable radios 6.a.2
Portable radio telephone ...6.a.2.a
Portable tape recorders 18.b
Posters, educational ... 7.d.4, 10.e
Power & lighting 3,8
Power failure alarm
   reporting systems 2.f.3
Power failure alarms 2.d.4
Power packs 2.i
Power supplies 8.a.1
Premise protection equipment 17.a
   to 17.p, 2, 9
Pressure mats 2.g, 2.g.5
Pressure sensors 2.c.6
Private telephone systems 6.e
Projectors, motion picture ... 4.g.3
Projectors, overhead display . 4.g.2
Projectors, slide 4.g.4
Property damage liability
   insurance 13.n
Property tags 20.c
Protective clothing/
   equipment 9.e, 10.c, 16.a
Psychological evaluation
   services 22.g
Psychological stress evaluators .14.j
Psychological tests 14.j
Public address systems 6.d
Pullboxes, fire 2.b.1
Pushbutton locks 1.a.2, 17.f

R

Radar intrusion alarms 2.c.2
Radar timing equipment 11.d
Radio communications 6.a to 6.a.11
Radio, alternators 6.a.9
Radio, amplifiers 6.a.7
Radio, antennas 6.a.8
Radio, mobile 6.a.3
Radio, portable 6.a.2
Radio receivers 6.a.6
Radio signaling alarm
   reporting systems 2.e.2

Radio, two-way, fixed station 6.a.1
Rainwear 21.a.2
Ranges, range equipment . . 21.b.2
Rate-of-rise fire detectors ... 2.a.3
Receivers, paging systems . .6.a.6.b
Receivers, radio 6.a.6
Recorders, audio .... 18.a to 18.g
Recorders, audio, accessories
........................18.g
Recorders, audio, general
purpose 18.a
Recorders, audio, miniature . . 18.c
Recorders, audio, portable ...18.b
Recorders, logging 18.e
Recording locks 17.g
Records destruction
equipment 15.d
Records, storage ... 9.c, 15.a, 20.e
Recreational vehicle alarms . . 2.d.1
Reference sources 7.a
Refrigeration failure
alarms 2.d.6, 2.f.3
Relays 2.g, 2.g.2, 26.b
Remote entrance control
systems 1.b.6
Remote lighting controls 17.m
Reports, topical 7.f
Rescue equipment 8.b.5
Residential fire/intrusion alarm
reporting systems 2.e.1, 2.e.2
Resuscitators 10.d
Rifles 21.b.1
Rust preventatives 24.d

S

Safes, burglary resistive 20.e
Safes, fire resistive 9.c
Safes, records storage,
permanent 15.a
Safety equipment .....10.a to 10.f
Scanners, CCTV 19.d
Schools 7.c
Scramblers 6.h.1
Screens, grilles, alarm
signaling 17.b
Screens, security 17.a
Search equipment, metal
detecting 14.g
Security consultant services ...22.b
Security education aids 7
Security training
films/videotape 7.d.1
Security training media 7.d to 7.d.4
Seismic intrusion detectors . 2.c.13
Seminars, security 7.c
Sequential switchers 19.d
Services .... 22.a to 22.h
Shirts, uniform 21.a.1
Shoplifting alarms 2.d.5, 20.g
Shoplifting prevention
equipment .2.d.5, 20.a, 20.f, 20.g,
20.h
Shredders 15.d
Signature authentication
systems 5.a

Signs 9.d.2, 10.e
Sirens, guard patrol
equipment 11.b
Sirens, alarm signaling . 2.g, 2.g.1
Slide projectors 4.g.4
Smoke activated fire detectors 2.a.4
Sonic alarms, audio 2.c.3
Sonic alarms, ultrasonic 2.c.1
Sound detecting alarms, audio 2.c.3
Sound discriminators 2.c.3
Special purpose alarms 2.d to 2.d.6,
17.a.1, 17.b, 17.k, 20.g, 20.h
Splints 10.a
Sprinkler system
supervisory devices 9.b.1
Standing microphones 6.a.10.a
Still cameras 4.e
Stress sensors 2.c.6
Stretchers 10.a
Surety bond insurance 13.o
Surveillance cameras, film 4.f
Surveillance systems, CCTV . . 19.f
Suspect identification 14.i
Swimming pool alarms 2.d.6, 17.p
Switchers, CCTV 19.d

T

Tags, property identification . 20.c
Tamper resistive fasteners ...20.d
Tap detecting devices 6.h.2
Tape dialers 2.f.2
Tape, magnetic, long play ...18.g
Tape recorders, audio 18.a to 18.g
Tape recorders, TV 19.c
Tear gas/dispensers 21.b.3, 21.b.3.a
Tear gas dispensers, intrusion
triggered 17.0
Telephone analyzers 6.h.2
Telephone answering/
recording 6.g, 18.f
Telephone dialing alarm
systems 2.f.2
Telephone locks 15.c
Telephone recorders 18.f
Telephone security 6.h
Telephone systems, private ...6.e
Telephones, mobile radio . .6.a.3.a
Telephones, portable radio 6.a.2.a
Teleprinters 6.f.2
Teletypewriter systems 6.f
Television cameras 19.a
Television cameras,
low-light-level 19.a.1
Television, closed circuit 19
Television monitors 19.b
Television, related equipment 19.d
Television tape recorders 19.c
Test equipment/instruments . . 24.a
Theft insurance 13.b
Theft & robbery preventive
equipment ......20.a to 20.h, 17
Thermal sensors 2.c.13
Time clocks & clock stations . . 17.j
Time locks 17.g.1
Time/date generators 19.d

Tools & instruments 24.a
Tool/instrument cases 24.c
Tools, installation and repair .24.b
Traffic mirrors 10.b
Training aids (not films) 7.d.4
Training films ......7.d.1 to 7.d.3
Training films, fire prevention
& protection 7.d.1
Training films, first aid 7.d.2
Training films, safety 7.d.2
Training films, security 7.d.1
Transmitter detectors 6.h.2
Transmitters 6.a.4
Transmitters, miniature ... 6.a.5
Truck alarms 2.d.1
Truth-, honesty-testing aids .. 14.j
Turnstiles 1.b.5
Two-way radios 6.a.1
Typewriter locks 15.b, 17.d.2

U

Ultraviolet equipment 14.b
Ultraviolet fire detectors 2.a.6
Ultrasonic alarms 2.c.1
Uniformed force
equipment 6, 11, 16, 21, 25
Uniformed force
equipment distributors 23.c
Uniforms 21.a.1

V

Vehicle alarms 2.d.1
Vehicle mounted lighting ... 8.b.2
Vehicle theft warning
systems 2.f.3, 20.h
Vehicles, armored 25.b
Vehicles, limited range 25.e
Vehicles, patrol 25.d
Vehicles, security &
safety ....25.a to 25.f
Vending machine alarms ... 2.c.7
Video motion detectors 19.e
Vidicon tubes 19.d
Visual control boards 15.f
Voice scramblers 6.h.1
Voice stress evaluators 14.j
Voiceprint equipment 14.j

W

Walkie-talkies 6.a.2
Warning lights & signals,
patrol equipment 11.c
Watchmen's clocks 17.j
Water flow sensors 2.a.5
Weapons .... 21b to 21.b.5
Window shock sensors 2.c.12
Windows, security 17.a
Wire & cable and accessories .26.a
Wired/wireless minature
microphones 6.a.10.b
Wireless alarm reporting
systems 2.e.2
Wiretap countermeasures ...6.h.2

Workmen's compensation
insurance 13.p

X

X-ray equipment for
detection 14.k, 15.e

PRODUCT DIRECTORY

ACCESS CONTROL
(see also 12)

Electronic/Mechanical Personnel ID Systems (1.a to 1.a.7)

1.a.1 Code card systems

ALARM LOCK CORP.
A.P.D. SECURITY SYSTEMS
AVANT INC.
A.V.I.D. ENTERPRISES
   (conversion device for key locks)
B-SAFE SYSTEMS INC.
BURNS INTERNATIONAL SECURITY
   SERVICES, INC.
CAMERAS FOR INDUSTRY (CFI)
CARDKEY SYSTEMS
COMPUGUARD CORP.
CONTINENTAL INSTRUMENTS CORP.
DETEX CORP.
ESTERLINE ELECTRONICS CORP.
FALCON UNITED INDUSTRIES, INC.
FEDERAL SIGNAL CORP.
HARCO INDUSTRIES, INC.
HONEYWELL
HOTELTRON SYSTEMS, INC.
   (hotel security system)
MANITOU SYSTEMS, INC.
MORGAN ELECTRONICS, INC.
MOSLER AIRMATIC & ELECTRONIC
   SYSTEMS
NATIONAL SECURITY SYSTEMS, INC.
PROMARK CORP.
ROBOT INDUSTRIES INC.
RUSCO ELECTRONIC SYSTEMS
SARGENT & CO.
SCHLAGE ELECTRONICS
SEALECTRO CORP.
SECOM
SECURA KEY
SECURITY SUPPLY SERVICE INC.
W. H. STEELE CO., INC.
TRINDEL SERVICE CLEMATIC
VISUAL METHODS INC.
WACKENHUT ELECTRONIC SYSTEMS

1.a.2 Code operated, pushbutton

ADMIC
ADVANCED SECURITY CO.
ALARM LOCK CORP.
A.P.D. SECURITY SYSTEMS
BURNS INTERNATIONAL SECURITY
   SERVICES, INC.
CARDKEY SYSTEMS
COMPUGUARD CORP.

CONTINENTAL INSTRUMENTS CORP.
CORBY INDUSTRIES, INC.
   (low power, no wire, touch tone,
   digital key)
DETEX CORP.
DTI SECURITY INC.
ELECTRONIC SECURITY SYSTEMS,
   INC.
FALCON UNITED INDUSTRIES, INC.
HARCO INDUSTRIES, INC.
HONEYWELL
MORGAN ELECTRONICS, INC.
MRL, INC.
PROMARK CORP.
REDCO INC.
RUSCO ELECTRONIC SYSTEMS
SARGENT & GREENLEAF, INC.
SECURA KEY
SECURITY PRODUCTS CO.
SECURTEC, INC.
SIMPLEX SECURITY SYSTEMS, INC.
W. H. STEELE CO., INC.
UNICAN SECURITY SYSTEMS CORP.
VERTEX SCIENCE INDUSTRIES, INC.
WACKENHUT ELECTRONIC SYSTEMS
WESTERN ALARM SUPPLY CO.

1.a.3 Data badge systems

CARDKEY SYSTEMS
HARCO INDUSTRIES, INC.
MANITOU SYSTEMS, INC.
MORGAN ELECTRONICS, INC.
NATIONAL SECURITY SYSTEMS, INC.
RUSCO ELECTRONIC SYSTEMS
SEALECTRO CORP.
VICON INDUSTRIES INC.

1.a.4 Electronic release locks

ADAMS RITE MFG. CO.
ALARM LOCK CORP.
CARDKEY SYSTEMS
CONTINENTAL INSTRUMENTS CORP.
CORBY INDUSTRIES, INC.
   (low power, no wire, touch tone,
   digital key)
FALCON UNITED INDUSTRIES, INC.
FOLGER ADAM CO.
HONEYWELL
MARDIX, INC.
ROBOT INDUSTRIES INC.
RUSCO ELECTRONIC SYSTEMS
SARGENT & GREENLEAF, INC.
SCHLAGE ELECTRONICS
SECURITRON MAGNALOCK CORP.
STANLEY VEMCO
TRINE MFG.
VON DUPRIN INC.
WICO CORP.

1.a.5 Special key devices

A.V.I.D. ENTERPRISES
   (key lock conversion device to
   code card system)
FACIT-ADDO, INC.
GERBER SECURITY PRODUCTS, INC.

1.a.6 Fingerprint and contour

CALSPAN TECHNOLOGY PRODUCTS,
   INC.
IDENTIMAT CORP.
   (hand geometry)
ROCKWELL INTERNATIONAL CORP.
TRINDEL SERVICE CLEMATIC

1.a.7 Other

COMPUGUARD CORP.
   (central monitoring control
   system)
LERRO ELECTRICAL CORP.
   (custom-designed)

Area, Passage and Remote Entrance Control Equipment (1.b to 1.b.8)

1.b.1 Booths (guards, traffic, etc.)

CHIC-SALES CO. INC.
ENDURE-A-LIFETIME PRODUCTS,
   INC.
KEENE CORP.
PAR-KUT INTERNATIONAL, INC.
PORTA-KING BLDG. SYSTEMS
PROTECTIVE MATERIALS CO.
ROBOT INDUSTRIES INC.
   (with turnstile/metal detector)

1.b.1.a Booth equipment

CHIC-SALES CO. INC.

1.b.2 Gate operating equipment

A.P.D. SECURITY SYSTEMS
CARDKEY SYSTEMS
FACIT-ADDO, INC.
HARCO INDUSTRIES, INC.
MORGAN ELECTRONICS, INC.
RICHARDS-WILCOX MFG. CO.
ROBOT INDUSTRIES INC.
RUSCO ELECTRONIC SYSTEMS
STANLEY VEMCO

1.b.3 Guardrails

ALVARADO MFG. CO., INC.

1.b.4 Parking control equipment

A.P.D. SECURITY SYSTEMS
CARDKEY SYSTEMS
FACIT-ADDO, INC.
FEDERAL SIGNAL CORP.
HARCO INDUSTRIES, INC.
MORGAN ELECTRONICS, INC.
RICHARDS-WILCOX MFG. CO.
ROBOT INDUSTRIES INC.
RUSCO ELECTRONIC SYSTEMS
SCHLAGE ELECTRONICS
STANLEY VEMCO

1.b.5 Turnstiles

ALVARADO MFG. CO., INC.
BEAVER TURNSTILES
FACIT-ADDO, INC.
HARCO INDUSTRIES, INC.
MORGAN ELECTRONICS, INC.

Perey Mfg. Co., Inc.
Qonaar Security Systems, Inc.
Robot Industries Inc.
Rusco Electronic Systems

1.b.6 Remote entrance control systems

Advanced Security Co.
(digital control system)
Avant Inc.
(split screen TV)
Corby Industries, Inc.
(low power, no wire, touch tone, digital key)
Crest Electronics Inc.
(split screen system)
Douglas Randall Div.
walter kidde & co., inc.
(systems)
Harco Industries, Inc.
(computer controlled mag stripe)
Honeywell
Kaba Security Locks, Inc.
(key activated switches)
Mardix, Inc.
(CCTV access control special system)
Rusco Electronic Systems
(central console, command capability)
Securitron Magnalock Corp.
(electromagnetic locks)
Speedcall Corp.
(tone signaling equipment for remote & supervisory control)
Stanley Vemco
(electric door & gate operators)
Visual Methods Inc.
(split screen television)
Von Duprin Inc.
(console & electric strikes)

1.b.7 Contraband detectors for walk-through control (see 14.g)

1.b.8 Other

Aarm Lock Corp.
(exit alarm lock)
Electro-Vox Industries Inc.
(telephone-controlled lobby entry system)
Extra Security Inc.
(telephone-controlled lobby entry system)
Marlee Electronics Corp.
(telephone-controlled lobby entry system)
Tele-Entry Security Inc.
(telephone-controlled lobby entry system)

ALARMS
(see also 23.a)

Alarms, Fire

Fire Detectors, Alarm Signaling (2.a to 2.a.6)

2.a.1 Combustion products

Ademco (Alarm Device Mfg. Co.)
ADT
Alarm Distributors
Alarm Supply Co. Inc.
Wm. B. Allen Security Supplies
American Electronics, Inc.
American Protection Systems
Aritech Corp.
A-T-O Inc.
BRK Electronics
B-Safe Systems Inc.
C.E.M. Security Products
Chloride Pyrotector
Conrac Corp.
Consolidated Security Products
"Controller Systems" Corp.
Crusader Security Corp.
Custom Alarm Products
W. S. Darley & Co.
Delta Products, Inc.
Douglas Randall Div.
walter kidde & co., inc.
Edwards Co., Inc.
Emergency Products Corp.
Empire Machines & Systems Inc.
Extra Security Inc.
Fenwal Inc.
(alarm/water release activating)
Fire Control Instruments, Inc.
Fire-Lite Alarms Inc.
Fried Brothers Inc.
Fyrnetics, Inc.
Gamewell/Alarmtronics
Graviner Inc.
Honeywell
Instant Alert
Jaybil Industries, Inc.
K-F Industries, Inc.
Lake Jackson Industries, Inc.
Moose Products Inc.
Morse Products Mfg.
MRL, Inc.
Napco Security Systems, Inc.
North Electric Co.
Nutone Div.
scovill
Poly-Sscientific Div.
litton systems, inc.
Pyr-A-Larm, Inc.
Qonaar Security Systems, Inc.
Reliable Fire Equipment Co.
Rixson-Firemark, Inc.
Rock-Land Industries, Inc.
Security Supply Service Inc.
Sensor-Tec, Inc.
Sentrol, Inc.
Spirig Ernest
Square D Co.
Statitrol Corp.

System Controls, Inc.
Unitec Inc.
Universal Security Instruments, Inc.
Wacenhut Electronic Systems
Wells Fargo Alarm Services
Western Alarm Supply Co.
Westinghouse Security Systems,Inc.

2.a.2 Fixed temperature

Ademco (Alarm Device Mfg. Co.)
Alarm Distributors
Wm. B. Allen Security Supplies
Aritech Corp.
C.E.M. Security Products
Chloride Pyrotector
Concepts-In-Alarms, Inc.
Conrac Corp.
"Controller Systems" Corp.
Controlonics Corp.
Crusader Security Corp.
Custom Alarm Products
W. S. Darley & Co.
Douglas Randall Div.
walter kidde & co., inc.
Edwards Co., Inc.
Fenwal Inc.
(alarm/water release activating)
Fire Control Instruments, Inc.
Fire-Lite Alarms Inc.
Gamewell/Alarmtronics
Graviner Inc.
Honeywell
Instant Alert
Morse Products Mfg.
North Electric Co.
Nutone Div.
scovill
The Peterzell Co.
Potter Electric Signal Co.
Pyr-A-Larm, Inc.
Rittenhouse
Spirig Ernest
Transcience Industries Inc.
Trine Mfg.
Wells Fargo Alarm Services

2.a.3 Rate-of-rise

Ademco (Alarm Device Mfg. Co.
Wm. B. Allen Security Supplies
Aritech Corp.
A-T-O Inc.
Conrac Corp.
"Controller Systems" Corp.
Custom Alarm Products
Douglas Randall Div.
walter kidde & co., inc.
Edwards Co., Inc.
Extra Security Inc.
Fenwal Inc.
(alarm/water release activating)
Fire Control Instruments, Inc.
Fire-Lite Alarms, Inc.
Gamewell/Alarmtronics

GRAVINER INC.
HOLMES PROTECTION, INC.
HONEYWELL
MORSE PRODUCTS MFG.
NORTH ELECTRIC CO.
NUTONE DIV.
  SCOVILL
POTTER ELECTRIC SIGNAL CO.
PYR-A-LARM, INC.
WELLS FARGO ALARM SERVICES

2.a.4 Smoke obscuration

ADCOR ELECTRONICS, INC.
ADEMCO (ALARM DEVICE MFG. CO.)
ADT
ALARM DISTRIBUTORS
WM. B. ALLEN SECURITY SUPPLIES
AMERICAN ELECTRONICS, INC.
ARITECH CORP.
B-SAFE SYSTEMS INC.
CHLORIDE PYROTECTOR
CONRAC CORP.
CUSTOM ALARM PRODUCTS
DOUGLAS RANDALL DIV.
  WALTER KIDDE & CO., INC.
EDWARDS CO., INC.
EMERGENCY PRODUCTS CORP.
EXTRA SECURITY INC.
FIRE BURGLARY INSTRUMENTS INC.
FIRE CONTROL INSTRUMENTS, INC.
FIRE-LITE ALARMS INC.
GAMEWELL/ALARMTRONICS
GRAVINER INC.
HONEYWELL
K-F INDUSTRIES, INC.
MORSE PRODUCTS MFG.
NAPCO SECURITY SYSTEMS, INC.
NUTONE DIV.
  SCOVILL
POTTER ELECTRIC SIGNAL CO.
PYR-A-LARM, INC.
RITTENHOUSE
SCAN SECURITY SYSTEMS INC.
SILENT KNIGHT SECURITY SYSTEMS
STATITROL CORP.
THREE B ELECTRONICS, INC.
TRINE MFG.
WACKENHUT ELECTRONIC SYSTEMS
WELLS FARGO ALARMS SERVICES

2.a.5 Water flow

ADEMCO (ALARM DEVICE MFG. CO.)
ARITECH CORP.
A-T-O INC.
FIRE-LITE ALARMS INC.
HONEYWELL
MORSE PRODUCTS MFG.
POTTER ELECTRIC SIGNAL CO.

2.a.6 Other

CHLORIDE PYROTECTOR
  (ultraviolet flame detectors)
CONTROLONICS CORP.
  (marine, explosive gases)
FENWAL INC.
  (ultraviolet)
K-F INDUSTRIES, INC.
  (gas, heat detectors)

Alarm Reporting Equipment, Fire (2.b to 2.b.1)

2.b Fire alarm reporting systems (see also 2.e to 2.e.2)

ADVANCED SIGNALING CO., INC.
BRASH INDUSTRIES
CONRAC CORP.
FIRE BURGLARY INSTRUMENTS INC.
HONEYWELL
POTTER ELECTRIC SIGNAL CO.
UNITEC INC.

2.b.1 Alarm components, fire (see also 2.g)

ADEMCO
  (manual pullboxes)
ALARM DISTRIBUTORS
  (break glass stations, manual
  pullboxes)
ALARM PRODUCTS INTERNATIONAL,
  INC.
  (fire controls)
WM. B. ALLEN SECURITY SUPPLIES
  (break glass stations)
AMERICAN ELECTRONICS, INC.
  (break glass stations, manual
  pullboxes)
ARITECH CORP.
  (break glass stations, manual
  pullboxes)
DOUGLAS RANDALL DIV.
  WALTER KIDDE & CO., INC.
  (break glass stations, manual
  pullboxes)
FIRE CONTROL INSTRUMENTS, INC.
  (break glass stations)
FIRE-LITE ALARMS, INC.
  (break glass stations, manual
  pullboxes)
GAMEWELL/ALARMTRONICS
  (break glass stations, manual
  pullboxes, two-way voice
  communication)
MORSE PRODUCTS MFG.
  (break glass stations, manual
  pullboxes)
SECURITY SUPPLY SERVICE INC.
  (break glass stations, manual
  pullboxes, two-way voice
  communication)
UNITEC INC.
  (control panels)
WESTERN SECURITY PRODUCTS
  (break glass stations, manual
  pullboxes)

Alarms, Intrusion/Special Purpose

Intrusion Detectors, Alarm Signaling (2.c to 2.c.13)

2.c.1 Ultrasonic

AB TELEKONTROLL
ADEMCO (ALARM DEVICE MFG. CO.)
ADVANCED DEVICES LABORATORY,
  INC.

ALARM DISTRIBUTORS
ALARM PRODUCTS INTERNATIONAL
  INC.
ALARM SUPPLY CO., INC.
WM. B. ALLEN SECURITY SUPPLIES
APS DIV.
  SECURITY TECHNOLOGY SYSTEMS
  CO.
ARITECH CORP.
ARROWHEAD ENTERPRISES INC.
ATRONIC
B-SAFE SYSTEMS INC.
COGNETICS CORP.
CONRAC CORP.
CONSOLIDATED SECURITY
  PRODUCTS
"CONTROLLOR SYSTEMS" CORP.
CONTRONIC CONTROLS LTD.
CUSTOM ALARM PRODUCTS
DELTA PRODUCTS, INC.
DETECTION SYSTEMS, INC.
DETECTRON SECURITY SYSTEMS,
  INC.
DOUGLAS RANDALL DIV.
  WALTER KIDDE & CO., INC.
EMERGENCY PRODUCTS CORP.
EMPIRE MACHINES & SYSTEMS INC.
FUNCTIONAL DEVICES INC.
HOLMES PROTECTION, INC.
HONEYWELL
INSTANT ALERT
INTERARMS
  (portable)
KOLIN INDUSTRIES INC.
MASSA CORP.
MORSE PRODUCTS MFG.
MSS ELECTRONICS, INC.
NEWBRITE ALARMS, INC.
NORTH ELECTRIC CO.
ON GUARD SECURITY SYSTEMS,
  INC.
  (self-contained)
PROTECTRON, INC.
SCAN SECURITY SYSTEMS INC.
SECURITY SUPPLY SERVICE INC.
SIGMA ELECTRONICS INC.
SIGNALARM INC.
SONTRIX
SPIRIG ERNEST
SYSTEM CONTROLS, INC.
THREE B ELECTRONICS, INC.
UNISEC, INC.
WESTERN ALARM SUPPLY CO.
WESTERN SECURITY PRODUCTS
WESTINGHOUSE SECURITY
  SYSTEMS, INC.

2.c.2 Microwave

ADEMCO (ALARM DEVICE MFG. CO.)
ADVANCED DEVICES LABORATORY,
  INC.
ALARM SUPPLY CO., INC.
WM. B. ALLEN SECURITY SUPPLIES
ARITECH CORP.
A.S.E. PROTECTIVE SYSTEMS &
  SERVICES
  (human vs. mechanical
  discrimination)

B-Safe Systems Inc. .
Consolidated Security
  Products
Crest Electronics Inc.
Detect-All Security Systems,
  Inc.
Detectron Security Systems,
  Inc.
Gamewell/Alarmtronics
Honeywell
Lucco Security Products Co.
Microwave Associates, Inc.
Microwave Sensors, Inc.
Mountain West Alarm Supply
  Co.
North Electric Co.
On Guard Security Systems,
  Inc.
  (self-contained)
Peak Technologies, Inc.
Potter Electric Signal Co.
Racon, Inc.
Security General
Security Supply Service Inc.
Shorrock Inc.
Signalarm Inc.
Solfan Systems Inc.
Spirig Ernest
Titan Security Systems
  (portable)
Transicoil Consumer Products,
  Inc.
Western Alarm Supply Co.
Western Security Products

2.c.3 Audio

Acron Corp.
  (sound discriminator)
Alarm Supply Co., Inc.
American Protection Systems
  (sound discriminator)
Andover Sensing Device Corp.
APS Div.
  security technology systems
  co.
Aritech Corp.
Atlas Sound
Audio Sentry Corp.
Audio Transport Systems
Audiotech Corp.
  (sound discriminator)
Betco Electronics
"Controllor Systems" Corp.
  (sound discriminator)
Dal Industries Inc.
  (sound discriminator)
E. E. Industries, Inc.
Emergency Products Corp.
Gamewell/Alarmtronics
Grandin Industries Inc.
Guardian Electronics Inc.
Honeywell
Instant Alert
International Alarm Research
Kenco Inc.
King Research Labs, Inc.
  (sound discriminator)

Lake Jackson Industries, Inc.
Magnum Products Inc.
MGI, Inc.
Mosler Airmatic & Electronic
  Systems
MRC Alarm Systems & Devices
  Co.
MRL, Inc.
North Electric Co.
Nutone Div.
  scovill
Potter Electric Signal Co.
Richmond Enterprises Inc.
Securitone, Inc.
Sensor-Tec, Inc.
Sigma Electronics Inc.
Technology Systems Corp.
  (sound discriminator)
Transcience Industries Inc.
Transicoil Consumer Products,
  Inc.
  (sound discriminator)
Vertex Science Industries, Inc.
  (listen-in capability)
World Wide Mktg. & Research,
  Inc.

2.c.4 Infrared
(see also 2.c.13)

Advanced Devices Laboratory,
  Inc.
Alarm Distributors
Alarm Supply Co., Inc.
Wm. B. Allen Security Supplies
Aritech Corp.
B-Safe Systems Inc.
C.E.M. Security Products
Colorado Eectro-Optics
Emergency Products Corp.
F & W Alarm Systems, Inc.
Fire-Lite Alarms Inc.
Honeywell
Morse Products Mfg.
Mosler Airmatic & Electronic
  Systems
North Electric Co.
Nutone Div.
  scovill
Peak Technologies, Inc.
Raytek
Scan Security Systems Inc.
Security General
Sentry Watch, Inc.
  (portable)
Signalarm Inc.
Silent Watchman Corp.
Spirig Ernest
Trans-Air Mfg. Co., Ltd.
Victory Eengineering Corp.
Western Alarm Supply Co.
Western Security Products

2.c.5 Photoelectric

Ademco (Alarm Device Mfg. Co.)
ADT
Air-Ways Distributors Inc.
Alarm Supply Co., Inc.
Wm. B. Allen Security Supplies

American Electronics, Inc.
Aritech Corp.
Arrowhead Enterprises Inc.
B-Safe Systems Inc.
Colorado Electro-Optics
Conrac Corp.
"Controllor Systems" Corp.
Contronic Controls Ltd.
Detection Systems, Inc.
F & W Alarm Systems, Inc.
Fire Burglary Instruments Inc.
Honeywell
Morse Products Mfg.
Napco Security Systems, Inc.
North Electric Co.
Nutone Div.
  scoville
Qonaar Security Systems, Inc.
Spirig Ernest
Three B Electronics, Inc.
Western Security Products

2.c.6 Pressure sensing

Ademco (Alarm Device Mfg.
  Co.)
Alarm Supply Co., Inc.
Wm. B. Allen Security Supplies
Aritech Corp.
Cable Switch Corp.
"Controllor Systems" Corp.
Emergency Products Corp.
Nutone Div.
  scovill
Recora Co., Inc.
Signal-U Mfg. Co.
Snyder Eelectronics, Inc.
United Security Products, Inc.

2.c.7 Video alarms

Wm. B. Allen Security Supplies
Aritech Corp.
Atronic
Crest Electronics Inc.
GBC Closed Circuit Television
  Corp.
Gyyr Products
Impossible Electronic
  Techniques, Inc.
RCA Electro-Optics & Devices
SC Electronics, Inc.
Vicon Industries, Inc.
Video Tek, Inc.
Visual Communication
  Specialists

2.c.8 Exit

Alarm Lock Corp.
Alpha Electronics Mfg. Ltd.
Aritech Corp.
Continental Instruments Corp.
Dal Industries Inc.
Detectron Security Systems,
  Inc.
Detex Corp.
Door Alarm Devices Corp.
Doppler Corp.
E. E. Industries, Inc.

PRO-TECH SECURITY SYSTEMS INC.
  (door/window)
SE-KURE CONTROLS, INC.
SENTATEK CORP. OF AMERICA
SILENT WATCHMAN CORP.
UNITED SECURITY PRODUCTS, INC.
VON DUPRIN INC.

2.c.9 Capacitance

ADEMCO (ALARM DEVICE MFG. CO.)
WM. B. ALLEN SECURITY SUPPLIES
ARITECH CORP.
GTE SYLVANIA SECURITY SYSTEMS
MOSLER AIRMATIC & ELECTRONIC
  SYSTEMS

2.c.10 Radar
  (see 2.c.2)

2.c.11 Glass breakage

ADEMCO (ALARM DEVICE MFG. CO.)
ADVANCED DEVICES LABORATORY,
  INC.
ALARM SUPPLY CO., INC.
WM. B. ALLEN SECURITY SUPPLIES
ANDOVER SENSING DEVICE CORP.
ARITECH CORP.
BETCO ELECTRONICS
"CONTROLLOR SYSTEMS" CORP.
EMERGENCY PRODUCTS CORP.
GAMEWELL/ALARMTRONICS
GRANDIN INDUSTRIES INC.
KING RESEARCH LABS., INC.
LASSEN ELECTRONICS CORP.
MORSE PRODUCTS MFG.
NAPCO SECURITY SYSTEMS, INC.
NUTONE DIV.
  SCOVILL
PRO-TECH SECURITY SYSTEMS INC.
SECURITY INSTRUMENTS, INC.
SIGNALARM INC.
SNYDER ELECTRONICS, INC.
SPIRIG ERNEST
TECHNOLOGY SYSTEMS CORP.
UNITED SECURITY PRODUCTS, INC.

2.c.12 Window shock

ADEMCO (ALARM DEVICE MFG. CO.)
ADVANCED DEVICES LABORATORY,
  INC.
ALARM SUPPLY CO., INC.
DETECTRON SECURITY SYSTEMS,
  INC.
KING RESEARCH LABS., INC.
LASSEN ELECTRONICS CORP.
NAPCO SECURITY SYSTEMS, INC.
POLY-SCIENTIFIC DIV.
  LITTON SYSTEMS, INC.
SECURITY INSTRUMENTS, INC.
SPIRIG ERNEST
TECHNOLOGY SYSTEMS CORP.
UNITED SECURITY PRODUCTS, INC.

2.c.13 Other

AEL-EMTECH CORP.
  (proximity)

CRUSADER SECURITY CORP.
  (non-electric, pneumatic)
DETECTRON SECURITY SYSTEMS,
  INC.
  (stress)
INTRUSION DETECTION SYSTEMS,
  INC. (I.D.S. INC.)
  (buried seismic system)
ROSSIN CORP.
  (passive infrared thermal
  sensors)
SHORROCK INC.
  (seismic)
TAPESWITCH CORP. OF AMERICA
  (window sill alarm)
TRANS-AIR MFG. CO., LTD.
  (thermal)

Alarms, Special Purpose (2.d to 2.d.6)

2.d.1 Vehicle alarms

ADEMCO (ALARM DEVICE MFG. CO.)
  (auto, truck)
AEROLARM
  (auto)
AIR-WAYS DISTRIBUTORS INC.
  (auto)
ALARM DISTRIBUTORS
  (auto, truck, motor home)
ALARM SUPPLY CO., INC.
  (auto)
WM. B. ALLEN SECURITY SUPPLIES
  (auto, truck, boat, recreational
  vehicle, motor home)
ALPHA ELECTRONICS MFG. LTD.
  (truck, motor home)
ANDOVER SENSING DEVICE CORP.
  (recreational vehicle, motor
  home)
APS DIV.
  SECURITY TECHNOLOGY SYSTEMS
  CO.
  (recreational vehicle, motor
  home)
ARITECH CORP.
  (auto)
ATLAS SOUND
  (auto, truck)
AUDIOTECH CORP.
  (auto, truck, recreational vehicle,
  motor home)
B-SAFE SYSTEMS INC.
  (auto, truck, boat, recreational
  vehicle, motor home)
BURGLAR BUG MFG.
  (auto, truck, recreational vehicle,
  motor home)
CALIFORNIA ELECTRONIC
  INDUSTRIES, INC.
  (auto, truck, with pocket pager
  theft warning system)
C.C.U. INC.
  (auto, truck, boat, recreational
  vehicle, motor home)
CITIZEN AMERICA CORP.

  (auto, truck, boat, recreational
  vehicle, motor home)
DON COCHRAN & ASSOCIATES
  (auto, ultrasonic)
COGNETICS CORP.
  (auto, truck, boat, recreational
  vehicle, motor home)
"CONTROLLOR SYSTEMS" CORP.
  (auto, truck, boat, recreational
  vehicle, motor home)
DAL INDUSTRIES INC.
  (auto, truck, boat, recreational
  vehicle, motor home)
DELTA PRODUCTS, INC.
  (auto, truck, boat, recreational
  vehicle, motor home)
DEPEND-ALARM
  (auto, truck, boat, recreational
  vehicle, motor home,
  motorcycle)
DETECTION SYSTEMS, INC.
  (auto, truck, boat, recreational
  vehicle, motor home)
DETECTRON SECURITY SYSTEMS,
  INC.
  (auto, truck, boat, recreational
  vehicle, motor home)
DIRECT SAFETY CO.
  (truck)
E.E. INDUSTRIES, INC.
  (auto, truck, boat, recreational
  vehicle, motor home)
ELK-ROUTEMASTER, INC.
  (truck)
EMPIRE MACHINES & SYSTEMS INC.
  (auto, recreational vehicle, motor
  home)
EVER-GUARD ALARM CO.
  (auto, truck, recreational vehicle,
  motor home, tractor)
GARD-A-CAR, INC.
  (auto: ignition immobilizer)
GUARD AWARE, INC.
  (auto, truck, recreational vehicle,
  motor home)
GUARDIAN ELECTRONICS INC.
  (boat, recreational vehicle, motor
  homes)
HARCOR INTERNATIONAL INC.
  (auto, truck, recreational vehicle,
  motor home)
INTERARMS
  (auto, truck, boat, recreational
  vehicle, motor home)
INTERNATIONAL IMPORTERS, INC.
  (auto)
KING RESEARCH LABS, INC.
  (auto, truck, boat, recreational
  vehicle, motor home)
KOLIN INDUSTRIES INC.
  (auto, truck, boat, recreational
  vehicle, motor home)
LAW ENFORCEMENT ASSOCIATES,
  INC.
  (auto, truck, boat, recreational
  vehicle)

MAGNA DIGITRONICS, INC.
(auto, truck, boat, recreational vehicle, motor home)
MONROE TIMER CO. INC.
(auto, truck, boat, recreational vehicle, motor home)
MOUNTAIN WEST ALARM SUPPLY CO.
(auto)
NEWBRITE ALARMS, INC.
(boat, recreational vehicle)
THE NIGHT EYE CORP.
(auto, truck, boat, recreational vehicle, motor home)
PAGE ALERT SYSTEMS, INC.
(auto, truck, boat, recreational vehicle, motor home)
THE PETERZELL CO.
(recreational vehicle, motor home)
PRO-COM SYSTEMS, INC.
(radio decoder)
PRO-TECH SECURITY SYSTEMS INC.
(auto, truck, boat, recreational vehicle, motor home: ignition immobilizer)
QUALICOMP SECURITY PRODUCTS
(auto)
SCAN SECURITY SYSTEMS INC.
(boat)
SECURITONE, INC.
(truck, boat, recreational vehicle, motor home)
SECURITY RESEARCH INC.
(auto, truck, boat, recreational vehicle, motor home)
SECURITY SUPPLY SERVICE INC.
(auto, truck)
SE-KURE CONTROLS, INC.
(auto, truck, boat, recreational vehicle, motor home)
SIGMA ELECTRONICS INC.
(auto, truck, boat, recreational vehicle, motor home)
SIGNALARM INC.
(auto, truck, recreational vehicle, motor home)
SILENT WATCHMAN CORP.
(truck)
TAYLOR MARKETING INT'L.
(auto, truck with engine shutoff)
THREE B ELECTRONICS, INC.
(auto)
T.P.S. INC.
(auto, truck, recreational vehicle, motor home)
UNITED SECURITY PRODUCTS, INC.
(auto, truck, boat, recreational vehicle, motor home)
UNIVERSAL SECURITY INSTRUMENTS, INC.
(auto, truck, boat, recreational vehicle)
WESTERN ALARM SUPPLY CO.
(auto)
WHOLESALE SECURITY DEVICES

(auto, truck, boat, recreational vehicle, motor home)
WILCO CORP.
(truck, recreational vehicle, motor home)
WOLO MFG. CORP.
(auto, truck, boat, recreational vehicle, motor home)

2.d.2 Portable alarms

ALPHA ELECTRONICS MFG. LTD.
ANDOVER SENSING DEVICE CORP.
APS DIV.
  SECURITY TECHNOLOGY SYSTEM CO.
BEI ELECTRONICS, INC.
(radio frequency)
DETECTION SYSTEMS, INC.
DETECTRON SECURITY SYSTEMS, INC.
ESTERLINE ELECTRONICS CORP.
GRANDIN INDUSTRIES INC.
GUARDIAN ELECTRONICS INC.
INTERARMS
INTRUSION DETECTION SYSTEMS, INC. (I.D.S. INC.)
(outdoor buried seismic system)
KOLIN INDUSTRIES INC.
LAW ENFORCEMENT ASSOCIATES, INC.
THE NIGHT EYE CORP.
ON GUARD SECURITY SYSTEMS, INC.
THE PETERZELL CO.
RICHMOND ENTERPRISES INC.
SECURITONE, INC.
SENTRY WATCH, INC.
SHORROCK INC.
(microwave fence system)
SIGNALARM INC.
SILENT WATCHMAN CORP.
SPIRIG ERNEST
TECHNOLOGY SYSTEMS CORP.
TITAN SECURITY SYSTEMS
TRANS-AIR MFG. CO., LTD.

2.d.3 Personal emergency (see also 2.g.6)

WM. B. ALLEN SECURITY SUPPLIES
ARITECH CORP.
ATRONIC
EXTRA SECURITY INC.
LAW ENFORCEMENT ASSOCIATES, INC.
MULTI-ELMAC CO.
NAPCO SECURITY SYSTEMS, INC.
THE PETERZELL CO.
QONAAR SECURITY SYSTEMS, INC.
TRINE MFG.
UNISEC, INC.

2.d.4 Power failure

APS DIV.
  SECURITY TECHNOLOGY SYSTEMS CO.
AUDIOTECH CORP.
FUNCTIONAL DEVICES INC.

MAGNA DIGITRONICS, INC.
(refrigeration failure)

2.d.5 Shoplifting alarms (see also 20.g)

AEROLARM
CHECKPOINT SYSTEMS, INC.
(walk-thru & portable detection devices)
DELTA PRODUCTS, INC.
(display, loop)

2.d.6 Other

ADMIC
(swimming pool alarm)
CRAFTOR INC.
(residential gas leak detector)
FOREWARN INC.
(swimming pool alarm)
HYDRO-TEMP CONTROLS, INC.
(water leakage/flooding, climate change alarms)
K-F INDUSTRIES, INC.
(gas, poisonous fumes detector)
MRL, INC.
(noxious gas detector)
POOL GUARD, INC.
(swimming pool alarm)
PRO-COM SYSTEMS, INC.
(stake-out alarm, radio controlled)
PREFERRED SECURITY COMPONENTS, INC.
(vehicle detection for driveways)
RASCO REFRIGERATION ALARM SYSTEMS CORP.
(refrigeration failure/temperature monitoring system)
STD, INC.
(rising/falling water level alarm)
VAN LOCK CO.
(door and lock tamper alarm)

Alarms, Reporting Equipment (Fire/Intrusion)

Alarm Reporting Systems (2.e to 2.e.2)

2.e.1 Alarm reporting systems, hardware

ADEMCO (ALARM DEVICE MFG. CO.)
(commercial, residential: direct wire, loop)
ADMIC
(commercial, multiplex)
ADVANCED SIGNALING CO, INC.
(commercial, residential)
AEROLARM
(commercial, residential)
WM. B. ALLEN SECURITY SUPPLIES
(commercial, residential: direct wire)
AMCEST CORP.
(commercial, residential)

ARITECH CORP.
(commercial, residential, direct wire: loop, multiplex)

ARROWHEAD ENTERPRISES INC.
(commercial, residential: direct wire)

ATRONIC
(commercial, residential: multiplex)

AUDIO SENTRY CORP.
(commercial, residential: direct wire)

BETCO ELECTRONICS
(commercial, residential: multiplex)

BRASH INDUSTRIES
(commercial, residential: direct wire, loop, multiplex)

C.C.U. INC.
(commercial, residential: direct wire, loop, multiplex)

COMPUGUARD CORP.
(commercial, residential: multiplex)

CONRAC CORP.
(commercial, residential: loop)

CONTINENTAL INSTRUMENTS CORP.
(commercial, residential: direct wire, loop)

"CONTROLLOR SYSTEMS" CORP.
(commercial, residential: direct wire, loop)

DETECT-ALL SECURITY SYSTEMS, INC.
(commercial, residential: direct wire)

DIGITAL COMMUNICATIONS, INC.
(residential, commercial)

DOOR ALARM DEVICES CORP.
(commercial)

DOPPLER CORP.
(commercial, residential: direct wire)

DOUGLAS RANDALL DIV.
WALTER KIDDE & CO., INC.
(commercial, direct wire: multiplex)

DTI SECURITY INC.
(commercial, residential: direct wire)

E.E. INDUSTRIES, INC.
(commercial, residential: direct wire, loop)

EMERGENCY DATA COMPUTER CENTER
(commercial, residential)

EMERGENCY PRODUCTS CORP.
(commercial, residential: direct wire, loop, multiplex)

ESTERLINE ELECTRONICS CORP.
(commercial, multiplex)

EXTRA SECURITY INC.
(residential)

FIRE-LITE ALARMS INC.

(commercial, residential: direct wire, loop)

FRANKLIN SIGNAL CORP.
(commercial, residential)

GAMEWELL/ALARMTRONICS
(commercial: direct wire, loop, multiplex)

GRAY SECURITY
(commercial, residential: direct wire, multiplex)

GUARD AWARE, INC.
(commercial, residential: direct wire)

HOLMES PROTECTION, INC.
(commercial, residential: multiplex)

HONEYWELL
(commercial, residential: multiplex)

INTERNATIONAL ALARM RESEARCH
(commercial, residential: direct wire)

KELTRON CORP.
(commercial, residential: direct wire, multiplex)

KENCO INC.
(commercial, residential: direct wire)

MESA SECURITY GROUP
(commercial, residential: direct wire, loop)

MGI, INC.
(commercial, residential: direct wire)

MORSE PRODUCTS MFG.
(commercial, residential: direct wire, multiplex)

MOSLER AIRMATIC & ELECTRONIC SYSTEMS
(commercial: direct wire, multiplex)

MRL, INC.
(commercial, residential: direct wire, loop)

NATIONAL SECURITY SYSTEMS, INC.
(direct wire: multiplex)

NEWBRITE ALARMS, INC.
(commercial, residential)

NORTH ELECTRIC CO.
(commercial, residential: multiplex)

NUTONE DIV.
SCOVILL
(residential)

POLY-SCIENTIFIC DIV.
LITTON SYSTEMS, INC.
(commercial, residential: loop)

POTTER ELECTRIC SIGNAL CO.
(commercial, residential)

PROTECT-ALARM SECURITY PRODUCTS CO.
(commercial, residential: direct wire)

PRO-TECTION PRODUCTS INC.

(commercial: direct wire, multiplex)

REDCO INC.
(commercial, residential: direct wire)

REMOTE CONTROL DEVICES CORP.
(commercial, residential: direct wire)

RICHMOND ENTERPRISES INC.
(residential: direct wire)

ROTHENBUHLER ENGINEERING CO.
(commercial: direct wire, loop, multiplex)

SADETO INC.
(commercial, residential: direct wire, loop, multiplex)

SECURITY COMMUNICATIONS CORP.
(SECUR-COM)
(commercial, residential: multiplex)

SECURITONE, INC.
(commercial, residential)

SECOM
(commercial)

SIGMA ELECTRONICS INC.
(commercial, residential: direct wire, loop)

SILENT KNIGHT SECURITY SYSTEMS
(commercial, residential: multiplex)

STELLAR SYSTEMS, INC.
(multiplex)

TIE SECURITY SYSTEMS
(commercial, residential: direct wire, multiplex)

TRANS-AIR MFG. CO., LTD.
(commercial, residential: direct wire)

TRINE MFG.
(residential)

UNITED SECURITY PRODUCTS, INC.
(residential)

VARITECH SECURITY SYSTEMS, INC.
(commercial, residential: direct wire, multiplex)

VINDICATOR CORP.
(commercial, multiplex)

VON DUPRIN INC.
(commercial, direct wire)

WACKENHUT ELECTRONIC SYSTEMS
(commercial)

WELLS FARGO ALARM SERVICES
(commercial, residential)

WESTERN ALARM SUPPLY CO.
(commercial)

WESTINGHOUSE SECURITY SYSTEMS, INC.
(commercial, residential)

WHOLESALE SECURITY DEVICES
(commercial, residential: direct wire, loop)

2.e.2 Alarm reporting systems, wireless

AB TELEKONTROLL

(radio frequency)

ADT
(commercial, proprietary,
residential: radio frequency, line
carrier)

ALPHA ELECTRONICS MFG. LTD.
(self-contained)

AMERICAN ALERT SYSTEMS
(commercial, proprietary,
residential: radio frequency)

ATLANTIC HOME SECURITY
SYSTEMS, INC.
(residential, radio signaling)

BEI ELECTRONICS, INC.
(commercial, proprietary,
residential: radio frequency, line
carrier)

B-SAFE SYSTEMS INC.
(commercial, proprietary,
residential: radio frequency)

COMPUGUARD CORP.
(commercial, proprietary,
residential: radio frequency, line
carrier)

"CONTROLLOR SYSTEMS" CORP.
(proprietary, residential: radio
frequency)

CRIMINALISTICS INC.
(radio frequency)

DAL INDUSTRIES INC.
(residential: radio frequency)

EXTRA SECURITY INC.
(residential)

FUNCTIONAL DEVICES INC.
(commercial, residential: line
carrier)

INTELATEX
(proprietary: radio frequency)

LINEAR CORP.
(residential: radio frequency)

F.G. MASON ENGINEERING, INC.
(portable: radio frequency)

MOTOROLA COMMUNICATIONS &
ELECTRONICS, INC.
(commercial, proprietary: radio
frequency)

MULTI-ELMAC CO.
(commercial, residential: radio
frequency)

NORTH ELECTRIC CO.
(commercial, proprietary,
residential: radio frequency)

ON GUARD SECURITY SYSTEMS,
INC.
(residential: line carrier, radio
frequency)

PAGE ALERT SYSTEMS, INC.
(radio frequency)

PLECTRON CORP.
(commercial, proprietary: radio
frequency)

PRO-COM SYSTEMS, INC.
(commercial, proprietary,
residential: radio frequency)

PRO-TECTION PRODUCTS INC.
(proprietary: radio frequency,
line carrier)

QONAAR SECURITY SYSTEMS, INC.
(residential, radio frequency)

ROCK-LAND INDUSTRIES, INC.
(commercial, proprietary,
residential: radio frequency)

SENTATEK CORP. OF AMERICA
(residential, radio frequency)

SPEEDCALL CORP.
(commercial: radio frequency)

TIE SECURITY SYSTEMS
(commercial, residential: line
carrier)

TRANSCIENCE INDUSTRIES INC.
(commercial, proprietary,
residential: radio frequency)

VINDICATOR CORP.
(commercial, proprietary: radio
frequency)

Alarm Reporting/Annunciating Systems (2.f to 2.f.3)

2.f.1 Central stations, complete

ADC TELECOMMUNICATIONS
(incl. remote, unmanned sites)

ADEMCO (ALARM DEVICE MFG. CO.)
(commercial)

ADT
(commercial, proprietary)

AEROLARM
(commercial, proprietary)

ARROWHEAD ENTERPRISES INC.
(commercial, proprietary)

AMCEST CORP.
(nationwide alarm monitoring
service)

ARITECH CORP.
(commercial, proprietary)

ARROWHEAD ENTERPRISES INC.
(commercial, proprietary)

ATRONIC
(commercial, proprietary)

AUDIO SENTRY CORP.
(commercial, proprietary)

BEI ELECTRONICS, INC.
(commercial, proprietary: radio
alarm transmission)

BETCO ELECTRONICS
(commercial, proprietary)

BRASH INDUSTRIES
(commercial, proprietary)

BURNS INTERNATIONAL SECURITY
SERVICES, INC.
(commercial, proprietary)

COMPUGUARD CORP.
(commercial, proprietary)

DAHILL ELECTRONICS CORP.
(commercial, residential)

DELTA PRODUCTS, INC.
(proprietary)

DIGITAL COMMUNICATIONS, INC.
(commercial, proprietary)

DOUGLAS RANDALL DIV.
WALTER KIDDE & CO., INC.
(proprietary)

EMERGENCY DATA COMPUTER
CENTER
(nationwide alarm monitoring
service)

EMERGENCY PRODUCTS CORP.
(commercial, proprietary)

ESTERLINE ELECTRONICS CORP.
(commercial, proprietary)

FIRE-LITE ALARMS INC.
(commercial, proprietary)

FRANKLIN SIGNAL CORP.
(commercial, proprietary)

GRAY SECURITY
(commercial, proprietary)

HOLMES PROTECTION, INC.
(commercial, proprietary)

HONEYWELL
(commercial, proprietary)

ICC, INC.
(commercial, proprietary)

KELTRON CORP.
(commercial, proprietary)

KENCO INC.
(commercial, proprietary)

LAKE JACKSON INDUSTRIES, INC.
(commercial, proprietary)

MGI, INC.
(commercial, proprietary)

MICROWAVE ASSOCIATES, INC.
(commercial, proprietary)

MORSE PRODUCTS MFG.
(commercial, proprietary)

MOUNTAIN WEST ALARM SUPPLY
CO.
(commercial, proprietary)

MRL, INC.
(proprietary)

NATIONAL SECURITY SYSTEMS, INC.
(commercial, proprietary)

NEWBRITE ALARMS, INC.
(proprietary)

PLECTRON CORP.
(commercial, proprietary)

POTTER ELECTRIC SIGNAL CO.
(commercial, proprietary)

PRO-COM SYSTEMS, INC.
(commercial, proprietary: radio
frequency)

SADETO INC.
(commercial, proprietary)

SECURITONE, INC.
(commercial, proprietary)

SECURITY COMMUNICATIONS CORP.
(SECUR-COM)
(commercial, proprietary)

SENTRY TECHNOLOGY, INC.
(commercial, proprietary)

SESCOA (SECURITY SCIENCES CORP.
OF AMERICA)
(commercial, proprietary)

SHORROCK INC.

(commercial)

SILENT WATCHMAN CORP.
(commercial)

UNICAN SECURITY SYSTEMS CORP.
(proprietary)

VARITECH SECURITY SYSTEMS, INC.
(commercial, proprietary)

VERTEX SCIENCE INDUSTRIES, INC.
(commercial, proprietary)

VINDICATOR CORP.
(commercial, proprietary)

WACKENHUT ELECTRONIC SYSTEMS
(commercial, proprietary)

WELLS FARGO ALARM SERVICES
(commercial, proprietary)

2.f.1.a Central station equipment components

ADMIC
(central station and remote terminals for control and monitoring of mechanical equipment)

ADVANCED SIGNALING CO., INC.
(police station receivers, adaptable for police station interconnect)

ALARM PRODUCTS INTERNATIONAL, INC.
(modular)

CONRAC CORP.
(receivers, registers, power supplies)

FRANKLIN SIGNAL CORP.
(receivers, printers, power supplies)

GRAY SECURITY
(computerized central station information retrieval system)

INTERBORO TIME CLOCK CORP.
(consecutive print signal receiving clock)

INTERNATIONAL ALARM RESEARCH
(receivers)

INTERNATIONAL MICROWAVE CORP.
(data transmission microwave system)

KELTRON CORP.
(computerized central station information retrieval system)

NAPCO SECURITY SYSTEMS, INC.
(digital McCulloh transmitter)

RADIONICS INC.
(digital receiver)

REMOTE CONTROL DEVICES CORP.
(sending module, reverseing relay)

RICHMOND ENTERPRISES INC.
(reversing relay)

SESCOA (SECURITY SCIENCES CORP. OF AMERICA)
(printers, power supplies, accessories)

VERSA-LITE SYSTEMS, INC.
(visual alarm display board)

2.f.2 Automatic communicators (telephone dialers)

ACRON CORP.
(tape)

ADCOR ELECTRONICS, INC.
(tape, digital)

ADEMCO (ALARM DEVICE MFG. CO.)
(tape, digital)

ALARM DISTRIBUTORS
(tape, digital)

ALARM PRODUCTS INTERNATIONAL, INC.
(tape)

ALERT INTERNATIONAL CORP.
(tape, self-programmable)

WM. B. ALLEN SECURITY SUPPLIES
(tape, digital)

AMERICAN ELECTRONICS, INC.
(tape, digital)

THE ANSWERLINE ASSOCIATES INC.
(tape)

ARITECH CORP.
(tape, digital)

BETCO ELECTRONICS
(digital)

BRASH INDUSTRIES
(digital)

B-SAFE SYSTEMS INC.
(tape, digital)

C.E.M. SECURITY PRODUCTS
(digital)

CONRAC CORP.
(tape)

"CONTROLLOR SYSTEMS" CORP.
(tape)

DELTA PRODUCTS, INC.
(digital)

DETECT-ALL SECURITY SYSTEMS, INC.
(tape)

DIGITAL COMMUNICATIONS, INC.
(digital)

DIGITAL PRODUCTS CORP.
(digital)

DYTRON INC.
(tape)

FIRE BURGLARY INSTRUMENTS INC.
(tape, digital)

FRANKLIN SIGNAL CORP.
(digital)

LATAH, INC.
(digital)

MICROWAVE ASSOCIATES, INC.
(digitial, remote interrogation capability)

MOUNTAIN WEST ALARM SUPPLY CO.
(tape, digital)

NAPCO SECURITY SYSTEMS, INC.
(tape, digital)

NEWBRITE ALARMS, INC.
(tape, digital)

NORTH ELECTRIC CO.
(tape, digital)

PROTECTION & LOSS CONTROL (PLC) ELECTRONICS
(tape)

RADIONICS INC.
(digital)

RICHMOND ENTERPRISES INC.
(tape)

SCAN SECURITY SYSTEMS INC.
(tape)

SEABOARD ELECTRONICS CO.
(digital)

SECURITY SUPPLY SERVICE INC.
(tape, digital)

SENTRY TECHNOLOGY, INC.
(digital)

SENTRY WATCH, INC.
(tape)

SESCOA (SECURITY SCIENCES CORP. OF AMERICA)
(digital)

SIGHT & SOUND SYSTEMS
(tape)

SILENT KNIGHT SECURITY SYSTEMS
(digital)

SILENT WATCHMAN CORP.
(tape)

THREE B ELECTRONICS, INC.
(tape)

UNIVERSAL SECURITY INSTRUMENTS, INC.
(tape)

VARITECH SECURITY SYSTEMS, INC.
(digital)

VERTEX SCIENCE INDUSTRIES, INC.
(digital)

WESTERN ALARM SUPPLY CO.
(digital)

WESTERN SECURITY PRODUCTS
(tape, digital)

WESTINGHOUSE SECURITY SYSTEMS, INC.
(tape, digital)

WHOLESALE SECURITY DEVICES
(tape, digital)

2.f.3 Alarm reporting systems, special purpose

AB TELEKONTROLL
(personal emergency)

ADMIC
(power failure, climate control, equipment failure)

ADVANCED SIGNALING CO., INC.
(line security)

ALERT INTERNATIONAL CORP.
(personal emergency)

WM. B. ALLEN SECURITY SUPPLIES
(personal emergency)

AMERICAN ALERT SYSTEMS
(personal emergency, power failure)

AMERICAN ELECTRONICS, INC.
(personal emergency, power
failure)
ARROWHEAD ENTERPRISES INC.
(personal emergency)
ATRONIC
(personal emergency)
CERBERUS SYSTEMS
(holdup)
COMPUGUARD CORP.
(personal emergency)
"CONTROLLOR SYSTEMS" CORP.
(personal emergency)
CONTROLONICS CORP.
(marine, explosive gases)
DEPEND-ALARM
(vehicle theft warning & pocket
paging system, radio signaling)
ESTERLINE ELECTRONICS CORP.
(personal emergency)
FRANKLIN SIGNAL CORP.
(personal emergency, power
failure)
FUNCTIONAL DEVICES INC.
(power failure)
GRAY SECURITY
(personal emergency, power
failure)
HYDRO-TEMP CONTROLS, INC.
(water leakage/flooding, climatic
change/hazards alarms)
KELTRON CORP.
(personal emergency, power
failure)
MAGNA DIGITRONICS, INC.
(refrigeration failure)
PAGE ALERT SYSTEMS, INC.
(vehicle theft warning & pocket
paging system, radio signaling)
RASCO REFRIGERATION ALARM
SYSTEMS CORP.
(refrigeration failure/
temperature monitoring system)
RICHMOND ENTERPRISES
(personal emergency)
GEORGE RISK INDUSTRIES, INC.
(for coin-operated vending
machines)
ROBOT RESEARCH, INC.
(telephone line TV verification)
SADETO INC.
(personal emergency, power
failure)
SCAN SECURITY SYSTEMS INC.
(power failure)
SENTRY WATCH, INC.
(portable)
SIGNAPLEX, INC.
(personal emergency)
SPEEDCALL CORP.
(personal emergency, power
failure)
TRANSCIENCE INDUSTRIES, INC.
(holdup/emergency radio

frequency alerting system for
cooperating businesses)

Alarms, Components

Alarm System Components (2.g
to 2.g.7)

2.g Alarm system components
(multiple products)
ADEMCO (ALARM DEVICE MFG.
Co.)
ALARM DISTRIBUTORS
ALARM SUPPLY CO., INC.
WM. B. ALLEN SECURITY SUPPLIES
ARITECH CORP.
B-SAFE SYSTEMS INC.
"CONTROLLOR SYSTEMS" CORP.
EMERGENCY PRODUCTS CORP.
MOUNTAIN WEST ALARM SUPPLY
Co.
NORTH ELECTRIC CO.
NUTONE DIV.
SCOVILL
SECURITY SUPPLY SERVICE INC.
WESTERN SECURITY PRODUCTS

2.g.1 Sirens, bells, buzzers,
chimes, horns, etc. (see also
2.g)
ABCOR ELECTRONICS, INC.
(sirens, bells)
AEROLARM
(sirens, horns)
ALARM CONTROLS CORP.
(horns)
ALARM PRODUCTS INTERNATIONAL,
INC.
(sirens, bells)
ALPHA ELECTRONICS MFG., LTD.
(sirens, buzzers)
AMERICAN ELECTRONICS, INC.
(sirens, bells, buzzers, horns)
AMERICAN PROTECTION SYSTEMS
(sirens)
AMERICAN SECURITY EQUIPMENT
Co. (AMSECO)
(sirens, bells, buzzers, horns)
ANDOVER SENSING DEVICE CORP.
(horns)
APS DIV.
SECURITY TECHNOLOGY SYSTEMS
CO.
(sirens)
ARISTO-CRAFT
(sirens, buzzers, horns)
ATLAS SOUND
(sirens, horns)
AUDIO SENTRY CORP.
(sirens)
BEAVER ELECTRONICS
(sirens)
BURGLAR BUG MFG.
(sirens)
C.C.U. INC.

(sirens)
CONRAC CORP.
(bells, horns)
CONTINENTAL INSTRUMENTS CORP.
(sirens)
DELTA ELECTRIC
(sirens, horns)
DEPEND-ALARM
(sirens)
DETECTRON SECURITY SYSTEMS,
INC.
(sirens, bells)
DOPPLER CORP.
(sirens)
DOUGLAS RANDALL DIV.
WALTER KIDDE & CO., INC.
(bells, horns)
DTI SECURITY INC.
(sirens)
EDWARDS CO., INC.
(sirens, bells, buzzers, chimes,
horns)
EMPIRE MACHINES & SYSTEMS INC.
(sirens, bells)
FIRE BURGLARY INSTRUMENTS INC.
(sirens, horns)
FIRE-LITE ALARMS INC.
(bells, horns)
FRANKLIN SIGNAL CORP.
(sirens, buzzers)
FUNCTIONAL DEVICES INC.
(buzzers, horns)
GAMEWELL/ALARMTRONICS
(sirens, bells, buzzers, chimes,
horns)
GUARD AWARE, INC.
(sirens, horns)
GUARDIAN ELECTRONICS INC.
(sirens)
HARCOR INTERNATIONAL INC.
(sirens)
KOLIN INDUSTRIES INC.
(sirens, buzzers)
LASSEN ELECTRONICS CORP.
(sirens)
LUMENITE ELECTRONICS CO.
(bells, buzzers, horns)
MONROE TIMER CO. INC.
(sirens)
MOOSE PRODUCTS INC.
(sirens, horns)
MORSE PRODUCTS MFG.
(bells)
MRL, INC.
(sirens, bells, buzzers, horns)
NAPCO SECURITY SYSTEMS, INC.
(sirens)
POTTER & BRUMFIELD DIV.
AMF DIV.
(buzzers)
POTTER ELECTRIC SIGNAL CO.
(bells, horns)
PROJECTS UNLIMITED
(horns)

PROTECT-ALARM SECURITY
   PRODUCTS CO.
   (sirens)
PROTECTION & LOSS CONTROL
   (PLC) ELECTRONICS
   (sirens, bells)
REDCO INC.
   (sirens)
REMOTE CONTROL DEVICES CORP.
   (sirens)
RITTENHOUSE
   (sirens, bells, chimes, horns)
SENSOR-TEC, INC.
   (sirens, horns)
SENTROL, INC.
   (sirens)
SESCOA (SECURITY SCIENCES
   CORP. OF AMERICA)
   (sirens, horns)
SIGMA ELECTRONICS INC.
   (sirens, bells, buzzers)
SIGNAL-U MFG. CO.
   (chimes)
SILENT KNIGHT SECURITY SYSTEMS
   (sirens)
SILENT WATCHMAN CORP.
   (sirens)
SNYDER ELECTRONICS, INC.
   (chimes)
SPIRIG ERNEST
   (sirens)
TRANS-AIR MFG. CO., LTD.
   (sirens)
TRINE MFG.
   (bells, buzzers, chimes, horns)
UNITED SECURITY PRODUCTS, INC.
   (sirens, bells, buzzers, horns)
UNIVERSAL SECURITY
   INSTRUMENTS, INC.
   (sirens, bells, buzzers, horns)
VON DUPRIN INC.
   (bells, buzzers, horns)
WESTERN ALARM SUPPLY CO.
   (sirens)
WHEELOCK SIGNALS, INC.
   (bells, chimes, horns)
WICO CORP.
   (sirens, bells)
WOLO MFG. CORP.
   (sirens, horns)

**2.g.2 Switches, contacts, relays
   (see also 2.g)**

AEROLARM
   (mechanical, magnetic contacts)
ALARM PRODUCTS INTERNATIONAL
   INC.
   (relays)
AMERICAN ELECTRONICS, INC.
   (switches, mechanical & magnetic
   contacts, relays)
AMERICAN SECURITY EQUIPMENT
   CO. (AMSECO)
   (switches, mechanical & magnetic
   contacts)

AMERICAN ZETTLER, INC.
   (relays)
ARROW-M CORP.
   (relays)
CALIFORNIA SWITCH & SIGNAL
   (switches)
C.E.M. SECURITY PRODUCTS
   (magnetic contacts)
CITIZEN AMERICA CORP.
   (buzzers)
CONRAC CORP.
   (switches, magnetic contacts)
CONTROL DEVICES INC.
   (magnetic switches, concealed)
CORBY INDUSTRIES, INC.
   (relays)
CUSTOM ELECTRONICS
   (switches)
DELTA ELECTRIC
   (switches)
EDWARDS CO., INC.
   (switches, magnetic contacts,
   relays)
ELECTRONIC RELAYS INC.
   (magnetic contacts, relays)
EMPIRE MACHINES & SYSTEMS INC.
   (switches, mechanical & magnetic
   contacts, relays)
FIRE BURGLARY INSTRUMENTS INC.
   (magnetic contacts)
FLAIR ELECTRONICS, INC.
   (switches, magnetic contacts,
   relays)
FUNCTIONAL DEVICES INC.
   (contacts)
KABA SECURITY LOCKS, INC.
   (lockswitches)
LUMENITE ELECTRONICS CO.
   (time switches)
MONROE TIMER CO. INC.
   (switches)
MOOSE PRODUCTS INC.
   (switches, magnetic contacts)
MORSE PRODUCTS MFG.
   (magnetic contacts)
NAPCO SECURITY SYSTEMS, INC.
   (magnetic contacts)
NORTH AMERICAN PHILIPS
   CONTROLS CORP.
   (magnetic contacts, relays)
THE PETERZELL CO.
   (switches)
POTTER & BRUMFIELD DIV.
AMF INC.
   (switches, relays)
POTTER ELECTRIC SIGNAL CO.
   (switches, mechanical & magnetic
   contacts)
PREFERRED SECURITY
   COMPONENTS, INC.
   (switches, magnetic contacts,
   relays)
RELAYMATIC INC.
   (relays)

GEORGE RISK INDUSTRIES, INC.
   (switches, magnetic contacts)
RITTENHOUSE
   (switches, magnetic contacts,
   relays)
SECURITY INSTRUMENTS, INC.
   (switches, mechanical & magnetic
   contacts)
SENTROL, INC.
   (switches, magnetic contacts)
SHORROCK INC.
   (mechanical, magnetic contacts)
SIGMA ELECTRONICS INC.
   (switches, magnetic contacts)
SIGNALARM INC.
   (switches)
SIGNAL-U MFG. CO.
   (switches)
SONAR SECURITY MFG. CO.
   (switches, mechanical contacts)
SPIRIG ERNEST
   (switches)
SQUARE D CO.
   (switches, relays)
STANLEY HARDWARE
   (magnetic contacts)
TAPESWITCH CORP. OF AMERICA
   (switches)
TELSAR CORP.
   (magnetic contacts)
TRINE MFG.
   (switches, mechanical & magnetic
   contacts)
UNICAN SECURITY SYSTEMS CORP.
   (magnetic contacts)
UNITED SECURITY PRODUCTS, INC.
   (switches, mechanical & magnetic
   contacts, relays)
VON DUPRIN INC.
   (switches, mechanical & magnetic
   contacts)
WOLO MFG. CORP.
   (switches, relays)

**2.g.3 Control panels
   (see also 2.g)**

AAMES SECURITY CORP.
   (fire)
ACRON CORP.
ADC TELECOMMUNICATIONS
   (incl. remote, unmanned sites)
ADCOR ELECTRONICS, INC.
ADVANCED SECURITY CO.
AEROLARM
ALARM CONTROLS CORP.
ALARM PRODUCTS INTERNATIONAL
   INC.
ALERT INTERNATIONAL CORP.
ALPHA ELECTRONICS MFG. LTD.
AMERICAN ELECTRONICS, INC.
AMERICAN SECURITY EQUIPMENT
   CO. (AMSECO)
APS DIV.
   SECURITY TECHNOLOGY SYSTEMS
   CO.

ARROWHEAD ENTERPRISES INC.
A.S.E. PROTECTIVE SYSTEMS &
   SERVICES
ATRONIC
AUDIO SENTRY CORP.
BEAVER ELECTRONICS
BEI ELECTRONICS, INC.
BRASH INDUSTRIES
CADDI (CONVERTIBLE ALARM
   DETECTION DEVICES, INC.)
C.C.U. INC.
C.E.M. SECURITY PRODUCTS
CONCEPTS-IN-ALARMS, INC.
CONRAC CORP.
CONTINENTAL INSTRUMENTS CORP.
CONTINENTAL TELECOM
   (digital counter for)
   CUSTOM ALARM PRODUCTS
DAL INDUSTRIES INC.
DETECTRON SECURITY SYSTEMS,
   INC.
DIVERSIFIED SECURITY SYSTEMS
DOPPLER CORP.
DOUGLAS RANDALL DIV.
   WALTER KIDDE & CO., INC.
DTI SECURITY INC.
DYTRON INC.
EDWARDS CO., INC.
E.E. INDUSTRIES, INC.
ELECTROLARM INC.
FIRE BURGLARY INSTRUMENTS INC.
FIRE-LITE ALARMS INC.
FRANKLIN SIGNAL CORP.
GAMEWELL/ALARMTRONICS
GRAVINER INC.
   (fire)
GUARD AWARE, INC.
GUARDIAN ELECTRONICS INC.
HOLMES PROTECTION, INC.
HYDRO-TEMP CONTROLS, INC.
KING RESEARCH LABS., INC.
MAGNA DIGITRONICS, INC.
MAYDAY ALARMS, INC.
MESA SECURITY GROUP
MICROWAVE ASSOCIATES, INC.
MOOSE PRODUCTS MFG.
MRL, INC.
NAPCO SECURITY SYSTEMS, INC.
NATIONAL SECURITY SYSTEMS, INC.
NEL-TECH DEVELOPMENT, INC.
NEWBRITE ALARMS, INC.
THE NIGHT EYE CORP.
PENINSULA ALARM PRODUCTS
POLY-SCIENTIFIC DIV.
   LITTON SYSTEMS, INC.
POTTER ELECTRIC SIGNAL CO.
PROTECT-ALARM SECURITY
   PRODUCTS CO.
PROTECTION & LOSS CONTROL
   (PLC) ELECTRONICS
PRO-TECTION PRODUCTS INC.
REDCO INC.
REMOTE CONTROL DEVICES CORP.
RITTENHOUSE
SCAN SECURITY SYSTEMS INC.

SECURTEC, INC.
SENTROL, INC.
SESCOA (SECURITY SCIENCES CORP.
   OF AMERICA)
SIGHT & SOUND SYSTEMS
SIGMA ELECTRONICS, INC.
SIGNALARM INC.
SILENT KNIGHT SECURITY SYSTEMS
SNYDER ELECTRONICS, INC.
TRANS-AIR MFG. CO., LTD.
TRANSCIENCE INDUSTRIES INC.
UNITEC INC.
   (fire)
UNITED SECURITY PRODUCTS, INC.
VON DUPRIN INC.
WHOLESALE SECURITY DEVICES
   (vehicle)
WORLDWIDE SECURITY PRODUCTS

2.g.4 Annunciators
   (see also 2.g)

AAMES SECURITY CORP.
   (fire)
AEROLARM
ALPHA ELECTRONICS MFG. LTD.
ARROWHEAD ENTERPRISES INC.
ATRONIC
AUDIO SENTRY CORP.
BRASH INDUSTRIES
C.C.U. INC.
CONCEPTS-IN-ALARMS, INC.
CONTINENTAL INSTRUMENTS CORP.
DAL INDUSTRIES INC.
DOOR ALARM DEVICES CORP.
DOUGLAS RANDALL DIV.
   WALTER KIDDE & CO., INC.
DTI SECURITY INC.
EDWARDS CO., INC.
FUNCTIONAL DEVICES INC.
GAMEWELL/ALARMTRONICS
GRAVINER INC.
   (fire)
MORSE PRODUCTS MFG.
NATIONAL SECURITY SYSTEMS, INC.
NORTH ELECTRIC CO.
PENINSULA ALARM PRODUCTS
POTTER ELECTRIC SIGNAL CO.
PRO-TECTION PRODUCTS INC.
SESCOA (SECURITY SCIENCES
   CORP. OF AMERICA)
SNYDER ELECTRONICS, INC.
SOLFAN SYSTEMS INC.
TAPESWITCH CORP. OF AMERICA
UNITED SECURITY PRODUCTS, INC.
VERSA-LITE SYSTEMS, INC.
VINDICATOR CORP.
VON DUPRIN INC.

2.g.5 Pressure mats
   (see also 2.g)

CONRAC CORP.
DAL INDUSTRIES INC.
DETECT-ALL SECURITY SYSTEMS,
   INC.
PROTECTION & LOSS CONTROL
   (PLC) ELECTRONICS

RECORA CO., INC.
RITTENHOUSE
SENTROL, INC.
SIGMA ELECTRONICS INC.
SIGNAL-U MFG. CO.
SNYDER ELECTRONICS, INC.
TAPESWITCH CORP. OF OF AMERICA
TRINE MFG.
UNITED SECURITY PRODUCTS, INC.

2.g.6 Panic buttons
   (see also 2.g)

AMERICAN ALERT SYSTEMS
AMERICAN SECURITY EQUIPMENT
   CO. (AMSECO)
ATLANTIC HOME SECURITY
   SYSTEMS, INC.
AUTOMATIC FIRE & BURGLAR
   CONTROL CORP.
BEAVER ELECTRONICS
CONCEPTS-IN-ALARMS, INC.
CONRAC CORP.
CORBY INDUSTRIES, INC.
CUSTOM ELECTRONICS
DAL INDUSTRIES INC.
DTI SECURITY INC.
FIRE BURGLARY INSTRUMENTS INC.
FLAIR ELECTRONICS, INC.
FUNCTIONAL DEVICES INC.
HARCOR INTERNATIONAL INC.
LINEAR CORP.
MORSE PRODUCTS MFG.
MULTI-ELMAC CO.
NAPCO SECURITY SYSTEMS, INC.
NEL-TECH DEVELOPMENT, INC.
POTTER ELECTRIC SIGNAL CO.
ROCK-LAND INDUSTRIES, INC.
ROTHENBUHLER ENGINEERING CO.
   (holdup)
SCAN SECURITY SYSTEMS INC.
SENTROL, INC.
TRANS-AIR MFG. CO., LTD.
TRANSCIENCE INDUSTRIES INC.
TRINE MFG.
UNITED SECURITY PRODUCTS, INC.

2.g.7 Alarm components, other

ADVANCED SECURITY CO.
   (alarm control, digital)
ADVANCED SIGNALING CO., INC.
   (line security)
ALPHA ELECTRONICS MFG. LTD.
   (exit/entry delays, automatic
   shutoff)
AMERICAN SECURITY EQUIPMENT
   CO. (AMSECO)
   (foil blocks, door cords, bell/siren
   boxes)
CONTINENTAL TELECOM
   (digital counter)
CUSTOM ELECTRONICS
   (holdup switch)
DAL INDUSTRIES INC.
   (siren modules)
DOPPLER CORP.
   (zone indicator panels)

E.E. INDUSTRIES, INC.
(bell cutoff timers, control panel reset timers, exit/entrance delay timers)
FIRE BURGLARY INSTRUMENTS INC.
(entry/exit delays, bell cutoffs)
INTRUSION DETECTION SYSTEM, INC. (I.D.S. INC.)
(timers/lights)
MONROE TIMER CO. INC.
(auto alarm accessories incl. timers)
MOOSE PRODUCTS INC.
(housing)
NEL-TECH DEVELOPMENT, INC.
(entry/exit delay)
PENINSULA ALARM PRODUCTS
(bell cutoff with alarm reset)
PERMA PACK INC.
(time delay, foil protector tape)
PROTECTRON, INC.
(sirens)
RADIONICS INC.
(digital/tap dialer tester)
RIXSON-FIREMARK, INC.
(electromechanical security pivot)
SALCO INDUSTRIES, INC.
(zone annunciator)
SECURA KEY
(car activated on/off switch)
SIGMA ELECTRONICS, INC.
(alarm shutoff timer)
SIMPLEX SECURITY SYSTEMS, INC.
(lockswitches for shunt locks)
STANLEY HARDWARE
(electric hinges)
STD, INC.
(water switch)
TECHNOLOGY SYSTEMS CORP.
(halogen lights)
TRANS-AIR MFG. CO., LTD.
(exit/entry delays)

**2.h Electronic parts
(see also 26.b)**
WM. B. ALLEN SECURITY SUPPLIES
(multi-line distributor)
AMERICAN ELECTRONICS, INC.
(siren modules)
ARISTO-CRAFT
(rectifiers)
CADDI (CONVERTIBLE ALARM DETECTION DEVICES, INC.)
(components for control panels)
COGNETICS CORP.
(ultrasonic transducers)
CORBY INDUSTRIES, INC.
(light emitting diodes, relays, equipment housings)
DIVERSIFIED SECURITY SYSTEMS
(digital key locks)
ELECTRONIC DEVICES INC.
(rectifier bridge)
ELECTRONIC RELAYS INC.
(solid state/sensitive relays)

LINDEN LABORATORIES, INC.
(ultrasonic air transducers, piezoelectric ceramics)
POTTER & BRUMFIELD DIV. AMF Div.
(circuit breakers, solenoids)
THREE B ELECTRONICS, INC.
(electronic siren boards)
WOLO MFG. CORP.
(current sensing timers)

2.i Alarm power packs
ACRON CORP.
ADCOR ELECTRONICS, INC.
AEROLARM
ALARM CONTROLS CORP.
ALARM PRODUCTS INTERNATIONAL INC.
AULT INC.
C.C.U. INC.
CENTURY 500 PRODUCTS, INC.
COLORADO ELECTRO-OPTICS
CONRAC CORP.
"CONTROLLOR SYSTEMS" CORP.
DOOR ALARM DEVICES CORP.
E.E. INDUSTRIES, INC.
ELPOWER CORP.
F & W ALARM SYSTEMS, INC.
FRANKLIN SIGNAL CORP.
GOULD INC.
GUARD AWARE, INC.
KENCO INC.
MOOSE PRODUCTS INC.
MORSE PRODUCTS MFG.
PERMA PACK INC.
PROTECT-ALARM SECURITY PRODUCTS CO.
PROTECTION & LOSS CONTROL (PLC) ELECTRONICS
REMOTE CONTROL DEVICES CORP.
SCAN SECURITY SYSTEMS INC.
SENTRY TECHNOLOGY, INC.
SIGNALARM INC.
SONTRIX
TECHNOLOGY SYSTEMS CORP.
TRANS-AIR MFG. CO., LTD.
WESTERN SECURITY PRODUCTS
WICO CORP.

**ALARM EQUIPMENT DISTRIBUTORS
(see 23.a)**

**ASSEMBLY COMPONENTS
(see 26.b)**

**BATTERIES AND BATTERY CHARGERS
(see also 8)**

3.a Batteries, rechargeable
ADEMCO (ALARM DEVICE MFG. CO.)
AIR-WAYS DISTRIBUTORS INC.
ALARMS CONTROLS CORP.
ALARM PRODUCTS INTERNATIONAL INC.

WM. B. ALLEN SECURITY SUPPLIES
ARISTO-CRAFT
ARITECH CORP.
DETECTRON SECURITY SYSTEMS, INC.
DUAL-LITE INC.
EAGLE-PICHER INDUSTRIES, INC.
ELECTROCON, INC.
ELPOWER CORP.
FIRE BURGLARY INSTRUMENTS INC.
GENERAL ELECTRIC CO.
IMAGING SYSTEMS OPERATION
GLOBE-UNION INC.
GOULD INC.
GUARD AWARE, INC.
MOOSE PRODUCTS INC.
MORSE PRODUCTS MFG.
MOUNTAIN WEST ALARM SUPPLY CO.
NUTONE DIV.
SCOVILL
PERMA PACK INC.
POWER-SONIC CORP.
PROTECT-ALARM SECURITY PRODUCTS CO.
REPCO INC.
(for communications equipment)
SANYO ELECTRIC INC.
Battery Div.
SECURITY SUPPLY SERVICE INC.
SESCOA (SECURITY SCIENCES CORP. OF AMERICA)
SONTRIX
TECHNICAL ELECTRONIC DISTRIBUTORS INC.
TRANS-AIR MFG. CO., LTD.
UNION CARBIDE CORP.
VSI/PRO-LIGHT
WESTERN SECURITY PRODUCTS
YARDNEY ELECTRIC CORP.
YUASA BATTERY (AMERICA) INC.
ZYGO INDUSTRIES, INC.

3.b Battery rechargers
AEROLARM
ALARM CONTROLS CORP.
WM. B. ALLEN SECURITY SUPPLIES
ARISTO-CRAFT
ARITECH CORP.
AULT INC.
BASLER ELECTRIC CO.
DETECTRON SECURITY SYSTEMS, INC.
DUAL-LITE INC.
EAGLE-PICHER INDUSTRIES, INC.
ELECTROCON, INC.
ELPOWER CORP.
GENERAL ELECTRIC CO.
IMAGING SYSTEMS OPERATION
GOBE-UNION INC.
GOULD INC.
GUARD AWARE, INC.
MOOSE PRODUCTS INC.
NUTONE DIV.
SCOVILL
PENINSULA ALARM PRODUCTS

Power-Sonic Corp.
Protect-Alarm Security
    Products Co.
Repco Inc.
    (for communications equipment)
Sanyo Electric Inc.
    battery div.
Spirig Ernest
Technical Electronic
    Distributors Inc.
Trans-Air Mfg. Co., Ltd.
Union Carbide Corp.
VSI/Pro-Light
Yuasa Battery (America), Inc.
Zygo Industries, Inc.

3.c Batteries, primary

Wm. B. Allen Security Supplies
Aritech Corp.
Detectron Security Systems,
    Inc.
Dual-Lite Inc.
Guard Aware, Inc.
Mallory Battery Co.
Sanyo Electric Inc.
    battery div.
Technical Electronic
    Distributors Inc.
Trans-Air Mfg. Co., Ltd.
Union Carbide Corp.
Western Security Products
Yardney Electric Corp.
Zygo Industries, Inc.

CAMERAS
(see also 19.23.b)

4.a Cameras, check cashing

ADT
Cameras for Industry (CFI)
Filmdex Inc.
Lucco Security Products Co.
Mosler Airmatic & Electronic
    Systems
Optics of Kansas, Inc.
Philips Audio Video Systems
    Corp.
Regiscope Corp. of America
Richmond Enterprises Inc.

4.b Cameras, identification

Avant Inc.
Filmdex Inc.
General Binding Corp.
Holmes Protection, Inc.
Identatronics, Inc.
Identicard Systems, Inc.
Identification Systems, Inc.
Industrial Photo Products,
    Inc.
Marvel Photo
Optics of Kansas, Inc.
Phillips Audio Video Systems
    Corp.
Polaroid Corp.
Regiscope Corp. of America

Richmond Enterprises
Seal In Plastic Co., Inc.

4.c Cameras, miniature

Marvel Photo
Philips Audio Video Systems
    Corp.
Visual Methods Inc.
Zoomar, Inc.

4.d Cameras, motion picture

Air-Ways Distributors Inc.
Canon U.S.A., Inc.
    (8, 16 mm)
Gimbel Security Cameras, Inc.
    (8, 16, 35 mm)
Richmond Enterprises
    (8 mm)
Yashica, Inc.
    (8 mm)

4.e Cameras, still

Electrophysics Corp.
    (intensifier cameras, custom-
    designed)
Gimbel Security Cameras, Inc.
Industrial Photo Products,
    Inc.
Marvel Photo
Yashica, Inc.

4.f Cameras, surveillance and holdup (film only)

ADT
Burns International Security
    Services, Inc.
Cameras for Industry (CFI)
    (16, 35 mm)
Carol Products Co. Inc.
    (concealed)
D/A General, Inc.
Filmdex Inc.
Frisco Bay Industries of
    Canada Ltd.
    (8, 16 mm)
Gimbel Security Cameras, Inc.
Holmes Protection, Inc.
Law Enforcement Associates,
    Inc.
Mosler Airmatic & Electronic
    Systems
Mountain West Alarm Supply
    Co.
Optics of Kansas, Inc.
Richmond Enterprises
Rothenbuhler Engineering Co.
    (35 mm)

Camera-Related Equipment (4.g to 4.g.6)

4.g.1 Lenses

Wm. B. Allen Security Supplies
Aritech Corp.
Canon U.S.A., Inc.
Cosmicar Lens Div.
    asahi precision co., ltd.

Lenzar Optics Corp.
Questar Corp.
Smith & Wesson
Video Components, Inc.
Visual Components, Inc.
Visual Methods Inc.
Yashica, Inc.
Zoomar, Inc.

4.g.2 Projectors, overhead display

Cosmicar Lens Div.
    asahi precision co., ltd.

4.g.3 Projectors, motion picture

Cosmicar Lens Div.
    asahi precision co., ltd.
Video Components, Inc.
Yashica, Inc.

4.g.4 Projectors, slide

Cosmicar Lens Div.
    asahi precision co., ltd.
Video Components, Inc.

4.g.5 Film and film processing equipment

Cameras for Industry (CFI)
D/A General, Inc.
Poloroid Corp.

4.g.6 Camera equipment, other

Cosmicar Lens Div.
    asahi precision co., ltd.
D/A General, Inc.
    (automated bank teller
    transaction cameras)
Optics of Kansas, Inc.
Video Components, Inc.

CAMERA EQUIPMENT DISTRIBUTORS
(see 23.b)

CHECK/DOCUMENT AND CREDIT CARD PROTECTION

5.a Check verification and signature authentication systems
(see also 4.a)

Alden Electronic & Recording
    Equipment Co., Inc.
Authentiprint Identification
    Systems
Electrophysics Corp.
    (infrared viewer, infrared
    microscope viewers)
Javelin Electronics
Optics of Kansas, Inc.
Philips Audio Video Systems
    Corp.
Regiscope Corp. of America
Rockwell International Corp.
Ultra-Violet Products, Inc.
Visual Methods Inc.

5.b Credit card verification systems

ADMIC
AVANT INC.
HARCO INDUSTRIES, INC.
REGISCOPE CORP. OF AMERICA
ROCKWELL INTERNATIONAL CORP.
SEALECTRO CORP.

5.c Other

DECALS, INC.
  (decals, point of sale
  information)
3M CO.
  (document transparent ID film
  and viewers)
WRIGHT LINE INC.
  (portable code punch device for
  internal use credit cards)

COMMUNICATIONS

Radio Communications (6.a to 6.a.11)

6.a.1 Two-way, fixed station

ADT
AEROTRON, INC.
GENERAL ELECTRIC CO.
  MOBILE RADIO DEPT.
E. F. JOHNSON CO.
MOTOROLA COMMUNICATIONS &
  ELECTRONICS, INC.
SONAR RADIO CORP.
STANDARD COMMUNICATIONS
  CORP.

6.a.2 Portable

ADT
AEROTRON, INC.
GENERAL ELECTRIC CO.
  MOBILE RADIO DEPT.
E. F. JOHNSON CO.
LAW ENFORCEMENT ASSOCIATES,
  INC.
MOTOROLA COMMUNICATIONS &
  ELECTRONICS, INC.
REPCO INC.
SONAR RADIO CORP.
STANDARD COMMUNICATIONS
  CORP.

6.a.2.a Portable radio telephone

MOTOROLA COMMUNICATIONS &
  ELECTRONICS, INC.
SONAR RADIO CORP.
STANDARD COMMUNICATIONS
  CORP.

6.a.3 Mobile

ADT
AEROTRON, INC.
GENERAL ELECTRIC CO.
  MOBILE RADIO DEPT.
E. F. JOHNSON CO.
MOTOROLA COMMUNICATIONS &
  ELECTRONICS, INC.

REPCO INC.
SONAR RADIO CORP.
STANDARD COMMUNICATIONS
  CORP.

6.a.3.a Mobile radio telephone

AEROTRON, INC.
MOTOROLA COMMUNICATIONS &
  ELECTRONICS, INC.

6.a.4 Transmitters

E. F. JOHNSON CO.
MOTOROLA COMMUNICATIONS &
  ELECTRONICS, INC.
REPCO INC.
STANDARD COMMUNICATIONS
  CORP.
TRANSCIENCE INDUSTRIES INC.
WILSON ELECTRONICS

6.a.5 Transmitters, miniature

LAW ENFORCEMENT ASSOCIATES,
  INC.
MORGAN ELECTRONICS, INC.
MOTOROLA COMMUNICATIONS &
  ELECTRONICS, INC.
REPCO INC.
STANDARD COMMUNICATIONS
  CORP.

6.a.6 Receivers

E. F. JOHNSON CO.
MOTOROLA COMMUNICATIONS &
  ELECTRONICS, INC.
PLECTRON CORP.
REACH ELECTRONICS, INC.
REPCO INC.
STANDARD COMMUNICATIONS
  CORP.
TRANSCIENCE INDUSTRIES INC.
WILSON ELECTRONICS

6.a.6.a Alerting systems

MULTITONE ELECTRONICS INC.
PAGE ALERT SYSTEMS, INC.
PLECTRON CORP.
  (disaster warning device)
REACH ELECTRONICS INC.
STANDARD COMMUNICATIONS
  CORP.
VINDICATOR CORP.

6.a.6.b Paging systems, portable

WM. B. ALLEN SECURITY SUPPLIES
GENERAL ELECTRIC CO.
  MOBILE RADIO DEPT.
ISTANT ALERT
LAW ENFORCEMENT ASSOCIATES,
  INC.
MOTOROLA COMMUNICATIONS &
  ELECTRONICS, INC.
MULTITONE ELECTRONICS INC.
PLECTRON CORP.
REACH ELECTRONICS, INC.
SONAR RADIO CORP.
STANDARD COMMUNICATIONS
  CORP.

6.a.7 Amplifiers

WM. B. ALLEN SECURITY SUPPLIES
BELL P/A PRODUCTS CORP.
MICROWAVE ASSOCIATES, INC.
STANDARD COMMUNICATIONS
  CORP.

6.a.8 Antennas

WM. B. ALLEN SECURITY SUPPLIES
SONAR RADIO CORP.

6.a.9 Alternators

ADT
MOTOROLA COMMUNICATIONS &
  ELECTRONICS, INC.

Microphones (6.a.10 to 6.a.10.b)

6.a.10.a Handheld, lavaliere, standing

WM. B. ALLEN SECURITY SUPPLIES
BELL P/A PRODUCTS CORP.
E. F. JOHNSON CO.
SC ELECTRONICS, INC.

6.a.10.b Miniature

WM. B. ALLEN SECURITY SUPPLIES
  (wired/wireless)
A.M.C. SALES, INC.
  (wireless)
LAW ENFORCEMENT ASSOCIATES,
  INC.
  (wired/wireless)
LINDIN LABORATORIES, INC.
  (wireless)
MOTOROLA COMMUNICATIONS &
  ELECTRONICS, INC.
  (wireless)
SC ELECTRONICS, INC.
  (wired)

6.a.11 Radio equipment, other

ATLAS SOUND
  (microphone stands)
REACH ELECTRONICS, INC.
  (system connection to telephone
  lines; identification, status
  reporting systems for mobile use)

Communications Equipment/ Systems, General (6.b to 6.g)

6.b Facsimile transmitters/ receivers

ALDEN ELECTRONIC & IMPULSE
  RECORDING EQUIPMENT CO., INC.
  (hard-copy photos)
INTERNATIONAL MICROWAVE
  CORP.
  (microwave transmission of data,
  images)

6.c Loudspeakers (audio amplifiers)

WM. B. ALLEN SECURITY SUPPLIES
ATLAS SOUND
BELL P/A PRODUCTS CORP.

ELECTRO-VOX INDUSTRIES INC.
EMPIRE MACHINES & SYSTEMS INC.
ISL PRODUCTS LTD.
MICROWAVE ASSOCIATES, INC.
SC ELECTRONICS, INC.

6.c.1 Loudspeakers, mobile

WM. B. ALLEN SECURITY SUPPLIES
ATLAS SOUND
MICROWAVE ASSOCIATES, INC.

6.c.2 Loudspeakers, portable

WM. B. ALLEN SECURITY SUPPLIES
ATLAS SOUND
MICROWAVE ASSOCIATES, INC.

6.d Public address systems

AIPHONE U.S.A., INC.
WM. B. ALLEN SECURITY SUPPLIES
BELL P/A PRODUCTS CORP.
ELECTRO-VOX INDUSTRIES INC.
MICROWAVE ASSOCIATES, INC.
SC ELECTRONICS, INC.

6.e Telephone systems, private

AIPHONE U.S.A., INC.

6.e.1 Intercom systems

AIPHONE U.S.A., INC.
ALARM SUPPLY CO., INC.
WM. B. ALLEN SECURITY SUPPLIES
ELECTRO-VOX INDUSTRIES INC.
MARLEE ELECTRONICS CORP.
MORGAN ELECTRONICS, INC.
RITTENHOUSE

6.f Teleprinters

MOTOROLA COMMUNICATIONS &
  ELECTRONICS, INC.
  (mobile)

6.g Telephone answering/ recording equipment (see also 18.f)

THE ANSWERLINE ASSOCIATES INC.

Communications Security Equipment (6.h to 6.h.3)

6.h.1 Scramblers

E.A. BRADLEY CO.
  (voice)
CERBERUS SYSTEMS
  (voice)
COM/TECH SYSTEMS INC.
  (data)
CONTROLONICS CORP.
DATOTEX, INC.
  (data/voice, base/telephone)
LAW ENFORCEMENT ASSOCIATES,
  INC.
  (voice)
MIECO
  (voice: mobile/base, radio/
  telephone)
SECURITY RESEARCH INC.
  (voice)

TECHNICAL COMMUNICATIONS
  CORP.
  (data/voice, radio/telephone)

6.h.2 Electronic measures and countermeasures

ASHBY & ASSOCIATES
  (telephone security system)
E.A. BRADLEY CO.
  (transmitter detectors, telephone
  analyzers)
THE CLIFTON CO.
  (transmitter detectors)
COMMUNICATION CONTROL
  SYSTEMS INC.
  (transmitter detectors, telephone
  analyzers, line tap defeat system)
DEKTOR COUNTER INTELLIGENCE &
  SECURITY, INC.
  (digital telephone analyzer)
INTELATEX
  (transmitter detectors)
LAW ENFORCEMENT ASSOCIATES,
  INC.
  (transmitter detectors, telephone
  analyzers)
F.G. MASON ENGINEERING, INC.
  (transmitter detectors, telephone
  analyzer)
SECURITY RESEARCH INC.
  (transmitter detectors, telephone
  analyzers, spectrum analyzers)

6.h.3 Other

COM LOG CO., INC.
  (dial number recorder)
INTERNATIONAL MICROWAVE
  CORP.
  (microwave video, audio, & data
  information transmitters, intra-
  city)
LAW ENFORCEMENT ASSOCIATES,
  INC.
  (impedience analyzer)
SECURITY RESEARCH INC.
  (acoustic noise generator)
SENTRY TECHNOLOGY, INC.
  (telephone line fault monitor)

DISTRIBUTORS AND IMPORTERS (see 23)

EDUCATIONAL AIDS

7.a Reference sources

THE BUREAU OF NATIONAL
  AFFAIRS, INC.
  (newsletters re: Federal
  regulations & legislation, OSHA,
  court decisions, etc.)
DAVIS PUBLISHING CO., INC.
VICTOR GREEN PUBLICATIONS LTD.
LIBRARY JOURNAL
MERIDIAN PUBLISHING CO.
  (custom-designed publications)

THE MERRITT CO.
  (OSHA, risk management,
  reference manual)
SECURITY DISTRIBUTING &
  MARKETING MAGAZINE
  Div. Security World Publishing
  Co., Inc.
SECURITY (JAPAN)
SECURITY WORLD BOOKS
  Div. Security World Publishing
  Co., Inc.
SECURITY WORLD MAGAZINE
  Div. Security World Publishing
  Co., Inc.
CHARLES C. THOMAS, PUBLISHER
20th CENTURY SECURITY
  EDUCATION LTD.

  (periodical)
UNISAF PUBLICATIONS LTD.
  (fire/security publications)
UNIVERSITY MICROFILMS
  INTERNATIONAL
  (Security World/Security
  Distributing & Marketing
  periodicals covered)

7.b Associations and organizations

AMERICAN BLDG. CONTRACTOR'S
  ASSN.
AMERICAN LAW ENFORCEMENT
  OFFICERS ASSN.
AMERICAN POLYGRAPH ASSN.
AMERICAN SOCIETY FOR
  AMUSEMENT PARK SECURITY/
  SAFETY
AMERICAN SOCIETY FOR
  INDUSTRIAL SECURITY
AMERICAN SOCIETY FOR
  NONDESTRUCTIVE TESTING, INC.
AMERICAN SOCIETY FOR TESTING &
  MATERIALS
AMERICAN SOCIETY OF
  MECHANICAL ENGINEERS
AMERICAN SOCIETY OF SAFETY
  ENGINEERS
ASSOCIATED LOCKSMITHS OF
  AMERICA, INC.
ASSN. OF TRANSPORTATION
  SECURITY OFFICERS
BUILDING OWNERS & MANAGERS
  ASSN. INTERNATIONAL
BUREAU OF NATIONAL AFFAIRS
CANADIAN SOCIETY FOR
  INDUSTRIAL SECURITY
COUNCIL OF INTERNATIONAL
  INVESTIGATORS
INDEPENDENT ARMORED CAR
  OPERATORS ASSN. INC.
INDUSTRIAL & COMMERCIAL
  SECURITY ASSN.
INSTITUTE OF ELECTRICAL &
  ELECTRONICS ENGINEERS
INTERNATIONAL ASSN. FOR
  HOSPITAL SECURITY
INTERNATIONAL ASSN. OF BOMB

TECHNICIANS & INVESTIGATORS
INTERNATIONAL ASSN. OF CHIEFS
  OF POLICE
INTERNATIONAL ASSN. OF COLLEGE
  & UNIVERSITY SECURITY
  DIRECTORS
INTERNATIONAL ASSN. OF CREDIT
  CARD INVESTIGATORS
INTERNATIONAL ASSN. OF FIRE
  CHIEFS
ITERNATIONAL COUNCIL OF
  SHOPPING CENTERS
INTERNATIONAL SOCIETY OF STRESS
  ANALYSIS
MASS RETAILING INSTITUTE
NATIONAL ASSN. OF SCHOOL
  SECURITY DIRECTORS
NATIONAL BURGLAR & FIRE ALARM
  ASSN.
NATIONAL COUNCIL OF
  INVESTIGATIVE & SECURITY
  SERVICES
NATIONAL CRIME PREVENTION
  INSTITUTE
NATIONAL ELECTRICAL
  MANUFACTURERS ASSN.
NATIONAL FIRE PROTECTION ASSN.
NATIONAL LOCKSMITHS SUPPLIERS
  ASSN.
NATIONAL RETAIL MERCHANTS
  ASSN.
NATIONAL SAFETY COUNCIL
RISK & INSURANCE MANAGEMENT
  SOCIETY, INC.
SECURITY EQUIPMENT INDUSTRY
  ASSN.
TRANSPORTATION ASSN. OF
  AMERICA
WORLD ASSN. OF DETECTIVES

7.c Schools and educational seminars

ADEMCO (ALARM DEVICE MFG. CO.)
  (for dealers, distributors,
  installers)
BANK ADMINISTRATION INSTITUTE
  (bank security conference)
COMMUNICATION CONTROL
  SYSTEMS INC.
  (countersurveillance seminars)
GENERAL MOTORS CORP.
  (on-site seminar packages with
  videotape in fire & security
  techniques)
GUARDSMARK, INC.
INTERMARKET CONSULTANTS INC.
  (European conference)
INTERNATIONAL LOSS CONTROL
  INSTITUTE
  (safety/loss control conference)
INTERNATIONAL SECURITY
  CONFERENCE
  (conference, workshops,
  certificated seminars)

LOS ANGELES INSTITUTE OF
  POLYGRAPH
NATIONAL TRAINING CENTER OF
  POLYGRAPH SCIENCE
JOHN E. REID & ASSOCIATES
SMITH & WESSON
  (training academy)
UNITED STATES SCHOOL OF LAW
  ENFORCEMENT

Security Training Media (7.d to 7.d.5)

7.d.1 Security training films/videotape

AIMS INSTRUCTIONAL MEDIA
  SERVICES, INC.
  (legal aspects, uniformed force)
GENERAL MOTORS CORP.
  (videotape fire/security controls/
  bombs/sabotage/legal, etc.)
HIGHWAY SAFETY FILMS, INC.
THE LITTLE RED FILMHOUSE
  (crime prevention)
MOTOROLA TELEPROGRAMS INC.
SECURITY FILMS, INC.
  (security officer training films)

7.d.2 First aid and safety films

AIMS INSTRUCTIONAL MEDIA
  SERVICES, INC.
  (rescue, injured persons/
  community education for)
HIGHWAY SAFETY FILMS, INC.
  (traffic safety)
MOTOROLA TELEPROGRAMS INC.

7.d.3 Films, other

AIMS INSTRUCTIONAL MEDIA
  SERVICES, INC.
  (crime prevention, community,
  employee)
DETECTION SYSTEMS, INC.
  (sales, management skills)

7.d.4 Training aids (not films)

AEROLARM
  (electronic trainers)
AIMS INSTRUCTIONAL MEDIA
  SERVICES INC.
  (filmstrips/slides and cassettes)
JOHN V. DUNIGAN STUDIOS
  (cassette loss prevention
  programs; audio-visual guard/
  store detective training
  programs)
MOTOROLA TELEPROGRAMS INC.
  (training programs for crisis
  response)
SECURITY WORLD PUBLISHING CO.,
  INC.
  (audio tapes of security subjects)
SIERRA ENGINEERING CO.
  (human body simulator for
  rescue training)

STANDARD SECURITY SYSTEMS
  (posters, government security)
TRAINING CONSULTANTS, INC.
  (security officer training
  manuals)

7.e Law enforcement training media

AIMS INSTRUCTIONAL MEDIA
  SERVICES, INC.
  (law briefs, fire arms/riot, bombs
  etc./traffic-films & filmstrips)

7.f Topical reports

ASHBY & ASSOCIATES
  (electronic surveillance report)
THE MERRITT CO.
  (manual & subscription update
  "Protection of Assets")

EMERGENCY AND DISASTER EQUIPMENT

Power, Emergency/Backup (8.a to 8.a.5) (see also 3)

8.a.1 Power supplies

WM. B. ALLEN SECURITY SUPPLIES
ARISTO-CRAFT
  (miniature motors)
ARITECH CORP.
AULT INC.
BASLER ELECTRIC CO.
CHLORIDE SYSTEMS USA
COLORADO ELECTRO-OPTICS
ELGAR CORP.
  (uninterruptible)
F & W ALARM SYSTEMS, INC.
  (regulated)
GLOBE-UNION INC.
KENCO INC.
POWER-SONIC CORP.
SONTRIX
TECHNICAL ELECTRONIC
  DISTRIBUTORS INC.
TRANS-AIR MFG. CO., LTD.
UNION CARBIDE CORP.

8.a.2 Battery systems, emergency

ADVANCED SECURITY CO.
ARISTO-CRAFT
CHLORIDE SYSTEMS USA
DUAL-LITE INC.
EAGLE-PICHER INDUSTRIES, INC.
ELECTROCON, INC.
ELGAR CORP.
ELPOWER CORP.
GLOBE-UNION INC.
GOULD INC.
POWER-SONIC CORP.
SANYO ELECTRIC INC.
  BATTERY DIV.
TECH LABORATORIES, INC.

8.a.3 Generators

AIR-WAYS DISTRIBUTORS INC.
KOHLER CO.

8.a.4 Inverters

WM. B. ALLEN SECURITY SUPPLIES
BASLER ELECTRIC CO.
CHLORIDE SYSTEMS USA
DUAL-LITE INC.
ELECTROCON, INC.
ELGAR CORP.
TECH LABORATORIES, INC.

8.a.5 Transformers

ARITECH CORP.
AULT INC.
BASLER ELECTRIC CO.
  (plug-in)

**Emergency Lighting and Rescue
Equipment (8.b to 8.b.5)**

8.b.1 Automatic/backup

CHLORIDE SYSTEMS USA
W. S. DARLEY & CO.
DUAL-LITE INC.
INSTANT ALERT

**8.b.2 Portable and vehicle
    mounted**

W. S. DARLEY & CO.
PICHEL INDUSTRIES INC.
RACON, INC.
  (portable strobe beacon)
UNION CARBIDE CORP.

8.b.3 Handlamps and flashlights

WM. B. ALLEN SECURITY SUPPLIES
AMERICAN CYANAMID CO.
  (chemical lightsticks)
W. S. DARLEY & CO.
DELTA ELECTRIC
FARALLON INDUSTRIES
  (variable beam, rechargable)
ORECK CORP.
  (high/low intensity, cordless,
  rechargable)
PICHEL INDUSTRIES INC.
  (high intensity)
F. MORTON PITT CO.
UNION CARBIDE CORP.
VSI/PRO-LIGHT
  (high intensity)
YARDNEY ELECTRIC CORP.
  (high intensity)

8.b.4 Exit signs, lighted

CHLORIDE SYSTEMS USA
  (self-powered exit)
DUAL-LITE, INC.

**8.b.5 Rescue equipment
    (see also 10, 25)**

A-T-O INC.
  (escape ladders, air packs)
W. S. DARLEY & CO.
  (escape ladders)
EXTRA SECURITY INC.
  (escape ladders)

M & G SHEET METAL CORP.
  (escape ladders)

**FIRE PROTECTION AND
EMERGENCY EQUIPMENT**

(see also 2.a, 2.b, 2.e, 8.b.5, 10)

9.a Fire extinguishers, portable

ADEMCO (ALARM DEVICE MFG. CO.)
AIR-WAYS DISTRIBUTORS INC.
A-T-O INC.
W. S. DARLEY & CO.
DIRECT SAFETY CO.
GRAVINER INC.
JAYBIL INDUSTRIES, INC.
WALTER KIDDE & CO., INC.
  BELLEVILLE DIV.
MOUNTAIN WEST ALARM SUPPLY
  CO.
MRL, INC.
STOP-FIRE, INC.
WHOLESALE SECURITY DEVICES

9.b Fire extinguishing systems

ADMIC
A-T-O INC.
FENWAL INC.
GRAVINER INC.
WALTER KIDDE & CO., INC.
  BELLEVILLE DIV.
STOP-FIRE, INC.

**9.b.1 Sprinkler systems,
    supervisory devices**

ADMIC
A-T-O INC.
HONEYWELL
NORTH ELECTRIC CO.
POTTER ELECTRIC SIGNAL CO.

**9.c. Fire resistive containers,
    including safes and files (see
    also 15.a, 20.e)**

INTERCONTINENTAL SECURITY
  PRODUCTS INC. (INTERSEC)
MOSLER AIRMATIC & ELECTRONIC
  SYSTEMS

9.d Automatic fire doors

AMWELD BUILDING PRODUCTS
CORNELL IRON WORKS, INC.
RICHARDS-WILCOX MFG. CO.

9.d.1 Fire exit equipment

AB TELEKONTROLL
  (magnetic locks)
ALARM LOCK CORP.
  (exit locks, panic exit device)
CHLORIDE SYSTEMS USA
  (exit signs, lighted)
DETEX CORP.
  (panic exit device)
DUAL-LITE INC.
  (exit signs, lighted)

EXTRA SECURITY INC.
  (exit signs, lights)
KABA SECURITY LOCKS, INC.
  (emergency exit locks)
KANE MFG. CORP.
  (panic exit device for screens)
RICHARDS-WILCOX MFG. CO.
  (panic exit device)
SARGENT & CO.
  (panic exit device, exit locks)
SILENT WATCHMAN CORP.
  (panic exit device, exit locks)
W.H. STEELE CO., INC.
  (panic exit device, automatic
  smoke detecting door closer)
VON DUPRIN INC.
  (panic exit devices, exit locks)
WICO CORP.
  (fire exit hardware)

**9.e Protective clothing/
    equipment**

LION UNIFORM, INC.
3M CO.
  (fluorescent reflective fabrics)

**9.f Fire retardant doors/
    partitions**

RICHARDS-WILCOX MFG. CO.
UNITED STATES GYPSUM

9.g Fire protection, other

G.W. DAHL CO., INC.
  (heat-activated shutoff valve)
FIRESAFE
  (trash containers, self-
  extinguishing)
M & G SHEET METAL CORP.
  (escape ladders)
MORSE PRODUCTS MFG.
  (waterflow switch)
SAFE-T-WAY SAFETY CANS
  (non-explosive filling cans)

FIRST AID AND SAFETY

10.a First aid kits and supplies

A-T-O INC.
DIRECT SAFETY CO.
  (incl. splints, stretchers)
PRO-TECTION PRODUCTS INC.
TECHNI-TOOL, INC.
ZEE MEDICAL PRODUCTS CO., INC.
  (incl. splints, stretchers)

10.b Mirrors, traffic

BELL DETECTION MIRRORS
DELTA ELECTRIC
DETECTOR INDUSTRIES
DIRECT SAFETY CO.

**10.c Protective clothing/
    equipment
    (see also 9.e, 16.a)**

AIR SPACE DEVICES
  (fall protection)

DIRECT SAFETY CO.
(protection for head, face, eyes,
ears, hands, feet)
LION UNIFORM, INC.
(clothing)
SIERRA ENGINEERING CO.
(protection for head, eyes, face,
incl. ballistic helmets)
TECHNI-TOOL, INC.
(protection for head, face, eyes,
ears, hands, feet)
3M CO.
(fluorescent reflection fabrics)

**10.d Resuscitators and oxygen
equipment**

ADD SALES CO., INC.
A-T-O INC.
DIRECT SAFETY CO.
ZEE MEDICAL PRODUCTS, INC.

10.e Signs, posters

ARTHUR BLANK & CO., INC.
DIRECT SAFETY CO.

10.f Safety, other

AIR SPACE DEVICES, INC.
(ladder safety devices)
AMERICAN CYANAMID CO.
(chemical lightsticks)
EDWARDS CO., INC.
(backup alarms)
M & G SHEET METAL CORP.
(escape ladders)
UNITED STATES GYPSUM CO.
(noise absorbers, safety grating)

**GUARD PATROL
EQUIPMENT
(see also 6, 10, 16, 21, 23.c, 25)**

11.a Flashers and signs

C.C.U. INC.

11.b Sirens

C.C.U. INC.
W. S. DARLEY & CO.
EMPIRE MACHINES & SYSTEMS INC.
KOLIN INDUSTRIES INC.
LAW ENFORCEMENT ASSOCIATES,
INC.
THE PETERZELL CO.
F. MORTON PITT CO.
SMITH & WESSON

11.c Warning lights and signals

C.C.U. INC.
LAW ENFORCEMENT ASSOCIATES,
INC.
F. MORTON PITT CO.
SMITH & WESSON

11.d Radar timing equipment

F. MORTON PITT CO.

**11.e Guard patrol equipment,
other**

CENTRAL METAL PRODUCTS, INC.

(folding cages for security dog
transit)
PRO-COM SYSTEMS, INC.
(stake-out equipment)
SENTRY TECHNOLOGY, INC.
(electronic guard supervision
equipment)

IDENTIFICATION

**12.a Badges, identification
(plastic laminated) (see also
21.a.4)**

A.P.D SECURITY SYSTEMS
AVANT INC.
ARTHUR BLANK & CO., INC.
CARDKEY SYSTEMS
GENERAL BINDING CORP.
HARCO INDUSTRIES, INC.
THE I.D. CO.
IDENTATRONICS, INC.
IDENTIFICATION SYSTEMS, INC.
MANITOU SYSTEMS, INC.
MARVEL PHOTO
POLAROID CORP.
RUSCO ELECTRONIC SYSTEMS
SEAL IN PLASTIC CO., INC.
SECURA KEY

12.b Badge and ID equipment

AVANT INC.
ARTHUR BLANK & CO., INC.
CARDKEY SYSTEMS
GENERAL BINDING CORP.
HARCO INDUSTRIES, INC.
THE I.D. CO.
IDENTICARD SYSTEMS, INC.
IDENTIFICATION SYSTEMS, INC.
MANITOU SYSTEMS, INC.
MARVEL PHOTO
F. MORTON PITT CO.
POLAROID CORP.
RUSCO ELECTRONIC SYSTEMS
SEAL IN PLASTIC CO, INC.

12.c Identification card supplies

AVANT INC.
ARTHUR BLANK & CO., INC.
CARDKEY SYSTEMS
GENERAL BINDING CORP.
HARCO INDUSTRIES, INC.
THE I.D. CO.
IDENTATRONICS, INC.
IDENTICARD SYSTEMS, INC.
IDENTIFICATION SYSTEMS, INC.
INDUSTRIAL PHOTO PRODUCTS,
INC.
LAW ENFORCEMENT ASSOCIATES,
INC.
MANITOU SYSTEMS, INC.
MARVEL PHOTO
POLOROID CORP.
RUSCO ELECTRONIC SYSTEMS
SEAL IN PLASTIC CO., INC.

12.d Laminating equipment

AVANT INC.

ARTHUR BLANK & CO., INC.
GENERAL BINDING CORP.
HARCO INDUSTRIES, INC.
THE I.D. CO.
IDENTATRONICS, INC.
IDENTIFICATION SYSTEMS, INC.
INDUSTRIAL PHOTO PRODUCTS,
INC.
MANITOU SYSTEMS, INC.
MARVEL PHOTO
RUSCO ELECTRONIC SYSTEMS
SEAL IN PLASTIC CO., INC.

**12.e Personnel ID nameplates &
tags**

ARTHUR BLANK & CO., INC.
EVERSON ROSS CO.
GENERAL BINDING CORP.
THE C. H. HANSON CO.
THE I.D. CO.
MARVEL PHOTO
MEYER & WENTHE
RUSCO ELECTRONIC SYSTEMS
SEAL IN PLASTIC CO., INC.

**12.f Property ID nameplates,
tags, and decals**

DECALS, INC.
(vehicle decals, striping)
DE GROOT ALARM DECALS
THE I.D. CO.
IDENTATRONICS, INC.
MARVEL PHOTO

**12.g ID making equipment,
miscellaneous**

AVANT INC.
GENERAL BINDING CORP.
THE I.D. CO.
IDENTIFICATION SYSTEMS, INC.
INDUSTRIAL PHOTO PRODUCTS,
INC.
MARVEL PHOTO
POLOROID CORP.
RUSCO ELECTRONIC SYSTEMS

12.h Identification, other

DECALS, INC.
(bicycle & vehicle licenses:
parking validation, permits, etc.
for law enforcement only)
IDATA, INC.
(centralized equipment for
custom-made ID)
IDENTIFICATION SYSTEMS, INC.
(microfilm ID card storage/
retrieval system)
IDENTIMAT CORP.
(prevents false acceptance of
access control cards, time cards,
ID, etc.)
ROBOT RESEARCH, INC.
(image transmission by
telephone)
WRIGHT LINE INC.
(portable code punch devices)

INSURANCE

13.a Auto, physical damage
AMERICAN INTERNATIONAL GROUP INC.

13.b Burglary and theft
W.H. BROWNYARD CORP.

13.c Business interruption
AMERICAN INTERNATIONAL GROUP INC.
W.H. BROWNYARD CORP.

13.d Commercial multiple peril
AMERICAN INTERNATIONAL GROUP INC.
W.H. BROWNYARD CORP.

13.e Errors and omissions
AMERICAN INTERNATIONAL GROUP INC.
W.H. BROWNYARD CORP.
NORTH SUBURBAN, INC.

13.f Extended coverage
AMERICAN INTERNATIONAL GROUP INC.
W.H. BROWNYARD CORP.

13.g False arrest
AMERICAN INTERNATIONAL GROUP INC.
W.H. BROWNYARD CORP.
NORTH SUBURBAN, INC.

13.h Fidelity bonds
W.H. BROWNYARD CORP.
NORTH SUBURBAN, INC.

13.j Fire insurance
AMERICAN INTERNATIONAL GROUP INC.
W.H. BROWNYARD CORP.

13.j Guard insurance
W.H. BROWNYARD CORP.
NORTH SUBURBAN, INC.

13.k Inland marine
AMERICAN INTERNATIONAL GROUP INC.
W.H. BROWNYARD CORP.

13.1 Kidnap insurance
AMERICAN INTERNATIONAL GROUP INC.

13.m Miscellaneous body injury liability
W.H. BROWNYARD CORP.
NORTH SUBURBAN, INC.

13.n Miscellaneous property damage liability
W.H. BROWNYARD CORP.
NORTH SUBURBAN, INC.

13.o Surety bonds
AMERICAN INTERNATIONAL GROUP INC.
W.H. BROWNYARD CORP.
NORTH SUBURBAN, INC.

13.p Workmen's compensation
AMERICAN INTERNATIONAL GROUP INC.
W.H. BROWNYARD CORP.

13.q Other
THE MERRITT COMPANY
risk management reference manual)

INVESTIGATIVE AIDS

14.a Binoculars
LAW ENFORCEMENT ASSOCIATES, INC.

14.b Black light equipment
SECURITY RESEARCH INC.
TECHNI-TOOL, INC.
ULTRA-VIOLET PRODUCTS, INC.

14.c Bomb, explosives detectors
E.A. BRADLEY CO.
FEDERAL LABORATORIES, INC.
(letter bomb detector)
HOTELTRON SYSTEMS, INC.
(letter bomb detector)
LAW ENFORCEMENT ASSOCIATES, INC.
(letter bomb detector; portable/walk-thru systems)
PHILIPS ELECTRONIC INSTRUMENTS, INC.
TORR X-RAY CORP.
(for letters, parcels)

14.d Breathtesting equipment
SMITH & WESSON

14.e Fingerprinting equipment
AUTHENTIPRINT IDENTIFICATION SYSTEMS
(inkless, thumbprinting system)
CRIMINALISTICS INC.
LAW ENFORCEMENT ASSOCIATES, INC.
F. MORTON PITT CO.
SECURITY RESEARCH INC.

14.f Magnifiers
QUESTAR CORP.
(telescopes)
TECHNI-TOOL, INC.

14.g Metal detecting equipment
E.A. BRADLEY CO.
THE ELECTRO-MECHANICS CO.
FEDERAL LABORATORIES, INC.
INTELATEX
INTEX INC.
SENTRIE DIV.
(walk-thru, handheld)

LAW ENFORCEMENT ASSOCIATES, INC.
F. MORTON PITT CO.
SECURITY RESEARCH INC.
S.P. INTERNATIONAL U.S.A., INC.
(walk-thru, handheld)

14.h Night viewing devices
ELECTROPHYSICS CORP.
FJW INDUSTRIES
(handheld & head-mounted)
IMPOSSIBLE ELECTRONIC TECHNIQUES, INC.
JAVELIN ELECTRONICS
LAW ENFORCEMENT ASSOCIATES, INC.
F. MORTON PITT CO.
SECURITY RESEARCH INC.
SMITH & WESSON
STANDARD LAW ENFORCEMENT SUPPLY CO.
ZOOMAR, INC.

14.i Suspect identification
ROBOT RESEARCH, INC.
(picture transmission by telephone)
SMITH & WESSON

14.j Truth-, honesty-testing aids
A-T-O INC.
(psychological stress evaluator)
B & W ASSOCIATES
(electrodermal response evaluator)
DEKTOR COUNTERINTELLIGENCE & SECURITY, INC.
(psychological stress evaluator)
LAW ENFORCEMENT ASSOCIATES, INC.
(polygraph, psychological stress evaluator, voice stress evaluator)
NATIONAL TRAINING CENTER OF POLYGRAPH SCIENCE
(polygraph)
F. MORTON PITT CO.
(polygraph)
JOHN E. REID & ASSOCIATES
(polygraph, paper-and-pencil psychological honesty tests)

14.k X-ray equipment for detection
ASTROPHYSICS RESEARCH CORP.
(for luggage, parcels, containers)
LAW ENFORCEMENT ASSOCIATES, INC.
PHILIPS ELECTRONIC INSTRUMENTS, INC.
TORR X-RAY CORP.
X-RAY INDUSTRIAL DISTRIBUTORS
(for baggage, letters)

14.l Voiceprint equipment (sound spectrograph)
LAW ENFORCEMENT ASSOCIATES, INC.

14.m Other

THE ELECTRO-MECHANICS CO.
(magnetic object detector)
ELECTROPHYSICS CORP.
(infrared viewers, infrared
microscope viewers)
HOTELTRON SYSTEMS, INC.
(counterfeit bill/certificates
detector)
ROBOT RESEARCH, INC.
(telephone transmission of image
for fingerprint/schematics/
gauges/surveillance, etc.)

MAINTENANCE SUPPLIES
(see 24)

OFFICE AND BUSINESS EQUIPMENT
(see also 6.e, 6.e.1, 18, 24)

15.a Records storage, permanent, incl. safes and files (see also 9.c, 20.e)

INTERCONTINENTAL SECURITY
PRODUCTS INC. (INTERSEC)
MOSLER AIRMATIC & ELECTRONIC
SYSTEMS
WICO CORP.

15.b Locks, anti-theft for typewriters, office machines, portable equipment (see also 17.d.2, 20.d)

ANCHOR PAD INTERNATIONAL, INC.
APC, INC.
S.P. INTERNATIONAL U.S.A., INC.
STANDARD SECURITY SYSTEMS
(lockbars for file cabinets)

15.c Telephone locks

LOXEM MFG. CORP.

15.d Records destruction equipment

CUMMINS-ALLISON CORP.
DATATECH INC.
(for paper, microfilm, x-rays)
ELECTRIC WASTEBASKET CORP.
INDUSTRIAL SHREDDER & CUTTER
CO.
SECURITY ENGINEERED MACHINERY
SHREDMASTER DIV.
GENERAL BINDING CORP.

15.e X-ray inspection equipment for letters, parcels

LAW ENFORCEMENT ASSOCIATES,
INC.
PHILIPS ELECTRONIC
INSTRUMENTS, INC.
TORR X-RAY CORP.
X-RAY INDUSTRIAL DISTRIBUTORS

15.f Other

AB TELEKONTROLL
(telephone automatic personnel
locater)
CUMMINS-ALLISON CORP.
(perforators, check signers)
ELECTRIC WASTEBASKET CORP.
(baler)
GENERAL BINDING CORP.
(binders)
HOTELTRON SYSTEMS, INC.
(letter bomb detector)
INTERBORO TIME CLOCK CORP.
(time stamping machine)
LITTLE GIANT INDUSTRIES, INC.
(telescoping ladders)
MAGNETIC SHIELD DIV.
PERFECTION MICA CO.
(shielded carrying cases for
magnetic tapes)
NIK-O-LOK CO.
(dollar bill & coin changers)
STANDARD SECURITY SYSTEMS
(government inventory control
systems: documents, marking
devices)
VERSA-LITE SYSTEMS, INC.
(electronic visual display boards)
ZERO CORP.
(aluminum carrying cases)

PERSONNEL PROTECTIVE EQUIPMENT
(see also 21.b, 25.b)

16.a Protective wearing apparel (see also 9.e)

ARMORED VEHICLE BUILDERS, INC.
(shields)
LAW ENFORCEMENT ASSOCIATES,
INC.
(ballistic vests, body armor, riot
jackets)
F. MORTON PITT CO.
(body armor)
POINT BLANK BODY ARMOR, INC.
(ballistic vests, body armor)
PROTECTIVE MATERIALS CO.
(ballistic vests, body armor, riot
jackets)
SMITH & WESSON
(ballistic vests)
STANDARD LAW ENFORCEMENT
SUPPLY CO.
(ballistic vests, materials)

16.b External aids (see also 21.b)

AB TELEKONTROLL
(silent personnel locators)
CENTRAL METAL PRODUCTS, INC.
(folding cages for security dog
transit)

CRIMINALISTICS INC.
(bomb handling equipment)
LAW ENFORCEMENT ASSOCIATES,
INC.
(bomb handling equipment,
bomb blankets, remote car
starter)
PROTECTIVE MATERIALS CO.
(shields, bomb handling
equipment, bomb blankets)

POLICE EQUIPMENT
(see 11, 16, 21, 25)

POLICE EQUIPMENT DISTRIBUTORS
(see 23.c)

PREMISE PROTECTION
(see also 2, 9, 19, 20)

17.a Perimeter barriers (see also 17.1)

AMWELD BUILDING PRODUCTS
(steel, glass doors; door frames)
A.P.D. SECURITY SYSTEMS
(gates, doors)
ARMORED VEHICLE BUILDERS, INC.
(windows, doors, glass,
partitions)
CORNELL IRON WORKS, INC.
(gates, grilles, rolling doors/
grilles)
EQUIPMENT CO. OF AMERICA
(steel folding gates)
GRANDIN INDUSTRIES INC.
(basement window bars)
HARTFORD WIRE WORKS CO.
(grilles, fencing, rolling doors/
grilles, window guards, screens,
steel folding gates, wire
partitions)
KANE MFG. CORP.
(screens, doors)
MORGAN ELECTRONICS, INC.
(gates, rolling doors)
RICHARDS-WILCOX MFG. CO.
(gates, grilles, rolling doors,
doors, partitions)
ROBOT INDUSTRIES INC.
(gates, fencing, rolling doors)
ROLL-O-MATIC CHAIN CO.
(chain closure gates)
SECURITY IRON CO.
(iron gates, grilles)
SONAR SECURITY MFG. CO.
(rolling doors, windows, glass
partitions)
SPIRIG ERNEST
(fencing)
SUPERIOR SECURITY IRON
(gates)
UNITED STATES GYPSUM CO.

(expanded metal, doors &
frames)
WHOLESALE SECURITY DEVICES
(gates)
WICO CORP.
(gates, rolling doors)

17.a.1 Fence alarms
AIR SPACE DEVICES, INC.
AIR-WAYS DISTRIBUTORS INC.
ALARM SUPPLY CO., INC.
WM. B. ALLEN SECURITY SUPPLIES
ARITECH CORP.
B-SAFE SYSTEMS INC.
COMMODORE AVIATION INC.
DOPPLER CORP.
ELECTRONIC SURVEILLANCE FENCE
SECURITY, INC.
EMERGENCY PRODUCTS CORP.
FLAIR ELECTRONICS, INC.
GTE SYLVANIA SECURITY SYSTEMS
INTERNATIONAL FENCE ALARM
CORP.
MORSE PRODUCTS MFG.
MOUNTAIN WEST ALARM SUPPLY
CO.
PRO-TECH SECURITY SYSTEMS INC.
SELLERS SECURITY & ELECTRONICS
STELLAR SYSTEMS, INC.
T.P.S. INC.
UNITED SECURITY PRODUCTS, INC.

**17.b Screens, grilles, alarm
signaling**
CUSTOM ALARM PRODUCTS
IMPERIAL SCREEN CO., INC.
MORSE PRODUCTS MFG.

17.c Automatic closures
CORNELL IRON WORKS, INC.
(roll down)
ROBOT INDUSTRIES INC.
STANLEY VEMCO
(electric door & gate operators)

17.d Locks
AB TELEKONTROLL
(magnetic)
ABLOY, INC.
ADAMS RITE MFG. CO.
ALARM DISTRIBUTORS
ALARM LOCK CORP.
WM. B. ALLEN SECURITY SUPPLIES
AMERICAN LOCK CO.
A.V.I.D. ENTERPRISES
BRINK'S LOCKING SYSTEMS, INC.
(electromechanical)
CARDKEY SYSTEMS
(card activated)
FOLGER ADAM CO.
KABA SECURITY LOCKS, INC.
LUCCO SECURITY PRODUCTS CO.
MAGLOK, INC.
(magnetic deadbolt lock)
MEDECO SECURITY LOCK INC.

GOODLOE E. MOORE, INC.
MOUNTAIN WEST ALARM SUPPLY
CO.
MUL-T-LOCK CORP.
(multi-deadbolt lock)
NIK-O-LOK CO.
(token & coin operated)
PHELPS TIME RECORDING LOCK
CORP.
P.T.I.-DOLCO
(sliding door/window)
RUSSWIN DIV.
EMHART CORP.
SARGENT & CO.
SARGENT & GREENLEAF, INC.
SCHLAGE ELECTRONICS
(electronic)
SECURITRON MAGNALOCK CORP.
(electromagnetic)
SECURITY ENGINEERING INC.
(electromagnetic)
STANLEY VEMCO
(electric gate locks)
VON DUPRIN INC.
WICO CORP.

17.d Lock working equipment
A.V.I.D. ENTERPRISES
FACIT-ADDO, INC.
FOLGER ADAM CO.
KEY MASTER SALES CO.
(key making equipment)
STANDARD SECURITY SYSTEMS
(lockbars for file cabinets)

**17.d.2 Locks, portable equipment
(see also 15.b)**
ANCHOR PAD INTERNATIONAL, INC.
APC, INC.

17.e Lock cylinders
ABLOY, INC.
ADAMS RITE MFG. CO.
A.V.I.D. ENTERPRISES
FOLGER ADAM CO.
KABA SECURITY LOCKS, INC.
LOXEM MFG. CORP.
MEDECO SECURITY LOCKS INC.
SARGENT & CO.

17.e.1 Cylinder guards
ADAMS RITE MFG. CO.
ADEMCO (ALARM DEVICE MFG. CO.)
KABA SECURITY LOCKS, INC.

17.f Locks, combination
ADVANCED SECURITY CO.
(pushbutton)
ALARM LOCK CORP.
(pushbutton)
WM. B. ALLEN SECURITY SUPPLIES
(mechanical, pushbutton)
AMERICAN LOCK CO.
(mechanical)
A.P.D. SECURITY SYSTEMS
(mechanical, pushbutton)

B-SAFE SYSTEMS INC.
(pushbutton)
CAMPBELL CHAIN CO.
(mechanical)
CONTINENTAL INSTRUMENTS CORP.
(pushbutton)
CORBY INDUSTRIES, INC.
(pushbutton)
ELECTRONIC SECURITY SYSTEMS,
INC.
(pushbutton)
KABA SECURITY LOCKS, INC.
(mechanical)
MEDECO SECURITY LOCKS INC.
(mechanical)
PROMARK CORP.
(pushbutton)
ROBOT INDUSTRIES INC.
(pushbutton)
SARGENT & GREENLEAF, INC.
(mechanical, pushbutton)
SECURITY PRODUCTS CO.
(pushbutton)
SECURTEC, INC.
(pushbutton)
SIMPLEX SECURITY SYSTEMS, INC.
(pushbutton)
UNICAN SECURITY SYSTEMS CORP.
(pushbutton)
WOLO MFG. CORP.
(electrical/mechanical)

17.g Locks, recording
FACIT-ADDO, INC.
PHELPS TIME RECORDING LOCK
CORP.
SILENT WATCHMAN CORP.

17.g.1 Time locks
FACIT-ADDO, INC.
SARGENT & GREENLEAF, INC.

17.h Padlocks
ABLOY, INC.
WM. B. ALLEN SECURITY SUPPLIES
AMERICAN LOCK CO.
CAMPBELL CHAIN CO.
KABA SECURITY LOCKS, INC.
MAGLOK, INC.
(magnetic)
MEDECO SECURITY LOCKS INC.
SARGENT & CO.
SARGENT & GREENLEAF, INC.
THE WHITMAN CO.

17.i Key control systems
COMMERCIAL PASTICS & SUPPLY
CORP.
FACIT-ADDO, INC.
KABA SECURITY LOCKS, INC.
KE-MASTER
SQUARE D CO.
TELKEE INC.

17.i.1 Key cabinets and carriers

KE-MASTER

TELKEE INC.

17.j Time clocks and clock stations

DETEX CORP.

DOUGLAS RANDALL DIV.

  WALTER KIDDE & CO., INC.

FACIT-ADDO, INC.

INTERBORO TIME CLOCK CORP.

PINKERTON'S, INC.

SARGENT & GREENLEAF, INC.

SENTRY TECHNOLOGY, INC.

17.j.1 Central clock station reporting systems

INTERBORO TIME COCK CORP.

SENTRY TECHNOLOGY, INC.

17.k Outdoor, ground space protection

ADVANCED DEVICES LABORATORY, INC.

  (microwave)

ARROWHEAD ENTERPRISES INC.

  (photoelectric)

COLORADO ELECTRO-OPTICS

  (photoelectric)

CREST ELECTRONICS INC.

  (microwave)

DOPPLER CORP.

  (piezoelectric)

F&W ALARM SYSTEMS, INC.

  (photoelectric)

INTRUSION DETECTION SYSTEM, INC.

  (I.D.S. INC.)

  (buried seismic system)

MORGAN ELECTRONICS, INC.

  (electric field)

MORSE PRODUCTS MFG.

  (photoelectric)

RACON, INC.

  (microwave)

SHORROCK INC.

  (microwave)

STELLAR SYSTEMS, INC.

  (electrostatic field)

17.1 Glazing materials, burglary/bullet resistive

ARMORED VEHICLE BUILDERS, INC.

E.I. DU PONT DE NEMOURS & CO.

ROHM AND HAAS CO.

SAFELITE INDUSTRIES

  (laminated glass)

17.1.1 Doors, walls, partitions: burglary/bullet resistive

ARMORED VEHICLE BUILDERS, INC.

HARTFORD WIRE WORKS CO.

PROTECTIVE MATERIALS CO.

RICHARDS-WILCOX MFG. CO.

17.m Lighting controls, remote

GUARDIAN ELECTRONICS INC.

INTRUSION DETECTION SYSTEM, INC.

  (I.D.S. INC.)

SQUARE D CO.

17.n Signs, warning security

BURNS INTERNATIONAL SECURITY SERVICES, INC.

DE GROOT ALARM DECALS

  (decals)

17.o Tear gas dispensers, intrusion triggered

FEDERAL LABORATORIES, INC.

PROTECTION & SECURITY EQUIPMENT CORP.

17.p Premise protection equipment, other

ADMIC

  (swimming pool alarm)

AIR-FLO CO. INC.

  (tamper proof door latch protector)

CHAMBERLAIN MFG. CORP.

  (electronic garage door openers, radio frequency)

CREATIVE INDUSTRIES INC.

  (pass-through transaction trays for bulletproof windows)

DETROIT MINI-SAFE CO.

  (deposit safes)

FLAIR EECTRONICS, INC.

  (overhead garage door alarm)

FOREWARN INC.

  (swimming pool alarm)

THE GANNON MFG. CORP.

  (door hinges and hardware)

KABA SECURITY LOCKS, INC.

  (selective multiplex key systems)

KANE MFG. CORP.

  (panic exit devices for screens, locks for detention screens)

LINEAR CORP.

  (electronic garage door openers, radio frequency)

LOXEM MFG. CORP.

  (190° optical viewer, sliding glass door locks, window locks, door chains)

LUMENITE ELECTRONICS CO.

  (time signal program clock)

GOODLOE E. MOORE, INC.

  (in-door wide angle door viewer)

NEWSTAMP

  (in-door observation window)

THE PETERZELL CO.

  (chain locks)

PHELPS TIME RECORDING LOCK CORP.

  (sequence locking system)

POOL GUARD, INC.

  (swimming pool alarms)

R-BAR INDUSTRIES, INC.

  (high vantage fixed observation posts)

RECORA CO., INC.

  (doorway announcer mat)

ROBOT RESEARCH, INC.

  (telephone transmission system for CCTV image)

SIGNAL-U MFG. CO.

  (doorway floormat announcer; driveway signals for banks, gas stations)

SILENT WATCHMAN CORP.

  (sequence locking system)

SQUARE D CO.

  (overhead door control and lock)

STANLEY HARDWARE

  (spring hinges, electric hinges)

TAPESWITCH CORP. OF AMERICA

  (doorway announcer mat)

VAN LOCK CO.

  (door and lock tamper alarm)

WOLO MFG. CORP.

  (vehicle hood/trunk locks)

RECORDERS, AUDIO

18.a General purpose

THE ANSWERLINE ASSOCIATES INC.

  (cassette)

AUDIOTRONICS CORP.

  (cassette)

PANASONIC CO.

  (tape, cassette)

SC ELECTRONICS, INC.

  (cassette)

18.b Portable

THE ANSWERLINE ASSOCIATES INC.

  (cassette)

AUDIOTRONICS CORP.

  (cassette)

GYYR PRODUCTS

  (cassette, courtroom recording/transcription applications)

LAW ENFORCEMENT ASSOCIATES, INC.

  (cassette)

PANASONIC CO.

  (tape, cassette)

SC ELECTRONICS INC.

  (cassette)

18.c Miniature

INTELATEX

LAW ENFORCEMENT ASSOCIATES, INC.

18.d Dictating equipment

THE ANSWERLINE ASSOCIATES INC.

  (cassette)

18.e Logging recorders (12 hours and up)

THE ANSWERLINE ASSOCIATES INC.
(cassette)
LAW ENFORCEMENT ASSOCIATES,
INC.

18.f Telephone recorders

THE ANSWERLINE ASSOCIATES INC.
INTELATEX
LAW ENFORCEMENT ASSOCIATES,
INC.
PANASONIC CO.

18.g Accessories and components for recording/playback

ATLAS SOUND
(microphone stands)
INTELATEX
(special purpose)
INTERNATIONAL AUDIO VISUAL,
INC.
(tape transports)
LAW ENFORCEMENT ASSOCIATES,
INC.
(monitors, couplers, patch cords)
PANASONIC CO.

TELEVISION, CLOSED CIRCUIT

19.a Cameras (see also 19.a.1, 20.f)

ADEMCO (ALARM DEVICE MFG. CO.)
AIR-WAYS DISTRIBUTORS INC.
WM. B. ALLEN SECURITY SUPPLIES
ARITECH CORP.
ATV RESEARCH
COHU, INC.
COLUMBIA VIDEO SYSTEMS
CREST ELECTRONICS INC.
DAGE-MTI, INC.
GBC CLOSED CIRCUIT TELEVISION
CORP.
GENERAL ELECTRIC CO.
IMAGING SYSTEMS OPERATION
GENERAL ELECTRIC CO.
TUBE PRODUCTS DEPT.
GENERAL ELECTRODYNAMICS CORP.
GYYR PRODUCTS
HOLMES PROTECTION, INC.
HONEYWELL
IKEGAMI ELECTRONICS (U.S.A.)
INC.
IMPOSSIBLE ELECTRONIC
TECHNIQUES, INC.
JAVELIN ELECTRONICS
KOYO INTERNATIONAL INC. OF
AMERICA
M.M.S., INC.
MORGAN ELECTRONICS, INC.

MOTOROLA COMMUNICATIONS &
ELECTRONICS, INC.
NEC AMERICA, INC.
NORTH ELECTRIC CO.
PANASONIC CO.
PHILIPS AUDIO VIDEO SYSTEMS
CORP.
RCA ELECTRO-OPTICS & DEVICES
SANYO ELECTRIC INC.
SECURITY SUPPLY SERVICE INC.
TELEMATION, INC.
VISUAL METHODS INC.
WELLS FARGO ALARM SERVICES

19.a.1 Cameras, low-light-level

WM. B. ALLEN SECURITY SUPPLIES
ARITECH CORP.
COHU, INC.
COLUMBIA VIDEO SYSTEMS
CREST ELECTRONICS INC.
DAGE-MTI, INC.
ELECTROPHYSICS CORP.
(custom-designed)
GBC CLOSED CIRCUIT TELEVISION
CORP.
GENERAL ELECTRIC CO.
IMAGING SYSTEMS OPERATION
GENERAL ELECTRIC CO.
TUBE PRODUCTS DEPT.
GENERAL ELECTRODYNAMICS CORP.
IKEGAMI ELECTRONICS (U.S.A.)
INC.
IMPOSSIBLE ELECTRONIC
TECHNIQUES INC.
JAVELIN ELECTRONICS
KOYO INTERNATIONAL INC. OF
AMERICA
LENZAR OPTICS CORP.
M.M.S., INC.
MOTOROLA COMMUNICATIONS &
ELECTRONICS, INC.
PANASONIC CO.
PHILIPS AUDIO VIDEO SYSTEMS
CORP.
RCA ELECTRO-OPTICS & DEVICES
TELEMATION, INC.
VENUS SCIENTIFIC INC.
WELLS FARGO ALARM SERVICES

19.b Monitors

ADEMCO (ALARM DEVICE MFG. CO.)
WM. B. ALLEN SECURITY SUPPLIES
ARITECH CORP.
ATV RESEARCH
COHU, INC.
COLUMBIA VIDEO SYSTEMS
CREST ELECTRONICS INC.
DAGE-MTI, INC.
ELECTROHOME LTD.
GBC COSED CIRCUIT TELEVISION
CORP.
GENERAL ELECTRIC CO.
IMAGING SYSTEMS OPERATION

GENERAL ELECTRIC CO.
TUBE PRODUCTS DEPT.
GYYR PRODUCTS
HOLMES PROTECTION, INC.
HONEYWELL
IKEGAMI ELECTRONICS (U.S.A.)
INC.
JAVELIN ELECTRONICS
KOYO INTERNATIONAL INC. OF
AMERICA
M.M.S., INC.
MOTOROLA COMMUNICATIONS &
ELECTRONICS, INC.
NEC AMERICA, INC.
PANASONIC CO.
PHILIPS AUDIO VIDEO SYSTEMS
CORP.
RCA ELECTRO-OPTICS & DEVICES
SANYO ELECTRIC INC.
SC ELECTRONICS, INC.
WELLS FARGO ALARM SERVICES

19.c Video tape recorders

WM. B. ALLEN SECURITY SUPPLIES
ARITECH CORP.
ATV RESEARCH
COLUMBIA VIDEO SYSTEMS
CREST ELECTRONICS INC.
GBC CLOSED CIRCUIT TELEVISION
CORP.
GYYR PRODUCTS
(inc. time lapse)
HOLMES PROTECTION, INC.
HONEYWELL
JAVELIN ELECTRONICS
KOYO INTERNATIONAL INC. OF
AMERICA
M.M.S., INC.
NEC AMERICA, INC.
(incl. time lapse)
PANASONIC CO.
PHILIPS AUDIO VIDEO SYSTEMS
CORP.
RCA ELECTRO OPTICS & DEVICES
SANYO ELECTRIC INC.
TEKNEKRON, INC.
(disc)
WELLS FARGO ALARM SERVICES

19.d CCTV related equipment

ADEMCO (ALARM DEVICE MFG. CO.)
(lenses, housings, switchers,
scanners, pan & tilt, vidicon
tubes, mounts)
ALDEN ELECTRONICS & IMPULSE
RECORDING EQUIPMENT CO., INC.
(TV image storage and hard-
copy print-out system)
WM. B. ALLEN SECURITY SUPPLIES
(lenses, housings, switches,
scanners, pan & tilt, vidicon
tubes, time/date generator,
remote control mounts)

AMPEREX ELECTRONIC CORP.
(vidicon tubes, pyroelectric vidicon tubes)

ARITECH CORP.
(lenses, night viewing devices, housings, switchers, scanners, pan & tilt, vidicon tubes, time/date generator, remote controls)

ATV RESEARCH
(lenses, vidicon tubes, wall/ceiling mounts, etc.)

AVANT INC.
(split screen with access control)

CANON U.S.A. INC.
(lenses)

COHU, INC.
(lenses, night viewing devices, pan & tilt, vidicon tubes, remote controls)

COLUMBIA VIDEO SYSTEMS
(lenses, night viewing devices, housings, switchers, scanners, pan & tilt, vidicon tubes, time/date generator, remote controls, mounts)

COSMICAR LENS DIV.
ASAHI PRECISION CO., LTD.
(lenses)

CREST ELECTRONICS INC.
(lenses, housings, switchers, scanners, pan & tilt, vidicon tubes, time/date generator, remote controls, split screen system)

CROSSPOINT LATCH CORP.
(low-light-level amplifier)

DAGE-MTI, INC.
(switchers)

DYNAIR ELECTRONICS, INC.
(switcher)

ELECTRO-MECHANICAL IMAGINEERING, INC.
(housings, mounts)

ELECTROPHYSICS CORP.
(night viewing devices)

GBC CLOSED CIRCUIT TELEVISION CORP.
(lenses, night viewing devices, housings, switches, pan & tilt, vidicon tubes, time/date generator, remote controls, mounts)

GENERAL ELECTRIC CO.
Imaging Systems Operation
(lenses, night viewing devices, housings, switchers, scanners, pan & tilt, vidicon tubes, time/date generator, remote controls, mounts)

GENERAL ELECTRIC CO.
TUBE PRODUCTS DEPT.
(lenses, night viewing devices, housings, switchers, scanners, pan & tilt, vidicon tubes, time/date generator, remote controls, mounts)

GENERAL ELECTRODYNAMICS CORP.
(vidicon tubes, remote control)

GYYR PRODUCTS
(lenses, time/date generator)

IKEGAMI ELECTRONICS (U.S.A.) INC.
(lenses, switchers)

IMPOSSIBLE ELECTRONIC TECHNIQUES, INC.
(lenses, time/date generators)

INTERNATIONAL AUDIO VISUAL, INC.
(infrared LED for wireless TV transmission)

INTERNATIONAL MICROWAVE CORP.
(microwave transmission of video information)

JAVELIN ELECTRONICS
(lenses, night viewing devices, housings, switchers, pan & tilt, time/date generator, scanners, vidicon tubes, remote controls, mounts)

KAPCO ENTERPRISES, INC.
(switchers, character generators, audio controls, etc.; control panels, B/W or color)

KOYO INTERNATIONAL INC. OF AMERICA
(lenses, housings, switchers, scanners, pan & tilt, vidicon tubes, time/date generator, remote controls, mounts)

LENZAR OPTICS CORP.
(lenses, night viewing devices)

MERET INC.
(complete systems for transmission of CCTV signals over IR beams via fiber optics & free space line-of-sight)

M.M.S., INC.
(lenses, housings, switchers, pan & tilt, vidicon tubes, time/date generator, remote controls, mounts, video transmission over telephone or intercom)

MOTOROLA COMMUNICATION & ELECTRONICS, INC.
(housings, switchers, pan & tilt, remote controls)

NEC AMERICA, INC.
(lenses)

PANASONIC CO.
(lenses, night viewing devices, housings, switchers, pan & tilt, vidicon tubes, time/date generator, remote controls, mounts)

PELCO SALES INC.
(lenses, housings, switches, scanners, pan & tilt, time/date generator, remote controls, mounts)

PHILIPS AUDIO VIDEO SYSTEMS CORP.
(lenses, night viewing devices, housings, scanners, pan & tilt, vidicon tubes, remote controls, mounts)

PICHEL INDUSTRIES INC.
(infrared illuminators)

PORTAC CO.
(switchers, time/date generator, remote controls, split screen camera systems)

POWER-OPTICS, INC.
(lenses, pan & tilt, remote controls)

QUESTAR CORP.
(lenses)

QUICK-SET INC./CUNNINGHAM
(lenses, housings, switchers, scanners, pan & tilt, vidicon tubes, time/date generator, remote controls, low voltage relay system)

RCA ELECTRO-OPTICS & DEVICES
(lenses, housings, switchers, scanners, pan & tilt, vidicon tubes, time/date generator, remote controls, mounts)

RIVERS PROTECTION SYSTEMS INC.
(universal mounting bracket for cameras, motion detectors, etc.)

ROBOT RESEARCH, INC.
(telephone line image & recorder)

SANYO ELECTRIC INC.
(lenses, vidicon tubes)

SNYDER ELECTRONICS, INC.
(scanners, brackets)

TELEMATION, INC.
(lenses, switchers, source identifiers, video distribution amplifiers)

THALNER ELECTRONIC LABORATORIES INC.
(screen splitter, video message generator, video distribution amplifier)

VICON INDUSTRIES INC.
(lenses, housings, switchers, scanners, pan & tilt, time/date generator, remote controls, mounts, video amplifiers)

VIDEO COMPONENTS, INC.
(lenses, night viewing devices, switchers, vidicon tubes, time/date generator, mounts)

VIDEOLARM INC.
(outdoor, all-weather housings, mounts)

VISUAL METHODS INC.
(lenses, night viewing devices,

housings, switchers, time/date
generator)
WELLS FARGO ALARM SERVICES
(lenses, night viewing devices,
housings, switchers, scanners,
pan & tilt, vidicon tubes, time/
date generator, remote controls,
mounts)
ZOOMAR, INC.
(lenses, night viewing devices,
remote controls)

19.e Video motion detector

ATRONIC
COLUMBIA VIDEO SYSTEMS
CREST ELECTRONICS INC.
GBC CLOSED CIRCUIT TELEVISION
CORP.
GYYR PRODUCTS
HONEYWELL
IMPOSSIBLE ELECTRONIC
TECHNIQUES, INC.
INTELATEX
JAVELIN ELECTRONICS
KOYO INTERNATIONAL INC. OF
AMERICA
M.M.S., INC.
PELCO SALES INC.
RCA ELECTRO-OPTICS & DEVICES
SANYO ELECTRIC INC.
SC ELECTRONICS, INC.
VICON INDUSTRIES INC.
VIDEO TEK, INC.
VISUAL COMMUNICATION
SPECIALISTS

19.f CCTV surveillance systems

ADEMCO (ALARM DEVICE MFG. CO.)
ADT
ARITECH CORP.
COLUMBIA VIDEO SYSTEMS
CREST ELECTRONICS INC.
DAGE-MTI, INC.
FRISCO BAY INDUSTRIES OF
CANADA LTD.
GBC COSED CIRCUIT TELEVISION
CORP.
GENERAL ELECTRIC CO.
IMAGING SYSTEMS OPERATION
GENERAL ELECTRODYNAMICS CORP.
GYYR PRODUCTS
HONEYWELL
IKEGAMI ELECTRONICS (U.S.A.)
INC.
IMPOSSIBLE ELECTRONIC
TECHNIQUES, INC.
INTELATEX
JAVELIN ELECTRONICS
KAPCO ENTERPRISES, INC.
(custom-designed)
KOYO INTERNATIONAL INC. OF
AMERICA
LERRO ELECTRICAL CORP.
(custom-designed)

MARDIX, INC.
(special access control system)
M.M.S., INC.
MORGAN ELECTRONICS, INC.
MOSLER AIRMATIC & ELECTRONIC
SYSTEMS
MOTOROLA COMMUNICATIONS &
ELECTRONICS, INC.
NORTH ELECTRIC CO.
PANASONIC CO.
PHILIPS AUDIO VIDEO SYSTEMS
CORP.
PINKERTON'S, INC.
POWER-OPTICS, INC.
(series telemetry systems, remote
controlled)
QUESTAR CORP.
(custom-designed)
SANYO ELECTRIC CO.
VENUS SCIENTIFIC INC.
VICON INDUSTRIES INC.
VIDEO TEK, INC.
VISUAL COMMUNICATION
SPECIALISTS
VISUAL METHODS INC.

THEFT AND ROBBERY PREVENTIVE EQUIPMENT
(see also 2.c, 4.f, 17, 19)

20.a Mirrors (two-way, convex, etc.)

ADD SALES CO., INC.
(convex)
ALARM SUPPLY CO., INC.
(convex)
WM. B. ALLEN SECURITY SUPPLIES
(convex)
BELL DETECTION MIRRORS
(incl. indoor/outdoor use,
circular/rectangular, convex/
flat)
BEST INDUSTRIES INC.
(convex)
DETECTOR INDUSTRIES
(convex)
OPTICS OF KANSAS, INC.
SE-KURE CONTROLS, INC.
(convex, plexiglas, one-way)
SNYDER ELECTRONICS, INC.
(convex)

20.b Booths, cashiers'

ARMORED VEHICLE BUILDERS, INC.
ENDURE-A-LIFETIME PRODUCTS,
INC.
KEENE CORP.
PAR-KUT INTERNATIONAL, INC.
PORTA-KING BLDG. SYSTEMS
PROTECTIVE MATERIALS CO.
ROBOT INDUSTRIES INC.

20.c Property tags, nameplates, and decals

ARTHUR BLANK & CO., INC.

DE GROOT ALARM DECALS
(decals)

20.d Fasteners, tamper resistive
(see also 15.b, 17.d.2)

AMERICAN LOCK CO.
(hasps)
APC, INC.
(desk-top office/audio visual
equipment locking devices)
E.J. BROOKS CO.
(plastic seals)
LOXEM MFG. CORP.
(lockbars)
SPENCER PRODUCTS CO.
STANDARD SECURITY SYSTEMS
(lockbars)
STOFFEL SEALS CORP.
(plastic, metal)

20.e Safes, burglary resistive (see also 9.c, 15.a)

WM. B. ALLEN SECURITY SUPPLIES
IN-A-FLOOR SAFE CO.
(steel floor-embedded safes)
INTERCONTINENTAL SECURITY
PRODUCTS INC. (INTERSEC)
MOSLER AIRMATIC & ELECTRONIC
SYSTEMS
WICO CORP.

20.f Dummy CCTV cameras

BEST INDUSTRIES INC.
CREST ELECTRONICS INC.
JAVELIN ELECTRONICS
KOYO INTERNATIONAL INC. OF
AMERICA
M.M.S., INC.
OPTICS OF KANSAS, INC.
RCA ELECTRO-OPTICS & DEVICES
RICHMOND ENTERPRISES INC.
S.P. INTERNATIONAL U.S.A., INC.
SURVEILLANCE VIDEO SYSTEMS
TEL-GARD INDUSTRIES

20.g Shoplifting alarms

AEROLARM
(for business machines, TV,
stereo equipment)
ANCHOR PAD INTERNATIONAL, INC.
(desk top equipment locks)
CHECKPOINT SYSTEMS, INC.
(walk-through & portable
detection systems for retail
stores, libraries, etc.)
DELTA PRODUCTS, INC.
(display, loop)
FRISCO BAY INDUSTRIES OF
CANADA LTD.
GLENCO SECURITY ELECTRONICS
INC.
(display alarm, loop)
LPS INTERNATIONAL, LTD.
RONALD MILLER INC.
(anti-holdup currency time lock
safe)

SE-KURE CONTROLS, INC.
(display alarm, showcase alarm)
SPIRIG ERNEST
TAPESWITCH CORP. OF AMERICA
(detector cells for displayed
objects)

20.h Theft preventive equipment, other

ASTROPHYSICS RESEARCH CORP.
(x-ray inspection systems)
CALIFORNIA ELECTRONIC
INDUSTRIES, INC.
(pocket pager vehicle theft
alerting system)
CAMPBELL CHAIN CO.
(anti-theft chain & cable)
DETROIT MINI-SAFE CO.
(deposit safes)
ELK-ROUTEMASTER INC.
(truck anti-hijacking and theft
preventive system)
INTERCHECK CORP.
(coat/display merchandise chain
locking system, coin operated
coat check system)
INTEX INC.
SENTRIE DIV.
(weapons detection; anti-
pilferage walk-thru/hand held
systems)
LAW ENFORCEMENT ASSOCIATES,
INC.
(anti-theft portable alarms,
wireless, concealed weapons/
object detectors)
LPS INTERNATIONAL, LTD.
(anti-theft sensitized label walk-
thru system for retail stores,
libraries, museums, etc.)
LUCCO SECURITY PRODUCTS CO.
(money clip alarm)
PAGE ALERT SYSTEMS, INC.
(anti-vehicle theft warning
system, radio signaling)
PRO-TECH SECURITY SYSTEMS INC.
(anti-theft device for vehicle
tires)
QONAAR SECURITY SYSTEMS INC.
(parking meters with anti-theft
coin collection systems, cash
drawer alarm)
RECORA CO., INC.
(cash register locking floor mat)
GEORGE RISK INDUSTRIES, INC.
(anti-theft alarm for vending
machines incl. laundromats; anti-
theft alarms for car CB, stereo,
etc.; anti-theft alarms for TV
sets, hotel/motel & residential
application)
SCANDUS INC.
(anti-holdup counter minisafe)
SNYDER ELECTRONICS, INC.
(photoelectric announcing

systems, pressure mat
announcing systems)
SOLFAN SYSTEMS INC.
(anti-holdup armored cash
control system)
SUNSHINE RECREATION INC.
(anti-theft bicycle station locking
system, parking meter mounted
bicycle locking system)
TAPESWITCH CORP. OF AMERICA
(cash register protector mat)
VISUAL METHODS INC.
(cash register surveillance
system)
WOLO MFG. CORP.
(anti-theft vehicle hood/trunk
locks)
ZERO CORP.
(aluminum carrying cases for
valuables)

TOOLS AND INSTRUMENTS (see 24)

UNIFORMED FORCE, SUPPLIES AND ANCILLARY AIDS (see also 6, 11, 16, 23.c, 25)

Uniforms and Accessories (21.a to 21.a.8)

21.a.1 Uniforms

CONE MILLS
GERBER MFG. CO., INC.
(coats, pants, jackets)
LION UNIFORM, INC.
(jackets, shirts, trousers)
MAGSON UNIFORM CO.
MERSON UNIFORM CO.
(shirts, trousers, accessories)
MT. PLEASANT MFG. CO.
(shirts)
RIVERSIDE MFG. CO.
(shirts, trousers, jackets,
accessories)
SLALOM UNIFORM CO.
(jackets)
HORACE SMALL MFG. CO.
(jackets, coats, skirts, slacks,
shirts)

21.a.2 Rainwear

LION UNIFORM, INC.
MAGSON UNIFORM CO.
RIVERSIDE MFG. CO.

21.a.3 Caps & hats

GERBER MFG. CO., INC.
MAGSON UNIFORM CO.
MIDWAY CAP CO.
RIVERSIDE MFG. CO.
HORACE SMALL MFG. CO.
STRATTON HATS, INC.

21.a.4 Badges, metal (see also 12.a)

EVERSON ROSS CO.
THE C. H. HANSON CO.
MAGSON UNIFORM CO.
MEYER & WENTHE
MIDWAY CAP CO.

21.a.5 Emblems

EVERSON ROSS CO.
THE C. H. HANSON CO.
MAGSON UNIFORM CO.
MEYER & WENTHE
RIVERSIDE MFG. CO.

21.a.6 Holsters, leather goods

J.M. BUCHEIMER CO.
COURTLANDT BOOT JACK CO. INC.
(incl. holsters, badge/flashlight
holders, belts)
THE C. H. HANSON CO.
(badge holders)
INTERARMS
MAGSON UNIFORM CO.
MIDWAY CAP CO.
VSI/PRO-LIGHT

21.a.7 Handcuffs

COURTLANDT BOOT JACK CO., INC.
MAGSON UNIFORM CO.

21.a.8 Other

WEST COAST CHAIN MFG. CO.
(key chain reels)

Weapons (21.b to 21.b.5)

21.b.1 Firearms and parts

CHARTER ARMS CORP.
(handguns)
H.K.S. TOOL PRODUCTS CO.
(gun parts incl. speed loader)
INTERARMS
(handguns, rifles, rifle scopes)
LAW ENFORCEMENT ASSOCIATES,
INC.
(handguns, rifles, laser sights)
SMITH & WESSON
(handguns, shotguns)
STURM, RUGER & CO. INC.
(revolvers, pistols, rifles, selective
fire weapons)
VSI/PRO-LIGHT
(combat pistol grips)
DAN WESSON ARMS, INC.

21.b.1.a Ammunition

INTERARMS
SMITH & WESSON

21.b.2 Firearms training materials, ranges/ equipment

SMITH & WESSON

21.b.3 Tear gas

MIDWAY CAP CO.

F. MORTON PITT CO.
PROTECTION & SECURITY
EQUIPMENT CORP.
SMITH & WESSON

21.b.3.a Tear gas dispensers
CHEMLITE INC.
(flashlights)
FEDERAL LABORATORIES, INC.
PROTECTION & SECURITY
EQUIPMENT CORP.
SMITH & WESSON

21.b.4 Batons and nightsticks
COURTLANDT BOOT JACK CO., INC.
FEDERAL LABORATORIES, INC.
MAGSON UNIFORM CO.
SMITH & WESSON

21.b.5 Weapons, other
SMITH & WESSON
WEAPONS CORP. OF AMERICA
(non-lethal)

SERVICES, SECURITY

22.a Alarm services
ADT
E.A. BRADLEY CO.
BURNS INTERNATIONAL SECURITY
SERVICES, INC.
EMERGENCY DATA COMPUTER
CENTER
(nationwide alarm dialers
monitoring service)
HONEYWELL
NATIONAL SECURITY SYSTEMS, INC.
SILENT WATCHMAN CORP.
STANLEY SMITH SECURITY, INC.
UNIVERSAL SECURITY
CONSULTANTS, INC.
WELLS FARGO ALARM SERVICES

22.b Consultant services
ADVANCE INDUSTRIAL SECURITY
A-T-O INC.
E.A. BRADLEY CO.
BURNS INTERNATIONAL SECURITY
SERVICES, INC.
COM/TECH SYSTEMS INC.
GUARDSMARK, INC.
INTELATEX
KBI SECURITY SERVICE INC.
NATIONAL SECURITY SYSTEMS, INC.
NUSAC, INC.
PINKERTON'S, INC.
STANLEY SMITH SECURITY, INC.
UNIVERSAL SECURITY
CONSULTANTS, INC.

22.c Employment services
GUARDSMARK, INC.
STANLEY SMITH SECURITY, INC.

22.d Guard services
ADVANCE INDUSTRIAL SECURITY

A-T-O INC.
BURNS INTERNATIONAL SECURITY
SERVICES, INC.
GUARDSMARK, INC.
KBI SECURITY SERVICE INC.
PINKERTON'S, INC.
STANLEY SMITH SECURITY, INC.

22.e Investigative services
ADVANCE INDUSTRIAL SECURITY
A-T-O INC.
BURNS INTERNATIONAL SECURITY
SERVICES, INC.
GUARDSMARK, INC.
INTELATEX
KBI SECURITY SERVICE INC.
PINKERTON'S, INC.
STANLEY SMITH SECURITY, INC.
UNIVERSAL SECURITY
CONSULTANTS, INC.

22.f Polygraph services
ADVANCE INDUSTRIAL SECURITY
GUARDSMARK, INC.
KBI SECURITY SERVICE INC.
PINKERTON'S, INC.
JOHN E. REID & ASSOCIATES
STANLEY SMITH SECURITY, INC.

**22.g Psychological stress
evaluation services**
ADVANCE INDUSTRIAL SECURITY
A-T-O INC.
DEKTOR COUNTERINTELLIGENCE &
SECURITY, INC.
INTELATEX
LAW ENFORCEMENT ASSOCIATES,
INC.
STANLEY SMITH SECURITY, INC.

22.h Other
AMCEST
(nationwide alarm monitoring
system)
EMERGENCY DATA COMPUTER
CENTER
(nationwide alarm monitoring
service)
FORTRESS HILL ELECTRONICS
(selected equipment repair
service)
IDATA, INC.
(centralized equipment for
custom-made ID)
LANGUAGE TRANSLATION
SERVICES, INC.
(language translation services for
international marketing
communications)
LAW ENFORCEMENT ASSOCIATES,
INC.
(electronic countermeasure
services)
F.G. MASON ENGINEERING, INC.
(electronic countermeasures)
NUSAC, INC.

(security, management &
planning services)
PINKERTON'S, INC.
(electronic countermeasure
services)
JOHN E. REID & ASSOCIATES
(Reid Report testing for honesty)
STANLEY SMITH SECURITY, INC.
(armored car, courier patrol
services)

DISTRIBUTORS AND
IMPORTERS

23.a Alarm equipment
WM. B. ALLEN SUPPLY CO., INC.
ADEMCO (ALARM DEVICE MFG. CO.)
AIR-WAYS DISTRIBUTORS INC.
ALARM CRAFT, INC.
ALARM DISTRIBUTORS
ALARM SUPPLY CO., INC.
ALARMTRONICS OF ILLINOIS INC.
WM. B. ALLEN SECURITY SUPPLIES
ARITECH CORP.
B-SAFE SYSTEMS INC.
CALIFORNIA ALARM & TELEGRAPH
CITIZEN AMERICA CORP.
(alarm components)
CONSOLIDATED SECURITY
PRODUCTS
CONTROL INSTRUMENT ASSOCIATES
"CONTROLLOR SYSTEMS" CORP.
CREST ELECTRONICS INC.
CUSTOM ALARM PRODUCTS
DAL INDUSTRIES INC.
DEFENSIVE SECURITY CORP.
DEFENSIVE SECURITY SOUTHWEST
DETECT-ALL SECURITY SYSTEMS,
INC.
DIVERSIFIED SECURITY SYSTEMS
GARD-A-CAR, INC.
HARCOR INTERNATIONAL INC.
HYDRO-TEMP CONTROLS, INC.
INTERARMS
LIBERTY SECURITY DISTRIBUTORS
M.M.S., INC.
NATIONAL SECURITY SYSTEMS, INC.
NEWBRITE ALARMS, INC.
NORTH ELECTRIC CO.
PAGE ALERT SYSTEMS, INC.
PETERS INDUSTRIES, INC.
THE PETERZELL CO.
POTTER ELECTRIC SIGNAL CO.
PRO-TECTION PRODUCTS, INC.
QONAAR SECURITY SYSTEMS, INC.
QUALICOMP SECURITY PRODUCTS
REMLIN PRODUCTS INC.
S & B DISTRIBUTORS
SECURITY PRODUCTS CO.
SENTRY WATCH, INC.
SIGMA ELECTRONICS INC.
SIGNALARM, INC.
SILMAR ELECTRONICS, INC.
SPECTROGARD INC.
SPIRIG ERNEST

SYSTEM CONTROLS, INC.
VERSA-LITE SYSTEMS, INC.
WESTERN ALARM SUPPLY CO.
WESTERN SECURITY PRODUCTS
WHOLESALE SECURITY DEVICES
WICO CORP.

23.b Camera equipment

AIR-WAYS DISTRIBUTORS INC.
WM. B. ALLEN SECURITY SUPPLIES
B-SAFE SYSTEMS INC.
CAMERAS FOR INDUSTRY (CFI)
CAROL PRODUCTS CO. INC.
  (concealed surveillance cameras)
CREST ELECTRONICS INC.
GBC CLOSED CIRCUIT TELEVISION
  CORP.
GIMBEL SECURITY CAMERAS, INC.
THE I.D. CO.
KOYO INTERNATIONAL INC. OF
  AMERICA
MARVEL PHOTO
M.M.S., INC
NATIONAL SECURITY SYSTEMS, INC.
NORTH ELECTRIC CO.
  (CCTV)
PETERS INDUSTRIES, INC.
STANDARD LAW ENFORCEMENT
  SUPPLY CO.
VIDEOLARM INC.
ZOOMAR, INC.
  (CCTV)

23.c Uniformed force equipment

CAKE/DAVIS CO.
  (police equipment)
W. S. DARLEY & CO.
INTERARMS
LAW ENFORCEMENT ASSOCIATES,
  INC.
MAGSON UNIFORM CO.
F. MORTON PITT CO.
PRO-TECTION PRODUCTS, INC.
PROTECTIVE MATERIALS CO.
SENTRY WATCH, INC.
  (police equipment)

23.d Other

DEKTOR COUNTERINTELLIGENCE &
  SECURITY, INC.
  (psychological stress evaluator,
  digital telephone analyzer)
LAW ENFORCEMENT ASSOCIATES,
  INC.
  (voice analyzers, countermeasure
  equipment)
NATIONAL TRAINING CENTER OF
  POLYGRAPH SCIENCE
  (polygraph)
THE PETERZELL CO.
  (residential security devices)
SCANDUS INC.
  (counter minisafes)
TECHNI-TOOL, INC.
  (tools, testers)

TOOLS AND INSTRUMENTS AND MAINTENANCE SUPPLIES

24.a Tools and instruments

BURNWORTH TESTER CO.
  (circuit tester, low voltage tester)
COM/TECH SYSTEMS INC.
  (data link checking system)
M.E. HANSEN & ASSOCIATES
  (dual circuit analyzer for dialer
  output verification)
NORTH ELECTRIC CO.
  (hand tools)
RADIONICS INC.
  (digital/tape dialer tester)
SALCO INDUSTRIES, INC.
  (automatic dialer test set)
SECURITY INSTRUMENTS, INC.
  (circuit tester)
SHUFRO ENGINEERING LABS
  (loop testers)
TECHNI-TOOL, INC.
  (hand tools, testers)

24.b Installation and repair

ADEMCO (ALARM DEVICE MFG. CO.)
  (wiring tools & meters)
ARROW FASTENER CO., INC.
  (staple guns for wire & cable
  installation)
ATRONIC
  (cable fault locator)
BUILDEX
  (concrete fastening tool)
DIVERSIFIED MFG. & MKTG. CO.,
  INC.
  (wire retrieving & installation
  tool)
NORTH ELECTRIC CO.
  (hand tools)
OK MACHINE & TOOL CORP.
  (wire-wrapping tool)
PERMA PACK INC.
  (trouble shooting meter)
SECURITY INSTRUMENTS, INC.
  (foiling devices, tools, &
  maintenance equipment)
SPENCER PRODUCTS CO.
  (screws, screwdrivers)
SPIRIG ERNEST
  (special soldering irons, de-
  soldering braids)
TECHNI-TOOL, INC.
  (hand tools & testers)

24.c Tool/instrument cases

PLATT LUGGAGE, INC.
  (tool cases)
ZERO CORP.
  (aluminum carrying cases)

24.d Maintenance supplies

DIRECT SAFETY CO.
  (ladders)

EQUIPMENT CO. OF AMERICA
  (rolling ladders)
LITTLE GIANT INDUSTRIES, INC.
  (telescoping ladders)
LPS RESEARCH LABORATORIES,
  INC.
  (lubricants, cleaners, penetrants,
  rust inhibitors, ultrasonic
  cleaners)
MULTI-PURPOSE LADDER CO. INC.
  (ladders)
RICHARDS-WILCOX MFG. CO.
  (ladders)
TECHNI-TOOL, INC.
  (lubricants, cleaners, penetrants,
  rust inhibitors)

VEHICLES, SECURITY AND SAFETY

25.a Ambulances

CUSHMAN, OMC-LINCOLN
  (electric)
TAYLOR-DUNN MFG. CO.
  (electric in-plant)

25.b Armored vehicles

ARMORED VEHICLE BUILDERS
  (cars, trucks)
LAW ENFORCEMENT ASSOCIATES,
  INC.
PROTECTIVE MATERIALS CO.
TETRADYNE CORP.
  (autos, vans)
WICO CORP.

25.c Fire trucks

A-T-O INC.
W. S. DARLEY & CO.
  (electric)
TAYLOR-DUNN MFG. CO.
  (electric, in-plant)

25.d Plant patrol vehicles

ARMORED VEHICLE BUILDERS, INC.
CUSHMAN, OMC-LINCOLN
  (electric)
TAYLOR-DUNN MFG. CO.
  (electric, in-plant/shopping
  center)

25.e Vehicles, limited range

CUSHMAN, OMC-LINCOLN
  (twin-tracked, meter, accident
  patrol)

25.f Vehicles, other

ARMORED VEHICLE BUILDERS, INC.
  (detention vehicles)

WIRE AND CABLE AND ASSEMBLY COMPONENTS

26.a Wire and cable and accessories

ADEMCO (ALARM DEVICE MFG. CO.)

ALARM SUPPLY CO., INC.
WM. B. ALLEN SECURITY SUPPLIES
BELDEN CORP.
B-SAFE SYSTEMS INC.
CALIFORNIA SWITCH & SIGNAL
CLIFFORD OF VERMONT, INC.
COLUMBIA ELECTRIC CABLES
DEARBORN WIRE & CABLE CO.
EASTMAN WIRE & CABLE CO.
HARCOR INTERNATIONAL INC.
LINDEN LABORATORIES, INC.
   (cable assemblies)
MERET INC.
   (fiber optic cables & terminals)
SIGNAL CABLE CO.
TECHNI-TOOL, INC.
   (handling tools)
WESTAMERICA COMMUNICATIONS
SUPPLY CO., INC.

26.b Assembly components

BASLER ELECTRIC CO.
   (plug-in transformers)
C.C.U. INC.
   (control modules)
CORBY INDUSTRIES, INC.
   (snap lid lock covers)
ELECTRONIC RELAYS INC.
   (microprocessors)
LINDEN LABORATORIES, INC.
   (ultrasonic air transducers,
   piezoelectric ceramics)
MERET INC.
   (supplier of transmitter &
   receiver modules for IR alarm
   system)
PROJECTS UNLIMITED
   (solid state audio indicators)
SQUARE D CO.
   (breakers, switchers,
   transformers, relays, etc.)
TDK CORP. OF AMERICA
   (piezoelectric elements,
   ultrasonic transducers, electronic
   components)
WHOLESALE SECURITY DEVICES
   (hard wire master controls)

MANUFACTURERS AND DISTRIBUTORS

AAMES SECURITY CORP.
1141 E. Market St.
Long Beach, CA 90805
(213) 423-0414

AB TELEKONTROLL
Box 466
S-401 27 Goteborg 1, Sweden
031/23 51 30

ABLOY, INC.
6212 Oakton St.
Morton Grove, IL 60053
(312) 965-1500

ACRON CORP.
1095 Towbin Ave.
Corporate Park
Lakewood, NJ 08701
(201) 364-7200
(800) 631-2144

ADAMS RITE MFG. CO.
4040 S. Capitol Ave.
City of Industry, CA 91749
(213) 699-0511

ADC TELECOMMUNICATIONS
4900 W. 78th St.
Minneapolis, MN 55435
(612) 835-6800

ADCOR ELECTRONICS, INC.
349 Peachtree Hills Ave., N.E.
Atlanta, GA 30305
(404) 261-0245
(800) 241-2470

ADD SALES CO., INC.
P.O. Box 376
Manitowoc, WI 54220
(414) 682-6188

ADEMCO (ALARM DEVICE MFG. CO.)
Div. Pittway Corp.
165 Eileen Way
Syosset, NY 11791
(516) 921-6700

ADMIC
Div. Adaptive Microelectronics
Ltd.
2-33 Glen Cameron Rd.
Thornhill, Ont., Can. L3T 1N9
(416) 881-4112

ADT
One World Trade Ctr.
New York, NY 10048
(212) 558-1100

ADVANCE INDUSTRIAL SECURITY
Sub A-T-O Inc.
3330 Peachtree Rd., N.E.
Atlanta, GA 30326
(404) 231-1210
(800) 241-2460

ADVANCED DEVICES LABORATORY, INC.
520 S. Rock Blvd.
Reno, NV 89502
(702) 329-3188

ADVANCED SECURITY CO.
3010 Lawrence Exp'y
Santa Clara, CA 95051
(408) 733-5555

ADVANCED SIGNALING CO., INC.
P.O. Box 5841
Arlington, TX 76011
(817) 261-6070

ADVISOR SECURITY
(see Aritech Corp.)

AEL-EMTECH CORP.
Sub. American Electronic
   Laboratories, Inc.
P.O. Box 507
Lansdale, PA 19446
(215) 368-2440

AEROLARM
Div., Aerolite Electronics Corp.
2207 Summit Ave.
Union City, NJ 07087
(201) 863-2562

AEROTRON, INC.
P.O. Box 6527
U.S. Hwy. 1 North
Raleigh, NC 27628
(919) 876-4620

AIMS INSTRUCTIONAL MEDIA SERVICES, INC.
626 Justin Ave.
Glendale, CA 91201
(213) 240-9300

AIPHONE U.S.A., INC.
2116 N. Pacific
Seattle, WA 98103
(206) 634-3040

AIR SPACE DEVICES, INC.
Sub. Norton Co.
Safety Products Div.
P.O. Box 197
Paramount, CA 90723
(213) 774-4905

AIR-FLO CO. INC.
P.O. Box 705
Elkhart, IN 46514
(219) 293-9581

AIR-WAYS DISTRIBUTORS INC.
1456 Middle Country Rd.
Centereach, NY 11720
(516) 698-7447

ALARM CONTROLS CORP.
151-22 W. Industry Ct.
Deer Park, NY 11729
(516)586-4220

ALARM CRAFT INC.
153-11 Northern Blvd.
Flushing, NY 11354
(212) 886-0090

ALARM DISTRIBUTORS
6307 S. Dixie Hwy.
West Palm Beach, FL 33405
(305) 588-6449

ALARM LOCK CORP.
5411 Telegraph Rd.
Los Angeles, CA 90040
(213) 726-9811

ALARM PRODUCTS INTERNATIONAL, INC.
24-02 40th Ave.
Long Island City, NY 11101
(212) 937-4900
(800) 221-3548

ALARM SUPPLY CO., INC.
12551 Globe Rd.
Livonia, MI 48150
(313) 425-2500
(800) 521-5222

ALARMTRONICS OF ILLINOIS INC.
4410 W. Irving Park Rd.
Chicago, IL 60641
(800) 621-4113

ALDEN ELECTRONIC & IMPULSE RECORDING EQUIPMENT CO., INC.
Washington St.
Westboro, MA 01581
(617) 366-8851

ALERT INTERNATIONAL CORP.
203 Orchard St.
Mills, MA 02054
(617) 376-8679

WM. B. ALLEN SECURITY SUPPLIES
Div. Wm. B. Allen Supply Co., Inc.
1601 Basin/Orleans
New Orleans, LA 70116
(504) 525-8222
(800) 535-9593

ALPHA ELECTRONICS MFG. LTD.
527 E. Liberty St.
Ann Arbor, MI 48104
(313) 995-0210

ALVARADO MFG. CO., INC.
10626 E. Rush St.
S. El Monte, CA 91733
(213) 444-9268

A.M.C. SALES, INC.
9335 Lubec St.
Downey, CA 90241
(213) 869-8519

AMCEST CORP.
333 W. St. George Ave.
Linden, NJ 07036
(800) 631-7370
(800) 492-4051

AMERICAN ALERT SYSTEMS
1648 10th St.
Santa Monica, CA 90404
(213) 394-5410

AMERICAN BLDG. CONTRACTOR'S ASSN.
2476 Overland Ave., Ste. 205
Los Angeles, CA 90064
(213) 559-6664

AMERICAN CYANAMID CO.
Chemical Light Dept.
Bound Brook, NJ 08805
(201) 356-2000

AMERICAN ELECTRONICS, INC. ("AMECO")
40 Essex St.
Hackensack, NJ 07601
(201) 489-1585

AMERICAN INTERNATIONAL GROUP INC.
102 Maiden Ln.
New York, NY 10006
(212) 791-7000

AMERICAN LAW ENFORCEMENT OFFICERS ASSN.
4005 Plaza Towers
New Orleans, LA 70113
(504) 688-0901

AMERICAN LOCK CO.
Exchange Rd.
Crete, IL 60417
(312) 534-2000

AMERICAN POLYGRAPH ASSN.
P.O. Box 74
Linthicum Heights, MD 21090

AMERICAN PROTECTION SYSTEMS
Div. A.CTIVE P.ROTECTION S.YSTEMS, INC.
33 Courtland St.
Nashua, NJ 03060
(603) 883-1001

AMERICAN SECURITY EQUIPMENT CO. (AMSECO)
Div. Kobishi America Inc.
153 E. Savarona Way
Victoria Business Park
Carson, CA 90746
(213) 538-4670

AMERICAN SOCIETY FOR AMUSEMENT PARK SECURITY/SAFETY
c/o Lloyd Warren, Pres.
Opry Land
P.O. Box 2138
Nashville, TN 37214
(615) 899-6600

AMERICAN SOCIETY FOR INDUSTRIAL SECURITY
2000 K St., N.W.
Suite 651
Washington, DC 20006
(202) 331-7887

AMERICAN SOCIETY FOR NON-DESTRUCTIVE TESTING, INC.
3200 Riverside Dr.

Columbus, OH 43221
(614) 488-7921

AMERICAN SOCIETY FOR TESTING & MATERIALS
1916 Race St.
Philadelphia, PA 19103
(215) 299-5478

AMERICAN SOCIETY OF MECHANICAL ENGINEERS
c/o Clapp & Poliak, Inc.
245 Park Ave.
New York, NY 10017
(212) 752-6800

AMERICAN SOCIETY OF SAFETY ENGINEERS
850 Busse Hwy.
Park Ridge, IL 60068
(312) 692-4121

AMERICAN ZETTLER, INC.
16881 Hale Ave.
Irvine, CA 92714
(714) 540-4190

AMF ELECTRICAL PRODUCTS DEVELOPMENT DIV.
3001 Centreville Rd.
Herndon, VA 22070
(703) 471-3111

AMPEREX ELECTRONIC CORP.
A North American Philips Co.
Slatersville, RI 02876
(401) 762-3800

AMWELD BUILDING PRODUCTS
Div. The American Welding & Mfg. Co.
100 Plant St.
Niles, OH 44446
(216) 652-9971

ANCHOR PAD INTERNATIONAL, INC.
3731 Robertson Blvd.
Culver City, CA 90230
(213) 559-7111

ANDOVER SENSING DEVICE, CORP.
Shetland Industrial Park
Haverhill St.
Andover, MA 01810
(617) 475-5900

THE ANSWERLINE ASSOCIATES INC.
124 W. Lincoln Ave.
Mt. Vernon, NY 10550
(914) 667-2220

APC, INC.
5421 S. 101st E. Ave.
Tulsa, OK 74145
(918) 664-8484

A.P.D. SECURITY SYSTEMS
24700 Crestview Ct.
Farmington, MI 48024
(313) 477-2703

APS DIV.
Security Technology Systems Co.
110 Hayward Ave.
San Mateo, CA 94401
(415) 347-3850

ARISTO-CRAFT
314 5th Ave.
New York, NY 10001
(212) 279-9034

ARITECH CORP.
25 Newbury St.
Framingham, MA 01701
(617) 620-0800

ARMORED VEHICLE
BUILDERS, INC.
343 Pecks Rd.
Pittsfield, MA 01201
(413) 445-4541

ARROW FASTENER CO., INC.
271 Mayhill St.
Saddle Brook, NJ 07663
(201) 843-6900

ARROWHEAD ENTERPRISES
INC.
Anderson Ave.
New Milford, CT 06776
(203) 354-9381

ARROW-M CORP.
Member Matsushita Group
250 Sheffield St.
Mountainside, NJ 07092
(201) 232-4260

A.S.E. PROTECTIVE SYSTEMS
& SERVICES
P.O. Box 5051
Huntsville, AL 35805
(205) 453-1779

ASHBY & ASSOCIATES
Systems Div.
Ste. 511, 1730 M St.
Washington, DC 20036
(202) 296-3840

ASSOCIATED LOCKSMITHS
OF AMERICA, INC.
3003 Live Oak St.
Dallas, TX 75204
(214) 827-1701

ASSN. OF TRANSPORTATION
SECURITY OFFICERS
Robert Hurley, Dir. of Security
Services
Spector Freight Systems, Inc.
205 W. Wacker Dr.
Chicago, IL 60606
(312) 236-7220

ASTROPHYSICS RESEARCH
CORP.
1526 W. 240th St.
Harbor City, CA 90710
(213) 534-4370

ATLANTIC HOME SECURITY
SYSTEMS, INC.
Rt. 1
Emerald Isle
Morehead City, NC 28557
(919) 326-3149

ATLAS SOUND
Div. American Trading &
Production Corp.
10 Pomeroy Rd.
Parsippany, NJ 07054
(201) 887-7800

A-T-O INC.
4420 Sherwin Rd.
Willoughby, OH 44094
(216) 946-9000

ATRONIC
2065 Martin Ave.
Santa Clara, CA 95050
(408) 984-0812

ATV RESEARCH
13-S Broadway
Dakota City, NB 68731
(402) 987-3771

AUDIO SENTRY CORP.
31807 Utica Rd.
Fraser, MI 48026
(313) 294-2941

AUDIO TRANSPORT
SYSTEMS
985 Pleasant St.
Bridgewater, MA 02324
(617) 697-3322

AUDIOTECH CORP.
P.O. Box 152
Watertown, NY 13601
(315) 782-1151

AUDIOTRONICS CORP.
7428 Bellaire Ave.
North Hollywood, CA 91605
(213) 765-2645

AULT INC.
1600-H Freeway Blvd.
Minneappolis, MN 55430
(612) 560-9301

AUTHENTIPRINT
IDENTIFICATION SYSTEMS
4710 Woodman Ave.
Sherman Oaks, CA 91423
(213) 986-4090

AUTOMATIC FIRE &
BURGLAR CONTROL CORP.
3338 Olive Blvd.
St. Louis, MO 63103
(314) 652-5756

AVANT INC.
Box A
Lincoln, MA 01773
(617) 259-9260

A.V.I.D. ENTERPRISES
8622 Bellanca Ave.
Los Angeles, CA 90045
(213) 670-5545

B & W ASSOCIATES
1428 E. Olive Ave.
Fresno, CA 93728
(209) 486-7973

BANK ADMINISTRATION
INSTITUTE
P.O. Box 500
Park Ridge, IL 60068
(312) 693-7300

BASLER ELECTRIC CO.
Box 269
Highland, IL 62249
(618) 654-2341

BEAVER ELECTRONICS
P.O. Box 284
Beaverton, OR 97005
(503) 646-8519

BEAVER TURNSTILES
Div. LCN Closers of Canada, Ltd.
P.O. Box 100
Port Credit Post Office
Mississauga, Ont., Can. L5G 4L5
(416) 278-6128

BEI ELECTRONICS, INC.
1101 McAlmont St.
Little Rock, AR 72203

BELDEN CORP.
Electronic Div. P.O. Box 1327
Richmond, IN 47374
(317) 966-6661

BELL DETECTION MIRRORS
Div. Bell Glass & Mirror Co.
1328 Flatbush Ave.
Brooklyn, NY 11210
(212) 859-2223

BELL P/A PRODUCTS CORP.
1200 N. Fifth St.
Columbus, OH 43201
(614) 299-1487

BEST INDUSTRIES INC.
564 W. Randolph St.
Chicago, IL 60606
(312) 263-2413

BETCO ELECTRONICS
15504 Old Columbia Pike
Burtonsville, MD 10730
(301) 421-9760

ARTHUR BLANK & CO., INC.
119 Braintree St.
Boston (Allston), MA 02134
(617) 254-4000

E.A. BRADLEY CO.
1810 Pot Spring Rd., Ste. 5B
Timonium, MD 21093
(301) 252-8219

BRASH INDUSTRIES
P.O. Box 9250
Marina Del Rey, CA 90291
(213) 821-5076

BRINK'S LOCKING SYSTEMS, INC.
Naperville Rd.
P.O. Box 233
Plainfield, IL 60544
(815) 436-7530

BRK ELECTRONICS
Div. Pittway Corp.
780 McClure Ave.
Aurora, IL 60507
(312) 851-7330

E.J. BROOKS CO.
164 N. 13th St.
Newark, NJ 07107
(201) 483-0335

W.H. BROWNYARD CORP.
One Merrick Ave.
Westbury, NY 11590
(212) 343-3333
(800) 645-3122

B-SAFE SYSTEMS INC.
6427 Roswell Rd., N.E.
Atlanta, GA 30328
(404) 256-1343
(800) 241-5555

J.M. BUCHEIMER CO.
A. Tandy Brands, Inc. Co.
P.O. Box 280
Airport Rd.
Frederick, MD 21701
(301) 662-5101

BUILDEX
Div. Illinois Tool Works Inc.
2500 Brickvale Dr.
Elk Grove Village, IL 60007
(312) 595-3500

BUILDING OWNERS & MANAGERS ASSN. INTERNATIONAL
224 S. Michigan Ave.
Chicago, IL 60604
(312) 922-0210

THE BUREAU OF NATIONAL AFFAIRS, INC.
1231 25th St., N.W.
Washington, DC 20037
(202) 452-4200

BURGLAR BUG MFG.
16A Eaton Square
Needham, MA 02192

BURNS INTERNATIONAL SECURITY SERVICES, INC.
Sub. Burns Electronic Security Services, Inc.
320 Old Briarcliff Rd.
Briarcliff Manor, NY 10510
(914) 762-1000

BURNWORTH TESTER CO.
815 Pomona Ave.
El Cerrito, CA 94530
(415) 525-7599

CABLE SWITCH CORP.
P.O. Box 72 DF
West Long Branch, NJ 07764
(201) 531-4935

CADDI (CONVERTIBLE ALARM DETECTION DEVICES, INC.)
824 E. Methvin St.
Longview, TX 75601
(214) 753-8734

CAKE/DAVIS CO.
1200 5th St.
Berkeley, CA 94710
(415) 526-9124

CALIFORNIA ALARM & TELEGRAPH
220 N. State College Blvd.
Anaheim, CA 92806
(714) 635-7573

CALIFORNIA ELECTRONICS INDUSTRIES, INC.
2005 S. Ritchey Ave.
Santa Ana, CA 92705
(714) 835-4522

CALIFORNIA SWITCH & SIGNAL
13717 S. Normandie Ave.
Gardena, CA 90249
(213) 770-2330

CALSPAN TECHNOLOGY PRODUCTS, INC.
Sub. Calspan Corp.
4455 Genesee St.
Buffalo, NY 14221
(716) 632-7500

CAMERAS FOR INDUSTRY (CFI)
A Schirmer-National Div.
100 Ricefield Ln.
Hauppauge, NY 11787
(516) 864-3224

CAMPBELL CHAIN CO.
3990 E. Market St.
York, PA 17402
(717) 755-2921

CANADIAN SOCIETY FOR INDUSTRIAL SECURITY
co Bill Heggie, National Secretary-Treasurer

926 Connaught
Ottawa, Ont., Can. K2B 5MB

CANON U.S.A., INC.
10 Nevada Dr.
Lake Success, NY 11040
(516) 488-6700

CARDKEY SYSTEMS
Div. Greer Hydraulics, Inc.
20339 Nordhoff St.
Chatsworth, CA 91311
(213) 882-8111

CAROL PRODUCTS CO. INC.
1560 Springfield Ave.
Maplewood, NJ 07040
(201) 761-7749

C.C.U. INC.
Creative Concepts Unlimited, Inc.
1068 Hope St.
Stamford, CT 06907
(203) 329-8448

C.E.M. SECURITY PRODUCTS
1916-H Old Middlefield Way
Mountain View, CA 94043
(415) 965-9000

CENTURY 500 PRODUCTS, INC.
2737 W. Lincoln
Phoenix, AZ 85009
(602) 278-1521

CENTRAL METAL PRODUCTS, INC.
P.O. Box 305
Windfall, IN 46076
(317) 945-7677

CERBERUS SYSTEMS
Sub. Metallurgical Research Inc.
P.O. Box 66508
Scotts Valley, CA 95066
(408) 438-0330

CHAMBERLAIN MFG. CORP.
845 Larch Ave.
Elmhurst, IL 60126
(312) 279-3600

CHARTER ARMS CORP.
430 Sniffens Ln.
Stratford, CT 06497
(203) 377-8080

CHECKPOINT SYSTEMS INC.
110 E. Gloucester Pike
Barrington, NJ 08007
(609) 546-0100

CHEMLITE INC.
4611 N. Scottsdale Rd.
Scottsdale, AZ 85252
(602) 946-3322

CHIC-SALES CO., INC.
P.O. Box 373
Costa Mesa, CA 92627
(714) 646-0293

CHLORIDE PYROTECTOR
333 Lincoln St.
Hingham, MA 02043
(617) 749-3466

CHLORIDE SYSTEMS USA
Unit Chloride Inc.
Mallard Ln.
North Haven, CT 06473
(203) 777-6351

CITIZEN AMERICA CORP.
1710 22nd St.
Santa Monica, CA 90404
(213) 829-3541
(800) 421-6516

**CLIFFORD OF VERMONT,
INC.**
187 Clifford St.
Bethel, VT 05032
(800) 451-4381
(802) 234-9921

THE CLIFTON CO.
11500 N.W. 7th Ave.
Miami, FL 33168
(305) 688-0911

**DON COCHRAN &
ASSOCIATES**
12 Andrew St.
Greenville, SC 29610
(803) 269-9605

COGNETICS CORP.
Hwy. No. 1, Box 48
Caguas, Puerto Rico 00625
(809) 743-9377

COHU, INC.
Electronics Div.
5725 Kearny Villa Rd.
San Diego, CA 92112
(714) 277-6700

**COLORADO ELECTRO-
OPTICS, INC.**
1880 S. Flatirons Ct.
Boulder, CO 80301
(303) 494-3200

**COLUMBIA ELECTRONIC
CABLES**
11 Cove St.
New Bedford, MA 02744
(617) 999-4451

COLUMBIA VIDEO SYSTEMS
1805 St. Johns Ave.
Highland Park, IL 60035
(312) 433-6010

COM LOG CO., INC.
2959 W. Fairmont Ave.
Phoenix, AZ 85017
(602) 248-0769

**COMMERCIAL PLASTICS &
SUPPLY CORP.**
Insulgard Div.
1642 Woodhaven Dr.

Cornwells Hts., PA 19020
(215) 638-0800

**COMMODORE AVIATION
INC.**
505 Park Ave.
New York, NY 10022
(212) 486-5919

**COMMUNICATION
CONTROL SYSTEMS, INC.**
605 3rd Ave.
New York, NY 10016
(212) 682-4637

COMPUGUARD CORP.
4907 Baum Blvd.
Pittsburgh, PA 15213
(412) 622-6200

COM/TECH SYSTEMS, INC.
44 Beaver St.
New York, NY 10004
(212) 425-0733

CONCEPTS-IN-ALARMS, INC.
3359 Ocean Ave.
Oceanside, NY 11572
(516) 678-3444

CONE MILLS
1440 Broadway
New York, NY 10018
(212) 565-4600

CONRAC CORP.
Cramer Div.
Mill Rock Rd.
Old Saybrook, CT 06475
(203) 388-3574

**CONSOLIDATED SECURITY
PRODUCTS**
1393 Baker Rd.
Virginia Beach, FL 23455
(804) 460-2671

**CONTINENTAL
INSTRUMENTS CORP.**
170 Lauman Ln.
Hicksville, NY 11801
(516) 938-0800

CONTINENTAL TELECOM
6600 W. 90th St.
Overland Park, KS 66212
(913) 341-2121

CONTROL DEVICES INC.
4108 N. Nashville Ave.
Chicago, IL 60634
(312) 181-1522

**CONTROL INSTRUMENT
ASSOCIATES**
377 Rockaway Ave.
Valley Stream, NY 11581
(516) 825-5550
(800) 645-2255

**"CONTROLLOR SYSTEMS"
CORP.**
21363 Gratiot Ave.

E. Detroit, MI 48021
(313) 772-6100
(800) 521-6220

CONTROLONICS CORP.
One Adam St.
Littleton, MA 01460
(617) 486-3571

**CONTRONIC CONTROLS
LTD.**
7611 Bath Rd.
Mississauga, Ont., Can. L4T 3T1
(416) 678-1032

CORBY INDUSTRIES, INC.
1747 MacArthur Rd.
Whitehall, PA 18052
(215) 433-1412

CORNELL IRON WORKS INC.
Crestwood Industrial Park
Mountaintop, PA 18707
(717) 474-6773

COSMICAR LENS DIV.
Asahi Precision Co., Ltd.
424, Higashi-Oizumi
Nerima-Ku, Tokyo, Japan 177
921-1441

**COUNCIL OF
INTERNATIONAL
INVESTIGATORS**
P.O. Box 5646
Baltimore, MD 21210
(301) 323-3100

**COURTLANDT BOOT JACK
CO., INC.**
270 Lafayette St.
New York, NY 10012
(212) 966-5686

CRAFTOR INC.
Craft-Alarm Div.
1237 Central Ave.
Albany, NY 12205
(518) 459-2135

CREATIVE INDUSTRIES INC.
959 N. Holmes
Indianapolis, IN 46222
(317) 632-7471

CREST ELECTRONICS INC.
4921 Exposition Blvd.
Los Angeles, CA 90016
(213) 731-1105

CRIMINALISTICS INC.
13830 N.W. 27th Ave.
Miami, FL 33054
(305) 688-0822

CROSSPOINT LATCH CORP.
316 Broad St.
Summit, NJ 07901
(201) 273-1090

CRUSADER SECURITY CORP.
KnightGuard Div.

P.O. Box 1488
Salisbury, NC 28144
(704) 636-7010

CUMMINS-ALLISON CORP.
Office Products Div.
800 Waukegan Rd.
Glenview, IL 60025
(312) 724-8000

CUNNINGHAM CORP.
(see Quick-Set Inc.)

CUSHMAN, OMC-LINCOLN
Div. Outboard Marine Corp.
1115 Cushman Dr.
Lincoln, NB 68501
(402) 475-9581

CUSTOM ALARM PRODUCTS
13863 N.W. 19th Ave.
Miami, FL 33054
(305) 681-7400

CUSTOM ELECTRONICS
1905 Wynnefield Terr.
Philadelphia, PA 19131
(215) 879-5254

D/A GENERAL, INC.
47 Kearney Rd.
Needham, MA 02192
(617) 449-1533

DAGE-MTI, INC.
108 Wabash St.
Michigan City, IN 46360
(219) 872-5514

**DAHILL ELECTRONICS
CORP.**
1714 Dahill Rd.
Brooklyn, NY 11223
(212) 336-7314

G.W. DAHL CO., INC.
86 Tupelo St.
Bristol, RI 02809
(401) 253-9500

DAL INDUSTRIES, INC.
3954 N.E. 5th Ave.
Ft. Lauderdale, FL 33334
(305) 566-0109

W.S. DARLEY & CO.
2000 Anson Dr.
Melrose Park, IL 60160
(312) 345-8050

DATATECH INC.
Trimex Bldg.
Mooers, NY 12958
(514) 735-5356

DATOTEK INC.
13740 Midway Rd.
Dallas, TX 75240
(214) 233-1030

DAVIS PUBLISHING CO., INC.
250 Potrero St.

Santa Cruz, CA 95060
(408) 423-4968

**DEARBORN WIRE & CABLE
CO.**
9299 Evenhouse Ave.
Rosemont, IL 60018
(312) 696-1000

DECALS, INC.
4850 Ward Rd.
Wheat Ridge, CO 80033
(303) 425-0510

DEFENSIVE SECURITY CORP.
158 Eileen Way
Syosset, NY 11791
(516) 364-0970

**DEFENSIVE SECURITY
SOUTHWEST**
Div. LaMarCo Associates
104 N. Bowie
Jasper, TX 75951
(713) 384-9569

DE GROOT ALARM DECALS
434 Parkinson Terr.
Orange, NJ 07050
(201) 672-9209

**DEKTOR COUNTER-
INTELLIGENCE &
SECURITY, INC.**
5508 Port Royal Rd.
Springfield, VA 22151
(703) 321-9333

DELTA ELECTRIC
Div. Halle Industries, Inc.
3302 S. Nebraska St.
Marion, IN 46952
(317) 674-2293

DELTA PRODUCTS, INC.
P.O. Box 1147
Grand Junction, CO 81501
(303) 242-9000

DEPEND-ALARM
2021 W. Carroll
Chicago, IL 60612
(312) 733-2504

**DETECT-ALL SECURITY
SYSTEMS, INC.**
Unit Detect-All Security Mfg. Co.
21141 Governor's Hwy.
Matteson, IL 60443
(312) 481-6555

DETECTION SYSTEMS, INC.
400 Mason Rd.
Fairport, NY 14450
(716) 223-4060

DETECTOR INDUSTRIES
Div. Binswanger Mirror Co.
1355 Lynnfield R., Ste. 205
Memphis, TN 38117
(901) 761-3150

**DETECTION SECURITY
SYSTEMS, INC.**
Bay St.
Sag Harbor, NY 11963
(516) 725-2600

DETECTRONICS, INC.
(see Aritech Corp.)

DETEX CORP.
4147 N. Ravenswood Ave.
Chicago, IL 60613
(312) 348-3377

DETROIT MINI-SAFE CO.
13660 Elmira Ave.
Detroit, MI 48227
(313) 931-7720

**DIGITAL
COMMUNICATIONS, INC.**
10205 Colvin Run Rd.
Great Falls, VA 22066
(703) 759-3900

DIGITAL PRODUCTS CORP.
4028 N.E. 6th Ave.
Ft. Lauderdale, FL 33334
(305) 564-0521

DIRECT SAFETY CO.
Div. Goldblatt Tool Co.
A. Bliss & Laughlin Industry
511 Osage
Kansas City, KS 66110
(913) 281-0504
(800) 255-4416

**DIVERSIFIED MFG. & MKTG.
CO., INC.**
P.O. Box 2260
Burlington, NC 27215
(919) 227-7012

**DIVERSIFIED SECURITY
SYSTEMS**
Div. Diversified Electronics Inc.
8507 Speedway
San Antonio, TX 78230
(512) 344-2386

**DOOR ALARM DEVICES
CORP.**
20 Lucon Dr.
Deer Park, NY 11729
(516) 586-2400

DOPPLER CORP.
2401 University Ave.
St. Paul, MN 55114
(612) 647-0707

DOUGLAS RANDALL DIV.
Walter Kidde & Co., Inc.
6 Pawcatuck Ave.
Pawcatuck, CT 02891
(203) 599-1750

DTI SECURITY INC.
1034 Keil Ct.
Sunnyvale, CA 94086
(408) 744-1200

DUAL-LITE, INC.
Simm Ln.
Newtown, CT 06470
(203) 426-2585

JOHN V. DUNIGAN STUDIOS
108 Fifth Ave.
New York, NY 10010
(212) 889-7594

**E.I. DU PONT DE NEMOURS &
CO.**
1007 Market St.
Wilmington, DE 19898
(302) 744-2421

DYNAIR ELECTRONICS, INC.
5275 Market St.
San Diego, CA 92114
(714) 263-7711

DYTRON INC.
241 Crescent St.
Waltham, MA 02154
(617) 891-9029

**EAGLE-PICHER INDUSTRIES,
INC.**
Commercial Products Dept.
P.O. Box 130
Seneca, MO 64865
(417) 776-2256

EASTMAN WIRE & CABLE CO.
Box 139
Mays Landing & Piney Hollow Rds.
Winslow, NJ 08095
(609) 567-1252

EDWARDS CO., INC.
Unit General Signal
90 Connecticut Ave.
Norwalk, CT 06856
(203) 838-8441

E.E. INDUSTRIES, INC.
75 Sheer Plaza
Plainview, NY 11803
(516) 694-4884

**ELECTRIC WASTEBASKET
CORP.**
145 W. 45th St.
New York, NY 10036
(212) 582-2900

ELECTROCON, INC.
701 Deerfield Rd.
Deerfield, IL 60015
(312) 948-0320

ELECTROHOME LTD.
809 Wellington St. No.
Kitchener, Ont., Can. N2G 4J6
(519) 744-7111

ELECTROLARM INC.
7171 Torbram Rd.
Unit 32A
Mississauga, Ont., Can. L4T 1G7
(416) 677-9397

**ELECTRO-MECHANICAL
IMAGINEERING, INC.**
812 N. Normandie Ave.
Los Angeles, CA 90029
(213) 660-1175

**THE ELECTRIC-MECHANICS
CO.**
P.O. Box 1546
Austin, TX 78767
(512) 451-8273

ELECTRONIC DEVICES INC.
21 Gray Oaks Ave.
Yonkers, NY 10710
(914) 965-4400

ELECTRONIC RELAYS INC.
7106 W. Toohy Ave.
Niles, IL 60648
(312) 647-7727

**ELECTRONIC SECURITY
SYSTEMS, INC.**
P.O. Box 61403
Sunnyvale, CA 94088
(408) 737-1343

**ELECTRONIC
SURVEILLANCE FENCE
SECURITY, INC.**
P.O. Box 406
Long Lake, MN 55356
(612) 475-3363

ELECTROPHYSICS CORP.
48 Spruce St.
Nutley, NJ 07110
(201) 667-2262

**ELECTRO-VOX INDUSTRIES
INC.**
60 Walnut St.
Boston, MA 02122
(617) 282-7475

ELGAR CORP.
8225 Mercury Ct.
San Diego, CA 92111
(714) 565-1155

ELK-ROUTEMASTER INC.
136 6th St.
Jersey City, NJ 07302
(201) 963-7601

ELPOWER CORP.
Sub. Eldon Industries, Inc.
2117 S. Anne St.
Santa Ana, CA 92704
(714) 540-6155

**EMERGENCY DATA
COMPUTER CENTER**
4410 W. Irving Park Rd.
Chicago, IL 60641
(800) 621-4113

**EMERGENCY PRODUCTS
CORP.**
25 Eastmans Rd.

Parsippany, NJ 07054
(201) 386-1510

**EMPIRE MACHINES &
SYSTEMS INC.**
Shore Rd.
Glenwood Landing, NY 11547
(516) 671-8200

**ENDURE-A-LIFETIME
PRODUCTS, INC.**
7500 N.W. 72nd Ave.
Miami, FL 33166
(305) 885-9901

**EQUIPMENT CO. OF
AMERICA**
1075 Hialeah Dr.
Hialeah, FL 33010
(305) 887-1772
(800) 327-0681

**ESTERLINE ELECTRONICS
CORP.**
3501 N. Harbor Blvd.
Costa Mesa, CA 92626
(714) 540-1234

EVER-GUARD ALARM CO.
512 W. 20th St.
New York, NY 10011
(212) 242-3310

EVERSON ROSS CO.
15 West St.
Spring Valley, NJ 10977
(914) 356-8835

EXTRA SECURITY INC.
1235 Capri Dr.
St. Louis, MO 63126
(314) 821-7666

F & W ALARM SYSTEMS, INC.
5510 17th Ave.
Brooklyn, NY 11204
(212) 851-6351

FACIT-ADDO, INC.
66 Field Point Rd.
Greenwich, CT 06830
(203) 622-9150

**FALCON UNITED
INDUSTRIES, INC.**
7129 Gerald Ave.
Van Nuys, CA 91406
(213) 873-3621

FARALLON INDUSTRIES
1333 Old County Rd.
Belmont, CA 94002
(415) 592-8484

**FEDERAL LABORATORIES,
INC.**
Saltsburg, PA 15681
(412) 639-3511

FEDERAL SIGNAL CORP.
Security Products Div.

291 Frontage Rd.
Hinsdale, IL 60521
(312) 887-6999

FENWAL INC.
400 Main St.
Ashland, MA 01721
(617) 881-2000

FILMDEX INC.
15500 Lee Hwy.
Centreville, VA 22020
(703) 631-0600

**FIRE BURGLARY
INSTRUMENTS INC.**
Sub. A.T.A. Control Systems Inc.
999 A Stewart Ave.
Garden City, NY 11530
(516) 222-9030

**FIRE CONTROL
INSTRUMENTS, INC.**
149 California St.
Newton, MA 02158
(617) 965-2010

FIRE-LITE ALARMS INC.
40 Albert St.
New Haven, CT 06504
(203) 777-7861

FIRESAFE
Div. Huggins Engineering
2070 Walsh Ave.
Santa Clara, CA 95050
(408) 249-1766

FJW INDUSTRIES
215 E. Prospect Ave.
Mt. Prospect, IL 60056
(312) 259-8100

FLAIR ELECTRONICS, INC.
600 W. Foothill Blvd.
Glendora, CA 91740
(213) 963-6077

FOLGER ADAM CO.
700 Railroad St.
Joliet, IL 60436
(815) 723-3438

FOREWARN INC.
34 Tower St.
Hudson, MA 01749
(617) 562-9057

**FORTRESS HILL
ELECTRONICS**
Rt. 3
Browerville, MN 56438
(612) 594-6429

FRANKLIN SIGNAL CORP.
370 Third Ave.
Clear Lake, WI 54005
(715) 263-2448
(800) 826-6608

FRIED BROTHERS INC.
467 N. 7th St.
Philadelphia, PA 19123
(800) 523-2924

**FRISCO BAY INDUSTRIES OF
CANADA LTD.**
1050 Beaulac St.
Montreal, Que., Can. H4R 1R7
(514) 332-3370

FUNCTIONAL DEVICES INC.
310 S. Union St.
Russiaville, IN 46979
(317) 883-5538

FYRNETICS INC.
1021 Davis Rd.
Elgin, IL 60120
(312) 742-5215

GAMEWELL/ALARMTRONICS
Div. Gulf + Western Mfg. Co.
91 Bartlett St.
Marlborough, MA 01752
(617) 481-6800

THE GANNON MFG. CORP.
142 Deer Hill Ave.
Danbury, CT 06810
(203) 792-5250

GARD-A-CAR, INC.
27201 Lexington
Grosse Ile, MI 48138
(313) 671-0478

**GBC CLOSED CIRCUIT
TELEVISION CORP.**
74 Fifth Ave.
New York, NY 10011
(212) 989-4433

GENERAL BINDING CORP.
And Subsidiaries
1101 Skokie Blvd.
Northbrook, IL 60062
(312) 272-3700

GENERAL ELECTRIC CO.
Imaging Systems Operation
Electronics Park
Bldg. 7, Rm. 301
Syracuse, NY 13201
(315) 456-3210

GENERAL ELECTRIC CO.
Mobile Radio Dept.
P.O. Box 4197
Lynchburg, VA 24502
(804) 846-7311

GENERAL ELECTRIC CO.
Tube Products Dept.
316 E. 9th St.
Owensboro, KY 42301
(502) 683-2401

**GENERAL
ELECTRODYNAMICS CORP.**
4430 Forest Ln.
Garland, TX 75042
(214) 276-1161

GENERAL MOTORS CORP.
Education & Training Dept.
1700 W. 3rd Ave.
Flint, MI 48502
(313) 766-2982

GERBER MFG. CO., INC.
1655 E. 12th St.
Mishawaka, IN 46544
(219) 259-2481

**GERBER SECURITY
PRODUCTS, INC.**
15627 Forest Blvd.
Hugo, MN 55038
(612) 426-1852

**GIMBEL SECURITY
CAMERAS, INC.**
915 Township Line Rd.
Elkins Park, PA 19117
(215) 635-4945

**GLENCO SECURITY
ELECTRONICS INC.**
P.O. Box 11663
Winston-Salem, NC 27106
(919) 924-6212

GLOBE-UNION INC.
Battery Div.
5757 N. Green Bay Ave.
Milwaukee, WI 53201
(414) 228-2393

GOULD INC.
Portable Battery Div.
931 N. Vandalia
St. Paul, MN 55114
(612) 645-8531

GRANDIN INDUSTRIES INC.
2469 Grandin Rd.
Cincinnati, OH 45208
(513) 662-7463

GRAVINER INC.
1121 Bristol Rd.
Mountainside, NJ 07092
(201) 654-6800

GRAY SECURITY
1950 E. Watkins St.
Phoenix, AZ 85034
(602) 257-1970

**VICTOR GREEN
PUBLICATIONS LTD.**
106 Hampstead Rd.
London, England NW1 2LS
01-3887661

GTE SYLVANIA SECURITY SYSTEMS
P.O. Box 188
Mountain View, CA 94042
(415) 966-2210

GUARD AWARE, INC.
98 Westgate Dr.
Brockton, MA 02403
(617) 588-2246

GUARDIAN ELECTRONICS INC.
3133 Via Colinas
Westlake Village, CA 91361
(213) 889-1414

GUARDSMARK, INC.
40 W. 57th St., Ste. 415
New York, NY 10019
(212) 586-1017

GYYR PRODUCTS
Div. Odetics Inc.
1341 S. Claudina St.
Anaheim, CA 92805
(714) 635-9100

M.E. HANSEN & ASSOCIATES
4637 W. 132nd St.
Hawthorne, CA 90250
(213) 673-3693

THE C. H. HANSON CO.
303 W. Erie St.
Chicago, IL 60610
(312) 787-1130

HARCO INDUSTRIES, INC.
10802 N. 21st Ave.
Phoenix, AZ 85029
(602) 944-1565

HARCOR INTERNATIONAL INC.
774 W. Algonquin Rd.
Arlington Heights, IL 60005
(312) 956-7121

HARTFORD WIRE WORKS CO.
P.O. Box 327
Hartford, CT 06101
(203) 522-0296

HB ENGINEERING
(see Security Communications Corp.)

HIGHWAY SAFETY FILMS, INC.
890 Hollywood Ln.
Mansfield, OH 44907
(419) 756-5593

H.K.S. TOOL PRODUCTS CO.
132 Fifth St.
Dayton, KY 41074
(606) 581-5600

HOLMES PROTECTION, INC.
370 Seventh Ave.
New York, NY 10001
(212) 868-6400

HONEYWELL
Protection Services Div.
Mail Station MN 12-2194
Honeywell Plaza
Minneapolis, MN 55408
(612) 870-5200

HOTELTRON SYSTEMS, INC.
135 New York Ave.
Huntington, NY 11743
(516) 549-1711

HYDRO-TEMP CONTROLS, INC.
203 Carondelet St., Ste. 817
New Orleans, LA 70130
(504) 522-0541

ICC, INC.
7895 Convoy Ct.
Ste. IX
San Diego, CA 92111
(714) 279-7230

THE I.D. CO.
728 Calle Clavel
Thousand Oaks, CA 91360
(805) 497-2959

IDATA, INC.
1120 Goffle Rd.
Hawthorne, NJ 07506
(201) 423-3335

IDENTATRONICS, INC.
425 Lively Blvd.
Elk Grove Village, IL 60007
(312) 437-2654

IDENTICARD SYSTEMS, INC.
630 E. Oregon Rd.
Lancaster, PA 17601
(717) 569-5797

IDENTIFICATION SYSTEMS, INC.
73 Lowell Rd.
Concord, MA 01742
(617) 369-1118

IDENTIMAT CORP.
135 W. 50th St.
New York, NY 10020
(212) 371-3300

IKEGAMI ELECTRONICS (U.S.A.) INC.
29-19 39th Ave.
L.I., NY 11101
(212) 932-2577

IMPERIAL SCREEN CO., INC.
5336 W. 145th St.
Lawndale, CA 90260
(213) 772-7465

IMPOSSIBLE ELECTRONIC TECHNIQUES, INC.
121 Pennsylvania Ave.
Wayne, PA 19087
(215) 687-5400

IN-A-FLOOR SAFE CO.
1416 So. Los Angeles St.
Los Angeles, CA 90015
(213) 749-2448

INDEPENDENT ARMORED CAR OPERATORS ASSN. INC.
c/o Ernest Moreau, Sec'y-Treasurer
254 Scholes St.
Brooklyn, NY 11206
(212) 366-8103

INDUSTRIAL & COMMERCIAL SECURITY ASSN.
210 Lyndhurst
Johannesburg, South Africa 2001
40-6339 Johannesburg

INDUSTRIAL PHOTO PRODUCTS, INC.
Industrial Security Div.
74 Fifth Ave.
New York, NY 10011
(212) 255-6505

INDUSTRIAL SHREDDER & CUTTER CO.
510 S. Ellsworth Ave.
Salem, OH 44460
(216) 332-0024

INSTANT ALERT
9551 Cresta Dr.
Los Angeles, CA 90035

INSTITUTE OF ELECTRICAL & ELECTRONICS ENGINEERS
345 E. 47th St.
New York, NY 10017
(212) 832-8277

INTELATEX, INC.
1201 Bethleham Pike
Flourtown, PA 19031
(215) 836-1111

INTERARMS
Special Products Div.
10 Prince St.
Alexandria, VA 22313
(703) 548-1400

INTERBORO TIME CLOCK CORP.
126 W. 26th St.
New York, NY 10001
(212) 741-7200

INTERCHECK CORP.
1350 E. 4th Ave.
Vancouver, BC, Can. V5N 1J5
(604) 255-5178

**INTERCONTINENTAL
SECURITY PRODUCTS INC.
(INTERSEC)**
1901 N.W. 20th St.
Miami, FL 33142
(305) 324-4014

**INTERMARKET
CONSULTANTS INC.**
141 Founders Rd.
Glastonbury, CT 06033
(203) 633-0644

**INTERNATIONAL ALARM
RESEARCH**
31807 Utica Rd.
Fraser, MI 48026
(313) 294-2941

**INTERNATIONAL ASSN. FOR
HOSPITAL SECURITY**
Merchandise Mart Station
P.O. Box 3776
Chicago, IL 60545

**INTERNATIONAL ASSN. OF
BOMB TECHNICIANS &
INVESTIGATORS**
7th & Mission Sts.
San Francisco, CA 94101

**INTERNATIONAL ASSN. OF
CHIEFS OF POLICE**
11 Firstfield Rd.
Gaithersburg, MD 20760
(301) 948-0922

**INTERNATIONAL ASSN. OF
COLLEGE & UNIVERSITY
SECURITY DIRECTORS**
James L. McGovern, Exec. Sec'y
P.O. Box 98127
Atlanta, GA 30329
(404) 261-8136

**INTERNATIONAL ASSN. OF
CREDIT CARD
INVESTIGATORS**
1620 Grant Ave.
Novato, CA 94947
(415) 897-8800

**INTERNATIONAL ASSN. OF
FIRE CHIEFS**
1329 18th St., N.W.
Washington, DC 20006
(202) 833-3420

**INTERNATIONAL AUDIO
VISUAL, INC.**
15818 Arminta St.
Van Nuys, CA 91406
(213) 787-4400

**INTERNATIONAL COUNCIL
OF SHOPPING CENTERS**
445 Park Ave.
New York, NY 10022
(212) 421-8181

**INTERNATIONAL FENCE
ALARM CORP.**
175 Greeley Ave.
Sayville, L.I., NY 11782
(516) 567-4907

**INTERNATIONAL
IMPORTERS, INC.**
2244 S. Western Ave.
Chicago, IL 60608
(312) 847-6363

**INTERNATIONAL LOSS
CONTROL INSTITUTE**
P.O. Box 345
Loganville, GA 30249
(404) 466-2576

**INTERNATIONAL
MICROWAVE CORP.**
33 River Rd.
Cos Cob, CT 06807
(203) 661-6277

**INTERNATIONAL SECURITY
CONFERENCE**
Security World Publishing Co., Inc.
2639 S. La Cienega Blvd.
Los Angeles, CA 90034
(213) 836-5000

**INTERNATIONAL SOCIETY
OF STRESS ANALYSTS**
96 Colchester Ave.
Burlington, VT 05401

INTEX INC.
SENTRIE Div.
6935 Wisconsin Ave.
Chevy Chase, MD 20015
(301) 654-4550

**INTRUSION DETECTION
SYSTEMS, INC. (I.D.S. INC.)**
414 Pendleton Way
Airport Business Park
Oakland, CA 94621
(415) 562-3550

ISL PRODUCTS LTD.
1757 Merrick Ave.
Merrick, NY 11566
(516) 623-1141

JAVELIN ELECTRONICS
6357 Arizona Circle
Los Angeles, CA 90045
(213) 641-4490

JAYBIL INDUSTRIES, INC.
700 Woodfield Rd.
West Hempstead, NY 11552
(212) 341-1300

E.F. JOHNSON CO.
Land Mobile Radio Div.
299 10th Ave. S.W.
Waseca, MN 56093
(507) 835-6222

KABA SECURITY LOCKS, INC.
One Oliver Plaza
Pittsburgh, PA 15222
(412) 765-1405

KANE MFG. CORP.
515 N. Fraley St.
Kane, PA 16735
(814) 837-6464

KAPCO ENTERPRISES, INC.
947 Janesville Ave.
Ft. Atkinson, WI 53538
(414) 563-8441

KBI SECURITY SERVICE INC.
680 E. 233rd St.
New York, NY 10466
(212) 325-9111

KEENE CORP.
Porta-FAb Div.
2319 Grissom Dr.
St. Louis, MO 63141
(800) 325-3781

KELTRON CORP.
225 Crescent St.
Waltham, MA 02154
(617) 894-0525

KE-MASTER
300 S. Pennell Rd.
Media, PA 19063
(215) 459-1129

KENCO INC.
1386 Wall Ave.
Ogden, UT 84401
(801) 399-9621

KEY MASTER SALES CO.
Div. Clark Security Products Co.
P.O. Box 17610
San Diego, CA 92117
(714) 565-0101

K-F INDUSTRIES INC.
230 W. Dauphin St.
Philadelphia, PA 19133
(215) 425-7710

WALTER KIDDE & CO., INC.
Belleville Div.
675 Main St.
Belleville, NJ 07109
(201) 759-5000

KING RESEARCH LABS., INC.
801 S. 11th Ave.
Maywood, IL 60153
(312) 344-7877

KOHLER CO.
High St.
Kohler, WI 53044
(414) 457-4441

KOLIN INDUSTRIES INC.
P.O. Box 357

Bronxville, NY 10708
(914) 961-5065

KOYO INTERNATIONAL INC. OF AMERICA
1114 Ave. of the Americas
New York, NY 10036
(212) 869-1919

LAKE JACKSON INDUSTRIES, INC.
1830 Massachusetts Ave.
McLean, VA 22101
(703) 538-4677

LANGUAGE TRANSLATION SERVICES, INC.
P.O. Box 4042
Lexington, KY 40504
(606) 277-7350

LASSEN ELECTRONICS CORP.
37427 Centralmont Pl.
Fremont, CA 94536
(415) 792-0709

LATAH, INC.
Box 8128
Boise, ID 83707
(208) 375-4305

LAW ENFORCEMENT ASSOCIATES, INC.
88 Holmes St.
Belleville, NJ 07109
(201) 751-0001

LENZAR OPTICS CORP.
210 Brant Rd.
Lake Park, FL 33403
(305) 844-0263

LERRO ELECTRICAL CORP.
3127 N. Broad St.
Philadelphia, PA 19132
(215) 223-8200

LIBERTY SECURITY DISTRIBUTORS
6037 Liberty Rd.
Baltimore, MD 21207
(301) 944-4193

LIBRARY JOURNAL
1180 Ave. of the Americas
New York, NY 10036
(212) 764-5247

LINDEN LABORATORIES, INC.
BOX 920
State College, PA 16801
(814) 355-5491

LINEAR CORP.
347 S. Glasgow Ave.
Inglewood, CA 90301
(213) 649-0222

LION UNIFORM, INC.
2735 Kearns Ave.
Dayton, OH 45414
(513) 278-6531

LITTLE GIANT INDUSTRIES, INC.
31 S. 100 West
American Fork, UT 84003
(801) 756-7656

THE LITTLE RED FILMHOUSE
119 S. Kikea Dr.
Los Angeles, CA 90048
(213) 655-6726

LOS ANGELES INSTITUTE OF POLYGRAPH
5410 Wilshire Blvd. Ste. 912
Los Angeles, CA 90036
(213) 936-8233

LOXEM MFG. CORP.
Welch, Inc.
1201 Exchange Dr.
Richardson, TX 75080
(214) 238-7845

LPS INTERNATIONAL, LTD.
6065 Roswell Rd.
Atlanta, GA 30328
(404) 256-0297

LPS RESEARCH LABORATORIES, INC.
2050 Cotner Ave.
Los Angeles, CA 90025
(213) 478-0095

LUCCO SECURITY PRODUCTS CO.
P.O. Box 34851
Los Angeles, CA 90034

LUMENITE ELECTRONIC CO.
2331 N. 17th Ave.
Franklin Park, IL 60131
(312) 455-1450

M & G SHEET METAL CORP.
100 White St.
Brooklyn, NY 11206
(212) 497-7316

MAGLOK, INC.
1684 Medina Rd., Rt. 18
Medina, OH 44256
(216) 239-1951

MAGNA DIGITRONICS INC.
2740 S.E. Marine Dr.
Vancouver, BC, Can. V5S 2H1
(604) 438-7471

MAGNETIC SHIELD DIV.
Perfection Mica Co.
740 N. Thomas Dr.
Bensenville, IL 60106
(312) 766-7800

MAGNUM PRODUCTS, INC.
2189 N.W. 53rd St.
Ft. Lauderdale, FL 33309
(305) 484-1550

MAGSON UNIFORM CO.
279 New Britain Rd.
Kensington, CT 06037
(203) 225-8641

MALLORY BATTERY CO.
Div. P.R. Mallory & Co. Inc.
S. Broadway
Tarrytown, NY 10591
(914) 591-7000

MANITOU SYSTEMS, INC.
722 Foster Ave.
Bensenville, IL 60106
(312) 595-0020

MARDIX, INC.
900 Stierlin Rd.
Mountain View, CA 94043
(415) 961-3030

MARLEE ELECTRONICS CORP.
3346 S. La Cienega Blvd.
Los Angeles, CA 90016
(213) 993-9595

MARVEL PHOTO
Box 2464
Tulsa, OK 74101
(918) 582-1454

FG. MASON ENGINEERING, INC.
1700 Post Rd.
Fairfield, CT 06430
(203) 255-3461

MASS RETAILING INSTITUTE
570 Seventh Ave.
New York, NY 10018
(212) 354-6600

MASSA CORP.
280 Lincoln St.
Hingham, MA 02043
(617) 749-4800

MAXWELL ALARM SCREEN MFG. CO. OF CALIFORNIA, INC.
1670 20th St.
Santa Monica, CA 90404
(213) 829-1967

MAYDAY ALARMS, INC.
Sub. Security Exchange, Inc.
561 Atlantic Ave.
East Rockaway, NY 11518
(516) 599-5128

MEDECO SECURITY LOCKS INC.
P.O. Box 1075
Salem VA 24153
(703) 387-0481

MERET INC.
1815 24th St.
Santa Monica, CA 90404
(213) 828-7496

MERIDIAN PUBLISHING CO.
P.O. Box 4231
Hialeah, FL 33014
(305) 621-2161

THE MERRITT CO.
Dept. #16
1661 9th St.
Santa Monica, CA 90406
(213) 451-0725

MERSON UNIFORM CO.
254 Canal St.
New York, NY 10013
(212) 226-5959

MESA SECURITY GROUP
6656 W. 87th Pl.
Los Angeles, CA 90045
(213) 645-5509

MEYER & WENTHE
Div. Consolidated Foods Industry
7220 Wilson Ave.
Harwood Heights, IL 60656
(312) 867-7575

MGI, INC.
1930 E. Pembroke Ave.
Hampton, VA 23663
(804) 723-3381

**MICROWAVE ASSOCIATES,
INC.**
South Ave.
Burlington, MA 01803
(617) 272-3000

MICROWAVE SENSORS, INC.
2378 E. Stadium Blvd.
Ann Arbor, MI 48104
(313) 971-9231

MIDWAY CAP CO.
2301 W. St. Paul Ave.
Chicago, IL 60647
(312) 276-4300

MIECO
Div. Polarad Electronics Corp.
109 Beaver Ct.
Cockeysville, MD 21030
(301) 667-4660

RONALD MILLER INC.
6427 Bay Club Dr.
Ft. Lauderdale, FL 33308
(305) 772-6427

M.M.S., INC.
Mfrs. Mktg. Service, Inc.
3665 W. 240th St.
Torrance, CA 90505
(213) 378-8403

MONROE TIMER CO. INC.
3044 Westchester Ave.
Bronx, NY 10461
(212) 931-2530

GOODLOE E. MOORE, INC.
2811 N. Vermilion St.
Danville, IL 61832
(217) 446-7900

MOOSE PRODUCTS INC.
1014 3rd Ave. N.W.
Hickory, NC 28601
(704) 322-2333

**MORGAN ELECTRONICS,
INC.**
20700 Corsair Blvd.
Hayward, CA 94545
(415) 785-7200

MORSE PRODUCTS MFG.
12960 Bradley Ave.
Sylmar, CA 91342
(213) 367-5951

**MOSLER AIRMATIC &
ELECTRONIC SYSTEMS**
415 Hamburg Turnpike
Wayne, NJ 07470
(201) 881-4000

**MOTOROLA
COMMUNICATIONS &
ELECTRONICS, INC.**
1301 E. Algonquin Rd.
Schaumburg, IL 60172
(312) 397-1000

**MOTOROLA
TELEPROGRAMS INC.**
4825 N. Scott St.
Schiller Park, IL 60176
(312) 671-1565

MT. PLEASANT MFG. CO.
105 Jordan Ave.
Mt. Pleasant, TN 38474
(615) 379-7731

**MOUNTAIN WEST ALARM
SUPPLY CO.**
4215 N. 16th St.
Phoenix, AZ 85016
(602) 263-8831

**MRC ALARM SYSTEMS &
DEVICES CO.**
700 W. Virginia St.
Milwaukee, WI 53204
(414) 271-4343

MRL, INC.
7644 Fullerton Rd.
Springfield, VA 22153
(703) 569-0195

MSS ELECTRONICS, INC.
37 Fulton St.

White Plains, NY 10606
(914) 948-1414

MULTI-ELMAC CO.
22700 Heslip Dr.
Novi, MI 48050
(313) 349-3990

**MULTI-PURPOSE LADDER
CO. INC.**
1280 N. Grove Ave.
Anaheim, CA 92806
(714) 630-6611

**MULTITONE ELECTRONICS
INC.**
One Cornell Pkwy.
Springfield, NJ 07081
(201) 467-1800

MUL-T-LOCK CORP.
167 Madison Ave.
New York, NY 10016
(212) 889-9545

**NAPCO SECURITY SYSTEMS,
INC.**
6 DiTomas Ct.
Copiague, NY 11726
(516) 842-9400

**NATIONAL ASSN. OF
SCHOOL SECURITY
DIRECTORS**
1320 S.W. 4th St.
Fort Lauderdale, FL 33312
(305) 765-6201

**NATIONAL BURGLAR & FIRE
ALARM ASSN.**
1730 Pennsylvania Ave., N.W.
Washington, DC 2006
(202) 785-0500

**NATIONAL COUNCIL OF
INVESTIGATIVE &
SECURITY SERVICES**
1730 Pennsylvania Ave., N.W.
St. 1150
Washington, DC 20006
(202) 785-0500

**NATIONAL CRIME
PREVENTION INSTITUTE**
University of Louisville
Shelby Campus
Louisville, KY 40222
(502) 425-0653

**NATIONAL ELECTRICAL
MANUFACTURERS ASSN.**
155 E. 44th St.
New York, NY 10017
(212) 682-1500

**NATIONAL FIRE
PROTECTION ASSN.**
470 Atlantic Ave.

Boston, MA 02210
(617) 482-8755

**NATIONAL LOCKSMITHS
SUPPLIERS ASSN.**
95 E. Valley Stream Blvd.
Valley Stream, NY 11580
(516) 825-6673

**NATIONAL RETAIL
MERCHANTS ASSN.**
100 W. 31st St.
New York, NY 10001
(212) 244-8780

**NATIONAL SAFETY
COUNCIL**
444 N. Michigan Ave.
Chicago, IL 60611
(312) 527-4800

**NATIONAL SECURITY
SYSTEMS, INC.**
20 Beechwood Ave.
Port Washington, NY 11050
(516) 883-2444

**THE NATIONAL TRAINING
CENTER OF POLYGRAPH
SCIENCE**
57 W. 57th St.
New York, NY 10019
(212) 755-5241

NEC AMERICA, INC.
Sub. Nippon Electric Co., Ltd.
160 Martin Ln.
Elk Grove Village, IL 60007
(312) 593-8750

**NEL-TECH DEVELOPMENT,
INC.**
10815 S.W. Cascade Blvd.
Portland, OR 97223
(503) 620-1911
(800) 547-1884

NEWBRITE ALARMS, INC.
166 Laurel Rd.
E. Northport, NY 11731
(516) 757-8600

NEWSTAMP
Div. New England Stamping &
Fabricating Works
227 Bay Rd.
North Easton, MA 02356
(617) 238-7071

THE NIGHT EYE CORP.
Rural Rt. 6, Box 260A
Interstate 80 & North Dubuque
Iowa City, IA 52240
(319) 351-5827

NIK-O-LOK CO.
Affil. Standard Change-Makers
422 E. New York St.

Indianapolis, IN 46202
(317) 639-3516

**NORTH AMERICAN PHILIPS
CONTROLS CORP.**
Husky Park
Frederick, MD 21701
(301) 663-5141

NORTH ELECTRIC CO.
Supply Div.
10951 Lakeview Ave.
Lenexa, KS 66219
(913) 888-9800

NORTH SUBURBAN INC.
5828 N. Lincoln Ave.
Chicago, IL 60659
(312) 769-2800

NUSAC, INC.
7926 Jones Branch Dr.
McLean, VA 22101
(703) 893-6004

NUTONE DIV.
Scovill
Madison & Red Bank Rds.
Cincinnati, OH 45227
(513) 527-5100

OK MACHINE & TOOL CORP.
3455 Conner St.
Bronx, NY 10475
(212) 994-6600

OMNI SPECTRA INC.
Security Products Div.
2626 S. Hardy Dr.
Tempe, AZ 85282
(602) 966-1471

**ON GUARD SECURITY
SYSTEMS, INC.**
P.O. Box 129
Pleasantville, NJ 08232
(609) 646-4488

OPTICS OF KANSAS, INC.
612 Kansas Ave.
Kansas City, KS 66119
(913) 342-2424

ORECK CORP.
100 Plantation Rd.
New Orleans, LA 70123
(504) 733-8761

PAGE ALERT SYSTEMS, INC.
23840 Madison St.
Torrance, CA 90505
(213) 378-8596

PANASONIC CO.
Div. Matsushita Electric Corp. of
America
One Panasonic Way
Secaucus, NJ 07094
(201) 348-7000

**PAR-KUT INTERNATIONAL,
INC.**
25500 Joy Blvd.
Mt. Clemens, MI 48043
(313) 468-2947

PEAK TECHNOLOGIES, INC.
543 Old County Rd.
San Carlos, CA 94070
(415) 592-2479

PELCO SALES INC.
351 E. Alondra Blvd.
Gardena, CA 90248
(213) 321-5591

**PENINSULA ALARM
PRODUCTS**
309 Laurelwood Rd., Ste. 13
Santa Clara, CA 95050
(408) 988-2401

PEREY MFG. CO. INC.
Perey Turnstiles Div.
101 Park Ave.
New York, NY 10017
(212) 679-6080

PERMA PACK INC.
118 W. 29th St.
New York, NY 10001
(212) 736-9580

PETERS INDUSTRIES, INC.
1600 Cowart St.
Chattanooga, TN 37401
(615) 267-7673
(800) 251-6415

THE PETERZELL CO.
951 N. Pennsylvania Ave.
Winter Park, FL 32789
(305) 628-4758

**PHELPS TIME RECORDING
LOCK CORP.**
New York, NY 10007
(212) 732-3791

**PHILIPS AUDIO VIDEO
SYSTEMS CORP.**
91 McKee Dr.
Mahwah, NJ 07430
(201) 529-3800

**PHILIPS ELECTRONIC
INSTRUMENTS, INC.**
85 McKee Dr.
Mahwah, NJ 07430
(201) 529-3800

PICHEL INDUSTRIES INC.
28007 Front St.
Temecula, CA 92390
(714) 676-5721

PINKERTON'S, INC.
100 Church St.
New York, NY 10007
(212) 285-4856

F. MORTON PITT CO.
1444 S. San Gabriel Blvd.
San Gabriel, CA 91776
(213) 283-5176

PLATT LUGGAGE, INC.
2301 S. Prairie Ave.
Chicago, IL 60616
(312) 225-6670

PLECTRON CORP.
Overton, NB 68863
(308) 987-2416

POINT BLANK BODY ARMOR, INC.
14 W. 17th St.
New York, NY 10011
(212) 929-3220

POLAROID CORP.
549 Technology Sq.
Cambridge, MA 02139
(617) 864-6000

POLY-SCIENTIFIC DIV.
Litton Systems, Inc.
1213 N. Main St.
Blacksburg, VA 24060
(703) 552-3011

POOL GUARD, INC.
11005 Indian Trail
Dallas, TX 75229
(214) 243-1518

PORTAC CO.
4115 Marina Dr.
Santa Barbara, CA 93110
(805) 967-2170

PORTA-KING BLDG. SYSTEMS
4133 Shoreline Dr.
Earth City, MO 63045
(314) 291-6600

POTTER & BRUMFIELD DIV.
AMF Inc.
200 Richland Creek Dr.
Princeton, IN 47671
(812) 386-1000

POTTER ELECTRIC SIGNAL CO.
2081 Craig Rd.
St. Louis, MO 63141
(314) 878-4321
(800) 325-3936

POWER-OPTICS, INC.
1055 W. Germantown Pike
Fairview Village, PA 19409
(215) 539-5300

POWER-SONIC CORP.
3106 Spring St.
Redwood City, CA 94063
(415) 364-5001

PREFERRED SECURITY COMPONENTS, INC.
1605 Ayre St.
Newark, DE 19804
(302) 995-6158

PRO-COM SYSTEMS INC.
11411 Landan Ln.
Cincinnati, OH 45246
(513) 771-4240

PROJECTS UNLIMITED
3680 Wyse Rd.
Dayton, OH 45414
(513) 890-1918

PROMARK CORP.
39 W. Brother Dr.
Greenwich, CT 06830
(203) 869-1106

PRO-TECH SECURITY SYSTEMS INC.
29830 Beck
Wixom, MI 48096
(313) 624-6470

PROTECT-ALARM SECURITY PRODUCTS
Div. New Mexico Alarm Co. Inc.
714 Calle Grillo
Sante Fe, NM 87501
(505) 988-4722

PROTECTION & LOSS CONTROL (PLC) ELECTRONICS
39-50 Crescent St.
Long Island City, NY 11101
(212) 937-2605
(800) 221-0174

PROTECTION & SECURITY EQUIPMENT CORP.
5089 Lampglow Ct.
St. Louis, MO 63129
(314) 892-9005

PRO-TECTION PRODUCTS INC.
10961 Bloomfield St.
Los Alamitos, CA 90720
(213) 598-9474

PROTECTIVE MATERIALS CO.
York St.
Andover, MA 01810
(617) 475-6397

PROTECTRON, INC.
7 Rose St.
Branford, CT 06405
(203) 488-1657

P.T.I.-DOLCO
13401 S. Main St.
Los Angeles, CA 90061
(213) 538-2710

PYR-A-LARM, INC.
A Baker Industries Co.
8 Ridgedale Ave.
Cedar Knolls, NJ 07927
(201) 267-1300

PYROTECTOR, INC.
(see Chloride Pyrotector)

QONAAR SECURITY SYSTEMS, INC.
Sub. QONAAR Corp.
100 Lively Blvd.
Elk Grove Village, IL 60007
(312) 593-8453

QUALICOMP SECURITY PRODUCTS
308 E St.
Michigan City, IN 46360
(219) 872-0569
(800) 348-3261

QUESTAR CORP.
P.O. Box C
New Hope, PA 18938
(215) 862-2000

QUICK-SET INC./ CUNNINGHAM
3650 Woodhead Dr.
Northbrook, IL 60062
(312) 498-0704

RACON, INC.
Boeing Field Int'l
8490 Perimeter Rd. So.
Seattle, WA 98108
(206) 762-6011

RADIONICS INC.
546-F Hartnell
Monterey, CA 93940
(408) 649-8877

RASCO REFRIGERATION ALARM SYSTEMS CORP.
26-35 Pettit Ave.
Bellmore, NY 11710
(516) 221-2500

RAYTEK
Div. Optical Coating Laboratory, Inc.
325 E. Middlefield Rd.
Mountain View, CA 94043
(415) 961-1650
(800) 227-8074

R-BAR INDUSTRIES, INC.
1884 Columbia Rd., N.W.
Ste. 122
Washington, DC 20009
(202) 667-7446

RCA ELECTRO-OPTICS & DEVICES
Closed Circuit Video Equipment
New Holland Ave.

Lancaster, PA 17604
(717) 397-7661

REACH ELECTRONICS, INC.
P.O. Box 308
W. 13th St.
Lexington, NB 68850
(308) 324-5641

RECORA CO., INC.
Powis Rd.
St. Charles, IL 60174
(312) 584-3000

REDCO INC.
5515 Westfield Ave.
Pennsauken, NJ 08110
(609) 662-4774

**REGISCOPE CORP. OF
AMERICA**
7 E. 43rd St.
New York, NY 10017
(212) 661-1730

JOHN E. REID & ASSOCIATES
215 N. Dearborn St.
Chicago, IL 60601
(312) 782-0800

RELAYMATIC INC.
Main St.
Sag Harbor, NY 11963
(516) 725-1669

**RELIABLE FIRE EQUIPMENT
CO.**
12845 S. Cicero Ave.
Alsip, IL 60658
(312) 597-4600

REMLIN PRODUCTS INC.
40 Essex St.
Hackensack, NJ 07601
(201) 489-1580

**REMOTE CONTROL DEVICES
CORP.**
7835 Manchester Ave.
St. Louis, MO 63143
(314) 647-8167

REPCO INC.
Sub. SCOPE Inc.
1940 Lockwood Way
Orlando, FL 32804
(305) 843-8484

RICHARDS-WILCOX MFG. CO.
788 Third St.
Aurora, IL 60507
(312) 897-6951

**RICHMOND ENTERPRISES
INC.**
7835 Manchester Ave.
St. Louis, MO 63143
(314) 781-1645

**RISK & INSURANCE
MANAGEMENT SOCIETY,
INC.**
205 E. 42nd St., Ste. 1504
New York, NY 10017

**GEORGE RISK INDUSTRIES,
INC.**
G.R.I. Plaza
Kimball, NB 69145
(308) 235-4645

RITTENHOUSE
Unit Emerson Electric Co.
Honeoye Falls, NY 14472
(716) 624-1400

**RIVERS PROTECTION
SYSTEMS**
5841 Irving Ave. So.
Minneapolis, MN 55419
(612) 920-0337

RIVERSIDE MFG. CO.
P.O. Box 460
Moultrie, GA 31768
(912) 985-5210

RIXSON-FIREMARK, INC.
Sub. Conrac Corp.
9100 W. Belmont Ave.
Franklin Park, IL 60131
(312) 671-5670

ROBOT INDUSTRIES INC.
7041 Orchard St.
Dearborn, MI 48126
(313) 846-2623

ROBOT RESEARCH, INC.
7591 Convoy Ct.
San Diego, CA 92111
(714) 279-9430

**ROCK-LAND INDUSTRIES,
INC.**
P.O. Box 135
Edison, NJ 08817
(201) 548-1800

**ROCKWELL
INTERNATIONAL CORP.**
Autonetics Group
Identification Systems Div.
3370 Miraloma Ave.
Anaheim, CA 92803
(714) 632-8111

ROHM AND HAAS CO.
Independence Mall West
Philadelphia, PA 19105
(215) 592-3000

ROLL-O-MATIC CHAIN CO.
200 Wyandotte St.
Kansas City, MO 64105
(816) 221-4416

ROSSIN CORP.
1411 Norman Firestone Rd.
Goleta, CA 93017
(805) 967-5606
(800) 235-6961

**ROTHENBUHLER
ENGINEERING CO.**
Rhodes Rd.
Sedro Woolley, WA 98284
(206) 856-0836

**RUSCO ELECTRONIC
SYSTEMS**
1840 Victory Blvd.
Glendale, CA 91201
(213) 240-2540

RUSSWIN DIV.
Emhart Corp.
225 Episcopal Rd.
Berlin, CT 06037
(203) 225-7411

S & B DISTRIBUTORS
416 Scott St.
Michigan City, IN 46360
(219) 872-0569
(800) 348-3261

SADETO INC.
Sub. Electronic Relays, Inc.
71 Regent Dr.
Oak Brook, IL 60521
(312) 887-9522

SAFELITE INDUSTRIES
801 S. Wichita
Wichita, KS 67201
(316) 267-3276
(800) 835-2092

SAFE-T-WAY SAFETY CANS
Div. Cooper Industries, Inc.
P.O. Box 188
Canfield, OH 44406
(216) 533-5535

SALCO INDUSTRIES, INC.
572 Broadway
Long Branch, NJ 07740
(201) 222-3781

SANYO ELECTRIC INC.
1200 W. Artesia Blvd.
Compton, CA 90220
(213) 537-5830

SANYO ELECTRIC INC.
Battery Div.
51 Joseph St.
Moonachie, NJ 07074
(210) 641-2333

SARGENT & CO.
100 Sargent Dr.
New Haven, CT 06509
(203) 562-2151

SARGENT & GREENLEAF, INC.
1 Security Dr.
Nicholasville, KY 40356
(606) 885-9411

SC ELECTRONICS, INC.
Sub. Audiotronics Corp.
530 5th Ave., N.W.
New Brighton, MN 55112
(612) 633-3131

SCAN SECURITY SYSTEMS INC.
472 Suffolk Ave.
Brentwood, NY 11717
(516) 273-1444

SCANDUS INC.
Turn-O-Matic Div.
2470 El Camino Real
Palo Alto, CA 94306
(415) 327-2160

SCHLAGE ELECTRONICS
Sub. Schlage Lock Co.
1135 Arques Ave.
Sunnyvale, CA 94086
(408) 736-8430

SEABOARD ELECTRONICS CO.
70 Church St.
New Rochelle, NY 10805
(914) 235-8053

SEAL IN PLASTIC CO., INC.
20739 Dearborn St.
Chatsworth, CA 91311
(213) 882-8171

SEALECTRO CORP.
225 Hoyt St.
Mamaroneck, NY 10543
(914) 698-5600

SECOM
P.O. Box 2074
Culver City, CA 90230
(213) 649-1185

SECURA KEY
6300 Variel Ave.
Woodland Hills, CA 91367
(213) 883-6221

SECURTEC, INC.
P.O. Box 4454
Scottsdale, AZ 85258
(602) 966-6201

SECURITONE, INC.
23W223 Black Cherry Ln.
Glen Ellyn, IL 60137
(312) 858-6060

SECURITRON MAGNALOCK CORP.
21806 S. Vermont Ave.
Torrance, CA 90502
(213) 320-1625

SECURITY COMMUNICATIONS CORP. (SECUR-COM)
200 E. Wyomissing Ave.
Park Manor
Schillington, PA 19607
(215) 777-6581

SECURITY DISTRIBUTING & MARKETING MAGAZINE
Div. Security World Publishing Co., Inc.
2639 S. La Cienega Blvd.
Los Angeles, CA 90034
(213) 836-5000

SECURITY ENGINEERED MACHINERY
5 Walkup Dr.
Westboro, MA 01581
(617) 366-1488

SECURITY ENGINEERING INC.
P.O. Box 265
Plantsville, CT 06479
(203) 621-6757

SECURITY EQUIPMENT INDUSTRY ASSN.
2639 S. La Cienega Blvd.
Los Angeles, CA 90034
(213) 838-3193

SECURITY FILMS, INC.
400 N. Michigan Ave.
Chicago, IL 60610
(312) 467-0330

SECURITY GENERAL
P.O. Box 11455
Reno, NV 89510
(702) 786-3778

SECURITY INSTRUMENTS, INC.
4519 White Plains Rd.
Bronx, NY 10470
(212) 324-4062

SECURITY IRON CO.
1201 S. Broad St.
New Orleans, LA 70125
(504) 821-0524

SECURITY (JAPAN)
Security World Co., Ltd.
Daini Nakada Bldg.
3-15, Akasaka 1-chome
Minato-ku, Tokyo, Japan

SECURITY PRODUCTS CO.
14915 Woodworth Ave.
Cleveland, OH 44110
(216) 249-4600

SECURITY RESEARCH INC.
P.O. Box 5913
Lighthouse Point, FL 33064
(305) 561-8401

SECURITY SUPPLY SERVICE INC.
285 Newtonville Ave.
Newtonville, MA 02160
(617) 965-3400
(800) 852-3015
(800) 225-3278

SECURITY WORLD BOOKS
Div. Security World Publishing Co., Inc.
2639 S. La Cienega Blvd.
Los Angeles, CA 90034
(213) 836-5000

SECURITY WORLD MAGAZINE
Div. Security World Publishing Co., Inc.
2639 S. La Cienega Blvd.
Los Angeles, CA 90034
(213) 836-5000

SECURITY WORLD PUBLISHING CO., INC.
2639 S. La Cienega Blvd.
Los Angeles, CA 90034
(213) 836-5000

SE-KURE CONTROLS, INC.
5685 N. Lincoln Ave.
Chicago, IL 60659
(312) 728-2435

SELLERS SECURITY & ELECTRONICS
7009 Argyle Ave.
San Bernardino, CA 92404
(714) 862-2016

SENSOR-TEC, INC.
P.O. Box 31
Goshen, KY 40026
(502) 228-8333

SENTATEK CORP. OF AMERICA
3412 Enterprise Ave.
Naples, FL 33942
(813) 775-2211

SENTROL, INC.
Sub. Kentrox Industries, Inc.
10950 S.W. 5th St.
Beaverton, OR 97005
(503) 646-7174
(800) 547-5741

SENTRY TECHNOLOGY, INC.
222 Mt. Hermon Rd.
Santa Cruz, CA 95066
(408) 438-3311

SENTRY WATCH, INC.
1105 S. Chapman St.
Greensboro, NC 27402
(919) 273-8103

SESCOA (SECURITY SCIENCES CORP. OF AMERICA)
3621 Wells Fargo
Scottsdale, AZ 85251
(602) 994-9351

SHORROCK INC.
9730 George Palmer Hwy.
Lanham, MD 20801
(301) 459-6166

SHREDMASTER DIV.
General Binding Corp.
1101 Skokie Blvd.
Northbrook, IL 60062
(312) 272-3700

SHUFRO ENGINEERING LABS
4200 Washington St.
Roslindale, MA 02131
(617) 327-0547

SIERRA ENGINEERING CO.
Div. CapTech Inc.
123 E. Montecito Ave.
Sierra Madre, CA 91024
(213) 681-1141

SIGHT & SOUND SYSTEMS
5619 St. John Ave.
Kansas City, MO 64123
(816) 483-4612

SIGMA ELECTRONICS INC.
5402 Alhambra Ave.
Los Angeles, CA 90032
(213) 225-8147

SIGNAL CABLE CO.
2325 Davis
N. Chicago, IL 60064
(312) 689-9090

SIGNALARM INC.
Div. Spirig International
357 Cottage St.
Springfield, MA 01104
(413) 788-0224

SIGNAL-U MFG. CO.
250 Railroad St.
Canfield, OH 44406
(216) 533-5535

SIGNAPLEX, INC.
833 Union St.
Brooklyn, NY 11215
(212) 622-5321

SILENT KNIGHT SECURITY SYSTEMS
Div. Waycrosse, Inc.
2930 Emerson Ave. So.
Minneapolis, MN 55408
(612) 827-2681

SILENT WATCHMAN CORP.
4861 McGaw Rd.
Columbus, OH 43207
(614) 491-5200

SILMAR ELECTRONICS
133 S.W. 57th Ave.
Miami, FL 33144
(305) 266-1910

SIMPLEX SECURITY SYSTEMS, INC.
Front & Main Sts.
Colinsville, CT 06022
(203) 693-8391

HORACE SMALL MFG. CO.
350 28th Ave., No.
Nashville, TN 37202
(615) 383-8001

SMITH & WESSON
2100 Roosevelt Ave.
Springfield, MA 01101
(413) 781-8300

STANLEY SMITH SECURITY, INC.
3355 Cherryridge
San Antonio, TX 78230
(512) 349-6321

SNYDER ELECTRONICS, INC.
2082 Lincoln Ave.
Altadena, CA 91001
(213) 794-7139

SOLFAN SYSTEMS INC.
665 Clyde Ave.
Mountain View, CA 94043
(415) 964-7020

SONAR RADIO CORP.
73 Wortman Ave.
Brooklyn, NY 11207
(212) 649-8000

SONAR SECURITY MFG. CO.
Div. Sonar Mfg. Co.
1 W. 182nd St.
Bronx, NY 10453
(212) 584-7800

SONTRIX
Div. Pittway Corp.
4593 N. Broadway
Boulder, CO 80302
(303) 449-3700

S.P. INTERNATIONAL U.S.A. INC.
20235 Nordhoff St.
Chatsworth, CA 91311
(213) 996-1715

SPECTROGARD INC.
200 Ross Rd.
Bridgeport, PA 19405
(215) 265-3550

SPEEDCALL CORP.
2020 National Ave.
Hayward, CA 94545
(415) 783-5611

SPENCER PRODUCTS CO.
22841 Aurora Rd.
Bedford Heights, OH 44146
(216) 475-8700

SPIRIG ERNEST
Security Div.
P.O. Box 160
CH8640 Rapperswil, Switzerland
(055) 274403

SQUARE D CO.
Executive Plaza
Park Ridge, IL 60068
(312) 774-9200

STANDARD COMMUNICATIONS CORP.
P.O. Box 92151
Los Angeles, CA 90009
(213) 532-5300

STANDARD LAW ENFORCEMENT SUPPLY CO.
9240 N. 107th St.
Milwaukee, WI 53224
(414) 355-9730

STANDARD SECURITY SYSTEMS
5515 Cahuenga Blvd.
North Hollywood, CA 91603
(213) 769-4947

STANLEY HARDWARE
Div. the Stanley Works
195 Lake St.
New Britain, CT 06050
(203) 225-5111

STANLEY VEMCO
Div. The Stanley Works
5740 E. Nevada
Detroit, MI 48234
(313) 366-1300

STATITROL CORP.
140 S. Union Blvd.
Lakewood, CO 80228
(303) 986-1581

STD, INC.
Standard Telephone Design, Inc.
8250 S.W. Tonka St.
Tualatin, OR 97062
(503) 638-7331

W.H. STEELE CO., INC.
2622 N. Main St.
Los Angeles, CA 90031
(213) 223-3831

STELLAR SYSTEMS, INC.
3020 Olcott St.
Santa Clara, CA 95051
(408) 244- 8161

STOFFEL SEALS CORP.
68 Main St.
Tuckahoe, NY 10707
(914) 961-8500

STOP-FIRE, INC.
P.O. Box 9
Monmouth Junction, NJ 08852
(201) 297-3600

STRATTON HATS, INC.
3200 Randolph
Bellwood, IL 60104
(312) 544-5220

STURM, RUGER & CO., INC.
Dept. SW
Southport, CT 06490
(203) 259-7843

SUNSHINE RECREATION INC.
22713 Ventura Blvd., Ste. A
Woodland Hills, CA 91364
(213) 884-1732

SUPERIOR SECURITY IRON
5037 N. Union
St. Louis, MO 63115
(314) 382-3081

SURVEILLANCE VIDEO SYSTEMS
4710 Woodman Ave.
Sherman Oaks, CA 91423
(213) 784-2626

SYSTEM CONTROLS, INC.
3231 1st Ave. So.
Seattle, WA 98134
(206) 682-7116

TAPESWITCH CORP. OF AMERICA
100 Schmitt Blvd.
Farmingdale, NY 17735
(516) 694-6312

TAYLOR MARKETING INT'L
917 W. Manchester Ave.
Los Angeles, CA 90044
(213) 751-9091

TAYLOR-DUNN MFG. CO.
2114 W. Ball Rd.
Anaheim, CA 92804
(714) 956-4040

TDK CORP. OF AMERICA
Sub. TDK Electronics Co., Ltd.
931 S. Douglas St.
El Segundo, CA 90245
(213) 644-8625

TECH LABORATORIES, INC.
Bergen & Edsall Blvds.
Palisades Park, NJ 07650
(201) 944-2221

TECHNICAL COMMUNICATIONS CORP.
56 Winthrop St.
Concord, MA 01742
(617) 862-6035

TECHNICAL ELECTRONIC DISTRIBUTORS INC.
16 Foster St.
Bergenfield, NJ 07621
(201) 384-3643

TECHNI-TOOL, INC.
Apollo Rd.
Plymouth Meeting, PA 19462
(215) 825-4990

TECHNOLOGY SYSTEMS CORP.
18 Perimeter Park
Atlanta, GA 30341
(404) 455-3007

TEKNEKRON, INC.
Div. Trax
2020 Milvia St.
Berkeley, CA 94704
(415) 843-0606

TELE-ENTRY SECURITY SYSTEMS INC.
375 N.W. 170th St.
North Miami Beach, FL 33169
(305) 652-7822

TELEMATION, INC.
P.O. Box 15068
Salt Lake City, UT 84115
(801) 972-8000

TEL-GARD INDUSTRIES
Drawer D
Carmen, OK 73726
(405) 987-2220

TELKEE INC.
Rt. 452
Glen Riddle, PA 19037
(215) 459-1100

TELSAR CORP.
1010 Park Ave.
San Jose, CA 95126
(408) 287-0366

TETRADYNE CORP.
1681 S. Broadway
Carrollton, TX 75006
(214) 242-1512

THALNER ELECTRONIC LABORATORIES INC.
7235 Jackson Rd.
Ann Arbor, MI 48103
(313) 761-4506

CHARLES C. THOMAS, PUBLISHER
301-327 E. Lawrence Ave.
Springfield, IL 62717
(217) 789-8980

THREE B ELECTRONICS, INC.
5404 8th Ave.
Brooklyn, NY 11220
(212) 854-7005

3M CO.
Safety Systems Div.
3M Center, Bldg. 223-3N
St. Paul, MN 55101
(612) 733-0094

TIE SECURITY SYSTEMS
Glidden St.
Newcastle, ME 04553
(207) 563-3806

TITAN SECURITY SYSTEMS
600 E. Ocean Blvd.
Long Beach, CA 90802
(213) 436-5569

TORR X-RAY CORP.
Sub. Xonics, Inc.
6837 Hayvenhurst Ave.
Van Nuys, CA 91406
(213) 787-7380

T.P.S. INC. (THEFT PREVENTION SYSTEMS)
2930 College Ave.
Costa Mesa, CA 92626
(714) 545-8249

TRAINING CONSULTANTS, INC.
P.O. Box 81
Knoxville, TN 37901
(615) 522-1421

TRANS-AIR MFG. CO. LTD.
835 N. Salina St.
Syracuse, NY 13208
(315) 478-3285

TRANSCIENCE INDUSTRIES INC.
17 Irving Ave.
Stamford, CT 06902
(203) 327-7810
(800) 243-3495

TRANSPORTATION ASSN. OF AMERICA
1100 17th St., N.W.
Ste. 1107
Washington, DC 20036
(202) 296-2470

TRANSICOIL CONSUMER PRODUCTS INC.
Trooper Rd.
Worcester, PA 19490
(215) 277-1300
(800) 523-1262

TRINDEL SERVICE CLEMATIC
44, Rue de Lisbonn
75008 Paris, France
522.19.09

TRINE MFG.
Div. Square D Co.
1430 Ferris Pl.

Bronx, NY 10461
(212) 829-4796

**20TH CENTURY SECURITY
EDUCATION LTD.**
293 Kingston Rd.
Leatherhead, Surrey, Eng. KT22
7NJ
Leatherhhead 74505

**ULTRA-VIOLET PRODUCTS,
INC.**
5100 Walnut Grove Ave.
San Gabriel, CA 91778
(213) 285-3123

**UNDERWOOD SERVICE
ASSOCIATES**
13238 D Fiji Wy.
Marina Del Rey, CA 90291
(213) 823-8585

**UNICAN SECURITY SYSTEMS
CORP.**
P.O. Box 307
Plattsburgh, NY 12901
(518) 563-4690

UNION CARBIDE CORP.
Battery Products Div.
270 Park Ave.
New York, NY 10017
(212) 551-2345

UNISAF PUBLICATIONS LTD.
Unisaf House
32-36 Dudley Rd.
Tunbridge Wells, Kent, Eng.
(0892) 23184-6

UNISEC, INC.
2251 Bancroft Ave.
San Leandro, CA 94577
(415) 352-5610

UNITEC INC.
3910 S. Mariposa St.
Englewood, CO 80110
(303) 761-8391

**UNITED SECURITY
PRODUCTS, INC.**
6843 Dublin Blvd.
Dublin, CA 94566
(415) 829-1180

UNITED STATES GYPSUM
Metal Products Div.
101 S. Wacker Dr.
Chicago, IL 60606
(312) 321-4000

**UNITED STATES SCHOOL OF
LAW ENFORCEMENT**
1417 Georgia St.
Los Angeles, CA 90013
(213) 747-6201

**UNIVERSAL SECURITY
CONSULTANTS, INC.**
Div. Executive Protection, U.S.A.,
Inc.
426 Via Corta, Ste. 303
Palos Verdes Estates, CA 90274
(213) 373-6948

**UNIVERSAL SECURITY
INSTRUMENTS, INC.**
2829 Potee St.
Baltimore, MD 21225
(301) 355-9000

**UNIVERSITY MICROFILMS
INTERNATIONAL**
300 N. Zeeb Rd.
Ann Arbor, MI 48106
(313) 761-4700

VAN LOCK CO.
3609 Church St.
Cincinnati, OH 45244
(513) 561-9692

**VARITECH SECURITY
SYSTEMS, INC.**
1220 Broadway
New York, NY 10001
(212) 695-4460

VENUS SCIENTIFIC INC.
399 Smith St.
Farmingdale, NY 11735
(516) 293-4100

VERSA-LITE SYSTEMS, INC.
5834 Kirby Rd.
Clinton, MD 20735
(301) 297-7710

**VERTEX SCIENCE
INDUSTRIES, INC.**
401 N. Bowser Rd.
Richardson, TX 75080
(214) 231-9491

VICON INDUSTRIES INC.
125 E. Bethpage Rd.
Plainveiw, NY 11803
(516) 293-2200

**VICTORY ENGINEERING
CORP.**
Victory Rd.
Springfield, NJ 07081
(201) 379-5900

VIDEO COMPONENTS, INC.
601 S. Main St.
Spring Valley, NY 10977
(914) 356-3700

VIDEO TEK, INC.
8 Morris Ave.
Mountain Lakes, NJ 07046
(201) 335-1628

VIDEOLARM INC.
5931 Sutcliffe Sq.
Lithonia, GA 30058
(404) 981-9228

VINDICATOR
3520 Victor St.
Santa Clara, CA 95050
(408) 246-8686

VISITRAK CORP.
8 Saw Mill River Rd.
Hawthorne, NY 10532
(914) 592-6230

**VISUAL COMMUNICATION
SPECIALISTS**
7162 Convoy Ct.
San Diego, CA 92111
(714) 560-9156

VISUAL METHODS INC.
5 Wortendyke Ave.
Montvale, NJ 07645
(201) 391-7383

VON DUPRIN INC.
400 W. Maryland St.
Indianapolis, IN 46225
(317) 637-5521

VSI/PRO-LIGHT
1410 E. Walnut Ave.
Fullerton, CA 92631
(714) 870-9600

**WACKENHUT ELECTRONIC
SYSTEMS**
1742 N.W. 69th Ave.
Miami, FL 33126
(305) 592-3278

**WEAPONS CORP. OF
AMERICA**
2131 Kingston Ct.
Ste. 103
Marietta, GA 300367
(404) 427-8018

**WELLS FARGO ALARM
SERVICES**
Div. Baker Protective Services, Inc.
1901 N. Fort Myer Dr.
Suite 600
Arlington, VA 22209
(703) 524-8210

DAN WESSON ARMS, INC.
293 Main St.
Monson, MA 01057
(413) 267-4081

**WEST COAST CHAIN MFG.
CO.**
Key-Bak Div.
P.O. Box 5060
Pasadena, CA 91107
(213) 681-6358

**WESTAMERICA
  COMMUNICATIONS SUPPLY
  CO., INC.**
4408 Menan, N.E.
Albuquerque, NM 87110
(505) 265-7621
(800) 545-6500

**WESTERN ALARM SUPPLY
  CO.**
1414 Blake St.
Denver, CO 80202
(303) 534-3087

**WESTERN SECURITY
  PRODUCTS**
Signal Wire & Cable Co. Sub.
20800 S. Belshaw Ave.
Carson, CA 90746
(213) 774-2395

**WESTINGHOUSE SECURITY
  SYSTEMS, INC.**
200 Beta Dr.
Pittsburgh, PA 15238
(412) 782-1730

WHEELOCK SIGNALS, INC.
273 Branchport Ave.
Long Branch, NJ 07740
(201) 222-6880

THE WHITMAN CO.
P.O. Box 1105
Linden Hill Station
Flushing, L.I., NY 11354
(212) 353-6011

**WHOLESALE SECURITY
  DEVICES**
21415 W. 8 Mile Rd.
Detroit, MI 48219
(313) 537-5204

WICO CORP.
6400 W. Gross Point Rd.
Niles, Il 60648
(312) 647-7400

WILSON ELECTRONICS
4288 Polaris
Las Vegas, NY 89103
(702) 739-1931

WOLO MFG. CORP.
46 Cain Dr.
Plainview, NY 11803
(516) 293-0333

**WORLD ASSN. OF
  DETECTIVES**
c/o Norman J. Sloan, Exec. Dir.
P.O. Box 36172
Cincinnati, OH 45236

**WORLD WIDE MFG. &
  RESEARCH, INC.**
990 Washington St.
Dedham, MA 02026
(617) 326-0240

**WORLDWIDE SECURITY
  PRODUCTS**
Hwy. H-58
P.O. Box 623
Munising, MI 49862
(906) 387-3161

WRIGHT LINE INC.
160 Gold Star Blvd.
Worcester, MA 01606
(617) 852-4300

**X-RAY INDUSTRIAL
  DISTRIBUTORS**
338 Delawanna Ave.
Clifton, NJ 07014
(201) 773-9400

YARDNEY ELECTRIC CORP.
Yardney Electric Div.
82 Mechanic St.
Pawcatuck, CT 02891
(203) 599-1100

YASHICA, INC.
411 Sette Dr.
Paramus, NJ 07652
(201) 262-7300

**YUASA BATTERY (AMERICA),
  INC.**
P.O. Box 2905
Santa Fe Springs, CA 90670
(213) 698-2275

**ZEE MEDICAL PRODUCTS,
  INC.**
16641 Hale Ave.
Irvine, CA 92714
(714) 556-1660

ZERO CORP.
777 Front St.
Burbank, CA 91503
(213) 846-4191

ZOOMAR, INC.
55 Sea Cliff Ave.
Glen Cove, NY 11542
(516) 676-1900

ZYGO INDUSTRIES, INC.
Sole Distributor & U.S. Rep. for
  Yuasa Battery Co.
P.O. Box 1008
Portland, OR 97207
(503) 292-4695

Appendix B

Directory of
Security Consultants

Excerpted from "Directory of Security Consultants"

prepared for the National Institute of Law Enforcement and
Criminal Justice, Law Enforcement Assistance
Administration, U.S. Department of Justice, by
Elizabeth Robertson and John V. Fechter,
Center for Consumer Product Technology, National Bureau
of Standards

This directory was developed from information provided by the consultants themselves, submitted in response to a press release published in the Commerce Business Daily and a number of trade publications. In addition, letters were directed to several thousand individuals and organizations identified from various special mailing lists. The number of responses was far less than anticipated, and some which were received did not fall within the intended scope of the directory, and were excluded from this document.

Once information was obtained from the consultant, it was verified by telephone or letter, and the descriptions of technical services and experience were edited to best describe that resource. It should be noted that this information was not verified by field inspection, and no attempt was made to evaluate technical capability or substantiate previous experience. Inclusion in the directory does not constitute endorsement or imply recommendation of the individuals and organizations listed. Conversely, failure to list a resource in this directory should not be construed as a criticism or rejection of that resource.

The information about each entry in the directory constitutes a separate entry. Each entry contains the following information: (1) the full title of the organization and its acronym, where applicable; (2) the mailing address; (3) the telephone number;

(4) a description of the services which are provided and a brief summary of experience; (5) a list of publications; (6) the year when operations were started; (7) the number of man years of specialized security experience within the organization; (8) the number of persons on the staff; (9) the geographical area of operation and; (10) the dates and locations of annual meetings, where applicable. The entries are grouped alphabetically into three general categories: private consultants; consultants associated with colleges or universities; and specialized resources—associations, institutes, schools, authors, publishers and film producers concentrating on the security field.

In many cases, the individual resource listed in this directory will provide additional information or specific references upon request. The data are correct as of the fall of 1974.

I. CONSULTANTS IN THE INDUSTRIAL/ COMMERCIAL ENVIRONMENT

Advanced Technology Systems, Inc.
2425 Wilson Boulevard
Arlington, Virginia 22201
Phone: (703) 525-2664
This company provides system engineering services for security and law enforcement communications to local, state, and Federal government agencies, and to private organizations. After determining a user's communication needs, an appropriate system is described, applying such techniques as wire, radio, or digital signal transmission, computers, acoustics, and optics.

Experience in computer switched, wide-area, point-to-point digital transmission networks includes: state police information networks; metropolitan area/county integrated communications systems; correctional facility communications systems; emergency medical communications and others. The company does not sell or represent sellers of equipment.

Staff specialists have experience in communications engineering practice and theory, and have made contributions to Federal Communications Commission decisions governing the development and use of law enforcement and other communications.
Started operations: 1969
Man years of experience: 210
No. of persons on staff: 10
Geographic operation: Nationwide

Alarm Security Konsultants
Division of Security Architects, Inc.
P.O. Box 182
Medford, NJ 90955
Phone: (609) 654-5333
This firm provides analysis and assessment of security problems. For residential, institutional, educational, industrial, and commercial applications, recommendations, supportive specifications and drawings are prepared for use in the solicitation of competitive bids from equipment installers.

Experience includes burglary and fire protection systems for local, proprietary, central or police control; surveillance systems for employee access identification and perimeter control using closed circuit television, remote monitoring, random access control and other techniques; and protection of electronic data processing rooms and equipment.
Started operations: 1970
Man years of experience: 18
No. of persons on staff: One full-time employee
Geographic operation: Delaware Valley (Penn., N.J., and Delaware)

American Justice Institute
1007 7th Street, Suite 406
Sacramento, CA 95814
Phone: (916) 444-3096
This organization designs and implements surveys, and observational methodologies, and analyzes training requirements, and develops training programs. Experience includes analysis of

the roles of persons interacting in the front line with criminal justice offenders, e.g., police, public defender, prosecutor, judge, correctional worker, and probation officer. Techniques such as the mock trial are used in training judges, prosecutors and public defenders in their attitudes toward the offender. Community reactions to problem situations are also analyzed to propose solutions, and to implement programs. Community reaction analysis has included the effect of innovations in the criminal justice system as felt by the parents, the clients, bail bondsmen, etc. This private, non-profit group has done research on the development of offender classification systems for rehabilitation purposes and a master plan for the delivery of an offender through the criminal justice system. State plans, as required by the Omnibus Crime Control Act, are also developed.

Publications, 16 available; sample titles are: *Crime and Its Correction, California Correctional Information System: Preliminary Information System Requirements.*

Started operations: 1959

Man years of experience: 576

No. of persons on staff: 32

Geographic operation: United States

American Society for Industrial Security (ASIS)
National Office
2000 K Street, N.W., Suite 651
Washington, DC 20006
Phone: (202) 331-7887

This society is comprised of those officials in industry who are responsible for the security and loss prevention functions of their companies, and those in government who are professionally employed in security work. The Society maintains a library of several hundred volumes on security and related topics; compiles information on security and maintains a placement service for members.

Committees are: Banking and Finance, Budget and Finance, Computer Security, Credit Cards, Drug Abuse, Education Services, Insurance, Investigations, Physical Security, Professional Development and Education, Public Relations, Public Utilities, Restaurant and Lodging, Retail, Safeguarding Proprietary Information, Transportation, U.S. Government Security, Emergency Planning and Safety, Fire Prevention and Protection.

Publications: *Security Management*, bimonthly; Directory of Members, annual.

Convention/Meeting: Annual, always in September; 1976 Boston, MA; 1977 Orlando, FL; 1978 Los Angeles, CA

Started operations: 1955

Man years of experience: approximately 75,000 in the field of security

Geographic operation: International membership of 5,000, with 60 chapters in states and cities of the United States and in countries overseas

Anacapa Sciences, Incorporated
P.O. Drawer Q
2034 De La Vina
Santa Barbara, CA 93102
Phone: (805) 966-6157

This company provides research, training, and consulting services in the behavioral and engineering sciences. Interest in law enforcement involves: evaluation of systems, equipment, and procedures from the human user viewpoint, evaluation of crime reduction programs, development of law-enforcement techniques and methods, the conduct of pertinent training programs and law enforcement information processing systems. Classes and research emphasize: white-collar crime, urban terrorism, burglary, intelligence analysis and management and tactical decision making. Services are rendered to government agencies, industries, and commercial concerns.

Started operations: 1969

Man years of experience: 13 professional

No. of persons on staff: 27

Geographic operation: National and international

Analytical Systems Engineering Corporation
25 Ray Avenue
Burlington, MA 01803
Phone: (617) 272-7910
This company has experience in law enforcement, criminal justice consulting and security systems, including the specific areas of sensor applications, human factors considerations and data base management. The company specializes in objective studies and analyses designed to solve a user's specific problems. Systems have been devised to prevent pilferage of inventory and physical plant items as well as the loss of proprietary data and secrets through the activities of business intelligence and espionage operatives. Electromagnetic and acoustic intrusion detection devices have been designed, tested, and evaluated. A special sensor system for identifying and tracking hijacked trucks in a metropolitan environment was developed for police use. Completed projects include a Joint Operations Center (JOC) Simulation Facility for the U.S. Strike Command; an information system for the Rhode Island Department of Social and Rehabilitative Services; assistance with the preparation of a grant application for an information system and a Haverhill Police Department project to identify and deal with behavioral vocational training and future job placement problems of convicts.
Started operations: 1969
Man years of experience: (unavailable)
No. of persons on staff: 43 (additional specialized consultants are tapped as necessary)
Geographic operation: International

Anticipation, Inc.
410 Jericho Turnpike
Jericho, NY 11753
Phone: (516) 922-8338
This company provides consultation services specializing in internal theft; designs and sells burglary and fire alarm systems and metal (weapons) detectors. The staff works with first line supervisors, presents talks, and prepares reports. Internal theft reduction programs include the design of CCTV monitoring equipment, pilferage control devices, and cargo security systems. Systems are tailored to meet individual needs of each client, such as local banks and New York State.
Started operations: 1973
Man years of experience: 25
No. of persons on staff: 2
Geographic operation: New York City area

A-Sonic Guard, Inc.
Central Station and Consulting Services
745 South Sixth Street
Louisville, KY 40203
Phone: (502) 584-3117
This company provides recommendations for off-the-shelf security equipment and systems to meet individual client needs, and can install, monitor, and maintain such equipment if desired. Service on local, proprietary, police connect and central station fire and burglar systems is available to small businesses, homes, government buildings, and industry. Experienced staff members are available for lectures to such firms. Supplemented by films, these lectures are "no charge" for groups of 12 or more and the public is encouraged to visit the central station. Specialization is in ultrasonic, infrared and proximity detectors and interfaces; sound monitoring systems transmitted over leased lines; door traps and line security. Future plans call for a computer multiplexing service.
Started operations: 1963
Man years of experience: 120
No. of persons on staff: 25
Geographic operation: Louisville, Kentucky, area

Barnes Engineering Company
30 Commerce Road
Stamford, CT 06904
Phone: (203) 348-5381
This company, in addition to off-the-shelf sales, undertakes the custom design and fabrication of sophisticated security devices meeting unique government and industrial specifications.

Previous customers include the Atomic Energy Commission and the U.S. Army. Specialization is in the area of passive infrared intrusion alarms and includes the following instrumentation for industry and research: Infrared detectors, thermal imaging systems, non-contact thermometers, precision radiometers, infrared (IR) microscopes and microscanners, portable IR thermometers and black bodies, and collimators. The firm has government clearances for highly classified work.

Started operations: 1950
Man years of experience: unavailable
No. of persons on staff: 450
Geographic operation: Customers served nationally

Bellaire Associates
331 Madison Avenue
New York, NY 10017
Phone: (212) 682-2128

This firm specializes in management consulting and performs security surveys. The staff is comprised of professional engineers who have designed security systems for major real estate organizations in the eastern U.S. and consulted with Federal agencies. Specialization is in the field of electronic alarms and communication systems, custom designed access identification systems, volumetric (infrared) alarms, and personal portable emergency transmitters (emergency alarm systems). The security systems for the World Trade Center in New York City were designed by this company. Associates conduct security seminars on such topics as the security of high-rise buildings (an annual seminar attended by managers, owners, and builders).

The Security Systems Institute (founded by Bellaire Associates in 1972) is an independent testing institute for industrial alarm equipment and locking devices; it provides reports and develops handbooks for use by its clients.

Publications: Many specific articles in trade journals
Started operations: 1968
Man years of experience: 100
No. of persons on staff: 10
Geographic operation: Sections of the U.S. and several foreign countries

Benedict & Myrick, Inc.
Office of Special Services
4332 Rhoda Drive
Baton Rouge, LA 70816
Phone: (504) 293-4260 (Baton Rouge)
      (504) 581-4222 (New Orleans)

This company provides consultation and installs equipment for specific security needs, and will custom design and manufacture security items and systems. Staff personnel have formal training in many areas of security, communications, engineering, electronics and business administration and management. Surveillance equipment, CCTV, parking access control, and communications systems are used for deterrence, detection, and control. Guard services are available on a contract basis. The firm develops security planning for new operations, assists in policy planning and prepares manuals of security procedures and personnel training for "turn-key" programs. Officers of the firm are available for speaking engagements on security matters. Previous experience includes U.S. Army intelligence and security. Customers include financial institutions, residences, civic groups, government, commerce, and industry.

Started operations: 1969
Man years of experience: 28
No. of persons on staff: 4
Geographic operation: Louisiana and Southern Mississippi

Braddock, Dunn, and McDonald, Inc.
1920 Aline Avenue
Vienna, VA 22180
Phone: (703) 893-0750
      (505) 266-5711

This corporation performs security system design and installation, operational test and vulnerability evaluation, and system operation and maintenance. It has in-depth experience in the development of requirements and specifications for building and site security systems including hardware, procedures and operations; evaluation of security equipment for both

operational effectiveness and equipment modification; and in the integration of security systems with company methods of operation. The firm is experienced in assuming the "threat" role for system penetration tests.
Started operations: 1960
Man years of experience: 40
No. of persons on staff: 12–15 in security areas with a staff of 700 in other fields
Geographic operation: Offices in Virginia and New Mexico, plus 11 offices nationwide

Bureau of Social Sciences Research Inc.
National Office
1990 M Street, N.W.
Washington, DC 20034
Phone: (202) 223-4300

This organization was originally established as part of The American University, and is now an independent, non-profit, social science research organization with a staff of sociologists, psychologists, and other behavioral scientists. Most of the work done is sponsored by public agencies through contracts and grants. Research programs have dealt with poverty, criminology, education and attitude change—household victimization surveys having been one area of interest. A current large-scale project assesses the effects of financial assistance and employment on recidivism among ex-prisoners. A subsidiary organization, Washington Survey, conducts sample and periodic surveys in the Washington area.
Regular Publications: *BSSR Newsletter* (free)
Recent Publication: *An Inventory of Surveys of the Public on Crime, Justice and Related Topics*
Started operations: 1956
Man years of experience: unavailable
No. of persons on staff: 90
Geographic operation: National and international

J. R. Burris & Associates
Division of Sentinel Security Inc.
700 N. Alabama—Suite 1516
Indianapolis, IN 46284
Phone: (317) 632-6944

This firm consults in security administration and trains personnel of organizations such as hospitals, universities, contract guard services, airport authorities, etc. Manuals have been developed and lectures, on magnetic tape, include five training categories: administration, line personnel, investigation, medical, and general information. A management guidebook is furnished with the instructional materials containing tests, supervisor's guide, evaluation forms, and answer sheets.

The staff has education and field experience in police administration, law, education, journalism and economics. It is not necessary to buy products in order to obtain services.
Started operations: 1970
Man years of experience: 62
No. of persons on staff: 8
Geographic operation: Continental U.S.

Cal Crim Security, Inc.
3625 Hauck Road
P.O. Box 444
Cincinnati, OH 45241
Phone: (513) 554-0500

This company provides security services to commercial organizations on an annual comtract/retainer basis for criminal investigations, embezzlement interrogations, polygraph examinations, undercover operation, pre-employment checking, background investigation, debugging, camera/CCTV surveillance, fingerprinting, personal protection, shopping service, patrol car service, security/safety surveys. Uniformed security officers are also available on request.
Started operations: 1913
Man years of experience: 1000
No. of persons on staff: 130
Geographic operation: Greater Cincinnati, Ohio area and the counties of Butler, Warren and Clermont, Ohio

CES Telecommunications
511 Golf Mill
Niles, IL 60648
Phone: (312) 297-2366
This company offers architectural and engineering support services for the design fo security systems for new buildings or for the remodeling of older structures. Staff capabilities include communication engineering, systems analysis, architectural consultation, telephone and micro-wave engineering, radio, telephone, and microwave data communications, and communications integration. Security systems may be linked to police, fire and other safety agencies. Services include the survey of facilities in order to determine security problems. Recommendations are made for system installation which include engineering specifications, accompanied by inspec-tion of work and acceptance testing.
Started operations: 1969
Man years of experience: 70 or more years
No. of persons on staff: 7
Geographic operation: Eastern, Midwestern and Southern United States

Continental Security Guards, Inc.
4010 North 27th Avenue
Phoenix, AZ 85017
Phone: (602) 264-4193
This firm provides security and consulting services for residences, small business, manufactur-ers, retailers, construction firms and banking institutions. The firm provides uniformed security guards, mobile patrol service, armored car and courier service, and "U.L. Approved" alarm systems. Commercial polygraph services are available for pre-employment tests and criminal investigations. Pilferage control services include undercover observation and loss prevention surveillance for factories and warehouses. Consultation and installation services include review of premises, cost estimate, and bid specifications.
Started operations: 1956
Man years of experience: 160
No. of persons on staff: 450
Geographic operation: Arizona, western New Mexico, and southern California

Cooper VideoCommunications, Inc.
Box 597
South Orange, NJ 07079
Phone: (201) 763-6147
This company specializes in the design of training systems which use audiovisual media. Recent projects have included teaching truck drivers how to prevent and combat pilferage. The services of the firm are available to law enforcement agencies seeking to understand the motivation of criminals and petty thieves from a psychological standpoint. A self-interviewing technique has been developed to strengthen personnel selection procedures.
Started operations: 1970
Man years of experience: 75
No. of persons on staff: 12
Geographic operation: United States, Canada, and Europe

Crime-Specific
P.O. Box 96
Aptos, CA 95003
Phone: (408) 475-0535
This company assists law enforcement personnel in felony control by giving consulting services and seminars in five areas: creation of new crime control programs and implementation of proven methods; planning security measures; upgrading the efficiency and effectiveness of existing operations by training personnel in new methods and how to evaluate their success; improving the "image" of law enforcement activities and the development of programs to secure citizen support, cooperation, and involvement; and the creation of successful public liaison programs.
Consultants with this company are knowledgeable in: law enforcement, felony control tech-niques and strategies, systems analysis, research techniques, program evaluation, resources allocation and planning, drug abuse control, the activities of organized crime, intelligence

methods, and the organization and regulations governing both state planning agencies and LEAA.
Started operations: 1973
Man years of experience: 37
No. of persons on staff: 3 consultants available for specific need
Geographic operation: United States

D-CO-Inc.
P.O. Box 5362
Santa Fe, NM 87501
Phone: (505) 983-1594

This firm provides consulting, planning and assessment services for high level security applications. Capabilities include: electronic engineering, engineering analysis, planning and layout, cost estimates, and report documentation. Security equipment recommendations are made on the basis of product performance and reliability; essential items can be fabricated when proper off-the-shelf components are not available. Clients have included the U.S. Army, National Guard, pipeline firms and institutions such as museums.
Started operations: 1970
Man years of experience: 75
No. of persons on staff: 6-8
Geographic operation: New Mexico and adjoining states, California, and the East Coast

Eastman Middleton Associates, Inc.
1748 Elm Drive
Kent, OH 44240
Phone: (216) 678-1346

This firm provides public management and criminal justice consulting services to public and private sectors. The firm provides: coordination and consolidation of records and communications systems for police departments; grantsmanship service—aiding agencies and non-profit groups to secure state and federal monies; training of personnel in the techniques of law enforcement as they are applicable to the private security field; security policy and personnel management when client needs such help; and can design automated systems to provide security, accounting, budgeting, telecommunications, and statistical processing of management information.
Recent Publications: *The Citizen and the Police in Scotts Bluff County, Nebraska—An Opinion Study and Analysis. 1972.*
Started operations: 1957
Man years of experience: 280–300 years
No. of persons on staff: 15
Geographic operation: National

Tom Kinley & Associates
1511 K Street, N.W., Suite 410
Washington, DC 20005
Phone: (202) 293-4327

This company provides consulting services on the problems of cargo theft and pilferage for industrial and government installations such as airports. Services include the development of methods for approaching the problem, hardware recommendations, monitoring of installations, and the training of employees on new security equipment. The firm is affiliated with three companies which sell an anti-hijacking device, but specialization lies in electronic surveillance equipment.
Started operations: 1962
Man years of experience: 300
No. of persons on staff: 18
Geographic operation: Nationwide

Gage-Babcock & Associates Inc.
9836 W. Roosevelt Road
P.O. Box 270
Westchester, IL 60153
Phone: (312) 345-8541

This firm specializes in integrating fire protection, safety and security into systems design. Criteria for the security of buildings and premises are developed for architects, along with

competitive bid specifications and evaluations. Problems such as personnel, equipment, and physical structure (but not private detective work) are examined in risk analyses of present buildings. Loss control recommendations generally cover external theft opportunities rather than employee dishonesty.
Started operations: 1952
Man years of experience: 200
No. of persons on staff: 24
Geographic operation: Nationwide, with local offices. The firm is independent of suppliers, contractors, or insurance affiliations.

General Nucleonics, Inc.
Sentronic International Division
P.O. Box 116
Brunswick, OH 44212
Phone: (216) 225-3029
  This company designs industrial security systems to reduce internal theft, shoplifting, and pilferage. Specific equipment recommendations are made, evaluation, equipment installation, and personnel training are provided. Custom fabrication is available for specific client needs. For example, physical controls (turnstiles) are fabricated for unique commercial and industrial situations, and electronics have been applied to a system to deter hijacking and prevent counterfeiting of copyrighted, patented, secret and trademarked materials. Past projects have included the installation of minicomputer systems, development of library loss controls, and the design of a secure industrial park.
Started operations: 1961
Man years of experience: 100
No. of persons on staff: 21
Geographic operation: National and international. This firm does sell equipment manufactured by company affiliates.

Ben Goldberg
R & D Management Consultant
8717 Sundale Drive
Silver Spring, MD 20910
Phone: (301) 588-9430
  An independent consultant on matters dealing with the selection and assessment of systems or devices for security purposes, with special emphasis in optical and electro-optical techniques. Experience has included extensive R & D work in the sophisticated equipment used for operation and surveillance at night. Equipment developed under Mr. Goldberg's directorship of the Night Vision Laboratory at Ft. Belvoir, Virginia (retired 1973) included searchlights, image intensifiers, active infrared and thermal viewers as well as intrusion detection devices employing magnetic induction, acoustic and ultrasonic techniques, and various types of radiation beam breakers.
Started operations: 1973
Man years of experience: 25
No. of persons on staff: Principal only
Geographic operation: Nationwide

Gulf South Research Institute
800 GSRI Avenue
Baton Rouge, LA 70808
Phone: (504) 766-3300
  Carries out feasibility and action research projects in the social sciences, with strong emphasis on the criminal justice system aspects. Research is chiefly for courts, corrections institutions and law enforcement agencies. Research has included telecommunications studies, custom-designing of computer programs for jury selection, computerization of criminal histories, systems analysis of courts and corrections agencies, case load management and projection, and evaluation of existing physical security to prevent illegal access to computer areas.
Started operations: 1965
Man years of experience: A team for a given project has an average of 6 years professional experience.
No. of persons on staff: 99 professionals
Geographic operation: United States

James P. Hackett
7240 N. Olcott Avenue
Chicago, IL 60648
Phone: (312) 774-5220

This organization consults for private plants needing loss prevention control and improved physical security. Services include system design, equipment specifications for electronic hardware items, identification cameras, sensors, CCTV systems, management and organization security surveys, incentive programs, and analysis of guard service needs.

As a consultant for the Service Bureau of the Illinois Chiefs of Police services are provided to rural and suburban police agencies for LEAA-funded management and organization surveys. Expertise is applied to improve central dispatch communications and manpower response capability. Electronic work and fire estimates are contracted to other firms.

Previous experience includes civilian, U.S. Navy and detective security professional work with the Illinois Chiefs of Police, and teaching of law enforcement.

Started operations: 1971
Man years of experience: 70
No. of persons on staff: 2
Geographic operation: Northern Illinois

Harris & Walsh Management Consultants, Inc.
P.O. Box 698 (271 North Avenue)
New Rochelle, NY 10802
Phone: (914) 576-0820

This firm offers comprehensive consulting services on security vulnerability studies, including risk appraisals, dollar loss, critical loss ratios; countermeasures selection and design, comprising alarms, fences, lights, and other electronic devices; and crime prevention through proper staffing and training of security personnel. Plant protection, fire and disaster control, emergency preparedness, fraud and theft prevention, and the overall protection of physical and informational assets are also areas of capability. Services are rendered internationally to industrial, mercantile, other commercial organizations and government agencies.

Publications: "Protection of Assets Manual" (comprehensive subscription service supplemented monthly). *Industrial Security Management,* 1971 by American Management Association. *Protecting Your Business Against Espionage,* 1973 by American Management Association.

Started operations: 1964
Man years of experience: 75
No. of persons on staff: 3 plus other consultants required
Geographic operation: International

John H. Herder Associates, Inc.
P.O. Box 5473
Hamden, CT 06518
Phone: (203) 248-9817

This firm provides consulting services to business and industry, with specialization on problems of security. Makes recommendations on improvement of managerial effectiveness, management reporting and information, cost effectiveness, performance evaluation, goalsetting, and management training and coaching. Among the techniques used to focus the attention of management on the need for security are role playing, group discussion and case analysis. Specifications for equipment are not provided.

Publications: *The Herder Report*
Started operations: 1970
No. of persons on staff: 4 (varies depending upon project)
Geographic operation: United States

IData, Inc.
63 East 64th Street
New York City, NY 10021
Phone: (212) 472-8818

This firm offers a customized credentials identification service to banks, small police departments, social service organizations, utilities, investigators and special agents. Service users complete an information form along with a passport quality photograph. IData manufactures the ID card and returns it to the applicant directly or thru a sponsoring organization. The

original photograph and signature card remain on file for revision or reissue purposes. Consulting services are offered for forged identification paper problems.
Started operations: 1972
Man years of experience: unavailable
No. of persons on staff: share staff w/a sister organization varies from 2–9
Geographic operation: National and international

IMMCO (Inventive Manufacturing and Marketing Co.)
949 South East Street
P.O. Box 6334
Anaheim, CA 92806
Phone: (714) 533-0800
   This company is primarily a research and development organization. Capabilities include prototype development and production, electronic assembly, design and testing, and research and engineering of electrical, electro-mechanical and mechanical equipment and systems including those intended primarily for security purposes. Services are available to state and Federal governments, major commercial/industrial firms and small business. Among the security and monitoring devices or technologies developed have been skyjack prevention methods, armor plating of police and commercial car fleets, sniper-locating devices, freeway safety systems, fire suppression systems, anti-intrusion alarms, remote monitoring security systems, ammunition bunker security screens, vehicle/camper anti-theft devices, and a universal missile control console. Customers include the U.S. Navy, Air Force, Coast Guard, and commercial concerns.
Started operations: 1970
Man years of experience: 640
No. of persons on staff: 31
Geographic operation: Nationwide

International Art Registry (U.K.) Ltd.
111 John Street, Room 1508
New York, NY 10038
Phone: (212) 374-6371
   This company offers a patented process to create an individual, one-of-a-kind, "fingerprint" profile for works of art which identifies but does not alter the work of art. The program includes recording the art object at the Registry's Central File Library, and at ARTCENTRAL, a public service which receives information from verifiable sources about the thefts and possibilities for recovery of fine art pieces irrespective of whether such items have or have not been filed with the Registry.
Started operations: 1971
Man years of experience: 75
No. of persons on staff: 14
Geographic operation: United States

Kelly Scientific Corporation
3900 Wisconsin Avenue, N.W.
Washington, DC 20016
Phone: (202) 966-6800
   This firm specializes in the design and evaluation of communications equipment required by police, correctional facilities and the criminal justice community. Work has included command and control systems for fire and police departments, configuration and design of communications for county jails and lock-up facilities; and development of electronic and mechanical security systems for the educational and training facilities in correctional and rehabilitation programs. Currently, the firm is developing equipment for the automation and telecommunication of law enforcement records for police, investigative, detention, and court activities.
Started operations: 1966
Man years of experience: 120
No. of persons on staff: 15
Geographic operation: East of the Mississippi

Kliever & Thomas Securi-T-Systems
Box 136
Gates Mille, OH 44040
Phone: (216) 432-4440
   This firm consults in the design of electronic security and emergency systems which provide silent alarms for identifying fire, loss and attack against persons, small businesses, homes and their contents. The specified systems include such equipment as ultrasonic detectors, heat and smoke detectors, microwave detection systems, strain gages, CCTV and still cameras, infrared devices, automatic telephone dialers, and pilferage detection devices. Systems planning covers selection, installation and testing of sensors, controls and communications. Staff has experience and training in physics, making sophisticated measurements, developing instrumentation, designing security systems and digital control. Holds several patents for security devices.
Started operations: 1971
Man years of experience: 25
No. of persons on staff: 2
Geographic operation: Nationwide

Koepsell-Girard and Associates, Inc.
Two-Ten East Broad Street
Falls Church, VA 22046
Phone: (703) 532-7737
   This organization provides a variety of planning and research services in the security and crime prevention fields. It serves police departments, state criminal justice planning agencies, college and universities; specializing in crime prevention program development, training and evaluation. Recent projects include the preparation of a five -year program plan for the National Crime Prevention Institute and the development of an 80-hour training curriculum for the Texas Crime Prevention Institute. It has also evaluated the programs of several local crime prevention bureaus and is updating a state in-service crime prevention training program.
Started operations: 1970
Man years of experience: unavailable
No. of persons on staff: 12
Geographic operation: Nationwide

Jay Mallin
406 Savona Avenue
Coral Gables, FL 33146
Phone: (305) 667-3832
   An independent consultant providing program development, security evaluation, and lectures to U.S. individuals or firms desiring protection from terrorist activities abroad. Experience includes 20 years as a journalist abroad, specializing in news of military affairs and terrorism, and staff work at the University of Miami Center for Advanced International Studies.
Publications: *Terror in Viet Nam, Terror and Urban Guerrillas*
Started operations: 1970
Man years of experience: 4 (related to security)
No. of persons on staff: principal
Geographic operation: Latin America

Management Safeguards, Inc.
National Headquarters, Two Park Avenue
New York, NY 10016
Phone: (212) 532-7150
   The Consulting Division of Management Safeguards offers surveys of physical security, operational procedures and accounting controls to identify exposures to loss, and to enable development and implementation of security plans. Physical security planning defines the need for alarm and locking devices, employee and visitor controls, communications, lighting, access controls, shipping and receiving dock protection, annunciator consoles, manpower deployment, and security requirements in new buildings or existing facilities. Operational security considerations include the redesign of procedures to protect the company from dishonest executives, collusive theft by employees, embezzlement by accounting personnel, inventory manipulation by department heads, kickbacks to purchasing agents, or loss of operational procedures and cash and information flow. Other services available include undercover investigations, guard and patrol services, polygraph examinations, special investigations, and crime laboratory analysis.

"Loss Prevention Institute," an affiliate of Management Safeguards, Inc., was established to train and motivate middle management to spot and minimize security hazards. Seminars, booklets and a supervisory training film are among the teaching aids employed.
Started operations: 1958
Man years of experience: over 2,000
Geographic operation: New York, New Jersey, New England, Chicago, Atlanta, and Miami

Mankind Research Unlimited, Inc.
1325 1/2 Wisconsin Avenue, N.W.
Washington, DC 20007
Phone: (202) 337-7270
This company deals essentially with scientifically-oriented research and development, for publications and products. It provides consulting services in the areas of psychological screening and stress evaluation (using the voice analysis polygraph), technical expertise in tracking objects or vehicles and wire-tapping detection. The firm is also agent for the sale of a metal-detector device produced by an associate organization.
Man Started operations: 1972
Man years of experience: unavailable
No. of persons on staff: 150
Geographic operation: United States and Europe

Marlborough Intelligence
P.O. Box 13
Upper Marlboro, MD 20870
Phone: (301) 952-0909
This firm offers a variety of services, including security consulting and general intelligence investigations. Procedures consist of investigation of undercover activities such as espionage, internal theft, embezzlement, and pilferage; consulting services are available for the design of internal controls for personnel, equipment, and premises. Recommendations for security systems are made for business and industry after surveys of premises and operations. Staff personnel are authors of *Security Management Systems*.
Started operations: 1970
Man years of experience: 50
No. of persons on staff: 2 and associates as required
Geographic operation: Maryland, New Jersey and licensed under Maryland State Private
  Detective License

McManis Associates, Inc.
1120 Connecticut Avenue, N.W.
Washington, DC 20036
Phone: (202) 296-1355
This firm employs systems engineering methodology to develop pre-architectural specifications for operational configurations including security. Attention is given to security program planning and evaluation, defining objectives, identifying protective needs, and allocating resources.
Management information systems through computer technology applications are designed as needed. Management by objectives is the philosophy governing recommendations made for changes in operational procedures. Specialists are employed on an as-needed basis. Clients have included city and Federal government, associations and colleges.
Started operations: 1964
Man years of experience: 1975
No. of persons on staff: 22
Geographic operation: Nationwide

The Mentoris Company
55 Capitol Mall
Sacramento, CA 95814
Phone: (916) 444-2956
        (408) 286-3515
This firm provides management/engineering consulting services in building security, particularly communications/alarm systems and prison equipment problems. Special skills include study and design of communications, alarm control and dispatch systems in manufacturing and

commercial sites; test, evaluation and comparison of sophisticated security equipment; systems/equipment trouble shooting, working at the staff/hardware interface to uncover reasons for failure or non-optimum functioning; one-of-a-kind hardware design and build-for-concept evaluation; and preparation of statements of work and specifications for equipment and systems. Security problems are analyzed using threat analyses, and software and hardware is developed to counter identified threats. The firm has carried out a study of Corrections and Youth Authority facilities of California. New products are being developed such as "SCAN," an ultra-sonic personal alarm system, and the "Automated Attendance Management System" to provide real-time monitoring of personnel work stations which should be manned.
Started operations: 1970
Man years of experience: 100
No. of persons on staff: 4 senior staff plus consultants on standing agreements
Geographic operation: United States

Morgan Electronics
20700 Corsair Blvd.
Hayward, CA 94540
Phone: (415) 785-7200
  This company specializes in the design, engineering, installation, and service of both perimeter and internal access control systems. Typical products are automatic gate and door operators used in apartment house and industrial perimeter security. Additional capability includes the design of card access systems for central control, multiplexing, perimeter laser systems, and security intercom equipment (as used in apartment complexes).
Started operations: 1953
Man years of experience: 175
No. of persons on staff: 25-30
Geographic operation: The 11 Western states, with national coverage on a selective basis

National Data Systems, Inc.
210 Summit Avenue
Montvale, NJ 07645
Phone: (201) 391-0400
  This firm offers consulting, systems analysis, design and implementation of micro- and minicomputer systems for use in the security field. Typical applications include: automated remote sensor monitoring, validity checking of signals, threat evaluation (based on sequence and pattern of sensor changes), data logging, access control automatic message composition and distribution, data base storage, retrieval and update of security related information, credit card validation, teleprocessing information to other locations, and a simplified method of transmitting secure data via telephone.
Started operations: 1950
Man years of experience: 95
No. of persons on staff: 5
Geographic operation: New Jersey, New York, and other specific requests

North American Systems Corporation
Grenier Industrial Village, Box 375
Londonderry, NH 03053
Phone: (603) 669-0794
  This firm provides consulting services in support of research and development in the field of security devices and systems, with major expertise in infrared and radio frequency devices. The company has developed an infrared intrusion alarm (not yet in production), an article surveillance system, and is presently engaged in the development of a mathematical model for evaluation of programs and activities in the criminal justice field. Testing and evaluation of security systems and components is also a specialty.
  A systems approach is used to examine technical/social systems with the purpose of establishing an objective (quantitative) basis for judgement. Services are available to Federal, state and local government as well as to private industry.
Started operations: 1968
Man years of experience: 28
No. of persons on staff: 3, up to 20 additional available
Geographic operation: National and international

Odgen Security, Inc.
111 Waldenmar Avenue
P.O. Box 81
East Boston, MA 02128
Phone: (617) 569-6400

This company provides a full range of security services including consultation, investigation, supplying guard and patrol personnel, staff training and technical advice. The company management is comprised of former FBI agents and administrators of major city police departments. Clients include financial, insurance, business, industrial, institutional, government, commercial and professional sports interests.

Services offered include review and evaluation of architectural specifications to determine measures needed to maximize the total security environment of buildings and complexes, administrative analysis and equipment system planning for police agencies, training of security forces, patrolling, recommendations for bank security, loss prevention control and employee investigations, countermeasures, and provisions of administrative and technical experts in law enforcement fields.

Started operations: 1972
Man years of experience: unavailable
No. of persons on staff: 950
Geographic operation: Local offices in many major cities

James W. O'Neil, Inc.
25 Massachusetts Avenue
Braintree, MA 02184
Phone: (617) 843-8653

An independent consultant specializing in preventing losses from burglary, employee theft, robbery, vandalism, espionage and other criminal activities. Consultation is available for help with problem assessment, analysis of procedures and techniques, improvement in security equipment and service, supervision of acquisition and installation of systems and devices and review of overall security conditions. Surveys include the evaluation of physical security arrangements, review of personnel hiring and training in security; comparison of security policies versus actual practices and recommendations for developing and implementing security programs.

Loss prevention systems analysis covers the study of internal control procedures through discussion with employees, improvement of employee attitudes toward security and development of measures to insure prevention system integrity. Investigations cover assembling of evidence and statement for use in criminal prosecutions. Technical equipment and undercover agents are available.

Started operations: 1973
Man years of experience: 24
No. of persons on staff: Principal only
Geographic operation: Greater Boston area and nationwide

Henry L. Orwitz/Investigations
P.O. Box 1353
Santa Cruz, CA 95061
Phone: (408) 426-4466

This firm specializes in one-time problem solving and recommendations. Clients include law enforcement agencies, courts, industry and individuals. Investigations may employ electronic surveillance or countermeasures; determination of the presence of phone taps; analysis of audio aircraft crash tapes, ground-to-aircraft tapes, and records from personal recording devices; consultations on surveillance of information-recording both audio and visual; and the location of missing persons. Other services include consultation on the security of both premises and personnel, security in new buildings, reduction of internal theft, security hardware selection and planning the protection of confidential company information and communications.

Started operations: 1970
Man years of experience: 48
No. of persons on staff: 5
Geographic operation: San Francisco Bay area and throughout the world

PRC Public Management Services, Inc.(PRC/PMS)
7600 Old Springhouse Road
McLean, VA 22101
Phone: (703) 893-1830
(Formerly SSDC - Systems Science Development Corporation)

This company provides services to public and private agencies for organization and management analysis, program evaluation, resource allocation, information systems design and implementation, facilities design, crime-specific planning, evaluation of anti-crime countermeasures, design of correctional systems, and the training of personnel for administration, fiscal control and reporting. Through the variety of its project experience, PRC/PMS has acquired an extensive background and staff capability in the disciplines of the criminal justice system. In addition to their project experience, key management and consulting staff members have contributed to the professional criminal justice literature.

Publications: Maintains facility to store documents and reports generated
Started operations: 1964
Man years of experience: 846
No. of persons on staff: 90–100
Geographic operation: Nationwide

Pacemaker Planning
3617 Lexington Road
Louisville, KY 40207
Phone: (502) 987-5756
          (502) 454-0225

This firm analyzes, evaluates, and makes recommendations to wholesale or retail business chains on how to reduce the loss of cash and high-value merchandise due to employee theft, shoplifting, armed robbery and burglary.

Crime reduction recommendations emphasize environmental redesign through attention to lighting arrangements, display techniques, interior design, exterior landscaping and control of parking patterns, aisle and customer-flow control, and management and employee training. Recommendations focus on changes in business procedures and physical plant modifications rather than on installation of hardware devices or use of sentry personnel.

Services also include the preparation of plans and the evaluation of programs for state and local criminal justice offices and other agencies in the areas of crime prevention, allocation or training of patrols, reorganization of resources, and specific crime-reducing tactics. Community-based juvenile or adult correctional programs are developed, and existing community-based treatment programs are evaluated.

Started operations: 1973
Man years of experience: 60
No. of persons on staff: 4 part-time and 4 full time
Geographic operation: Midwest and Southern United States

Per Mar Security & Research Corporation
P.O. Box 4227
Davenport, IA 52808
Phone: (319) 326-6291

This firm, in addition to guard service, provides security assistance to reduce shoplifting and internal theft; performs pre-employment polygraph examination, personnel background-investigations, undercover services; and completes alarm systems engineering using off-the-shelf equipment. Most applications of these services are one time, in response to specific problems recognized by the client.

Other services include central station supervision of burglar, robbery, and emergency alarm systems such as watchman reporting systems, industrial process and boiler supervision and automatic fire and evacuation alarms.

Started operations: 1952
Man years of experience: 250
No. of persons on staff: 9 key staff plus 841 guards, investigators and other staff
Geographic operation: Iowa, Illinois, Minnesota, Nebraska, Kansas, Missouri

Perkin Private Police
211 N. California Street
P.O. Box 1627
Stockton, CA 95201
Phone: (209) 948-1201

This company provides consulting, protective, and surveillance services to small businesses and industry. Capabilities in consulting include: general security surveys, hardware evaluation, training program recommendations and services recommendations. Protective services include installation and maintenance of leased and individually owned equipment, guard and patrol service, guard dogs, and underwater security and recovery. Central alarm service is not available from this company.
Started operations: 1970
Man years of experience: unavailable
No. of persons on staff: 10
Geographic operation: California San Joaquin Delta area; holder of a state license

Photo Security Systems, Inc.
Subsidiary of Cir-Tech, Inc.
3905 California Street, N.E.
Minneapolis, MN 55421
Phone: (612) 788-8611

This firm provides security consultation and system design services for government, industry and businesses desiring visual surveillance systems to combat pilferage, shoplifting and unauthorized entry and to provide employee protection in parking lot areas. Check protection is provided for banks, retail stores, rental agencies, freight terminals, truck terminals and airline credit card/travel cards. Services include surveys of business practices such as check cashing procedures and analysis of problems with bad checks; security recommendations and specifications; seminars and training by means of slides and lectures; and on-the-job training for police, community, merchant and bank organizations. Other specialization is in CCTV, video, film and low-light level systems for access/entry control or surveillance support and photo and photo-optical equipment. Electronic, mechanical and systems engineering services are also provided. The firm also has dealerships for a variety of equipment.
Started operations: 1958
Man years of experience: 23
No. of persons on staff: 3 professional consultants
Geographic operation: Minneapolis/St. Paul and Central Minnesota area; covers 5-state area
Member American Society for Industrial Security

Richard S. Post & Associates
901 Williams Boulevard
Springfield, IL 62704
Phone: (217) 753-2049

This organization develops security policy for corporate clients. Analysis includes company philosophy toward prosecution, control of operations, its use of discretion in making security audits, and the company goals and objectives. Game theory and simulation techniques are applied to the training of management personnel in security/loss prevention; and instructional materials such as videotapes and slides are used. Location-specific presentations are prepared for security guard training programs.

In its crime prevention activities, the firm specializes in improving the working relationship and exchange of resources among private police and law enforcement agencies within a community. Public education materials and concepts are also provided. Mr. Post is a consultant to IACP (International Association of Chiefs of Police) for Public Education.

Published work includes several texts on security and crime prevention. One publication, *Security Education Briefs,* can be obtained from Nickerson-Collins Publishers, Des Plaines, Illinois.
Started operations: 1973
Man years of experience: 75
No. of persons on staff: 7
Geographic operation: Nationwide, with an emphasis on Midwestern states

John W. Powell Consultants, Inc.
4400 Whitney Avenue
Hamden, CT 06518
Phone: (203) 248-2985
   This firm specializes in the security problems of large, complex installations such as college and school campuses, utility and insurance companies, atomic power stations, business and industrial establishments and computer centers. Experience includes the development of proprietary control systems and the training and organization of back-up security personnel. Assistance is also provided to architects in the planning and design of security systems and programs for new facilities such as civic centers, large shopping/office complexes, high rise apartments and condominiums. All services include analysis, study, recommendations for equipment and procedures, bid specifications, and training as required. This firm has no sales or product affiliations.
Started operations: 1968
Man years of experience: 100
No. of persons on staff: 4
Geographic operation: Primarily the Northeast, but available anywhere

Professional Investigations Company
5108 West Wells Street
Milwaukee, WI 53208
Phone: (414) 475-5585
   This firm conducts investigations in security areas such as: pre-employment screening, periodic background and follow-up checks of current employees and undercover assignment within client companies. Consultation is offered in loss control, business, industry, and some individuals. Guard services and private police are not provided.
Started operations: 1971
Man years of experience: 3
No. of persons on staff: varies with needs
Geographic operation: Limited by license to Wisconsin

Profitect Inc.
Professional Protection Consultants
At Wharfside, 680 Beach Street
San Francisco, CA 94109
Phone: (415) 283-3802
        (415) 283-0511
Los Angeles (213) 786-4605
   This firm provides consultation for comprehensive protection programs as well as systems and engineering guidance in equipment selection to architects, commerce, industry, hospitals, financial institutions and data centers. Recent projects include the following: nationwide survey of security practices of credit card associations; security guidance and educational program for a major eastern stock exchange; a continuing series of executive level law enforcement seminars for the California Department of Justice (LEAA funded); and security advice to architects for the Yerba Buena Convention Center and Sports Arena, San Francisco.
Started operations: 1960
Man years of experience: 65
No. of persons on staff: 3 (10 additional staff associates with special backgrounds)
Geographic operation: National

Protection Systems
10961 Bloomfield Street
Los Alamitos, CA 90720
Phone: (213) 430-0786
        (714) 826-0880
   This firm offers security consultation and design work for public utilities, major shopping centers, large professional buildings, government agencies, state prison and police agencies, with some custom design of equipment. Specialties include design-layout, installation, and maintenance of the following bank security systems, outdoor systems and access control, central alarms and closed circuit television.

A study done in 1972 was on "The Effect of Alarm Systems upon Residential Burglaries in the City of Seal Beach."
Started operations: 1967
Man years of experience: 50
No. of persons on staff: 10
Geographic operation: Greater Los Angeles area

Public Research and Management, Inc.
157 Luckie Street, N.W.
Atlanta, GA 30303
Phone: (404) 525-5687

This firm provides management and other consulting services in the area of public safety and protection (police and fire). The firm prepares and publishes organization and management studies, manuals, statutes and ordinances for legislative, executive and judicial branches. Projects are usually carried out at city and county levels on subjects such as reorganization of court systems.
Started operations: 1967
Man years of experience: 100
No. of persons on staff: 15
Geographic operation: Southeastern United States

Public Safety Systems Incorporated (PSSI)
P.O. Box 30410
Santa Barbara, CA 93105
Phone: (805) 964-6737

This company provides assistance to municipal. county, state, and Federal government in the solution of public safety problems. Specific examples include: resource management, communications, command and control, activity analysis, long-range and contingency planning. information systems design and development, evaluation and treatment of drug and alcohol abuse. Recent projects: South Bay Cities Regional/Communications Study; Command and Control System Design for the City of Portland/Multnomah County, Oregon; and Long-range Planning Study for the Los Angeles Sheriff's Department.

The firm will design systems, write specifications, and evaluate or oversee system implementation bids. It does not manufacture or sell products.
Started operations: 1969
Man years of experience: 350
No. of persons on staff: 35
Geographic operation: Nationwide

Raytheon Service Company
Subsidiary of Raytheon Company
12 Second Avenue
Burlington, ME 01803
Phone: (617) 272-9300

This company provides systems engineering services in security analyses and the design, development, and installation of protection systems, including those operated completely on the "turn-key" principle. Analysis includes comprehensive review of the facilities, evaluation and recommendation of system elements, development of specifications for equipment procurement and installation of the equipment. Documentation and specific personnel indoctrination and training are provided for turn-key systems.

Projects have been completed for major U.S. utilities, correctional institutions, and highrise Federal Centers in major cities. The Service Company sells no equipment.
Started operations: 1968
Man years of experience: 50
No. of persons on staff: 5
Geographic operation: Nationwide

John E. Reid Associates
Suite 1208
600 South Michigan Ave.
Chicago, IL 60605
Phone: (312) 922-1800
   This firm utilizes a psychological test, The Reid Report, designed to identify dishonest job applicants by means of a pencil-and-paper test. Three main sections are included in the test: a measure of punitiveness, attitudes and behavior related to theft; a detailed biographical section; and a list of questions to which a specific response constitutes an admission of committed theft or other embezzlement or defaulting. Polygraph examinations for criminal, civil and preemployment cases are also performed. Seminars are offered on a nationwide basis which place emphasis on the principles and legality of interrogations. The Reid College of Polygraph, part of the firm, offers a degree in polygraph science.
Publications: Books—*Truth and Deception: Polygraph (Lie Detector) Techniques* (1966 and 1974)
Started operations: 1947
Man years of experience: 250
No. of persons on staff: 25
Geographic operation: International

Saber Laboratories, Inc.
1150 Bryant Street
San Francisco, CA 94103
Phone: (415) 431-4707
   This firm manufactures security countermeasure systems for detecting industrial spies who utilize illegal, clandestine eavesdropping devices. Countermeasure surveys (sweeps or searches for hidden listening devices) are performed for persons or companies who do not have their own personnel or equipment for such work. Service is available in Western States only.
Publications: Various articles in newspapers, magazines, periodicals
Started operations: 1965
Man years of experience: 40
No. of persons on staff: 8
Geographic operation: U.S. and foreign countries friendly to the U.S.

Sachs/Freeman Associates, Inc.
7515 Annapolis Road
Hyattsville, MD 20784
Phone: (301) 577-8630
   This firm provides consulting services and independent equipment evaluations to organizations interested in antipilferage and CCTV surveillance systems. Major emphasis is on the design of two-way radio systems which includes the coordination of frequency assignments for police, fire, or other public safety service such as emergency medical services and reducing radio frequency interference. Specialization is in the area of design and evaluation of these systems and in specification development. Installations are subcontracted. In addition to the engineering services offered, the management sciences area provides assistance in project control, cost benefit ratios, and PERT charts, while the computer sciences branch offers programming support.
Started operations: 1969
Man years of experience: 40
No. of persons on staff: 4
Geographic operation: Washington, D.C. area

Security Communications, Inc.
251-12 Hillside Avenue
Bellerose, NY 11426
Phone: (212) 343-4400
   This company provides consulting services for small businesses, private homes, and apartments in need of security protection during working and non-working hours. Capabilities include home and business security surveys, hardware recommendations and installation, equipment leasing and maintenance for central station use and systems design when necessary. Specialization is in the area of ultrasonic detectors, proximity detectors, closed circuit television, interfaces with central station and police alarm systems, and armed guard response.

Started operations: 1967
Man years of experience: 132
No. of persons on staff: 23
Geographic operation: New York, New Jersey, Connecticut, and Pennsylvania

Security Consultants
5670 Wilshire Boulevard
Los Angeles, CA 90054
Phone: (213) 937-2123

This firm provides consulting services for large and small businesses including systems analysis and bid specifications for the physical security of various kinds of facilities, stock and pilferage "shrinkage" control, employee investigations through polygraph examination and other techniques, as well as general investigations including anti-wiretapping and debugging. Two security awareness films have been prepared for use by police departments, industry, commerce and security firms: "A Happy Family Is," which looks at the apartment dweller and homeowner, and "Do You Want to Think It Over Again," which looks at small business crime problems. Custom training films are also produced.

Started operations: 1971
Man years of experience: 25
No. of persons on staff: 4 full-time employees and specialists as needed
Geographic operation: U.S. and Europe

Security Perception Unlimited, Inc.
181 Old Post Road
Southport, CT 06490
Phone: (203) 259-7490

This firm provides consultation in industrial espionage, employee theft, and security system planning and application. An extensive security library is maintained which includes many out-of-print and unpublished works, crime and security literature and related doctoral theses. The firm president is the author of current texts, for example, *Library Security and Combatting Terrorism.* Past experience includes the design and presentation of courses for the International Association of Chiefs of Police (IACP) covering terrorism, school security, and risk management.

Started operations: 1971
Man years of experience: 80
No. of persons on staff: 4
Geographic operation: Eastern U.S., and some international clients

Sentor Security Group, Inc.
17 Battery Place
New York, NY 10004
Phone: (212) 425-8555

The Security Consulting Division of Sentor Security Group performs analyses of assets, operations and possible threats in the surrounding environment to identify security needs, establish security policy and define the security program. Assistance is provided in implementing security programs in areas such as: management, auditing, electronic equipment, maintenance planning, data processing security, internal controls, document controls, education programs and emergency action planning.

Experience includes communications, computer science, and vehicle location techniques. The Engineering Division provides computer based command and control systems for law enforcement agencies. Other divisions engineer, specify and procure electronic devices; train personnel; perform both general pre-employment and specific personnel investigations; conduct research; do complete investigations; and provide guard service.

Publications: A senior staff member is principal author of the Federal Information Processing Standards Publication 31 "Guidelines for Automatic Data Processing: Physical Security and Risk Management."

Started operations: 1967
Man years of experience: unavailable
No. of persons on staff: 300
Geographic operation: Nationwide

Stanley Smith Security, Inc.
211 Olmos Drive West
San Antonio, TX 78212
Phone: (512) 824-0564
   This company provides consultation, planning and the implementation of security measures through audits, surveys, and protection of the point-of-sales. Hardware recommendations and security system design are also available. The specific services available include: executive protection, pre-employment polygraph screening, civil and criminal investigations, expert witness testimony, night patrol and guard service, and shopping service (to assess customer treatment, employee attitudes, demeanor and appearance). Implementation of services involves installation, maintenance and monitoring of local, central and proprietary alarms.
Started operations: 1928
Man years of experience: unavailable
No. of persons on staff: 1000
Geographic operation: National and international

Stanford Research Institute (SRI)
(Office of Research Operations)
333 Ravenswood Avenue
Menlo Park, CA 94025
Phone: (415) 326-6200 x2756
   This institute provides security systems research, consultation, and engineering services. Past work has included the following projects: assessment of client security posture; analysis, design, and development of security systems; development of security organization structure, policies, operating procedures, training and equipment; and market analyses of security services and hardware. Specialist consultation is provided in such areas as: criminal motivation and methodology; law enforcement operations; security system hardware; computer systems; architectural aspects of security; behavioral and physical sciences; electronics and communications engineering; urban and social systems; and economics. The Institute also has the capability to develop prototype devices and systems.
Started operations: 1946
Man years of experience: 270
No. of persons on staff: 18 senior professionals; support available from 1450 scientists and
   engineers
Geographic operation: United States and overseas; offices in Washington, D.C. Huntsville,
   Alabama, Great Britain, Switzerland, and elsewhere

Systech Corporation
Codd Professional Building
Severna Park, MD 21146
Phone: (301) 647-6668
   This company specializes in techniques to interface communications systems with security-related telemetry for remote surveillance; monitors equipment and premises to provide protection from sabotage or natural causes (e.g. wind) using visual, audio, or digital display. Communications/security systems planning includes system design, technical specifications, bid package development, procurement negotiations, and installations. Other services available are clinics to improve client operational procedures and equipment status, analyses of requirements through interviews, onsite inspections and review of past procedures. Alternative systems are offered to meet the needs of individual clients. Past projects have included airports, civil defense, highways, universities, small industries and schools. The firm has developed material for symposia conferences, publications and client reports.
Started operations: 1968
Man years of experience: 40
No. of persons on staff: 12
Geographic operation: National and international

System Development Corporation
2500 Colorado Avenue
Santa Monica, CA 90406
Phone: (213) 393-9411
            (703) 820-2220
   This company designs computer supported systems for telecommunications, the evaluation of major crime prevention programs and large scale physical security systems. It also designs and

installs custom systems for the protection of information in computers and communication networks.

Applications include: implementations of interactive data retrieval systems for courts, probation offices, law enforcement and criminal justice agencies; data management consulting for electronic data processing; and development of transportation dispatching systems. Training is offered for the use, operation, and maintenance of equipment. All systems design work includes specifications for equipment, functions, procedures, information flow and analysis and reporting requirements.

Major crime prevention programs evaluated include: the burglary prevention programs of six California police departments, an evaluation of the Police Foundation field interrogations program including an analysis of the burglary and offender reports developed in the course of the interrogations. A handbook was developed which police could use in evaluating their own procedures.

Training is provided for criminal justice and law enforcement personnel. Teachers with FBI and CIA backgrounds provide both academic and field instruction to classes of twenty-five to forty students.

Customers ranged from private corporations to Federal, state, and local government agencies.
Started operations: 1957
Man years of experience: unavailable
No. of persons on staff: more than 3500 professional employees
Geographic operation: National and international, offices located regionally and overseas

Richard Thayer Associates
465 Woodford Street
Portland, ME 04103
Phone: (207) 774-8766
This firm provides consulting services concerned with the prevention of the theft of antiques. Antiques are identified with a mark which does not detract from the value of the piece; devices for making the marks are sold for use by individual owners or the firm can be engaged to do all marking for the client; housing of collections is surveyed and recommendations for needed security equipment are made; fine arts appraisal service is offered. Collectors, dealers, law enforcement agencies, security firms and museums are most likely to benefit from the services of this firm.
Started operations: 1973
Man years of experience: 80
No. of persons on staff: 5
Geographic operation: Northeastern United States

Thompson Enterprises
P.O. Box 271
Odenton, MD 21113
Phone: (301) 569-9373
An independent consultant and polygraph examiner provides expert witness testimony for criminal and civil trials; specific polygraph testing of persons charged with crimes; pre-employment screening examinations; and personnel examinations aimed at reducing/deterring internal theft and recovery of property. Other services include coordination of seminars and talks for association meetings.
Started operations: 1971
Man years of experience: 12
No. of persons on staff: self-employed, principal only
Geographic operation: Baltimore, Maryland and Washington, D.C. area

John D. Tippit
650 Edgewood Drive
Goleta, CA 93017
Phone: (805) 967-4003
This firm provides consultation on security and loss prevention to business, industry, law enforcement, and public administrators located in the United States and its possessions. Typical services provided are: design or evaluation of trade secret or proprietary information programs; security alarm systems; development of security education, personnel security and crime prevention programs; and evaluation of the vulnerability to theft or espionage of client facilities.
Started operations: 1968
Man years of experience: 45

No. of persons on staff: 2
Geographic operation: Not limited

Ultrasystems, Inc.
2400 Michelson Drive
Irvine, CA 92664
Phone: (714) 833-0482

This company provides security consulting services to businesses, institutions, homeowners, and criminal justice agencies. The company will evaluate proposals, recommend detection and communications equipment, propose needed services, and design systems. Staff personnel are knowledgeable in how to reduce false alarms through proper equipment use, development and use of proper decision-making by security and other personnel, and security procedure changes. Interfaces between the client's security system and police are offered along with expertise in the application of small-computers and individualized programming for unique situations.

Criminal justice projects for police agencies, courts, and correction facilities cover the areas of training, information system programming, organization management and the development of written and audiovisual training material on security subject matter.
Started operations: 1968
Man years of experience: 80
No. of persons on staff: 200
Geographic operation: Nationwide, with special emphasis on Southwestern states

Urban Systems Research & Engineering, Inc.
1218 Massachusetts Avenue
Cambridge, MA 02138
Phone: (617) 661-1550

This company researches and designs comprehensive crime control models for urban residential areas. Techniques used in developing models include: literature searches, problem definition, data analysis, attitude studies, interviews, field observation, crime control modeling, and implementation and validation of models. Reports and technical manuals are also developed.

Projects have included a study of residential crime patterns in Hartford, Connecticut, with the goal of reducing the incidence of burglary, assault and robbery and level of citizen fear; other studies have concentrated on the nature and pattern of stranger-to-stranger crimes committed on residential premises.
Publications: *Crime and Housing in a Metropolitan Area: A Study of the Patterns of Residential Crime*
Started operations: 1969
Man years of experience: 50
No. of persons on staff: approximately 50
Geographic operation: Eastern Seaboard area

Ralph V. Ward, Ltd.
1309 Oberon Way
McLean, VA 22101
Phone: (703) 356-5266

An independent consultant provides services including surveys of basic security measures in use at the client's establishment, vulnerability assessment for procedural policy changes, procurement specifications and drawings, construction supervision, and acceptance tests. The use of electronic security devices and the development of security policy and organization are emphasized. Associates with other capabilities are available to meet specific needs of clients. Services are provided to government, industrial, and commercial sponsors. Particular fields of application include: museums, banks, hospitals, computer areas, high rise buildings, and real estate developments.
Publications: Brochure to prospective clients
Started operations: 1972
Man years of experience: 16
No. of persons on staff: Principal
Geographic operation: Primarily in the East, with some national accounts

Warner Consultants
75-A G Street, S.W.
Washington, DC 20024
Phone: (202) 737-0255

This company engages in research and development of security systems for residential and

light commercial buildings. Work includes site evaluation system design and development. The firm has carried out studies of this kind for industrial and commercial organizations, associations, and government agencies, emphasizing the effect of building design and location on residential security. Current work includes the development of a residential security planning and design guide, drafting a compendium of building concepts, a projection of the near future of the building industry, and a feasibility study for the establishment of a modular housing firm.
Publications: *Residential Security: A Planning and Design Guide;* other client-directed reports are available upon request.
Started operations: 1969
Man years of experience: 20 in building research, 1 in security systems (total)
No. of persons on staff: 4-8, depending on work volume
Geographic operation: Limited to the United States and developed countries

Thad L. Weber and Associates, Inc.
P.O. Box 207
Wenoah, NJ 08090
Phone: (212) 972-0270
**   (212) 687-0328**
This firm provides consultation services which include planning and selection of physical security components; designing electronic systems for detecting, signalling and deterring criminal activity; and advice on related security measures. Programs of improved security through better pre-employment personnel policies, security training for personnel and continuing security advice are additional services offered to clients. Selection and application of alarm systems and personnel procedures to high risk areas such as banks, jewelry stores, warehouses, liquor and drug businesses is a specialty.
Publications: *Alarm Systems and Theft Prevention,* 1973, SDM Publishing Co.
Started operations: 1970
Man years of experience: 25
No. of persons on staff: 2 full-time, plus associates as required to meet clients' needs
Geographic operation: National

Westinghouse Electric Corporation
1111 Schilling Road
Hunt Valley, MD 21030
Phone: (301) 667-5234
This company designs and integrates large scale, computer-controlled security systems for industrial plant sites, corrections and mental health institutions, sensitive government operations and airports. Work includes consultation to define the threat, constraints of the site, security response requirements, performance specifications, installation assistance, maintenance and service, and training of personnel for security operation and equipment maintenance. Although the firm manufactures pressure-sensitive detectors, low light cameras, metal detectors, and annunciator/interface units, it will integrate other manufacturers' components to design the system needed. Emphasis is on electronic protection of perimeters and surveillance of areas such as military bases, gas and oil pumping and storage areas, electrical substations and switchyards, sites involved with nuclear material and nuclear energy (major area of work), airport weapons detection, parking lots, museums, and government radio security systems.
Publications: *Developing an Integrated Security Plan for Plant Protection*
Started operations: 1968
Man years of experience: 100 years
No. of persons on staff: 10 (plus 50-60 professionals in manufacturing/engineering)
Geographic operation: National and international

Hubert Wilke, Inc.
Communications Facilities Consultants
280 Park Avenue
New York, NY 10017
Phone: (212) 557-0650
This company specializes in the planning, design and specifications of audiovisual communications systems for board rooms, conference rooms and training rooms; auditoriums; lecture halls, and closed-circuit TV studios. Additional services include the design and bid specification of security/surveillance systems, and programming services to assist clients with software. Expertise in electronic security/surveillance includes a range of applications for verification card readers,

audio and proximity detectors, two-way radio facilities, closed-circuit television and computerized monitoring systems and telecommunications using existing computer facilities. Projects include a planned television and audio surveillance system in addition to an extensive alarm and reporting system for the new Library of Congress, and a Command Control Center for New York City Police Department.

Started operations: 1965

Man years of experience: Principals and associates average 25 years

No. of persons on staff: 32

Geographic operation: Nationwide and international, with branches in Los Angeles, Brussels, and New York

II. CONSULTANTS IN THE COLLEGE/ UNIVERSITY ENVIRONMENT

Andres Inn Research Center
School of Law, Southern Methodist University
Dallas, TX 75275
Phone: (214) 692-3380

    This organization offers a research capability for police and industrial security forces, including examination of the criteria needed for security personnel selection and deployment. Deployment criteria development includes examining the response time and visibility level of security personnel using such techniques as cost/benefit analysis and statistical sampling. Evaluation programs are offered, involving both the selection of a system and the design of evaluation instruments such as rating scales. Implementation and research is combined in the information retrieval systems areas. Associates are experienced in accounting, law, operations research, advertising campaigns, and building flow pattern design. Technical reports and publications are available.

Started operations: 1968

Man years of experience: 40

No. of persons on staff: 5

Geographic operation: Nationwide

Center for Research in Criminal Justice
University of Illinois at Chicago Circle
Box 4348
Chicago, IL 60680
Phone: (312) 996-5665

    This organization conducts social science research in the field of criminal justice. It specializes in evaluating the impact of programs designed to prevent, control or treat crime problems and offenders, as well as in empirical research related to the field. Currently the Center is evaluating "Operation Identification" in the state of Illinois.

Started operations: 1966, at the Chicago Circle location in 1972

Man years of experience: 35

No. of persons on staff: 3-10 persons, with additional staff available as necessary

Geographic operation: Concentrated in Illinois

Center for the Study of Crime, Delinquency, and Corrections
Southern Illinois University at Carbondale
Carbondale, IL 62901
Phone: (618) 453-2836

    This organization provides staff members to consult on the development of curricula, the preparation of proposals, and other activities in which they are knowledgeable. Faculty has experience in training, research, higher education, and consultation to criminal justice agencies in crime prevention matters.

    Publications include films, periodicals, and reports in the areas of correctional training, social sciences, juvenile delinquency, general education and law enforcement.

Started operations: 1961

Man years of experience: includes academic and practical experience

No. of persons on staff: 20

Geographic operation: National

Commission on Peace Officer Standards and Training (POST)
Crime Prevention Training Program
Department of Justice, State of California
7100 Bowling Drive, Suite 240
Sacramento, CA 95823
Phone: (916) 445-4515

This organization is currently operating under a federal grant to conduct a Crime Prevention Training program to accomplish three goals: establish and present crime prevention institute seminars to local law enforcement officers who have primarily crime prevention responsibilities; establish a centralized repository of crime prevention information and programs; recommend crime prevention training curricula to be incorporated into California POST-certified pre-service and in-service courses.

The program was funded initially for one year—1974–1975.
Started operations: 1974
Man years of experience: 16
No. of persons on staff: 2 staff
Geographic operation: California

Criminal Justice Program
Institute for Social Research and Development
Vandelier West
Albuquerque, NM 87131
Phone: (505) 277-3422

The Program branch of the Institute for Social Research and Development conducts exploratory and demonstration research projects in the criminal justice field. Public awareness and motivation, juvenile justice, and computer simulation of the workload in a criminal justice system are among the subject areas studied. Demonstration projects are conducted on occasion for the police, probation systems, courts or corrections systems. The organization has special capabilities in the evaluation and planning of criminal justice research assignment, the application of technology to research problems and the evaluation of the effectiveness and results of various methods of correction.
Publication: an annotated bibliography is available.
Started operations: 1971
Man years of experience: 52
No. of persons on staff: 10
Geographic operation: New Mexico

Illinois State University
Program In Corrections
Schroeder Hall, Room 401
Normal, IL 61761
Phone: (309) 438-5173

The University offers consulting services to criminal justice agencies, governmental units and business firms, and offers academic training for entry-level positions in the law enforcement field. Consultation services offered have included administration, staff development and training for the Illinois Department of Corrections; development of criminal justice programs for city managers, other programs on community crime prevention directed at juveniles and adults, with pre- and post-project analysis; loss prevention; hiring and integration of ex-offenders in civilian jobs; and tailoring job training to meet the needs of security firms, police agencies, and corrections departments.
Started operations: 1970
Man years of experience: 90
No. of persons on staff: 5, able to expand staff from univeristy as required
Geographic operation: Illinois and surrounding Midwestern states

Institute for the Study of Change
406 Savona Avenue
Coral Gables, FL 33146
Phone: (305) 667-3832

This institute provides consulting services to private firms wishing to increase company personnel individual awareness of the need to protect both themselves and company installations

abroad, particularly against terrorism. Technical advisory services are provided by staff members having security police, journalistic, or academic expertise on Latin America. Outside speakers are obtained when necessary to complement staff seminar presentations. Past projects have required research and the development of written and audiovisual materials. Assistance to police departments is expected to be a major area of effort in the future.
Started operations: 1971
Man years of experience: 1–2 years per man in institute
No. of persons on staff: 15 members
Geographic operation: Latin American

International Association of College and University Security Directors
4400 Whitney Avenue
Hamden, CT 06518
Phone: (203) 288-3094
   This association, comprised of over five hundred universities and colleges, seeks to improve campus security and render it more nearly professional through research and an exchange of ideas and programs setting higher training and performance standards. A number of regional seminars and workshops is convened each year in addition to the regular June conference held annually on the campus of a member institution.
Publications: *Campus Law Enforcement Journal*
Started operations: 1958

Lewis H. Irving, Consultant
Department of Sociology
Central State University
Edmond, OK 73034
Phone: (405) 2980 x2533
   An independent consultant, providing social survey research to government agencies and businesses. Areas of specialization are: questionnaires, attitude survey design, interviewing techniques and statistical analyses. Previous activities required participation and consultation with the Oklahoma Department of Corrections and State Courts. This consultant specializes in defining the human factors approach, both in defining the environment necessary to produce social change and social integration, and in identifying types and kinds of equipment needed to work on the problem. Publications have been in areas related to law enforcement and corrections (e.g. a 1972 study, sponsored by LEAA), and articles on female criminals and the typology of offenders in general.
Started operations: 1970
Man years of experience: See above
No. of persons on staff: 4
Geographic operation: Oklahoma

Louisiana State University
Law Enforcement Training Program
Pleasant Hall
Baton Rouge, LA 70803
Phone: (504) 388-5115
   This organization convenes an annual Industrial Security Seminar for the region. Led by experts in each field, participants examine topics such as white-collar theft, blue-collar theft, gambling at industrial locations, and compromise of computer privacy. New electronic equipment/devices/systems provided by invited companies are available for review.
   The University is responsible for statewide law enforcement training including: regular curricula; response to special requests from within and outside the state; provision of expert advice in the field on demand; research assistance; analysis of state agencies; pamphlets for updating law enforcement skills (police report writing for example); and the conduct of special schools such as a Command School for heads of traffic departments.
Started operations: 1953
Man years of experience: 200
No. of persons on staff: 19
Geographic operation: Southeastern United States

Macomb County Criminal Justice Training Center
Macomb County Community College
16500 Hall Road
Mt. Clemens, MI 48043
Phone: (313) 465-4626

The Training Center is responsible for training the new crime prevention personnel of Macomb County and teaching these officers the basic fundamentals and theories of locks, lighting techniques, glass usage, alarm systems, etc. At the conclusion of training, each officer is required to carry out a security survey of three local businesses. The Center also offers advanced training to evidence technicians and supervisory, business, and security personnel. Seminars are convened for the private citizen on methods for the physical reduction of crime.

Four criminal justice specialists in the areas mentioned above as well as numerous part-time instructors have extensive experience in specific areas of criminal justice.
Started operations: 1971
Man years of experience: 54
No. of persons on staff: 4
Geographic operation: Michigan

Modesto Junior College, West
Regional Criminal Justice Training Center
P.O. Box 4065
Modesto, CA 95342
Phone: (209) 526-5440

This Center has developed and implemented a comprehensive program of education and training which encompasses the entire spectrum of the criminal justice system. Training emphasizes corrections, judicial process and law enforcement, both as preperformance and inservice programs. Seminars, institutes, and workshops are available to meet the needs of various segments of the criminal justice system. An Outreach program has been designed to provide education and training to criminal justice agencies without ready access to the training center facility at Modesto.
Started operations: 1971
Man years of experience: 60–75
No. of persons on staff: Teaching and instructional staff of 11
Geographic operation: California regions K & L of California—Counties of Alpine, Amador, Calaveras, Maripos, Merced, San Joaquin, Stanislaus, and Tuolumne

Mt. San Antonio College
Department of Public Safety and Service
110 North Grand Avenue
Walnut, CA 91789
Phone: (213) 339-7331
**   (714) 595-2211 x252, x324**

This organization provides staff personnel who analyze and interpret research data from the vantage point of past experience. The findings are then applied to the design and development of security-related programs, implemented through community action programs, speakers' bureaus or formal instruction. Staff experience is based upon many years of actual work in law enforcement, security and corrections. External advisory committees are used to develop cooperation and better communciations between elements of the security-system and the formal educational program.
Started operations: 1948
Man years of experience: unavailable
No. of persons on staff: 40 faculty members
Geographic operation: California

National Crime Prevention Institute (NCPI)
School of Police Administration
University of Louisville—Shelby Campus
Louisville, KY 40222
Phone: (800) 626-3550 (Toll Free)

This institute is federally funded to train professional police officers in modern crime prevention techniques. The prime objective of the program is to reduce criminal opportunities

by establishing local Crime Prevention Bureaus on a nationwide scale. Approximately 700 police officers have been trained in the four-week sessions on Crime Prevention Theory and Practice while an additional 200 law enforcement administrators and criminal justice planners were trained in shorter sessions. Schooling in private security measures is also offered to industry, commerce and private police organizations. This instruction includes courses in transportation and cargo security, retail and industrial security and crime and loss prevention for the insurance industry. Each student receives a current issue of the NCPI Implementation Manual for establishing crime prevention bureaus. Other programs are available to give help to businesses in surveying their security needs and lighting systems, to citizen groups to familiarize them with security problems and instruct them in the design of anti-shoplifting programs and Neighborhood Watch programs.
Started operations: 1971
Man years of experience: 125
No. of persons on staff: 5, plus support personnel
Geographic operation: Students represent U.S., Canada, Puerto Rico

Southeast Florida Institute of Criminal Justice
Miami-Dade Community College
11380 N.W. 27 Avenue
Miami, FL 33167
Phone: (305) 685-4505
   The Institute is a cooperative effort of Federal, state, county, and local governmental agencies located in the Miami area. It provides a centralized facility for instruction and training needed by the various criminal justice personnel in Dade and Monroe Counties. Student/trainee-community interactions is encouraged and developed for both institute and college programs and courses.
Started operations: 1972
Man years of experience: unavailable
No. of persons on staff: 220 (includes 200 part-time instructors)
Geographic operation: Dade and Monroe counties in Florida

III. CONSULTANTS WITH SPECIALIZED FUNCTIONS

Adams Rite Manufacturing Company
4040 South Capitol
City of Industry, CA 91749
Phone: (213) 699-0511
   This firm has developed an Anti-burglary and Security Seminar as a community relations program to alert and inform the public about burglary methods and security products commercially available which delay and discourage theft. This program is intended to help police departments in enlisting the public cooperation necessary to "harden targets" against burglary. The program presents demonstrations of devices such as locks, safes, alarms, closed-circuit television, burglary-resistant glass, protective bars, specialized lighting, and means of property identification. The roles of law enforcement and insurance in loss prevention are stressed, and a pamphlet entitled *Burglary Prevention* is available to session attendees. Seminar is available at cost to sponsoring police departments, civic groups, insurance and locksmith associations as well as to representatives of the security products industry. Local representatives are available to help organize attendance.
   The program has been presented with the help of police in Syracuse, Miami, Cincinnati, Seattle, Vancouver, Kansas City, Shreveport, San Jose, Los Angeles, and Orange County, California.
Started operations: 1955
Man years of experience: 100
No. of persons on staff: 6, plus local participants
Geographic operation: U.S., Canada, England

Alarm Industry Committee for Combating Crime (AICCC)
1776 K Street, N.W.-Suite 900
Washington, DC 20006
Phone: (202) 293-6260

The Committee was formed in 1969 in response to a report on crime against small businesses issued by the Senate Committee on Small Business. Members of this *ad hoc* group come from the Central Station Electrical Protection Association (CSEPA), which represents most of the burglar and fire alarm central stations in the United States which have been approved by the Underwriters' Laboratories, and the National Burglar and Fire Alarm Association (NBFAA), the trade association for firms that manufacture, install, service and maintain security systems and equipment. Several of the members represented through the AICCC also provide private watchman and guards.

The Committee serves as a clearinghouse for its members to consider and express their views on matters of common interest. It meets about every six weeks to review pertinent activities of the Federal government and Congress, and of private organizations such as Underwriters' Laboratories, the National Alliance for Safer Cities, and the American Society for Testing Materials. A permanent committee was established in 1974 to promote better liaison between the International Association of Chiefs of Police and the AICCC.
Started operations: 1969

American Society for Testing and Materials (ASTM)
1916 Race Street
Philadelphia, PA 19096
Phone: (215) 569-4200

This organization, a non-profit corporation, develops voluntary consensus standards for the characteristics and performance of materials, products, systems and services. Standards are developed by over 14,000 members serving on 120 main technical committees and 1200 subcommittees.

ASTM Committee F-12, Security Systems and Equipment, was organized in 1972 for the development of standards (definitions, specifications, methods of test, and recommended practices) "for the security of property and safety of life." This committee has members representing business, industry, government agencies and the consumer. Standards developed will apply to financial premises, commercial, institutional and industrial buildings, homes and apartments, communications, shipping and transportation. The committee will coordinate its work with other organizations which have developed security standards and will reference such work where it is appropriate.
Related publications: *ASTM Annual Book of Standards* (over 5000 standards published in 47
 volumes; updated yearly). *Standardization News* (published monthly). *ASTM Journal of Testing
 and Evaluation* (published six times yearly). *Journal of Forensic Sciences* (published quarterly).
Started operations: 1898
No. of persons on staff: 22,000

Aptos Film Productions, Inc.
Box 225
Aptos, CA 95003
Phone: (408) 475-0535

This company produces films on various aspects of crime and crime prevention. For example, "An Ounce of Prevention" narrated by Glenn Ford uses an inspection approach to help the viewer evaluate his home security. In "The Plastic Criminal" Chuck Connors tells how to prevent credit card fraud. Using on-the-spot shots of a variety of commercial enterprises, Henry Ford shows businessmen how to protect their establishments against burglary. "Invitation to Burglary," starring Raymond Burr, tells homeowners and tenants about burglary prevention. Films are intended for use by law enforcement agencies, in cooperation with service clubs, schools, crime prevention organizations, government at all levels and security and insurance groups.
Started operations: 1971

Associated Locksmiths of America, Inc. (ALOA)
11 Elmendorf Street
Kingston, NY 12401
Phone: (914) 338-5906
This organization of 3000 participating firms, with members in the United States, Canada, and fifteen other countries, gives service and advice on security matters to individual homeowners, apartment dwellers, and businesses. Publications include a monthly bulletin called *KEY-NOTES,* security equipment standards bulletins and pamphlets on home and business security. Local members or representatives work with crime prevention units of law enforcement agencies.
Started operations: 1956
Geographic operation: National and international

Association of Management Consultants, Inc.
811 East Wisconsin Avenue
Milwaukee, WI 53202
Phone: (414) 272-5222
This non-profit organization of professional management consultants has as objectives: to provide professional management consultants with the benefits of a formal association; to establish standards of professional practice; to provide a means of co-operation among consultants; to establish a criterion upon which business concerns may select competent consultants; to promote the general interests of mangement consulting as a profession and to co-operate with other organizations. Any management consulting firm meeting membership requirements and operating in a manner consistent with the code of professional practice is eligible for membership.
Started operations: 1959
Man years of experience: Depends on the particular consultants
Geographic operation: Varies with each consultant

CONtact, Inc.
P.O. Box 81826
Lincoln, NE 68501
Phone: (402) 464-0602
This referral/clearinghouse group locates and refers clients to experts in criminal justice, crime prevention and security, as well as organizations who provide volunteer services for specific problems. The identification of resources, programs, materials and consulting services is available without charge. Recent projects on a national scale include helping to implement the Neighborhood Watch Program throughout the United States as it is supported by the National Sheriff's Association, and consulting to the U.S. Jaycees on the Community Crime Prevention Task Force of the National Commission on Criminal Justice Standards and Goals. With contacts in over nine thousand communities, CONtact also makes referrals for problems in areas other than security.
Started operations: 1971
Man years of experience: 40
No. of persons on staff: 13
Geographic operation: United States, Canada, and 30 foreign countries

Criminal Justice Press
P.O. Box 159
Kennedale, TX 76060
Attn: Robert M. Platt, General Editor
(no telephone)
This firm publishes and distributes educational materials in the theoretical and practical aspects of police science and corrections. A six-volume set focused on police-community relations, and a series of training manuals based on the National Advisory Commission Criminal Justice Standards Goals have been issued. These books include test questions and suggested techniques for classroom use.

Richard J. Healy
Building C101, Mail Station 592
The Aerospace Corporation
P.O. Box 92957
Los Angeles, CA 90009
Phone: (213) 648-5362

An independent consultant providing services to define the expected hazards to security, and design a defense which applies modern methods and equipment to raise the security level and reduce protection costs. All aspects of potential designs are covered, from plant layout to locks to alarms and lighting. Threats to organizations from riots, explosions, bombs, and other acts of violence are reduced by emergency planning for facilities, assets and personnel protection. Management is further aided in cost effective loss control methods by application of modern management techniques and skills to the security program and assistance in development of staffing requirements. Additional expertise is applied in industrial espionage protection problems.

Publications: *Design for Security, Emergency and Disaster Planning, Industrial Security Management, Protecting Your Business Against Espionage, Protection of Assets Manual*
Started operations: Independent consultant
Man years of experience: 20
No. of persons on staff: Principal
Geographic operation: International

Highway Safety Foundation
890 Hollywood Lane
P.O. Box 3563
Mansfield, OH 44907
Phone: (419) 756-5593

The Foundation was originally incorporated to produce traffic safety, motion pictures in cooperation with the Ohio State Highway Patrol. In 1964 the program was expanded to include crime prevention motion pictures. Films emphasize realism, showing law enforcement officials performing their duties in situations where actual crimes have occurred. Current film titles include: "The Child Molester," "The Shoplifter," "Plant Pilferage," "The Paperhangers," and "You & The Bank Robber." Some films are restricted to use by merchandisers and police.
Started operations: 1960
No. of persons on staff: Production crews called in as needed. Distribution handled by mail or telephone.
Geographic operation: United States, Canada, Australia

International Association of Chiefs of Police, Inc. (IACP)
Eleven Firstfield Road
Gaithersburg, MD 20760
Phone: (301) 948-0922

This association is incorporated as a tax-exempt, non-profit, professional organization of ten thousand members in fifty-five nations, devoted to advancing the science and art of police service. The association gives assistance to local police agencies on all phases of law enforcement activity and community support services. IACP conducts comprehensive management surveys of police agencies, in which it collects, analyzes, and then makes available information about weapons systems and protective equipment, training requirements and tactical applications. Publications have been issued on police attitudes and behavior, bombs and explosives, chemical agents, campus and civil disturbances, communications, community relations, criminal investigation, criminal statistics, education, highway safety, juvenile delinquency, labor relations/personnel administration, management and organization, police facilities, organized crime, patrol operations, police ethics, law and legislation, and management case studies. *The Police Chief* is published monthly, but other titles issued at intervals include a Police Reference Notebook, a training series, and the *Proceedings of the Annual IACP Conference*.
Started operations: 1893
Man years of experience: over 1000
No. of persons on staff: 140
Geographic operation: Nationwide and international

Law Enforcement Association on Professional Standards, Education and Ethical Practice (LEAPS)
8001 Natural Bridge Road
St. Louis, MS 63121
Phone: (314) 453-5592

This association seeks to develop high professional standards in education, research and ethical practice in law enforcement. The organization conducts small regional workshops and symposia on police policies and methods such as lateral entry, team policing, law enforcement management, police ethics, and other special topics. Consultants are available through LEAPS for speaking engagements. Members are from local, state, and Federal law enforcement agencies, the administrative staffs of these offices and from the academic world.

Publications: *Proceedings of the National Symposium on Police Ethical Practice, and Ethical Standards of Law Enforcement*
Started operations: 1971
Man years of experience: 34
No. of persons on staff: 3
Geographic operation: 5 chapters nationwide

Law Enforcement Standards Laboratory (LESL)
National Bureau of Standards
Physics B150
Washington, DC 20234
Phone: (301) 921-3167

This organization was established in January, 1971 by the National Bureau of Standards, at the request of the U.S. Department of Justice. It is funded primarily by the National Institute of Law Enforcement and Criminal Justice. The mission of the Laboratory is to develop voluntary performance standards, specifications, and procurement guidelines for equipment to be used by U.S. law enforcement and criminal justice personnel in addition to assisting Federal, state, and local law enforcement organizations in the selection and procurement of equipment suitable for their needs. The Laboratory is currently developing methods for measuring performance levels of protective equipment and clothing, communications and security systems, weapons, emergency equipment, investigative aids and vehicles.
Started operations: 1971
No. of persons on staff: 10 (Program Level Personnel)

Lomond Systems, Inc.
Mt. Airy, MD 21771
Phone: (301) 829-1633)

This firm publishes a newsletter, *Systems, Technology and Science for Law Enforcement and Security,* an annotated bibliography of current literature in the field, a report on current news, and abstracts of government reports.
Started operations: 1968
Man years of experience: 10
No. of persons on staff: 2
Geographic operation: Nationwide distribution

Master Lock Company
2600 N. 32nd Street
Milwaukee, WI 53210
Phone: (414) 444-2800

This manufacturer offers a variety of public service material on home security and gun safety. In conjuction with the Madison, Wisconsin Safety Council, for example, the company developed two public service television announcements on bicycle registration and security and an 8 minute (16 mm) film on bicycle security entitled, *Wheelin' & Stealin'.* The firm works with civic groups to put together educational displays of padlocks and other security devices in their product line. Publications are made available to interested communities.

Since the company does not employ a staff for this purpose alone, contact Mr. Edson Allen, Director of Public Affairs, for information.

Middle Department Inspection Agency, Inc.
1800 Davis Street
Camden, NJ 08103
Phone: (609) 962-6815

This firm examines and certifies installations of fire and alarm systems, although it neither tests nor certifies the equipment itself. The Security Verification Division checks on the location, quality and type of devices needed for a system, the wiring and reaction of the circuitry to test conditions, etc. Independent of both manufacturers and installers, conclusions about an inspection are made in accordance with applicable state public utility commission regulations, the Agency's own standards for residences, standards of the National Fire Protection Association or insurance company requirements. Inspection of contractors' installations of fire and alarm systems in nursing homes is typical of the work carried on by the Security Verification Division. The firm is recognized by the Insurance Service Organization.

Started operations: 1883
Man years of experience: unavailable
No. of persons on staff: 205 in Security Verification Division
Geographic operation: Delaware, Maryland, New Jersey, New York, Ohio, Pennsylvania, Virginia, and West Virginia

National Alliance for Safer Cities
165 East 56 Str-et
New York, NY 10022
Phone: (212) 751-4000

This organization is a coalition of 70 national organizations and 14 local alliances. The aim of the Alliance is to discourage casual crime at community and local levels through the cooperation of labor unions, industry, government and local citizens. It uses a grass roots approach to help residents meet the crisis of fear and crime in their own neighborhoods. The Law Enforcement Assistance Administration (LEAA) and national and local foundations often fund local groups of this association. Its activities include endorsing minimum building security codes, a project to demonstrate that crimes against the elderly in public housing can be reduced to zero, developing educational programs about crime for presentation on radio and television, and procuring jobs for ex-offenders. National Alliance publications include discussions of such well-known programs as *Crime Watch, Block Mothers,* and *Neighborhood Police Teams.*

Publications: *Twenty-two Steps to Safer Neighborhoods,* issued for national distribution
Started operations: 1970
No. of persons on staff: 4 staff on national level
Geographic operation: Nationwide

National Association of School Security Directors (NASSD)
1320 Southwest 4th Street
Fort Lauderdale, FL 33312
Phone: (305) 765-6201

This association is the meeting ground for school security directors who must deal with the many and varied problems of protecting elementary and secondary schools. It serves as a forum for the exchange of ideas and useful approaches, for improved security, primarily through sessions at its annual meeting where in-depth programs and workshops are held on specific topics. Programs and papers are presented on subjects such as assaults on school personnel, weapons in school, bomb threats, arson, vandalism, thefts, drug abuse, community and police involvement, bus transporation problems, architectural planning for better security, and athletic events. The organization will also assemble testimony for state legislatures and the U.S. Congress when appropriate. Members of the organization represent 180 cities throughout the United States.

Started operations: 1970
Geographic operation: Annual Meetings: 1977, Dallas, TX; 1978, Alberquerque, NM

National Burglar and Fire Alarm Association (NBFAA)
1730 Pennsylvania Avenue, N.W., Suite 1150
Washington, DC 20006
Phone: (202) 785-0500

This organization is a non-profit trade association of firms engaged in the installation and servicing of all types of burglar and fire alarm systems. Local members are available to cooperate and participate in community crime prevention/reduction programs and activities. The NBFAA is active in national liaison efforts with the International Association of Chiefs of Police, the National Fire Protection Association, the National Crime Prevention Institute, the Alarm Industry Committee for Combating Crime, Underwriters' Laboratories the Law Enforcement Assistance Administration, and other related groups.

Publications: *NBFAA Signal* (quarterly trade journal); *Considerations When Looking for a Burglar Alarm System Signal/Gram Newsletter* (membership newsletter)

Started operations: 1948

The National Criminal Justice Reference Service
U.S. Department of Justice
Law Enforcement Assistance Administration
Washington, DC 20531
Phone: (202) 755-9704

This organization was established under the Law Enforcement Assistance Administration (LEAA). The National Criminal Justice Reference Service (NCJRS) serves as a central information reference source for the nation's law enforcement and criminal justice community. NCJRS seeks to cover all aspects of law enforcement and criminal justice including LEAA research and development and action grant project reports and studies.

Users are provided with NILECJ publications, books, tapes, and other material from both government and nongovernment sources. An information exchange is maintained with other reference and documentation services. Abstracts and bibliographic data are entered into the system for each item.

Two types of users are served: General users, who receive selected or intermittent services and registered users who receive all products and services. There is no charge for NCJRS materials or services. When users are referred to other sources they may anticipate normal charges from those sources. Services are briefly summarized as:

1. The Document Retrieval Index—describes each item, cross-referenced by documents, grants, author and subject list
2. A Thesaurus describing the law enforcement and criminal justice community
3. A Selective Notice of Information which relates subjects to selected interests of system users
4. Referral Services
5. User Orientation
6. Current Awareness Material
7. Selected Topic Digests
8. In-Center Services

Registration for services is accomplished by filling out the "Registration for Services" available at the above address.

National Institute of Law Enforcement and Criminal Justice (NILECJ)
Law Enforcement Assistance Administration
U.S. Department of Justice
Washington, DC 20531
Phone: (202) 376-3606

This Institute funds grants and contracts as authorized by the Omnibus Crime Control and Safe Streets Act of 1968, Public Law 90-351, amended by the Omnibus Crime Control Act of 1970; Public Law 91-644; 72 U.S.C. 3741-3743. The organization encourages and supports research and development to improve and strengthen all activities pertaining to crime prevention or reduction and the enforcement of criminal law. Objectives and priorities are specified annually in the National Institute's Program Plan. Funds are given or contracted out by NILECJ to develop new or improved approaches, techniques systems, equipment and devices for crime control; and for programs of behavioral research on: the causes of crime, means of preventing crime and evaluations of correctional procedures. Final reports are published through various sources including the Government Printing Office and the National Technical Information Service. (See also National Criminal Justice Reference Service.)

Started operations: 1968

No. of persons on staff: 80

Nickerson & Collins Co., Publishers
Security Education Division
2720 Des Plaines Avenue
Des Plaines, IL 60018
Phone: (312) 298-6210
This company publishes magazines, newsletters and texts in the security field:
Magazines:
  Locksmith Ledger—for professional locksmiths, wholesalers and other distributors
  Security Register—for security managers, administrators, directors
Newsletters:
  Security Education Briefs—for security officers
  Alternatives—for security administrators
  Specifications—for security designers and engineers
Textbooks:
  Paine, David, *Basic Principles of Industrial Security*
  Post, Richard S., *Determining Security Needs*
  A directory of equipment manufacturers and trade associations is published annually.
Started operations: 1973 (Security Education Division)

Schlage Security Institute
P.O. Box 3324
San Francisco, CA 94119
Phone: (415) 467-1100
  This public service institute cooperates with law enforcement agencies, security and insurance industries to develop educational programs which will make citizens more aware of the need for home security.
  Seminar presentations from the Institute staff are augmented by local experts. Literature covering all aspects of crime prevention is made available at the seminars—alarm systems, perimeter protection, vaults, door and windows, and locking devices. The institute assists in developing and revising the security provisions of state, county and local building ordinances and has produced and distributed in cooperation with the International Association of Chiefs of Police a home security film, *The Door Was Locked;* and also is active in national organizations interested in security ordinances.
Started operations: 1963
Man years of experience: 150
No. of persons on staff: 7, varies with area and is supplemented by sales staff in the area and other industry staff
Geographic operation: Nationwide

Security Distributing & Marketing Magazine (SDM)
Division of Security World Publishing Co., Inc.
2639 So. La Cienega Blvd.
Los Angeles, CA 90034
Phone: (213) 836-5000
  This company publishes the magazine *SDM* on a monthly basis for manufacturers, sales representatives, distributors, retail dealers, and installers of loss prevention equipment. Crime/fire detection and prevention equipment as well as security products and services are covered in the text and advertising. Regular monthly features present new products and literature, and "selling security" philosophy. Special issues include a directory of manufacturers (August), three "show issues" (January, April and October) and an advertisers and editorial directory (December). *Security Mart,* a postcard-type advertising publication published quarterly, is mailed to approximately fifty thousand end users, dealers, distributors, manufacturers, and consultants. Subscriptions to this are not available to individual consumers.
Started operations: 1971
Man years of experience: 6 years in fields of advertising, marketing, and public relations in security.
No. of persons on staff: editor (plus 5 staff)

Smith & Wesson Academy
Charles L. Smith, Director
Box 2208
Springfield, MA 01101
Phone: (413) 736-0323

The Academy gives specialized technical training at Basic, Advanced and Instructor levels in the areas of judicious use of firearms and nonlethal weapons, night surveillance, alcohol detection and security training. Students (to date over 1400) are accepted from all law enforcement agencies and security personnel firms. Staff members have had experience in FBI and state police assignments. Instruction techniques feature lectures, seminars, audiovisual presentations and demonstrations, indoor and outdoor target ranges, and close supervision of small classes. Courses may be given at users' locations and are tailored to their particular needs. Extra services include weaponry training; development and production of special topic curricula, manuals, audiovisuals and other training aids; and assistance in the development of specialized training programs. For training sessions held at Springfield, transporation and lodging information is provided in the Academy pamphlet.
Started operations: 1969

Society of Professional Investigators
Box 1197, Church Street Station
New York, NY 10008
Phone: (212) 653-2715

This Society is open to persons having at least five years' investigative experience with an official or quasi-official government agency devoted to law enforcement or related activities. The mission of the Society is to enhance knowledge of the science and technology of professional investigation, law enforcement, and police science; to maintain high standards and ethics among members of the profession; and to promote the effectiveness of the individual investigator. An annual award is presented for outstanding law enforcement achievement. As a service to members and clients the organization maintains a library of books and studies on law enforcement and operates a placement service and speakers' bureau.
Publications: 1) Bulletin, Annually - 14 October; 2) Roster, Triennial
Started operations: 1955
No. of persons on staff: 375
Geographic operation: New York City area

Texas Association of Licensed Investigators and Security Services (TALISS)
P.O. Box 12565
Austin, TX 78711
Phone: (713) 721-0126

This association is a non-profit, professional organization of licensed private investigative, security and alarm companies, organized to promote the public image of the profession in Texas, strengthen ethical service standards, and develop improved cooperation and communication with law enforcement agencies. The association also works to obtain equipment, educational material, and related items, and encourage the exchange of business between members and out-of-state agencies. Members who violate the established Bylaws and Code of Ethics are suspended from membership. Speaker services and the TALISS NEWS are available from the Association.
Started operations: 1971
No. of persons on staff: 100
Geographic operation: Primarily the state of Texas

Charles C Thomas Publisher
301-327 East Lawrence Avenue
Springfield, IL 62717
(no telephone)

This publisher specializes in technical fields which are of interest to small but very select audiences. Contributing authors are usually considered to be expert by peers in the field of interest. Thirteen publications (1970-1973) are available on security; other subject fields include: police science, criminology, criminal law (152 titles), law enforcement (66 titles), alcoholism, drug addiction, toxicology, delinquency, penology, parole and probation. Available titles are summarized in announcements sent in response to written requests or inquiries. Approval copies of texts are available and sales are not restricted.

Publications: *Fundamentals of Protective Systems; Locks, Safes and Security; Shoplifting and Shrinkage Protection for Stores*

U.S. Naval Surface Weapons Center
White Oak
Silver Springs, MD 20910
Phone: (202) 394-1142

This organization is the principal RDT&E (Development Test, and Evaluation) laboratory of the U.S. Navy for ordinance technology and weapon systems development. Located in convenient proximity to most Federal agencies in the greater Washington, D.C. area, the activities at NOL range from basic research to the fielding of an operational system. Research covers the design, development and test of surface and underwater weapon systems. Technicians and personnel are experienced in a wide variety of field operations and equipment applications.

Publications: A recent report is entitled "Law Enforcement Application of Magnetic Sensors."
No. of persons on staff: 2800
Geographic operation: United States, U.S. Government Laboratory

United Research & Training, Inc.
Police Science Productions
5107 Hollywood Blvd.
Hollywood, CA 90027
Phone: (213) 666-5636

This firm produces and distributes law enforcement training films (16 mm) and publications, some in foreign language editions. Custom films will be produced for individuals or organizations on any subject. Among the currently available film subjects are those on narcotics, patrol situations, safety, public information, explosives, self-defense, crowd control and other law enforcement problems. The films have been used by criminal justice and law enforcement organizations and colleges throughout the world.

Publications: *Recognizing Explosives; Prowler; Hot Car*
Started operations: 1957
Man years of experience: 125
No. of persons on staff: 5
Geographic operation: International

Western Burglar and Fire Alarm Association (WBFAA)
8500 Wilshire Boulevard, Suite 614
Beverly Hills, CA 90211
Phone: (213) 652-0490

This association includes 80 percent of the local and central station fire and burglar alarm firms in Oregon, Nevada, California, Arizona, and Washington. The technical committee of this Association conducts performance tests of newly developed equipment and systems; other committees have primary interest in government liaison (state and local), or with telephone liaison (leased circuits). In its capacity as a nonprofit corporation, the Association provides seminars on request for insurance company personnel, police and community representatives. Past activities have been instrumental in reducing proposed rates for telephone lines used for security purposes, in drafting city alarm ordinances, and in negotiating a labor agreement with a major union. Current projects for WBFAA involve a proposed state-wide alarm statute, and alarm agent licensing at the state level.

Started operations: 1967
No. of persons on staff: 45 member companies

Zonn Institute of Polygraph, Inc.
Colony Square Building, Suite 510
1175 Peachtree Street, N.E.
Atlanta, GA 30309
Phone: (404) 892-0105

This firm offers a six-week training course (284 hour) in the theory and operation of the polygraph. Instruction concentrates in the four areas of breathing, galvanic skin response, cardiovascular measurement and plethysmograph. Training covers interrogation, chart analysis, wording of questions and pre-test interviews. Students conduct actual examinations as part of their laboratory practicum. Certificates of competence are awarded after the Institute evaluation and approval of the first 30 student cases. Refresher courses are available.

The faculty includes members with Army polygraph experience and police backgrounds and guest lecturers. Applicants are required to take a polygraph examination before admission. The course also prepares students for the professional examinations required by the various states.
Started operations: 1972
Man years of experience: 75
No. of persons on staff: 4 supplemented by guest lecturers and Zonn operations staff
Geographic operation: Nationwide

"40,000 Pairs of Eyes"
Freeport Police Department
Anthony Elar, Chief
40 North Ocean Avenue
Freeport, NY 11520
Phone: (516) 378-0700
This security program was established by the Freeport Police Department with the active support of the community and local business, based on the concept of "being your brother's keeper." Members of the community are asked to be on the alert for suspicious activities, accidents, crimes, etc., which warrant investigation by a uniformed officer. Participating citizens are cautioned not to take enforcement action themselves but to serve as the eyes and ears of the police. A second, concurrent program, "Operation I.D.," encourages community residents to apply identifying numbers to their personal possessions to discourage theft and subsequent efforts to sell the stolen goods. Marking equipment is available free of charge at the local library.

Both of the above approaches are general and can be applied by other cities with only minor modification of publicity releases and instruments.
Started operations: 1956
No. of persons on staff: Police Department and citizens of Freeport
Geographic operation: Freeport, NY

Bibliography

Reprinted by permission from Technical Leaflet # 83,
"Security for Museums and Historic Houses," by John E.
Hunter, American Association for State and Local History,
1400 Eighth Avenue South, Nashville, TN 37203.

General Works

The Application of Security Systems and Hardware. Richard B. Cole. Springfield, Ill.: Charles C. Thomas, 1970. 251 pp.
Thorough discussion of basics in lock application, truck protection, lighting, and general premises protection techniques. Treats analysis of risk and evaluation of burglar resistance of buildings.

Being Safe. Mel Mandell. New York: Saturday Review Press, 1972. 314 pp.
Mainly about security in the home, but the chapter "Security on the Job" can be of use to museums. Contains good information on selecting locks and alarm systems.

"The Burglar Isn't Your Friend—Don't Be His." Ivan Berger. *Popular Mechanics,* January 1975, pp. 97–104.
Discusses simple, inexpensive ways to protect a residence from burglary by proper selection and installation of locks and alarm systems. Museums in converted residences will find the article helpful.

Burglary Prevention. Los Angeles Police Department, n.d. 8 pp.
A basic checklist of actions that can be taken to reduce the likelihood of burglary. Also tells how to report thefts.

Design for Security. Richard J. Healy. New York: John Wiley and Sons, 1968. 309 pp.
Definition of the nonbusiness losses that threaten industrial organizations, with recommendations for deterrence through physical and security devices.

Fundamentals of Protective Systems: Planning, Evaluation, Selection. Albert J. Mandelbaum. Springfield, Ill.: Charles C. Thomas, 1973, 272 pp.
A guide to planning, evaluating, and selecting the most effective and eocnomic protective systems.

Industrial Security Management—A Cost-Effective Approach. Richard J. Healy and Timothy J. Walsh. New York: American Management Association, 1971. 274 pp.
Guidelines for defensive planning and a systems approach to all aspects of the security problem.

"*Museums and the Theft of Works of Art.*" Entire issue of UNESCO Museum, Vol. 26, No. 1 (1974). 64 pp.
Includes these articles (selected): "Museums and the Theft of Works of Art," Michael Clamen. "Psychoanalytic Notes on the Theft and Defacement of Works of Art," Guy

Rosolato. "The Ethics of Museum Acquisition," William A. Bostick. "Museum Attendants," Georges Sportouch. "An International Meeting on Museum Security," Norman Pegden. "The Need for a Systematic Approach to the Protection of Museums," A.F. Noblecourt. "A Comparison of National Laws Protecting Cultural Property" (with a selective bibliography), Norman Pegden.

Practical Ways to Prevent Burglary and Illegal Entry. V. Moolman. New York: Cornerstone Library, Inc., 1970. 192 pp.
Concise and practical descriptions of security hardware and measures for burglary protection and prevention.

A Primer on Museum Security. Caroline K. Keck, Huntington T. Block, Joseph Chapman, John B. Lawton, and Nathan Stolow. Cooperstown, N.Y.: New York State Historical Association, 1966. 85 pp.
Chapters: "Physical Security"; "Insurance"; "Environmental Security"; "Light and Its Effect on Museum Objects." Bibliography and sources of supplies.

Protection of Assets Manual. Timothy J. Walsh and Richard J. Healy. Santa Monica: The Merritt Co., 1974, with periodic supplements. Two volumes.
Looseleaf in ring binders. Chapters on all aspects of protecting assets from money to merchandise.

"Security." Frank Francis. *Museums Journal,* Vol. 63, Nos. 1 and 2 (June and September 1963), pp. 28–32.

"Security." Robert J. McQuarie. *Museum News,* Vol. 49, No. 7 (March 1971), pp. 25–27.
Good suggestions on preventive measures; information on fire prevention.

Security Administration—An Introduction. Arthur A. Kingsbury. Springfield, Ill.: Charles C. Thomas, 1973. 368 pp.
History and philosophy of security, legal basis for governmental and proprietary security, organizations concepts, and security procedures and techniques.

"Security and Protection in a Museum." Michael J. Pakalik. *Curator,* Vol. 1, No. 4 (1958), pp. 89-93.
Discusses what needs to be protected in a museum. Touches on the public relations factor.

"Security and the Museum." A.F. Michaels. *Museum News,* Vol. 43, No. 3 (November 1964), pp. 11–16.
Discusses security at the Smithsonian. General presentation, many useful ideas.

"Security Depends on People." Caroline K. Keck. *Curator,* Vol. 10, No. 1 (1967), pp. 54–59.
Primarily a review of how museum environments can adversely affect collections and how museums must depend upon conservators to correct damage; some mention of preventive measures.

Security for Business and Industry. Charles E. Hemphill. Homewood, Ill.: Dow Jones-Irwin Publishers, 1971. 328 pp.
Methods for reducing business losses due to theft, vandalism, fire, burglary, embezzlement, and other problems.

"Security of Museums and Art Galleries." J. Mannings. *Museums Journal,* Vol. 70, No. 1 (June 1970), pp. 7–9.
General, comprehensive treatment of procedural and physical steps that can be taken to improve security in an existing museum building. Discusses good housekeeping, structural alterations, better locks, searching of premises after closing, outside lighting, and alarms.

Security Subjects: An Officer's Guide to Plant Protection. Thomas W. Wathen. Springfield, Ill.: Charles C. Thomas, 1972, 172 pp.
A thorough discussion of everything a private guard force member needs to know. Useful in planning a security program, especially operating procedures.

"What Is the State of Museum Security?" William A. Bostick, *Museum News,* Vol. 46, No. 5 (January 1968), pp. 13–19.
Details of a survey of security measures used in several large U.S. and European museums. Excellent ideas presented, along with one of the best discussions of protection from riots and civil disturbances.

"Winterthur: Security in a Decorative Arts Museum." Stephen Weldon. *Museum News,* Vol. 50, No. 5 (January 1972), pp. 36–37.
Emphasis on guards and their training, emergency preparedness plans, and positive attitudes of security preparations.

"Your Security Questions Answered." Joseph Chapman. *Museum News,* Vol. 50, No. 5 (January 1972), pp. 22–25.

Questions and answers at the security sessions of the 1971 AAM Regional Conferences. Suggestions on how staff personnel who are not guards can cope with apparent thieves or vandals.

Alarm and Communications Systems

Accident, Automotive, Burglary Protection Equipment Lists. Chicago: Underwriters' Laboratories, Inc., 1973. 114 pp.
A listing of all companies manufacturing protection equipment who have qualified to use the Listing Mark of Underwriters' Laboratories, Inc. on or in connection with their products.

Alarm Systems and Theft Prevention. Thad L. Weber. Los Angeles: Security World Publishing Co., 1973. 385 pp.
A definitive text on the realities of physical protection today, on alarm systems as they are in fact (and not necessarily in the words of their manufacturers), on little-known security weaknesses, and on the methods by which criminals are successfully evading alarm protection.

A Brief Guide to Security Alarm Systems for Financial Institutions. Hamilton, Ohio: Mosler, 1970. 30 pp.
A guide to the types of alarm systems applicable to safes and vaults; many of the principles and types of equipment discussed have wider applicability as well.

Building Security Systems: Applications and Functions. Commercial Division, Honeywell, Inc., Honeywell Proprietary Information [Form No. 74-2800 (1-69) D.L./D.E.L.]. 85 pp.
In addition to information about electronic security equipment manufactured by Honeywell, discusses in general terms the operating principles and applications of many types of equipment. Well illustrated.

"Computer Protects 1,020-Unit Building." E. Paul Robsham. *Security World,* Vol. 10, No. 10 (November 1973), p. 16.
How a central computer handles multiple detection points for intrusion, fire, and equipment malfunction at low cost because it was planned for the building.

"Dictionary of Anti-Intrusion Devices for Architects and Builders." J. E. Thorsen. *Security World,* Vol. 10, No. 10 (November 1973), p. 30.
Basic information on fundamental categories of anti-intrusion devices, their principles and methods of operation, cost and general parameters in application, possible usefulness to building planners, owners, and managers in construction and remodeling.

"Electronic Eyes and Ears on Guard." Tom Probst. *Museum News,* Vol. 44, No. 3 (November 1965), pp. 11–16.

Electronic Security Systems. Leo G. Sands. Indianapolis: Theodore Audel & Co., 1973. 281 pp.
Technical treatment of how electronic security equipment works; explanation of basic circuitry and operation.

Evaluation of Small Business and Residential Alarm Systems, Vol. 1. T.P. Chleboun and K.M. Duvall, Springfield, Va.: National Technical Information Service, 1972. 295 pp.
Role of alarm systems in reducing burglary, robbery, and related crimes; development of cost-effective alarm systems with minimum false alarms and failure rates.

"A Glossary of Common Security Terms." Timothy J. Walsh and Richard J. Healy. *Security World,* Vol. 11, No. 10 (November 1974), pp. 26–28.
A valuable reference list of security terms relating primarily to alarm systems.

"Handbook of Modern Alarm Systems." Eugene L. Fuss. *Security World,* Vol. 11, Nos. 6, 8, 9 (June, September, October, 1974).
An in-depth look at the operation and application of modern, technically improved commercial and industrial alarm systems. Omits systems whose worth has not been proved.

"An Inexpensive Alarm System for Small Museums." Robert L. Strickland, *Museum News,* Vol. 43, No. 10 (June 1965), pp. 24–26.
How to build and use a simple system for signaling to a central location that a protected object has been removed.

"A Low-Cost System of Protecting Paintings." Richard S. Carroll. *Museum News,* Vol. 41, No. 10 (June 1963), pp. 27–29.
How to build and use a low-cost system for protecting paintings.

"Magnetometers for Museum Theft Control." William J. O'Rourke. *Curator,* Vol. 16, No. 1 (1973), pp. 56-58.

How museums can employ passive magnetometers similar to those used in airport security to deter theft. Magnetized plastiform or other signals are attached unobtrusively to objects on display; these signals are detected by the magnetometer.

"Practical Solutions to Entrance Security for Large Area, Multiple Buildings." Floyd G. Miller. *Security World,* Vol. 11, Nos. 9 and 10 (October and November 1974).

Describes one institution's security equipment application, including 24-hour access control for a 31-building complex regulated from one control room. System described can be used in other situations.

"The Protection of Museums Against Theft." Andre F. Nobelcourt. UNESCO *Museum,* Vol. 17, No. 4 (1964), pp. 184–96, 211-32.

An exhaustive study of many types of alarm systems and mechanical devices to prevent, or detect theft, robbery, and attacks. Highly recommended.

Protect Your Property: The Application of Burglar Alarm Hardware. Richard B. Cole. Springfield, Ill.: Charles C Thomas, 1971. 180 pp.

Discusses the applicative advantages and disadvantages and estimated cost of various detection devices. Deals with the concepts of burglar alarm protection in an attempt to have the purchaser of alarm systems properly invest his protection dollar on a "cost versus risk" basis,

"Security Applications, Needs and Trends." J.E. Thorsen. *Security World,* Vol. 10, No. 9 (October 1973), p. 18.

A prediction of equipment improvement and how security electronics can be applied more widely over the next decade.

Security Control: External Theft. Bob Curtis. New York: Chain Store Age Books, 1971. 372 pp.

Contains useful information on the selection, location, and operation of intrusion detection devices; safes and vaults; locks and keys; and protective lighting.

"Security Devices, Systems, and Electronic Technology." J.E. Thorsen. *Security World,* Vol. 10, No. 9 (October 1973), p. 20.

Defines electronic security systems and predicts increasingly sophisticated uses of closed circuit television, electronic access control, and minicomputers.

Security Electronics. John E. Cunningham. Indianapolis: Howard W. Sams & Co., 1973. 159 pp.

A treatment of the electrical principles upon which electronic security systems operate. Some discussion of applications.

Selection and Application of Joint-Services Interior Intrusion Detection System (JSIIDS). Washington, D.C.: Department of the Army, February 1974. Technical Bulletin 5-6350-262. 53 pp.

J-SIIDS is an intrusion detection system composed of a number of compatible components from which the user may select to form an alarm system package to suit his needs. Though J-SIIDS is not available outside the military service, museums will find this bulletin a concise, easy-to-understand explanation of how alarm system sensors and controls operate, how they may be applied, what they will and will not do. Especially useful is the chapter on selecting components.

"Should Management Invest in Electronic Security?" Saul Astor. *Security World,* Vol. 11, No. 1 (January 1974), pp. 30–33.

Discusses the virtue of pre-purchase appraisal of cost and personnel factors important in long-range success of electronic security installations. Stresses the need for continuing training of personnel in using and responding to installation.

"Small Computer Boosts Surveillance Security." George Keener. *Security World,* Vol. 11, No. 4 (April 1974), p. 22.

How a computer in a control center simultaneously monitors sensors of different types, including intrusion, fire, and mechanical equipment, and prints a log of activity of the sensors.

"Television—Museums Watchdog." Albert J. Grossman. *Museum News,* Vol. 44, No. 3 (November 1965), pp. 22–24.

Security of Buildings through Proper Construction

All About Locks and Locksmithing. Max Alth. New York: Hawthorn Books, Inc., 1972. 180 pp.

A history of the types and development of locks and keys. Some information about re-keying and picking of locks.

American National Standard Practice for Protective Lighting. New York: Illuminating Engineering Society, June 1970. American National Standard A85.1 1956 (R197). 20 pp.
Sets forth the principles involved in outdoor protective lighting, the points to be lighted, and the minimum degree of illumination considered necessary.

Architectural Design for Crime Prevention. Oscar Newman. Washington D.C.: U.S. Government Printing Office, 1971.

"The Decision to Masterkey." Robert L. Robinson. *Security World,* Vol. 11, Nos. 8 and 9 (September and October 1974). An overview of the problems of security and management as they relate to masterkeying, with a step-by-step look at the many considerations in key security.

Designing for Security. Richard B. Gale. West Caldwell, N.J.: Loss Prevention Diagnostics, Inc., n.d. 6 pp.
How to design an office area for adequate security. Many good ideas for museums, especially concerning locks.

"Door Locks." *Consumer Reports,* Vol. 36, No. 2 (February 1971), pp. 93–103.
Detailed discussion and ratings of tested locks by type (key-in-knob, mortise, vertical-bolt auxiliary), high-security cylinders, and special-purpose locks. Useful.

"The Doors That Locks Must Go On." Edwin F. Toepfer. *Security World,* Vol. 11, No. 10 (November 1974), p. 22.
Describes doors and door frames, their types of construction, their importance to building security and relationship to secure lock installation.

Locks, Safes, and Security: A Handbook for Law Enforcement Personnel. Marc Weber Tobias. Springfield, Ill.: Charles C. Thomas, 1971, 338 pp.
A "how-to-do-it" book for those who need to be familiar with locking and security devices. Includes detailed information on the basic types of locking mechanisms.

Lock Security. K.C. Freimuth. Santa Cruz: Davis Publications, Inc., n.d. 13 pp.
Operating principles and limitations of key and combination locks.

"Lock Security: Cylinders, Keys, and Keying." Edwin Toepfer. *Security World,* Vol. 2, Nos. 7, 8, 9 (July-August, September, October 1965).
A thorough discussion of the uses, applications, strengths, and weaknesses of locks and locking devices. Discusses pros and cons of masterkeying and the need for proper key control and security.

"A New-Building Look at Locks and Keys." Edwin F. Toepfer. *Security World,* Vol. 11, No. 10 (November 1974), pp. 20–21.
Describes selection of door locks, proper installation, handling of keys—all vital components of building security.

"Planned Security for High-Rise Buildings." Walter M. Strobl. *Security World,* n.d. Good discussion of basic principles of limiting access and key control.

"Planning Ahead—The Registrar's Role in a Building Program." David Vance. Article 16 in *Museum Registration Methods,* edited by Dorothy H. Dudley and Irma B. Wilkinson. Washington, D.C.: American Association of Museums and the Smithsonian Institution, 1968.
How to plan for security of collections while a museum building is being designed. "Zone of safety" is presented.

Protect Your Business From Burglary. Los Angeles Police Department, n.d. 15 pp.
Helpful guidance on potential points of entry for burglars and how to improve security at those points.

The Technical Requirements of a Small Museum. Raymond O. Harrison. Ottawa, Ontario: The Canadian Museums Association, 1969. Technical Paper No. 1. 27 pp.
Brief presentation on space organization to meet the zone of safety requirements of a small museum. Other useful concepts not dealing with security also presented.

Fire Prevention and Detection

"Basic Information on Fire Detection Devices." W.J. Christian and P.M. Dubivsky. *Security World,* Vol. 11, No. 3 (March 1974), pp. 71–73.
A non-technical overview of the kinds, functions, applications, and operating requirements of commonly used fire detection devices.

"The Consultant's Role in Fire Protection." Gerald L. Maatman. *Fire Journal,* Vol. 64, No. 2 (March 1970). NFPA reprint FJ70-10.

How fire prevention specialists can prevent loss from fire by inspection of existing premises and by participating in the design of new construction.

"Fire." Joseph Chapman. *Museum News,* Vol. 50, No. 5 (January 1972), pp. 32–35.

A brief overview of how to prevent and detect fire in the museum.

Fire Protection Equipment List. Chicago: Underwriters' Laboratories, Inc., January 1974. 202 pp.

The names of companies who have qualified to use the Listing Mark of Underwriters' Laboratories, Inc. on or in connection with their products.

"Halon 1301 Total Flooding System for Winterthur Museum." John H. Dowling and Charles Burton Ford. *Fire Journal,* Vol. 63, No. 6 (November 1969), p. 10. NFPA reprint FJ69-17.

How a museum of decorative arts uses the Halon 1301 flooding system to put out fires in enclosed spaces.

"Housekeeping Practices." Section 6 of *Fire Protection Handbook* (13th edition). Boston: National Fire Protection Association, 1969, pp. 6-117 through 6-126.

Discusses housekeeping and orderliness as basic factors in fire prevention.

"Protecting Historical Buildings from Fire." *Environmental Design,* Winter 1969/70. Industrial Publications, Inc. 3 pp.

Discusses the use of early warning ionization detectors recessed in ceilings of historic buildings to provide fire protection while maintaining aesthetic appeal.

Protecting Our Heritage, A Discourse on Fire Protection and Prevention in Historic Buildings and Landmarks. Joseph F. Jenkins, editor. Boston: NFPA, 1970. 39 pp.

"Talking Extinguishing Equipment: The Halons." James M. Hammack. *Fire Journal,* Vol. 64, No. 3 (May 1970). NFPA reprint FJ70-27.

A history of the use of halogenated hydrocarbons (Halons) as fire extinguishants and the status of modern halons, especially Halon 1301 (bromotrifluoromethane), in fire protection.

The following are Standards and Recommended Practices published by the National Fire Protection Association.

Archives and Record Centers. 1972. NFPA 232AM.

Auxiliary Protective Signaling Systems. 1972. NFPA 72B.

Cellulose Nitrate Motion Picture Film. 1967. NFPA 40.

Central Station Protective Signaling Systems. 1972. NFPA 71.

Installation of Portable Fire Extinguishers. 1972. NFPA 10.

Life Safety Code. 1970. NFPA 101.

Local Protective Signaling Systems. 1972. NFPA 72A.

Maintenance and Use of Portable Fire Extinguishers. 1972. NFPA 10A.

National Fire Codes. (Contains all standards listed here, among others.) Fifteen volumes. NFPA FC-1-15.

Proprietary Protective Signaling Systems. 1973. NFPA 72D.

Protection of Library Collections. 1970. NFPA 910.

Protection of Museum Collections. 1969. NFPA 911.

Protection of Records. 1970. NFPA 232.

Remote Station Protective Signaling Systems. 1972. NFPA 72C.

Standard for Fumigation. 1973. NFPA 57.

Tentative Recommendations for Evaluating Fire Protection at a New Facility. 1970. NFPA 5A-T.

Tentative Standard on Automatic Fire Detectors. 1972. NFPA 72E-T.

Vandalism, Civil Disturbances, and Natural Disasters

"Blueprint for Industrial Disaster Readiness." Virgil L. Couch. *Environmental Control and Safety Management.* February 1971, pp. 33–36. Available from the Office of Civil Defense.

How to plan for peacetime and wartime emergencies. Includes a bibliography of Civil Defense publications.

"Bomb Threats and Disasters—A Guide to Corporate Planning." Virgil L. Couch. *Environmental Control and Safety Management,* May 1971, pp. 14–19. Available from the Office of Civil Defense. How to prepare for and cope with bomb threats and actual bombings.

Emergency and Disaster Planning. Richard J. Healy. Hew York: John Wiley and Sons, Inc., 1969.

"Emergency Measures and Museums." Neal FitzSimmons. *Museum News*, Vol. 43, No. 6 (February 1965), pp. 23–24.

Asks questions about disaster preparedness that should be asked by museum directors; suggests some answers and gives references to sources of answers.

Industrial Defense Against Civil Disturbances, Bombing, and Sabotage. Washington, D.C.: Office of the Provost Marshal General, Department of the Army, 1971. 50 pp.

A guide to developing and writing a disaster plan; includes suggested format. Contains Office of Civil Defense bibliography.

The Protection of Cultural Resources Against the Hazards of War. Washington, D.C.: Committee on Conservation of Cultural Resources, National Resources Planning Board, February 1942. 46 pp. Available from the Office of U.S. Government Printing Office.

Slightly dated, but still an excellent guide on how to plan and execute protection for museum properties in time of war and civil disturbances.

Protection of Vital Records. A Special Report by the Association of Records Executives and Administrators. Washington, D.C.: Office of Civil Defense, July 1966. 24 pp.

Describes what records deserve protection and how to provide protection.

Vandalism and Violence. An Education U.S.A. Special Report (No. 29). Washington, D.C.: National School Public Relations Association, 1971. 57 pp.

Especially useful information on how to curb vandalism. Includes an appendix on security preparedness.

Crime Prevention Surveys

"Do-It-Yourself Security Evaluation Checklist." Henry S. Ursic and Leroy E. Pagano. *Security World*, Vol. 11, No. 7 (July-August 1974), pp. 38–41.

A self-evaluation checklist for the security manager to use in analyzing the strengths and weaknesses of his security program.

Introduction to Security and Crime Prevention Surveys. Arthur A. Kingsbury. Springfield, Ill.: Charles C Thomas, 1973. 364 pp.

A basic procedural manual presenting the predominate methods and techniques utilized in planning and conducting a crime prevention survey.

Selected List of Publishers

American Association of Museums
2233 Wisconsin Avenue, NW
Washington, DC 20007
Publishes *Museum News*

American Museum of Natural History
Central Park West at 79th Street
New York, NY 10024
Publishes *Curator*

British Museums Association
87 Charlotte Street
London WIP 2BX
ENGLAND
Publishes *Museums Journal*

Los Angeles Police Department
Attn.: Crime Prevention Unit
P.O. Box 30158
Los Angeles, CA 90030

The Merritt Company
P.O. Box 1256
Santa Monica, CA 90406
Publishes *Protection of Assets Manual*

National Fire Protection Association
470 Atlantic Avenue
Boston, MA 02210
Publishes *Fire Journal, Fire Command!*

New York State Historical Association
Box 391
Cooperstown, NY 13326

Security World Publishing Company
2639 South La Cienega Boulevard
Los Angeles, CA 90034
Publishes *Security World*

Charles C Thomas—Publisher
301 East Lawrence Avenue
Springfield, IL 62717

Underwriters' Laboratories, Inc.
207 East Ohio Street
Chicago, IL 60611

UNIPUB, Inc.
650 First Avenue
New York, NY 10016
Distributes UNESCO Museum

Index

Academic libraries, 28-2
Access areas, public, 26-18
Access control, 9-12, 11-12, 16-13, 21-26, 21-33, 25-12, 27-5
Acrylics, 12-3
Activator, footrail, 21-20
Air duct openings, 4-17
Air flow in smoke control, 26-7
Air supply systems, 26-6 to 26-8
Alarm(s), 22-13
  activating devices, 21-19
  audio sounding devices, 11-12
  check valves, 20-8, 20-12
  dedicated lines, 11-4
  outside connections, 21-33
  pressure switches, 20-9
  radar unit, 21-11
  security of, 21-35
  silent, 4-8, 4-17, 21-18
  sounding devices, 11-4
  wiring for, 21-12
Alarm annunciation, 11-13
  access system controls, 11-14
  audio systems, 11-14
  remote controls, 11-14
  video monitors and controls, 11-14
Alarm systems:
  central-station, 11-4
  failures of, 11-5
  local, 11-4
  proprietary, 11-4
  redundancy in, 11-5 to 11-7
  reliability of, 11-5 to 11-8
"All call" voice communications, 26-9
Alpide Belt, 6-6
American Library Association, 28-1, 28-17
American Society for Industrial Security, 1-10
American Society for Testing and Materials, 1-10
Anterooms, 29-18
Anti-shim device, 15-10

Area protection, 21-11, 21-14, 26-14
Assets, protection of, 9-4
Atmospheric pressures, forces induced by, 7-15
ATS (automatic transfer switches), 23-6
Audio systems, 21-14
  alarm annunciation and, 11-14
Automatic synchronization, 23-10
Automatic teller machine, 21-7, 21-16
Automatic transfer switches (ATS), 23-6

Back plate, 15-10
Bacon, Francis, 6-4
Badge readers, 26-13
Ballasts, maintenance of, 14-21
Bank Protection Act of 1968, 16-1, 21-3, 21-33, 21-39
Bank vault classifications, 21-4, 21-8, 21-9
Banks, 21-3
  drive-in, 21-31
Barrel key, 15-10
Barriers, 10-4, 22-3, 22-11
  bandit, 21-18, 21-20
  natural, 27-2
  perimeter, 27-1
  structural, 27-2
Batch processing, 23-2
Batteries, 19-24
Beam lumens, 14-12
Bit key, 15-10
Bit key mortise lock, 15-2
Blank key, 15-10
Bolt, 15-10
Bombs, 30-5
Book mutilation, 28-18
Book-return slots, 28-12
Book theft, 28-17
Bored (cylindrical) lock, 15-2, 15-3
Bottom pin, lock, 15-10
Boundaries, 29-9, 29-15, 30-3
Bow of key, 15-10

Box strike for bolt, 15-10
BPA (Bank Protection Act), 21-4, 21-7
Brooks, Jared, 6-10
Brooks earthquake intensity scale, 6-10
Brownsville Homes, Brooklyn, New York, 29-5
Building control center, 26-16
Building exterior surfaces, lighting, 14-1
Building security, 21-11
Building security codes, 4-1 to 4-19
Building security programs, 1-9
    federal government, 1-10
    local government, 1-9
    private action, 1-10
Buildings:
    interconnecting, 10-6
    new, 30-2
    public (*see* Public buildings)
    recommended specifications for, 22-8
Bullet-resisting enclosures, 17-8, 17-9, 21-22, 21-23
Bullet-resisting materials, 21-24, 21-27
Burglary:
    capabilities of doors and windows against specific threats, 13-5, 13-6
    distance from scene to offender's residence, 1-7
    perpetrator of, 31-2
    premises and tools used for, 1-5, 1-6
    protection against, 21-4, 26-12
Burglary arrests in California, 1-6
Burglary offenders by age, 1-7
Burglary rate per 1000 establishments, 1-8

Cadmium sulfide cells, 19-17
California Crime Technological Research Foundation (CCTRF), 1-5, 13-1, 31-3
    door striker plate design of, 13-8, 13-9
    exterior door design of, 13-9 to 13-11
Cam, 15-11
Cameras:
    activator for, 21-20
    automatic holdup camera systems, 21-28
    for bank use, 21-37
    closed-circuit television, 21-37
        continuous-surveillance, 21-33
        sequence, 21-29
    holdup, 21-29, 21-35
    motion-picture, 21-29
    programmed sequence, 21-29
    surveillance (*see* Surveillance cameras)
    wiring, 21-12
Campus, "open," 24-3
Campus lighting, 24-12
Campus parking lots, 24-13
Campus residence halls, 24-13
Campus security, 24-1
    magnitude of the problem, 24-1
Candlepower, 14-12, 22-6

Card access control console, 21-39
Card access control systems, 21-25, 21-34, 26-13
Card catalog, library, 28-10
Cargo, high-risk specifications for, 22-11
Cargo security checklist, 22-11
Cargo storage, 22-1
Cashiers, 25-12
    hospital, 25-6
CCTV (closed-circuit television), 14-15, 26-14, 26-17
    cameras, 21-37
    communications, 21-26
    continuous-surveillance, 21-33
    security system conduit, 21-38
    sequence cameras, 21-29
    surveillance (*see* Surveillance cameras)
    videotape recorder, 21-39
Ceiling systems, 6-24
Central console station, 24-15
Central station system, 21-34, 26-3
Change key, 15-11
Chimneys and flues, 6-23
Clevis, padlock, 15-11
Closed-circuit television (*see* CCTV)
Closed-circuit television cameras, 21-37
Codes, building security, 4-1 to 4-19
    chief purpose of, 4-2
Coin-operated equipment, 28-14
Colleges and universities, 24-11 to 24-14
    campus lighting, 24-12
    entrances to, 24-12
    high-rise vs. low-rise buildings, 24-11
    landscaping, 24-12
    locking hardware for, 24-12
    residence halls of, 24-11
Combinations, 15-11
Commercial entrances, exterior sliding, 4-7
Communications, 22-13
    emergency, 26-9
    with guests, 29-21
Communications console, 21-39
Communications systems, 11-13
    social, 29-9
Community, the, design and, 3-2
Compression wave, 6-9
Computer(s):
    access control, 6-9
    air conditioning for, 30-5
    categories of, 23-1
    security of, 30-5
Computer centers:
    large, 23-3, 23-11
    medium, 23-3, 23-8
    small, 23-2, 23-3
    suppliers of, 26-1
Computer electricity requirements, 23-2
Computer installation, 10-5

Computer operation factors, 23-2
  disturbances, 23-2
Computer power security, 23-1
Computer power source, 30-5
  support loads and, 23-5
  typical power system, 23-6 to 23-8
Computerized records, protection of, 17-13
Concord, California, 4-1
  municipal code of, 4-14 to 4-19
Connecting screw, 15-11
Consultants, security:
  government agencies, 5-2
  manufacturers and distributors, 5-2, A-35
    to A-54
  personal recommendations, 5-2
  publications, 5-2
  security associations, 5-2
  selecting, 5-1
    checklist of needs, 5-1
    credentials, 5-3
    directory, 5-3, B-1 to B-40
    interviewing, 5-3
Continental drift, 6-4
Control center, building, 26-16
Control desks in libraries, 28-6 to 28-9
Control units:
  auxiliary, 19-3
  central-station, 19-5, 21-36, 21-40
  proprietary, 19-4
  remote-station, 19-3
Controlled areas, 20-2
Corridors, 29-18
Corrugated key, 15-11
Cost of crime, 1-9
Countermeasures, multiple, 9-6
CPTED (crime prevention through
  environmental design), 3-4
Crime(s):
  in buildings, 29-4
  burglary rate, 1-5
  cost of, 1-9
  felony, 1-4
  prevention of, 29-2
Crime deterrence, 29-9
Crime environment features, 29-9
Criminal justice theory, 29-3
CRT (cathode-ray tube) display, 19-5
Crustal movements, 6-4
Current, 14-19
Custodial rooms, 28-14
Cyclones, tropical, 7-7
Cylinder deadbolt locks, 31-8
Cylinder guard, 4-11, 4-15, 15-11
Cylinder set screw, 15-11
Cylinders:
  protection of, 4-7
  removable-core, 15-7
  special high-security, 15-8

Danger, freedom from, 2-2
Data processing and distribution:
  audio distribution, 11-17
  line supervision, 11-7
  radio spectrum, 11-17
  system power distribution, 11-17
  threshold of sensed current, 11-17
  video distribution, 11-17
Deadbolt, 4-11, 4-15
  cylindrical-type, 15-4
  rim lock, 15-4
Deadlatch, 4-11, 4-15
Deadlocks, 4-9, 15-3
  mortise-type, 15-4
Death and Life of Great American Cities, The (Jane
  Jacobs), 3-3
De Ballore, de Montessus, 6-3
Defense lines, 9-4
Defensible space, 3-4, 29-3
Delivery entrance, library, 28-11
DeRossi earthquake intensity scale, 6-10
Design:
  and the community, 3-2
  and security relationship, 10-8
Detection devices, reliability of, 19-23
Detection systems, fire, 26-2
Detectors:
  application considerations for, 19-25
  breakwire, 11-10
  combination, 19-12
  condensation nuclei type, 19-20
  conductive foil, 11-10
  duct, 26-8
  flame-flicker, 19-19
  heat, 19-23
  heating and air-conditioning effects on, 19-22
  infrared, 19-19, 21-11
  ion chamber alarm signal, 19-16
  light sources and photocells, 19-23
  locations and background levels and, 19-21
  maintenance of, 19-24
  microwave, 11-11
  multiple, 9-7
  particle counter, 19-25
  passive infrared, 11-11
  photocell, 11-11
  photoelectric, 19-17, 19-23
  pneumatic-type, 19-12
  positive beam interrupt, 11-10
  pressure-sensitive, 11-12
  rate-compensation, 19-14
  rate-of-rise, 19-12
    fixed-temperature-type, 19-13
  redundant design of, 9-7
  reliability levels of, 9-7
  response of, 19-21
  selection of, 19-24
  spot-type, 19-17
  submicrometer-size particle, 19-20

Detectors (*Cont.*):
  thermoelectric, 19-14
  ultrasonic motion, 11-11
  ultraviolet type, 19-20
  vibration, 11-11
Developers, responsibilities of, 29-8
Digital encoding, 9-10
Dimming, 14-19
Direct wire circuit, 19-7
Door and window controls, 10-5
Door or window switches, 11-9
Door locks, 27-4
  (*See also* Locks)
Door viewers, 29-11, 31-6
Doors, 31-3
  active, 15-10
  construction of, 31-5
  edge reinforcement of, 13-9
  equipment for, ANSI standards, 15-10
  equipment room, 30-3
  exterior (*see* Exterior doors; Exterior single-
    door systems)
  fire, exterior, 30-4
  frames of, 31-3
  framing of, standard FHA, 13-6, 13-7
  front, 30-4
  garage, 4-10, 29-13, 31-6
  with glass panels, 4-7
  inswinging, 4-7
  interior, 30-4
    closure, 29-12
  metal accordion grate, 4-13
  overhead, 4-7
  overhead and sliding, 4-13, 4-19
  restroom, 30-4
  single, framing of, 31-4
  sliding glass (*see* Sliding glass doors)
  sliding glass patio, 13-12
  sliding patio, 4-9, 4-10
  striker plate on, 13-9
  swinging, 4-10, 4-12, 4-18
  turreted, 29-12
  wooden, 4-7
Doors and windows, 13-1
Drive-in facilities, 21-31
Drive-in windows, 21-25
Driver pins, 15-11
Duct detectors, 26-8
Dynamic analysis, 6-20

Earthquake Engineering Research Institute, 6-
  3
Earthquake wave motions, 6-6
Earthquakes:
  causes of, theories of, 6-4
  construction and, 6-25
  deep-focus, 6-6
  design criteria and, 6-15

Earthquakes (*Cont.*):
  distribution of, with depth, 6-6
  elastic-rebound theory of, 6-9
  ground movement, 6-14
  historical aspects of, 6-3
  location considerations and, 6-13
  major zones of, 6-8
  nonstructural design elements and, 6-21
  plate boundaries and, 6-5
  structural elements and, 6-16
  types of waves, 6-6
Educational facilities, 24-1
  access control in, 24-8
  after-hours protection of, 24-7
  crime prevention in, 24-5
  glazing, 24-10
  new, planning for security in, 24-3
  roof access control in, 24-10
  security consultants for, 24-4
    (*See also* Consultants, security)
  security planning process for, 24-4
  site selection for, 24-6
  special requirements of, 24-6
Elastic rebound theory of earthquake
  causation, 6-4
Electronic backup systems, 27-4
Electronic equipment:
  failure rates for, 11-6
  protection of, 26-19
Electronic security products, 11-1
Electronic security systems:
  making the best choice, 11-1
  remote-control, 11-12
  remote equipment, 11-6, 11-8
Elevator bank locations, 26-5
Elevator cars, 6-22
  guide rails for, 6-22
Elevator safety systems, 29-12
Elevator sounds, 29-22
Elevators, 28-15, 30-4
  capture of, 26-4
  counterweights for, 6-21
  driving mechanism for, 6-22
  fire use of, 26-5
  "locking out," 26-5
Emergency communications, 26-9
Emergency Flood Insurance Program, 8-4
Emergency light and power, 28-15
Emergency power, 14-19
Emergency power system, random-access, 23-10
Emergency-room entrance, 25-4
Emergency voice communications, 26-10, 26-11
Enclave and access control, 29-2
Energy level, equivalent, 6-12
Energy releases, 6-11
Entrances, 22-4, 29-14, 29-15, 30-3
Entries, 29-16
Environmental design:
  crime prevention through (CPTED), 3-4
  physical security through, 31-2

Equipment room doors, 30-3
 (*See also* Doors)
Equivalent static force, 6-18
 seismic design requirements, 6-17
Equivalent static lateral force analysis, 6-20
Escutcheon plate, 15-11
Eutectic metal, 19-13
Evacuation plans, 30-5
Evacuation stairwells, 26-18
Exclusion areas, 22-2
Executive protection, 26-19
Exit devices, 15-4, 15-5
 electrically or air-operated, 15-9
Exits:
 fire, 25-4
 secondary, 29-12
Exterior building surfaces, lighting, 14-1
Exterior doors, 4-6, 4-7, 4-9, 4-10, 30-4
 securing, 4-15
 specific threats to, 13-1 to 13-3
Exterior single-door dynamic load tests, 13-15
 to 13-17
Exterior single-door dynamic test
 configurations, 13-13
Exterior single-door systems, 13-6
 resistance capabilities of, 13-13
 static lateral-load tests of, 13-6
 static load failure tests of, 13-14
External security, 30-3
Extinguishing agents, 20-1
Extreme winds, 7-1
 best available space in, 7-17
 building survey, 7-17
 emergency planning for, 7-15
 load combinations, 7-15
 location of shelters in, 7-15
 missiles in, 7-15
 shelters for protection from, 7-10
  concept, 7-11
  future innovations, 7-14
  modifying existing space, 7-12
  new construction, 7-12
  residential, 7-11
  spaces to avoid as, 7-17
  upgrading construction, 7-13
  venting, 7-15
Extreme windstorms, 7-10

Facades, 29-20
Face plates, 15-11
Factory Mutual Engineering Association, 20-15
Failure of security devices, 4-3
Farnsworth House, Plano, Illinois, 8-14
Federal Insurance Administration, 8-4
Fencing, 22-3, 30-3
 maximum security, 27-3
 medium security, 27-3
 minimum security, 27-4
Fencing classifications, 27-2

Fire alarm communications, 19-1
 control units, 19-1
 local, 19-2
Fire alarm sounds, 26-9
Fire alarm system:
 auxiliary, 19-3
 local, 19-3
 proprietary, 19-5
 remote-station, 19-4
Fire considerations, 26-3
Fire destruction of libraries, 28-16
Fire detection systems, 26-2
 heat-actuated devices, 9-7
Fire doors:
 exterior, 30-4
 labeled, locks for, 15-4
Fire endurance, "measuring stick" for, 17-12
Fire exits, 25-4
Fire extinguishers, 28-15
Fire protection, 26-1
Fire pumps, 20-5
Firemen's communication panel, 26-9
Fixtures, pendant and surface-mounted, 6-24
Flame detector, 9-7, 19-18, 19-25
Flat key, 15-11
Flood losses:
 annual, 8-1
 distribution of, 8-2
 estimates of damage in, 8-3
Flood shields, 8-16, 8-19
Floodlights, 14-11, 14-12, 14-15
Floodproofed building program, 8-20
Floodproofed structures, 8-22
 essential systems in, 8-20
Floodproofing, insurance rates and, 8-6 to 8-13
Floodproofing alternatives, construction costs of,
 8-11
Floodproofing decisions, 8-4
Floodproofing procedure(s):
 for preventing water entry, 8-14
 site planning as, 8-13
Floods, 6-14, 8-1
 Emergency Flood Insurance Program, 8-4
 Flood Hazard Boundary Map, 8-4
 Flood Insurance Manual, 8-7
 Flood Insurance Rate Map, 8-4
 National Flood Insurance Rules and
  Regulations, 8-6
Floor warden station, 26-9
Flues and chimneys, 6-23
"Foehn" winds, 7-1
Foil tape, 21-17
Footcandles, 14-12, 22-6
Footrail activator, 21-20
Force, use of, 18-4
Forel earthquake intensity scale, 6-10
Fresnel lens, 14-1
Front door, 30-4
 (*See also* Doors)

Garage doors, 4-10, 29-13, 31-6
Garages, 29-19
Gardens, urban, 29-15
Gatehouses, 22-9, 27-5
Gates, recommended specifications for, 22-9
Glare barrier, 14-1
Glass:
   bullet-resistant, 12-1, 12-2
   categories of, 12-1
   durable, 29-11
   laminated, 12-4 to 12-7
   laminated security, 12-1, 12-2
   laminated transparent, 12-8
   manufacturers of, 12-7, 12-8
   origins of, 12-1
   tempered, 12-4 to 12-7
   tempered transparent, 12-7, 12-8
   transparent wired, 12-8
   wired, 12-3 to 12-7
Glass systems, threats to, 13-3, 13-4
Glass windows, 4-7, 4-16
Glazing, consumer safety and, 12-4
Gondwanaland, earthquake theories and, 6-4
Grates, metal accordion, 4-16
Gravity tanks, 20-4
Greenwich Village, New York City, 29-2
Ground-fault detection, 23-9
Ground movement, 6-14
Groups, spontaneous anonymous, 29-8
Guard orders, 18-4
Guard patrols, 18-11
Guard schedules, 18-5
Guardianship, 2-2
Guards (*see* Security guards)

Hardy-Cross formula for sprinkler systems, 20-12
Hasp, 15-11
Hatchway opening, 4-17
Hatchways and scuttles, 4-10
Health care facilities (*see* Hospitals)
Health care security checklist, 25-12
Heat-actuated devices, 9-7
Heat detectors, 19-24
Heel, padlock, 15-11
High-rise buildings, 26-1, 29-10
   communications in, 19-26
   proprietary fire alarm systems in, 19-6
Hinges, 31-5
   outside, 4-7, 4-16
Holdup cameras, 21-29, 21-35
Honeywell as supplier of computer centers, 26-1
Hospitals, 25-1
   access controls, 25-1
   cashiers, 25-6
   elevators, 25-2
   employee entrance, 25-4
   lobby, 25-2

Hospitals (*Cont.*):
   outpatient clinic, 25-3
   stairwells, 25-4
   visitor control desk, 25-1
Housing developments, scale of, 29-9
Hurricanes, 7-1, 7-7
   landfall probabilities, 7-10
   movement of, 7-9
   size of, 7-9
Hydraulic sprinkler system design, 20-12
Hydropneumatic tanks, 20-4

Illumination:
   computing levels, 14-12
   horizontal, 22-6
   vertical, 22-6
   (*See also* Lamps; Lighting)
Improved Risk Mutuals, 20-15
Indicating devices, 19-26
Industrial plants, 27-1
Industrial revolution, 2-2
Industrial Risk Insurers, 20-15
Infrared alarm systems, 21-16
Institutional libraries, 28-3
Insurance:
   Broad Form, 17-6
   Mercantile Safe, 17-6
Insurance rates and floodproofing, 8-6 to 8-13
Insurance Services Office, 20-15, 21-4, 21-6, 21-7
Intensity scales, earthquake, 6-10
Intercoms, apartment, 29-22
Interior courts, 29-14
Interior doors, closure, 29-12
Internal line security, 21-11
Internal security, 30-3
International Conference of Building Officials, 1-11
Intrusion detection devices, 4-17
   (*See also* Detectors)
Ion chamber, 19-15
   unipolar and bipolar, 19-18
Ionization of chamber air space, 19-14
ISO (*see* Insurance Services Office)

Jacobs, Jane, 29-2, 3-3
Jimmy-resistant locks, 15-11
Johnson Controls as supplier of computer centers, 26-1

Kemper Group, 2-15
Key:
   code for, 15-11
   control of, 15-1, 15-7
   cuts in, 15-11
   glossary, 15-10
   manipulation, 15-12

Key (*Cont.*):
  system updating, 15-7
  tryout, 15-13
  (*See also* Locking devices; Locks)
Key and lock control systems, 22-5, 25-10, 25-13
Key locks, 22-4
Keying, 15-6, 15-8, 15-11
  change key, 15-6
  construction master, 15-7
  grandmaster key, 15-7
  great grandmaster key, 15-7
  great great grandmaster key, 15-7
  master key, 15-7, 15-12
Keyway, 15-11
  restricted, 15-12
  selection of, 15-7
Kitchen views, 19-17
Krupp, House of, 18-6

Labeled fire doors, locks for, 15-4
Ladders, 4-17
Lamps:
  arc discharge, 14-3
  bulb finish, 14-4
  dimming, 14-4
  fluorescent, 14-3, 14-5
  gaseous discharge, 22-7
  high-intensity discharge, 14-3
  high-pressure sodium, 14-3, 14-7, 14-8
  incandescent, 14-3, 14-4, 22-7
  interchangeability of, 14-3
  low-pressure sodium, 14-3, 14-8, 14-9
  maintenance of, 14-20
  mercury, 14-3, 14-6, 14-7
  mercury-vapor, 22-7
  metal halide, 14-3, 14-4, 14-7
  phosphor, 14-4
  restrike time, 14-2
  sodium-vapor, 22-7
  types of, 14-3
  warmup and restrike, 14-3
Landscaping, 30-3
Landslides and lurching, 6-14
Latch, 4-11, 15-2, 15-3
Lateral force coefficients, 6-17
Laundry and linen storage, 25-13
Law Enforcement Assistance Administration
  (LEAA), 1-10, 18-9
Letter and bag night depositories, 21-7
Lexan plastic sheet, 12-4
Lexgard, 12-2, 12-3
Libraries, 28-1
  academic, 28-2
  book stacks, 28-9
  building protection, 28-4
  card catalog, 28-10
  collection security, 28-15
  control desks in, 28-6 to 28-9

Libraries (*Cont.*):
  entrances to, 28-5
    delivery, 28-11
  fire destruction of, 28-16
  institutional, 28-3
  public, 28-2
  public restrooms in, 28-10
  school, 28-3
  security systems in, 28-3
  service areas of, 28-9
  special, 28-3
  special security for, 28-5
  staff areas in, 28-11
  staff security in, 28-19
  types of, 28-1
  vaults and safes in, 28-13
  water damage to, 28-16
Light-emitting diodes, 19-23
Light fixtures, 6-23
Light loss factors, 14-21
Lighted way, 29-13
Lighting, 4-13, 10-5, 22-6, 22-12, 26-14, 30-3
  campus, 24-12
  circuit design, 27-7
  continuous, 22-6
  controlled, 22-7
  electrical systems, 14-18
  emergency, 22-7
  exterior, 26-18
    building, 14-1
  floodlights, 14-11, 14-12, 14-15
  glare protection, 22-7
  lamps (*see* Lamps)
  levels of illumination, 14-2
  light fixtures, 6-23
  light sources, 14-2 to 14-15
  luminaire (*see* Luminaire)
  movable, 22-7
  of parking lots, 4-19
  recommended specifications, 22-10
  residential, 31-7
  security, 14-1
  standby, 22-7
  system maintenance, 14-20
  typical equipment for protective, 14-11
  (*See also* Illumination)
Limit switches, 11-9
Limited area for cargo storage, 22-2
Liquefaction, 6-14
Loading docks, 26-18
Lobbies, 29-16
Lobby security, 30-3
Local protective systems, 26-2
Lock and key control systems, 22-5, 25-10, 25-13
Lock and keying checklists, 15-10
Lock-in-knob, 15-12
Locking devices, 31-10
  automatically time controlled, 15-8

Locking devices (*Cont.*):
  at bottom or top rail of doors, 4-7
  electric and air-activated, 15-8
  glossary, 15-10
  lock systems and circumvention, 13-4
  lock systems tests, 13-19
  locking dog, 15-12
  picking, 15-12
  relocking, 22-5
  (*See also* Keying)
Locks, 15-1, 22-4, 31-8
  ANSI standards, 15-10
  change key operated, 15-11
  combination, 15-11, 17-14, 22-4, 22-5
  consideration of, 15-1
  cylinder, 31-8, 31-11
  defeating, 13-14
  door, 27-4
  functions of, 15-2 to 15-5
  glossary, 15-10
  magnetic, 15-9
  manipulation, 15-12
  master keyed, 15-12
  permutation, 15-12
  positive, 29-11
  recommended specifications, 27-10
  resistance to attack, 13-4
  strikes, 31-12
  system controls, 27-6
  tubular, 15-3
  tumbler, 15-12
  unit (*see* Unit lock)
  window, 29-11
  (*See also* Key)
Loiding locks, 15-12
Long Beach, California, earthquake, 6-17
Loop circuit, 9-9
Loop circuit faults, 9-9
Los Angeles County security provisions, 4-11 to 4-14
Loss event, 9-3
Loudspeaker location, 26-9
Louvered windows, 4-7
Love waves, 6-9
Low-hazard properties, 20-3
Lumes, 14-3
Luminaire:
  coefficient of utilization, 14-18
  enclosure, 14-9
  Hi-Mast, 14-14
  lamp position, 14-9
  light distribution, 14-10
  location, 14-2
  location and mounting, 14-10
  low-pressure sodium, 14-13
  maintenance, 14-20
  mountings, maintenance of, 14-21
  optical system, 14-9
  roadway, 14-14, 14-17

McCulloh circuit, 9-9, 19-8
Magnetic reed switch, 11-8, 11-9
Magnetic switches, 21-18
Magnitude scales, earthquake, 6-11
Mailboxes, 29-23
Maisonettes, 29-17
Manker Patten Tennis Center, University of Chattanooga, 8-14
Marking and numbering, 27-6
Master key, 15-7, 15-12
Master pins, 15-12
Mechanical systems in earthquakes, 6-22
Mercalli earthquake intensity scale, 6-10
Metal accordion grate doors, 4-7
Mid-ocean ridges, 6-4
Mobile libraries, 28-15
Model code, development of, 4-5
Modified Mercalli earthquake intensity scale, 6-10
Money clip, 21-19
Money safes, 17-1
  burglary-resistant, 17-1
  improving protection of, 17-6
  insulated, 17-14
  (*See also* Safes)
Mortise cylinder, 15-12
Mortise latch, 15-3
Mortise lock, 15-2, 15-12
Mortise lock trim, 15-4
Motion-picture cameras, 21-29
  (*See also* Surveillance cameras)
Mount Vesuvius, 2-1
Multiple housing, 29-1
Multiple-housing prototypes, 29-3
Multiplexing circuits, 9-10
Mushroom pins, 15-12

National Bureau of Standards Security Program, 1-10
National Crime Prevention Institute, 1-10
National Flood Insurance Rules and Regulations, 8-6
National Flood Insurers Association, 8-7
National Institute for Law Enforcement and Criminal Justice, 1-10
National Oceanic and Atmospheric Administration, 7-6
National Severe Storms Forecast Center, 7-5
National Severe Storms Laboratory, 7-3
Needs analysis, security, 2-3, 30-2
Neighborhoods, 3-1, 30-3
  concept of, 3-1
  definition of, 3-2
  design and planning of, 3-3
  security in, 3-1 to 3-6
  urban frame, 3-3
  user characteristics, 3-2
New buildings, 30-2

New York City Housing Authority, 29-3, 29-4
Newman, Oscar, 3-4, 29-3, 29-5
NFPA (National Fire Protection Association), 20-14, 26-2
Night depositories, 21-7, 21-14, 21-15

Oakland Model Burglary Security Code, 4-5 to 4-11
Oakland Municipal Code, 1-9
Object protection, 21-11, 26-14
Occupancy, low-hazard, 20-2
Occupational Safety and Health Administration (OSHA), 10-6
Office building considerations, 26-16
Older buildings, 30-2
Operational needs, planning for, 10-7
"Opting out" opportunities, 29-9
Outpatient clinic, 25-3
Overhead doors, 4-7

Pacific Rim Belt, 6-6
Padlock, 15-12
Panic bolts, 15-12
Parking, 25-9, 25-13
  recommended specifications, 22-9
Parking lot(s):
  campus, 24-13
  location of, 10-6
Patio-type doors, 4-9
  (See also Doors)
Patrol, exterior and interior, 18-2
Peachtree Plaza Hotel, Atlanta, 26-1
Perimeter barriers, 27-1
Perimeter protection, 21-14, 26-14
Perimeter security systems, 21-16
Personnel movement, 26-4
Personnel protection, 26-12
Pharmaceutical storeroom, 25-6
Pharmacy, 25-12
Pharmacy counter, 25-6
Phones, communal, 29-22
Photoelectric cells, 21-16
Physical controls, site, 10-4
Physical security standards, 22-8
Pin tumblers, 25-12
Piping:
  copper, 20-6
  and fittings, 20-6
  galvanized, 20-6
  welded, 20-6
Piping layout drawings, 20-12
Piping systems, 6-23
Placet, P., 6-4
Planning, coordination of, 30-2
Plastic safety sheet:
  acrylic, 12-8
  polycarbonate, 12-3, 12-8

Plastics, 12-3
  Lexan, 12-4
  Lexgard, 12-2, 12-3
  manufacturers of, 12-7 to 12-8
Plate boundaries, 6-4
Plate tectonics, 6-4
Plug, lock, 15-12
Point protection, 21-11
Point security systems, 21-14
Police connection, direct, 21-34
Polycarbonate sheets, 12-3, 12-8
Post indicator valves, 20-5
Power factor, 14-19
Power failure, electronic security systems, 11-8
Power sources, 22-7
  standby, 11-17
Powers as supplier of computer centers, 26-1
Pressure pump, excess, 20-9
Pressure tanks, 20-4
Pressurization, 26-7
Private Security Task Force to the National Advisory Committee on Criminal Justice Standards and Goals, 18-9
Property and person, security of, 2-1 to 2-7
Property line protection, 9-4
Proprietary security systems, 21-35, 21-40
Protection, 2-3
  area, 21-11, 21-14, 26-14
  of assets, 9-4
  against burglary, 21-4, 26-12
  of computerized records, 17-13
  crime and the need for, 1-4
  executive, 26-19
  fire, 26-1
  identifying kinds of, 9-6
  object, 21-11, 26-14
  perimeter, 21-14, 26-14
  personnel, 26-12
  point, 21-11
  property line, 9-4
  of records, 17-9
  sensitive-area, 21-21
  space, 21-11
  of utilities, 10-8
Protection systems, 9-3, 9-8
Proximity sensors, 21-14
Public access areas, 26-18
Public buildings, 30-1
  definition of, 30-2
  security checklist for, 30-6
  security planning for, 30-2
  shelters in, 7-14
Public libraries, 28-2
Public processes and neighborhood security, 3-6
Public zones in multiple housing, 29-13
Pull button, 21-19

Rayleigh theory, 19-18
Rayleigh waves, 6-9

Real-time processing, 23-1
Receiving and storage, 25-8, 25-13
Record containers, insulated, 17-13
Records, protection of, 17-9
Reflector, lighting, 14-11
Refuge areas, 26-8
Reid, H. F., 6-4
Relocking devices, 22-5
Remote equipment switches, 11-8, 11-9
Remote teller stations, 21-28, 21-31
Remote transaction systems, 21-19, 21-21
Reporting stations, security guard, 18-11
Residential project security checklist, 3-5
Response spectrum analysis, 6-20
Restrooms, library, 28-10
Retard chambers, 20-9
Return air systems, 26-6 to 26-8
Richter, C. F., 6-11
Richter earthquake magnitude scale, 6-11, 6-12
Riley Act, 6-17
Rim cylinder, 15-12
Rim devices, 15-5
Rim lock, 15-2 to 15-4, 15-13, 31-11
Risk, freedom from, 2-2
Risk analysis, 9-5
Risk logic tree, 9-5
Robbery:
    armed, 17-7
    protection against, 21-18
Robertshaw as supplier of computer centers,
    26-1
Roof openings, 4-8, 4-16
Rose, lock, 15-13
Rossi-Forel earthquake intensity scale, 6-10

Safe deposit boxes, 21-7
Safe Manufacturers National Association, 17-4,
    17-5
Safe Schools Act, 24-3
Safes, 4-8, 10-6, 17-1
    alarms for, 17-7
    auxiliary, 21-7
    burglary- and robbery-resistive, 17-4
    in commercial establishments, 4-17
    dual-purpose, 17-13
    fire-resistive, 17-5
    floor-installed, 17-2
    with key-locking dials, 17-3, 17-8
    record, 17-6
    tested, 17-2
        time element involved in, 17-3
    tool-resistant, 17-3
    untested, 17-2
    (See also Vaults)
Safety in definition of security, 2-2
Safety glass products, 12-4 to 12-7
San Fernando, California, earthquake, 6-14, 6-
    15, 6-19

Santa Barbara, California, earthquake, 6-17
São Paulo, Brazil, fire, 26-5
Scattering principle, light-, in smoke detection,
    19-18, 19-19
Searchlight, 14-11
School libraries, 28-3
Schools, 24-1
    shelters in, 7-14
    within multiple housing, 29-13
    (See also Educational facilities)
Scuttles and hatchways, 4-10
Sea-floor spreading, 6-4
Sea wave warning systems, 6-15
Security:
    of alarms, 21-35
    building, 21-11
    computer, 30-5
    definition of, 1-3, 2-2
    external and internal, 30-3
    neighborhood, 3-1 to 3-6
    of property and person, 2-1 to 2-7
    sociotechnical, 29-9
Security center, 11-13 to 11-15
    data processing and distribution in, 11-15
    primary, 11-6
Security checklist:
    health care, 25-12
    residential project, 3-5
Security codes (see Building security codes)
Security consultants (see Consultants, security)
Security department:
    hospital, 25-5
    location of, 24-13
Security devices, weaknesses of, 4-3
Security guards, 18-1
    armed or unarmed, 18-8
    communications with, 18-11
    company vs. contract, 18-10
    component tasks of, 18-3
    contract or in-house, 18-9
    duties of, 18-1
    human relationships, 18-6
    modern concept of, 18-1
    physical capability, 18-4
    qualifications of, 18-2
    shifts of, 10-1
    skills and qualifications of, 18-3
        visual acuity, 18-3
    specific job descriptions, 18-3
    summary of tasks of, 18-2
    tour reporting stations, 11-13
    tour stations, 26-15
Security hardware, 31-3
Security personnel, 18-1
Security procedures:
    planning, 2-3
    surveying the need for, 2-3, 30-2
Security stations, 27-5
Security survey model, 2-4
Security survey outline, 2-5

Security systems:
  area, 21-14
  costs of, 9-12
  designer's guide to, 9-10
  key points, 9-11
  perimeter, 21-16
  planning, 24-14
  point, 21-14
  proprietary, 21-35, 21-40
  specifying, 9-11
  tasks of, 9-11
Security technology review, 9-9
Seismic belts, 6-4
Seismic risk map, 6-13
Seismicity, locations of high, 6-6
Seismological Society of America, 6-3
Selenium cells, 19-17
Sensitive-area protection, 21-21
Sewer systems in floods, 8-20, 8-21
Shackle, lock, 15-13
Shear line, lock, 15-13
Shear wave in earthquake wave motions, 6-9
Shelters in schools and public buildings, 7-14
Sidewalks, 30-3
Signal-to-noise ratio, 19-16
Signals, audible, 19-2
Silent alarm, 4-8, 4-17, 21-18
Silicon cells, 19-17
Single-door framing, 31-4
  (See also Doors)
Single-family homes, 31-1
Site, 30-3
  location of facilities on the, 10-6
Site hardening, 9-12
Site planning, 10-4
Site protection considerations, 10-1
Site selection factors, 10-2, 10-3
Sliding glass doors, 4-13, 4-18, 4-19, 31-6
  tests of, 4-11, 4-18, 13-18
  (See also Doors)
Sliding glass patio doors, 13-12
Sliding glass windows, 13-19, 31-6
Sliding patio-type doors, 4-9, 4-10
Smoke control, 26-6
  air flow in, 26-7
  block diagram, 26-6
Smoke detectors, 19-25
  beam-type light attenuation, 19-17
  ionization chamber type, 19-15
  ionization principle in, 19-14
  light-scattering principle in, 19-18, 19-19
  photoelectric principle in, 19-14, 19-25
  photoresistive cell, 19-17
  photovoltaic, 19-17
  projected-beam, 19-17
Snider, Antonio, 6-4
Social communications systems, 29-9
Social control theory, 29-2
Sociotechnical security, 29-9
Solar radiation interference, 19-19

Sound waves, 21-14
Space protection, 21-11
Spatial boundaries, 29-9
Special flood hazard areas, 8-4
Spindle, lock, 15-13
Spring bolt, 15-13
Sprinkler(s), 20-1
  approvals, 20-14
  check valves, 20-6
  control valves, 20-5
  deflectors, 20-7
  deluge systems, 20-11
  design considerations, 20-11
  dry systems, 20-10
  pipe and fittings, 20-6
  risers, 20-5, 20-10, 20-11, 20-13
  standard spray, 20-8
  standard upright, 20-7
  wet systems, 20-8
Sprinkler equipment approval, 20-15
Sprinkler fitters, 20-14
Sprinkler heads, 20-7
  dry pendant, 20-8
  sidewall, 20-8
  special, 20-8
  temperature ratings of, 20-7
  tests of, 20-8
Sprinkler installers, 20-13
Sprinkler layout shop drawings, 20-15
Sprinkler rules, 20-14
Sprinkler standards, 20-14
Sprinkler supervisory devices, 19-26
Sprinkler systems:
  acceptance, 20-15
  components of, 20-2, 20-5
  definition of, 20-1
  functions of, 20-1
  Hardy-Cross formula for, 20-12
Staff areas, library, 28-11
Stairwells, 29-16
  emergency, 30-5
  evacuation, 26-18
Standby power source, 11-17
Stanley House, La Grange, Illinois, 8-15
Staple, hasp, 15-13
Stile of paneled door, 15-13
Storage and receiving, 25-8, 25-13
Streetlights, 14-11
Strike plate, 15-13
Structural Engineers Association of California,
  6-16
Subduction zones, 6-6
Suction tanks, 20-4
Suess, Eduard, 6-4
Surveillance by guards, 18-2
Surveillance cameras, 11-12, 16-1, 21-18, 21-28
  applications for, 16-1
  closed-circuit television (see CCTV)
  costs of, 16-12, 16-13
  demand cameras, 16-3

Surveillance cameras (*Cont.*):
film for: handling and storage of, 16-6
processing, 16-7
size of, 16-4
type of, 16-5
lens aiming and focusing, 16-9
lens selection, 16-9, 16-10
lighting and exposure for, 16-11
locations of, 16-7
maintenance of, 16-11
sequence cameras, 16-3
site survey, 16-13
surveillance purpose, 16-14
when and where needed, 16-1
Survey, security, 2-3, 2-4
Surveying the need for security procedures, 2-3, 30-2
Switches:
door or window, 11-9
magnetic, 21-18
remote equipment, 11-8, 11-9
toe, 21-19
Switching, 14-19

Tail piece, lock, 15-13
Tanks, 6-23, 20-4
Taylor, F. B., 6-4
Television-equipped transaction stations, 21-21
(*See also* CCTV)
Teller stations:
bullet-resistant, 21-22
remote, 21-28, 21-31
Tellers, automatic, 21-7, 21-16
Temperatures, melting, of various substances, 17-12
Time-history response analysis, 6-20
Toe, lock, 15-13
Toe switch, 21-19
Tornado days, frequency of, 7-8
Tornadoes, 7-1
damage characteristic, 7-3
damage path, 7-6
debris, 7-3
design basis, 7-2
funnel, 7-2
geographical distribution and intensity of, 7-4
intensity distribution, 7-10
meteorological conditions, 7-4
missiles, 7-3
occurrence map, 7-6
physical description of, 7-2
radial velocity, 7-2
seasonal distribution, 7-7
striking probability, 7-6
values of wind forces, 7-3
Transaction stations, 21-21
Transaction systems, remote, 21-19, 21-21

Transoms, accessible, 4-7, 4-16
Transportation linkages, 29-21
Tropical storms, 7-9
Tsunami, 6-15
Turnagain Arm slide, Anchorage, Alaska, 6-14
TV cameras, continuous-surveillance, 21-33
(*See also* CCTV)

Ultrasonic building security systems, 21-15
Underwriters' Laboratories, Inc. (UL), 17-2, 17-3, 21-35
classifications of, 21-4
fire endurance test of, 17-11
paper record categories of, 17-10
Uniform Building Code loading, 6-19
Uninterruptible power system (UPS), 23-3 to 23-5
Unit lock, 15-2, 15-3
door stile for, 15-4
preassembled, 15-4
United Association of Journeymen and Apprentices, 20-14
United States Coast and Geodetic Survey, 6-9
Universities (*see* Colleges and universities)
UPS (uninterruptible power system), 23-3 to 23-5
Urban gardens, 29-15
Utilities, location and protection of, 10-8

Van Dyke Houses, Brooklyn, New York, 29-5
Vaults, 10-6, 17-1, 21-4
classifications for, 21-4, 21-8, 21-9
doors for, 21-6
heating, ventilating, and electrical systems for, 21-6
library, 28-13
wall opening details for ventilation unit, 21-10
(*See also* Safes)
Vehicle control, 22-2
Vermin destruction, 28-18
Vertical streets in multiple-housing design, 29-20
Vibrating structures, 6-18
Voltages, 14-18

Walled cities, 2-1
Wallpack, 14-16
Walls in high-security areas, 30-4
Watch tours, 26-15
Watchman (*see* Security guards)
Water:
demand for, 20-3
effects of, 6-14
freeze protection, 20-4
natural bodies of, 20-5

Water (*Cont.*):
  sources of, 20-2
  storage of, 20-4
  supplies of, 20-2
Water damage to libraries, 28-16
Water flow, 20-3
Water motor gong, 20-9
Water supply:
  adequacy of, 20-2
  improvements to, 20-4
  on-site, 20-4
Watertower Place, Chicago, 26-1
Wattage, 14-19
Wegener, Alfred L., 6-4
Wet-floodproofed structure, 8-6
Wind damage, reducing, 7-13
Wind-induced forces, 7-14

Windows:
  door and window controls, 10-5
  door or window switches, 11-9
  drive-in, 21-25
  locking devices for, 4-19
  locks for, 29-11
  louvered, 4-7
  protection of, 4-9, 4-10
  sliding glass, 13-19, 31-6
Windows and doors, 13-1
Wiring:
  alarm, 21-12
  camera, 21-12
World Trade Center, New York City, 26-1

Zone selection, 26-9